LAW AND ORDER IN ANGLO-SAXON ENGLAND

Law and Order in Anglo-Saxon England

TOM LAMBERT

OXFORD
UNIVERSITY PRESS

OXFORD

UNIVERSITY PRESS

Great Clarendon Street, Oxford, OX2 6DP,
United Kingdom

Oxford University Press is a department of the University of Oxford.
It furthers the University's objective of excellence in research, scholarship,
and education by publishing worldwide. Oxford is a registered trade mark of
Oxford University Press in the UK and in certain other countries

© Tom Lambert 2017

The moral rights of the author have been asserted

First Edition published in 2017
Impression: 1

Published in the United States of America by Oxford University Press
198 Madison Avenue, New York, NY 10016, United States of America

British Library Cataloguing in Publication Data
Data available

Library of Congress Control Number: 2016949767

ISBN 978–0–19–878631–3

Printed in Great Britain by
Clays Ltd, St Ives plc

For Ruth

Preface

This book began with the urgent need to get my 2009 PhD thesis into print. Seven years on, the book is a different project entirely; only the pervasive sense of urgency remains unchanged. They have been highly enjoyable if sometimes rather fraught years. I suspect I will mainly remember them for both the remarkable generosity with which I was welcomed into professional academic life and the tension, sometimes scarcely bearable, created by my precarious employment. I did not find writing this book easy, and I have valued the much-needed (and largely unexpected) friendship and support that have come my way all the more highly as a result, so I am glad to have the opportunity to express my gratitude here, however inadequately.

First, though, it might be helpful to explain something of how this book came to take the form that it does, and why it took so long to find its final shape. Its transformation from a 'book-of-the-thesis' stemmed from the realization that although my work had suggested some revisions to an established interpretative tradition, arguing that it could not make sense of the evidence at a few potentially important points, I had not offered an alternative framework which could accommodate my findings. I found that readers and seminar audiences often interpreted my arguments in ways that made me uncomfortable. By arguing that late Anglo-Saxon kings did not prohibit feuding, for instance, I did not intend to argue for any weakness in the late Anglo-Saxon 'state', but it was understandable that I was construed in this way: I had no coherent model to offer in which strong centralized political authority sat easily alongside a legal order that accepted vengeance killings. Because publishing quickly was my top priority I initially resisted the idea of attempting to articulate such a model myself, instead trying to write a bland additional chapter that could quickly be tacked onto the thesis to push its coverage back to the seventh century. Yet on close inspection I found this early material was much more fascinating than I had anticipated; one chapter became three; their greater breadth then revealed gaps in my existing late Anglo-Saxon material; and so it continued. Regardless of my intentions I was in fact working on this new project, and I was much happier when I finally stopped pretending otherwise, though the reality of what that meant—repeatedly discarding and rewriting vast swathes of material whenever some new insight meant my argument outgrew the structure intended to contain it—was often incredibly frustrating, and rather unhelpful in career terms.

The institutions which have employed me through this stimulating but painfully drawn-out process thus have my sincere thanks for making it possible: the Past and Present Society; the Institute of Historical Research; Oxford University History Faculty; Balliol College, Brasenose College, and Exeter College, Oxford; and now Sidney Sussex College, Cambridge. Exeter College, where most of what appears here was written, has my particular gratitude for providing the enlightened mix of

teaching responsibilities and research time that allowed it to happen. My immediate colleagues have been uniformly supportive throughout, and share responsibility with several generations of students for making this mildly peripatetic
period a happy one. I would also like to thank David Rollason and Christian
Liddy for supervising the thesis from which this book grew. Paul Dresch, George
Molyneaux, and Chris Wickham each read and commented on drafts of the entire
manuscript, some chapters several times over, and I found their comments—
particularly their criticisms—invaluable. I have not followed all of their advice but
it is a much better book for their efforts. Similarly, I am grateful to Oxford
University Press's three anonymous readers, especially the one who read the
manuscript twice; I was so close to the text that I struggled to see it clearly (as
I still do), and I found their perspectives very helpful in revising it. I am also
indebted to Carolyne Larrington for responding patiently to my pleas for help
with legal Old English (in spite of my invariably managing to bother her while on
holiday). Finally, I would like to thank all those who at one point or another have
been kind enough to share unpublished work with me: Graham Barrett, Thomas
Charles-Edwards, Miriam Czock, Ros Faith, John Hudson, Paul Hyams, John
Maddicott, Alyx Mattison, George Molyneaux, Rory Naismith, David Pratt,
Richard Purkiss, Susan Reynolds, Alice Rio, Rick Sowerby, Alice Taylor, and
Chris Wickham, as well as all those who have pre-circulated their work for various
workshops (particularly those of the Oxford 'Legalism' project, a truly formative
influence for me for the last six years).

There are many others I would like to thank here, far more than it would be
practical to list by name. Although on a couple of memorable occasions my work
has drawn cool or even hostile reactions from other historians, who have (to my
considerable dismay) regarded my attempts at revisionism as displays of disres-
pectful arrogance, the experience of communicating the ideas contained in this
book to the world has been overwhelmingly positive. Many of the people I have
met in the process have become friends, and their friendship has not only
enriched my life but contributed meaningfully to this book, albeit in ways that
would be difficult to describe succinctly and are certainly impossible to quantify. I
hope they already have a good sense of how much they are appreciated. I am
grateful also to the much wider pool of people who have extended me the
compliment of engaging seriously with my work and discussing it with me in
all manner of contexts (over email after discovering it in print, or in person
following research presentations at conferences and seminars, but also in tutorials
and over college lunches, even in job interviews). Some of these often rather
fleeting interactions significantly shaped my thinking—I remember Chapters 2
and 5 evolving as I pondered two fairly brief conversations with non-medievalists
following seminar presentations in 2010—and collectively they did a great deal to
sustain my belief that the project as a whole was worth something: no small
contribution.

Most of all, however, this book owes its existence to my wife, Ruth. She has
suffered for it, both in my absences (physical and mental) and in my highly-strung
presence, to the extent that she has more than once professed to hate it. I, on the

other hand, have always found sanctuary with her, sheltered from the book by her healthy lack of interest in academic history of all forms, my work in particular. I cannot express how much I have valued this refuge. Whether or not she wants to read it, this book is dedicated to her.

Sidney Sussex College, Cambridge
November 2016

Contents

Contents

Abbreviations

Most of the abbreviations below relate to laws. This book follows the standard system of citation for Anglo-Saxon and Anglo-Norman legal texts established by Felix Liebermann in his *Die Gesetze der Angelsachsen* (Halle, 1903–16), and slightly extended by the Early English Laws project, which provides a comprehensive list here: <http://www. earlyenglishlaws.ac.uk/laws/texts/>. For most texts Liebermann's *Gesetze* remains the most authoritative edition. There are, however, other editions and a number of different translations available. These are indicated here, with the first reference indicating the primary edition. For the sake of brevity, the following abbreviations have been adopted for this section only:

Attenborough, *Laws*	F. L. Attenborough, *The Laws of the Earliest English Kings* (Cambridge, 1922).
EHD i	Dorothy Whitelock, ed., *English Historical Documents, 1, c.550–1042*, 2nd edn (London: Eyre Methuen, 1979).
EHD ii	D. C. Douglas and G. W. Greenaway, eds., *English Historical Documents, 2, 1042–1189* (2nd edn, London: Eyre Methuen, 1981).
Liebermann, *Gesetze*	Felix Liebermann, ed., *Die Gesetze der Angelsachsen*, 3 vols. (Halle, 1903–16).
Oliver, *Beginnings*	Lisi Oliver, *The Beginnings of English Law* (Toronto, 2002).
Robertson, *Laws*	A. J. Robertson, *The Laws of the Kings of England from Edmund to Henry I* (Cambridge, 1925).

KEY TO ABBREVIATIONS

The abbreviations listed below are used throughout the book.

Abt	Laws of Æthelberht. Edited: Oliver, *Beginnings*; Liebermann, *Gesetze*; Attenborough, *Laws*. English translations: Oliver, *Beginnings*; Attenborough, *Laws*; *EHD* i, no. 29. Though Oliver, *Beginnings* introduced a new system of numbering the clauses, Liebermann's is retained here because of its presence in all the other editions.
Af	Laws of Alfred. Edited: Liebermann, *Gesetze*; Attenborough, *Laws*. English translations: Attenborough, *Laws*; *EHD* i, no. 33.
AGu	Treaty of Alfred and Guthrum. Edited: Liebermann, *Gesetze*; Attenborough, *Laws*. English translations: Attenborough, *Laws*; *EHD* i, no. 34.
Anglo-Saxon Chronicle	The Anglo-Saxon Chronicle. Edited: David Dumville and Simon Keynes, general eds., *The Anglo-Saxon Chronicle: A Collaborative Edition*, 9 vols. (Cambridge, 1983-). English translations: D. Whitelock, D. C. Douglas and S. I. Tucker, trans., *The*

	Anglo-Saxon Chronicle: A Revised Translation (London, 1961); Michael Swanton, *The Anglo-Saxon Chronicles* (revised edn, London, 2000). Cited by corrected year and, where significant, by a letter to indicate the relevant manuscript.
[I–VI] As	Laws of Æthelstan. Edited: Liebermann, *Gesetze*; Attenborough, *Laws*. English translations: Attenborough, *Laws*; *EHD* i, nos. 35–7 (II, V, and VI As).
ASD	Joseph Bosworth and T. Northcote Toller, eds., *An Anglo-Saxon Dictionary* (London, 1898). An online version is now available: <http://bosworth.ff.cuni.cz/>.
Ass Clar	Assize of Clarendon. William Stubbs and H. W. C. Davis, eds., *Select Charters and Other Illustrations of English Constitutional History* (9th edn, Oxford, 1921), pp. 170–3. English translation: *EHD* ii, no. 24. Online edition and translation available at <http://www.earlyenglishlaws.ac.uk>.
Ass Nor	Assize of Northampton. William Stubbs and H. W. C. Davis, eds., *Select Charters and Other Illustrations of English Constitutional History* (9th edn, Oxford, 1921), pp. 179–81. English translation: *EHD* ii, no. 25. Online edition and translation available at <http://www.earlyenglishlaws.ac.uk>.
[I–X] Atr	Laws of Æthelred. Edited: Liebermann, *Gesetze*; Robertson, *Laws*. English translations: Robertson, *Laws*; *EHD* i, nos. 42–6 (II, III, V, VII, and VIII Atr).
Að	The anonymous legal text 'Að'. Edited: Liebermann, *Gesetze*.
Blas	The anonymous legal text 'Be Blaserum'. Edited: Liebermann, *Gesetze*; Attenborough, *Laws*. English translation: Attenborough, *Laws*.
[I–II] Cn	Laws of Cnut. Edited: Liebermann, *Gesetze*; Robertson, *Laws*. English translations: Robertson, *Laws*; *EHD* i, no. 50.
Cn 1018	Cnut's law code of 1018. Edited Liebermann, *Gesetze* (as MS D of I Cnut). Edited and translated: A. G. Kennedy, 'Cnut's Law-Code of 1018' *Anglo-Saxon England* 11 (1982), pp. 57–81. Online edition and translation available at <http://www.earlyenglishlaws.ac.uk>.
Cn 1020	Cnut's letter to the English of 1020. Edited: Liebermann, *Gesetze*; Robertson, *Laws*. English translations: Robertson, *Laws*; *EHD* i, no. 48.
Cn 1027	Cnut's letter to the English of 1027. Edited: Liebermann, *Gesetze*; Robertson, *Laws*. English translations: Robertson, *Laws*; *EHD* i, no. 49.
Cons Cn	*Consiliatio Cnuti*. Edited: Liebermann, *Gesetze*.
DB	*Domesday Book*. Entries are cited by folio. The standard editions of the text are A. Farley, ed., *Domesday Book* (London, 1783), and, county by county, John Morris et al., eds., *Domesday Book*, 39 vols. (Chichester, 1975–86).
DOE	Angus Cameron, Ashley Crandell Amos, and Antonette diPaolo Healey, eds., *Dictionary of Old English: A-G Online* (Toronto, 2007): <http://www.doe.utoronto.ca>.
Duns	The Ordinance Concerning the *Dunsæte*. Edited: Liebermann, *Gesetze*.
Ecclesiastical History	Bede, *Ecclesiastical History of the English People*. Bertram Colgrave and R. A. B. Mynors, eds., *Bede's Ecclesiastical History of the English People* (Oxford, 1969).

ECf	*Leges Edwardi Confessoris*. Edited: Bruce R. O'Brien, *God's Peace and King's Peace: The Laws of Edward the Confessor* (Philadelphia, 1999); Liebermann, *Gesetze*. English translation: O'Brien, *God's Peace and King's Peace*.
[II–IV] Eg	Laws of Edgar. Edited: Liebermann, *Gesetze*; Robertson, *Laws*. English translations: Robertson, *Laws*; *EHD* i, nos. 40–1.
EGu	The legal text known as 'The Laws of Edward and Guthrum'. Edited: Liebermann, *Gesetze*; Attenborough, *Laws*. English translation: Attenborough, *Laws*.
[I–III] Em	Laws of Edmund. Edited: Liebermann, *Gesetze*; Robertson, *Laws*. English translations: Robertson, *Laws*; *EHD* i, no. 38 (II Em).
[I–II] Ew	Laws of Edward. Edited: Liebermann, *Gesetze*; Attenborough, *Laws*. English translations: Attenborough, *Laws*.
Ger	The anonymous tract known as *Gerefa*. Edited: Liebermann, *Gesetze*. Online edition and translation available at <http://www.earlyenglishlaws. ac.uk>.
Geþyncðo	The anonymous legal text 'Geþyncðo'. Edited: Liebermann, *Gesetze*. English translation: *EHD* i, no. 51.
Grið	The anonymous legal text 'Grið'. Edited: Liebermann, *Gesetze*.
Hl	Laws of Hlothere and Eadric. Edited: Oliver, *Beginnings*; Liebermann, *Gesetze*; Attenborough, *Laws*. English translations: Oliver, *Beginnings*; Attenborough, *Laws*; *EHD* i, no. 30. Though Oliver, *Beginnings* introduced a new system of numbering the clauses, Liebermann's is retained here because of its usefulness for all previous editions.
Hn	*Leges Henrici Primi*. Edited: L. J. Downer, *Leges Henrici Primi* (Oxford, 1972); Liebermann, *Gesetze*. English translations: Downer, *Leges Henrici Primi*; *EHD* ii, no. 57.
Hu	The Hundred Ordinance. Edited: Liebermann, *Gesetze*; Robertson, *Laws*. English translations: Robertson, *Laws*; *EHD* i, no. 39.
In Cn	*Instituta Cnuti*. Edited: Liebermann, *Gesetze*.
Ine	Laws of Ine. Edited: Liebermann, *Gesetze*; Attenborough, *Laws*. English translations: Attenborough, *Laws*; *EHD* i, no. 32.
Leis Wl	*Leis Willelme*. Edited: Liebermann, *Gesetze*; Robertson, *Laws*. English translation: Robertson, *Laws*; *EHD* ii, no. 18.
Mirce	The anonymous legal text 'Mircna laga'. Edited: Liebermann, *Gesetze*. English translation: *EHD* i, no. 51.
Northu	Northumbrian Priests' Law. Edited: Liebermann, *Gesetze*. English translation: *EHD* i, no. 53.
Norðleod	The anonymous legal text 'Norðleoda laga'. Edited: Liebermann, *Gesetze*. English translation: *EHD* i, no. 51.
Ordal	The anonymous legal text 'Ordal'. Edited: Liebermann, *Gesetze*; Attenborough, *Laws*. English translation: Attenborough, *Laws*.
Quadr	*Quadripartitus*. Edited: Liebermann, *Gesetze*.
S	Anglo-Saxon charters are usually referred to by their 'Sawyer numbers', from P. H. Sawyer, ed., *Anglo-Saxon Charters: An Annotated List and Bibliography* (London, 1968). An updated version is now available online at <http://www.esawyer.org.uk>.
Wer	The anonymous legal text 'Wergeld'. Edited: Liebermann, *Gesetze*.

Wi   Laws of Wihtred. Edited: Oliver, *Beginnings*; Liebermann, *Gesetze*;
                            Attenborough, *Laws*. English translations: Oliver, *Beginnings*;
                            Attenborough, *Laws*; *EHD* i, no. 31. Though Oliver, *Beginnings*
                            introduced a new system of numbering the clauses, Liebermann's is
                            retained here because of its usefulness for all previous editions.

Wl art   The 'Ten Articles' of William the Conqueror. Edited: Liebermann,
                            Gesetze; Robertson, *Laws*. English translation: Robertson, *Laws*.

Introduction
Approaching Law and Order in the Early Middle Ages

LAW, ORDER, AND 'THE STATE'

It is probably the case that all traditions of law contain within them an implicit vision of good order. Although these visions are not always sharply defined and are subject to subtle changes over time, which can introduce inconsistencies, most individual laws can be understood as part of a broadly coherent framework of rules and categories which, in defining rightful and wrongful conduct, constitutes an idealized moral order.[1] The intellectual core of this book is an attempt to recover the vision of order that underlies England's early medieval legal tradition. Its fundamental argument is that we cannot properly comprehend early medieval law unless we do this; if we approach this period assuming that we know what law is for—the form of order it naturally aims to achieve—we will distort and misunderstand it. Recovering early medieval ideals of order requires us to pay close attention to the categories and priorities within our evidence, particularly our texts of laws themselves. These rather unfashionable texts may not be perfect sources for the reconstruction of behaviour— though given the scarcity and narrowness of our evidence for legal behaviour in the period, the tendency of modern scholarship to dismiss laws in this context seems short-sighted[2]—but they have a great deal to tell us about what good order meant to contemporaries and how they expected it to be maintained. This book's central premise is that Anglo-Saxon law will be much more readily comprehensible if we frame our understanding of it with reference to these contemporary (largely native and secular) ideals and try our utmost to avoid imposing conceptual frameworks derived from other places and periods.

---

[1] See Paul Dresch, 'Legalism, Anthropology and History: a View from the Part of Anthropology', in Paul Dresch and Hannah Skoda, eds., *Legalism: Anthropology and History* (Oxford, 2012), pp. 1–37; Donald R. Davis Jr, 'Rules, Culture and Imagination in Sanskrit Jurisprudence', in Paul Dresch and Judith Scheele, eds., *Legalism: Rules and Categories* (Oxford, 2015), pp. 29–52; Fernanda Pirie, *The Anthropology of Law* (Oxford, 2013), ch. 7.

[2] See, for example, Patrick Wormald, 'Introduction', in Wendy Davies and Paul Fouracre, eds., *The Settlement of Disputes in Early Medieval Europe* (Cambridge, 1986), pp. 1–5, at 3; Warren C. Brown and Piotr Górecki, 'What Conflict Means: The Making of Medieval Conflict Studies in the United States, 1970–2000', in Warren C. Brown and Piotr Górecki, eds., *Conflict in Medieval Europe: Changing Perspectives on Society and Culture* (Aldershot, 2003), pp. 1–35, at 7–9, 34–5; Chris Wickham, *Courts and Conflict in Twelfth-Century Tuscany* (Oxford, 2003), pp. 3–6.

Consciously or not, most historians approaching early medieval law come equipped with modern models. The most important is that of 'the state'. The legal systems of modern states are far from identical but they offer little variety in terms of the idealized visions of order implicit within them. There is a common set of ideas about the state's duty to maintain order by protecting its citizens from harm, by suppressing activities judged harmful to society generally, and by providing peaceful and fair mechanisms for the resolution of disputes between individuals or groups. The maintenance of order is the state's responsibility, not that of private citizens. States alone have the authority to establish laws, to make judgements about how those laws should be applied in specific cases, and to resort to violence so as to compel individuals to submit to such judgements. Importantly, from an early medieval perspective, the order that modern states maintain is non-violent. With a few minor exceptions, modern legal systems reserve legitimate violence to the state, formally prohibiting all significant violent acts by private citizens. This categorization of violence is not only a legal matter, it is embedded in our use of language: the very word 'violence' has strong connotations of illegitimacy. We generally accept that the state has a legitimate right to commit violent acts in the context of law enforcement as well as in warfare, but when speaking of acts of violence which we judge to have made a positive contribution to order we often avoid the word 'violence' entirely and resort to blander euphemisms—'the use of force', for example. In the modern world, law is something that states create and administer so as to maintain a fundamentally non-violent moral order.[3]

If historians have tended to bring modern assumptions about the nature and purpose of law with them as they approach the early Middle Ages, they have done so primarily because of the lack of established alternative frameworks. To take the most obvious example, the prominence of feuding in laws and other sources from the period is widely acknowledged, but interpreting it is problematic: how does one go about imagining a legal system that does not attempt to assert a state monopoly on legitimate violence? While modern anthropology offers multiple examples of feuding cultures, the models offered by such studies necessarily derive from the observation of activities formally prohibited by the states within which they occur. In contrast to the early medieval period, in the modern world violent feuding has to take place with minimal reference to, or even in direct opposition to, the formal legal structures of the state. Feuding is thus extra-legal almost by definition, and

[3] For the basic acceptance of this vision of the state by early medieval historians, see Chris Wickham, _Framing the Early Middle Ages: Europe and the Mediterranean, 400–800_ (Oxford, 2005), p. 57, where 'the centralisation of legitimate enforceable authority (justice and the army)' is one the key criteria identified. For its influence on the interpretation of Anglo-Saxon law, see Patrick Wormald, 'Giving God and King Their Due: Conflict and Its Regulation in the Early English State' repr. in and cited from Wormald, _Legal Culture in the Early Medieval West: Law as Text, Image and Experience_ (London, 1999), pp. 333–57, at 342. For debate about the appropriateness of the term 'state' in the medieval period, see Susan Reynolds, 'The Historiography of the Medieval State', in Michael Bentley, ed., _Companion to Historiography_ (London, 1997), pp. 117–38; Rees Davies, 'The Medieval State: The Tyranny of a Concept?', _Journal of Historical Sociology_ 16 (2003), 280–300; Susan Reynolds, 'There Were States in Medieval Europe: A Response to Rees Davies', _Journal of Historical Sociology_ 16 (2003), pp. 550–5.

strongly associated with what might reasonably, in some senses at least, be termed 'stateless' environments. Such modern ethnographic parallels are far from useless—through them we can see honour cultures in action and they offer us a way of thinking about order that does not depend on formal law and legal institutions[4]—but they cannot provide a model to help early medieval historians understand legitimate feuding *within* a legal system.[5] Thanks to the influence of anthropological models feuding is no longer written off as an entirely negative or illegitimate phenomenon, but—perhaps in part because of those models—it still tends to be treated as marginal to, or even entirely separate from, formal legal processes. Even Paul Hyams, who has done more than anyone to rehabilitate feuding as an important and relevant aspect of English legal history, represents aggrieved parties as having to *choose* between feuding and using legal structures.[6] The implicit assumption in most modern work is that early medieval kings tolerated the existence of this violent quasi-legal option because, like weak states in the modern world, they lacked the power to force their people to pursue their grievances through legal avenues.[7]

---

[4] Max Gluckman, 'Peace in the Feud', in Gluckman, *Custom and Conflict in Africa* (Oxford, 1955), pp. 1–26, has been highly influential; its analysis is based on E. E. Evans-Pritchard, *The Nuer: A Description of the Modes of Livelihood and Political Institutions of a Nilotic People* (Oxford, 1940), ch. 4. More modern examples, which have informed my thinking in this book, include Paul Dresch, *Tribes, Government and History in Yemen* (Oxford, 1989), chs. 2–4; Michael Gilsenan, *Lords of the Lebanese Marches: Violence and Narrative in an Arab Society* (Berkeley, 1996), chs. 10–14; Fernanda Pirie, 'Order, Individualism and Responsibility: Contrasting Dynamics on the Tibetan Plateau', in Keebet von Benda-Beckmann and Fernanda Pirie, eds., *Order and Disorder: Anthropological Perspectives* (Oxford, 2007), pp. 54–73.

[5] This problem is noted in Simon Roberts, 'The Study of Disputes: Anthropological Perspectives', in John Bossy, ed., *Disputes and Settlements: Law and Human Relations in the West* (Cambridge, 1983), pp. 1–24, at 9: 'anthropologists should find very interesting what [social historians] have to say . . . about the treatment of feud where central government has been established. On the whole anthropologists have assumed that fighting is seldom an approved mode of handling disputes under central government. Rulers tend to object strongly to sustained fighting among their subjects, to present themselves as authoritative agents of dispute settlement and to do their best to make sure they are treated as such. Where significant resort to retaliatory violence and fighting between groups has been found in association with central government, this has been taken as an indication of the uncertain extent to which government is established.'

[6] Indeed, he does so in the course of criticizing extra- or anti-legal interpretations of feuding: Paul R. Hyams, *Rancor and Reconciliation in Medieval England* (Ithaca, 2003), p. 4. A similar situation, in which the juxtaposition of official legal process and extra-judicial conflict resolution frames an analysis which undermines this distinction, is visible in P. S. Barnwell, 'The Early Frankish *Mallus*: Its Nature, Participants and Practices', in Aliki Pantos and Sarah Semple, eds., *Assembly Places and Practices in Medieval Europe* (Dublin, 2004), pp. 233–46 at 239–41. See also, Lisi Oliver, *The Body Legal in Barbarian Law* (Toronto, 2011), pp. 46–7.

[7] Most recently and authoritatively, see John Hudson, *The Oxford History of the Laws of England*, vol. 2: *871–1216* (Oxford, 2012), pp. 11, 171–5, 395–6. Feuding appears here as a violent 'impulse' which could be 'channelled' by kings who wished to punish wrongdoing, but which otherwise was only 'permitted within certain narrowing limits'. Hudson does not specify when those narrowing limits became a complete prohibition, but he notes the scarcity of evidence for extended feuds after 1066 and does not discuss feuding at all in the Angevin period. The implication seems to be that this practice died out under increasingly strong post-Conquest kings, and—perhaps more significantly—that it had been so marginal to legitimate legal practice in the first place that its passing scarcely warrants legal historians' attention. A more detailed but fundamentally similar picture, explicitly linking the suppression of feud to increasing royal power, is painted in John Hudson, 'Feud, Vengeance and

In the modern world, then, the status of feuding and the power of the state are clearly connected issues, and historians have tended to assume the same applies to the early medieval period. Frederic William Maitland regarded feuding as a characteristic feature of law up to, and indeed beyond, the Norman Conquest. Though 'the law'—at times basically synonymous with 'the state' in Maitland's usage— naturally had a theoretical monopoly on the legitimate use of violence, in practice kings were incapable of enforcing this, so he envisaged the law 'conceding' to the relatives of slain men 'the right to revenge themselves'.[8] For Maitland, the evidence for the acceptance of feuding in Anglo-Saxon law was not problematic: this was simply 'a time when law was weak'.[9] However, the twentieth century saw a shift towards increasingly optimistic assessments of the strength of late Anglo-Saxon government, and it is striking how this seems to have affected assumptions about feuding. Rather than examining the evidence in detail, historians have tended to reason that so strongly governed a kingdom as pre-Conquest England must have been powerful enough to outlaw feuding. The first signs of this are surprisingly early: Julius Goebel asserted that this was the case in a brief aside in 1937, offering no evidence to justify his view.[10] Naomi Hurnard did something similar in 1949, building a far-reaching argument against the existence of significant aristocratic legal privileges (and thus in favour of the centralization of legal power in the hands of the king) on the assumption that homicide was a 'royal crime' in the eleventh century. She clearly felt this assumption was unlikely to provoke controversy, as she made only a cursory effort to justify it in a footnote.[11] Her instinct proved to be correct: her seemingly radical departure from the orthodoxy of the late nineteenth century drew no significant criticism.[12]

Violence in England from the Tenth to the Twelfth Centuries', in Belle S. Tuten and Tracey A. Billado, eds., *Feud, Violence and Practice: Essays in Medieval Studies in Honour of Stephen D. White* (Farnham, 2010), pp. 29–53, especially at 51–2. My intention here is to establish that historians generally have tended to think about feuding in this way; I am focusing on Hudson because of his work's great authority: it is the best guide available to current historiographical 'common sense' assumptions. This collectively constructed 'common sense', which until very recently underpinned my own thought on this issue (and doubtless still does on many others) is the target of my critique here, not any specific historian's articulation of it. See T. B. Lambert, 'Theft, Homicide and Crime in Late Anglo-Saxon Law', *Past and Present* 214 (2012), pp. 3–43 at 42.

[8] Frederick Pollock and Frederic William Maitland, *The History of English Law Before the Time of Edward I*, 2 vols. (2nd edn, Cambridge, 1898), ii, p. 472.

[9] Ibid., p. 471. For some perceptive comments on Maitland's understanding of the nature and purpose of law, see Paul R. Hyams, 'Maitland and the Rest of Us', in John Hudson, ed., *The History of English Law: Centenary Essays on 'Pollock and Maitland'* (Proceedings of the British Academy 89; Oxford, 1996), pp. 215–41, especially at 234, 238.

[10] Julius Goebel, *Felony and Misdemeanor: A Study in the History of Criminal Law* (2nd edn, Philadelphia, 1976), p. 436.

[11] Naomi Hurnard, 'The Anglo-Norman Franchises', *English Historical Review* 64 (1949), pp. 289–327 and 433–60, at 300.

[12] The most direct critique is Helen M. Cam, 'The Evolution of the Mediaeval English Franchise', *Speculum* 32 (1957), pp. 427–42, at 431. Cam points out that Hurnard uses the term criminal without defining its meaning within eleventh-century justice, and points out its incompatibility with the legitimacy of feuding. However, at the same time she implicitly accepts Hurnard's argument that homicide was punished by the king by 1066, characterizing the broader case founded on that argument

In the late twentieth century the strength of late Anglo-Saxon government became a major historiographical theme. James Campbell and Patrick Wormald, in particular, pointedly and forcefully argued that the late Anglo-Saxon kingdom was sufficiently centralized and powerful to deserve the label 'state'.[13] Though the appropriateness of the term itself can be debated, there can be no question that eleventh-century England conforms to our expectations of a state in a number of important ways: it was divided up into a coherent administrative hierarchy of shires and hundreds; it was capable of imposing heavy taxes on its population and for a time did so annually, using the proceeds to fund a standing army; it had a system for maintaining a standardized currency through periodic re-coinages; and its laws show considerable ingenuity in their attempts to identify, convict, and severely punish thieves.[14] The general impression that late Anglo-Saxon kings had a sophisticated administrative system at their disposal and were capable of imposing harsh burdens on their people made it very difficult to imagine that 'the state' (or whatever term is judged appropriate) was weak in this period, lacking the power to force people to resolve their disputes through legal avenues. And if the late Anglo-Saxon state was capable of suppressing feud, is it really plausible to imagine that it failed to do so?

A strong indication that there is a flaw in this logic is that the evidence relating specifically to feuding seems to contradict it: late Anglo-Saxon laws accept the legitimacy of feuding reasonably frequently. Cnut's laws, for instance, are perfectly explicit in stating that even priests could be legitimate targets for vengeance killings.[15] In 1997 Wormald tackled this issue head-on, constructing a much more compelling case than Hurnard's for the view that such passages are deceptive, and that the state had in fact prohibited and punished homicide outright from the mid-tenth century.[16] His case is too richly nuanced to summarize here (it is discussed in more detail and refuted in Chapter 4, alongside Hurnard's earlier argument),[17] but it is important to note that he framed his analysis explicitly in terms of statehood and statelessness, envisaging these two modern models as occupying opposite ends of a spectrum.[18] This spectrum maps onto the common-place historiographical distinction between 'horizontal' and 'vertical' justice.[19]

---

as 'good' and perhaps also implying that considerable steps had been taken in outlawing feuding between Alfred's time and the Norman Conquest.

[13] In particular, James Campbell, 'The Late Anglo-Saxon State: A Maximum View' repr. in and cited from Campbell, *The Anglo-Saxon State* (London, 2000), pp. 1–30; Patrick Wormald, 'Pre-Modern 'State' and 'Nation': Definite or Indefinite?', in Stuart Airlie, Walter Pohl, and Helmut Reimitz, eds., *Staat im frühen Mittelalter* (Vienna, 2006), pp. 179–89; Wormald, 'God and King'.

[14] The essential overview is now George Molyneaux, *The Formation of the English Kingdom in the Tenth Century* (Oxford, 2015), which reviews the extensive literature and offers a critical reassessment.

[15] I Cn 5:2b.   [16] Wormald, 'God and King', pp. 331–42.

[17] See Chapter 4, pp. 191–2, 169–9.   [18] Wormald, 'God and King', p. 336.

[19] See, for example, Jay Paul Gates and Nicole Marafioti, 'Introduction: Capital and Corporal Punishment in Anglo-Saxon England', in Jay Paul Gates and Nicole Marafioti, eds., *Capital and Corporal Punishment in Anglo-Saxon England* (Woodbridge, 2014), pp. 1–16 at 9–10; Paul R. Hyams, 'Afterword: Neither Unnatural nor Wholly Negative: The Future of Medieval Vengeance', in Susanna A. Throop and Paul R. Hyams, eds., *Vengeance in the Middle Ages: Emotion, Religion and Feud* (Farnham, 2010), pp. 203–20 at 218; and (questioning the usefulness of the distinction) Alice

On one end there are stateless societies, characterized by the (horizontal) 'kin-based' justice associated with feuding; on the other there were states, characterized by a (vertical) 'top-down' approach to crime and punishment, in which (vertical) bonds of lordship were dominant and (horizontal) kinship structures of marginal importance. Wormald argued that the late Anglo-Saxon evidence suggests an overall picture that is ambitiously and impressively punitive—overwhelmingly vertical—and he presented arguments that sought to minimize more horizontal themes such as feuding. This general picture, he in effect argued, is so compelling that we ought to accept some very limited hints that homicide was in practice punished by the state, in spite of the apparent acceptance of feuding in certain laws from the period.[20] Again, this proved remarkably uncontroversial. Although Hyams directly criticized Wormald's attempts to minimize the significance of feud in the period, he did not challenge the central conclusion.[21]

I have dwelt on the historiography of feuding here not just because the issue is important—it matters a great deal that we understand it as central to legitimate legal practice rather than as some sort of marginal and undesirable folk custom—but because it provides a clear example of the influence of the model of the modern state.[22] Widely accepted assumptions about the legal status of feuding changed radically between Maitland's day and Wormald's, but this change did not arise from detailed analysis of the evidence for feuding. Attitudes shifted largely without debate and roughly in line with assessments of the general capabilities of Anglo-Saxon government. This is a striking illustration of modern assumptions about the nature and purpose of law: it is something created and administered by states with the goal of realizing a non-violent ideal of order. If we accept that all states naturally want to prohibit feuding, and that the only reason a state would fail to do this is its own weakness, assessments of the Anglo-Saxon kingdom's generic 'strength' become relevant to the question of whether it outlawed feud. Evidence of the centralization of power in matters unrelated to violence, and indeed unrelated to law, thus seems to support the conclusion that feuding was illegal. Conversely,

Taylor, 'Crime Without Punishment: Medieval Scottish Law in Comparative Perspective', *Anglo-Norman Studies* 35 (2013), pp. 287–304 at 288–90. Daniela Fruscione, 'Beginnings and Legitimation of Punishment in Early Anglo-Saxon Legislation from the Seventh to the Ninth Century', in Gates and Marafioti, *Capital and Corporal Punishment*, pp. 34–47 at 35, sets up essentially the same opposition, postulating a 'progression between two methods of dealing with offences: restitutive, which is typical of family-centred societies; and punitive, which is typical of civilizations where a central power is emerging'.

[20] This interpretation is most explicit in Wormald's 'God and King', but the analytical framework underpinning it, in effect juxtaposing horizontal and vertical justice, is a broad theme in his scholarship. This is most notable in '"Inter Cetera Bona Genti Suae": Law-Making and Peace-Keeping in the Earliest English Kingdoms', repr. in and cited from Wormald, *Legal Culture*, pp. 179–98, especially at 194–8 (with the dichotomy between horizontal and vertical justice referenced at 196) and Wormald, 'Charters, Law and the Settlement of Disputes in Anglo-Saxon England' repr. in and cited from Wormald, *Legal Culture*, pp. 289–310, especially at 306–7.

[21] Hyams, *Rancor and Reconciliation*, ch. 3.

[22] Another example is the assumption that formal legal structures represent the state's administrative power. This is addressed in Chapters 3 and 6. An excellent discussion is Matthew Innes, *State and Society in the Early Middle Ages: The Middle Rhine Valley, 400–1000* (Cambridge, 2000), ch. 7.

attempts to argue for the continued legitimacy of feuding are easily misconstrued as arguments for more general governmental 'weakness'.

The important point here is not that some specific historians' arguments are mistaken; it is that a fundamentally anachronistic interpretative framework, inherited from the nineteenth century, still shapes our understanding of Anglo-Saxon law. I suggest this needs to be replaced. We cannot assume early medieval law was attempting to realize a non-violent idealized order similar to that of modern law, nor that the early medieval state's role in the maintenance of order necessarily approximates that of the modern state. We need to begin with an open mind on these issues, to investigate our evidence for early medieval law without assuming we already know the broad outlines of what it was aiming to achieve. This book is an attempt to do that. It aims to show that implicit in our evidence from the period is a coherent alternative to the model of the modern state. If we pay close attention to the laws themselves we find a different way of imagining a legal system, one characteristic feature of which is that rather than being in tension (as the conventional dichotomy between vertical and horizontal justice would suggest) harsh royal punishment and legitimate feuding are understood to play complementary roles in the maintenance of order.

THE APPROACH

Three features of this book's approach are worth highlighting. First, I have tried to respect basic chronology, constructing my arguments by starting with earliest evidence and working forwards from there. Later evidence often offers more detail than early sources can supply, and it is sometimes reasonable (and always tempting) to use it to fill in blanks. I have not shunned such back-projections entirely but I have tried to use them cautiously, using early sources to establish as clear picture as possible *before* turning to later evidence to see if it can enrich this picture without substantially altering its outlines. Second, I have tried as much as possible to derive important concepts and categories from the evidence, rather than imposing modern ones. This means beginning with basic questions about the shape of our evidence. Why do laws from this period discuss some subjects and not others? Did contemporaries distinguish between different categories of law? What offences did kings try to punish? What links those offences? Ultimately, the answers to these questions will allow us to build up a picture of the ideals implicit in our evidence—of the moral order which England's early medieval laws were aiming to uphold. Third, I have tried to think through the practicalities of law in detail, even when the evidence makes this difficult. I have not, that is to say, confined my attention to those aspects of legal practice which we can see in our very limited records of actual cases, but instead have tried to build up a broad understanding of legal practice by, again, starting with basic questions. How were compensation payments enforced? What was the point of bringing a legal case to an assembly? How did assemblies reach their final judgments? How did kings ensure their legislation was transmitted to and applied by local assemblies? Even if there is little evidence to go on, interrogating practicalities in this way is valuable in that it keeps our understanding of law grounded in participants' decision-making. These three features are closely interrelated. They all stem from the same desire to understand the Anglo-Saxon legal order on its own terms and not impose modern or later medieval expectations on early medieval thoughts and actions. All three are both rooted in recent historiographical trends and reactions against certain aspects of them.

A cautious approach to retrospective inferences drawn from later evidence is perhaps the most fundamental of these. On one level, this no more than basic historical method: it is obvious enough that it is dangerous to start from the assumption that any source is a reliable guide to the realities of a century—sometimes several centuries—earlier. However, it is often the case in this period that early evidence on a given subject is sparse and difficult to interpret whereas later sources are comparatively plentiful and seemingly well understood, and historians of Anglo-Saxon England have a well-established tradition of working backwards from later evidence. Maitland, famously, approached the period by grounding himself in the known (or, as he put it, 'the knowable') of Domesday Book and from there exploring the unknown past that lay 'beyond'.[23] The enduring value of his work is a testament to the potential of this approach when used cautiously, but it ought not to blind us to its dangers. George Molyneaux's recent study of late Anglo-Saxon administrative structures has highlighted these very effectively, and demonstrated that scrupulously grounding analysis in contemporary source material can yield a much more precise sense not just of the timing of important changes, but also of their significance.[24]

Too great a reliance on late evidence can naturally lead to the unwarranted back-projection of specific ideas and institutions, but the greatest problem with a broadly retrospective approach is that it militates against interpretations rooted in contemporary concepts. Beginning with later conditions and working backwards means taking an interpretative framework appropriate to a later period and trying to fit earlier evidence into it, making whatever minor adjustments seem warranted, and in theory discarding it entirely when the evidence ceases to fit. The problem is that this process colours the way we read the early evidence. If ambiguities can be resolved in a way which makes them fit with the later interpretative framework, such convenient readings inevitably seem the most plausible.[25] It seems to make

[23] Frederic William Maitland, *Domesday Book and Beyond: Three Essays in the Early History of England* (Cambridge, 1897), p. xix.

[24] Molyneaux, *Formation*.

[25] When it is noted that later conceptual categories do not fit earlier evidence, the natural response is a minor adjustment to the accepted framework, assuming that everything was basically the same except for the absence of a particular distinction, such as that between crime and tort or that between fact and law. Cumulatively, arguments of this type create the impression that before the explicit articulation of various important learned distinctions people tended not to classify things at all, and that one of the characteristic features of the early medieval legal world was the absence of important conceptual categories. This is a particularly striking feature of Hyams's scholarship, with its emphasis on 'undifferentiated wrongs' and 'undifferentiated procedures' (see *Rancor and Reconciliation*, pp. 108, 218–24), but it is a more general pattern. See, for example, the way difficulties with projecting the category 'crime' backwards from the late twelfth century are dealt with in John Hudson, *The Formation of the English Common Law: Law and Society in England from the Norman Conquest to Magna Carta*

sense to regard more problematic evidence, providing it is not too abundant, as a minor exception, and thus of peripheral significance. Moreover, in practice backward-looking approaches tend to have horizons beyond which they are not pursued—the assumption of broad continuity pushes really fundamental change backwards, so it always seems to take place just before the period under consideration—meaning that serious problems with the interpretative frameworks employed rarely have to be confronted.[26]

Traditions of retrogressive analysis are common throughout early medieval history—it is perhaps inevitable whenever a period rich in evidence follows a period of scarcity—but it is a particularly pronounced and problematic feature of scholarship on Anglo-Saxon law. English legal history is a sub-discipline that has fundamentally been shaped by the concerns of lawyers interested in the common law, which took shape in the late twelfth and thirteenth centuries. The need to take serious account of the Anglo-Saxon past within the grand narrative of the common law's origins is not necessarily obvious, although Wormald in particular did much to press the late Anglo-Saxon period's claims to relevance.[27] The important point here is not whether he was right to do so, but that that this generally is the context within which Anglo-Saxon law is interpreted in this legal historical tradition. Wormald, in fact, is exceptional for engaging seriously (if relatively briefly) with both Æthelberht's laws and those of the late seventh and early eighth century. English laws from before Alfred's reign (871–99) generally lie beyond the horizons

(London, 1996), p. 56. It almost certainly is the case that the emergence of a learned legal profession led to much sharper conceptual distinctions being drawn in the thirteenth century than had been the case in, say, the tenth—Susan Reynolds, *Kingdoms and Communities in Western Europe, 900–1300* (2nd edn, Oxford, 1997), chs. 1–2, and Reynolds, 'The Emergence of Professional Law in the Long Twelfth Century', *Law and History Review* 21 (2003), pp. 347–66, provide wide-ranging discussion— and it is of course valuable to pin down what these new (or newly sharp) distinctions were and when they emerged. But although doing so reveals a great deal about the far-reaching changes of the late twelfth and thirteenth centuries, the knowledge that distinctions prominent in other times and places were absent can only contribute so much to understanding how people thought in the Anglo-Saxon period. Crucially, it does not follow that they lacked conceptual categories of a more fuzzy-edged sort, nor is there any reason to assume that categories with hazy boundaries are less important than the finely honed distinctions produced by intellectuals' debates. In broad social and cultural terms, at least, the opposite is surely more likely.

[26] Hence the obscurity surrounding the issue of when feuding was first prohibited in English law: until Wormald grasped the nettle in 1997 (in 'God and King') the literature had no clear line on this fundamental issue. Hudson, *Oxford History* still does not, as is noted above, p. 9, n. 7. For an attempt to pin it down, see T. B. Lambert, 'Protection, Feud and Royal Power: Violence and Its Regulation in English Law, c.850–c.1250' (University of Durham PhD thesis, 2009), ch. 4. The discussion of jurisdiction in Chapter 7, pp. 301–6, provides another example of this process at work.

[27] Unfortunately he did not do so in published form, but his core arguments are discussed and critiqued in John Hudson, '*The Making of English Law* and Varieties of Legal History', in Stephen Baxter et al., eds., *Early Medieval Studies in Memory of Patrick Wormald* (Farnham, Surrey, 2009), pp. 421–32. Wormald's unpublished papers have recently been made available online, and they render the trajectory of his argument much clearer: Patrick Wormald, *Papers Preparatory to the Making of English Law: King Alfred to the Twelfth Century*, vol. 2: *From God's Law to Common Law*, ed. Stephen Baxter and John Hudson (University of London, 2014) <http://www.earlyenglishlaws.ac.uk/reference/ wormald/>, especially chs. 7b, 15, and appendix 1. In his draft introduction, for example, he characterized his second volume as an exploration of 'the *prima facie* relevance for English law's later history of the vigorous tradition of English royal legislation between 890 to 1020' (pp. 4–5).

of mainstream legal history, as is strikingly illustrated by the fact that the recently published earliest volume on secular law in the monumental *Oxford History of the Laws of England* series covers the period 871–1216. This is a sensible chronological range within which to analyse the emergence of the common law, but it is problematic for those wishing to understand Anglo-Saxon law on its own terms.[28] It is not simply that the development of law in the earlier period both deserves attention in its own right and is crucial context for developments under Alfred and his successors; it is also that the tradition of studying late Anglo-Saxon law as part of a development leading towards the common law distorts our analytical priorities, focusing attention on ideas and institutions relevant to that development in a way that need not align with their contemporary significance.[29] The risk is that we take a set of questions formulated for the late twelfth century and apply them to late Anglo-Saxon evidence, rather than reflecting on whether these questions are the most revealing ones we could be asking, or indeed whether the conceptual framework which formed them is appropriate at all.[30]

My point is not that historians have been blind to the hazards of retrogressive analysis; the potential problems are obvious and those who deliberately adopt this approach tend to make significant efforts to counteract them. The issue is that such conscious efforts are necessarily concentrated where writers are aware that an-achronism is a danger, and there are so many ways that later frameworks and assumptions might shape one's thinking that even the most diligent analyst could not possibly anticipate all of them. It would be hubris to imagine that this book can avoid the problem, but it does seem to me that our best chance of securing some level of immunity lies in beginning with our very earliest evidence. The laws of King Æthelberht of Kent were written down in the late sixth or early seventh century but, as we shall see, are best understood as a snapshot of an existing pre-Christian oral tradition. It may be possible to analyse the eleventh and even tenth centuries within a late twelfth-century conceptual framework without stretching that framework to breaking point, but for the sixth century the anachronism would

---

[28] Hudson acknowledges this problem in general terms ('To talk only in terms of continuing lines and dead-ends is to present legal development as metaphorical genealogy rather than plausible history'—*Oxford History*, p. 251) and makes an effort to compensate by highlighting features of late Anglo-Saxon law which did not persist in later centuries. Nonetheless, this quotation comes in the context of a section on 'the place of the late Anglo-Saxon period in the development of English law', and the book's blurb in particular makes it clear that the work as a whole was envisaged as an account of the common law's emergence: 'This is the first full-length treatment since the late nineteenth century of all aspects of the early development of the English common law'; 'this book examines the particular contributions of Anglo-Saxon period to the development of English law'; 'Laying out in exhaustive detail the origins of the English common law through the ninth to the early thirteenth centuries, this book will be essential reading for all legal historians and a vital work of reference for academics, students and practitioners'.

[29] For instance, Chapter 5, pp. 210–13, argues that Wormald's interest in identifying the pre-Conquest roots of common law felony led him to overstate the ideological significance of loyalty to the king in a late Anglo-Saxon context.

[30] A case in point is the long-running historiographical controversy over whether jurisdiction was commonly held by lords or reserved to the king in the late Anglo-Saxon period: Chapter 7, pp. 301–6, argues that 'jurisdiction' was not a contemporary concept.

be hard to ignore. It simply does not work to project the state's exclusive responsibility to create and administer law so as to maintain a non-violent moral order onto Æthelberht's Kent.[31] In other areas of Europe this is more plausible because of the considerable continuities with the Roman past, but Roman Britain was unusual for its catastrophic economic collapse. The currently dominant strand in the scholarship sees this as resulting in complete disintegration of political structures and social hierarchies, such that the Germanic migrants of the mid- to late fifth century entered a materially very poor but essentially egalitarian world of subsistence farmers, from which kings and associated social elites subsequently developed.[32] It would be truly remarkable if late sixth-century Kentish society regarded its kings as nascent versions of 'the state', expecting them to be responsible for the maintenance of order; its laws certainly do not suggest this when taken on their own terms. If we engage seriously with our earliest evidence, in short, the inappropriateness of later assumptions rapidly becomes apparent: our methodology *forces* us to reassess the nature and purpose of law.

The other two aspects of this book's methodology highlighted above follow from this. Rethinking our approach to law means questioning both conventional conceptual categories and the terms in which we describe legal practices and structures. There is no other way to do this than by testing these ideas against sources from the period, starting with basic questions and building up from there. To claim that this approach is in some way specifically anthropological would be both inaccurate (so basic a methodology can hardly be pinned to a single discipline) and, as an exaggerated claim to exotic interdisciplinarity, somewhat pretentious. Nonetheless, anthropologists have a strong tradition of subjecting the conceptual frameworks scholars impose on the people they study to critical scrutiny, and of making sense of their chosen societies by building locally important categories into their analyses. Though I am sure other disciplines could provide equally good examples,[33] I did in fact spend a considerable amount of time in the company of anthropologists in the period when this book was taking shape and I am conscious that this feature of its analysis owes much to their influence. This debt needs to be acknowledged, but it should also be noted that admiration for anthropology's rigorous approach to conceptual frameworks and respect for local categories does not imply adherence to specific theories or doctrines. Standard narratives of the development of the historiography of early medieval legal culture tend to emphasize two key anthropological influences: Max Gluckman's theory of 'peace in the feud', which was famously taken up by his Manchester colleague Michael Wallace-Hadrill, and the enthusiastic adoption of a 'processual approach' to studying dispute settlement

---

[31] Though something along these lines is, perhaps, visible in A. W. B. Simpson, 'The Laws of Ethelbert' in M.S. Green et al., eds., *On the Laws and Customs of England: Essays in Honor of Samuel E. Thorne* (Chapel Hill, 1981), pp. 3–17.

[32] See discussion in Chapter 1, pp. 27–8. Egalitarianism should not be exaggerated: free men may have been broadly equal but we should not forget that they could own slaves.

[33] Early medieval history certainly can. An excellent example is T. M. Charles-Edwards, 'Kinship, Status and the Origin of the Hide', *Past and Present* 56 (1972), pp. 3–33.

from the early 1980s onwards.[34] While each of these had a positive impact, stimulating historians to engage with legal themes in new ways, neither is uncontroversial among anthropologists—both have recently been subjected to scathing criticism by Paul Dresch[35]—and other than as background influences neither has been a significant factor in my thinking here. Indeed, insofar as the 'processual approach' carries with it a dogmatic hostility to the analysis of explicit rules, I find it unhelpful.

THE SOURCES

This book's basic method, then, is to start with our earliest sources and use them to build up an interpretation of law and order rooted in both contemporary ideas and practices. A potential objection to this is that this early evidence cannot bear the strain thus placed on it: it cannot provide reliable answers to the basic questions about ideas and practices we need to ask, so the attempt to establish a new framework for thinking about law in this period will necessarily fall at the first hurdle. Source material of most types is scarce for the first few centuries covered by this book, and throughout the period the bulk of the evidence bearing on most aspects of legal culture and practice takes the form of written laws. Although significant cracks have begun to appear recently,[36] the clear consensus among early medieval historians for at least the last three decades—influenced by a number of intersecting intellectual trends including the anthropologists' 'processual approach'—has been that laws are deeply problematic evidence because the considerations that actually govern people's thoughts and actions tend to be different from those expressed in explicit rules. To have any real hope of understanding legal culture and practice we need access to sources which provide examples of legal behaviour.[37]

[34] For the influence of peace in the feud see Stephen D. White, '"The Peace in the Feud" Revisited: Feuds in the Peace in Medieval European Feuds', in Conrad Leyser and Kate Cooper, eds., *Making Early Medieval Societies: Conflict and Belonging in the Latin West, 300–1200* (Cambridge, 2016), pp. 220–43. Also: Hyams, *Rancor and Reconciliation*, 14–16 (esp. n. 31) and Wormald, 'Frederic William Maitland and the Earliest English Law' repr. in and cited from Wormald, *Legal Culture*, pp. 45–69, at 63. Specifically on Gluckman and Wallace-Hadrill, see Ian Wood, '"The Bloodfeud of the Franks"': a Historiographical Legend', *Early Medieval Europe* 14 (2006), pp. 489–504. On the processual approach, see Roberts, 'The Study of Disputes'; John L. Comaroff and Simon Roberts, *Rules and Processes: The Cultural Logic of Dispute in an African Context* (Chicago, 1981); Brown and Górecki, 'What Conflict Means', pp. 7–9.
[35] Dresch, 'Legalism, Anthropology and History', pp. 3–15 (especially at p. 9, n. 15: 'we should all be better off if we admitted that Gluckman's idea is not coherent'; and p. 11: 'talk of 'what really happened' omits the fact that the world is classified morally by those involved, who are aware in some degree of what they are doing.')
[36] See in particular Alice Taylor, '*Lex Scripta* and the Problem of Enforcement: Anglo-Saxon, Scottish and Welsh Law Compared', in Judith Scheele and Fernanda Pirie, eds., *Legalism: Community and Justice* (Oxford, 2014), pp. 47–75; Alice Rio, 'Introduction', in Alice Rio, ed., *Law, Custom, and Justice in Late Antiquity and the Early Middle Ages: Proceedings of the 2008 Byzantine Colloquium* (London, 2011), pp. 1–22; Matthew Innes, 'Charlemagne, Justice and Written Law', in Rio, *Law, Custom, and Justice*, pp. 155–203.
[37] See, for example, Wormald, 'Introduction', pp. 1–5, at 3; Brown and Górecki, 'What Conflict Means', pp. 7–8; Wickham, *Courts and Conflict*, pp. 3–6.

Indeed, as Chris Wickham explains, the relative weakness of early medieval states exacerbates the problem, as we have even less reason than usual to believe that the rules articulated in normative texts were actually imposed on the ground.

> The regionalization of social development, joined to the weakness of most states and external powers, permitted a notable fluidity in most of our local societies. Of course, even the rigidities of the late empire did not prevent flexibility of practice, as has been true of every society in history, no matter how regulated. But the late Roman state did at least legislate to keep people in their place . . . Flexibility thus marked the early middle ages by comparison both with preceding and with subsequent periods. It makes our task harder in many ways, but also more interesting: it forces us to look at social practice on every occasion, rather than simply at rules—which tell us little enough in any period, but which are close to meaningless as a guide to real social behaviour in ours.[38]

If we were to accept this line this book's entire enterprise would be hopeless. We have very few sources which allow us to construct narratives of legal practice before the tenth century, and even after that point those which do exist are patently unrepresentative. They focus heavily on land disputes involving the ecclesiastical institutions that recorded them, with a small minority of narratives recounting the misdeeds of secular lords who themselves held legal privileges (and whose forfeited lands and privileges ultimately came into the possession of churches which kept the relevant written records). Even in the later Anglo-Saxon period, then, if we accept conventional wisdom and reject laws, the best we can hope for is a partial understanding of some aspects of late Anglo-Saxon elite legal culture and practice. The only way to expand our field of vision is to examine how people behaved in a later, better-documented age and project it backwards.[39] Starting at the beginning *and* taking a holistic approach seems an impossible combination.

My own view is that laws in general are much richer sources than conventional wisdom would suggest, and that a great deal of value can be teased out of them if we approach them sensitively and imaginatively. Rejecting laws because they provide an idealistic and hence distorted picture of real-life behaviour—because they prescribe how the world ought to be rather than describing it as it actually is— strikes me as short-sighted. That early medieval historians have tended to do this is somewhat odd, as while this trend took place they also came to embrace other types of evidence which had previously been rejected on similar grounds, turning to the analysis of entirely fictional or partially fictionalized sources and skilfully drawing out the concepts, values, and assumptions implicit in them.[40] Though perhaps it is

---

[38] Wickham, *Framing*, p. 830.

[39] This is essentially the message of Hudson, *Formation*, p. 57.

[40] Some examples: T. M. Charles-Edwards, 'Honour and Status in some Irish and Welsh Prose Tales', *Ériu* 29 (1978), pp. 123–41; William Ian Miller, *Bloodtaking and Peacemaking: Feud, Law and Society in Saga Iceland* (Chicago, 1990); Wendy Davies, 'Adding Insult to Injury: Power, Property and Immunities in Early Medieval Wales', in Wendy Davies and Paul Fouracre, eds., *Property and Power in the Early Middle Ages* (Cambridge, 1995), pp. 137–64; Stephen D. White, 'Kinship and Lordship in Early Medieval England: The Story of Cynewulf and Cyneheard', *Viator* 20 (1989), pp. 1–18; Stephen D. White, 'Protection, Warranty, and Vengeance in *La Chanson De Roland*', in T. B. Lambert and

not immediately obvious, laws can be just as abundant as literature in this regard, and it is possible to use them in a similarly broad and imaginative way. That is, just as we can fruitfully analyse fictional narratives without fretting about the fact that the events they describe never actually took place, so too can we analyse laws without agonizing about the extent to which they were enforced and obeyed.[41]

It is important to note that we are often reasonably well informed about the contexts in which laws were produced. Each set of laws needs to be assessed on its own merits, of course. The circumstances surrounding them can vary considerably, but many of them contain prologues explaining that their contents represent the decisions of a particular king in conjunction with an assembly of leading noblemen, and well over a century of rigorous editorial scholarship has confirmed that most of these statements are broadly trustworthy.[42] Not all our texts can be pinned to specific reigns or safely be linked to an assembly context in this way, and even for those which can much remains uncertain about how our written record relates to the actual business conducted in the assemblies they purport to record. Nevertheless, we have good reason to think that our law texts represent part of the discourse of great royal assemblies—that the laws as we have them would have made sense to the aristocrats present, many of whom may well have participated in formal and informal discussions about them even if they did not directly shape what was written down and preserved. The access to this oral assembly discourse provided by the written discourse of the surviving laws is, clearly, indirect—mediated by the perspective of our texts' original authors, by the generic conventions that shaped their writing, and possibly by changes introduced by subsequent copyists—but it is valuable access nonetheless.

Thus contextualized, the discourse of the laws can be interrogated productively. It is a discourse which contains both prescriptive and descriptive elements, and while it is true that the former tend to dominate this need not be understood as an insurmountable obstacle. Indeed, it can be regarded as a significant analytical opportunity. For precisely the reasons Wickham outlines, we can never safely assume that the rules prescribed by laws in this period were obeyed or enforced,

---

David Rollason, eds., *Peace and Protection in the Middle Ages* (Toronto, 2009), pp. 155–67; Peter S. Baker, *Honour, Exchange and Violence in Beowulf* (Cambridge, 2013).

[41] It should be noted that my objections to the blanket rejection of laws are very close to those articulated in T. M. Charles-Edwards, *Early Irish and Welsh Kinship* (Oxford, 1993), pp. 3–20. Indeed, swimming against the historiographical tide of the last few decades, Charles-Edwards's scholarship has repeatedly demonstrated that laws, sensitively analysed, have the potential to provide invaluable insights. It is also noteworthy that the use of laws has been less controversial for traditionally 'non-legal' topics. There is a strong tradition, for example, of using the laws to analyse Anglo-Saxon assumptions about gender roles: for example, Carole Hough, 'Women and the Law in Seventh-Century England' repr. in and cited from Carole Hough, *An Ald Recht: Essays on Anglo-Saxon Law* (Newcastle upon Tyne, 2014), pp. 46–72; Henrietta Leyser, *Medieval Women* (London, 1995), ch. 3. Reticence about using laws to study basic categories and assumptions, paradoxically, applies mainly to legal themes. See also the more recent discussions cited above, p. 12, n. 36.

[42] The essential reference points are Felix Liebermann, ed., *Die Gesetze der Angelsachsen*, 3 vols. (Halle, 1898–1916); Patrick Wormald, *The Making of English Law: King Alfred to the Twelfth Century*, vol. 1: *Legislation and Its Limits* (Oxford, 1999); and the 'Early English Laws' project: <http://www.earlyenglishlaws.ac.uk>.

but we can often be confident that they represent ideas about the improvement of society current among the Anglo-Saxon elite of particular kingdoms and decades. Through such prescriptive discourse we gain access to contemporary perceptions of disorder, contemporary ideals of good order, and contemporary assumptions about what types of changes might succeed in bringing about improvements to order. There are complications, of course—we should, for instance, be alert to the possibility that more self-interested motivations underlay the legislative activity recorded in our texts—but this is just to say that we need to be cautious when handling our evidence; there is no reason to suppose that such interpretative issues are so fundamental as to make analysis of laws futile, or indeed necessarily any more problematic than the analysis of any other textual genre. Even if we were to accept the received wisdom that laws have nothing whatsoever to offer us on real-life legal practice (which we should not), we would still be able to investigate them as idealized visions, subjecting the ideals implicit within them to close critical exam-ination and analysing the categories and concepts that shaped them. Laws, in short, may not be direct windows onto how contemporaries behaved but they are excellent sources for how Anglo-Saxon elites thought.[43]

Moreover, in the context of the source material that survives for the period, the corpus of laws has some particularly valuable features. Unlike most of our surviving examples of Anglo-Saxon elite discourse, that of the laws has a strong secular component: it provides rare and valuable access to a moral world which, though tinged by Christianity, was not fundamentally shaped by it. And importantly, it is quite possible that this moral world was inhabited not just by the aristocrats who attended royal assemblies but by non-elite society more generally, or at least by the legally free. A worthwhile observation here is that Anglo-Saxon legal discourse, as visible in our texts at any rate, generally does not seem to be that of a distinct group of legal experts.[44] There is little to suggest that it would have been beyond the comprehension of anyone who had the sort of basic legal knowledge accessible to those who attended local assemblies. That is to say, in looking at written law in

---

[43] This has been recognized in analyses of law as ideology, focusing on high-political and religious themes. Again, Wormald was most influential here, in particular Patrick Wormald, '*Lex Scripta* and *Verbum Regis*: Legislation and Germanic Kingship from Euric to Cnut' repr. in and cited from Wormald, *Legal Culture*, pp. 1–43. His arguments about late Anglo-Saxon legal ideology were expressed most clearly in print in Wormald, 'Frederic William Maitland', esp. at pp. 61–2, and are now accessible more fully expressed in Wormald, *Papers Preparatory*, chs. 8–9. Literary analyses, however, have been broader in their scope—a superb example is Miller, *Bloodtaking*, a wide-ranging excavation of social, economic and legal assumptions from Icelandic sagas.

[44] Anglo-Saxon England may have known legal experts of various sorts: people who knew compensation tariffs by heart, who could recall the way their local assembly judged cases decades previously, who had privileged knowledge of recent royal decrees (see Chapter 1, p. 34; Chapter 2, pp. 67–79; Chapter 3, pp. 136–49). However, there is almost nothing to suggest that professional Anglo-Saxon lawyers for whom law was a matter for intellectual debate ever existed—for discussion, see John Hudson, 'From the *Leges* to *Glanvill*: Legal Expertise and Legal Reasoning', in Stefan Jurasinski, Lisi Oliver and Andrew Rabin, eds., *English Law Before Magna Carta: Felix Liebermann and Die Gesetze der Angelsachsen* (Leiden, 2010), pp. 221–49; Reynolds, 'Emergence of Professional Law'. If they did their legal discourse has not left a significant imprint on our evidence, though we do catch a glimpse of something resembling lawyerly abstraction in Ine 43–43:1 (see Chapter 2, p. 89, n. 93).

England in this period—in contrast to, say, contemporary Ireland or England from the turn of the thirteenth century onwards—we do not seem to be looking at the technical discourse of a self-conscious body of legal professionals, potentially reflecting a vision of moral order particular to that group, but at ideas which we might *suspect* had wider currency.[45] For now I simply wish to note this possibility. We certainly cannot build an analysis on the supposition that the laws reflect generally held assumptions rather than those of an elite, or indeed that the idealized moral order underpinning them was not fundamentally Christian, but this book does try to argue these points (particularly in Chapters 1, 2, and 4).[46]

We must also acknowledge that laws are not just windows onto legal culture; they *can* tell us important things about legal practice. We obviously cannot assume that people lived their lives in rigid obedience to the laws that have survived for us to analyse but this does not make them useless. We can begin instead from the observation that when laws prescribe practices, they must usually be prescribing practices that made sense in the context of Anglo-Saxon elite understandings of existing legal customs, practices which at least some of those gathered in great assemblies thought they could realistically hope people would adopt. We need to be alert to the possibility that some legislators had unrealistic expectations—laws' statements about practice need to be approached on a case-by-case basis—but there is little reason to think that wildly impractical fantasies were the norm. More fundamentally, it would be perverse to assume that kings and aristocrats did not generally understand the functioning of law in their own societies, so even when we do have reason to doubt the practicality of new measures being proposed in laws we can still usefully try to identify the assumptions about existing practice that underlie them. If we engage with laws on this level—focusing on implicit assumptions about the legal environment rather than overt attempts to establish new rules—they are much less problematic sources for legal practice than is usually assumed.[47]

---

[45] This is not to say that elite intellectuals were uninterested in law; indeed, the laws only survive for us to read because they were interested—a point made in comprehensive detail in Wormald, *Making of English Law*. However, the fact that high-ranking churchmen took an interest in legal texts shows that they were a significant feature of elite intellectual culture, not that elite intellectual culture was a fundamental influence on these texts' contents, let alone the legislative discourse of major royal assemblies. That said, there are some texts—notably those known to have been composed by Archbishop Wulfstan II of York in the early eleventh century—where there are good reasons to worry that we are dealing with elite intellectual discourse, and thus a moral world that made a great deal of sense in high ecclesiastical circles but perhaps not to the wider population. See below, p. 21, n. 58.

[46] These contentions are far from uncontroversial; for a clear articulation of an alternative perspective, see Stefan Jurasinski, *The Old English Penitentials and Anglo-Saxon Law* (New York, 2015), pp. 9–21. Unfortunately, Jurasinski's book was published during the period when the manuscript for this one was already under review and it has not been possible fully to integrate it here.

[47] For a good example see Chapter 6, pp. 270–3: late tenth-century laws about the witnessing and reporting of transactions may have been unrealistic, but they represent an attempt to solve a practical legal problem—we can therefore proceed by analysing both this perceived problem and our texts' assumptions about how it could, and could not, legitimately be addressed. The issue of whether or not the state was able to enforce its legislative will is an analytical obstacle for some of the questions about practice we might ask of the laws, but not all of them. This is essentially to follow the logic articulated in Taylor, 'Lex Scripta', pp. 47–50.

More prosaically, and absolutely crucially, the reality is that the evidence which survives for this period means that there are many aspects of legal practice for which laws are our best source of information. The procedure known to legal historians as 'vouching to warranty', for instance, in which someone accused of possessing stolen goods calls on witnesses to prove that he bought them in good faith from a third party, and thereby transfers the accusation to this third party, is the subject of several fairly detailed discussions in laws. Next to these, we can place a single case narrative which shows us a privileged secular lord being convicted of theft through the procedure but provides no detail on how it worked.[48] The laws are not straightforward evidence for the practical operation of this procedure, but it would be difficult to deny that they *are* evidence, or to claim to that our single case narrative—certainly unrepresentative in some ways, perhaps in many—is actually more useful to us for this purpose. In practice, even the historians who make a point of their commitment to grounding their analyses in case narratives are frequently forced to rely on information derived from laws to fill in the blanks around them.[49]

Laws, then, are both rich sources for legal culture—for ideals, concepts, and categories—and quite often the best evidence we have for legal practice, in spite of the obvious interpretative problems they pose. Rather than denigrating them we ought to focus our energies on analysing them sensitively, so as to use them to their full potential. This is partly a matter of understanding the texts themselves, thinking carefully not only about what they say and mean but about the processes that led to their production, and indeed those which allowed for their preservation. It is difficult to exaggerate how fortunate we are to have good editions of the laws and a long tradition of detailed critical commentary. Felix Liebermann's monumental early twentieth-century edition remains the foundation on which any study of the laws must rest, though now necessarily in conjunction with Wormald's detailed reappraisal of the entire corpus in his *Making of English Law* and the thriving strand of modern textual scholarship represented by the Early English Laws project.[50] The achievements of this long scholarly tradition are such that crucial questions about the context of each individual text's production and subsequent copying invariably have well-thought-out answers. Rather than independently investigating these issues in depth here, I have for the most part been able to accept these established readings and move on—quite a luxury. Were it not for the foundations laid by generations of textual studies a book such as this one would have been inconceivable.

Interpreting laws sensitively, however, requires more than just a solid understanding of the texts and the immediate context of their production and preservation; we need to interpret them within their wider social, economic, cultural, and political contexts. Most obviously, we need to understand the socio-economic,

---

[48] I Ew 1–1:5; II Atr 8–9:4; II Cn 23–24:3; S 1447. This evidence is conveniently reviewed in Hudson, *Oxford History*, pp. 155–9.

[49] This is acknowledged in Wormald, 'Introduction', p. 3.

[50] See references above, p. 14, n. 42.

political and administrative structures which shaped what law meant in practice, which means not only thinking about issues ranging from the mechanisms of agricultural surplus extraction, through different forms of lordship and local communal organization, all the way up to high-political bonds linking client kings to their overlords, but about how they all fit together. Here again, it should be noted at the outset that this task would be impossible were we not able draw on the insights of decades of careful and thoughtful scholarship on these subjects.

Understanding structures, however, is not in itself sufficient. We need to construct a realistic picture of how people engaged with these structures. We obviously need to avoid the naive assumption that people generally adhered to the neatly ordered vision of legal practice presented by the laws. Explicitly reacting against this tendency, a generation of studies of dispute settlement based on charter material from throughout early medieval Europe has repeatedly shown that participants in disputes tended to pursue their own interests in ways that they judged most likely to bring success, drawing on whatever personal connections they had available; this did not always mean meek compliance with formal legal structures, nor did it mean acting in groups rigidly defined by legalistic understandings of social bonds such as kinship and lordship (though this is not to say that such bonds were unimportant).[51] These insights are valuable and they need to be taken into account. We may have to start with laws issued by kings, but we can and should try to interpret them in their practical context, focusing on the perspective of self-interested individuals seeking social and economic advantage and susceptible to political pressure.[52]

On the other hand, we need to be wary of taking this to extremes and imagining a society characterized by little more than ruthless self-interest, with people invariably pursuing courses determined only by cold calculations about personal gain. Cynicism is not realism. We need to leave room for emotions and ideals, and for the potentially complex mixtures of them which could inform people's behaviour. We also need to recognize that self-interest is subjective and rooted in contemporary value judgements, both those of individuals deciding how to act and those of communities assessing their decisions. It would be naive to assume that from our modern perspective we can understand early medieval people's motivations without making a significant effort to think through this interplay of personal emotions, social dynamics, and cultural assumptions.

The laws themselves can help us with some of these issues—they are excellent sources for ideals of a certain type—but only some of them. The behaviour they

---

[51] See Pauline Stafford, 'King and Kin, Lord and Community: England in the Tenth and Eleventh Centuries', in Pauline Stafford, *Gender, Family and the Legitimation of Power: England from the Ninth to the Early Twelfth Century* (Aldershot, 2006), VIII, pp. 1–33; Lorraine Lancaster, 'Kinship in Anglo-Saxon Society', *British Journal of Sociology* 9 (1958), pp. 230–50, 359–77; Henry Loyn, 'Kinship in Anglo-Saxon England', *Anglo-Saxon England* 3 (1973), pp. 197–209.

[52] Basically this means trying to adopt, as far as is possible, the approach outlined in Wormald, 'Introduction', p. 3. Though I am not primarily using charters, I too have tried to start with law in action, and aspire to be a 'realist', accepting 'political pressure and social advantage as integral (and not always unfair) parts of legal procedure'.

idealize is patient, moderate, considerate of the interests of the wider community. These socially responsible ideals were shaped in relation to others which had the potential to be more disruptive. Ideas about personal honour, most notably, were probably important in shaping and legitimizing violent emotional reactions and in promoting the single-minded pursuit of individual or group self-interest, but though the presence of such ideas is implicit in the laws they are rarely discussed directly. One strategy for dealing with this is to read against the grain of our sources—to be sensitive to signs that the laws are working around or against ideals that are not explicitly articulated. Another is to look elsewhere. Fortunately, honour is a major theme in early medieval literature, and there is a developed tradition of scholarship that can help us come to terms with it.[53] We can also call on modern studies of honour more generally, and on a range of comparative examples, anthropological and historical, to illustrate the diversity of the forms it can take.[54] None of this is ideal, of course—honour in literature is unlikely to correspond directly to honour in real life and the one thing comparative examples show clearly is that honour can mean different things in different societies—but it can still be helpful.

The broader point here is that to interpret laws sensitively we need to think through what they would mean in the context of real-life legal cases, and for that it is essential that we have as fully textured as possible an understanding of the factors which shaped participants' decision-making. In practice, this means attempting to synthesize conclusions from various strands of scholarship—work on social, political, and economic structures and their developments, dispute settlement studies focusing on the practical operation of patronage networks, analyses of honour as articulated in literary sources—some of which are rarely combined. This book's central methodological contention is that laws are a much more useful category of evidence than most recent historians have imagined, but to use them to their full potential we need to think about their context at least as carefully as we investigate the texts themselves.

SCOPE AND STRUCTURE

The scope and structure of this book are shaped by the approach it adopts and the available evidence. Most obviously, it works forwards, so that the late Anglo-Saxon analysis of the final four chapters is firmly grounded in the first three, which engage with the under-studied period from the late sixth to the early tenth centuries. The first chapter begins at the beginning, using Æthelberht's laws as a prism through which to view pre-Christian legal ideals and practices. The second builds on this, but focuses on ideas, using the rather different laws that survive from the late seventh and early eighth centuries to assess the impact of conversion to Christianity

---

[53] Most notably Baker, *Honour, Exchange and Violence*; Miller, *Bloodtaking*.
[54] Frank Henderson Stewart, *Honor* (Chicago, 1994); Elvin Hatch, 'Theories of Social Honor', *American Anthropologist* 91 (1989), pp. 341–53; Dresch, *Tribes*, ch. 2.

on English legal culture. The third chapter takes up the more practical elements of the first, looking at how kings tried to influence legal practice between the late seventh and early tenth centuries, using the laws which survive from either end of that period alongside the evidence of charter formulae from in between. The last four chapters examine the late Anglo-Saxon period (roughly 871–1066) against this background, the aim being to structure their analysis as much as possible around the themes that emerge from the earlier period rather than to engage in established historiographical debates. The fourth and fifth chapters pick up where the second left off, focusing mainly on ideas: Chapter 4 tries to pin down as precisely as possible the nature and extent of substantive legal change—arguing for substantial continuity in the basic shape of the legal system—and Chapter 5 uses our much richer late Anglo-Saxon source material to investigate in more detail the explicit ideological concepts and implicit cultural assumptions that shaped law in the period. Chapters 6 and 7 turn to practicalities, following on from Chapter 3 in, respectively, analysing how kings sought to influence local legal practice and arguing for an important eleventh-century shift in the balance of power between royal officials and aristocratic holders of formal legal privileges.

The main aim throughout the book is to pursue an agenda shaped by Anglo-Saxon categories and practicalities rather than accepting the established priorities of the literature (and especially those deriving from legal historical scholarship focused on the common law). This means that although the book's coverage is extensive in some respects it does not attempt to be comprehensive in its engagement with existing debates. Some readers will doubtless find it disappointing that certain historiographical controversies which are conventionally afforded a central place in discussions of the period receive scant coverage. This is unavoidable. Part of the book's argument is that existing historiographical priorities are skewed—to understand Anglo-Saxon law properly we need to pay much more attention to some topics and afford rather less weight to others—so it would not make sense to frame the analysis here around established points of contention. It also seems to me that frequent historiographical disputation inevitably distracts from the business of understanding the past on its own terms and risks turning what are really very broad points about the way historians generally have projected certain assumptions onto this period into rather unfair criticisms focused on specific individuals' work.[55] For these reasons I have tried to keep direct discussion of existing scholarship to a minimum, mostly confining it to the footnotes, but there are some points where the book's argument is so much at odds with established ideas that failing to discuss the discrepancy explicitly and in detail would only cause

---

[55] This is problematic as a general consideration, but it is particularly so in the context of Anglo-Saxon law because of the remarkable extent to which its modern scholarship is dominated by a single figure, Patrick Wormald, with a particular talent for pithily encapsulating and thereby defining his generation's thoughts on any given subject. I have been very concerned throughout the years spent writing this book to strike a balance between engaging with Wormald's ideas head on (and thus treating his work with the respect it undoubtedly deserves) and avoiding doing so too often, making the book seem like some sort of personal crusade against the ideas of one man. That this is even an issue is a tribute to the breadth and forcefulness of Wormald's scholarship.

confusion. On these points it has seemed most sensible to devote a section of a chapter to reviewing these ideas and justifying my departure from them, and then to move on.[56]

Another important consideration is that the book's chronological range necessitates a clearly defined thematic focus. Broadly, it follows the concerns of its main sources, the laws, which align reasonably well with the conceptual range of the modern collocation 'law and order'. That is, it focuses on acts that contemporaries perceived to be wrongful—which approximate, albeit imperfectly, to the offences that we would today categorize as crimes—and on the routine, local legal practice of relatively ordinary people rather than elite disputes. This means issues surrounding the inheritance of land, which are central to traditional legal history for good reasons, are a peripheral concern. It also means that the evidence of legal practice that can be gleaned from charters is less useful here than might be expected, not just because it tends to involve disputes over title to landed property but because even where we do find accounts of wrongdoing the people involved are almost invariably privileged lords, their treatment potentially unrepresentative of non-elite legal practice.[57] Again, the marginal status of this material here is a product of the book's thematic focus; it should not be construed as a dismissal of its usefulness in other contexts. Finally, a similar point needs to be made about the laws as texts: while laws are this book's main sources, its analytical focus is not on the texts themselves but on what they can reveal about legal culture and practice. This means that it exploits the fruits of the long tradition of textual scholarship noted above without any pretence of contributing to that tradition in return. Moreover, it does so primarily in order to understand the laws' original context, largely ignoring the questions about later manuscript context that occupied Wormald for much of the first volume of his *Making of English Law*. These are questions, it seems to me, which are fundamentally about the meaning and role of law within intellectual culture—a topic certainly worthy of attention in its own right but not a central concern of this book.[58]

[56] See Chapter 4, pp. 192–9; Chapter 7, pp. 295–310.

[57] It should be noted that although the validity of extrapolating from such aristocratic case narratives to draw more general conclusions about legal practice is always a concern, the potential problems are much greater for some issues than for others. The contention that these cases reflect broader ideas about rightful and wrongful conduct is relatively unproblematic, for instance, but we need to be much more cautious about the information they contain about the treatment of legal revenues: they usually concern men who in normal circumstances received fines rather than paying them.

[58] Wormald would probably have challenged the underlying logic here. One of his most ambitious contentions was that the intellectual culture which preserved the laws was precisely the culture which shaped the original texts, making questions about manuscript context essential to the interpretation of the laws themselves. This interpretation, with its implication that the laws represent the thought-world of elite intellectuals and were disconnected from the realities of legal culture and practice, allowed for arguments that late Anglo-Saxon England was much more state-like than the laws themselves suggest. This is the point underlying the subtitle of the first volume of his *Making of English Law*, 'legislation and its limits', and is the thrust of its conclusion, though its full implications are only hinted at in the final paragraph, which offers a tantalizing sketch of 'the central point of Volume II' (p. 483). The fullest statement of the case is in the draft introduction to this second volume (*Papers Preparatory*, pp. 7–12), which proceeds by juxtaposing two possible interpretations. In the first, that which Wormald was critiquing, written law was widely used—a practical genre familiar to those actively

The most obvious limitations on the book's scope are chronological and geographical. There is no coverage of law in Roman Britain here and little on England after 1066. Justifying this is not difficult: the lack of evidence for any direct continuity between Roman British and Anglo-Saxon legal systems, and the far-reaching changes that took place in century after the Norman Conquest, make the period in between as coherent a block as one could reasonably hope for. Desirable though it would be to connect the account of Anglo-Saxon law presented here with the emergence of the common law in the late twelfth century, doing so would be an ambitious research project in its own right: the sources available render the potentially rather complex changes of this period obscure, and it may well not be possible to comprehend them without coming to terms with wider European trends which may have influenced English developments (for example, the Peace and Truce of God, and the reception of Roman Law). Indeed, even for the period with which it is concerned, the book's limited geographical scope is not ideal: Anglo-Saxon law is clearly just one part of a broader early medieval legal culture which it would make sense to study as a whole.[59] The reason for not attempting this is pragmatic. Understanding even one early medieval legal tradition on the level for which I am aiming here requires deep engagement with not only its texts but with the social, economic, cultural and political contexts that formed it, and with the historiographical traditions that have shaped modern understandings. A comprehensive comparative study of early medieval legal systems, covering all the themes of this book in full detail, would be an immensely valuable contribution

engaged in legal administration—but our evidence for it happens to have been preserved by elite intellectuals who took an interest in this material: 'In sum, the extant state of legal texts is neither here nor there. It tells us only about the predilections of an unrepresentative intelligentsia' (p. 11). In the second reading, Wormald's own, written law was not integral to legal practice, but a textual genre created by and for elite intellectuals: 'Hence, the mentality that preserved law-codes was not at variance from that which issued and applied them. Instead, it is the best guide to that mentality' (p. 12). To my mind this is a sensible reading of a few specific texts—those of Alfred and Wulfstan are the best candidates—but I find it difficult to accept as a general principle. It appears to me that Wormald's argument conflates two issues which ought to be kept separate: whether laws were transmitted in a written or oral form need not bear on whether our texts originated in a specifically intellectual or more general elite discourse. As was argued above, many of our texts (whatever their subsequent manuscript histories) were composed as records of decisions made in great assemblies of lay and ecclesiastical aristocrats. If it is these assemblies' decisions that interest us, the question of whether they were expected to be disseminated in primarily written or oral form is largely immaterial. Even if we were to accept that *written* records of decisions made in great assemblies were of minimal relevance for legal practice (which is far from certain), this would not allow us to conclude that our texts fail to reflect the decisions actually taken (for this we would have to suppose a sustained effort to deceive on the part of their authors), nor that the decisions themselves were irrelevant (for that we would need to rule out all effective oral transmission). (This point is made T. M. Charles-Edwards, 'Law in the Western Kingdoms between the Fifth and Seventh Centuries', in Averil Cameron, Bryan Ward-Perkins and Michael Whitby, eds., *The Cambridge Ancient History Volume 14: Late Antiquity: Empire and Successors, AD 425–600* (Cambridge, 2001), pp. 260–87 at 277–8.) There are exceptions—sensitivity to differences between texts is crucial—but there is generally little reason to suspect our texts were shaped fundamentally by the mentalities of the intellectuals who wrote and copied them rather than by the broader mix of mentalities present in the assemblies whose decisions they purport to record.

[59] For a recent attempt at a broad-ranging reinterpretation, see Maurizio Lupoi, *The Origins of the European Legal Order*, trans. Adrian Belton (Cambridge, 2000).

but it would also be truly a formidable undertaking—a life's work or a major international collaboration rather than a first book by a single historian.

A potential benefit of such a project would be the establishment of a nuanced understanding of the significance of external influences in shaping English law in this period; the focus on England alone here means that this book cannot hope to address these influences in any systematic way, and I have been wary about assuming that they had a significant role. Similarities between legal systems, after all, could just reflect similar societies trying to solve similar problems in similar ways. To assume direct borrowings played a major part in shaping English legal culture is to assume that kings and their senior ecclesiastical subordinates— presumably the immediate recipients of such external influences—had the capacity to impose essentially foreign legal practices on their kingdoms' local assemblies. They may have done, but in my judgement this is not an assumption that should be made lightly, as a starting point for analysis; the development of kings' capacity to impose legal change is a subject which needs to be approached critically and cautiously. My aim here has been to construct an interpretation that can stand on the basis of Anglo-Saxon evidence alone, not relying on speculation about external influences. To some extent the existing literature (the conclusions of which I broadly accept) compensates for the lack of direct attention here: the earliest Anglo-Saxon laws are conventionally interpreted within a broader context of post-Roman 'barbarian' royal law-giving,[60] whereas the later laws are understood to reflect significant influences from Carolingian Francia.[61] Indeed, it seems to me that it is the extent of continuity with native (pre-Christian and, later on, pre-Carolingian) legal culture and practice which is most likely to be underrepresented in modern scholarship. In part, this book is an attempt to place existing arguments about external influences into their proper context, by paying close attention to the native ideas and practices with which they interacted.

It is also worth noting here that the book does not evenly cover what we would think of as 'England': its geographical coverage follows the evidence available, and is patchy as a result. In the late sixth century it focuses on Kent, in the late seventh on Kent and Wessex, for the 150 years in the eighth and ninth from which no laws survive it relies on charter material from Mercia and Wessex, and then for the late

---

[60] See Wormald, '*Lex Scripta*'; Wormald, 'The *Leges Barbarorum*: Law and Ethnicity in the Post-Roman West', in Hans-Werner Goetz, Jörg Jarnut, and Walter Pohl, eds., *Regna and Gentes: The Relationship Between Late Antique and Early Medieval Peoples and Kingdoms in the Transformation of the Roman World* (Leiden, 2003), pp. 21–53; Oliver, *Body Legal*.

[61] This is a pervasive feature of Wormald's scholarship. It was most clearly expressed in print in his arguments about oaths of loyalty (reviewed in detail in Chapter 5, pp. 210–13) but was significantly broader than that. It is one of the strongest themes running through his (previously) unpublished papers. For example, Wormald, *Papers Preparatory*, p. 188 ('The founders of the English kingdom were the most visible heirs to the Carolingian legacy. They did the most to preserve it through European law's "Dark Age"') or p. 250 ('England, not Normandy or Anjou, was the Carolingian successor-state *par excellence*'). More broadly, see James Campbell, 'Observations on English Government from the Tenth to the Twelfth Century' repr. in and cited from James Campbell, *Essays in Anglo-Saxon History* (London, 1986), pp. 155–70; Chris Wickham, *The Inheritance of Rome: A History of Europe from 400–1000* (London, 2009), ch. 19 ('"Carolingian" England'). For a critical re-evaluation, see Molyneaux, *Formation*, pp. 231–49.

Anglo-Saxon period it focuses on the West Saxon legal tradition (which eventually, in effect, becomes the 'English' one). Although we do have evidence for Danish law from this later period and it does feature in the broader analysis, I have chosen not to focus on it specifically here; there are distinctive features, but within a context of broad similarity, and it seemed to me that detailed discussion of relatively minor points of difference would not have made sense within the book's structure.

This patchiness is inevitable: the early medieval period is difficult to study because evidence is scarce. This is a significant part of what makes it such an attractive intellectual challenge: the need to make the most of what we have forces early medieval historians to approach their material in imaginative ways, and its relative sparseness means that in-depth studies of developments spanning five centuries are possible in a way that they are not in later periods. My hope is that, in conjunction with other recent reassessments,[62] this book will help persuade early medieval historians that there is room for a more imaginative (but no less critically cautious) approach to the interpretation of laws as evidence, and that the legal systems of the societies they study are at their most interesting when analysed broadly. The tendency to look in detail at specific texts, issues or practices is understandable, but the big picture is surely what is most valuable both for scholars studying early medieval societies more holistically and, indeed, for those with a general interest in legal systems. Implicit in our evidence for early medieval law is a vision of an ideal moral order and a set of ideas about how it ought to be maintained for which the modern world can offer no close analogues. Early medieval legal systems were neither state-like nor stateless. That this renders them difficult to understand makes it all the more important that we try.

---

[62] Particularly those cited above, p. 12, n. 36.

PART I

FOUNDATIONS OF THE ANGLO-SAXON LEGAL ORDER

1

Law before Æthelberht

INTRODUCTION

The beginnings of English history are deeply obscure. Britain south of Hadrian's Wall was part of the Roman Empire at the end of the fourth century, but what happened during the fifth and sixth is largely irrecoverable. We know that the Roman general Constantine III began his attempt to seize control of the Western Empire in Britain: he was declared emperor by the frontier army in early 407 and swiftly moved to Gaul in order to assert his claim, presumably taking a large portion of that army with him. After this, however, our written evidence for events in Britain is extremely sparse until roughly 597, when King Æthelberht of Kent received a group of Roman missionaries and converted to Christianity, by which point we are able to draw on the political narrative contained within the *Ecclesiastical History of the English People* written by the Northumbrian monk Bede in the early eighth century. Though the situation is not so dire as for written sources, the fifth and sixth centuries are also obscure in archaeological terms. Evidence for meaningful continuity with the Roman past—for coin use, the manufacture of pottery, the occupation of towns and villas—ceases swiftly and completely. We can be certain that the economy collapsed catastrophically, definitely by the mid-fifth century and possibly much more quickly than that, and it is likely that this was accompanied by the demise of most of what was Roman about Britain in social, political, and cultural terms too.[1]

---

[1] The fullest statement of this case remains A. S. Esmonde-Cleary, *The Ending of Roman Britain* (London, 1989), esp. ch. 4; though see the slight modifications in A. S. Esmonde-Cleary, 'The Ending(s) of Roman Britain', in Helena Hamerow, David A. Hinton, and Sally Crawford, eds., *The Oxford Handbook of Anglo-Saxon Archaeology* (Oxford, 2012), pp. 13–29. While archaeological evidence makes rapid economic collapse virtually indisputable, the extent and speed of social, political, and cultural changes in this period are more debatable. Scholars who, like Esmonde-Cleary, take a pessimistic view of the extent of Roman continuity often emphasize archaeology: see Chris Wickham, *Framing the Early Middle Ages: Europe and the Mediterranean, 400–800* (Oxford, 2005), pp. 47–50, 306–10; Chris Wickham, *The Inheritance of Rome: A History of Europe from 400 to 1000* (London, 2009), pp. 150–5; Bryan Ward-Perkins, *The Fall of Rome and the End of Civilization* (Oxford, 2005), 117–20 and ch. 7; Robin Fleming, *Britain After Rome: The Fall and Rise* (London, 2010), chs. 1–2. More optimistic (and usually more text-based) assessments allowing for an intermediate 'sub-Roman' period are possible, but they are essentially variations on a stable theme of extensive 'de-Romanization' across the fifth century: see K. R. Dark, *Civitas to Kingdom: British Political Continuity 300–800* (Leicester, 1994); Nicholas. J. Higham and Martin Ryan, *The Anglo-Saxon World* (New Haven, 2013), pp. 41–56; Ian Wood, 'The North-Western Provinces', in Averil Cameron, Bryan Ward-Perkins, and Michael Whitby, eds., *The Cambridge Ancient History Volume 14: Late Antiquity: Empire and Successors, AD 425–600*

How far this collapse, which was much more complete in Britain than in most of Western Europe, was prompted by Anglo-Saxon invaders is the subject of debate, but by the seventh century we can be certain that most of lowland Britain—much of what we now think of as England—was settled by people who spoke dialects of Old English (a Germanic language which owes little to those which had been spoken in Roman Britain). It is now accepted that many of these people—conventionally labelled the Anglo-Saxons or simply the English—must in fact have been descendants of the inhabitants of Roman Britain whose families had gradually assimilated, adopting Anglo-Saxon language and culture, including their pagan religion.[2] Politically, it is clear that by the late sixth century there was, relative to later periods, a large number of small English kingdoms, many of which included subordinate British populations. Inevitably, given the scarcity of reliable evidence, the origins of this state of affairs are debated, but at present the most widely accepted theory is that Anglo-Saxon migrants initially formed communities of subsistence farmers which were not ruled by kings. Ideas about kingship are thought to have developed gradually during this murky period, as these small communities coalesced into larger political units.[3]

Considering the general obscurity of the pre-Christian period in English history we are remarkably well informed about law: we have a law code apparently drawn up on the orders of King Æthelberht of Kent in the wake of his conversion to Christianity in 597. The Old English text survives only in a much later copy and contains no allusion to Æthelberht (his involvement is first mentioned by Bede over a century later) but scholarly analysis, in particular of its language, has done much to confirm the traditional attribution.[4] Crucially, it is now widely accepted that the

(Cambridge, 2001), pp. 497–524. A recent highly detailed discussion is T. M. Charles-Edwards, *Wales and the Britons, 350–1064* (Oxford, 2013), chs. 1–6.

[2] See Catherine Hills, *The Origins of the English* (London, 2003). Wickham, *Framing*, pp. 312–13 suggests as a 'bald guess' that Germanic migrants were outnumbered 10:1 by the indigenous population. Bryan Ward-Perkins, 'Why Did the Anglo-Saxons Not Become More British?', *English Historical Review* 115 (2000), pp. 513–33, argues at pp. 521–3 that even taking the lowest plausible estimates of the native population and the highest for the incomers it is likely that there were at least four natives for each migrant. Genetic studies are beginning to cast light on this issue but their implications are not yet clear. For a recent review, see Robert Hedges, 'Anglo-Saxon Migration and the Molecular Evidence', in Hamerow, Hinton, and Crawford, *Oxford Handbook of Anglo-Saxon Archaeology*, pp. 79–90.

[3] See Steven Bassett, 'In Search of the Origins of Anglo-Saxon Kingdoms', in Steven Bassett, ed., *The Origins of Anglo-Saxon Kingdoms* (Leicester, 1989), pp. 3–27; Helena Hamerow, 'The Earliest Anglo-Saxon Kingdoms', in Paul Fouracre, ed., *The New Cambridge Medieval History Volume I: c. 500–c. 700* (Cambridge, 2005), pp. 263–88; Fleming, *Britain After Rome*, chs. 3–4; Barbara Yorke, *Kings and Kingdoms of Early Anglo-Saxon England* (London, 1990), esp. ch. 1; Wickham, *Framing*, pp. 313–14, 325–6, 340–3; Wickham, *Inheritance*, pp. 150–8.

[4] For a full discussion see Lisi Oliver, ed., *The Beginnings of English Law* (Toronto, 2002), pp. 20–52. Minor doubts remain as to whether the code's opening clauses, which are the only ones to mention the Church and are syntactically distinct from the rest of the text, were composed in Æthelberht's day or a later accretion (at pp. 44–6). The code cannot be dated with certainty but the available evidence suggests that the period 599–600 is most likely; see Carole Hough, 'Legal and Documentary Writings' repr. in and cited from Carole Hough, *An Ald Recht: Essays on Anglo-Saxon Law* (Newcastle upon Tyne, 2014), pp. 2–24 at 4–6.

king's role was to have existing laws committed to writing.[5] Except for a small initial group of clauses dealing mainly with the Church, this was a written record of pre-Christian law. It provides us with an immensely valuable window into English culture generally in the sixth century and into legal matters in particular. Æthelberht's code is notable for being longer than many later English laws, and for being unusually coherent in terms of both content and structure. Its one over-riding concern is to specify the compensation payable for a range of offences; after the newly added clauses on the Church, it begins at the top of society with a section on the king and works methodically downwards society, discussing nobles, free-men, women, and two ranks of the unfree, dealing with offences committed by or against such people. Between the sections on freemen and women comes a long personal injury tariff, which again works methodically downwards, beginning at the top of the body with the appropriate compensation for hair-seizing and ending with that for the striking off of toenails.[6] Individual laws tend to be very terse: they rarely do more than describe the offence in question and state the compensation appropriate for it in monetary terms.

Making this material yield useful conclusions is not easy, but if we are to break with a retrospective approach to Anglo-Saxon law and instead work forwards it is with this text that we have to start. A traditional approach is comparative: law codes survive from many other parts of early medieval Europe and the information they provide is of a broadly similar type. Studying Æthelberht's laws alongside texts from Frankish Gaul, Visigothic Spain, and Lombard Italy leads to a series of questions about the commonalities and differences that emerge, and these can be taken a long

---

[5] The case is made most fully in Oliver, *Beginnings*, pp. 34–51, and is discussed below, pp. 32–3. For general acceptance, see Carole Hough, 'Legal and Documentary Writings', p. 4; T. M. Charles-Edwards, 'Law in the Western Kingdoms between the Fifth and Seventh Centuries', in Cameron, Ward-Perkins and Whitby, *Cambridge Ancient History Volume 14*, pp. 260–87 at 271; Patrick Wormald, '"Inter Cetera Bona Genti Suae": Law-Making and Peace-Keeping in the Earliest English Kingdoms', repr. in and cited from Patrick Wormald, *Legal Culture in the Early Medieval West: Law as Text, Image and Experience* (London, 1999), pp. 179–98, at 183–6; Patrick Wormald, *The Making of English Law: King Alfred to the Twelfth Century. Volume I: Legislation and Its Limits* (Oxford, 1999), pp. 95–101. Stefan Jurasinski, 'The Continental Origins of Æthelberht's Code', *Philological Quarterly* 80 (2001), pp. 1–15, argues the opposite case, concluding that stylistic and syntactical similarities between Æthelberht's text's Old English and the Latin of continental laws show that the code was dependent on 'one or several examples of lost Merovingian legislation' (p. 12). However, in the absence of demonstrable dependence on an extant text this conclusion is little more than a suggestion; it is not obvious that similarities of syntax—or indeed of structure and content—need imply direct borrowing rather than merely the linguistic and legal similarities of the cultures concerned. An argument for a Latin original is made in Patrizia Lendinara, 'The Kentish Laws', in John Hines, ed., *The Anglo-Saxons from the Migration Period to the Eighth Century: An Ethnographic Perspective* (Woodbridge, 1997), pp. 211–30. This argument, however, found little acceptance and has now been comprehensively refuted: Carole Hough, 'The Earliest English Texts? The Language of the Kentish Laws Reconsidered', in Bruce O'Brien and Barbara Bombi, eds., *Textus Roffensis: Law, Language and Libraries in Medieval England* (Turnhout, 2015), pp. 137–56. For more speculative arguments in favour of native pre-Christian written laws, perhaps in the runic alphabet, see Nicholas Brooks, 'The Laws of King Æthelberht of Kent: Preservation, Content and Composition', in O'Brien and Bombi, *Textus Roffensis*, pp. 105–36 at 111–12, 125–30; H. G. Richardson and G. O. Sayles, *Law and Legislation from Æthelberht to Magna Carta* (Edinburgh, 1966), pp. 1–10.

[6] Oliver, *Beginnings*, p. 36, provides a clause-by-clause breakdown of the text's structure.

way.[7] This was a major field of research in the late nineteenth and early twentieth centuries. Scholars such as H. M. Chadwick analysed the English evidence in this wider framework, attempting to understand the various monetary systems employed by these texts so as to render the information they provide comparable.[8] Possible explanations could then be offered for discrepancies, for example between the values of the wergilds of freemen (that is, the compensation payable for killing them) in different texts: Chadwick concluded that in real terms a West Saxon freeman's 200-shilling wergild was worth half the 100-shilling wergild which pertained to freemen in Kent, and suggested that this was because before their migration the Saxons had been conquered by the Danes, and the value of their wergilds had been reduced by a period of subjection.[9] Chadwick's conclusions now seem distinctly over-ambitious—the relative values of the monetary terms in the laws are far from settled and modern historians are generally less willing to assume the traditions revealed in laws derived from the distant past[10]—but in spite of the significant methodological challenges it presents, this comparative approach remains perhaps the most productive avenue of research into early medieval laws.[11] It is not, however, the approach adopted here. The questions on which this chapter focuses are not about how Kentish law relates to other legal traditions, but about how law functioned and what law meant within Kentish society.

Before we can approach these questions, however, we need to understand the evidence we are working with. The first issue to confront is the context for our text's production: why did Æthelberht want to have a written law code in the first place? Modern scholarship provides a clear and convincing answer to this, which derives mainly from the work of Patrick Wormald.[12] Æthelberht, having converted to

---

[7] An excellent recent overview is Charles-Edwards, 'Law in the Western Kingdoms'.

[8] H. M. Chadwick, *Studies on Anglo-Saxon Institutions* (Cambridge, 1905), pp. 1–75. See also, in particular, Frederic Seebohm, *Tribal Custom in Anglo-Saxon Law* (London, 1911). For a succinct review of this tradition of scholarship, see Rory Naismith, 'H. M. Chadwick and the Anglo-Saxon Monetary System', in Michael Lapidge, ed., *The Life and Writings of Hector Munro Chadwick* (Aberystwyth, 2015), pp. 143–56.

[9] Chadwick, *Anglo-Saxon Institutions*, pp. 400–11.

[10] The formidable difficulties of working out how the various monetary terms of early laws relate to one another are reviewed in Naismith, 'H. M. Chadwick'. For the argument that Kentish and West Saxon freemen in fact had equivalent wergilds: D. A. Bullough, 'Anglo-Saxon Institutions and Early English Society' repr. in and cited from David E. Pelteret, *Anglo-Saxon History: Basic Readings* (New York, 2000), pp. 1–19 at 3–5; Stewart Lyon, 'Historical Problems of Anglo-Saxon Coinage – (3) Denominations and Weights' *British Numismatic Journal* 38 (1969), pp. 204–22, at 204–12. For a new interpretation: John Hines, 'Units of Account in Gold and Silver in Seventh-Century England: *Scillingas*, *Sceattas* and *Pæningas*' *Antiquaries Journal* 90 (2010), 153–73.

[11] See Lisi Oliver, *The Body Legal in Barbarian Law* (Toronto, 2011); Patrick Wormald, 'The *Leges Barbarorum*: Law and Ethnicity in the Post-Roman West', in Hans-Werner Goetz, Jörg Jarnut, and Walter Pohl, eds., *Regna and Gentes: The Relationship Between Late Antique and Early Medieval Peoples and Kingdoms in the Transformation of the Roman World* (Leiden, 2003), pp. 21–53; Patrick Wormald, '*Lex Scripta* and *Verbum Regis*: Legislation and Germanic Kingship from Euric to Cnut' repr. in and cited from Wormald, *Legal Culture*, pp. 1–43; Maurizio Lupoi, *The Origins of the European Legal Order*, trans. Adrian Belton (Cambridge, 2000).

[12] See Wormald, *Making*, ch. 2; Wormald, '*Lex Scripta*'; Patrick Wormald, 'Kings and Kingship', in Fouracre, *New Cambridge Medieval History Volume I*, pp. 571–604, at 596–9; Patrick Wormald, *The First Code of English Law* (Canterbury, 2005), pp. 15–17. Wormald's interpretation represents a development of a line of thought already established by J. M. Wallace-Hadrill: J. M. Wallace-Hadrill,

Christianity, was motivated to produce a law code because producing law codes was an aspect of the model of Romano-Christian kingship that his more powerful Frankish in-laws (and the other Christian rulers of Western Europe) had adopted, and to which he aspired. This is how Bede understood it slightly over a century later: the converted king, with the advice of his councillors, established a law code 'according to the examples of the Romans.'[13] There is no reason to suspect, then, that by having laws written down Æthelberht intended to change their content in any significant way (beyond setting out how the Church would fit into existing structures in the text's initial clauses). It is also extremely unlikely that the code was written down in the expectation that it would henceforth be consulted as a part of routine legal procedure. (The shift from an oral to a literate legal culture was a long-term phenomenon, still far from complete by the end of the Anglo-Saxon period.)[14] The purpose of Æthelberht's act of codification was ideological: to demonstrate that he had joined the club of powerful Christian kings who, across Europe, ruled as the heirs of Roman emperors.

This leads to a second and much more difficult question. It is widely accepted that Æthelberht's code was based on existing Kentish law, but in what form did that law exist? There is nothing to suggest the existence of an earlier written code, so most historians have tended to assume that Æthelberht's code drew on existing oral legal traditions. This, however, could mean at least two different things. On the one hand we might envisage this earlier oral law as having been formally recorded: law existed in a set form of words that could be learnt by rote and recited. If this were the case, we could understand Æthelberht's code as a version of a 'text' of Kentish law that had previously existed in an oral form, remaining more or less stable (though probably not completely fixed) perhaps for several decades before Æthelberht had it committed to writing. On the other hand, we might imagine that law had not previously been recorded in a set form of words at all: old men would have known what the law was by virtue of their years of legal experience, and when asked about it they could explain it, but there was no set 'text' to be learnt and recited. If this were the case, we would have to understand Æthelberht's code as the result of an act of composition: we could speculate that a number of old and wise

---

The Long-Haired Kings (London, 1962), pp. 179–81; J. M. Wallace-Hadrill, *Early Germanic Kingship in England and on the Continent* (Oxford, 1971), pp. 32–44.

[13] *Ecclesiastical History*, ii.5.

[14] Exactly how far from complete, however, has been the subject of debate. See Wormald, '*Lex Scripta*'; Wormald, *Making*, esp. ch. 7; Patrick Wormald, 'The Uses of Literacy in Anglo-Saxon England and Its Neighbours', *Transactions of the Royal Historical Society* 27 (1977), pp. 95–114; Simon Keynes, 'Royal Government and the Written Word in Late Anglo-Saxon England', in Rosamond McKitterick, ed., *The Uses of Literacy in Early Mediaeval Europe* (Cambridge, 1990), pp. 226–57; Levi Roach, 'Law Codes and Legal Norms in Later Anglo-Saxon England', *Historical Research* 86 (2013), pp. 465–86; Catherine Cubitt, '"As the Lawbook Teaches": Reeves, Lawbooks and Urban Life in the Anonymous Old English Legend of the Seven Sleepers', *English Historical Review* 124 (2009), pp. 1021–49; David Pratt, 'Written Law and the Communication of Authority in Tenth-Century England', in David Rollason, Conrad Leyser and Hannah Williams, eds., *England and the Continent in the Tenth Century: Studies in Honour of Wilhelm Levison (1876–1947)* (Turnhout, 2010), pp. 331–50; Michael Clanchy, *From Memory to Written Record: England 1066–1307* (3rd edn., Chichester, 2013), pp. 30–5.

men were commissioned to come up with (perhaps with the king's personal input) a formal statement of law based on their extensive knowledge.

Until recently this issue was uncertain, but the painstaking and penetrating analysis provided by the text's modern editor, Lisi Oliver, has strengthened and clarified the case for the first of these two options.[15] Oliver argued that the text may contain 'traces of an elevated prose style, using the poetic device of alliteration as an aid to memory', and that its orderly structure (which is strikingly different from the more chaotic codes produced in later, more literate centuries) represents an 'architectural mnemonic' inherited from the days when it existed only in a memorized form.[16] The core of her case, however, lies in her analysis of syntax, from which she concluded that some parts of the code are likely to be older than others. Specifically, she identified an archaic 'dative of quantity' in the sections of the text concerned with personal injury and offences against freemen. This is a usage familiar in other West Germanic languages but, outside early Kentish law, unattested in the entire Old English corpus. Oliver argued that we should infer that these sections were first formulated at an earlier point than the rest of the code, fossilizing a syntactical construction that later fell out of use.[17] Her argument thus implies the existence of at least three stages in the evolution of the text we know as Æthelberht's laws: the earliest oral version, marked by the use of the dative of quantity, which covered offences against freemen and personal injury; a more elaborate oral version which included the material on kings, nobles, women, and the unfree which was current at the time of Æthelberht's conversion; and the written version, which added the initial clauses on the Church.[18]

Oliver's findings have far-reaching implications for the interpretation of Æthelberht's code, and her case is persuasive. The evidence on which it is based is limited but this is hardly surprising given the nature of the available sources. Taken individually, the features she identifies are susceptible to alternative readings: the code's orderly structure may make most sense interpreted as an 'architectural mnemonic', for instance, but it cannot be proven to be such; one might attempt to explain away the presence of the dative of quantity as a deliberate archaizing feature in a seventh-century composition rather than a relic of the fifth or early sixth century preserved by oral transmission;[19] the existence of three syntactically distinct sections could perhaps have resulted from textual emendations between the code's

---

[15] Oliver, *Beginnings*, pp. 34–51. This fleshes out the briefer argument for the same conclusion in Hough, 'Legal and Documentary Writings', p. 4. The discussion in Charles-Edwards, 'Law in the Western Kingdoms', pp. 270–1, also provides arguments in favour of a pre-existing oral 'text', although that conclusion is left implicit. Wormald's position is less clear: most of his discussion suggests the existence of an oral legal tradition involving memorized texts (e.g. Wormald, 'Inter Cetera', pp. 183–6; Wormald, *Making*, pp. 95–6) but he also argued that Æthelberht's text was modelled on Frankish examples, the matters which it was proper for the new text to discuss being those 'on which eminent Frankish legislators had pronounced' (Wormald, *Making*, p. 101).

[16] Oliver, *Beginnings*, pp. 34–41 (quotations at 41 and 37).

[17] Ibid., pp. 32–4, 41–51. The dative of quantity also appears in Hl 4.   [18] Ibid., p. 51.

[19] This is perhaps the most persuasive explanation for its presence in Hl 4. Oliver (*Beginnings*, pp. 32–3) suggests a different reading: that archaic oral custom is here being used to fill a gap in Æthelberht's text. For considerations that tell against such a reading, see Chapter 2, pp. 71–2.

composition under Æthelberht and the production of the twelfth-century manuscript in which it survives. Oliver's interpretation, however, has the virtue of
providing a simple, coherent and plausible explanation for all these features, and
in the absence of any reason to suspect her conclusions it would be perverse to
resort to elaborate interpretative contortions in order to avoid them. It would be
wrong to assert that Oliver's analysis constitutes proof that Æthelberht's code was a
version of an established (if evolving) pre-Christian oral 'text', but she has greatly
strengthened the already well-founded and widely accepted argument that this is
the most plausible interpretation available. And, as shall be seen in Chapter 2, it is
an interpretation that fits well with the way law is categorized in late seventh-
century texts.[20]

This chapter proceeds on the assumption that both Wormald and Oliver are
correct: Æthelberht wanted to produce a law code to demonstrate his credentials as
a Romano-Christian king, which in practice meant commissioning someone to
write down laws which already existed as an oral 'text'—a set form of words that
could be learnt by rote and recited[21]—deliberately modifying this text only by
appending a handful of clauses on the Church. These starting assumptions shape
the conclusions we draw from the code in important ways. It follows that we should
dismiss out of hand (as Wormald did) interpretations that understand Æthelberht's
laws' focus on compensation payments as a Christian attempt to pacify a pagan
society characterized by unrestrained vengeful bloodshed. If we accept that these

---

[20] See Chapter 2, pp. 67–82.

[21] Though probably understood by contemporaries as fixed, we should of course note the
possibility that oral 'texts' of this sort were prone to change in their transmission across generations.
One prominent scholarly trend has been to emphasize this malleability of memory in 'oral cultures',
almost to the point of denying the possibility of rote learning; see, in particular, Jack Goody, 'Memory
in Oral Tradition', in Patricia Fara and Karalyn Patterson, eds., *Memory* (Cambridge, 1998),
pp. 73–94 esp. at 93 ('it is with literacy that the notion of exact verbatim reproduction becomes
possible and valued'). A more balanced assessment is provided by Jan Vansina, *Oral Tradition as
History* (Oxford, 1985), ch. 2, which emphasizes the importance of context: 'The intent of the
performance greatly matters. Where, as in the case of tales, innovation on a stable theme is at a
premium, the pulse of change beats faster. Where, to the contrary, the performers intend to stick as
closely as possible to the message related and to avoid lapses of memory or distortions, the pace of
change can almost be stopped' (p. 41). Even Goody acknowledges this to a limited extent, noting
(p. 91) that 'short events such as proverbs and songs (where rhythms help)' and 'short narrative
sequences such as those in folk tales' are less prone to transformation than his primary example, the
Bagre—a West African myth of 'some 12,000 "lines"': see Jack Goody, ed., *The Myth of the Bagre*
(Oxford, 1972), p. 60. In our (much shorter) case, of course, there is every reason to think that accurate
recollection of a fixed form of words was prioritized, and creative improvisation much more severely
frowned upon than in any literary performance. Indeed, the derivation of the Old English verb
mathelian, to speak solemnly or weightily, from the word for an assembly, *mæthl*, implies that the
forums in which law was applied were solemn, formal gatherings in which a particular linguistic register
was appropriate (see Charles-Edwards, 'Law in the Western Kingdoms', p. 268; Aliki Pantos, '*In medle
oððe an þinge*: The Old English Vocabulary of Assembly', in Aliki Pantos and Sarah Semple, eds.,
Assembly Places and Practices in Medieval Europe (Dublin, 2004), pp. 181–201, at 184–5). Though we
should of course accept that many Anglo-Saxon oral traditions were malleable (for a useful discussion of
oral traditions in literary evidence see Andy Orchard, 'Oral Tradition', in Katherine O'Brien O'Keefe,
ed., *Reading Old English Texts* (Cambridge, 1997), pp. 101–23), there are good reasons to suspect
that the tradition of formalized oral law underlying Æthelberht's text lay on the more stable end of
the spectrum.

compensations were central to Kent's pre-Christian oral legal tradition, this reading is not only implausible but impossible.[22] It also follows that we need to be alert to the possibility that the strong royal association with law-making visible in later law codes was *not* a feature of Anglo-Saxon society in the pre-Christian period (something also hinted at by the fact that Æthelberht's name does not appear in his code). Accepting pre-Christian oral transmission means accepting that there were people in sixth-century Kent who had memorized the law and could recite it; by definition, these were the people who had the authority to make formal statements of law at this time.[23] Æthelberht's having laws written down can thus be read as the first tentative step in the erosion of these legal experts' authority and the establishment of the king's position as the primary source of law—a process of great long-term significance though not one that would have been apparent at the time.[24]

Such issues, however, are not the subject of this chapter. Our interpretation of Æthelberht's code will necessarily affect our understanding of the legal changes that followed, particularly those of the seventh century discussed in Chapter 2, but this is not the only context in which the text should be read. Carefully analysed, it can tell us a great deal about sixth-century Kentish society. On one level we can approach the text as a product of pre-Christian legal practice. We can think about the practical purpose that would have been served by fixing these particular laws in a set form of words and recording them in the memories of legal experts, and we can try to work from there to a broader model of the way sixth-century law might have worked in practice. This is the focus of the first half of this chapter. The second half considers the laws on the level of ideology. That Æthelberht's purpose in having the laws written down was to assert his status as a Romano-Christian king is well known. This, however, is the ideological significance of his post-conversion act of codification, not that of the existing oral laws. The laws' contents have been analysed frequently enough from one angle or another, but they have never been considered as an ideological whole. This is done here, first focusing on the laws' vision of social order, then on the role that they attribute to the king.

[22] See the summary discussions and dismissals in Wormald, '*Lex Scripta*', p. 8; Wormald, 'Inter Cetera', 186, n. 14; Wormald, *Making*, p. 96. For a statement of this case, see A.W.B. Simpson, 'The Laws of Ethelbert', in Morris S. Arnold et al., eds., *On the Laws and Customs of England: Essays in Honour of Samuel E. Thorne* (Chapel Hill, 1981), pp. 3–17 at 13–17.

[23] As Oliver (*Beginnings*, p. 35) points out, there are good comparative precedents (early medieval Germanic and otherwise) for oral legal traditions featuring specific figures whose duties included the proclamation of law. The most immediate parallels for sixth-century Kent are the Frankish *rachimburgii* of *Lex Salica* whose duty was to speak the law: Karl Augustus Eckhardt, ed., *Pactus Legis Salicae* (Monumenta Germaniae Historica, Legum sectio I, Leges Nationum Germanicarum 4.2, Hanover, 1962), cap. 57, pp. 215–17. For a clear exposition of their role, see Charles-Edwards, 'Law in the Western Kingdoms', pp. 267–9.

[24] Alice Taylor, *The Shape of the State in Medieval Scotland, 1124–1290* (Oxford, 2016), pp. 117–32, shows that such a process can be inferred from twelfth- and thirteenth-century Scottish evidence.

HONOUR AND THE COMPENSATION TARIFF

Let us turn to the laws as a product of legal practice. A crucial observation here is that Æthelberht's laws are strikingly uniform in their content. Virtually every clause of the code is concerned to define an affront and the compensation appropriate to it. The word 'affront' here is important. The code specifies compensations not only for offences that cause material harm (we are told that stealing from a freeman required compensation of triple the stolen goods' value, whilst breaking a rib would cost 3 shillings) but also for less tangible offences, more akin to insults, where the harm done is to the victim's social standing, his reputation, his honour.[25] (The term 'honour', as used here, is no more technical than this: it can be defined as 'the publicly declared valuation put upon a person by those who know him'.)[26] Thus, the wound to man's honour when someone breached his protection by lying with one of his top-ranking female dependants, or by killing someone in his home, is quantified financially in Æthelberht's code (for a nobleman 12 shillings for each of these offences, 6 shillings for a freeman).[27] Today we would tend to categorize these types of offence separately: intangible insult is something one can add to a material injury, but in most circumstances we would expect compensation only for the latter. The laws, however, do not make this distinction: both are to be compensated. This suggests that contemporaries regarded physical injuries as a species of insult; just as lying with a man's female slave was an affront to his honour, so too was breaking his rib.[28]

The context of honour is not something the laws discuss explicitly. The reason for this is surely that it did not need explication: an understanding of honour is assumed. There are a few places, however, where the effects of pervading assumptions about honour can be detected. Bruises which were black 'outside the clothing', for instance, are compensated at a higher rate than those which did not have to be displayed openly.[29] Similarly, as Oliver has rather ingeniously observed, the compensation specified for front teeth is much greater than that for molars, which can only be explained by their visibility (in practical terms the cutting function of front teeth can be performed with a knife, whereas the chewing function of molars cannot easily be replaced).[30] The disproportionately high compensation levels set for offences that touch directly on gender and status are also indicative of a context of honour. The actual harm done to a freeman by physically binding him is negligible, yet the required compensation of 20 shillings makes it the equivalent of a serious physical injury: a broken jaw, a chopped-off

---

[25] 'His' because the victim of an offence is generally presumed to be male. See the discussion of gender below, pp. 51–3.
[26] This definition is borrowed from T. M. Charles-Edwards, 'Honour and Status in Some Irish and Welsh Prose Tales' *Ériu* 29 (1978), pp. 123–41, at 123.
[27] Abt 13–14, 16–17.
[28] This point is nicely illustrated by the analysis of the later Icelandic *Story of Thorstein the Staff-Struck* in William Ian Miller, *Bloodtaking and Peacemaking: Feud, Law and Society in Saga Iceland* (Chicago, 1990), pp. 51–76.
[29] Abt 59–60.   [30] Abt 51. Oliver, *Beginnings*, pp. 100–1.

thumb, or an impaled abdomen.[31] Likewise, though violent castration is undoubtedly horrific, it cannot actually be three times worse than death, as the
triple wergild specified in compensation for it would suggest.[32] These offences are
treated severely relative to the physical harm they cause because they were potent
insults: forceful denials of a free man's freedom and masculinity.[33] The laws
recognize that the worst insults imaginable are not necessarily those that do most
physical harm—they acknowledge that wounds to honour can be more important
than bodily injury or material loss.[34]

The key point here is simple: almost every clause of Æthelberht's code defines
the precise compensation appropriate to a specific affront to honour. The code is
united by this single, overriding concern. By comparison with a lot of other early
medieval legal texts it is a remarkably coherent document. This in itself is analytically useful because it enables us to ask a question: why was it that Kent's legal
experts took the trouble to record *these* laws formally, fixing them in a particular
form of words that could be memorized and recited? Laws on compensation for
affront cannot, after all, have been the only customs that existed in sixth-century
Kent. There must have been a series of accepted ideas about, for example,
inheritance, the duties associated with kinship, the appropriate size of dowries
for women of various statuses, or the number of oaths necessary to deny various
accusations. Pre-Christian Kent must have had a lot of customs covering a lot of
subjects, but these particular customs are the only ones we find recorded
formally. They are certainly the only customs that were accorded the unusual
honour of being written down, and this is probably because they were the only
customs that had previously existed in a set form of words—as an oral 'text'.[35]

---

[31] Abt 24, 50, 54, 61:1.

[32] Abt 64. Oliver's suggestion that this is compensation 'for the lack of future children' does not
make sense in material terms. Only a single wergild would have been required if the victim had been
killed outright (Abt 24), and the harm suffered here is objectively greater: a slain man lacks not just
future children but any future at all. See Oliver, *Beginnings*, p. 99.

[33] Potentially relevant here is the argument made in Carole Hough, 'Two Kentish Laws
Concerning Women: A New Reading of Æthelberht 73 and 74' repr. in and cited from Hough, *An
Ald Recht*, pp. 87–110. If Hough is correct to read Abt 73–4 as specifying compensations to be paid by
women who commit violent acts, presumably in addition to the compensation paid for any wounds
inflicted, this would suggest that being physically attacked by a woman was regarded as particularly
shameful. Physical harm inflicted by a woman may have cast doubt on a man's masculinity to a much
greater degree than the same injuries inflicted by a man.

[34] Oliver, *Body Legal*, pp. 165–71 surveys parallel laws across early medieval Europe.

[35] It is logically possible that Æthelberht—who needed, as Wallace-Hadrill put it, to record 'just
that fraction of custom that seemed enough to satisfy royal pride in legislation' (*Germanic Kingship*,
p. 37)—in fact had a number of carefully memorized and orally transmitted sets of laws to choose
from, and just happened to alight upon this one. This is unlikely, however. Perhaps the most telling
consideration here is that Æthelberht's code is far from unique (Oliver, *Body Legal*, provides a
comprehensive survey of early medieval compensation tariffs): its concern with compensation
settlements is a well-known characteristic of the category of early medieval law known in the
literature as *lex* (as opposed to *capitularia*) or 'primary legislation'. (On these categories, see
Wormald, '*Lex Scripta*', pp. 6–8; Roger Collins, 'Law and Ethnic Identity in the Fifth and Sixth
Centuries', in Alfred P. Smyth, ed., *Medieval Europeans: Studies in Ethnic Identity and National
Perspectives in Medieval Europe* (Basingstoke, 1998), pp. 1–23 at 2.) As there is no reason to suppose
that compensation for affronts to honour was an issue high on the agendas of Christian missionaries,
we surely have to conclude that these texts reflect the priorities of pre-Christian societies. Even if we did

The implication must be that the rules we find in Æthelberht's code were unusually prestigious. Indeed, they were the most prestigious rules in pre-Christian Kentish society, the rules committed to the memories of legal experts, presumably so that they could be recited formally in a public setting.[36] Any explanation of Æthelberht's code, then, needs to explain why this particular type of law, specifying precise compensations for a range of affronts to honour, was so important in sixth-century culture.

Thinking about the problem of satisfying honour in compensation settlements provides a way forward here. A successful compensation settlement required a fine balance to be struck, such that each party could emerge with its honour intact and no reason to reopen the conflict. For this to work the compensation paid could not be too little (it needed to rectify the dishonour inflicted on the victim by the original affront), nor could it be too much (or it would dishonour the party that paid it): only if it was precisely right could both parties be free from reproach. Concern about honour made it important for there to be an authoritative statement of the proper compensation for any given affront. The orally transmitted laws which were eventually written down under Æthelberht make sense as products of this context. They provided exactly the precise and authoritative valuations necessary to reassure parties whose honour was at stake in compensation settlements. In theory a man who accepted 3 shillings in compensation for a broken rib could rest easy knowing that nobody could reproach him for doing so—all would recognize that he had taken exactly what an honourable man ought to take in such a situation, and no less. Likewise, the man who paid could be reassured that he had paid no more than precisely what was warranted by the injury he had inflicted: nobody could claim he had weakly given in to a stronger opponent's unreasonable demands. Compensation tariffs make sense in this sort of honour-bound context. Their basic purpose was to provide authoritative reassurance to the parties involved in a settlement that the amount they paid and accepted was exactly right, dishonouring neither side.[37]

Concern about honour made it important that there be an authoritative and precise definition of the proper compensation payable for an affront. That is, the social logic of honour made it important for a compensation tariff to exist,

---

postulate that the oral material recorded in Æthelberht's code represents only a fraction of the formal oral legal tradition of pre-Christian Kent, we would still have to explain why Æthelberht chose the rules in his code to be written down, leaving the others to languish in obscurity. Again, it should be stressed that this scenario is unlikely, but it would not significantly affect my argument if it were true. To explain it we would have to resort to the idea that the rules Æthelberht (and other early medieval rulers) chose were the most prestigious rules available, and the conclusions that follow from this are near-identical to those set out here.

[36] Clearly we cannot know this, but the alliterative passages noted by Oliver (*Beginnings*, pp. 38–9) hint at a context of recitation, albeit rather weakly, and it is difficult to imagine that people took the trouble to memorize these laws in order to recite them either privately or casually.

[37] This same point is made in a different context in Pauline Stafford, 'Kings, Kingships and Kingdoms', in Wendy Davies, ed., *From the Vikings to the Normans* (Oxford, 2003) pp. 11–39 at 31: 'Precise notions about levels of compensation were essential to the acceptance of a settlement as honourable and thus to its permanence.'

providing indisputable answers to questions about compensation levels.[38] This social logic is probably what lies behind the unusually high level of prestige that tended to be accorded to compensation tariffs in this period: they were prestigious because they *needed* to be prestigious in order to be effective. Their validity needed to be accepted without question if they were to help in the difficult business of negotiating compensation settlements that left neither party dishonoured. A crucial feature of this interpretation is that it requires us to imagine that compensation tariffs were actually *used*. It implies that, whoever they were, the legal experts who memorized Æthelberht's code's sixth-century precursors did so in the expectation that their knowledge would, at least occasionally, be referred to in the context of disputes. Though these laws can and should be regarded as ideological statements of a sort, we will misunderstand them unless we appreciate that in their original oral form they would have served a practical purpose.

We must not be naive about this, however. It is unlikely that in practice compensation settlements tended to adhere rigidly to what the laws specified. A plausible guess is that the laws were understood to provide authoritative state-ments of the compensation required for affronts in generalized terms, but that it was simultaneously held that every case had unique circumstances which needed to be taken into account in the compensation paid if the delicate equilibrium between both parties' honour were to be maintained. Accepting that the value of an ordinary freeman's life is 100 shillings need not imply acceptance that a particular individ-ual's life was worth precisely that amount: 'Ordinary freeman? My brother was no ordinary freeman!' The point of personal honour, after all, is that it is specific to a particular person. Even if the authority of the laws' statements was unquestioned there would have been room for disagreement about how they applied in any given case. Nonetheless, they could still be valuable in providing common ground—a starting point upon which everyone could agree from which discussions about the final sum to be paid could proceed—and as an authoritative resource to be called upon by those trying to persuade reluctant parties that it was right and honourable to agree once a settlement had been negotiated. To argue that these laws grew out of

---

[38] This social logic did not, however, make it important for the internal logic of the compensation tariff to revolve around the concept of honour. This is an important distinction to draw because, though the influence of ideas about honour can be detected in Æthelberht's code they are far from all-pervading; much of the time, as Oliver has emphasized, personal injuries seem to be assessed not with any clear reference to honour, but in relation to the level of suffering and disability a given wound would cause (Oliver, *Beginnings*, pp. 99–105; see also Oliver, *Body Legal*, chs. 3–5). That this internal logic is not fundamentally about honour does not undermine the interpretation of honour offered here. Indeed, the method by which the compensation tariff calculated its valuations did not really matter, except in that it had to be commensurate with the tariff's authority. If it were generally held that a particular tariff of compensations had been drawn up casually and carelessly, or by foolish people with a weak understanding of justice, or in accordance with some fundamentally foreign set of principles, people would simply not accept that what it said was correct. Part of what made any given valuation the *right* valuation might well be that it was rooted in a deep knowledge of relative levels of pain and inconvenience caused by various personal injuries (as Oliver's analysis suggests). The internal logic of compensation tariffs mattered, then, insofar as it was part of what gave those tariffs their authority, but it was the social logic of compensation settlements, rooted in concern for honour, that made it important for precise and authoritative compensation tariffs to exist.

legal practice, then, is not to argue that the nature of legal practice can be read from them in a simple way.[39]

IMAGINING LEGAL PRACTICE

It would be easy enough to leave the subject of legal practice with this warning against the facile assumption that it conformed directly to what the laws say. The evidence does not exist, even in later centuries, that would allow us to reconstruct practice reliably, and for the pre-Christian period we essentially have nothing beyond Æthelberht's code. Nonetheless, there are limits to what is plausible. Though the procedural information they contain is meagre, it is possible to make some deductions about practice from Æthelberht's laws and comparison with better-documented cultures whose laws are broadly similar can provide us with some guidance. In this section my aim is to set out a model for pre-Christian legal practice which I think is plausible, and the clearest way to illustrate the various dynamics at play is to work through an imaginary case.

Using imagination to make up for an absence of evidence is a risky enterprise but it is one that all historians coming to terms with the early medieval past engage in, albeit mostly in private. It is useful to do it in print both because openly displaying the assumptions underlying a given interpretation allows them to be scrutinized by others, and because these reconstructions are helpful for readers trying to imagine their way into a different cultural world. Such hypothetical discussions have a surprisingly sound pedigree. Chris Wickham's account of the imaginary early Anglo-Saxon village of Malling is an outstanding example of this sort of approach being used to good effect, but the direct inspirations for what follows are Lisi Oliver's analysis of the various courses that a hypothetical personal injury case might take in seventh-century Kent and Paul Hyams's 'thought experiments' concerning the options open to an 'average disputing thegn' in late Anglo-Saxon England.[40] Readers will have to make up their own minds as to how convincing they find the interpretation presented in this way. My aim is to persuade but if the ideas presented here stimulate debate, so much the better.

It may be useful at this point to be clear about the comparative material that in part shapes this account. A key influence has been early medieval literature, which has contributed a great deal to my understanding of what honour meant in this

---

[39] This paragraph owes much to conversations with Fernanda Pirie relating to Fernanda Pirie, 'Rules, Proverbs and Persuasion: Legalism and Rhetoric in Tibet', in Paul Dresch and Judith Scheele, eds., *Legalism: Rules and Categories* (Oxford, 2015), pp. 105–28. See also Fernanda Pirie, 'From Tribal Tibet: The Significance of the Legal Form', in Michael Freeman and David Napier, eds., *Law and Anthropology* (Current Legal Issues 12; Oxford, 2009), pp. 143–61, esp. at 146–9 and 154–5 (for the suggestion that law codes were invoked in the 'lengthy and sententious speeches' made by mediators to persuade reluctant tribal leaders to 'swallow their pride' and accept a proposed compromise).

[40] Wickham, *Framing*, pp. 428–34; Lisi Oliver, 'Protecting the Body in Early Medieval Law', in T. B. Lambert and David Rollason, eds., *Peace and Protection in the Middle Ages* (Toronto, 2009), pp. 60–77 at 70–7 (though now also see Oliver, *Body Legal*, pp. 61–9); Paul Hyams, *Rancor and Reconciliation in Medieval England* (Ithaca, NY, 2003), pp. 101–10.

period. Icelandic sagas, in particular, provide a rich vein of material on this subject, which has been analysed astutely and at length by William Ian Miller.[41] It is generally accepted that this Icelandic material makes sense as part of a wider early medieval family of texts in which ideas about honour are largely shared. Honour in the sagas looks very similar to honour in *Beowulf*—the Anglo-Saxon epic poem that was probably composed in the pre-Viking period—and this in turn looks not at all unlike the notion of honour that can sometimes be discerned in the work of Gregory of Tours, who wrote in late sixth-century Francia. Peter S. Baker's excellent recent study *Honour, Exchange and Violence in Beowulf* draws out the essential similarity of the world envisaged by these and many other texts very well.[42] Although it is probably safe to assume that the people of sixth-century Kent would have recognized the role of honour in this world, just as their descendants would in later centuries and their Frankish contemporaries clearly did, it needs to be acknowledged that this *is* an assumption.

I have also spent time in recent years discussing modern feuding cultures with anthropologist colleagues (in particular tribesmen in highland Yemen with Paul Dresch and nomads in eastern Tibet with Fernanda Pirie) and have found it useful to hear about how honour can affect people's behaviour outside the potentially exaggerated or over-neat context of literary portrayals.[43] I hope it will be clear in what follows that I have tried to imagine the period in a generic way, avoiding facile assumptions of similarity and unjustifiable specificity. It would obviously be wrong, for example, to assume that there were no significant differences between the thoughts and behaviour of ordinary people and fictional characters, though this is not to say the two were unrelated. Nor would it be right to think that broad similarities between early medieval societies and those studied by modern anthropologists in terms of honour, violence, and legal practice mean that they were similar in more specific terms. In this context, anthropology is useful primarily for expanding the limits of the imaginable: it can suggest ways of interpreting our sources that might otherwise not have occurred to us. It would be dangerous to assume that modern ethnography can provide ready-made models which can simply be applied to the early medieval past.[44]

---

[41] Miller, *Bloodtaking*; William Ian Miller, *Why is Your Axe Bloody? A Reading of Njál's Saga* (Oxford, 2014).

[42] Peter S. Baker, *Honour, Exchange and Violence in Beowulf* (Cambridge, 2013). See also William Ian Miller, 'Choosing the Avenger: Some Aspects of the Bloodfeud in Medieval Iceland and England', *Law and History Review* 1 (1983), pp. 159–204.

[43] See, for example, Paul Dresch, *Tribes, Government and History in Yemen* (Oxford, 1989); Paul Dresch, 'Aspects of Non-State Law: Early Yemen and Perpetual Peace', in Paul Dresch and Hannah Skoda, eds., *Legalism: Anthropology and History* (Oxford, 2012), pp. 145–72; Fernanda Pirie, 'Rules, Proverbs and Persuasion'; Fernanda Pirie, 'From Tribal Tibet'; Fernanda Pirie, *Tribe and State in Eastern Tibet: Feuding, Mediation and the Negotiation of Authority among the Amdo Nomads* (Working paper no. 72. Halle: Max Planck Institute for Social Anthropology, 2005).

[44] For an attempt to make a similar case in more depth, using anthropological and literary examples more directly, see Tom Lambert, 'Compensation, Honour and Idealism in the Laws of Æthelberht', in Stefan Esders, Han Nijdam, and Lukas Bothe, eds., *Wergild, Compensation and Penance: The Monetary Logic of Early Medieval Conflict Resolution* (Leiden, forthcoming 2017).

A Fictional Case

With this in mind, let us turn to our hypothetical scenario. Our starting point is that an imaginary Anglo-Saxon freeman named Ælfstan (A) has suffered a loss at the hands of the equally imaginary Berhtred (B). Our first question is what that loss means. A fundamental point is that Ælfstan's loss is not just inconvenient to him, it represents an affront to his honour. Internally Ælfstan might be angry about his loss or he might not really care very much but, whatever his inner feelings on the matter, when other people find out about the incident they will understand it as an affront. Socially, this is its meaning (and this will be one of the factors informing Ælfstan's emotional response to it). This is true regardless of what the original loss was: whether it be an eyeball or a chicken, a loss is an affront. Indeed, had Ælfstan been publicly offended in a way that caused no material loss or physical harm (for example, if Berhtred tied him up or lay with one of his female slaves without his permission) it would have been understood in the same way. The nature of Berhtred's offence against Ælfstan does not really matter so long as their peers believe it constitutes an affront.

Unless Ælfstan is willing to be known as someone who accepts such treatment without complaint he needs to do something about it. Doing something about it probably involved conforming to expected emotional models: Ælfstan might feign anger at the affront even if he were not feeling particularly enraged in order to show the world that he was taking the matter seriously.[45] Indeed, for serious affronts it may have been difficult for people in Ælfstan's position to climb down from their initial displays of anger and abandon the pursuit of vengeance unless powerful figures intervened to press the case for socially responsible restraint.[46] But ultimately Ælfstan's task is practical: he needs to make Berhtred pay for the affront. He needs, moreover, to make Berhtred pay in public and at a level which the wider community will accept as appropriate for the loss. Once this is achieved the stain on Ælfstan's honour will be wiped out and his social standing restored, perhaps even enhanced. Whether Berhtred is made to pay financially—in a compensation settlement—or through suffering a loss inflicted by Ælfstan as vengeance, the point of the exercise in social terms is to persuade Ælfstan's peers that he has restored his honour. Personally this could mean many things to Ælfstan: he might revel in the bloody task of chopping off an equivalent part of Berhtred's body, or be appalled by it; he might resent the killing of his brother even after a financial settlement or never have liked him in the first place; he might be satisfied with the return of his prized pig or he might boil with suppressed rage. But in social terms Ælfstan's private emotions are largely irrelevant: what matters is being known to have dealt firmly with Berhtred's initial affront.

---

[45] See Pirie, *Tribe and State*, p. 13, for Tibetan tribesmen 'having' to get angry in this situation. See Miller, *Bloodtaking*, pp. 61–8 for the same social pressure in a medieval Icelandic context.

[46] This is commonplace in comparative examples. See Pirie, *Feuding, Mediation and the Negotiation of Authority*, 14–20; Miller, *Bloodtaking and Peacemaking*, 264–5; Dresch, *Tribes, Government, and History*, 53, 68–9.

At this early point many different things could happen. Ælfstan could be hot-headed enough to set out immediately to take vengeance on Berhtred, perhaps even going beyond what his peers would consider justified by the original affront, which would add a new grievance to the conflict and complicate things considerably. Alternatively, Berhtred might regret his action and want to restore the breach with Ælfstan as soon as possible, apologizing for the offence and offering to pay compensation. If Ælfstan accepts, life is much simpler for all concerned. He would probably want to make sure his peers recognized that his honour was restored, so he might well insist that the deal struck with Berhtred is ratified in an assembly of his neighbours, but providing this happens all will be well—the feud ends without violence. One of the factors that might make Berhtred apologize and offer to pay in this way could be fear of a violent response from Ælfstan—the threat of violence could still have underpinned the transaction—but there is no reason to dismiss the idea that genuine regret and concern to maintain social harmony could play a role in such situations. In our scenario, however, Berhtred does not imme-diately offer to pay compensation. He is a stubborn man and miserly; he is not going to part with his wealth without a fight. So Ælfstan needs to take action. Ælfstan is, because it is useful for us to imagine him in this way, a level-headed man who wants to end the conflict peacefully if at all possible; his task is therefore to coerce Berhtred into payment of compensation.

One way of doing this would be to threaten him with violence directly. Ælfstan would need to gather a group of supporters sufficiently large and intimidating to make the threat seem serious. Most people in Berhtred's position would then probably capitulate rather than risk a violent confrontation. However, if that was going to be easy for Ælfstan to achieve, Berhtred would probably have apologized and paid up in the first place rather than further antagonizing a potentially dangerous enemy. Ælfstan, then, needs to attract supporters beyond the kinsmen and friends upon whose help everyone already knew he could rely, and to do this he needs to persuade other people to help him. A potentially important aspect of this would be for Ælfstan to convince them of the justice of his cause. If people did not accept that Ælfstan had been affronted and was unjustly being denied compensa-tion they would be much less likely to support him. To do this most efficiently, Ælfstan would need an assembly of the local population at which, among other things, it was customary to present legal claims for judgement. A favourable judgement from such an assembly would amount to a firm statement that in the eyes of the community as a whole Berhtred owed Ælfstan compensation.

Such a judgement could certainly be useful to Ælfstan, in that it would put a great deal of pressure on Berhtred. That pressure was partly a matter of political calculation: in the face of the settled will of the community some of the people who previously would have supported Berhtred may well now change their stance and refuse to do so. Even if they do not, the judgement in favour of Ælfstan would make it easier for him to persuade others, who previously would have remained neutral, to support his cause. A judgment might well change the balance of forces between Ælfstan and Berhtred, leading Berhtred to calculate that he would prob-ably lose in the event of a violent confrontation, and that he should therefore pay up. It is important to recognize, however, that much of the pressure on Berhtred would be moral: Ælfstan's favourable judgement is a forceful statement that paying compensation at a particular level was both the right thing to do and the will of the community as a whole. Less stubborn men than Berhtred might well give in to such pressure rather than alienate their neighbours. Indeed, judgement would have made it much easier for Berhtred to submit without losing face: rather than showing weakness by surrendering when threatened by Ælfstan, he could demonstrate his manliness by steadfastly refusing to do so until the wider community asserted that he ought, whereupon he could magnanimously bow to the will of his peers for the sake of maintaining social harmony. Judgements could be useful, then, even to those they did not favour, in that they provided a context in which a defeated party could capitulate without incurring dishonour.

Berhtred, though, is not the sort of man who gives in to moral pressure, and he badly underestimates Ælfstan's resolve. Ultimately he lapses into open defiance and Ælfstan, unwilling to accept dishonour, is forced to act. He gathers his supporters and they travel, armed, to Berhtred's farm. Even at this point a reconciliation may still have been possible in some cases: one later law envisages an Ælfstan figure besieging an opponent in his house for a week and sending word to his kinsmen, presumably in the hope that they would arrange an eleventh-hour settlement;[47] others offer the Berhtred figure the option of attempting to find sureties to guarantee that he will now pay what he owes.[48] Our scenario, however, was always destined to end in violence: Ælfstan is an unstoppable force and Berhtred an immovable object. Who ends up dying depends primarily on the balance of power. Given their personalities we can assume that Ælfstan is well liked by his neighbours in a way that Berhtred is not, and this could result in a bad end for Berhtred. But generalized liking need not translate into participation in a dangerous expedition onto Berhtred's home turf, and Berhtred could have other sources of support; he might be a valued man of a powerful lord, for instance, someone uninterested in Berhtred's neighbour's views and quite able to protect him from Ælfstan. The outcome is not a foregone conclusion.

A bloody denouement is inevitable here, and a prolonged and bitter enmity between the protagonists' families seems a distinct possibility, but this is because Ælfstan and Berhtred are fictional characters invented to illustrate the dynamics of early medieval legal practice. If our case had ended with Ælfstan simply accepting the dishonour of his ill-treatment by Berhtred, it would not have been much use to us, though this course of action (termed 'lumping it' by Miller and Hyams) must surely have been common enough.[49] The same goes for a case in which Berhtred immediately apologizes to Ælfstan and the two of them, with the help of friends and family, agree a settlement with a minimum of fuss. My guess would be that the majority of cases were either settled like this or immediately after a judgement in an assembly: people like Berhtred are not very common in real life. Violence may well have been relatively rare, and that which did occur was probably more likely to

---

[47] Af 42:1.   [48] II As 20–20:6; III Eg 7–7:1; I Atr 4.
[49] Miller, *Bloodtaking*, pp. 245, 274; Hyams, *Rancor*, p. x.

have been the product of hot-blooded anger than the climax of a process of gradually increasing pressure—people do not tend to be as coolly rational as Ælfstan in real life either. But this is not to say that violence was unimportant. Even if it never materializes, the threat of violence is hanging over this whole process, affecting the decision-making of everyone involved. Only a minority of real-life cases can have gone so far as Ælfstan and Berhtred's, but in large part that will be because many of those involved worked hard to prevent that happening. Eruptions may not have been that common but the potential for vengeful violence was fundamental to early medieval legal practice.

Discussion

Ælfstan and Berhtred are fictional but much of this sketch of the legal world they inhabit is implicit in the early evidence. It has already been argued that the existence of prestigious compensation tariffs such as Æthelberht's implies that affronts to honour were a central element of legal practice. That judgements given by assemblies were important aspects of legal practice is likewise suggested by the context of oral transmission: people surely memorized these laws in the expectation that they be applied and if not in assemblies of some sort, then where? Æthelberht's laws make the existence of assemblies explicit: they explain that breaching the peace of an assembly (*mæthl*) requires twofold compensation. Later seventh-century Kentish laws are similar in this: the code of Hlothere and Eadric distinguishes between two types of assembly, the *mæthl* and the *ðing*, though the significance of the distinction is unclear.[50]

One assumption I have been careful to avoid here is that kings played a significant role in people's disputes, using a network of agents either to control the assemblies in which judgements were made or to enforce those judgements. In the context of the sixth century—a period in which kingship itself may well have been in a nascent stage—it is surely sensible not to assume a high level of royal administrative control over local practice without evidence to demonstrate this. Moreover, there are plenty of comparative examples to show that local communal assemblies and enforcement led by affronted parties could function without royal input. Pre-thirteenth-century Iceland, where there were no kings, is the most obvious example, but we could equally turn to Wendy Davies's justly famous study of the early medieval charters of Redon in Brittany, which shows local communities running their own affairs in assemblies without royal involvement.[51] More broadly, we should remember that communities of farmers would have had practical reasons for assembling which had nothing to do with royal power: making arrangements for common grazing or for collective labour at harvest time, for

---

[50] Abt 1; Hl 8. See Pantos, '*In medlé*', pp. 182–4.

[51] See Miller, *Bloodtaking*, ch. 1; Wendy Davies, *Small Worlds: The Village Community in Early Medieval Brittany* (Berkeley, 1988) ch. 6. For a good modern example, see Judith Scheele, 'Community as an Achievement: Kabyle Customary Law and Beyond', in Fernanda Pirie and Judith Scheele, eds., *Legalism: Community and Justice* (Oxford, 2014), pp. 177–200.

instance.[52] Indeed, Æthelberht's laws (as discussed in the final section of this chapter) suggest that the king's financial interest in his people's disputes (and thus his incentive to become involved in enforcement action) was limited almost exclusively to cases in which he was an affronted party.

Æthelberht's code does not discuss enforcement but it does show that kings could call grand assemblies of their people. These, however, are distinct from the *mæthl*—presumably the more local assemblies at which most judgements in cases of wrongdoing would have been made. Harming someone at a royal assembly required twofold compensation to the victim and compensation to the king for breach of his protection; breaching the peace of the *mæthl*, by contrast, required only twofold compensation to the victim. The absence of any compensation due to an official presiding at a *mæthl* may well suggest that these assemblies were local communal affairs rather than parts of a royal administrative network. This is not much to go on but it aligns well with later evidence. As shall be seen in Chapters 3 and 6, there is little reason to imagine local assemblies were under close royal administrative control at any point in the Anglo-Saxon period: even our most detailed tenth-century sources are notable for not assuming that the men who presided at local assemblies were royal officials.[53] These chapters make a similar point for enforcement. Before the emergence of sheriffs in the late tenth century there is little to indicate that local royal officials were expected to play a major role in enforcing assembly judgements; until that point, when enforcement is discussed it either takes the form of vengeance by an affronted party or a communal expedition led by the senior men of an assembly.[54] (We have little evidence bearing on the size and shape of the areas from which Anglo-Saxon local assemblies drew their members before the late tenth century, so what exactly constituted a 'local' community in this period is necessarily rather vague.[55] The extent of local communality is also largely a matter of guesswork, but the clear evidence for the practice of assembling from Æthelberht's laws onwards does at least allow us to infer the existence of 'communities' of some sort.)[56]

[52] See Debby Banham and Rosamond Faith, *Anglo-Saxon Farms and Farming* (Oxford, 2014), pp. 158–61; George Molyneaux, *The Formation of the English Kingdom in the Tenth Century* (Oxford, 2015), pp. 102–3. There is a strong tendency in Anglo-Saxon historiography to see such assemblies in the context of royal government. See, for example, James Campbell, 'The Late Anglo-Saxon State: A Maximum View' repr. in and cited from James Campbell, *The Anglo-Saxon State* (London, 2000), pp. 1–30 at 1–7; James Campbell, 'The Significance of the Anglo-Norman State in the Administrative History of Western Europe', repr. in and cited from James Campbell, *Essays in Anglo-Saxon History* (London, 1986), pp.171–89 at 171–5. A more recent manifestation of this trend is the 'Landscapes of Governance' project, for a prospectus of which see Stuart Brookes and Andrew Reynolds, 'The Origins of Political Order and the Anglo-Saxon State', *Archaeology International* 13 (2011), pp. 84–93.

[53] Chapters 3 and 6, pp. 143–7, 246–50.

[54] Chapters 3 and 6, pp. 152–6, 274–6.

[55] The most plausible guess is that late tenth-century hundreds (which Domesday Book suggests varied considerably in size) were often based on existing assemblies and their associated districts. See Molyneaux, *Formation*, pp. 146–9. The significance of hundreds and wapentakes is discussed in Chapter 6, pp. 243–50.

[56] For a discussion of the slipperiness of the term community, see Fernanda Pirie and Judith Scheele, 'Justice, Community, and Law', in Fernanda Pirie and Judith Scheele, eds., *Legalism: Community and Justice* (Oxford, 2014), pp. 1–24 at 11–17. Scheele's scholarship in particular provides useful warnings

Although we cannot safely assume that kings had any routine involvement in the formation of judgements in local assemblies or in the enforcement of those judgements, it is important to emphasize that this does not mean they were incapable of involving themselves in legal cases if they wished. If Ælfstan happened to have an uncle who was close to the king it would make sense for him to try to use his contacts to secure royal support. If he succeeded this would probably prove decisive: a determined king could certainly enforce judgements against people living within his kingdom, and he would have been well placed to ensure local assemblies issued judgements that served his interests. However, we need not imagine kings took an active role in many of the compensation settlements within their kingdoms; the vast majority were probably beneath their attention.[57] Early kingdoms were relatively small, of course, so it may be that sixth-century kings took a greater interest in relatively petty matters than their successors in later centuries, but we have no reason to suspect that they felt obliged to do so as a matter of routine. They may sometimes have been willing to offend the men of a local assembly by bullying them into issuing a particular judgement, and they may sometimes have sent their own men into danger to enforce other people's compensation payments, but it is likely that they generally did these things only when they had political reasons for wanting to favour a particular party to a dispute.

Accepting the likelihood that kings and their agents had no direct involvement in most disputes is important because it demands that we think carefully about why people would want to submit their cases to formal judgement in assemblies. It is all too easy from a modern perspective to assume that their reasons for doing so related to the power of the 'state': that offended parties brought cases to assemblies either because they feared royal punishment for ignoring peaceful avenues and pursuing a violent feud, or because they wished to take advantage of the fact that assembly judgements were enforced by kings. Neither of these are safe assumptions to make

---

against assuming the universality of communities and communality: Scheele, 'Community as an Achievement'; Judith Scheele, 'In Praise of Disorder: Breaking the Rules in Northern Chad', in Paul Dresch and Judith Scheele, eds., *Legalism: Rules and Categories* (Oxford, 2015), pp. 153–76. For some useful reflection on the term in an early medieval context, see Alice Taylor, '*Lex Scripta* and the Problem of Enforcement: Anglo-Saxon, Scottish and Welsh Law Compared', in Scheele and Pirie, *Legalism: Community and Justice*, pp. 47–75 at 74. For a comparative review of early medieval communality on a larger scale, Chris Wickham, 'Consensus and Assemblies in the Romano-Germanic Kingdoms: A Comparative Approach', in Verena Epp and Christoph H. F. Meyer, eds., *Recht und Konsens im frühen Mittelalter* (Vorträge und Forschungen 82; Konstanz, 2016), pp. 387–424.

[57]　Indeed, it should be noted that coming to a king's personal attention did not guarantee that royal enforcement action would follow. One late tenth-century charter records King Æthelred repeatedly issuing judgements against a certain Wulfbald in a land dispute, and consistently being ignored, with the only attempt at enforcement seemingly coming in the form of a disastrous expedition mounted by Wulfbald's cousin. Wulfbald, then, represents a real-life Berhtred who successfully defies his opponents through repeated judgements, in spite of the king's personal involvement. See S 877 and discussions in Chapters 3 and 6, pp. 152–3 (for quotation of text), 275, 291. This case is discussed in Simon Keynes, 'Crime and Punishment in the Reign of King Æthelred the Unready', in Ian Wood and Niels Lund, eds., *People and Places in Northern Europe, 500–1600: Essays in Honour of Peter Hayes Sawyer* (Woodbridge, 1991), pp. 67–81 at 78–81.

and they can severely distort the way we imagine legal practice, leading us to separate feuding (based on illegitimate 'private' violence) from formal legal procedure (backed by the legitimate use of force by 'public' state power). If we are not careful we can easily imagine that aggrieved parties were faced with a choice: either to pursue their cases peacefully through formal assembly processes or to take up arms in a violent feud.[58]

The most important point I am trying to illustrate with the fictional Ælfstan and Berhtred case is that this separation is unnecessary and unhelpful. For men concerned to restore or maintain their personal honour in feuds it must often have been a sensible strategy to seek an assembly judgement, either as a means of recruiting additional support in a prospective violent confrontation or so as to provide way of climbing down from displays of ultra-masculine belligerence without significant loss of face. (It can be a noble thing to subordinate one's manly instincts to the community's formally expressed desire for peaceful settlement, but in the absence of such pressure the same decision could look like cowardice.) Moreover, unless we make the unjustifiable assumption that sixth-century kings had an extensive law-enforcement apparatus, we have little choice but to understand the threat of violent vengeance from victims and their supporters as central to how offenders were made to pay the compensations specified in assembly judgements. What I hope this hypothetical case has shown is that the temptation to look at violence as a phenomenon in its own right, artificially detaching it from seemingly more peaceful legal practice under the label 'feud', needs to be resisted.[59] It is central to this book's argument that in Anglo-Saxon England feuding was not a bloody and essentially extra-legal alternative to formal assembly procedures; rather, it ought to be understood as an integral part of legitimate legal practice. We cannot meaningfully separate the two.

---

[58] See Introduction, p. 3.

[59] Although he adopts a different position on the terminology, this is recognized in Guy Halsall, 'Violence and Society in the Early Medieval West: An Introductory Survey', in Guy Halsall, ed., *Violence and Society in the Early Medieval West* (Woodbridge, 1998), pp. 1–45. Starting from the premise that feuding is by definition separate from normal legal practice (necessarily encompassing a series of tit-for-tat vengeance killings), Halsall concluded that feuding was so rare as to be virtually non-existent in the early medieval period. Crucially, however, he recognized that the legitimate threat of vengeance was part of normal legal practice; he just labelled this 'customary vengeance' rather than calling it feuding. Perceptive as Halsall's analysis is, this terminological distinction strikes me as unhelpful in an early medieval context. It is easy to see how, if circumstances were unfavourable, the legitimate threat of vengeance inherent in normal legal practice could lead to the tit-for-tat series of revenge killings which he would understand as feuds. These may have been uncommon but they were products of exactly the same set of assumptions about honour and violence as more 'normal' legal practice, and drawing a qualitative distinction seems misleading in this context. Paul Hyams's usage of the term feud (*Rancour*, pp. 6–11, 32–3) is more sensitive on this point. For discussions that wrestle in detail with these definitional difficulties, see Jeppe Büchert Netterstrøm, 'Introduction: The Study of Feud in Medieval and Early Modern History', in Jeppe Büchert Netterstrøm and Bjørn Poulsen, eds., *Feud in Medieval and Early Modern Europe* (Aarhus, 2007), pp. 9–67; Helgi Þorláksson, 'Feud and Feuding in the Early and High Middle Ages: Working Descriptions and Continuity', in Netterstrøm and Poulsen, *Feud*, pp. 69–94.

AN IDEALIZED SOCIETY

Thus far the laws committed to writing during Æthelberht's reign have been considered primarily in terms of their practical function. A fundamental assumption underpinning this analysis has been that these laws were memorized and passed on because they were useful. Compensation settlements needed to strike a delicate balance between the parties involved, so that both could emerge with their honour intact. These laws, essentially a series of precise statements of the compensation appropriate to different affronts, could help achieve such settlements by providing a starting point for negotiations that everyone accepted. Because the practical value of these statements depended on their authority, they needed to be treated with reverence: it therefore makes sense that, of all the rules that must have existed in pre-Christian Kent, these were the ones that were recorded formally, set in a fixed form of words that could be memorized and recited. These laws existed because there was a practical need for the authoritative valuations of affronts they provided, and they need to be interpreted in this context.

Recognizing this, however, does not mean we have to ignore all other contexts. It is perfectly possible—indeed, wholly normal—for laws to be expressions of ideals at the same time as serving a practical purpose. It is, as we have seen, now widely accepted that Æthelberht's purpose in having these laws written down was ideological—an assertion of his credentials as a Romano-Christian king—but this observation tells us little about the sixth century. We can be confident that the laws as we have them (except the first clauses on the Church) represented a particularly prestigious and authoritative form of knowledge in pre-Christian Kent; they exist for us to study because they were understood to be significant in a way that other customs we would think of as legal were not. Indeed, it is a plausible guess that in the period before conversion these laws were sometimes recited in public, at assemblies. (This would make sense as an assertion of the laws' all-important authority, and indeed as a way for the people who took the trouble to memorize the laws to have their expertise recognized.) They certainly need to be treated as a repository for ideas about the proper ordering of society, and probably ought also to be understood as a key means by which those ideas were communicated to a general audience.

Community and Ethnicity

A basic message in almost any set of rules is that of belonging to a particular community, which is united by a shared set of moral standards. Though this is not explicit in Æthelberht's text, in most early medieval laws it is clear that this community is an ethnic community: the laws were probably understood as a manifestation of Kentishness.[60] This assertion of belonging to a community that

---

[60] For recent discussions, see Patrick Wormald, 'The *Leges Barbarorum* : Law and Ethnicity in the Post-Roman West', in Hans-Werner Goetz, Jörg Jarnut, and Walter Pohl, eds., *Regna and Gentes: The Relationship Between Late Antique and Early Medieval Peoples and Kingdoms in the Transformation*

extended beyond the local and specific is fundamental to the laws' practical usefulness: their authority to define what was honourable would be undercut if it were known that the people in neighbouring localities took a completely different view of things. Prestige and authority were important, and they came in part from a sense that the rules being articulated were of general validity, and that the solutions they offered to local disputes would be recognized as just by a much wider imagined community—not just everyone who mattered locally, but everyone who mattered.[61] Free Kentish men probably met other free Kentish men from outside their immediate locality on a reasonably regular basis, perhaps annually at royal assemblies or on military campaigns. The potential assessments of personal honour by such non-local peers presumably needed to be taken into account when negotiating compensation: a settlement which was acceptable locally but would elicit mockery in a wider context would not do. The existence of different local customs of inheritance or suretyship might have been expected and understood, but for matters which touched on personal honour it was important for there to be an accepted set of standards. The laws were thus probably understood as symbolic of the integration of various localities into a greater Kentish whole, unified by a common understanding of the conduct expected of honourable men.

It may not have been highly unusual for free Kentish men to meet people who were not themselves Kentish. Royal households were probably rather diverse places, featuring wives, retainers, and exiles from elsewhere; kingdoms were small and borders may well have been porous; people probably travelled for the purpose of trade; in many English kingdoms there was a resident British population. How foreigners assessed one's honour, however, may not have mattered much in an internal context: a visiting Frank's divergent opinion of the value of a thumb would probably have counted for little against the clear Kentish consensus. What may have mattered was that, if they encountered puzzlement from foreigners, Kentish men were able to assert that their laws were ancient and honourable, just as valid as anything the Franks or West Saxons or Irish had, which was essentially to assert Kentishness as valid identity. Having formalized (not necessarily written) laws, then, may well have been a collective claim to recognition as a people, distinct from but equal to others. For those concerned to assert Kent's place in the wider world to a foreign audience it was essential that the laws be both uniquely Kentish and similar enough to foreign laws as to be recognizably part of the same genre. It is questionable, however, how many people would have shared these macro-political concerns, or indeed understood this outward-facing aspect of the laws' ideological content at all. The absence of any explicit ethnic references in the text ought to caution us against attributing too much weight to this line of interpretation.

of the Roman World (Leiden, 2003), pp. 21–53; Charles-Edwards, 'Law in the Western Kingdoms', pp. 262–3; Oliver, *Body Legal*, pp. 11–14; and (more sceptically) Collins, 'Law and Ethnic Identity'.

[61] For a subtle exploration of this point in a modern context, see Judith Scheele, 'Rightful Measures: Irrigation, Land, and the Sharīʿah in the Algerian Touat', in Dresch and Skoda, *Legalism: Anthropology and History*, pp. 197–227.

Social Rank and Personal Freedom

One of the most striking aspects of Æthelberht's laws is their attention to social stratification. The text's very structure is hierarchical: after the newly added clauses on the Church, it begins with the king at the top of society and works methodically down to the slave at the bottom. The laws' main focus is on three ranks of free male—those of king, nobleman (*eorl*), and freeman (*ceorl*)—who are discussed at length, but they also set out three ranks of freedman, four ranks of widow, and two ranks of the unfree: the *esne* and the *þeow* (designated servant and slave in Oliver's translation).[62] The most obvious message conveyed, perhaps, is that of the super-iority of the king and the noble class, but we need to take care here for two reasons. The first is that if Oliver's conclusions about the text's development are correct, this was a relatively new feature: the oldest sections, marked by their unique use of the archaic dative of quantity, are those covering offences against freemen (including the very brief discussion of freedmen) and personal injury. The logical deduction is that at some early point—a reasonable guess might be in the early sixth century—these were the laws which were memorized and recited. Within this earliest iteration of the laws the vision of social stratification would have been radically different, its main message equality within a dominant class of fully free men. The hierarchical structure that now exists may thus be read as the result of a process in which this original material was added to and recast, creating a newly stratified vision of free society.

This leads on to the second point, that in some senses this original message of equality among free men remains a strong feature of the laws, in spite of the establishment of clear ranks. For the most part there is no qualitative difference between kings, nobles, and ordinary freemen: they are compensated for exactly the same types of offence, just at different levels. A nobleman is really just a grander species of freeman, and though (as we shall see shortly) there were aspects of the king's role which differentiated him from other free males, in most respects the same is true for him. Recasting the laws introduced status differentiation between different ranks of the free, but the free still had far more in common with one another than they did with the unfree. Virtually every clause of the laws involves the payment of compensation to a free recipient for an affront of some sort. The symbolic importance of freedom, as has been noted, was such that binding a freeman was judged to be an affront equivalent to breaking his jaw, chopping off his thumb or impaling his abdomen. By contrast, the unfree are never represented as recipients of compensation. If an unfree dependant is harmed the compensation

---

[62] Carole Hough, 'The Structure of English Society in the Seventh Century: A New Reading of Æthelberht 12', in Hough, *An Ald Recht*, pp. 74–86, suggests that the obscure compensation of 20 shillings associated with 'the king's *fedesl*' in Abt 12 refers to the *mundbyrd* ('protection-value') of a noble rank greater than that of the *eorl* that pertained to members of the king's household. The word *fedesl* relates to the verb *fedan*, 'to feed', one part of the compelling logic behind Hough's interpretation being that these figures were especially honoured because of their position within the king's inner circle, dining at his table. Unfortunately this interpretation came to my attention too late to be fully integrated into this book's analysis. It is discussed further below, p. 58, n. 84.

for that harm is owed to his master. If the foot or eye of an *esne* is struck off, we are told, the offender does not compensate him for the harm done according to the personal injury tariff, as he would for a freeman; rather, he has to pay his entire worth as compensation, presumably to the owner whose property has now been damaged almost to the point of uselessness.[63] The unfree can commit offences and seemingly they can owe compensation for them (and by implication own money), but they do not matter as people in their own right. Only the free could be affronted and require compensation in this society; only the free had their sense of honour recognized and affirmed by the laws.[64]

Gender and the Household

In many respects the distinction between male and female seems to align with that between free and unfree. The laws' discussion of marriage agreements apparently treats free women as property to be bought and sold by heads of household, whilst abduction and rape are treated as offences against a figure characterized as an owner (*agend*).[65] The apparent use of commercial language here may be misleading, however, as both *agan* ('to own') and *bicgan* ('to buy') have rather wider semantic ranges in Old English than their modern equivalents.[66] Nonetheless, even if women were not understood as commodities to be bought and sold, they were still akin to property in as much as they could be thought of as gifts to be given and reciprocated, or indeed stolen and compensated for. The general rule seems to be that, like the unfree, free women could commit offences and be liable for them, whilst offences committed against them were understood as affronts against the male heads of household upon whom they depended. It is possible that this does

[63] Abt 87.

[64] Abt 85 is a complication here. Oliver, following all previous editors, translates as follows: 'if a person lies with a servant's wife while the husband is alive, let him pay 2[-fold what he would have paid were she unmarried]'. This reading implies that singlefold compensation will be paid even for lying with an unmarried female *esne*, presumably to her owner. It is not obvious why the marital status of the *esne* should alter the degree of affront felt by her owner, however, and it is unusual for Æthelberht's laws not to specify the compensation due in monetary terms (except in cases of theft where the value is defined by the stolen goods). Carole Hough, 'Women and the Law in Seventh-Century England' repr. in and cited from Hough, *An Ald Recht*, pp. 46–72 at 69–70, suggests that the clause should be read 'let him pay 2 [shillings]' rather than 'let him pay 2[-fold]'. If this is correct, the natural reading is that the two shillings are due to the woman's husband, the *esne*—otherwise why no consideration of the scenario in which she is unmarried? This is all very uncertain, but it suggests that there may have been something rather anomalous about the *esne* in Kentish society. On the one hand he is someone else's property to the extent that it is his master, not he, who is compensated for serious bodily harm (Abt 87), but at the same time lying with a woman to whom he is married is recognized as an offence—either in its own right or as an aggravating factor which doubles the compensation required for lying with an equivalent unmarried woman. There is a tension here, it seems, between the *esne* as an owner's property and the *esne* as a married man—the head of a household, albeit an unfree one. *Esne* probably thus belongs among the ambiguous semi-free categories considered in Alice Rio, ' "Half-Free" Categories in the Early Middle Ages: Fine Status Distinctions Before Professional Lawyers', in Dresch and Scheele, *Legalism: Rules and Categories*, pp. 129–52.

[65] Abt 31, 77, 82. See *DOE*, s.v. 'agend'.

[66] See Christine Fell, *Women in Anglo-Saxon England* (Oxford, 1984), pp. 15–17; Hough, 'Women and the Law', pp. 64–5.

not apply offences directly against free women's persons—that the women them-selves were entitled to receive compensation for physical harm done to them, even if the heads of their households were also entitled to compensation for the breach of their protection—but the laws do not make this explicit. Indeed, it may be significant that the personal injury section includes no specifically female body parts whilst, as has already been noted, it makes it clear that to forcefully castrate a man was the worst affront imaginable in sixth-century Kent, a physical insult three times worse than death.[67] That the laws were in part an assertion of patriarchal gender roles has long been understood.

Important though this gender distinction clearly was, however, it may not have been quite so stark as that between free and unfree, because it may have been possible in some circumstances for free women to become heads of their own households. This is a significant position in the laws. Free householders are recognized as protectors of all permanent members of their households, as well as any guests who enter their houses temporarily. So, regardless of the identity of the victim, killing someone in a homes is an offence against the householder requiring compensation equivalent to the latter's *mundbyrd*, the value of his protection (*mund*): 50, 12, and 6 shillings for king, nobleman, and freeman.[68] The same compensations apply to illicit sexual intercourse with top-ranking female depend-ants, seemingly wherever this took place,[69] and in more general terms it is stated that if anyone kills the dependant (*hlafæta*, literally 'loaf-eater') of a freeman, the proper compensation is 6 shillings.[70] The head of household is clearly envisaged as a male role, but there is one passage which defines the value of the *mund* (protection) of four ranks of widow, and the most natural reading of this is that this *mund* belongs to the widow herself. This suggests that, in the sixth century just as in later periods, women could inherit the position of head of household on the death of their husbands, with its associated rights and duties. Widows thus occupied the protective role their husbands had previously performed for their household dependants, which could have included free males as well as women and the unfree. It seems, then, that in this capacity free women could be affronted and compensated in the same way as their free male equivalents.[71]

[67] See Abt 61:1, 64.

[68] Abt 5, 8, 13, 15. Note that there is no direct statement of *mundbyrd* for noblemen and no direct statement of compensation for killing in a house for freemen. Breaking into a freeman's house, however, requires 6 shillings in Abt 17.

[69] Abt 10–11, 14, 16. Three ranks of female dependant are imagined for both freemen and the king. The lowest two are explicitly said to be slaves, but the personal status of the top-ranking figure—the king's 'maiden' (*mægdenman*) or the freeman's 'cupbearer' (*birele*)—is unclear. See *ASD* s.v. 'mægdenman'; *DOE* s.v. 'byrle'.

[70] Abt 25.

[71] The text's editors have assumed that the *mund* here belongs to an unspecified guardian: Oliver, *Beginnings*, 111–12; Wormald, *First Code*, p. 9; F. L. Attenborough, ed., *The Laws of the Earliest English Kings* (Cambridge, 1922), p. 178; Felix Liebermann, ed., *Die Gesetze der Angelsachsen*, 3 vols. (Halle, 1898–1916), i., p. 7. However, the compensation payable for breaching *mund* normally varies with the status of the protector rather than the person being protected, and our text provides no reason to assume otherwise on this occasion. A full case for this reading is set out in Carole Hough, 'The Widow's *Mund* in Æthelberht 75 and 76' repr. in and cited from Hough, *An Ald Recht*, pp. 111–29.

The more general point to take from this is that household position had an important role in structuring relationships of domination and subordination. Women may have been regarded as inferior in an abstract sense—like the unfree, they did not matter in the way that free males mattered—but they are not absent from the laws. Rather, they are bound into this vision of society through their subordinate relationships to specific free men (their husbands and fathers), who would generally have been the heads of their households. In this respect they were similar not just to the unfree (whose owners would probably have been the heads of their households in some sense) but also to those, probably mostly young, free males who lived as household dependants of some sort, from military retainers to farmhands. The household was the structure through which specific relationships of domination and subordination were articulated, and the laws stress the validity of this structure just as strongly as they stress the importance of masculinity.[72] If we consider this as ideology, the primary message here is that (free) men are full members of society, and that as heads of household they both exercise authority over and protect their dependants, particularly their womenfolk. The anomalous position of widows as female householders is in tension with this, undercutting it slightly, but this is discussed so briefly that the tension is easily missed or ignored—we should not consider it part of the laws' ideological message.

Kinship and the Individual

There is a slightly more prominent tension in the laws between treating free males as autonomous individuals and assuming them to be bound by powerful obligations to their kinsmen. The laws are strongly individualistic. The most obvious manifestation of this is in verbs of compensation and payment, which invariably appear in the singular (*gebete, forgelde*): it is always 'let him pay', never 'let them pay'. Indeed, at one point it is explicitly stated that killers should pay compensation with their *own* money or unblemished property.[73] Kinship only comes up in the laws when it is absolutely necessary for it to do so: in contexts where a free male is killed. We are told that killing a freeman requires the payment of 100 shillings, of which 20 shillings must be paid at the open grave and the remainder within forty nights.[74] The compensation for killing one of three ranks of freedman (*læt*) is either

In practice, widows may often have been in vulnerable positions (as is implied by the discussion of their abduction in Abt 76) and probably would have needed male assistance to enforce payment of any *mundbyrd* owing to them. Women were almost certainly not expected to threaten to take vengeance for wrongs in person (though this is not to say it was impossible), but in this they were probably no different from other heads of household who would not have been expected to fight in person, such as elderly men. On later widows, see Henrietta Leyser, *Medieval Women* (London, 1995), ch. 8.

[72] On this point, it is well known but worth reiterating that the etymological roots of lordship are in early Anglo-Saxon household relationships: our word 'lord' comes from the Old English *hlaford*, which derives from *hlaf-weard*—the 'loaf-guardian' upon whom 'loaf-eaters' depended. See, for example, Oliver, *Beginnings*, p. 69.

[73] Abt 30.   [74] Abt 21–2.

40, 60, or 80 shillings.[75] That the victim's family are the expected recipients of this compensation is implied but it is not stated, let alone emphasized, in the laws. The responsibilities of kinship are in fact discussed explicitly only once, in the context of the kindred's duty to contribute to the compensation owed by a kinsman who had killed a freeman: if the killer departs the land, his relatives need pay only half the compensation he owed.[76]

The point here is not that kinship ties were unimportant in sixth-century Kentish society, but that the laws are emphasizing individual responsibility and seemingly playing down the duties of kinship. The few passages where kinship obligations are discussed make it clear enough that kinsmen had a central role to play in cases of homicide: the dead man's family's duty was plainly to pursue the killer and his family for either vengeance or payment of wergild, whilst the killer's family were just as plainly expected to contribute to the full payment of that wergild in normal circumstances. The laws seem to be reacting against the prospect of men behaving recklessly because they knew that their families had to support them: they stress that killers should pay wergilds with their *own* resources, and imply that if they cannot they should go into exile and thereby relieve their families of half the debt that had been foisted upon them. The laws' message was that individuals ought to bear responsibility for their own actions, paying for their own misdeeds and not burdening their wider families. This was the laws' ideal—their vision of how the world ought to be—but there is enough tension within them to suggest in reality there were strong expectations of kin solidarity.

An Ideal Society for Ideal Men

Kentish society must have been messier than the vision of it presented in the laws. Even within the laws themselves we can find passages which undercut their dominant ideological messages. The prevailing emphasis on the subordination of women to men is in tension with the one passage defining the *mund* of widows as heads of household, and the general stress on individual responsibility is in tension with the expectation of kindred solidarity visible in a few passages on homicide. The laws had a practical purpose: widows and homicide were important issues that could hardly be ignored. Because they were included we can deduce that in reality domestic hierarchies probably meant that gender roles were more complex than the laws' general impression of women's subordination to men would suggest, and that individuals expected rather more of their kinsmen than the laws would have liked. We might hypothesize that wives could hold considerable authority over their

---

[75] Abt 26. Note that these grades should probably be read as generational: a freed slave having a wergild of 40 shillings, his children 60 shillings, their children 80 shillings, and full freedom imagined as coming with the fourth generation. They are thus an indication of the importance of having free kinsmen to having free status; see Oliver, *Beginnings*, 91–2. For a detailed discussion, see T. M. Charles-Edwards, 'Kinship, Status and the Origin of the Hide', *Past and Present* 56 (1972), pp. 3–33.

[76] Abt 23.

husbands' household dependants, for example, or that kinsmen were expected to help pay compensations generally, rather than just in the context of homicide.

These are special cases, however, where the practical purpose of the laws meant that material cutting against their broader ideological grain had to be included. Our suspicions about the gap between ideal and reality should be more broadly based than this. Thinking about context is crucial here. Because it is likely that these laws had a practical function in compensation settlements we should, I think, be prepared to accept that in that in this context the distinctions around which they revolve were important. Gender, personal freedom, rank, and household position really did matter. This is not so say, however, that they always mattered in exactly the way the laws set out, or that other ideas (as we have seen for kinship) could not also have a role to play. We are safest imagining that in any given case the laws served as an authoritative starting point for discussions as to what should happen given that case's unique particularities, and keeping an open mind as to what those particularities could be. As was noted above, accepting that an ordinary freeman's life was worth 100 shillings leaves plenty of room for argument as to how much a specific individual's life is worth given his various merits and defects.

Even more importantly, we need to be very careful about taking laws which were relevant in the context of compensation settlements and extrapolating from them to draw more general conclusions about society. That we cannot safely assume the overriding importance of legal categories in social and economic terms is a point emphasized in recent scholarship on early medieval freedom and unfreedom. This has shown that in some contexts men treated their freedom as an economic resource to be bought and sold, and that in others the more important distinctions were those relating to a variety of 'grey area' categories between freedom and unfreedom, which are rather difficult to interpret in legal terms but could be important in the division of agricultural labour.[77] This is not to say that the categories which were important in disputes over labour are any more universally valid or 'real' than the categories which mattered for compensation settlements, just that we need to be aware that different distinctions could be prominent in different contexts. This could easily apply to distinctions of gender, rank and household position as well as to freedom. The distinction between freemen and noblemen may not have been particularly obvious or important outside the context of compensation settlements, for example, nor should we be too quick to conclude that because free women are treated as men's property in some contexts and senses in the laws, they were always treated in this way. The corollary of this is that social distinctions probably existed which were crucial in other contexts but relatively unimportant in compensation settlements, and hence absent from the laws. Æthelberht's code is our richest

---

[77] See Rio, '"Half-Free" Categories'; Alice Rio, 'Self-Sale and Voluntary Entry into Unfreedom', *Journal of Social History* 45 (2012), pp. 661–85; Alice Rio, 'High and Low: Ties of Dependence in the Frankish Kingdoms', *Transactions of the Royal Historical Society* 18 (2008), pp. 43–68; Alice Rio, 'Freedom and Unfreedom in Early Medieval Francia: The Evidence of the Legal Formulae', *Past and Present* 193 (2006), pp. 7–40; Wickham, *Framing*, esp. ch. 7.

written source for the social realities of sixth-century Kent, but its interpretation for this purpose is far from simple.

Accepting the likelihood that reality was much more complex and messy than the laws suggest serves to reinforce the value of reading them as ideological statements.[78] The fact that the laws promote a particular vision of society, which must have been at variance with social realities in a number of important ways, is significant in itself. Perhaps the main thrust of the laws was to define who mattered: this was a society consisting of free males. It was not a society of equals—free males could be kings, nobles or freemen, they could be householders or they could be dependants within other men's households—but freedom and masculinity were necessary and sufficient qualifications for full membership of society. When the laws use the word *leod*, 'people', they always seem to be referring to free men.[79] Women could perhaps partially qualify if as widows they inherited the character- istically masculine position of head of household from their husbands, but this exception aside, women and the unfree existed only as subordinate appurtenances of free male owners, husbands and fathers. The laws assert that this was how the world ought to be: it was right that the only full members of society be free and male, and that the unfree and female be considered in connection to them, as their property or at least under their protection. Though women and the unfree would of course have had their own sense of personal honour, and could certainly feel affronted by others' actions, the laws generally seem to assume (and thus implicitly assert) that honour was the preserve of free men. These are the only people whose feelings need to be taken into account. Indeed, in significant sense they *are* the Kentish people—the people who count. The laws are an assertion of the legitimacy of this group's dominance.

They also, however, convey a strong message about how people within this society of free Kentish men ought to interact. The ideal here is hardly non-violent. It accepts as its starting point that people will affront one another in a variety of deeply insulting and brutally violent ways. Their idealism relates to how those affronts will be dealt with: there will be compensation settlements exactly calibrated to the nature of the offence. No alternative is envisaged. This precision was to ensure that both parties to such settlements emerged with their honour intact, their conduct irreproachable because they had neither accepted too little compensation nor paid too much. The utopian vision of the laws is thus a society in which all free males maintain their honour in perfect equilibrium. Stomachs may be impaled, eyes gouged out and slaves raped, but proper compensation settlements would

---

[78] The next three paragraphs take their lead from Donald R. Davis Jr, 'Rules, Culture and Imagination in Sanskrit Jurisprudence', in Paul Dresch and Judith Scheele, eds., *Legalism: Rules and Categories* (Oxford, 2015), pp. 29–52.

[79] The people the king summons to a major assembly in Abt 2 are his *leod*; we cannot be sure that this was an exclusively male group but it is wholly plausible. That one had to be free to be a member of the *leod* is suggested by the fact that the compensation payable for a freeman's life is termed *medume leodgeld* in the laws (Oliver translates this as 'ordinary person-price'). The implication is that there are other ranks of *leodgeld* (lower for freedmen, higher for nobles and the king), but elsewhere (Abt 87) it is clear that the unfree do not qualify for *leodgeld*: if you kill or seriously maim an *esne*, you compensate his owner with the *esne*'s full value.

allow all free men to live together in a state of mutual respect and peaceful goodwill. This ideal could never be realized, as contemporaries would have understood far more fully than we ever will, but this does not mean it was any less likely to affect people's thoughts and behaviour. There is no reason to think that idealism was any less prominent in pre-Christian Kentish society than it is in the modern world.

Within this model of an ideal society of free males is a model of an ideal free man. He is strong and determined, in that he is willing and able do what is necessary to maintain his honour, insisting on being compensated in full for any affront. However, he is also level-headed and reasonable: his strength and determination are used to exact the compensation required to maintain his honour, and no more. He does not rush precipitately to avenge wrongs done to him, nor does he take advantage of his strength to dishonour his opponents by extorting more from them than is just. And he is careful not to impose obligations on others. He accepts full responsibility for all his own actions, personally paying compensation when it is right to do so, and he is certainly not so hot-headed and self-indulgent as to engage in reckless acts which might compel his family to use their wealth to bail him out. A proper man, the laws imply, is not just strong and determined, he exercises restraint because of his commitment to the ideal of a community of free men who respect one another's honour. The laws thus promote a particular construction of masculinity, one distinctly tinged by social responsibility.[80] Implicit in them is a message about how the free men who make up Kentish society ought to act to bring that society closer to its ideal form. The laws, then, can be considered not just as an important element in the practical business of reaching compensation settlements but as an expression of contemporary ideals of social order.

THE ROLE OF THE KING

So far in this chapter the king has been treated as essentially a very grand freeman: qualitatively the same as any other free male, but with quantitatively greater rights

---

[80] Peter S. Baker's recent discussion of the figure of the *ójafnaðarmaðr* ('man of no measure', 'unevenman') in the sagas makes a strikingly similar point: 'In the Icelandic saga, the type of character that best illustrates the disruptive effect of this warrior ethic away from the battlefield, on the farm, is the *ójafnaðarmaðr*, the man who refuses either to pay compensation for his own acts or to accept compensation from others, who insists on taking more than his due, and who bristles with hostility, signalling to all that he is not to be trifled with' (Baker, *Honour, Violence and Exchange*, p. 73). (On the *ójafnaðarmaðr* see Miller, *Bloodtaking*, p. 67; William Ian Miller, *Eye for an Eye* (Cambridge, 2006), p. 8.) Baker's ultimate argument here is that Grendel in *Beowulf*, who is specifically described as refusing to pay compensation for his killings, is another example of this literary type. I have no particular conclusion to advance here, but it does seem worthy of note that the idealized male behaviour in at least some early medieval laws corresponds closely with that in at least some early medieval literature. Broadly on the theme of tempering the violence inherent in certain models of masculinity with less destructive ideals, see D. M. Hadley, 'Introduction: Medieval Masculinities', in D. M. Hadley, ed., *Masculinity in Medieval Europe* (London, 1999), pp. 1–19 at 4–8; M. Bennett, 'Military Masculinity in England and Northern France, c. 1050–c.1225', in Hadley, *Masculinity*, pp. 71–88 at 85–7; Richard Kaeuper, 'Vengeance and Mercy in Chivalric *Mentalité*', in Lambert and Rollason, eds., *Peace and Protection*, pp. 168–80.

to reflect his more exalted status. This is not a misrepresentation; many royal rights are scaled-up versions of those of lesser men, and this needs to be emphasized. Stealing from the king requires ninefold compensation; for freemen it is three-fold.[81] The king's *mundbyrd* (protection-value) is 50 shillings, which is the same sum payable for killing in his house or for lying with a top-ranking female dependant. As has already been noted, the laws envisage noblemen and freemen being affronted in exactly the same ways but place less value on their protection: 12 and 6 shillings respectively.[82] There are, however, exceptions to this general rule: the king has some rights which are specifically kingly, and these can give us useful information about what it meant to be a king in the late sixth century. As Chapter 2 is concerned specifically with the development of English kings' legal roles in the century following Æthelberht's conversion, it makes sense to conclude this chapter with an examination of these distinctively royal rights.

Not all the pertinent passages here are particularly revealing or clear. We are told, for example, that the king was expected to have his own smith and someone called the *laadrincman* (literally something like 'lead-warrior-man'), whose particular significance is signalled by the compensation of 100 shillings owed to the king for killing them, twice what we might have expected.[83] We are also told that 20 shillings must be paid for the king's *fedesl*, which may or may not be our first evidence for one of the fundamental economic foundations of early medieval English kingship: the duty of the kingdom's free population to provide food for their king.[84] The king also has the right to summon his people to a great assembly

[81] Abt 4, 9.   [82] See above, p. 52.

[83] Abt 7. Given that the freeman's *mundbyrd* of 6 shillings applies to killing members of his household (Abt 15, 25), we would expect the figure here to be 50 shillings. That it is double this figure presumably implies that these two household members had a significance to kings beyond that of their other free dependants. It should be noted that there is some ambiguity in this passage: it is not clear whether the *ambiht smið oþþe laadrincman* means 'official smith or *laadrincman*' or 'official, smith or *laadrincman*'. It is thus plausible that a third figure, the *ambiht* ('official' or perhaps 'servant'), is also intended. See the discussion in Oliver, *Beginnings*, pp. 87–8.

[84] Abt 12. For this interpretation, see Lisi Oliver, 'Cyninges Fedesl: The King's Feeding in Æthelberht, ch. 12', *Anglo-Saxon England* 27 (1998), pp. 31–40. As is noted above (p. 50, n. 62), a different reading of this passage has recently been offered in Hough, 'Structure of English Society': a king's *fedesl* is the highest rank of nobleman, whose exalted status derives from his enjoyment of the king's food. He is thus, it is argued (pp. 83–6), a direct parallel for the 'king's *geneat*' of Ine 19, the term *geneat* being a derivative of the verb *neotan* ('to enjoy') just as *fedesl* derives from *fedan* ('to feed'). Hough argues that the Kentish king's *fedesl* and the West Saxon king's *geneat* were members of the king's household, and that the sum of 20 shillings for the king's *fedesl* in Abt 12 represents this figure's *mundbyrd* (protection-value). A potential problem here is that in Æthelberht's laws entitlement to *mundbyrd* is closely associated with heads of household rather than household dependants. This suggests a minor modification to Hough's theory, which links the passage to food renders in a different way from that suggested by Oliver: the *fedesl* here is a former member of the king's household who has been rewarded with a grant of the king's rights over a particular area of land, the most important of which was the entitlement to the king's food renders in that area for the support of his own household. As Thomas Charles-Edwards has shown, late seventh- and early eighth-century evidence implies the existence of a typical career pattern for noble males, involving a period serving in a royal household as a youth followed at around the age of twenty-five by a grant of land from the king, whereupon the young noble would marry and set up his own household, retiring from full-time attendance on the king. (See T. M. Charles-Edwards, 'The Distinction between Land and Moveable Wealth in Anglo-Saxon England', in P. H. Sawyer, ed., *Medieval Settlement: Continuity and Change*

at which, in addition to the usual doubling of compensation payments that applied at assemblies, all those attending were protected from harm by the king's *mundbyrd* of 50 shillings.[85] The laws suggest that under normal circumstances assemblies were not protected by a specific figure, which may imply that this ability to summon and protect an assembly was a peculiarly royal right.[86]

Kings, then, had a particular relationship with their people (meaning the free male population) which meant they were entitled to be fed by them and to command them to assemble. With this specifically royal authority went an equally royal duty of protection: the king protected those assembling at his orders from all forms of harm. This idea that kings have a particular protective relationship with their people is articulated even more forcefully and clearly in the rule that if one free male kills another, 50 shillings is to be paid to the king as *drihtinbeage*, which Oliver renders 'lord-payment' (more literally, 'lord-ring').[87] The figure of 50 shillings is equivalent to the king's *mundbyrd*, and the obvious and generally accepted inference is that the entire free male population was understood to be under the king's protection.[88] The king, then, was every free man's *dryhten*, his lord. He had some degree of authority over them and this came with a duty to protect them.[89]

There is one passage in the section of the laws devoted to the king's rights, however, which is much more difficult to interpret. 'If a freeman steals from a freeman, let him pay three[fold], and the king obtains the *wite* or all the [man's] goods'.[90] The most coherent reading of this is that the thief must pay threefold

(London, 1976), pp. 180–7 at 181–4; T. M. Charles-Edwards, 'Social Structure', in Pauline Stafford, ed., *A Companion to the Early Middle Ages: Britain and Ireland, c.500–1100* (Oxford, 2013), pp. 107–25 at 109–15; and Chapter 3, pp. 119–23). This passage may imply that this career path existed in Æthelberht's time, although if so the extreme brevity of the allusion to the *fedesl* could perhaps be taken as an indication of its relative novelty. This reading would align well with distinctions made between nobles with and without land in later laws, such as Ine 45, 51, VI As 11. On food renders: Ryan Lavelle, 'Ine 70.1 and Royal Provision in Anglo-Saxon Wessex', in Gale R. Owen-Crocker, ed., *Kingship, Legislation and Power in Anglo-Saxon England* (Woodbridge, 2013), pp. 259–73; Wickham, *Framing*, pp. 314–26.

[85] Abt 1, 2, 8.

[86] Our one reference to such assemblies (Abt 1) seems to imply that it was the collective (the *mæthl*) which had its own peace (*frið*).

[87] Abt 6. For an informative discussion of this term, see Daniela Fruscione, '*Drihtinbeag* and the Question of the Beginnings of Punishment', in O'Brien and Bombi, *Textus Roffensis*, pp. 157–74 at 160–1.

[88] Wormald, 'Inter Cetera', p. 193.

[89] There is a tempting analogy here with the role of the head of a household, who likewise has a duty to protect those under his authority. However, we should be wary of accepting this too easily. The king's household features in the laws in much the same way as other free households: if it really was imagined to encompass the entire kingdom this is not something the laws choose to emphasize. Indeed, it is noteworthy that the normal household relationship in which the householder provides food to his dependent loaf-eaters (*hlafætan*) is inverted if we consider the kingdom in this way: it is the free population who provide the king's food renders. The king's position may have been understood as in some ways resembling that of the head of a giant metaphorical household of all free Kentish men, but the roles of householder and king were clearly not identical.

[90] Abt 9. This translation is based on Oliver's, but with one important exception: she renders *cyning age þæt wite* as 'the king obtains that fine', seemingly implying that the fine the king receives is the threefold compensation due to the freeman. This does not make sense, so here I have followed earlier translators (e.g. Attenborough, *Laws*, p. 5; Wormald, *First Code*, p. 4) and rendered *þæt* as 'the'.

compensation to his victim and an unspecified *wite* to the king; should he fail to pay that *wite*, the king can seize his property.[91] In later laws *wite* is the standard term for a punitive fine, and in more general usage can mean simply 'punishment', 'pain that is inflicted as punishment', even 'torment'.[92] This is the only point in Æthelberht's text where this term is used, and indeed the only occasion when the amount to be paid for an offence is not defined in either absolute or relative terms. In a set of laws devoted to defining precisely the compensation proper to affronts, this is glaringly exceptional: it is neither precisely defined nor compensation for an affront. Theft is an affront requiring compensation, of course, and it is recognized as such in the passage: the affronted freeman is due three times the value of the stolen goods. The king, though, is not involved here as an affronted party, so in what capacity is he receiving this *wite* for theft?

Chapter 2, which examines the rise of royal punishment in seventh-century law, attempts to provide a full answer to this question. The most important point to make here is just how limited the inferences we can draw from Æthelberht's text are. The most revealing fact about this passage is where it appears: it mentions both compensation to an affronted freeman and a *wite* to the king, so it could conceivably have been placed in either the section on freemen or that on the king. That it appears in the list of the king's rights tells us that the royal *wite* was not added as an incidental detail (it also makes it unlikely that this exceptional reference to a punitive fine was a later emendation): we are told about this *wite* because it was understood to be worthy of inclusion in a list of major royal rights. It may thus be possible to infer that this *wite* for theft was the only significant punitive fine claimed by the king in Æthelberht's day. (There are two other passages in the section on women which could perhaps be understood as punitive royal fines, but the interpretation of each is vexed and their position in the text suggests they were not regarded as significant rights in the same way.)[93] This deduction is not certain

---

[91] Wormald, *First Code*, p. 14.   [92] ASD s.v. 'wite'.

[93] The obscurity of the scenarios these passages envisage offers some support to the idea that whatever royal rights they discuss were relatively insignificant. Abt 84 states that if *gængang* occurs 35 shillings are to be paid as compensation and 15 shillings to the king. The previous two clauses discuss the abduction of a *mægðman* ('maiden'). *Gængang* is a term that occurs only in this text, and its meaning is both obscure and contested. Various interpretations have been proposed. Oliver (*Beginnings*, pp. 108–9) suggests that *gængang* refers to the return of the woman and that the 15 shillings to the king represent something akin to a fine for robbery. Carole Hough, 'A Reappraisal of Æthelberht 84', repr. in and cited from Hough, *An Ald Recht*, pp. 150–7, argues that the term refers to an ambush on a road. This would make this an early equivalent to the later offence of *forsteal* and perhaps imply that the notion of royal protection of vulnerable travellers was rooted in the pre-Christian period (see Chapter 4, pp. 187–8; Chapter 5, pp. 233–4). Christine Fell, 'An Appendix to Carol Hough's Article "A Reappraisal of Æthelberht 84"', *Nottingham Mediaeval Studies*, 37 (1993), pp. 7–8, suggests *gængang* may here refer to a fight between the man to whom the *mægðman* had been promised and the man who had wrongfully taken her, and argues that the verb to take (*niman*) used in this context could imply wrongful sexual intercourse, or even rape, rather than abduction. Abt 73 has also been interpreted as a punitive fine: it states that if a lock-bearing free woman (*frewif locbore*) does something characterized as *leswæs* she is to pay 30 shillings. If *leswæs* refers in a generalized way to 'dishonest conduct' it is possible this represents a fine, but Hough, 'Two Kentish Laws', pp. 88–100, argues the sum represents additional compensation payable for violence committed by women, presumably to account for the added indignity of being subjected to a gender-inappropriate form of

but it is important: as shall be seen in the next chapter, late seventh-century kings asserted the right to receive significant fines for a range of offences which do not appear in Æthelberht's code. If it is correct to infer that the laws' section on the king was intended as a comprehensive list of all major royal rights, the absence of any reference to *wite*s other than that for theft is a significant absence—it would suggest that late seventh-century royal fines other than those for theft were innovations.

It is crucial, however, to recognize that Æthelberht's laws appear to have had a rather narrow agenda. Their fundamental purpose was to set out the proper level of compensation for a range of affronts to honour. A secondary purpose, it seems, was to list all the significant payments to which the king was entitled (hence the reference to the *wite* for theft and perhaps also to the king's right to food renders). It would therefore be wholly wrong to regard Æthelberht's code as anything approaching a comprehensive account of sixth-century legal customs. The fact that it does not mention inheritance customs does not mean sixth-century Kent lacked inheritance customs; the fact that it contains virtually no procedural rules does not mean assemblies had no procedural rules. The reason for emphasizing this here is that this applies to punishment too: the fact that Æthelberht's laws tell us about only one royal *wite* may tell us that this was the only significance *royal* punitive right but it does not imply that, with this one exception, punishment was absent from sixth-century legal culture. We must bear in mind the possibility that just as local communal assemblies probably had their own rules about procedure, they could well also have had traditions of collectively imposing punishment on people who breached such rules (and quite possibly other important behavioural norms). Recording such customs was not Æthelberht's laws' business: their absence from our text in no way precludes the possibility that they existed.

We should, then, at least be open to the possibility that punishment was a part of sixth-century legal culture but that it was primarily communal, its association with kingship still in its nascent stages. We could plausibly speculate, perhaps, that the practice of imposing a punitive *wite* on thieves developed independently in a lot of different locations, and that at some point the king claimed the right to receive all of these *wite*s. (It should be noted that local communities can be found receiving punitive fines in tenth-century laws.)[94] The fact that the laws do not specify the size of the *wite*, then, would be because it varied from place to place: what the king was actually doing was using his coercive power (the threat of seizing the thief's goods) to ensure that locally defined punitive fines were in fact paid, claiming the right to receive those fines in recompense for his role as an enforcer of communal norms. Æthelberht's laws neither support nor undermine this interpretation; at this stage I simply wish to highlight it as a possibility. (The only early evidence that

---

physical attack. For discussion: Oliver, *Beginnings*, 110–11; Christine Fell, 'A "Frewif Locbore" Revisited' *Anglo-Saxon England* 13 (1984), pp. 157–66.

[94] See Chapters 3 and 7, pp. 153–5, 315–17.

bears directly on it is archaeological: fifty-four decapitated skeletons spread across thirty-two primarily pre-Christian cemeteries.[95] Though there are other plausible contexts for decapitation, there is no reason to dismiss the possibility that some of these beheadings represent executions of people who had seriously transgressed communal morality.) We will return to this possibility in the next chapter, which tentatively argues that earlier communal traditions of punishment are implied by the shape of later evidence.

[95] Andrew Reynolds, *Anglo-Saxon Deviant Burial Customs* (Oxford, 2009), pp. 78–81, 263–4. Note that a minority of these burials have dating ranges stretching into the seventh century (p. 81). Reynolds, in the context of a broader analysis of 'deviant burial' in the Anglo-Saxon period, interprets these pre-Christian headless corpses as the result of post-mortem decapitations designed to prevent a suspected dead person from returning to haunt the living, but though he emphasizes this 'superstitious' context he acknowledges that we cannot discount a context of execution (p. 91). In the Christian period, by contrast, he strongly emphasizes a context of judicial execution for the ninety-nine possible instances of decapitation identified, giving very little weight to superstitious practices in spite of noting that the other key feature suggestive of execution—some indication that the dead person's hands had been bound—is not common (p. 166–9). Although Reynolds's emphasis on superstition in the pre-Christian period and royal punishment from the late seventh century aligns well with the currently dominant historiographical interpretation of the legal evidence (see discussions in Chapters 2 and 4, this volume, pp. 63–6, 169–71), it is not clear that the archaeological evidence offers any independent verification for it. A more cautious reading would be that in each period both contexts could have been important: some headless skeletons probably resulted from execution (though not necessarily in a judicial setting), and some may represent the practice of post-mortem decapitation. In later periods burial evidence has been used to argue specifically that serious breaches of sexual morality could result in execution. A context of homosexuality, at any rate, is suggested by Reynolds for some same-sex double burials in the late Anglo-Saxon period (p. 174), and that of bestiality for a number of burials involving animals (p. 172). Though he does not make this argument for the pre-Christian period he does note one burial in which two decapitated men were buried face-down and weighed down with stones, which could potentially be interpreted in the same way (p. 66). For an interpretation which emphasizes superstitious practices throughout the period, see John Blair, 'The Dangerous Dead in Early Medieval England', in Stephen Baxter et al., eds., *Early Medieval Studies in Memory of Patrick Wormald* (Farnham, 2009), pp. 539–59. See Chapter 5, pp. 220–3, for a suggestion about the ideological significance of what Reynolds (pp. 178–9) terms 'execution cemeteries'.

2

Kingship, Legislation, and Punishment in the Seventh Century

INTRODUCTION

The seventh century seems to have witnessed a major shift in the legal functions expected of English kings. If we accept that the laws of Æthelberht are a written version of laws that had previously existed in a memorized form, then they show that pre-Christian kings of Kent claimed the right to receive a *wite*—a punitive fine—from thieves. However, as we saw in Chapter 1, this reference is an isolated one. The laws' primary agenda was to define the proper levels of compensation for a range of affronts to honour. In the potentially problematic language of the historiography, our evidence for pre-Christian law focuses firmly on 'horizontal' justice, and this *wite* for theft is a rare 'vertical' exception.[1] Our next significant evidence for law in England is a cluster of texts from the late seventh century. We have two Kentish codes, one jointly in the names of Kings Hlothere and Eadric (dating between 679 and 686), the other in the name of King Wihtred, probably issued in September 695.[2] We also have our first evidence for English law outside Kent, in a set of laws attributed to King Ine of Wessex, the prologue of which can have been written no later than 694.[3] The balance between the 'horizontal' and the 'vertical' in these later texts is different. Laws about affront and compensation are still present, but they are no longer the main focus: there are many more royal punishments and a lot more rules about technical and procedural matters. Æthelberht's code and these three later texts are virtually our only evidence for law in this period. Superficially, at least, they suggest that an important shift took place: royal punishment became a part of English legal culture in a way that it had never been before.

This is a relatively obscure period in the historiography of English law. Whereas the tenth and eleventh centuries could be understood as necessary background to the common law, the seventh lies well beyond the interests of most modern legal

---

[1] See Introduction, pp. 5–6.

[2] On joint kingship in Kent, see Barbara Yorke, *Kings and Kingdoms of Early Anglo-Saxon England* (London, 1997), pp. 32–4.

[3] Although for the sake of simplicity the terms 'Wessex' and 'West Saxon' are used here throughout, it should be noted that until the late 680s the people known to historians as the West Saxons appear to have identified themselves as the 'Gewisse'. See H. E. Walker, 'Bede and the Gewissae: The Political Evolution of the Heptarchy and its Nomenclature', *Cambridge Historical Journal* 12 (1956), pp. 174–86.

historians. Patrick Wormald, however, was unusual in this regard. Though his main focus was the late Anglo-Saxon period, he ventured into the seventh century for long enough to establish what has become the standard interpretation of the legal changes it witnessed.[4] This interpretation places English developments in a wider European context, as part of a trend in which Germanic kingship was remoulded along Romano-Christian lines in the wake of religious conversion. The characteristically rich prose of his argument's concluding paragraph is worth quoting at length:

> Law-making itself was in all parts of Europe an increasingly serious matter.... Whether or not they made law in writing, kings were ever more active in the justice of the peoples they ruled. If Æthelberht gave Roman form to what was essentially traditional, Hlothere, Wihtred and Ine were beginning to use the Roman medium to put across what can be called the Roman message: that disturbances among their people were their business.... [T]he extent of actual change in seventh-century judicial process may have been less than the prescriptive texts make it seem. But the change in legislative approach is a fact, and one which, given the balance of social power in post-Roman society, can reasonably be expected to have had some effect at "ground level". Even, therefore, if Roman literary inspiration went off at half-cock, so that the impulse to make written law petered out, the Roman principle that justice was a ruler's affair did not. Anglo-Saxon kings no longer made written law through most of the eighth and ninth century; Bede's own Northumbrians never did. But nor, to judge from Ine's code or Bede's view of Æthelberht, did they any longer preside as essentially passive embodiments of harmony over a society that worked out its own discords by feud and compensation. "Parcere subiectis et debellare superbos" meant not merely committing law to script but exerting a vigorous and exploitative social control. It was a lesson that seventh-century Anglo-Saxon kings, like the other western legatees of Aeneas, were keen to learn.[5]

Æthelberht's laws, then, represent a newly converted king's attempt to assert his identity as a successor to the Roman emperors by having existing laws put into writing: 'the Roman medium'. Later kings, however, took this much further, making a genuine attempt to rule in more Roman fashion by asserting that the punishment of wrongdoing was the king's responsibility, and this resulted in a fundamental and lasting shift in English legal culture.

The core of this interpretation seems to me to be unassailable. It does appear likely that royal punishment had a relatively small role to play in Æthelberht's Kent: the laws he had written down do seem to be making an effort to list the king's principal financial rights, and (though certainty on this point is impossible) the absence of any fines beyond one *wite* for theft in that list is probably significant. The contrast between this and the later seventh-century laws shows that kings were much more aggressively punitive in their legislation from this point onwards,

---

[4] See discussion and references in Chapter 1, pp. 30–1.
[5] Patrick Wormald, '"Inter Cetera Bona Genti Suae": Law-Making and Peace-Keeping in the Earliest English Kingdoms', repr. in and cited from Wormald, *Legal Culture*, pp. 179–98, at 198. The Latin quotation is from Vergil's *Aeneid* (bk. 6, ln. 853), and refers to the duty of Roman conquerors to impose peace and, roughly translated, 'to forgive those who submit and vanquish the proud'.

and the best explanation for this is precisely the one Wormald offers. Bede's eulogy for King Edwin of Northumbria (d. 633) makes the point very clearly:

It is related that there was so great a peace in Britain, wherever the dominion of King Edwin reached, that, as the proverb still runs, a woman with newborn child could walk throughout the island from sea to sea and take no harm. The king cared so much for the good of the people that, in various places where he had noticed clear springs near the highway, he caused stakes to be set up and bronze drinking cups to be hung on them for the refreshment of travellers. No one dared to lay hands on them except for their proper purpose because they feared the king greatly nor did they wish to, because they loved him dearly. So great was his majesty in his realm that not only were banners carried before him in battle, but even in times of peace, as he rode about among his cities, estates and kingdoms with his thegns, he always used to be preceded by a standard bearer. Further, when he walked anywhere along the roads, there used to be carried before him the type of standard which the Romans call a *tufa* and the English call a *thuf*.[6]

It is quite possible Bede's portrayal of Edwin is entirely inaccurate: he is unlikely to have done anything of the sort with bronze drinking cups, and for all we know he may never have heard of a *tufa*. The passage is significant in this context as a representation of an ideal king written in the 730s.[7] Bede clearly associates Edwin's ostentatious *romanitas*—the *tufa*—with his impressive capacity to maintain order in his kingdom. Kings, as the heirs of Roman emperors, are responsible for ensuring peaceful conditions within their kingdoms, and an important aspect of this is making people fearful of their wrath should they do wrong. This early eighth-century expression of idealized Romano-Christian kingship aligns well with the punitive tenor of late seventh-century laws, and it seems much more likely than not that the two are connected in the way Wormald argued.

Accepting this explanation for the increased punitive ambitions of late seventh-century kings, however, only gets us so far. What impact these changing ideas about kings' legal responsibilities had on established legal culture and practice remains an open question. This was not a problem on which Wormald focused his attention, and in effect this means that there is no standard historiographical line. As he acknowledged in the quotation above, we cannot know for sure how far kings were able to mould existing legal culture to their new ideological model. Kings were the most powerful men of their day, but whether they were really able to exert 'vigorous

---

[6] *Ecclesiastical History*, ii.16.
[7] On this passage and its analogues, see Timothy Reuter, 'The Insecurity of Travel in the Early and High Middle Ages: Criminals, Victims and their Medieval and Modern Observers', in Timothy Reuter, *Medieval Polities and Modern Mentalities*, ed. Janet L. Nelson (Cambridge, 2006), pp. 38–71 at 42–5; Paul J. E. Kershaw, *Peaceful Kings: Peace, Power, and the Early Medieval Political Imagination* (Oxford, 2011), pp. 31–9; Alan Cooper, 'The Rise and Fall of the Anglo-Saxon Law of the Highway', *Haskins Society Journal* 12 (2002), pp. 39–69, at 39–45. Hints that this concern with security of travel on roads, and (albeit much less certainly) the notion of royal responsibility for ensuring it, may have been rooted in the pre-Christian past can perhaps be found in Æthelberht's laws' discussion of the offences of *wegreaf* (from *weg*, 'way', and *reaf*, 'robbery') and *gængang* (an obscure term which may refer to the offence of obstructing or attacking someone intent on travel). See Abt 19–20, 84, 89. On the interpretation of *gængang*, see Chapter 1, p. 60, n. 93.

and exploitative social control' over their people is uncertain. And as Chapter 1 emphasized, we need to be careful in the way we imagine pre-Christian English legal culture. Æthelberht's laws offer us an immensely valuable insight into the sixth century, but we should not forget that though they give a coherent and comprehensive account of a particularly prestigious category of legal rules—those defining compensations for affronts—they tell us next to nothing about legal rules beyond that category. When we find late seventh-century laws discussing 'new' types of law such as procedural rules and punishments, we need to keep an open mind as to how novel they really were. We should not automatically assume that our new 'vertical' punishments represent kings cutting against the grain of a purely 'horizontal' legal system.[8]

This chapter, ultimately, will argue the opposite. New royal punishments emerged in the late seventh century, but only in areas where punishment already made sense within native legal culture. Before we get to that point, however, we need to disentangle the substantive legal changes of the seventh century from the cultural assumptions and ideological agendas that pervade our sources. Most fundamentally, we need to understand our evidence. We naturally place Æthelberht's code and our three late seventh-century texts in a single category: 'law'. This is almost certainly not how contemporaries would have understood them, however, and unless we comprehend this we will misinterpret them. The first section of this chapter, then, tries to make sense of how the type of law represented by Æthelberht's code and that represented by the three later texts relate to one another, and what the emergence of this second genre tells us about seventh-century legal change. Much of this involves re-treading ground already covered by Wormald, largely accepting his conclusions (albeit sometimes with rather different emphasis) and exploring some of their implications more fully.

With this foundation laid, the second section turns to establishing precisely what new rights late seventh-century kings were trying to claim for themselves. For Kent, this is relatively simple as we have Æthelberht's laws as a baseline against which to compare those of Hlothere and Eadric and those of Wihtred. For Wessex we have only the laws attributed to Ine and this makes it much more difficult to work out whether the claims they make for the king are restatements of traditional rights, traditional rights dressed up in new ideologically tinged language, or entirely novel creations. This second section, building on the findings of the first, establishes

---

[8] At certain points this assumption informs Wormald's work in ways that strike me as problematic: see below, p. 108, n. 143. However, it should be noted that this is a more general feature of the historiography; I am focusing on Wormald here because his work has proven seminal. Carole Hough, 'Legal and Documentary Writings', repr. in and cited from Carole Hough, *An Ald Recht: Essays on Anglo-Saxon Law* (Newcastle upon Tyne, 2014), pp. 2–24 at 13, provides a relatively cautious summary, focusing her remarks on the changing emphasis of legal texts and only hinting that this reflects a broader shift in attitudes. By contrast, Daniela Fruscione, 'Beginnings and Legitimation of Punishment in Early Anglo-Saxon Legislation from the Seventh to the Ninth Century', in Jay Paul Gates and Nicole Marafioti, eds., *Capital and Corporal Punishment in Anglo-Saxon England* (Woodbridge, 2014), pp. 34–47 at 35, explicitly adopts the premise that the changing focus of the texts reflects a transition between different models of society—a process of fundamental socio-legal change driven by the emergence of a 'central power'.

a coherent account of the new punitive rights which Christianized kings claimed in the late seventh century. The third and final section examines how these new punitive rights fitted into existing legal culture. It tries to reconstruct the rationale underpinning kings' various punitive claims—what was it that made these offences worthy of punishment?—and argues that they are most plausibly interpreted as emerging from native understandings of good and bad conduct, perhaps even from existing communal punitive traditions. The chapter concludes by suggesting a new model for the relationship of feuding and punishment in early Anglo-Saxon law. Rather than representing a challenge to an existing 'horizontal' legal order, the new 'vertical' royal punishments complemented established law on affront and compensation. Because feuding was only an appropriate remedy for certain types of wrongdoing, there had always been room for punishment in English legal culture. The trend we see in the seventh century is kings moving to fill a punitive space that already existed: an important assertion of a new royal role but not the establishment of a fundamentally new legal order.

LAW AND LEGISLATION

Apart from a few useful passages in Bede's *Ecclesiastical History*, our evidence for the legal changes of the seventh century comes in the form of four law codes, three Kentish (those of Æthelberht, Hlothere and Eadric, and Wihtred) and one West Saxon (that of Ine). All survive as later copies. For the Kentish laws this presents relatively few problems: our only extant text for each appears in the same manuscript as Æthelberht's laws and there is little reason to believe that any of them were altered significantly during transmission from the seventh century to the twelfth.[9] Ine's laws, however, survive only as an appendix to the late ninth-century laws

---

[9] There are some complications, however. Carole Hough, 'Numbers in Manuscripts in Anglo-Saxon Law', repr. in and cited from Hough, *An Ald Recht*, pp. 251–71 at 262–3, argues that the differing treatment of numbers in the three Kentish texts (their different preferences on when to use numerals and words) not only show that the laws of Hlothere and Eadric were initially written down independently of the other texts, but also hint that the first few clauses of that code (Hl 1–4, where numbers are expressed exclusively in words) may have a different origin to the rest of the text (Hl 5–16:3, where numbers are primarily expressed as numerals). This bears on the uncertain but for present purposes relatively inconsequential issue of whether the code represents a legislative endeavour undertaken in the context of joint kingship or a compilation of two kings' legislation. For a suggestion that the final clauses of Wihtred's laws, which see a change in subject from ecclesiastical matters to theft (Wi 25–8), may represent borrowings from West Saxon law, see Wormald, *Making*, p. 102. Some textual relationship is certain because Wi 28 and Ine 20 are near-identical, but this could very easily have been a result of contemporary contact rather than later interpolation. For broader discussion of the manuscript, see Carole Hough, 'Palaeographical Evidence for the Compilation of *Textus Roffensis*', repr. in and cited from Hough, *An Ald Recht*, pp. 216–50 (especially at 233–4, for the conclusion that laws of Æthelberht circulated separately from those of his successors until 'a fairly advanced stage in [their] textual history'); Patrick Wormald, *The Making of English Law: King Alfred to the Twelfth Century*, vol. 1: *Legislation and Its Limits* (Oxford, 1999), pp. 244–53; Patrick Wormald, '*Laga Eadwardi*: The *Textus Roffensis* and its Context' repr. in and cited from Wormald, *Legal Culture*, pp. 115–38; Lisi Oliver, ed., *The Beginnings of English Law* (Toronto, 2002), pp. 20–34; Bruce O'Brien, '*Textus Roffensis*: An Introduction', in O'Brien and Bombi, *Textus Roffensis*, pp. 1–16.

of Alfred, which leaves more room for uncertainty. The fact that there are frequent discrepancies between Ine's laws and Alfred's shows that there was no comprehensive late ninth-century effort to update the older laws to bring them into line with Alfred's pronouncements. It was clearly not regarded as a problem that Alfred's laws were different in some respects from what had gone before, and this allows us to be fairly confident that our text of Ine's laws represents genuine early material.[10] It remains a possibility that our text includes some small-scale late ninth-century amendments to specific laws, made for reasons other than harmonizing them with Alfred's, but there is no strong reason to believe this is so, and if any such amendments were made they cannot now be detected.[11]

A crucial point, however, is that our text of Ine's laws looks like a compilation. It is disorderly and repetitious in a way that suggests it is a composite of several legislative edicts. Wormald, who first argued this, tentatively suggested that the text contains six distinct sets of laws. The prologue shows that one of them, probably the first, was promulgated no later than 694 but the rest could have been issued any time in Ine's reign (688–726).[12] Indeed, it is possible that laws issued by later kings—perhaps even earlier ones—have been falsely attributed to Ine here, though there is no obvious reason to suppose a late ninth-century compiler would have wanted to erase all other early kings' reputations as law-givers. A reasonable hypothesis, then, is that an Alfredian compiler has run together perhaps six legislative edicts from Ine's reign, excising all but one of their prologues so as to give a false impression of a single code.[13] Whether this represents all the early West Saxon written law available in the late ninth century is uncertain. It may have done, but we ought to remain open to the idea that the compiler chose these legislative edicts for a reason, deliberately omitting other laws.[14] The transmission of Ine's laws, then, is not as straightforward as that of the Kentish laws. Nonetheless, it seems likely that the laws we have are genuine products of the late seventh and early eighth centuries. The lack of a West-Saxon equivalent to Æthelberht's code makes deductions about what was new in late seventh-century law more uncertain for Wessex than for Kent. However, as we will see, there are good reasons to think that pre-Christian law was similar in both kingdoms. Providing we keep the uncertainties in mind, Ine's laws are valuable evidence, significantly richer than our Kentish material in some respects because of their greater length.

The main analytical obstacle to tracking legal change in the seventh century, in fact, applies just as much to Kentish as to West Saxon law: genre. All three of our later texts represent a different type of law from that visible in Æthelberht's code. We cannot compare our texts of late seventh-century law with our text of late sixth-century law and assume that the differences represent, in any simplistic way, changes which took place in the intervening decades. As we saw in Chapter 1,

[10] Wormald, *Making*, p. 278.
[11] The same can be said for amendments made between Ine's reign and Alfred's.
[12] Wormald, 'Inter Cetera', pp. 188–92; Wormald, *Making*, pp. 104–5.
[13] It is also possible that this composite text already existed in Alfred's time, having been compiled earlier.
[14] See below, p. 73, n. 29.

it is probable that Æthelberht's code was Æthelberht's only in the sense that he was responsible for having it written down. He was not legislating; he was codifying existing law. The laws represent the authoritative legal wisdom of the people of Kent, stored in the memories of a now deeply obscure group of legal experts. Hlothere and Eadric, Wihtred, and Ine, by contrast, were openly engaging in legislation: they were establishing new rules. Whereas the main source of legal authority underpinning Æthelberht's laws was presumably that of the legal experts in whose memories they had traditionally been kept, the authority underpinning the later seventh-century laws was that of the kings themselves, usually—perhaps always—acting in conjunction with large assemblies of their kingdoms' notables.[15] In the language of modern historiography, Æthelberht's laws represent *lex* or 'primary legislation' whereas the later texts are *capitularia* or 'secondary legislation', but these labels are not necessarily helpful.[16] Far more important is to understand the language contemporaries used to classify their own laws. The implications of this language need to be explored carefully.

Existing Law

Æthelberht's laws, unfortunately, lack a prologue: we have no direct evidence for the category of law to which contemporaries understood them to belong. As we saw in Chapter 1, however, they do seem to represent an attempt to provide a full list of the compensations appropriate for affronts to honour. We know that these rules about affront and compensation were prestigious not just because Æthelberht chose to write them down but because a lot of effort had previously been invested in their preservation: they appear to have been carefully articulated in a fixed form of words which was then then committed to the memories of legal experts. Though other types of legal rule must have existed in pre-Christian Kent, they were not written down and this is most likely because they had never been articulated and memorized in such a fixed form of words. People must have understood their inheritance customs, for instance, and the legal procedures of their local assemblies, but there is no sign that these rules were ever formalized in the same way. It is likely that alongside the prestigious rules about affront and compensation which the experts could recite, there was a host of well-known—though perhaps often more locally specific—rules about other things, which most people could describe but which did not exist in a form that could be learnt by rote. So, although we lack contemporary labels, Æthelberht's laws suggest the existence of two categories of legal rule: one formalized, prestigious, supposedly applied throughout Kent, and concerned almost exclusively with affront and compensation; the other a catch-all for legal

---

[15] The prologues of both Wihtred and Ine make the involvement of such assemblies explicit. The laws of Hlothere and Eadric make no reference to such an assembly but it remains possible that one (or more) took place. For a comparative review of the legislative and other roles of assemblies in early medieval Europe, see Chris Wickham, 'Consensus and Assemblies in the Romano-Germanic Kingdoms: A Comparative Approach', in Verena Epp and Christoph H. F. Meyer, eds., *Recht und Konsens im frühen Mittelalter* (Vorträge und Forschungen 82; Konstanz, 2016), pp. 387–424.

[16] See Chapter 1, p. 36, n. 35.

customs on other matters which were not formally memorized, and may have varied from locality to locality.

The late seventh-century laws provide evidence for the language contemporaries used to classify existing law. All three texts represent themselves in their prologues as additions to established legal rules, for which they use two different terms. The laws of Hlothere and Eadric and those of Ine use *æ* (plural: *æ*), 'law', which has connotations of lengthy and ongoing tradition and in later usage is often associated with the law of God.[17] The laws of Wihtred use *þeawas* (singular: *þeaw*), 'customs', other senses of which include 'conduct', 'practice' and 'behaviour'.[18] It is possible that these two terms, *æ* and *þeawas*, effectively mean the same thing in this context: that they are just different ways of referring to existing law. The vocabulary, however, strongly hints that *æ* was more formalized and prestigious than *þeawas*, and this makes it attractive to interpret the two terms in line with the distinction implicit in Æthelberht's laws between prestigious legal rules formally recorded in the memories of legal experts and those legal customs that were never recorded in this way. That is, the existing legal rules to which late seventh-century kings were adding consisted of both formalized and prestigious *æ* ('law'), and *þeawas* ('customs') which were well established but not recorded in a form that could be learnt by rote. *Æ* was concerned almost exclusively with the definition of the level of compensation appropriate for a range of affronts, and Æthelbert's code provides a valuable early snapshot of it, whereas *þeawas* ranged much more widely but are essentially invisible to us because (unlike *æ*) they did not exist in a set form of words which a king could order someone to write down.[19]

---

[17] Hl prol.; Ine prol.; DOE s.v. 'æ'. See Oliver, *Beginnings*, pp. 134–5; Wormald, *Making*, p. 95; Andreas Fischer, 'Lexical change in late Old English: from *æ* to *lagu*', in Andreas Fischer, ed., *The History and the Dialects of English: Festschrift for Eduard Kolb* (Heidelberg, 1989), pp. 103–14.

[18] Wi Prol 3; ASD s.v. 'þeaw'.

[19] The main reason for thinking *þeawas* were not recorded in this way—in an orally transmitted 'text'—is the likelihood that Æthelberht would have had such a text committed to writing had it existed. As was noted in Chapter 1 (p. 36, n. 35) there is no obvious reason to think that he would have chosen to have only one of several available sets of laws written down. And had prestigious oral rules on other subjects existed we would surely expect to find some hints of their existence in later written laws (as this chapter argues we do for the type of law represented by Æthelberht's code—see below, pp. 72–4). It is plausible, however, that formal sets of rules with limited applicability existed, perhaps defining procedures specific to particular assemblies (a later example would be the London rules in VI As 1–8:9). Although kings could have ordered someone to write such rules down, it is unlikely they would have wanted to associate themselves with rules that lacked general acceptance. That Æthelberht's code represents established law (*æ* or *þeawas*) rather than innovation is argued in Wormald, *Making*, pp. 94–6, where he points out that Bede's characterisation of the text as *decreta . . . iudicorum* ('decrees of judgements') almost certainly reflects contemporary assumptions about kings' legislative role rather than accurate information about Æthelberht's reign (see also Wormald, 'Inter Cetera', p. 186). Other commentators have tended to accept the accuracy of Bede's words rather less critically, and thus to assume Æthelberht legislated in an essentially late seventh-century manner. See A.W.B. Simpson, 'The Laws of Ethelbert', in Morris S. Arnold et al., eds., *On the Laws and Customs of England: Essays in Honour of Samuel E. Thorne* (Chapel Hill, 1981), pp. 3–17 at 5; H. G. Richardson and G. O. Sayles, *Law and Legislation from Æthelberht to Magna Carta* (Edinburgh, 1966), pp. 1–10; and also, albeit only implicitly, T. M. Charles-Edwards, 'Law in the Western Kingdoms between the Fifth and Seventh Centuries', in Averil Cameron, Bryan Ward-Perkins and Michael Whitby, eds., *The Cambridge Ancient History Volume 14: Late Antiquity: Empire and Successors, AD 425–600* (Cambridge, 2001), pp. 260–87 at 264–6. Speculation that Bede's

This interpretation of the way that existing law was categorized in the late seventh century law is impossible to prove, but it aligns well with the evidence. The later Kentish codes make good sense interpreted in this way. The laws of Hlothere and Eadric characterize themselves as additions to *æ*, and they do indeed fit that description if we accept that *æ* consisted of the rules about affront and compensation. Their overwhelming concern is with scenarios in which one party has affronted another and ought to pay compensation.[20] Wihtred's laws, on the other hand, have rather different concerns. With only one exception, they do not mention compensation at all: their main concern is with religious misconduct— with offences that had no direct victims and thus could not constitute affronts to honour.[21] The rules Wihtred made had little to do with the concerns of *æ*, in other words, and it therefore makes sense that they are presented as additions not to *æ* but to *þeawas*.

The laws of Hlothere and Eadric also convey a strong impression that they are building on and working around an established legal tradition. They assume existing knowledge of the type of basic laws about affront and compensation visible in Æthelberht's code. For example, they order that anyone who sheds blood in another man's house should pay that man his *mundbyrd* ('protection-value'), but they do not trouble to define how much that should be.[22] When they do mention established rules they do so in order to clarify new ones. So, in discussing a scenario in which an *esne* (an unfree dependant) has killed a free male and his owner owes compensation, the victim's status is defined with reference to his wergild: a man with a wergild of 100 shillings requires less compensation than one with a wergild of 300 shillings.[23] As additions to *æ*, these laws could refer to *æ* for illustrative purposes but it was not their business to alter or restate it.

It is important to be clear here about the form in which *æ* existed. It would be easy for us to assume that the authoritative statement of *æ* in late seventh-century

information was based on an original preamble, absent from the extant version of Æthelberht's code, may underlie this trend; see Felix Liebermann, ed., *Die Gesetze der Angelsachsen*, 3 vols. (Halle, 1898–1916), iii., p. 3.

[20] They deal with killings (Hl 1–4); theft of slaves (5); procedures for accusations about possession of stolen goods (7, 16–16:3); situations in which one man brings a claim for compensation against another (8–10); insults and violence in houses (11–14); and situations in which one man's guest harms another (15). The only clause which does not envisage a situation in which one party has affronted another (or at least is making an accusation relating to an affront) is Hl 6, which states that children under ten years of age should remain in the custody of their mothers should their fathers die, and that a kinsman should give surety to maintain his property for them.

[21] The exception is Wi 2, which states that the amount payable for breaching the Church's protection (its *mundbyrd*) is 50 shillings, like the king's. Otherwise they deal with the Church's liberties and obligations (Wi 1–1:1); unlawful unions (3–6); priests neglecting baptism (6); obligations to provide hospitality to clerics (7); manumission (8); working on the Sabbath (9–11); making offerings to devils (12–13); eating during fasts (14–15); oaths of exculpation (16–24); and theft (25–28). The passages on oaths of exculpation would of course apply to accusations relating to affronts, but they would apply to other types of offence too and a context of compensation is never made explicit (unlike in Hl 8–10). Thefts are affronts, but the situations envisaged in Wi 25–28 are those in which the thief is caught in the act and not permitted to pay compensation (unlike in Hl 5, 7, 16–16:3; or Abt 1, 4, 15, 82–3).

[22] Hl 14.   [23] Hl 1, 3.

Kent was Æthelberht's written code, but this is probably incorrect. There is no reason to assume that Æthelberht's attempt to codify an existing oral legal tradition brought that tradition to a close. It is likely that the *æ* people were aware of in the late seventh century continued to be oral, and that the authority to expound *æ* continued to lie with the legal experts who memorized it.[24] Indeed, a plausible guess is that the reference to *cantwara deman*—'the judges of the Kentish people'— in the laws of Hlothere and Eadric is a reference to this otherwise obscure group of legal experts.[25] Our expectation, then, ought to be that the *æ* around which these laws were working remained an oral tradition, not a written one. The texts themselves support this. Hlothere and Eadric allude to a nobleman's wergild of 300 shillings as though it is established law, but it does not appear in Æthelberht's code; they assume knowledge of the *mundbyrd* appropriate to various ranks of householders, but Æthelberht's code does not provide a complete list, missing out that of a nobleman.[26] The proper inference here is surely that these basic rules about compensation were a part of the oral tradition of *æ* which the compiler of Æthelberht's code happened to miss out. That these later codes show no sign of wanting to fill the gaps in the written text, assuming knowledge that it did not contain, suggests that they were constructed as additions to an oral tradition of *æ*, not a written one. We should thus understand *æ* as a continuous oral tradition, of which Æthelberht's laws provide an immensely valuable but imperfect snapshot.

Ine's laws make it clear that Wessex too had a tradition of *æ*, twice referring to it as something separate from but complemented by the king's new laws.[27] It is likely that, as in Kent, it was an oral tradition with pre-Christian roots. At one point Ine's laws envisage someone demanding justice before a *scirman* or another *dema*: it is again plausible that at least one of these figures, probably the *dema* ('judge'), was someone who had memorized *æ*.[28] Although we lack an early snapshot of this oral

---

[24] There are signs of something similar in Frankish evidence: several references survive to practices carried out 'according to Salic law' which do not correspond to our texts of *Lex Salica*. See Patrick Wormald, '*Lex Scripta* and *Verbum Regis*: Legislation and Germanic Kingship from Euric to Cnut' repr. in and cited from Patrick Wormald, *Legal Culture in the Early Medieval West: Law as Text, Image and Experience* (London, 1999), pp. 1–43 at 21–2.

[25] Hl 8. Their role in this passage is to specify the compensation that should be paid for an offence, which would be a suitable function for someone who had memorized a tariff of compensations.

[26] Hl 1; 14; Abt 8, 15. (We have to infer that a nobleman's *mundbyrd* was 12 shillings from a comparison of Abt 13–14 with Abt 15–16.)

[27] Ine Prol. Wormald's early suggestion ('*Lex Scripta*', p. 7) that Ine's laws represent 'the basic *lex* of the West Saxons' is thus problematic. He modified this later but only slightly, arguing that Ine's reference to 'just *æ* and just royal judgements' being *gefæstnode* throughout his people shows that 'accepted law and potentially innovatory judgements were both his business' (Wormald, *Making*, p. 104). I find this unconvincing. The distinction between *æ* and royal judgements (*cynedomas*) is drawn explicitly, and the same sentence goes on to characterise the laws that follow as *ure domas* ('our judgements'): the clear implication is that Ine's new laws are not *æ*. The confusion arises from the verb *gefæstnian* (DOE s.vv. 'fæstnian', 'ge-fæstnian', 'ge-fæstnod'). This is more likely to mean 'to make firm' or 'to fix in place' than 'to establish', as Wormald implies; the prologue is expressing the desire that both existing *æ* and the king's new *domas* be firmly adhered to—royal legislation certainly complements *æ*, reinforcing it, but it does not 'establish' it. We will come to *domas* shortly.

[28] Ine 8. The meaning of *scirman* in this passage is discussed in Chapter 3, pp. 143–4.

tradition equivalent to that provided by Æthelberht we may have one from a later period. The late ninth-century laws of Alfred, to which Ine's laws form an appendix, include a West Saxon personal injury tariff: a set of precisely the sort of basic rules about affront and compensation which, by analogy with Kent, we would expect to have been a key component of oral *æ* in the seventh century. Importantly, it is organized in a way that suggests periods of both oral and written transmission. The first half of the tariff has a head-to-toe structure of the type Oliver interprets in the laws of Æthelberht as a mnemonic device, and thus an indication of oral transmission. The second half of the tariff, by contrast, discusses body parts in a random order, which would have made the text much more difficult to memorize: it suggests a series of amendments made after the tariff had been committed to writing.[29] The most natural reading is that Alfred's personal injury tariff derives from oral *æ* which was first written down and then amended in that written form.

There are solid indications, then, that there was a West Saxon oral tradition of *æ* akin to the Kentish one we are lucky enough to find committed to writing under Æthelberht. The content of Ine's laws supports this: rather like the laws of Hlothere and Eadric, they seem to be working around an established set of basic rules about affront and compensation. Indeed, the *æ*-shaped hole in Ine's laws is much more pronounced because their greater length makes their omissions more striking. They do not mention core compensations for personal injury and theft, and (just as in the laws of Hlothere and Eadric) wergilds only appear incidentally as a means of defining rank in other contexts.[30] If we try to infer the value of the basic protections that householders of various ranks extended to their dependants and house-guests from Ine's laws, we struggle just as badly as we would if we were reading the later Kentish texts without the knowledge of *mundbyrd*s provided by Æthelberht's code.[31] It is not that rules about compensation are entirely absent, but that the rules which do come up are always peripheral issues, for which one can easily imagine there was no established *æ*. For example, Ine's laws set out the wergilds proper to Welshmen of differing ranks, and they specify the compensation due to a godfather or godson in the event of one or the other being killed. The latter would not have been an issue in the pre-Christian period, and the former may well reflect the aggressive extension of West Saxon rule to nearby British communities in the seventh century.[32] These examples of peripheral rules on affront and compensation

---

[29] If this reading is correct, it remains uncertain whether Alfred had access to *æ* in an oral form, which he had transcribed and subsequently modified, or whether there was an existing manuscript. A faint possibility is that, as well as issuing *domas*, Ine also commissioned a written statement of *æ* which Alfred drew upon liberally and chose not to include in his appendix because it would undermine his own code's authority.

[30] Incidental wergild references: Ine 19, 34:1, 70.

[31] The uncertainty surrounding the West Saxon king's *mundbyrd*, discussed below, pp. 86–7, illustrates this nicely.

[32] Ine 23:3, 24:2, 32–3, 74, 76–76:3. The discussion of *manbot* (compensation due to a lord when his man was killed) in Ine 70 may also belong in this category. Although this seems like a core compensation, and it certainly becomes one, it is noteworthy that there is no direct equivalent in Æthelberht's laws (or indeed in any of our Kentish texts). A possible interpretation, then, is that

throw the absence of core rules on this subject into relief. We may not have a direct record of an oral tradition of *æ* in seventh-century Wessex, but its presence can be detected in the shadow it casts on Ine's legislation.

Were there traditions of *æ* in other English kingdoms in the seventh century? There is no reason to think not. That no Mercian law code survives, and that Northumbrian and East Anglian kings seem never to have issued laws in writing, does not imply that an oral legal tradition was absent in those or any other kingdoms.[33] In early eleventh-century manuscripts, however, we do find short texts purporting to record Mercian and Northumbrian *laga* (singular: *lagu*), a Scandinavianism for 'law' which eventually comes to be used in a similar range of contexts to *æ*, and these focus on defining the wergilds of various ranks of society exactly as we would expect in *æ*.[34] In their current form these texts belong to the post-Viking period, but as Wormald notes they look 'decidedly old-fashioned' in that context—they use seemingly archaic units of value, for instance—and it is conceivable that they derived from Mercian and Northumbrian oral traditions of *æ*.[35] In some later evidence, particularly Domesday Book, we find references to groups of *lagemanni* ('lawmen') or *iudices* ('judges'), often associated with particular towns.[36] These are sometimes interpreted as manifestations of Scandinavian influence, but they are not confined to regions that were part of the 'Danelaw'. Most notably, the late tenth- or eleventh-century text known as the *Ordinance Concerning the Dunsæte*, which discusses legal arrangements pertaining to an unknown area towards the southern end of the Anglo-Welsh frontier, includes a reference to twelve *lahmen*.[37] It should also be noted that Domesday Book records twelve

---

manbot was not a feature of traditional West Saxon *æ* but a later addition, a reflection of seventh-century social changes which rendered personal lordship more significant and led to its legal recognition. We might imagine the idea that lords protected all their commended men evolving from the protection offered by heads of households to their household dependants (or 'loaf-eaters'), which is visible in Abt 25. See Chapter 1, pp. 52–3. If this reading is not accepted, Ine 70 must be regarded as an exception to the pattern identified here. For a clear discussion of commendatory lordship in the later period, Stephen Baxter, 'Lordship and Justice in Late Anglo-Saxon England: The Judicial Functions of Soke and Commendation Revisited', in Stephen Baxter et al., eds., *Early Medieval Studies in Memory of Patrick Wormald* (Farnham, 2009), pp. 383–419. On early West Saxon expansion see Barbara Yorke, *Wessex in the Early Middle Ages* (London, 1995), pp. 52–60.

[33] On the possible identity of the Mercian law code of King Offa, alluded to in Alfred's code (Af. Int. 49:7–49:9), see Patrick Wormald, 'In Search of King Offa's "Law-Code"' repr. in and cited from Wormald, *Legal Culture*, pp. 201–23. Cf. Hough, 'Legal and Documentary Writings', p. 12.

[34] ASD s.v. lagu; M. R. Godden, 'Ælfric's changing vocabulary' *English Studies* 61 (1980), pp. 206–23 at 214–17. The texts are *Mircna laga* and *Norðleoda laga*: see Wormald, *Making*, pp. 392–4.

[35] Wormald, *Making*, p. 393. The association of the number 30,000 with a royal wergild in both these texts (Mirce 2; Norðleod 1) fits with the royal wergild of 30,000 apparently paid to the West Saxons in 694 (*Anglo-Saxon Chronicle*, s.a. 694).

[36] Lincoln: DB i. 336r; Stamford: DB i. 336v; Cambridge: DB i. 189r and E. O. Blake, ed., *Liber Eliensis* (Camden Society Third Series 92, London, 1962), ii. 24; Chester: DB i. 262v; York: DB i. 298r and R. C. Van Caenegem, *English Lawsuits From William I to Richard I* (2 vols., Selden Society 106–7, London, 1990–1), no. 172A; involved in land disputes concerning the Bishop of Ely: Blake, ed., *Liber Eliensis*, ii. 8, ii. 11, ii. 33.

[37] Duns. 3:2. The essential discussion of this text is now George Molyneaux, 'The Ordinance Concerning the Dunsaete and the Anglo-Welsh Frontier in the Late Tenth and Eleventh Centuries' *Anglo-Saxon England* 40 (2012), pp. 249–72.

iudices in Chester, even though the other legal customs recorded there lack the apparently Scandinavian features of those listed for York or Lincoln.[38] While we cannot be sure as to their origins or level of formalization, it is likely that these groups of legal experts were bearers of oral legal traditions of some sort, and given that a Scandinavian root cannot readily explain all our examples we ought to remain open to the idea that they drew to some extent on pre-Viking practices.

It is thus plausible that oral traditions of *æ* were a feature of all Anglo-Saxon kingdoms. This would not be particularly surprising, as there is evidence that situations in which knowledge of the law rested with groups of legal experts were widespread in early medieval Europe. The *rachimburgii* who are envisaged 'speaking' the law in early Frankish texts are a well-known example, as is the Icelandic 'lawspeaker'.[39] In an incisive analysis, Alice Taylor has recently shown that the text known as *Leges inter Brettos et Scottos*, which has a similar focus on core compensation payments, is in fact one of a number of texts drawing on a broader corpus of material of this type circulating—possibly in oral form—in twelfth-century Scotland, most plausibly amongst an obscure group of legal specialists known as *iudices*.[40] It is also worth noting that legal expertise was particularly well developed in early medieval Ireland, with a distinct class of legal professionals claiming access to a wealth of intricate and prestigious specialist knowledge, much of which survives in the texts they produced.[41] Though in the literacy and self-conscious sophistication of its legal experts Ireland was exceptional, it fits within a broader European pattern. Indeed, the Carolingian writer Einhard seems to have assumed that all peoples who lacked written law had their own oral legal traditions: he explains that Charlemagne, on receiving the title of Emperor, had 'the unwritten laws of all the nations under his lordship written down and committed to letters'.[42] Except in areas of southern Europe where there is evidence for the consultation of written law in normal legal practice—Visigothic Spain, most notably—it may well be that in the early Middle Ages formalized law existed mainly in the memories of

[38] Chester does appear to have been the site of significant Hiberno-Norse settlement, but it was simultaneously a focal point of West Saxon political and military dominance: see 'Early Medieval Chester 400–1230', in C. P. Lewis and A. T. Thacker, eds., *A History of the County of Chester, Volume 5 Part 1: The City of Chester: General History and Topography* (London, 2003), pp. 16–33, http://www.british-history.ac.uk/vch/ches/vol5/pt1/pp16-33 [accessed 30 January 2015]. On law, the most notable Scandinavian absence are the large payments calculated in hundreds for the breach of the king's peace, which are a feature of York, Lincoln, and Nottingham (DB. i. 280v, 298v, 336v) and also appear in Æthelred's legislation for the Five Boroughs (III Atr 1–1:2). In Chester, by contrast, breaching the king's peace is said to require the standard payment of £5 (100 Norman shillings) associated with the West Saxon and Mercian legal traditions (see discussion in Chapter 7, pp. 333–6, and for the equation of Mercian and West Saxon law on this issue: II Cn 12–14).

[39] Charles-Edwards, 'Law in the Western Kingdoms', pp. 267–9; William Ian Miller, *Bloodtaking and Peacemaking: Feud, Law and Society in Saga Iceland* (Chicago, 1990), pp. 18–19.

[40] Alice Taylor, *The Shape of the State in Medieval Scotland, 1124–1290* (Oxford, 2016), pp. 117–32. Even if much of this material existed in written form in the twelfth century, it is quite plausible that this represents an evolution from an early medieval context in which its primary form was oral.

[41] See Fergus Kelly, *A Guide to Early Irish Law* (Dublin, 1988).

[42] Quoted in Wormald, *Making*, p. 45.

experts who had learnt their societies' most prestigious legal rules.[43] It would, then, be rather surprising if this were not the case in kingdoms such as Mercia, Northumbria, and East Anglia.

New Law

It is thus clear that when late seventh-century kings tried to enact new legislation they needed to contend with existing legal rules. Some of these rules, those concerned with specifying compensation for affront, were *æ*: formalized law rote-learnt by legal experts. Rules on other matters—the customary practices of assemblies—existed in people's memories as well, but probably not in a set form of words; these less formalized rules may have been known as *þeawas*. It was into this legal environment that late seventh-century kings tried to introduce new rules. All our texts agree that the proper term for this royal legislation was *domas* (singular: *dom*), usually translated 'judgements' or, more loosely, 'decrees'.[44]

Given that the most natural translation for *dom* is 'judgement', one way of understanding royal *domas* is as manifestations of the king's role as a judge. It is possible that pre-Christian kings had a judicial function of some sort: although we have no evidence to suggest that they did, it would perhaps be a natural role for a figure powerful enough to enforce his will on those below him to develop. We can be sure, however, that the king's role as judge is a feature of early medieval conceptions of Christian kingship, modelled both on Roman Emperors and on idealized royal judges in the Old Testament such as Solomon.[45] The seventh-century Irish text, *On the Twelve Abuses of the World*, for example, identifies just judgement as the key characteristic of kingship: an unjust king was the ninth of its abuses, liable to bring about dire consequences (poor harvests, plague, foreign invasion) for his entire kingdom.[46] It is possible that this is linked to the third element of our earliest description of the West Saxon royal inauguration ritual (which could have existed as early as the late seventh century but can only be securely dated to sometime prior to 856), which states that the king should 'order justice and mercy in all judgements so that, through that, the kind and merciful God may grant us his mercy.'[47] It is plausible that this role as a judge was one that kings assumed because of the Romano-Christian ideology of kingship which Wormald identified, and that the tradition of issuing *domas* was a manifestation

---

[43] See Wormald, '*Lex Scripta*', pp. 20–1; Graham Barrett, 'The Written and the World in Early Medieval Iberia' (University of Oxford D.Phil. Thesis, 2015), ch. 5.

[44] DOE s.v. 'dom'; Hl Prol.; Wi Prol 3; Ine Prol.

[45] See Wormald, *Making*, pp. 118–25.

[46] See Chapter 5, pp. 216–17. On the influence of this text, see Rob Meens, 'Politics, Mirrors of Princes and the Bible: Sins, Kings and the Well-Being of the Realm', *Early Medieval Europe* 7 (1998), pp. 345–57, at 353–7.

[47] See Chapter 5, pp. 205–6. For dating: Janet L. Nelson, 'The Earliest Royal *Ordo*: Some Liturgical and Historical Aspects', repr. in and cited from Nelson, *Politics and Ritual in Early Medieval Europe* (London, 1986), pp. 341–60, at 343–53. For the text: Nicholas Orchard, ed., *The Leofric Missal*, 2 vols. (London, 2002), ii, p. 432 (no. 2466).

of that role: a feature of kingship that was for the most part new in the seventh century.

A tempting possibility, therefore, is to read late seventh-century laws as records of royal judgements, something akin to modern 'case law'. A plausible reconstruction is as follows: a case raises an issue for which the law as it currently stands provides no clear answer; this case comes to the attention of the king in his capacity as judge because it cannot be resolved by normal means; the king makes a judgement (*dom*) resolving this legal uncertainty; and at some point this *dom* is collected together with *domas* prompted by similarly difficult cases and presented to an assembly so that the king's solutions to tricky legal issues can formally be added to existing law. Some late seventh-century laws are difficult to interpret except as the result of such a process. For example, this convoluted rule from Ine's laws:

> If anyone is accused and trial by ordeal is being forced upon him, and he has nothing to pay with, in order to escape the ordeal; and if another man goes and, on whatsoever terms he may be able to arrange, gives his goods instead, on condition that he [the accused] surrenders himself into his surety's hands, until he can restore to him the goods he has pledged; and then if he is accused a second time, and trial by ordeal is forced upon him, and he who had pledged goods for him will not continue to stand for him, and the accuser arrests him—he who had given [a pledge] for him shall lose his goods.[48]

It is inconceivable that anyone would have thought to legislate for this scenario alone, without articulating rules about more basic ordeal procedure, unless prompted by a specific case.

It is plausible that a lot of *domas* represent 'case law' of this sort. Few laws are as clear cut in this respect as the one just quoted, but a lot of them do seem to be dealing with gaps in existing laws' coverage—with unusual or complicated scenarios for which there was no established rule. These gaps must have been drawn to the king's attention somehow, and it is easy to imagine how requests for judgement in specific cases could have performed this function.[49] The laws of Hlothere and Eadric, for example, open with a series of laws defining the extent of an owner's liability if his *esne* (unfree dependant) kills someone, focusing in particular on how much that liability should increase if the *esne* escapes and therefore cannot be handed over to his victim's relatives.[50] It is perfectly plausible that the kings were driven to issue a *dom* on this point by a case in which an *esne* killed someone and escaped, leading to a dispute over the extent of his owner's liability that was insoluble within the existing legal framework.[51]

---

[48] Ine 62.
[49] The practicalities of royal judgement are discussed in Chapters 3 and 6, pp. 142–3, 265–6.
[50] Hl 1–4.
[51] Charles-Edwards, 'Law in the Western Kingdoms', pp. 264–9 argues for a slightly different interpretation of *dom*, arguing that the term encompasses 'both royal decree and judge's verdict' (p. 265). This is largely compatible with what is proposed here, though I would be reluctant to lose the sense in which the king's *domas* were—at least some of the time—literally judgements in themselves, not just templates for future judgements by local figures with specialist legal knowledge. The notion of a '*dom* type of decree' (p. 275) which emerges here in fact seems to arise from the phraseology of the Frankish *Lex Salica*, where of course the term *dom* is not used, and by analogy with Æthelberht's laws,

It would, however, be unnecessarily reductive to think that kings only ever issued *domas* in response to requests for judgement. Some laws clearly were ad hoc responses to those gaps in established law and custom which happened to come to the king's attention, but not all of them need have originated as specific cases.[52] Wihtred's laws, for example, explain that the value of the Church's protection—its *mundbyrd*—is 50 shillings, equivalent to that of the king.[53] It is possible that the absence of a *mundbyrd* for the Church was a gap in existing law that came to the king's attention through a specific case. However, given that it is part of a long series of laws on ecclesiastical matters it seems more likely that Wihtred was prompted to legislate by a more general desire to provide support to the Church in whatever ways seemed most appropriate. Likewise, Wihtred and Ine both offer rewards to men who capture thieves and hand them over to the king: this seems much more likely to be driven by a general desire to suppress theft through punishment than by a specific case.[54]

Kings could be driven to legislate by ideological agendas, then, as well as by specific cases which brought to light the inadequacy of existing rules. We might think of these, respectively, as 'proactive' and 'reactive' legislative modes. These are not always possible to tell apart in our texts—and there was probably a substantial grey area between the two ideal types in any case—but there are certain suggestive features. Context can be telling. Reactive legislation tends towards randomness. Kings responding to whatever issues happen to arise are likely to produce chaotic sets of judgements which jump unpredictably from subject to subject, something particularly noticeable in certain sections of Ine's laws (and in an even more pronounced form in Alfred's).[55] Proactive legislation, by contrast, is often more coherent, a single agenda leading to the establishment of a swathe of new rules, as in Wihtred's series of laws on ecclesiastical matters (and much tenth-century legislation). Another important feature is complexity. Reactive legislation tends to deal with unusual or complex scenarios, because these were the scenarios which highlighted legal issues that could not be resolved. Proactive legislation, on the other hand, had no particular reason to be complicated. This suggests that when we find

---

which almost certainly represent *æ* rather than being *domas*. While Charles-Edwards's insight that these laws' sentence structure corresponds to the way assembly judgements would in practice have been worded is extremely astute, the link between this insight and the late seventh-century Anglo-Saxon texts which describe themselves as *domas* is more problematic.

[52] The earliest example may be the ecclesiastical section appended to the start of Æthelberht's code (Abt 1). This was clearly designed to remedy the absence of rules integrating the Church into Kentish *æ*, but in the absence of any explicit statement of royal involvement in the composition of the code we cannot be sure that it represents *royal* legislation.

[53] Wi 2.   [54] Wi 26–26:1; Ine 28.

[55] For example, Ine 37 (theft), 38 (widows and fatherless children), 39 (secretly moving between districts), 40 (fencing of fields to prevent straying livestock), 41 (repudiating suretyship). Note that Wormald, 'Inter Cetera', p. 189 suggests these may all have been all part of a single legislative decree. On Alfred's laws: Af 13 (unintentional killing by felling trees), 14 (legal responsibility for the dumb and deaf), 15 (fighting in presence of bishops and ealdormen), 16 (stealing cows or mares and driving off their calves or foals), 17 (liability for deaths of vulnerable dependants), 18 (sexual assaults on nuns), and see Wormald, *Making*, p. 282.

kings making simple rules, they are more likely to be pursuing their own agendas than reacting to specific cases.

There is no particular pattern to legislation with strong reactive features: we find kings issuing *domas* to deal with perceived inadequacies in existing laws not just on affront and compensation but also on procedural and punitive matters. That is, they dealt with unprecedented legal questions regardless of whether those questions related to *þeawas* or *æ*.[56] There does, however, seem to have been some differentiation between *æ* and *þeawas* when legislating proactively: it is very unusual, as we have seen, to find kings making basic statements about affront and compensation. Kings could make additions to existing *æ* if the need arose (hence Ine's Welsh wergilds), but there is little to suggest they felt it their business to adjust traditional valuations of affronts. By contrast, we do find kings making simple rules on a variety of matters that would presumably have been covered by *þeawas* previously. Hlothere and Eadric give basic orders on the procedure for asserting ownership of allegedly stolen goods, known to legal historians as 'vouching to warranty': henceforth it is to be performed in the king's hall.[57] This probably represents an attempt to change existing legal custom. Wihtred's code includes a long section on oaths of denial, which focuses mainly on the clergy but ends by stating that a freeman must swear alongside three others of equal rank.[58] This too may represent an attempt to change basic practices that already existed, perhaps bringing the different customary procedures of various localities into line. It seems, then, that kings were much more constrained by existing *æ* than by existing *þeawas* when it came to making new law. This is what we might have expected: *æ* was a prestigious form of law, carefully recorded by men who learnt it by rote, whereas *þeawas* were customs that, though doubtless well established, were rarely if ever recorded formally and probably varied from locality to locality. It makes sense that the latter should have proved easier for kings to change.[59]

The Significance of Royal Legislation

It seems, then, that the *domas* issued by kings in the late seventh century had two purposes. As their kingdoms' leading judges, kings dealt with cases for which existing law and custom provided no clear answer, and they had at least some of their judgements in such cases formally recognized as law by great assemblies of their people. Kings also legislated on their own initiative, but here they needed to work around an existing oral legal tradition of considerable prestige: it seems to have been understood that kings could alter established customs—*þeawas*—on

---

[56] So, for instance, we find Ine issuing both a convoluted law on procedures for avoiding ordeal (Ine 62, quoted above p. 77) and detailed specifications on the compensation owed to spiritual kinsmen in homicide cases (Ine 76–76:2).

[57] Hl 7.   [58] Wi 21.

[59] This context, I would suggest, offers a useful perspective on the significance of the personal injury tariff in Alfred's code: it could be read as a major ideological statement, perhaps even as an aggressive attempt to extend royal legislative authority to a sphere of law—*æ*—which had previously been the preserve of legal experts. I intend to explore this idea further in a future article.

procedure and punishment, whereas there is little to suggest that they felt entitled to adjust the basic rules on affront and compensation with constituted *æ*.

Understanding how existing law and new legislation related to one another is important in its own right, but it is has a particular significance here because it helps us interpret our evidence. A large part of the difference between Æthelberht's laws and those of his successors is certainly genre: Æthelberht's code was a statement of established *æ*, whereas *æ* was the one thing that Hlothere and Eadric, Wihtred, and Ine did not engage with directly in their *domas*. If we do not bear this in mind we risk misreading our evidence and receiving an exaggerated impression of the difference between late sixth- and late seventh-century law. Crucially, the emphasis on *æ* in the prologues of the later texts suggests that the basic rules on affront and compensation remained just as authoritative and important as they had been a century earlier. This fundamental continuity of a prestigious and primarily oral legal tradition needs to be acknowledged.

It does, however, seem likely that the emergence of a new genre of law in the form of *domas* issued by the king in conjunction with great assemblies represents a significant shift in itself. It is possible that pre-Christian kings were doing something similar, without troubling to have their judgements committed to writing, but there are no signs that they were. The significance of this absence of evidence is debatable but if Æthelberht was accustomed to issuing his own *domas*, supplementing existing law in the way that his successors did, we might reasonably expect him to have had this quintessentially Roman activity recorded in writing. This is not much to go on, but all in all it seems most likely that the established interpretation is correct: as Wormald argued, late seventh-century kings were not just adopting Romano-Christian symbols—Æthelberht's written law—but trying to rule in a Romano-Christian way, and this included acting as their kingdoms' highest judges and issuing *domas* designed to augment existing traditions of *æ* and *peawas*.

We should be wary, however, of assuming that writing was a particularly important aspect of this royal role. Our earliest recorded instance of Kentish kings issuing new laws is Bede's statement that Eorcenberht of Kent (640–664) ordered idols to be abandoned and destroyed across his kingdom, and mandated the observance of Lent, prescribing heavy punishments for offenders.[60] There is nothing to suggest that his orders were written down. Though Eorcenberht's successors' *domas* were committed to writing it is likely that this was a fairly superficial act: the production of written records of a legislative process that for all practical purposes functioned orally.[61] We have no evidence to suggest that our texts were copied out and distributed to various corners of Kent and Wessex for reference purposes. Indeed, it is quite possible that one original copy was made and then consigned to a monastic or episcopal archive, ready to be copied again if any later churchmen, kings, or nobles happened to have an intellectual interest in matters legal.

---

[60] *Ecclesiastical History*, iii.8.　　　[61] Charles-Edwards, 'Law in the Western Kingdoms', p. 266.

Moreover, it is likely that the significance of committing law to writing was minimal even in ideological terms. Kings seem to have performed their role as judge-cum-legislator in front of large assemblies of their people, perhaps pronouncing their *domas* and, after suitably solemn discussion, having them confirmed formally by general acclamation. Those who witnessed this oral and visual performance were clearly on the receiving end of a potent display of royal ideology, but writing was not a fundamental part of it. The symbolic significance of committing law to 'the Roman medium' may have been apparent to a limited circle of ecclesiastical intellectuals, but how much a written document would have added for most of those who witnessed the theatre of law-making is questionable.[62] Perhaps the written record of Wihtred's great assembly of September 695 was formally presented to the king when it was completed and read aloud in front of all those gathered—it is certainly possible it contributed *something* to the public legislative performance, but it may well have been a relatively minor something.

If we accept that written records of royal *domas* had no practical legal purpose and were of relatively minor significance in terms of royal ideological display, then the sparseness of such records before the tenth century makes sense. The cessation of written law in Kent after Wihtred, the long break between Ine and Alfred in Wessex, and the apparent absence of a tradition of written law even in major kingdoms like East Anglia, Mercia, and Northumbria need not reflect a lack of royal interest in legislation. It is plausible that kings were issuing *domas* in oral form at great assemblies throughout these great silences in our source material, but not troubling to have them written down. Royal law-making could have been a continuous tradition in all Christianized English kingdoms, our texts from the late seventh-century representing an unusual period in which Kentish and West Saxon kings (or perhaps their ecclesiastical advisers) were enthusiastic about the image of written law.[63] That Mercian, Northumbrian and East Anglian kings may never have experimented with recording their law-making in writing in this way is unfortunate for us, but perfectly rational on their part: the benefits of having a written record made cannot have been significant.

Of course, the absence of written records need not mean these kings were any less invested in judging wisely in disputes that were brought before them, moulding local legal practice to a royal template, or asserting their rights to punish various types of wrongdoing. Indeed, our few bits of evidence suggest that Mercian and Northumbrian rulers, at least, were probably just as engaged with legal matters. Late eighth-century Mercian charters imply a legal world very similar to that visible in the laws of Wessex and Kent: a world with plenty of the royal punishments that

---

[62] Wormald, '*Lex Scripta*', p. 38, explicitly recognized this point: 'I use the word image rather than propaganda, because propaganda implies an audience, and we can neither know nor imagine enough about the circulation of our texts to talk confidently about their audience; whereas an image can be sufficient unto itself, and whoever else they were trying to impress I see barbarian kings as concerned primarily to impress themselves.'

[63] There are many broader similarities, of course, but the fact that Wi 28 and Ine 20 are near-identical provides the strongest evidence that the simultaneous efflorescence of written law in these two kingdoms was not coincidental.

kings such as Wihtred and Ine asserted in their *domas*. The most plausible explanation for this is that Mercian kings had previously asserted their punitive rights in the same way.[64] We lack charters for Northumbria, but Bede's writings are a solid early eighth-century Northumbrian source, and his assumptions about kingship and legislation, as we have already noted, are fundamentally very similar to those visible in late seventh-century *domas*.[65]

It is plausible, then, that towards the end of the seventh century Christianized English kings generally, not just those in Wessex and Kent, successfully claimed the right to legislate by issuing *domas* in major assemblies of their people. Not all *domas* need be understood as judgements in specific cases, but the term itself suggests that judgement and legislation were inextricably intertwined in this period and that kings' judicial functions may well lie behind their ability to make new law. Our meagre knowledge of pre-Christian kingship means we cannot be sure how big a break from tradition this was, but the few hints we have suggest that it may have been a major change. If so, its importance is hard to overstate. Although the right to legislate is now so central to our understanding of what 'government' entails that we find it rather difficult to imagine alternatives, we need to remember that it is neither obvious nor inevitable that those with political power should have exclusive authority to define the law.[66] This seventh-century assertion of legislative authority could represent a significant change to kings' roles: a fundamental shift in the meaning of kingship.

THE KING'S NEW RIGHTS

Kings, however, do not seem to have been content with their role as judge-legislator. It would, presumably, have been possible for them to have used their ability to make new laws in a relatively conservative way, clarifying legal ambiguities as they arose, and perhaps trying to make exemplary legal practices they found in particular localities standard across their kingdoms. In reality they did more than this: kings used their *domas* to assert new royal rights. In particular, we find them claiming a much wider range of rights to receive payments from, or to inflict violence on, wrongdoers of various kinds. The purpose of this section is simple: to set out as clearly as possible the nature of these rights, the types of offence to which they applied, and how they appear to have changed across the seventh century. Straightforward though this sounds, it is not something that any modern historian has attempted: whereas the previous section was re-treading ground already covered

---

[64] Wormald, *Making*, p. 108.   [65] See above, p. 65.

[66] Ireland provides the strongest contemporary example of this because of the literacy of its legal experts (see Kelly, *Guide*), but the example of Roman law jurists (see, for example, Mario Sbriccoli, 'Legislation, Justice and Political Power in Italian Cities, 1200–1400', in Antonio Padoa-Schioppa, ed., *Legislation and Justice* (Oxford, 1997), pp. 37–55) in the later medieval period ought to be sufficient to make this point. Medieval India provides another example: see Donald R. Davis Jr, 'Centres of Law: Duties, Rights, and Jurisdictional Pluralism in Medieval India', in Paul Dresch and Hannah Skoda, eds., *Legalism: Anthropology and History* (Oxford, 2012), pp. 85–113.

by Wormald, albeit with differences of emphasis, here we start venturing into new territory. This task, of course, is much easier for Kent than it is for Wessex. We have solid evidence for pre-Christian Kentish law against which to compare our late seventh-century texts, whereas for Wessex we have only the laws of Ine to work with. However, as we now have a reasonable idea of what a West Saxon tradition of *æ* probably looked like in this period, and of how Ine's *domas* related to it, we have the means to work around this absence of evidence. The development of Kentish kings' legal claims across the seventh century can also provide us with a helpful analogy. It makes sense, then, to analyse the Kentish evidence first and examine Ine's laws in the light of our findings.

Kent

We need to start by briefly reviewing the last chapter's conclusions about the rights of the king in Æthelberht's laws. Many of the king's rights are the same as those of other free males. Like other heads of household, he protects his household dependants as well as any guests who enter his home: killing or harming such people represents a breach of protection, an affront for which compensation must be paid. The compensation payable to the king for breaching his protection is much greater than that payable for breaching that of lesser figures, but it follows the same pattern. He is entitled to compensation when people steal his property: ninefold compensation rather than the threefold compensation to which freemen were entitled. Though this is not mentioned, we must presume that he is also entitled to share in wergilds paid for his relatives, like any other freeman, and—in theory at least—to compensation for any physical injuries inflicted on him.[67]

The king, however, is more than just a very grand freeman. His office means he has a special relationship with his kingdom's free population: he has a degree of authority over them (the extent of this is unclear, but he has the right to be given food and can command his people to assemble) and a duty to protect them. If someone kills a free man they owe the king 50 shillings, the value of the king's protection. The king, then, is entitled to a payment in homicide cases, but this payment is understood as compensation for an affront—a breach of his protection—and *not* a punitive fine. It is thus distinct from the king's right to a *wite* for thefts between free males. This is explicitly a punitive fine, and *not* compensation for an affront, but the evidence does not allow us to say much more about it than this. At this stage, then, the king's rights fall clearly into 'protective' and 'punitive' categories, with protective rights associated with violent offences and punitive rights associated with theft.

Late seventh-century Kentish laws suggest a clear expansion in royal claims, but they also show significant continuity in the way protective and punitive rights were used. Hlothere and Eadric provide an excellent example of the continued association of protective rights with violent offences:

---

[67] We have one reference to a royal wergild being paid: *Anglo-Saxon Chronicle*, s.a. 694.

11. If a person in another's house calls a person a perjurer or accosts him shamefully with mocking words, let him pay a shilling to him who owns the house, and 6 shillings to whom he spoke that utterance, and let him pay 12 shillings to the king.

12. If a person takes a cup from another where men are drinking without [the man from whom the cup was taken being at] fault, according to the established right let him give a shilling to him who owns that house, and 6 shillings to him from whom the cup was taken, and 12 shillings to the king.

13. If a person should draw a weapon where men are drinking and no harm is done there, a shilling to him who owns the house, and 12 shillings to the king.

14. If that house becomes bloodied, let him pay the man his *mundbyrd* [the value of his protection] and 50 shillings to the king.[68]

The main concept here is protection. All the offences are violations of the house-holder's protection of his guests, with the most serious—bloodshed—requiring payment of his *mundbyrd*. The king's demand of 50 shillings for this same offence is equivalent to the royal *mundbyrd*, which suggests that his involvement was conceived protectively too: a royal protection being used to reinforce the traditional protection a householder exercised over his own home.[69] This seems to represent a significant new royal claim. Æthelberht's laws show that kings had an established right to compensation of 50 shillings when one of their freemen was killed, but here they are claiming significant sums for cases that fall far short of that: incidents of non-lethal violence and insulting behaviour that happen to take place in other men's homes. Hlothere and Eadric, then, seem to be trying to use the king's right to protect his people in a new way, with the noble aim of reducing the risk of serious violence erupting while men drank together. There is change here, then, but the use of the king's protection to engage with violent offences remains constant.

There is also continuity in the association of punitive rights with theft. Wihtred's laws assert that any thief killed in the act should 'lie without wergild', meaning that his relatives were entitled to no compensation for his death.[70] Thieves who were caught in the act and taken alive were to be delivered to the king who would decide their fate, choosing from three options. The thief could be executed; he could be enslaved and sold 'across the sea'; or his life could be bought back from the king at the price of his wergild. If he were sold or his life redeemed, the proceeds were to be split between the king and the person who caught the thief, but if the king decided to execute the thief he would then pay the original captor 70 shillings, a strikingly large sum.[71] The laws, then, assume that the king would sometimes be prepared to

---

[68] Hl 11–14.
[69] On this theme, see Chapters 4 and 5, pp. 184–5, 232–3.   [70] Wi 25.
[71] Wi 26–26:1. The 70-shilling figure is remarkable because it is larger than the half-share of a freeman's 100-shilling wergild to which the captor might otherwise be entitled, which would presumably itself be more than the half share of any sum paid for the thief as a slave (for discussion, see Oliver, *Beginnings*, pp. 178–9). A possible explanation for this is that the larger sum was intended to reflect additional danger to the captor from the thief's kinsmen, who might hold him responsible if the

disburse his own money as a bounty, simply in order to inflict the ultimate punishment on a thief.[72] Wihtred even envisages men be slain for behaving in a thief-like way: strangers found away from the road who made no effort to announce their presence by shouting or blowing a horn could be treated as thieves and slain or captured.[73] (The point of this law, perhaps, was to allow for situations in which someone stumbled upon a thief before he had managed to steal anything: people ought not to have to wait for thieves to lay hands on their property before attempting to capture them.) Wihtred's laws thus go far beyond the *wite* for theft visible in Æthelberht's laws, but they probably did not displace it. We should note that Wihtred only discusses thieves who could not deny their offence because they had been caught either in the act of theft or immediately after, with stolen goods in hand. Theft laws from the late Anglo-Saxon period are similarly harsh with thieves caught in such circumstances but they tend to be more lenient with thieves who initially escape but are later identified and convicted, allowing them to pay a *wite*.[74] It is probable that this applied in Wihtred's Kent too. Late seventh-century theft law is thus just as clearly punitive as it had been a century earlier but, taken at face-value, significantly harsher.

Late seventh-century royal punishment, however, extended beyond theft. Kings claimed the right to receive fines for two additional categories of offence. The first category might be termed 'religious': kings prescribed punishments for failure to meet certain minimum standards of Christian observance. Wihtred's code lays out fines for entering illicit marriages, failing to observe the Sabbath or to fast when appropriate, and making offerings to devils.[75] The second category is slightly less straightforward. It consists of offences that might be characterized as 'procedural', in which offenders failed to fulfil their legal obligations in some way. As we shall see shortly, this is much more prominent in Ine's laws, but

---

king chose execution. This was a society in which people who did not participate personally in violence could still be held liable for it (as is well illustrated by, for instance, Abt 18–20).

[72] A similar law seems to exist for slaves caught stealing: the king can choose to execute the slave or allow his owner to redeem him, with the original captor entitled to either half the proceeds or a bounty of half the slave's value (Wi 27). The law does not quite say this explicitly and Oliver reads it differently (*Beginnings*, pp. 178–9), but this seems most likely to be what it implies (see Liebermann, *Gesetze*, iii, p. 30; Attenborough, *Laws*, p. 182).

[73] Wi 28.

[74] This distinction in treatment between those caught in the act and those who escape is clear in later laws (see Chapters 4 and 6, pp. 174–6, 254–5, 270–3), and it is implied in Ine's laws. For execution or mutilation for thieves caught in the act, see Ine 12, 16, 18, 35, 37. For the possibility of denial when not caught in such circumstances but later accused: Ine 35:1, 46–46:2; 53–53:1, 57, 75. It is even possible that Ine 28–28:2 is intended to illustrate the distinction. Ine 28 addresses captured thieves, offering a bounty to captors; Ine 28:1–28:2 then deal with a situation in which a thief escapes from sight, ordering that either a fine be paid or an oath of denial sworn. The passage is ambiguous: editors have assumed that the person paying the fine or denying the charge is the captor, who allowed the thief's escape, and this may be correct (see Liebermann, *Gesetze*, iii. p. 73; Attenborough, *Laws*, p. 186). However, it cannot be ruled out that the passage as a whole is a concise summary of contemporary theft law, Ine 28 being concerned with thieves who are captured and Ine 28:1–28:2 moving on to discuss thieves identified by other means.

[75] Wi 5–5:1, 11–15. Wormald, 'Inter Cetera', p. 193, notes that some of these punitive fines appear to be characterized as compensations; on this see below, p. 109.

Hlothere and Eadric's code contains one excellent example. It states that if one man accuses another at an assembly, the accused is to provide him with surety and agree to abide by the decision of the judges of Kent. If he did not do so he was to pay 12 shillings to the king.[76]

Grasping the substantive legal changes which took place in seventh-century Kent, then, is simple enough. Kings do seem to have become more ambitious in their engagement with wrongdoing across the board, but they articulated their new demands within a framework already visible in Æthelberht's time: protective rights were used for violent offences, and punitive rights for theft. However, we also find royal punishment clearly extending beyond theft for the first time, encompassing types of offence that might be characterized as religious and procedural.[77]

Wessex

The substantive legal changes that took place in seventh-century Wessex are much more difficult to assess. There are two principal issues. The most obvious has already been noted: we have no West Saxon equivalent to the laws of Æthelberht. This is not as great a difficulty as it may seem, mainly because Ine's use of the terms *æ* and *domas* implies that the basic conceptual framework of law and legislation in Wessex was the same as in Kent. We have good reasons for thinking that there was a West Saxon oral legal tradition of *æ*, and we know roughly what it might have looked like. What we lack are specific details. Most of these do not really matter: it will not affect our analysis much if we are ignorant of how much compensation was required for breaking a West Saxon rib, and if we really wanted to know we could turn to Alfred's personal injury tariff which seems likely, whether directly or indirectly, to have derived from traditional oral *æ*.

One particular detail is a problem, however: we do not know the value of a seventh-century West Saxon king's *mundbyrd*—the proper compensation for breach of his protection. Given the association of the king's protection with violent offences in Kentish law, this is a significant analytical obstacle. We cannot look to later law here because it seems that Alfred redefined the value of various royal rights: he doubled the full *wite* for theft from 60 to 120 shillings, for instance.[78] An established theory is that he doubled the value of the king's protection as well, taking it from an original 120 shillings to the £5 figure we find in late Anglo-Saxon laws (equivalent to 240 West Saxon shillings).[79] This theory, plausible in itself, gains some support from the possibility that 120 West Saxon shillings was the precise monetary equivalent of

---

[76] Hl 9.

[77] These punishments are just the ttips of more significant icebergs: kings used their *domas* to define people's legal and religious duties more generally, with punishments being used to give force to some, but not all, of what was specified. Though punishment is a key focus of this chapter, the laws themselves are rather broader in their concerns. See Chapter 4, pp. 179–81.

[78] Af 9:2; Ine 43.

[79] H. Munro Chadwick, *Studies on Anglo-Saxon Institutions* (Cambridge, 1905), pp. 115–26.

the 50 shillings that constituted a royal *mundbyrd* in Kent.[80] The figure of 120 shillings also tends to appear in Ine's laws in contexts where it would make sense as a manifestation of royal protection.[81] This is not a universal rule—in some instances it is not the case—but the same is true for the figure of £5 in our later texts, so this is probably to be expected.[82] There are, in any case, no other figures in Ine's laws that could plausibly be interpreted as a royal *mundbyrd*. Unless we are to assume the West Saxon king's *mundbyrd* either did not exist in the seventh century or left no impression whatsoever on Ine's laws, assuming that it was worth 120 shillings is our only option. Deductions based on this assumption can never be as solid as their equivalents for Kent or the late Anglo-Saxon period, but it is the best we can do with the evidence available.

The second issue exacerbates the first. Given that making deductions based on the value of the payments claimed by the king is uncertain, we might have hoped to be able to use the language in which they are expressed to distinguish between compensations for breached protections and punitive fines: verbs of compensation being limited to protective rights, perhaps, and the term *wite* reserved for punitive measures. Late seventh-century laws, however, are often unhelpfully loose in their language. For example, the first two subjects Ine's laws consider are religious offences. Men who make their slaves work on Sundays and those who fail to have their children baptized within 30 days of their birth each have to pay 30 shillings, but those 30 shillings are characterized as a *wite* for the Sunday work and treated as compensation for the neglected baptism (the verb used is *gebetan*—'to compensate' or 'to make good').[83] It is not plausible that this difference of vocabulary implies that these two offences were understood entirely differently. Wihtred's laws are just as prone to this issue but the effects are much more serious

---

[80] This is a key plank of the argument in Wormald, *Making*, p. 279, which comes to the same conclusion. It was first argued in D. A. Bullough, 'Anglo-Saxon Institutions and Early English Society' repr. in and cited from David E. Pelteret, *Anglo-Saxon History: Basic Readings* (New York, 2000), pp. 1–19 at 4, drawing on the unpublished Ford Lectures of Philip Grierson. For a review of the developments in numismatic scholarship that underpin this case, and of the methodological uncertainties involved in such deductions, see Rory Naismith, 'H. M. Chadwick and the Anglo-Saxon Monetary System', in Michael Lapidge, ed., *The Life and Writings of Hector Munro Chadwick* (Aberystwyth, 2015), pp. 143–56.

[81] Ine 6:1–6:4: the sum paid for fighting in various locations, possibly analogous to the king's protection in Abt 6 (see below, pp. 91–4); Ine 14: the sum paid to the king for belonging to a *hloð*, a raiding band of between seven and thirty-five men (for an interpretation linking this to royal protection, see below, p. 90, n. 96); Ine 45: the sum specified for the king's *burhbryce*, which Wormald renders 'enclosure penetration' (*Making*, p. 267), which would make sense as a payment for violating the protection the king exercised over whatever was meant by his *burh*; and possibly also Ine 70, where 120 shillings is the *manbot* of noblemen with wergilds of 1200 shillings (on the speculative theory that such men may generally, or perhaps even exclusively, have been characterized by their personal service to the king).

[82] Ine 13 (lying in the presence of a bishop), 51 (neglect of military service by a nobleman who had been granted land), 52 (making a secret agreement). The link between Ine 14 (on *hloðs*) and the king's protection is also rather speculative. But in the eleventh century we find the sum of £5, which is explicitly identified as the value of the king's *mundbyrd* (Af 3, 5; VIII Atr 5:1; I Cn 3:2), being used as the fine for harbouring outlaws (II Cn 13:2), for failing to pay a toll in London and subsequently lying about it (IV Atr 3:2), and probably also for neglect of military service (see Chapter 7, p. 336, n. 144).

[83] Ine 2, 3. DOE s.v. 'ge-betan'.

for Wessex because of the ambiguity about the king's protection. This terminological laxity may, of course, be a significant phenomenon in itself, not just an analytical inconvenience (a possible explanation for it is offered below).[84] It also presents some opportunities: when we find Ine's laws using this same language with precision it suggests that unusual care is being taken and that a particular point is being made.

Religious Misconduct, Procedural Offences, and Theft

If we steer clear of these difficulties initially, however, Ine's laws provide a very similar picture to that of the Kentish laws on religious and procedural offences, and on theft. On religious offences, they are relatively brief, prescribing penalties for those who fail to baptize their children within thirty days of their birth, refuse to pay church dues, or scorn to observe the Sabbath.[85] They also prohibit the sale of West Saxons overseas, no matter what their personal status or what wrong they have done, with offenders ordered to forfeit their wergild to the king and make amends to God.[86] The concern here is likely to be pastoral: Christians should not end up as slaves to pagans.[87] This is a different range of offences to Wihtred's laws which, strikingly, envisage the king himself selling captured thieves to foreign slave merchants.[88] The significance of the other differences—Wihtred does not try to enforce baptism or church dues, but does prescribe penalties for illicit marriages, failures to fast, and making offerings to devils[89]—is hard to assess. It is possible that this represents a genuine difference of practice between Kent and Wessex, but given our slender evidence it would be unwise to attribute much significance to this. It could be more a matter of emphasis.

On procedural matters, Ine's laws include a similar measure to Hlothere and Eadric's penalty for failing to provide surety when accused of an offence at an assembly, and they add fines for harbouring fugitives, making secret pacts, and seizing property before seeking a judgement.[90] This amounts to a broad attempt to ensure men pursued their legal claims in the proper way, with due respect to their local assemblies. They were to bring their cases to assemblies (rather than simply seizing what they thought they were owed or coming to private agreements which might deprive others of their rights); when accused they were to find sureties to guarantee in advance that they would accept their assembly's decision; and they were certainly not to harbour people who fled rather than submit to an assembly judgement. Another possible member of this category is the fine of 120 shillings for

---

[84] Wormald, 'Inter Cetera', p. 192–4 attributes considerable significance to this. There is a similar argument for the later period in Patrick Wormald, 'Frederic William Maitland and the Earliest English Law' repr. in and cited from Wormald, *Legal Culture*, pp. 1–69 at 61, and in slightly more detail in Patrick Wormald, *Papers Preparatory to the Making of English Law: King Alfred to the Twelfth Century. Volume II: From God's Law to Common Law*, ed. Stephen Baxter and John Hudson (University of London, 2014) http://www.earlyenglishlaws.ac.uk/reference/wormald/, pp. 159–60. My preferred reading, which is somewhat less ambitious, is set out below, p. 109.

[85] Ine 2–4.   [86] Ine 11.

[87] This is made explicit in late Anglo-Saxon laws: V Atr 2; VI Atr 9; II Cn 3.

[88] Wi 26.   [89] Wi 5–5:1, 11–15.   [90] Ine 8, 9, 13, 30, 52.

bearing false witness in the presence of a bishop, or repudiating a pledge given in his presence.[91] This does not seem to be punishment for perjury, in the sense of swearing a false oath, as the lies and broken promises involved are not characterized as oaths. It is possible that a legal procedural context is implied but this is not entirely clear: this might be better understood as a religious offence.[92]

It is important to note that open seizures of property ought to be regarded as procedural offences rather than as analogous to theft. The key characteristic of theft is secrecy: thieves not only take things which do not belong to them but try their utmost to hide their responsibility.[93] Open seizures of property in which the perpetrator freely and publicly acknowledged responsibility could be part of legitimate legal practice. If men defied assembly judgements, withholding payment of what they owed, it was proper for a band of men to assemble and seize their goods. Open seizures of property are only punished in the laws when the person doing the seizing does so precipitately. Ine's law against seizing property before seeking a judgement has already been noted: men who do so should give up what they took, compensate their victims, and pay a fine of 30 shillings.[94] This law, however, is immediately followed by one on men who commit *reaflac* ('rapine, robbery, spoliation') or *nidnæm* ('a taking by force, rapine'), which likewise orders that they should return what they had taken and pay a fine, this time of 60 shillings.[95] The laws make sense as a pair. Both impose fines on people who seize property without an assembly judgement entitling them to do so. The point seems likely to be that 30 shillings is the appropriate fine if the seizure can be justified retrospectively—if the offender merely pre-empted an assembly's judgement. The fine of 60 shillings, on the other hand, applies if the retrospective judgement is unfavourable to the perpetrator and his claims to the seized property are rejected.

---

[91] Ine 13.

[92] There are also fines for neglect of military service (Ine 51), which are probably best understood as belonging to a category of their own. On the separate status of military offences, see Chapter 3, pp. 124–36.

[93] This is a well-known and much more general point: theft is a secret offence across the early medieval world. A particularly useful discussion in a later medieval Welsh context is Dafydd Jenkins, 'Crime and Tort and the Three Columns of Law', in T. M. Charles-Edwards and Paul Russell, eds., *Tair Colofn Cyfraith: The Three Columns of Law in Medieval Wales. Homicide, Theft and Fire* (Bangor, 2005 [i.e. 2007]), pp. 1–25 at 3–5. However, it is worth noting that theft's essential secrecy is implicit in our seventh-century English evidence. The fact that the laws of both Ine and Wihtred allow people who wander off roads in a furtive or stealthy manner, without announcing their presence, to be regarded as thieves suggests that such behaviour was characteristic of thieves (Wi 28; Ine 20). Moreover, a rather odd passage in Ine's laws (Ine 43–43:1) on damaging other people's trees implies the same thing. Burning down a tree requires a larger fine than chopping them down with an axe because "fire is a thief" and "the axe is a *melda* and not a thief". A *melda* is "a narrator, an informer, announcer" (ASD s.v. "melda"): the metaphor makes sense if a thief is someone who does not act openly, failing to announce his presence at the time (as the noise of an axe does) or to tell people what he has done afterwards. This passage has a strong intellectual flavour to it: it may reveal something of what (apart from knowledge of compensation tariffs) specialist legal expertise entailed in the period. The notion that this is indeed law of a more intellectual than practical nature gains some support from the fact that Alfred seems to have felt the need to revise it, creating a new, much more readily comprehensible rule (Af 12) which makes a point of according identical treatment to the destruction of trees by fire and axe.

[94] Ine 9.   [95] Ine 10. ASD s.vv. 'nidnæm', 'reaflac'.

In that case he not only acted without an assembly's authorisation, he did so on the basis of an unlawful claim: a much more serious offence, worthy of a greater fine and condemnation as *reaflac* and *nidnæm*, but still rather more akin to a breach of legal procedure than to the secret offence of theft.[96]

On theft itself, Ine's laws have a great deal more to say than Wihtred's. They are similar in that they specify a bounty for captured thieves, albeit a much smaller one, and assert that those caught in the act could be killed without liability. Like Wihtred's laws, they envisage execution, enslavement (though not sale 'across the sea') and redemption for wergild as possible punishments for theft, but they also mention mutilation and payment of a *wite* as options. They contain an almost identically worded law to Wihtred's statement that strangers found away from roads who failed to announce their presence by shouting or blowing a horn could be slain as thieves.[97] Beyond this, Ine's laws extend punishment to men who captured thieves and subsequently failed to prevent their escape.[98] This could, of course, also be viewed as a procedural offence: men who captured thieves had a duty to hand them over to the king, it seems, and are here being threatened with punishment for negligently failing in that duty.

Violent Offences

For religious misconduct, procedural offences and theft, then, our West Saxon evidence tells essentially the same story as we found in Kent. In some important respects the same is true for violent offences. In Kent, as we have seen, Æthelberht's

---

[96] Another set of laws (Ine 13:1–15) deals with raiding bands, classifying them by size: up to seven men are termed thieves, a band of between seven and thirty-five is termed a *hloð*, and a larger party is a *here*—a term usually used to mean 'army'. Belonging to a *hloð* requires a 120-shilling payment to the king; those convicted of belonging to a *here* forfeited their lives to the king, to be redeemed by payment of their own wergilds. These are most convincingly read as royal attempts to suppress plundering raids within their kingdoms because they represented a threat to their political authority. Raiding for plunder was what kings did in war: a plundering raid within a kingdom was an act of war against its king—something akin to treason. Ravaging a king's country with something that could be termed an army could easily be regarded as an act of war for which the men involved forfeited their lives, whereas raiding in a smaller *hloð* was an analogous but slightly less serious affront to the king. These offences perhaps belong in a category of their own—treasonous offences, perhaps—but it is also possible that raiding in large bands was regarded as a breach of protection: the protection from being raided by their enemies that kings, with their military strength, were meant to provide for their people. This breach was serious enough to warrant forfeiture of life for belonging to a *here*, but for the lesser offence of belonging to a *hloð* it was sufficient to pay 120 shillings—quite possibly the traditional West Saxon royal *mundbyrd*. Laws about raiding bands, then, are more akin to laws about violence than theft. The language here is thus misleading. The characterisation of bands of up to seven men as 'thieves' was not meant to be taken literally: the fact that no penalty is specified for membership of such a band shows that such men were not actually to be punished, let alone treated as thieves and executed. However, contempt for their actions—morally reprehensible conduct so piffling as to be beneath the king's notice—was signalled by labelling them as such. We should not infer that members of small-scale armed expeditions were understood as thieves in a practical legal context. Likewise the fact that this passage chooses to use the term *here* to emphasise that violence by bands of thirty-six men constituted an insufferable affront to the king should not be taken to mean that contemporaries would have understood so small a force as an army in a practical military context.

[97] Ine 20; Wi 28.   [98] Ine 28:1 (though see above, p. 85, n. 74), 36, 72–3.

laws show that the king extended his protection to all free men, such that if any one of them was killed the king required compensation of 50 shillings: his *mundbyrd* or 'protection-value'.[99] The laws of Hlothere and Eadric go beyond this, claiming the right to be compensated for various offences that took place in other people's houses while men drank together—ranging from verbal insults and violations of drinking etiquette, through weapon-drawing, all the way up to bloodshed—with the most serious offence requiring payment of the king's 50-shilling *mundbyrd*.[100] Ine's laws have a passage covering similar ground. It also considers fighting in houses alongside the possibility of quarrels erupting while men drank together, and the payments demanded by the king revolve around the figure of 120 shillings— which, as was noted earlier, was probably the traditional value of a West Saxon king's *mundbyrd*. There are important differences in language and structure, however, so it is worth quoting the laws in full and analysing them in detail:

6. If anyone fights in the king's house, he shall forfeit all his property, and it shall be for the king to decide whether he shall be put to death or not.

6:1. If anyone fights in a monastery, he shall compensate (*gebete*) with 120 shillings.

6:2. If anyone fights in the house of an ealdorman, or of any other distinguished councillor, he shall compensate with 60 shillings and pay another 60 shillings as a fine (*to wite*).

6:3. If, however, he fights in the house of a *gafol*-payer or of a *gebur*, he shall pay 120 shillings as a fine and 6 shillings to the *gebur*.[101]

6:4. And even if it [the fight] takes place in the open, a fine of 120 shillings shall be paid.

6:5. If, however, two men quarrel while drinking together and one endures it patiently, the other shall pay a fine of 30 shillings.[102]

There are two important points to note here, which seem likely to be related. The first is that the language used is uncharacteristically precise: each payment to the king is a *wite*, whereas all payments to other parties use the verb *gebetan* ('to compensate'). This precision is unusual in Ine's laws and suggests that these terms are being used here with a particular purpose. The second is that the laws do not really make much sense. They imply that fighting, wherever it takes place,

---

[99] Abt 6, 8.   [100] Hl 11–14.

[101] The distinction here may be between free householders who held land (and thus paid the *gafol*—'tribute'—and other dues assessed on the number of hides held) and dependent freemen (*geburs*) who lived in their own households but lacked their own land (and thus did not owe *gafol*, as the land on which they worked pertained to other households). See Rosamond Faith, *The English Peasantry and the Growth of Lordship* (London, 1997), pp. 76–84, 105–6, and Chapter 3, pp. 119–21.

[102] Ine 6–6:5. Liebermann suggests correcting the text, adjusting the *wite* from 120 to 30 shillings (i.e. from cxx to "xxx") in both 6:3 and 6:4 on the grounds that Ine must have demanded less from offenders for these lesser offences (Liebermann, *Gesetze*, iii. p. 69). This attempt to impose logic on the text is understandable but misguided. The 120-shilling figure makes sense in if we look at West Saxon evidence in the light of what we know from Kent, and making an adjustment here removes that parallel. As there no strong grounds for accepting Liebermann's suggested emendation beyond this not wholly convincing logic, it is important to explore the possibility that the passage's incoherence can be explained by other means.

incurs the same liability to pay 120 shillings: it is no more costly to fight in a monastery than in an open field. This is odd taken in isolation, even odder if we consider that Anglo-Saxon laws usually aim for the opposite effect, with the payments prescribed for offences in buildings increasing with status.[103] The one exception to this flat rate of 120 shillings is even more bizarre. For fighting in the house of a *gebur*—the humblest of free householders—120 shillings must be paid to the king as a *wite* but a further 6 are owed to the *gebur*. It is thus, apparently, more expensive to fight in the lowliest of free dwellings than in the homes of the greatest secular nobles.

Both the incoherence of this scheme and the scrupulous use of language suggest that this passage was shaped—and distorted—by an ideological agenda. The point of insisting upon the label *wite* for payments to the king and the verb *gebetan* for those to other recipients, presumably, was to assert that the king's involvement in these cases was qualitatively different from that of lesser men. As a king in the Romano-Christian tradition, Ine had legal rights and responsibilities distinct from those of his people. They might require compensation for breach of the protection inhering in their houses; he, on the other hand, had a general duty to suppress wrongdoing through punishment. Though it seems very likely that, just as in Kent, the king's rights here were rooted in a traditional royal protection of freemen— hence the 120-shilling figure—this passage is trying to present those rights differently for ideological reasons.

The awkwardness of the scheme seems to result from an attempt—again presumably ideologically inspired—to recast the protective rights of major lay and ecclesiastical figures as delegated royal rights. Rather than protecting their own space, such figures are allowed to collect a proportion of the king's *wite* for fighting: monasteries can have all of it, ealdormen and other great nobles can take half. The king was not prepared to grant any proportion of his fine to lesser men, but this created a problem: even a *gebur* was clearly understood to be entitled to compensation for violence in his own home, so this compensation was made additional to the fine. This passage seems to be trying to recast existing protective rights into a scheme based on the assumption that all significant legal rights are delegated royal rights. This assumption, however, was essentially alien to the native Anglo-Saxon legal framework and the attempt results in absurdity.

The likely scenario, then, is that this passage is performing essentially the same task as the one in the laws of Hlothere and Eadric quoted above: reconciling the king's protective rights over violent offences with the protection householders exercised over guests in their own homes. It does so, however, in a much more ideologically charged way, recasting the king's right to compensation for breach of protection as a punitive fine so as to emphasize the qualitative difference between his legal role and those of his people, and treating the protective rights of his most senior aristocrats as delegated royal powers. Whether the substance of Ine's rights over violent offences differed significantly from those of Kentish kings is uncertain. A literal reading of the laws suggests that Ine claimed 120 shillings for any fighting

---

[103] For example, Abt 5, 13, 17, 27; Af 39:2, 40; I Cn 3:2. The one exception to this is *hamsocn*, on which see Chapters 4 and 5, pp. 184–5, 232–3.

whatsoever, whereas Æthelberht's claim to an equivalent sum only applied to homicides with free victims. But it has long been recognized that Ine's 'fighting' may well mean lethal fighting in this context—120 shillings would be a grossly disproportionate penalty for a fight that resulted in nothing worse than bruising.[104] And given the tendency of the laws to assume freemen are being discussed unless it is stated otherwise, we cannot be wholly confident that Ine's measure was meant to cover fighting involving the unfree: the implied context of collective drinking in free households may well suggest otherwise.

In the longer run the signs are that both Kentish and West Saxon laws were rather over-ambitious in asserting the king's right to be paid for non-lethal quarrelling in other people's houses. Alfred's laws discuss a very similar scenario and make no reference to a payment to the king, though they are clear that householders need to be compensated.[105] Ine does, however, seem to have been successful in rebranding what had probably once been a right to receive the 120-shilling West Saxon royal *mundbyrd* for breach of the protection the king extended to his kingdom's free population. All later laws follow him in referring to the payment due to the king in homicide cases as a punitive fine, sometimes terming it *fihtwite* ('fight-fine'). There are signs, however, that this re-labelling was cosmetic, in that *fihtwite* can be found behaving rather more like a protection than a punishment in later laws. Most fundamentally, in spite of its being formally prohibited and punished, it is clear from late Anglo-Saxon evidence that deliberately killing people remained in some senses a legitimate thing to do. There are passages which seem to imply that the *wite* applied in some circumstances but not in others, making it context-specific in a similar way to protections.[106] In later

---

[104] Frederic William Maitland, *Domesday Book and Beyond: Three Essays in the Early History of England* (Cambridge, 1897), p. 88, n. 3. The fact that Ine 6:1–6:4 do not discuss who should pay the fine, whereas this is set out in the definitely non-lethal scenario envisioned by Ine 6:5, could perhaps be taken as an indication that the person liable for the 'fighting' in the earlier clauses needed no identification, being the only one who survived the encounter. For a discussion of the problems with this view, which is contradicted in early twelfth-century evidence (Hn 94–94:1b.), see T. B. Lambert, 'Protection, Feud and Royal Power: Violence and Its Regulation in English Law, c.850–c.1250' (University of Durham PhD thesis, 2009), pp. 29–30.

[105] Af 39–39:2.

[106] See Chapters 4 and 5, pp. 181–99, 224–35. A passage in Alfred's laws (Af 42:5–42:7) which designates certain instances of homicide as *orwige* is particularly pertinent here. Men who kill when they find another man inappropriately secluded with one of their womenfolk (wife, mother, sister or daughter), when they fight on behalf of their lords or men, or when they fight alongside their wrongfully attacked kinsmen are said to do so *orwige*. People who fight against their lords in any circumstances, however, may not do so *orwige*. The term combines the prefix or- ('without') with the noun *wig* ('fight', 'battle', 'war', 'conflict'), and is conventionally interpreted as meaning something like 'without liability for vengeance in feud' (ASD s.vv. 'orwige', 'or', 'wig'; Attenborough, *Laws*, p. 198; Liebermann, *Gesetze*, ii, p. 168). It is difficult to reconcile this with the general principle of kin-responsibility visible in the laws (e.g. in II Em 1–1:3, on which see Chapters 4 and 5, pp. 191–2, 226–7): can we really imagine that men who fought and killed alongside their kinsmen were exempted from feud? I would suggest that modern historians have too readily dismissed the interpretation of this term given in the early twelfth-century Latin compilation known as the *Quadripartitus: sine wita* 'without fine' (*Gesetze*, i, p. 77). For this reading to work, we would have to understand the conflict (*wig*) from which these killers were exempt as the conflict with the king reflected in the *wite*, which seems plausible. This reading has the additional benefit of explaining the lack of penalties in the passage. If Alfred was really declaring that people who killed in these circumstances were not legitimate targets for vengeance

West Saxon grants of legal rights, *fihtwite* seems to pass to privileged lords along with the right to all other *wite*s and wergild forfeitures, but it is interesting to note that Cnut's laws state this is not the case in areas under Danish law.[107] There, *fihtwite* is reserved to the king to be conveyed to lords only by a specific grant, which puts it in the same category as the king's principal protective rights.[108] All this suggests that Ine was successful in renaming an existing right but that he was unable to change that right in a fundamental way.

THE ROOTS OF PUNISHMENT

Late seventh-century royal *domas* seem to have been driven by an ideological agenda in exactly the way Wormald described. In Wessex this even seems to have led Ine to relabel an established protective right as a punitive *wite*, a terminological change that was never reversed. The main substantive change we see, however, is the proliferation of royal punitive rights over theft, procedural offences and religious misconduct. The rise of royal punishment in these three categories is a major theme of seventh-century law. We should not forget that this rise seems to have roots in the pre-Christian period, as the reference to a *wite* for theft in Æthelberht's laws shows, but the surviving sources suggest that it accelerated sharply in the second half of the seventh century, probably for precisely the ideological reasons that Wormald identified. However, seventh-century kings were not operating in a vacuum. Wherever evidence survives, it shows that the societies they ruled had their own prestigious and formalized traditions of oral law, *æ*, and a much broader range of established legal customs (probably *þeawas*). If we are to understand the rise of royal punishment in the seventh century, we need to understand how new royal claims related to existing legal culture.

A central question, then, is how the new royal punishments of the late seventh century fitted in with existing ideas about good and bad conduct. Were kings simply proposing to punish behaviour that was already regarded as unacceptable, or did they try to use their punishments to introduce new standards of conduct? Answering this question is extraordinarily difficult with the evidence available. Æthelberht's laws are useful to an extent, but they tell us most about the type of law—*æ*—that kings left untouched in this period. As we have seen, when kings

(and therefore also owed no compensation for their actions), why did he not threaten people who took vengeance with penalties of some sort? This is not conclusive, but the passage makes more sense if the king is simply renouncing his own claim to a *wite*. For another passage which seems to imply that killings can be legitimate in certain circumstances, see IV Atr 4 and the discussions in Lambert, 'Protection, Feud and Royal Power', pp. 98–9 and Cooper, 'Law of the Highway', p. 54, n. 109. The passage perhaps implies that it was only in certain circumstances that kings claimed payments for violence: attacking someone in a house 'without licence' (*sine licentia*); attacking 'someone innocent' (*aliquis innocens*) on a road; and, less certainly, attacking someone in breach of the king's protection without bringing a case to an assembly (this relies on understanding the rather obscure phrase *de placito ungebendeo* as rendering the Old English verb *ungeboden*, which is used to mean 'to summon' in the context of assemblies: ASD, s.v. 'ungeboden').

[107] See Chapters 3 and 7, pp. 135–6, 332–6.   [108] II Cn 12–15.

legislated aggressively they did so in territory that would previously have been covered by *þeawas*, altering less prestigious customs that were probably never formally recorded and to which we have no direct access. We are often reduced to looking at what the late seventh-century *domas* say and thinking carefully about whether it is more likely they were rooted in existing ideas and practices or establishing something entirely new. This is obviously far from ideal but it is the best that we can do, and this is too important a question for us to ignore. To accept that Romano-Christian ideology impelled kings to claim a new and much more punitive legal role is one thing; to suppose that it fundamentally altered native legal culture, revolutionizing existing assumptions about what constituted wrongdoing, would be quite another. This section will take our three categories of offence in turn, trying to reconstruct the ideas which might have made them appear particularly worthy of punishment to contemporaries and assessing the origins of those ideas as far as possible.

Religious Misconduct

In some respects religious offences provide the most clear-cut answers here. Obviously enough, the specific standards of Christian observance which kings sought to enforce—such as failing to baptize children within thirty days of their birth, or working on the Sabbath—were not a part of pre-Christian legal culture. (It is possible they were well established by the time kings decided to enforce them with punishments, however.) The rationale for using royal punishments to impose minimum religious standards on the population was probably pastoral, at least in part. Ine's law that fathers should have their children baptized within thirty days shows a clear concern for the child's salvation: the fine of thirty shillings becomes forfeiture of all property if the child dies unbaptized.[109] Likewise, as has been noted, the prohibition on selling West Saxons as slaves overseas is almost certainly rooted in a pastoral concern for the fate of their souls should they end up sold to intolerant pagan masters.[110] Kings supported the Church in its pastoral mission in other ways too, both reinforcing episcopal authority—one of Wihtred's laws orders that incompetent, negligent or drunken priests be suspended from active duties pending a bishop's judgement—and looking after its economic interests by enforcing payment of ecclesiastical dues and exempting the Church from royal renders.[111]

Punishments for laymen who worked on Sundays and for marital irregularities could be read in this pastoral way too: the king forcing people to abstain from grievous sin so as to help the Church save their souls. We even have a contemporary and unimpeachably Romano-Christian articulation of this pastoral rationale for punishment. Bede records that Augustine, after being consecrated as the first archbishop of Canterbury, sent a series of nine questions to Pope Gregory, the third of which was on how someone who robbed the Church should be punished.

---

[109] Ine 2–2:1.   [110] Ine 11.   [111] Wi 1, 6; Ine 4.

Gregory's response, which Bede reproduced, included the following discussion of the proper purpose of punishment:

> And when the punishment is more severe, it must be administered in love and not in anger, for it is bestowed on the one who is punished so that he shall not be delivered up to hell-fire. We ought to maintain discipline among the faithful as good fathers do with their children according to the flesh: they beat them with stripes for their faults and yet the very ones they chastise, they intend to make their heirs; and they keep whatever they possess for those whom they appear to persecute in their anger. So we must always keep love in mind and love must dictate the method of correction, so that we do not decide on anything unreasonable.[112]

It is possible to read all royal punishments for religious offences in this framework. Indeed, it is compatible with all punishments that leave the offender alive to repent his sins and attain salvation.

An alternative reading of punishment for religious offences, however—and one which need not be incompatible with this pastoral approach—involves kings focusing not on saving individuals from the consequences of their own sin but on maintaining a favourable relationship between God and the people for whom they were responsible. The idea that terrible consequences could befall entire peoples if, through their collective sinfulness, they lost God's favour was clearly part of contemporary ecclesiastical thought. It is expressed particularly explicitly in this passage of Bede's *Ecclesiastical History* dealing with the Britons:

> With this affluence came an increase of luxury, followed by every kind of foul crime; in particular, cruelty and hatred of the truth and love of lying increased so that if anyone appeared to be milder than the rest and somewhat more inclined to the truth, the rest, without consideration, rained execrations and missiles upon him as if he had been an enemy of Britain. Not only were laymen guilty of these offences but even the Lord's own flock and their pastors. They cast off Christ's easy yoke and thrust their necks under the burden of drunkenness, hatred, quarrelling, strife, and envy and other similar crimes. In the meantime a virulent plague suddenly fell upon these corrupt people which quickly laid low so large a number that there were not enough people left alive to bury the dead. Yet those who survived could not be awakened from the spiritual death which their sins had brought upon them either by the death of their kinsmen or by fear of their own death. For this reason a still more terrible retribution soon afterward overtook this sinful people for their fearful crimes.[113]

Wihtred's demand that foreign men who refused to regularize their marriages 'depart from the land with their possessions and with [their] sins' is suggestive of the same sort of worldview.[114] The aim is to separate obdurately sinful men from

[112] *Ecclesiastical* History, i. 27.

[113] *Ecclesiastical* History, i. 14. James Campbell, 'Bede II', repr. in and cited from James Campbell, *Essays in Anglo-Saxon History* (London, 1986), pp. 29–48 at 38, argues that Bede personally shows very little inclination to interpret history in this way, reproducing such readings from his sources but not imposing them himself. This does not affect the important point here, which is that such ideas were part of contemporary thought more generally.

[114] Wi 4.

the community, which would make sense if the primary concern was to prevent the Kentish people's favourable place in God's esteem being jeopardized by individual sinfulness. This way of thinking about the divine was an established element of Christian thinking by this time. In the passage above Bede was drawing on the sixth-century British writer, Gildas, but their ultimate expression comes in a seventh-century Irish text, *On The Twelve Abuses of the World*, in which the maintenance of divine favour is linked directly to kings, particularly in their role as a judge.[115]

We have very little evidence bearing on pre-Christian religion in England, but what we do know suggests that kings had a religious significance of some sort. Royal genealogies universally trace kings' lineage back to a pagan god, usually Woden, and from Bede's narrative it is clear that kings were instrumental in decisions about religious conversion that affected entire peoples. Although it seems unlikely that pre-Christian kings had an equivalent of a pastoral role, there is a long scholarly tradition of speculation as to whether later ideas about kings' responsibility for maintaining divine favour were in fact inherited from the pre-Christian past. While the evidence used to support the idea is thin, it is possible that pagan Anglo-Saxon kings were held responsible for maintaining their people's 'luck' in a similar way.[116] It could be, then, that concern to maintain a people's favourable relationship with divine powers of some sort was a feature of pre-Christian culture, and that the notion that individuals could bring divine wrath down on an entire community through their reckless impiety would have been entirely comprehensible to Anglo-Saxons long before they came into contact with Christian missionaries. This is no more than a possibility, of course, but we ought to take it into account: the religious offences kings claimed to punish in the late seventh century were undoubtedly foreign introductions, but we cannot safely assume that they introduced the concept of socially threatening religious misconduct.

Procedural Offences

The core of our category of procedural offences is a series of duties related to legal practice in assemblies. The punishments the laws impose imply that men were expected to respect the judgements of assemblies in various ways: when they were accused they had to find sureties to guarantee they would pay what they were judged

[115] For the text, see Siegmund Hellmann, *Pseudo-Cyprianus De XII Abusivis Saeculi* (Leipzig, 1909); Aidan Breen, 'Towards a Critical Edition of *De XII Abusivis*: Introductory Essays with a Provisional Edition of the Text Accompanied by an English Translation' (Trinity College Dublin PhD thesis, 1988). For its influence, see Mary Clayton, '*De Duodecim Abusiuis*, Lordship and Kingship in Anglo-Saxon England', in Hugh Magennis and Stuart McWilliams, eds., *Saints and Scholars: New Perspectives on Anglo-Saxon Literature and Culture* (Cambridge, 2012), pp. 141–63 at 151–63. These assumptions are much more explicit in late Anglo-Saxon law and are discussed in Chapter 5, pp. 216–24.
[116] See William A. Chaney, *The Cult of Kingship in Anglo-Saxon England: The Transition from Paganism to Christianity* (Manchester, 1970), esp. ch. 1; Marita Blattman, '"Ein Unglück für sein Volk": Der Zusammenhang zwischen Fehlverhalten des Königs und Volkswohl in Quellen des 7.–12. Jahrhunderts', *Frühmittelalterliche Studien* 30 (1996), pp. 80–102.

to owe; they had to wait for judgements rather than seizing goods to which they believed they had a right; they were not meant to try to get around assembly judgements by making secret agreements with others;[117] and they certainly were not expected to harbour fugitives: people who fled instead of submitting to an assembly's judgement. It seems likely kings were inspired to take responsibility for enforcing these behavioural norms by Romano-Christian ideology in the way that Wormald argued. However, there is very little to suggest that the norms themselves represent Romano-Christian imports; indeed, it seems more or less certain that they derive from native Anglo-Saxon legal culture.

To some extent this can be confirmed through incidental references to pre-Christian legal practice in the laws which Æthelberht had committed to writing. These laws are not, of course, concerned directly with legal procedure, but they do allude to both assemblies and men who might be termed fugitives: sending a killer into exile is recognized as a way of relieving his kinsmen of half their liability for the wergild he incurred.[118] It is likely that oaths, suretyship, vouching to warranty, and all the other legal practices for which our first evidence survives in late seventh-century *domas*, were familiar in the sixth century as well. Their absence from Æthelberht's laws is not significant: it is almost certain that they are not mentioned because they were not the type of legal rule which counted as *æ*. In the absence of any plausible alternatives, we can safely assume that the basic legal practices which later kings made laws about were part of the native legal environment.

Moreover, the procedural offences which late seventh-century kings sought to punish would surely have been recognized as reprehensible conduct in the pre-Christian period. As the last chapter showed, the pre-Christian laws which Æthelberht had committed to writing are strikingly idealistic in some respects: good men, they imply, are concerned to maintain their own honour unsullied, but they are also restrained in their actions, demanding no more than is their due and accepting the precisely calibrated compensations defined by law, presumably as applied in assemblies. The procedural punishments visible in the late seventh-century *domas* seem designed to enforce exactly the sort of behaviour implicitly idealized in this sixth-century law. Æthelberht's laws may not state explicitly, for example, that it was unacceptable for men to refuse to pay the compensation which an assembly judged they owed, but this is because they refuse to envisage the possibility. The laws are concerned only to outline how people should behave, and their message is very clear: men should pay the correct compensation for any offences they commit.

---

[117] Ine 52. This fine for making secret agreements is obscure—one possible reading is that it has nothing to do with legal practice and reflects concern about treacherous political conspiracies—but if it does refer to men bypassing assemblies and reaching secret compensation settlements, this would only make sense in cases where an offender was liable to two or more parties. We might imagine him making a private deal with the most powerful party, neutralizing his most dangerous opponent in the hope that he could then avoid paying the others. In this sense, making a secret agreement is akin to harbouring a fugitive: both involve helping an offender to evade or disregard assembly judgements, thereby avoiding paying what he owes.

[118] Abt 1, 23.

All the behavioural norms about respect for assembly judgements just outlined are implicit in that message.[119]

It seems likely, then, that most of the procedural offences that late seventh-century kings tried to punish would have been recognized as reprehensible behaviour in the pre-Christian thought-world that produced Æthelberht's laws. It is possible that some of the specifics are new. Refusing to accept an assembly's judgement was doubtless regarded as very bad conduct in the sixth century, for instance, but it may be that finding sureties in advance to guarantee acceptance of such a judgement had previously been regarded as voluntary good practice rather than a compulsory duty. Ideologically motivated late seventh-century kings may well have tried to set higher standards of acceptable behaviour, but it seems likely that they did so in line with native ideals of good and bad conduct.

Theft

Theft has a special place in Anglo-Saxon law generally as an offence peculiarly worthy of harsh punishment. We see this clearly in late seventh-century laws but it is presaged in the *wite* for theft in Æthelberht's code and it remains the primary focus of kings' punitive endeavours throughout the late Anglo-Saxon period. That the Anglo-Saxons can consistently be found punishing theft over and above all other offences from Æthelberht's laws onwards in itself suggests that hatred of thieves was a deeply rooted aspect of native Anglo-Saxon legal culture, not something kings imposed on their people under the influence of new Romano-Christian ideas.

One of the clearest signs of this is the severity of late seventh-century rules on theft. If thieves were caught in the act of theft they could legitimately be killed on the spot.[120] This does not fit at all well with the pastoral rationale for punishment discussed above. Rather than helping a thief turn from his sinfulness and achieve salvation, killing him in the act of sinning would—by depriving him of the opportunity to undergo penance—deliver him up to the very hell-fire from which punishment was meant to save him. Concern about the death penalty consistent with this pastoral logic is visible in the laws of Ine, which—uniquely in the Anglo-Saxon legal corpus—state that anyone liable to the death penalty who flees to a church is to have his life spared.[121] Clearly, though, this logic has not influenced the harsher laws on theft. The severe punishment of thieves thus seems unlikely to result from the influence of Christian missionaries. We could speculate about the possible influence of more secular ideas from continental Europe, but though it is plausible there was some Frankish inspiration at work it is not necessary to explain late seventh-century English law in those terms. It is certainly possible to explain the harsh treatment of theft in Kent and Wessex without resorting to the

---

[119] See Chapter 1, pp. 54–7. [120] Wi 25; Ine 12, 16, 35.
[121] Ine 5.

idea that kings were imposing new and foreign punitive priorities against the grain of native legal culture.[122]

We need first to understand why theft might have been regarded as peculiarly threatening. The answer is almost certainly related to theft's key characteristic: its secrecy.[123] If thieves were successful their victims could not know for sure who had harmed and affronted them. This would mean that they could take no action against them; the victims of theft were left in a helpless situation unlike that of anyone who had been harmed openly. The evidence of rituals (probably late Anglo-Saxon though preserved only in a twelfth-century manuscript) designed to harness supernatural powers in order to return stolen property, thwart thieves' plans to hide their goods and 'bring [them] bound to judgement' illustrates their impotent position well.[124] This was unfortunate for the individual victim, but hostility to thieves was probably rooted in the wider effects they had on communities.[125] Inability to prove the identity of thieves would not stop people having their suspicions, breeding an atmosphere of mutual distrust that poisoned relationships between neighbours, weakening the community as a whole. The Anglo-Saxons' hatred of thieves may well reflect the high value they placed on communal solidarity.[126]

Thieves, as was noted above, can be identified and punished in two ways. They can be caught in the act of theft, or immediately afterwards with the stolen goods in hand, in which case their guilt is undeniable. If they escape with their stolen goods they can then be tracked down, formally accused in an assembly, and—if they are unable to deny the charge—convicted.[127] The second of these is less than ideal, in

---

[122] The strongest Frankish parallels can be found in the *Pactus Pro Tenore Pacis* promulgated by Childebert I and Chlothar I: Karl Augustus Eckhardt, ed., *Pactus Legis Salicae* (Monumenta Germaniae Historica, Legum sectio I, Leges Nationum Gemanicarum 4.2, Hanover, 1962), caps. 79–93, pp. 250–2. For example, caps. 80, 89 take a severe line with men who come to secret agreements with thieves, which aligns very well with Ine 36 (also Ine 52, 72–3). However, it is noteworthy that there are no known English parallels for many of these Frankish rules before the tenth century. The prologue to Childebert's decree, for example, orders that all proven thieves are to die, which is not echoed in England until Æthelstan's reign (see Chapter 4, pp. 174–7) and English 'hundreds' and 'hundredmen', clearly in some sense equivalents to the *centenas* and *centenarii* of Chlothar's decrees (caps. 84, 91–2), first appear in our sources sometime between the reigns of Edmund and Edgar (see Chapter 6, pp. 243–50). If Frankish models were fundamental to late seventh-century English legislation, it is odd that they were drawn on so selectively. It is likely that these were societies which understood theft to be problematic for similar reasons, and indeed shared a wide range of assumptions about law and order; similarities in the problems their law-makers identified and the solutions they proposed are therefore not very surprising, and need not indicate direct borrowing.

[123] See above, p. 89, n. 93.

[124] See Andrew Rabin, 'Ritual Magic or Legal Performance: Reconsidering an Old English Charm Against Theft', in Stefan Jurasinski, Lisi Oliver, and Andrew Rabin, eds., *English Law Before Magna Carta: Felix Liebermann and Die Gesetze der Angelsachsen* (Leiden, 2010), pp. 177–95 at 186.

[125] This sense that thieves pose a general threat is clearly articulated in VI As 8:9 when it is predicted that if people prove to be negligent in following the detailed anti-theft measure set down in that code 'these thieves will *rixian* still more than they have done in the past'. *Rixian* (ASD, s.v. 'ricsian') means 'to have power', 'to rule', 'to reign', particularly in the sense of supremacy secured or exercised by force, perhaps even 'to tyrannize' (as it is rendered in Attenborough, *Laws*, p. 167).

[126] This has recently been remarked upon in a different context: Wickham, 'Consensus and Assemblies', p. 416.

[127] See above, p. 85, n. 74.

that it requires a hunt for the thief, which is the very process that can upset communal harmony. It also seems that convictions of this type were regarded as less secure. It is only in the tenth century that we find kings trying to impose the death penalty on thieves who had not been caught in the act, and there are signs that they were unsuccessful. The norm in such cases seems to have been a fine.[128] The ideal scenario for unmasking thieves was to catch them in the act so that there could be no doubt, no socially corrosive witch-hunt.

Our late seventh-century rules about the treatment of thieves who were caught in the act are most plausibly explained as emerging from an existing legal culture which, for the reasons just outlined, prioritized catching thieves in circumstances where their guilt was undeniable. Capturing a thief could be a dangerous business. Some, presumably, would fight when they were confronted, and would be prepared to kill so as to avoid being unmasked. Any attempt to capture a thief had the potential to lead to a killing. To be confident in confronting thieves people had to know, at the very least, that if they ended up having to fight and kill a thief their local assembly would not judge that they had to pay a wergild. The rule that no wergild should be paid for thieves killed in such circumstances makes good sense, and is most plausibly interpreted as derived from practice. Men did kill thieves, thieves' kindreds did try to claim compensation for homicide, and at least some local assemblies—perhaps most of them—rejected those claims. It seems more likely than not that this rule was an established part of many assemblies' legal customs—*peawas*—before Wihtred and Ine included it in their *domas*.[129] The rule that men sneaking about away from roads could be captured or killed 'as thieves' could well be taken as a sign that this was so: that the notion thieves could be killed without penalty was so well established it could be applied to analogous situations.[130] As was noted earlier, however, this rule would make sense as an attempt to ensure that men caught just before an act of theft could be confronted with the same confidence as those found with stolen goods already in hand. Again, this seems like the sort of sensible rule that may well have existed in a customary form before kings put it into writing.

Rules about what people did with thieves once they had captured them, however, may well be new. Both Wihtred and Ine demand that they be handed over to the king, who claimed the right to decide their fate. We can only speculate about what men did with captured thieves before kings claimed them. The obvious choice would be to bring the thief to the local assembly for judgement, but it is possible that people tried to pass captured thieves onto kings and other powerful figures of their own accord, because it made sense for thieves to be held by someone who could not easily be intimidated by their kinsmen. Presumably, though, it was considered poor conduct simply to release the thief, either because of fear of reprisals or having accepted a bribe. The extremity of the measures taken to counteract this possibility suggests that late seventh-century kings were seriously worried about such conduct. Both Ine and Wihtred offer rewards to men who

---

[128] See Chapter 4, pp. 174–7.   [129] Wi 25; Ine 12, 16, 21, 35.   [130] Wi 28; Ine 20.

captured thieves and handed them to the king; it has already been noted that Wihtred's, at 70 shillings if the king chose to execute the thief, is staggeringly high.[131] Ine's laws also appear harsh, in that they seek to punish all captors from whom thieves escaped, not just those who deliberately let them go.[132] (Presumably it was often impossible to distinguish between the two.) It seems likely that these rewards and punishments were new, then, but that their purpose was to uphold standards of good conduct that were already well understood.

Punishment in Native Legal Practice

Late seventh-century kings' new punitive claims thus seem mostly to be rooted in native Anglo-Saxon legal culture. People already knew that theft was deeply wrong, that men who confronted and killed thieves ought not to be liable for their wergilds, and that men who captured thieves ought to be brave enough to hand them over for judgement and punishment, not allowing themselves to be bribed or blackmailed into letting them go. They must already have known that it was wrong to defy the authority of local assemblies by refusing to accept their judgements or helping others to do so. The available evidence is not sufficient to disprove it, but it is highly implausible that kings were trying to introduce completely new standards of behaviour with their new punishments. Even the religious norms may have been well established by the time kings asserted their right to punish breaches of them. It is far more likely that they were trying to use punishments to ensure their people lived up to their own ideals. Kings were asserting responsibility for maintaining good order within their kingdoms, certainly, but we need not imagine that they intended to change what was understood by good order. This process began before conversion to Christianity, as the *wite* for theft in Æthelberht's laws shows, but it seems to have accelerated sharply under the influence of Romano-Christian ideas about kingship in the late seventh century.

People would have understood what kings were trying to achieve with their new punishments, then, and it is possible that for the most part they approved, at least for secular offences. This was probably part of the point of royal legislation: by presenting themselves as leaders of a communal fight against a hated other, the thief, kings may well have been trying to win greater loyalty and support from their people. It could even be that the same can be said of punishments for religious offences—that the notion that individual impiety could provoke divine wrath from which all would suffer would have made just as much sense to pagan Anglo-Saxons as to their Christian descendants. Kings based most of their new claims on existing ideas; if they had not, they would have been incomprehensible to their people. But were these ideas just ideas, or were kings basing at least some of their new punishments on existing legal practices? It has already been argued that the rule permitting thieves caught in the act to be slain without liability for wergild makes

---

[131] Wi 26:1; Ine 28.

[132] Ine 72–3. Ine 36 (which explicitly envisages a scenario in which the captor not only releases the thief but hides the fact a theft had taken place) is similar but less harsh.

most sense as an established legal custom. It has also been suggested that other rules, such as the punishments for men who captured thieves that subsequently escaped, are not likely to have had a practical reality before kings became involved. For the majority we have no way of knowing, but it is at least worth considering the range of plausible options. There are three basic models.

The weakest model available is that the existing ideas on which royal punishments were based were idealized standards of good behaviour. People knew that good and honourable men would try their utmost to capture thieves and produce them for judgement, just as they knew that it was a very bad thing to refuse to accept a judgement given by an assembly, but when others failed to live up to these ideals there was little to be done about it. There was social and cultural pressure to behave well but little more. Kings understood these ideals but recognized that people often failed to live up to them, so they established royal punishments in an attempt to enforce them. The second, slightly stronger, model accepts the existence of these idealized standards and adds the assumption that they occasionally informed people's behaviour. When an offender refused to accept an assembly's judgement, for instance, this sometimes so outraged the men of the assembly that they banded together and helped his victim seize what he was owed, killing the offender if he dared to resist. They would perhaps then seize some additional property to punish the offender for the contempt he had shown for communal authority, and to recompense themselves for their trouble. Kings noted that this sometimes happened and were inspired to introduce new rules which formalized and standardized such practices. In the strongest model, finally, such ad hoc communal punishments for violations of accepted standards of behaviour ripened into custom without royal intervention. In some assemblies, though probably not all of them, the goods occasionally seized from men who defied judgements gradually became an established *wite* which the assembly demanded from all men who refused to provide sureties in advance of a judgement.[133] The main change of the seventh century, in this model, was kings asserting that they were the proper recipients of fines that already existed as part of some local assemblies' *peawas*.

All three models are plausible, and it may well be that each of them is accurate to an extent, for specific punishments in certain localities. If, as is perhaps likely, kings only started issuing *domas* in the mid-seventh century, there would have been no centralizing power pressing for standardization of local legal customs before that point, so it is probable that local practices had varied. Indeed, it may be that much of what we see in the late seventh century is the result of kings noting legal customs which had developed in particular areas and trying to make local assemblies throughout their kingdoms operate in the same way. This is speculation, however. The important point is that we need to keep an open mind here. We cannot reasonably assume that kings were responsible for dramatic innovation, introducing the very idea of the punitive fine to the astonishment of their people. Nor, however,

---

[133] That is, local communities in the sixth century behaved in roughly the way that local communities are often assumed to behave in tenth-century laws: independently enforcing fines as a collective body. See discussions in Chapters 3 and 7, pp. 152–6, 315–17.

can we safely assume that royal legislation lacked original thought—that nothing kings attempted was ambitious or experimental.

CONCLUSION

As we noted at the start of this chapter, the conventional reading of seventh-century legal developments—that developed by Patrick Wormald—stresses change. Kings were inspired by Romano-Christian ideology to claim a much more significant legal role, a legal role in which the punishment of wrongdoing was particularly prominent, and this represented a dramatic shift away from the feud-centric laws that Æthelberht's code suggests dominated the pre-Christian period. 'Vertical' punishments were introduced into a legal system that, in the evidence available, appears almost purely 'horizontal'. This was a great feat of royal power, a sign of newly centralized political authority. The horizontal justice of feuding was not yet displaced by the vertical justice of kings, of state power, but eventually it would be, and the seventh century represents a major step forward in this long-term process.[134] This chapter, however, suggests that we need to be careful here. Yes, Romano-Christian ideology does seem to have given kings important new legal ambitions—there is probably a major shift in conceptions of kingship—but there is also much that suggests continuity in legal culture, perhaps even in legal practice.

If we are attentive to the way contemporaries classified their own laws, it becomes apparent that many of the differences between Æthelberht's code and our three late seventh-century texts are differences between genres of law—the impression they give of radical seventh-century change is in some respects an illusion. Æthelberht's laws should be understood as a written record of a prestigious oral tradition of *æ*, which existed alongside well-established but unrecorded legal customs probably known as *þeawas*. This oral tradition of *æ* was very probably still living in the late seventh century; kings allude to it and seem to be working around it in their legislation, their *domas*. The different concerns of these *domas* from those of the laws written down at Æthelberht's behest may well arise from the fact that they engage with existing *þeawas* rather more fully than with existing *æ*. It was much more legitimate for kings to interfere with customs that had never been recorded formally than with an ancient and prestigious legal tradition, with laws expressed in a set form of words that experts had been learning by rote and passing down the generations for as long as anyone could recall. It seems unlikely that kings changed established *æ* very much with their *domas* and, given our complete ignorance of what established *þeawas* looked like, we cannot be confident that they changed them very significantly either.

What seems most certain to have changed in the seventh century is the establishment of the king's role in the punishment of wrongdoing. Kings claim that role in their *domas*, demanding that fines and captured thieves be given to them.

---

[134] See above, p. 64. The clearest articulation of this position is Wormald, 'Inter Cetera', pp. 192–8.

Æthelberht's laws show that the king claimed the right to a fine for theft, so this was not a revolutionary departure, but it seems likely that most of the king's punitive rights were new. Thieves must sometimes have been captured before and it is possible that, at least in some places, people paid punitive fines, but it had not previously been established that such fines and captured thieves belonged to the king. Some of the new royal claims, then, may well have been claims of responsibility for the oversight of, and therefore the right to profit from, established punitive customs. Others are likely to have been more ambitious: kings inventing fines for offences which had not previously been subject to fines. Even here, though, the signs are that the offences kings wished to punish would have been generally understood as wrongful conduct. There is little to suggest that new royal punitive claims represent the aggressive application of centralized political power— the top-down imposition of a new form of vertical justice which cut against the horizontal grain of an existing legal culture based on feuding.

A more plausible reading is that kings' new demands needed to work with the grain of existing legal culture if they were to work at all. Comparisons with later laws suggest that some of the more ambitious claims made by seventh-century kings could not be sustained in the long term. It has already been noted that although both Ine's laws and those of Hlothere and Eadric include royal demands for payment when men behaved provocatively while they drank together in other people's houses, Alfred's laws contain no sign of such royal demands when they discuss an essentially identical situation.[135] The obvious inference is that the earlier kings had been over-ambitious in their claims which, lacking popular legitimacy, proved impossible to enforce in the long term. Ine's laws also make some rather ambitious-seeming demands of those who took part in raiding bands, which again we find substantially ameliorated in Alfred's code.[136] Ine's attempt to impose severe punishments on those who, having captured a thief, failed to prevent his escape may well be another example: though they do not expressly contradict it, no later laws are as harsh in this context.[137] This seems to imply that popular legitimacy imposed practical limits on new royal legal claims: kings did sometimes try to assert rights which cut against the grain of established legal culture but, at least in the long term, they failed.

---

[135] Hl 11–13; Ine 6:5; Af 39:1.

[136] In Ine's laws each member of a *hloð*—which he defines as a raiding band of between seven and thirty-five people—must pay 120 shillings to the king (Ine 13:1–15). Alfred's laws require a significantly lower *hloðbot*, and seemingly only in the event of a *hloð* actually killing someone (Af 29–31:1).

[137] Ine 72–3 envisages a situation in which a thief escapes from his captors (as opposed to one in which they deliberately release him); a 'full fine' is imposed on the unfortunate captors for their oversight even if they succeed in recapturing the thief before one night has passed, and it is implied that the consequences will be even more dire if he is not recaptured within that time frame. By comparison, II Cn 29 only seeks to punish men who deliberately allow thieves to escape, knowing them to be thieves. This is not to say that late Anglo-Saxon laws are incapable of making seemingly unrealistic and perversely harsh demands: IV As 6:5 orders that eighty slaves be forced to participate in stoning to death any male slave found guilty of theft, requires that they each pay three pennies for the privilege, and orders that any slave who fails to hit the target three times be flogged.

All this tends to suggest that thinking in terms of horizontal and vertical legal cultures is unhelpfully crude. It is probably a drastic oversimplification to think of pre-Christian legal culture as purely based on feuding, and to see punishment as something introduced by kings as they grew in power and confidence. Rather, we should try to understand how a coherent legal culture could include both horizontal and vertical elements working in harmony with one another. Kings, after all, often represented their relatively punitive *domas* as complementary to established *æ*. They seem to have assumed that the vertical and the horizontal were compatible, that new punishments were not in tension with existing rules about affront and compensation in feud. The issue we need to address, then, is how this could have worked. What was this complementary relationship between two apparent opposites, feuding and punishment? The patterns formed by the new royal punishments of the late seventh century suggest an answer here: punishment and feuding applied to different types of offence. Offences against individuals—affronts to their honour in whatever form—were the province of feuding and compensation settlements. Offences against the community, however, could not be dealt with through feuding: if they were to be deterred effectively, punishment was necessary.

The dividing line between these two classes of offence is sometimes rather hazy, but there are places where it is sharply drawn. Two of the categories of offence which we find late seventh-century kings claiming to punish—religious and procedural offences—are very clearly *not* offences against individuals. Working on a Sunday or failing to have a child baptized were not offences which affronted an individual.[138] No one man's honour would suffer if he failed to pursue a claim for compensation; there was no claim to pursue. Indeed, it is notable that Wihtred has to offer a reward to persuade people to inform on their neighbours for Sunday work: because the offence affronted nobody directly and people would not be driven to take action by personal honour, they needed to be provided with artificial incentives to bring cases to assemblies.[139] Religious offences cannot be regarded as offences against individuals, then, but it is possible to read them as offences that endangered the community as a whole: sinful acts that risked provoking divine retribution in forms that would punish the innocent along with the guilty. The Church clearly had pastoral reasons for wanting to ensure minimum standards of Christian observance were maintained as well, but there are enough hints in our limited evidence to suggest that this communitarian rationale for punishing religious misconduct would have made sense to late seventh-century Anglo-Saxons (as it clearly did to their tenth-century descendants).[140]

Procedural offences are also fairly clear-cut examples of offences with no individual victims. To resurrect the fictional Ælfstan and Berhtred from Chapter 1 briefly, it would of course have mattered to Ælfstan if, when he tried to pursue a claim against Berhtred, Berhtred simply refused to agree to accept an assembly's

---

[138] The unbaptized child could be understood as the recipient of an affront, but in practice this would have been meaningless.
[139] Wi 11.   [140] See Chapter 5, pp. 216–24.

judgement.[141] It would have been far more convenient if Berhtred had provided sureties to guarantee he would abide by the assembly's decisions, but this non-cooperation with communal legal structures was not an affront to Ælfstan's personal honour. He had not been harmed, nor had his protection been breached, and if he did eventually prevail he would be entitled to no additional compensation. Berhtred's misconduct might frustrate Ælfstan, but it did not give him an additional claim to pursue. If there was an affront here it was an affront to the assembly—to the local community whose authority Berhtred had scorned. Harbouring fugitives, making secret agreements, and seizing compensation without a judgement are all, likewise, displays of contempt for the collective authority of communities expressed in assemblies.

Theft straddles the dividing line between our two classes of offence. It is both an offence against an individual—an affront to honour—and an offence against the community. The offence against the individual is obvious enough: thieves take people's property from them. This was an affront to honour, but it could be a relatively minor one: return of the goods, or their value, and payment of some additional compensation, would be sufficient to deal with it. This, however, was clearly not sufficient to deal with the grievous harm that thieves, through their secrecy, did to communal solidarity. The mutual distrust that successful thefts created was harmful to the very fabric of community, and this meant that when a thief was caught it was important for him to be dealt with disproportionately harshly. It was not enough for him simply to compensate the victim for the personal affront in proportion to the harm caused by this one act of theft; the thief needed to be severely punished, perhaps to reflect the harm done by many other more successful thefts beforehand, certainly so as to deter others from following his example in the future.

Violent offences, on the other hand, were understood to be offences against individuals. As was discussed in Chapter 1, violence was an affront to the honour of those who were harmed by it, and this meant they had to take action to secure either vengeance or compensation. It is important to remember that the direct victims of violent acts were not necessarily the people affronted by them. Indeed, it seems that the unfree and (at least in some circumstances) women were not understood to be personally affronted at all, the offence being against a free male protector—usually a head of household. Homicides with free victims represented not one but a series of individual affronts to honour. The victim's kinsmen were entitled to a wergild and thus honour-bound to take action to secure it, if not to avenge the killing. The victim might also have a personal lord—he certainly would if he was someone else's household dependant—who was considered to have been affronted by the death of his man, his 'loaf-eater'. Beyond that, all free men were under the personal protection of their king, which implied that if they were killed the king's protection had been breached and his honour affronted: he too required compensation. Ine's laws seem to relabel this right to compensation for a personal

---

affront as a punitive *wite*. This made good ideological sense—it turned what had been a personal affront akin to those suffered by any other free male into a punishment which reflected the king's supreme responsibility for the maintenance of order—but it did not mean that people suddenly began to think about violent offences, even killings, as offences against the community as a whole.

In fact, there is little to indicate violent offences were conceived in this way, either before or after Ine's day. Threatening to kill or harm people was an integral part of legitimate legal practice, and if an adversary refused to cooperate it was acceptable—probably admirable—to carry out that threat. Violence did not in itself cause harm to communities. It might do so if it led to bitter and divisive enmities, but if people pursued their claims relating to violence through the proper assembly procedures, and all parties accepted their judgements as they ought, peaceful compensation settlements would be reached and mutual goodwill restored. Feuding, properly conducted, was sufficient to deal with the potential harm to communal cohesion caused by violent offences, up to and including homicide. Providing there was no socially corrosive secrecy involved, there was no need for disproportionate punishment to serve as a deterrent: a precisely balanced compensation settlement that left all parties' personal honour intact was exactly what was needed to do away with a dangerous state of enmity. Such enmities could become a threat to communal cohesion, dividing a communicate against itself in a cycle of tit-for-tat vengeance spanning several generations, but this was only likely to come about if people flouted established legal procedures, ignoring judgements and taking precipitate or disproportionate vengeance. Violence in feud only became socially threatening when people offended the community by committing procedural offences.[142]

Feud and punishment thus occupied essentially separate spheres. Rather than imagining them as competitors, we should appreciate that they complemented one another. Properly conducted feuding could address types of wrongdoing which openly affronted specific individuals, bringing about compensation settlements that safeguarded communal interests; punishment was a way of dealing with forms of socially harmful behaviour that could not be addressed adequately in this way.[143]

---

[142] Late Anglo-Saxon evidence reinforces these conclusions. See Chapter 5, pp. 224.

[143] Though this chapter's analysis rests to a significant extent on Wormald's scholarship, its conclusions are thus a long way from his in some important respects. I do not, for instance, accept that the story of this period is one of 'kings' aggressive intervention in the dialogue of dispute' ('Inter Cetera', pp. 195–4). Nor do I think it right to suggest that this was 'a society whose deviants were being disciplined by it kings *instead* of settling its grievances by private transaction' (ibid., p. 197, my emphasis): this is to set up a false dichotomy, and probably also to underestimate the extent to which kings were reliant on local communal punitive practices for disciplining deviants. The idea that kings were 'beginning to take its [feud's] functions (and profits) unto themselves' (ibid. p. 196) is also problematic, because the functions kings seized had little to do with feuding—most of the offences they set out to punish did not even constitute affronts for which compensation would have been possible. J. M. Wallace-Hadrill, *Early Germanic Kingship in England and on the Continent* (Oxford, 1971), p. 43, comes much closer to the mark, albeit with reference to Æthelberht's Kent rather than the turn of the eighth century: 'The king is not consciously limiting the free play of feud for those many occasions when it is still the best solution; nor has he any moral objection to it. Rather, he supplements the procedure where it fails and perhaps makes something out of it for himself.'

There was some overlap in the offence of theft, and the necessity of balancing the rights of the offended individual and the needs of the offended community clearly caused law-makers some difficulty. People who stumbled upon thieves must often have had no pressing personal need to confront, capture and possibly kill them—doing so could lead to a dangerous personal enmity with the thief's kin—but the well-being of communities required that such opportunities to unmask thieves be seized whenever they arose. The disjunction between individual and communal interests in such overlapping cases must have been very hard for people to negotiate in practice, but the competing priorities are relatively easy for us to identify: they do not pose a significant analytical difficulty.

A much more troublesome point of overlap between the two spheres, from our perspective, is the person of the king. We ought, I think, to understand early medieval English kings as having two distinct legal roles. They were individuals who could be affronted and require compensation, when either they or (far more importantly) people under their protection were harmed. But they were also increasingly claiming a role as representatives of their people, the natural recipients of fines paid by men who had offended the community at large. They were affronted individuals, then, with respect to violent offences but embodiments of community when it came to theft, religious misconduct and procedural offences. This distinction, unfortunately, is obscured in our evidence. Partly this is a result of terminology: both Wihtred's and Ine's laws use the verb *gebetan* ('to compensate') and the term *wite* ('punitive fine') to refer to the same thing: sums paid by people who had committed offences against their communities. This makes sense if we understand punitive fines as in some sense compensation paid to an affronted community—this is quite probably how they originated—but it does not help us to distinguish them from compensations paid to individuals for affronts to their honour. Ine's laws muddy the water further with ideology, deliberately conflating the king's rights as an individual protector with his rights as an embodiment of community. This was a relatively superficial act which made no real difference to the nature of the king's rights—as will be seen, the king's two legal roles remain distinct for at least another three centuries, perhaps four[144]—but it has left the dividing line between our two spheres much more blurred in all the later evidence.

The legal shift we see in our seventh-century evidence, then, is a shift that takes place in only one of these two spheres. The laws about affront and compensation which defined offences against the individual remained essentially unchanged, enshrined in a prestigious oral tradition of *æ*. The big change was unrelated to feud: kings asserted their position as representatives of their people, with a duty to punish offences against the community and a right to profit from doing so. Though this was a process that seems to have started before the conversion—witness the *wite* for theft in Æthelberht's code—it is almost certain that it accelerated rapidly under the influence of the Romano-Christian ideology of kingship which Wormald identified. This ideology had radical effects on kings and their ambitions, but it is

---

[144] See Chapter 4.

much less clear that it made a substantial impact on legal culture. Rather, it seems that by claiming the right to punish offences which harmed not individuals but the community, kings were working within an established tradition of essentially communitarian legal thought, perhaps even seizing responsibility for an existing field of legal activity. They may well have tried to innovate in that field, introducing punishments which had not previously existed, but the later evidence suggests that they either worked with the grain of existing legal culture or, in the long term, they failed to change it.

3

Royal Administration and Legal Practice to the Early Tenth Century

INTRODUCTION

The evidence surveyed in the last two chapters suggests that the seventh century was a time of substantial change in the legal role of English kings. There is little to indicate that kings of the late sixth and early seventh centuries had much routine involvement in legal matters. The laws written down at the behest of Æthelberht of Kent suggest that formal law, known as *æ*, had until that point been the province of legal experts of some sort: men who had memorized long lists of compensations for affronts. Legal customs on other matters, probably termed *þeawas*, would have been well understood by the local assemblies that applied them but were not recorded in the same way: they are unlikely to have existed in a set form of words that could be learnt and recited. Although kings in this period had important legal rights and would have been involved in law because of them, our limited evidence suggests that by the time of conversion to Christianity they were only just beginning to claim a role in the punishment of wrongdoing. By the end of the seventh century, however, they had a much more prominent legal role. We find kings issuing new laws, termed *domas*, in which they claim extensive punitive rights: fines are to be paid to kings not just for theft (as in Æthelberht's laws) but for a wide range of offences. It is likely that the legal experts who had previously memorized *æ* remained important, but kings now claimed the right to shape all other aspects of legal practice to their specifications through their legislation. As far as we can tell they claimed overall responsibility for the legal order and its maintenance in a way that pre-Christian kings had not.

This chapter is an assessment of what this meant in practice. Kings' new claims presented them with new challenges. Making laws in great assemblies was relatively simple; ensuring that local assemblies throughout the kingdom thereafter judged in accordance with what had been decreed must have been much more difficult. Likewise, it was one thing to claim the right to receive a fine for a particular offence, but quite another to make sure that offenders paid up. We should not imagine that kings were faced with blank slates and had to invent entirely new legal structures for their kingdoms, of course. Rather, they had to find a way to implement their legal ambitions using their existing administrative resources in conjunction with existing legal practices and structures. Contemporaries would have had little difficulty in grasping how this worked. People understood their own legal institutions and the way the king's rights were administered on a local level, and it must have been fairly obvious how the two could sensibly be combined. For us, however, this is not the case. We need to think very carefully about both these established contexts if we are to understand how they fitted together.

Doing so presents two main challenges, which are interlinked. One is historiographical. The way kings exploited their non-legal rights on a local level in this period is, in fact, relatively well understood. There is a long tradition of careful scholarship on rural organization and surplus extraction, and since the publication of Rosamond Faith's seminal *The English Peasantry and the Growth of Lordship* in 1997, there has been broad scholarly consensus on these matters, for this period at least.[1] The modern literature on legal practice before the tenth century, however, is not of the same calibre. Part of the reason for this is historiographical: legal historians tend to be interested in the roots of the common law, and from that perspective this period can seem so distant as to be irrelevant. It is also, however, partly a consequence of the second of the two main challenges to studying the period: the relative poverty of the available evidence. We have late seventh-century laws from Kent and the West Saxon laws of Ine, which may well include material from the first quarter of the eighth century, but after that we have no texts of written law until Alfred's code from the last quarter of the ninth. From the intervening period, fortunately, we have some charters which show us Mercian and West Saxon kings transferring legal rights to aristocratic beneficiaries, but we

---

[1] Rosamond Faith, *The English Peasantry and the Growth of Lordship* (London, 1997). A clear critical overview of the historiography on this subject can be found in Chris Wickham, *Framing the Early Middle Ages: Europe and the Mediterranean, 400–800* (Oxford, 2005), pp. 314–26, which essentially accepts Faith's interpretation for the period with which we are concerned here, but diverges somewhat in the tenth century (pp. 323, 347–51). Broadly, Faith and Wickham argue that kings were not understood to own all the land in their kingdoms, but rather had 'superiority' or 'extensive lordship' over it, entitling them to dues that were more akin to taxes than to rents (though see Wickham, *Framing*, p. 70, for the argument that complex bureaucratic systems of 'taxation' ought to be distinguished from less developed 'tribute'). This position was established in the late nineteenth century by Frederic William Maitland, *Domesday Book and Beyond: Three Essays in the Early History of England* (Cambridge, 1897), pp. 272–90. For the opposing interpretation, which understands agricultural dues as rents paid by tenants, see H. M. Chadwick, *Studies on Anglo-Saxon Institutions* (Cambridge, 1905), pp. 367–77; T. H. Aston, 'The Origins of the Manor in England', *Transactions of the Royal Historical Society* 8 (1958), pp. 59–83. The significance of Faith's contribution lies in the convincing way she bridges the gap between the two models, integrating evidence for areas of intense exploitation of dependent free and unfree farmers—whose dues might reasonably be characterized as 'rent'—into a wider picture which accepts the existence of numerous free farming households whose relatively light dues ought to be understood as 'tribute'. This now needs some modification in the light of David Pratt, 'Demesne Exemption from Royal Taxation in Anglo-Saxon and Anglo-Norman England', *English Historical Review* 128 (2013), pp. 1–34, which challenges the evidential basis of one aspect of Faith's interpretation: the association of inlands with exemption from taxation. The most substantial challenge to Faith's model, in her own assessment (personal communication), is Richard Purkiss, 'Early Royal Rights in the Liberty of St Edmund' (unpublished), which uses Domesday evidence to demolish the retrospective inferences about royal 'hundredal' rights made in the introduction to R. H. C. Davis, ed., *The Kalendar of Abbot Samson of Bury St. Edmunds and Related Documents* (Camden Society Third Series 84, London, 1954), on which much subsequent scholarship is founded. Purkiss, currently a doctoral student at the University of Oxford, intends to publish a revised version of this essay as a journal article in the near future. I would like to thank him for allowing me advance access to it.

have almost nothing relevant to East Anglia or Northumbria, and very little that can tell us about the operation of ordinary legal disputes in practice. The scale of the problem is most clearly illustrated by the fact that Patrick Wormald's 'Handlist' of legal cases from the entire Anglo-Saxon period, which includes materials drawn from charters, chronicles and even miracle stories, contains only ten cases involving homicide and twenty-one involving theft.[2] Only one of these concerns events from the period before Alfred's reign—a theft in the reign of King Æthelheard of Wessex (726–40) reported in a charter supposedly issued by King Æthelstan (924–39)—but even this is probably an eleventh-century fabrication.[3]

We should not, however, be overawed by either of these difficulties. Our pre-tenth-century sources are sparse by comparison with the late Anglo-Saxon period, but they exist: we have some good evidence available for the central themes of this chapter and there is no reason not to exploit it. Once we get into the early tenth century, moreover, there is more to work with, and—although of course we have to be very careful not to make unjustifiable assumptions—it is not unreasonable to think that ideas and structures visible there can cast light on what came before. The lack of sustained attention to this period from modern legal historians is also helpful, in a sense, in that readers are less likely to come it with firmly engrained assumptions. The need for extended historiographical discussion is relatively minimal.

This chapter consists of four sections. The first is concerned to establish as clearly as possible the way kingdoms were structured in this period: how kings and their primarily military endeavours were supported by the vast majority of the population, whose own endeavours were mainly agricultural. This was a period of substantial change—kingdoms became fewer and larger—so this is not as straightforward a task as it may sound. But it is vital. The last two chapters have provided substantial background on the communal legal structures and feuding practices with which kings had to work; the background on the non-legal structures through which kings ruled provided by this section is the necessary counterpoint to that. The second section considers legal revenues. The right to receive royal legal revenues from particular areas was routinely held by people other than the king, and this meant that in different localities there were different people with an incentive to implement royal legislation. Understanding the distribution of legal revenues is thus fundamental to comprehending the practicalities of law on a local level. The third section considers the transmission of royal legislation to the localities: how did kings ensure that local assemblies made their judgements in accordance with royal law? To answer this question we need to think through the workings of assemblies in detail. Finally, the fourth section examines legal practice outside assemblies, the processes by which accusations relating to punishable

---

[2] Patrick Wormald, 'A Handlist of Anglo-Saxon Lawsuits', repr. in and cited from Patrick Wormald, *Legal Culture in the Early Medieval West: Law as Text, Image and Experience* (London, 1999), pp. 253–87. Homicides: nos. 50, 54, 58, 60, 61, 71, 145, 148, 161, 173. Theft: nos. 23, 25, 31, 37, 41, 45, 54, 56, 100, 102, 124, 127, 129, 132, 155, 156, 157, 158, 169, 173, 178.
[3] Wormald, 'Handlist', no. 32; S 443.

offences arrived at assemblies for consideration, and the means by which the judgements that arose from assemblies were enforced. A key issue here is how the processes by which offenders were identified and punished related to the dynamics of feuding.

THE PRACTICALITIES OF ROYAL POWER

Before we turn to specifically legal matters it is important to establish some broader context for how kings ruled their kingdoms. We need to understand the structures through which kings engaged with their people and ultimately drew their power. The vast majority of the people who lived at this time were farmers. The main things they had to offer those who ruled them were the agricultural surpluses they produced and their own bodies, as either workers or warriors. Kings, on the other hand, had two main requirements. Their most basic function was military leadership: they frequently needed men to fight, and they also had military infrastructure to maintain (fortifications, bridges, roads). For this they needed fighters and labourers. Even more fundamentally, they had the same basic need for food and shelter as anyone else. Kings were not farmers or labourers: they needed other people to provide their households with food and maintain the buildings they stayed in. (They also had a range of high-ranking subordinates who needed to be supported in the same way because they too were engaged in activities other than agriculture: various forms of warrior and churchman.) Our evidence implies that kings had essentially separate systems by which they met these military and non-military needs.[4]

Political and Military Networks

Everything we know about English kings throughout this period—and indeed for many subsequent centuries—suggests that their primary function was military leadership. There were a lot of kingdoms in seventh-century lowland Britain, not

---

[4] What follows leans heavily on the excellent literature on kingship and social structure in this period, much of which draws productively on comparisons with contemporary Irish and British evidence. See James Campbell, 'Bede's *Reges* and *Principes*', repr. in and cited from James Campbell, *Essays in Anglo-Saxon History* (London, 1986), pp. 85–98; Thomas M. Charles-Edwards, 'Social Structure', in Pauline Stafford, ed., *A Companion to the Early Middle Ages: Britain and Ireland, c.500–c.1100* (Chichester, 2009), pp. 107–25; Barbara Yorke, 'Kings and Kingship', in Stafford, *Companion to the Early Middle Ages*, pp. 76–90; Barbara Yorke, *Kings and Kingdoms of Early Anglo-Saxon England* (London, 1997), esp. ch. 7; Thomas Charles-Edwards, 'Nations and Kingdoms: A View from Above', in Thomas Charles-Edwards, ed., *After Rome* (Oxford, 2003), pp. 23–58; Thomas Charles-Edwards, 'Early Medieval Kingship in the British Isles', in Steven Bassett, ed., *The Origins of Anglo-Saxon Kingdoms* (Leicester, 1989), pp. 28–39; Pauline Stafford, 'Kings, Kingships and Kingdoms', in Wendy Davies, ed., *From the Vikings to the Normans* (Oxford, 2003) pp. 11–39; George Molyneaux, *The Formation of the English Kingdom in the Tenth Century* (Oxford, 2016), chs. 1–3; George Molyneaux, 'Why Were Some Tenth-Century English Kings Presented as Rulers of Britain?', *Transactions of the Royal Historical Society* 21 (2011), pp. 59–91.

all of them English and some of them very small.[5] Their kings seem to have been engaged in a complex, violent, and unstable game of often unequal political alliances. Overlord kings used their military power to dominate the rulers of lesser kingdoms, who would often rather accept their subordination than risk being attacked. The most successful kings were overlords who dominated numerous client kings by these means. The degree of these client kings' subordination varied. Some paid tribute, some did not; the loyalty of some, but not others, was ensured by hostages.[6] Generally, though, client kings were expected to express their political loyalty by providing military support, raising their own armies and marching with their overlords when they went to war. Great overlords could thus lead armies consisting of numerous contingents led by other rulers who acknowledged their domination. This is what Bede is referring to when he tells us that Penda of Mercia led an army made up of forces led by thirty *duces regii* (a rather ambiguous term conventionally translated as 'royal ealdormen'), among whom were kings of East Anglia and Deira, when he was finally defeated in 655.[7]

Warfare could be extremely profitable. The winners of a pitched battle could strip the bodies of their fallen enemies of weaponry, armour and probably jewellery (it is not unlikely that high-status warriors wore much of their wealth). However, while pitched battles feature strongly in our narratives they were probably relatively rare. Military aggression may well usually have taken the form of great plundering raids for slaves and livestock. Successful warfare, either way, was a major source of income, its spoils providing kings with the means to give rich rewards to their followers, maintaining their loyalty.[8] Marching with a dominant overlord king like Penda would usually have been a very profitable venture, the prospect of sharing in the spoils of such expeditions being a key incentive for lesser kings to accept their subordination to such figures. The kings of the seventh century thus ruled relatively small kingdoms—there were often separate kings of east and west Kent—but there was nothing petty about the warfare they engaged in. The armies dominant overlord kings assembled from their subordinate rulers were formidable, their raids long-ranging and probably devastating. Northumbrian armies raided into Ireland, Pictland, and Wales during this period, as well as other English kingdoms

---

[5] The clearest illustration of this situation is the text known as the Tribal Hidage, on which see: David Dumville, 'The Tribal Hidage: An Introduction to its Texts and their History', in Bassett, *Origins*, pp. 225–30; Wendy Davies and Hayo Vierck, 'The Contexts of the Tribal Hidage: Social Aggregates and Settlement Patterns', *Frühmittelalterliche Studien* 8 (1974), pp. 223–93; Yorke, *Kings and Kingdoms*, pp. 9–15; James Campbell, 'Archipelagic Thoughts: Comparing Early Medieval Polities in Britain and Ireland', in Stephen Baxter et al., eds. *Early Medieval Studies in Memory of Patrick Wormald* (Farnham, 2009), pp. 47–63 at 54–5 (for a succinct review of the earlier literature).

[6] Particularly helpful here is the scheme of seven levels of overlordship set out in T. M. Charles-Edwards, *Wales and the Britons, 350–1064* (Oxford, 2013), pp. 326–7. For Ecgfrith, future king of Northumbria, spending time as a hostage in Mercia, see Ecclesiastical History, iii.24.

[7] *Ecclesiastical History*, iii.24. Œthelwald of Deira, however, is said to have abandoned Penda, withdrawing his force at the last minute and sitting out the battle in a place of safety.

[8] The point is generally accepted but most cogently argued in a Frankish context: Timothy Reuter, 'Plunder and Tribute in the Carolingian Empire', repr. in and cited from Timothy Reuter, *Medieval Polities and Modern Mentalities*, ed. Janet L. Nelson (Cambridge, 2006), pp. 231–50.

as far south as Wessex.[9] Kings in the seventh century were predators who often hunted in packs led by overlords. As long as they were successful these packs held together, and could seem unstoppable, but they disintegrated quickly when they encountered defeat. Early seventh-century figures like Æthelberht of Kent and Rædwald of East Anglia, for example, were the greatest kings of their day, exercising overlordship over all their neighbours, but Kentish and East Anglian dominance collapsed rapidly upon their deaths, never to re-emerge.[10]

Over subsequent centuries power became more stable. Many client kings lost their positions, or at least their royal status: their kingdoms were absorbed into those of their overlords. If fortune favoured them these formerly royal families could maintain something close to their old power. The kingdom of the Hwicce in the West Midlands provides a particularly clear example of this. It was already under Mercian overlordship by the time of our first reference to it, in the late seventh century, and by the end of the eighth it had been fully absorbed into Mercia. Ealdred, a member of the Hwiccian royal family, is described in a charter of King Offa of Mercia of 778 as his *subregulus*, and as 'ealdorman (*dux*) of his own people, the Hwicce'.[11] The Hwicce continue to have their own ealdormen into the early ninth century, though perhaps not from the same family.[12] The line between the highest form of secular aristocrat, the ealdorman, and the lowest form of client king was thus not very clearly defined. It is not simply that someone who looked royal from one perspective could seem like an ealdorman from another (though this is demonstrably true); Offa's description of Ealdred shows that it was possible to be both at once.[13]

The essential similarity of ealdormen and client kings in functional terms warrants emphasis. The powerful kings of the seventh century led conglomerations of smaller rulers, each of whom was expected to provide them with military support when required. If we accept that the practical functions of ealdormen and client kings were basically the same, later kingdoms can be described in exactly the same way. The greater solidity of ninth-century kingdoms did not result from the removal of a tier of subordinate rulers (though some were removed), but from a shift in the way kings related to the regional military leaders who acknowledged their domination and contributed contingents to their armies. Bede tells us that the

---

[9] *Ecclesiastical History*, ii.9 (Edwin campaigns in Wessex), iv.26 (Ecgfrith sends raiders to Ireland and attacks Pictland, albeit only to be defeated and killed, seemingly bringing an end to the period of clear Northumbrian dominance).

[10] *Ecclesiastical History*, ii.5 (both for the extent of these kings' dominance and for the collapse following Æthelberht's death, culminating in defeat by the West Saxons), ii.12 (for Rædwald's defeat of the Northumbrians in battle and ability to impose his own candidate as king), ii.15 (for Edwin of Northumbria inducing Earpwald of East Anglia, Rædwald's son, to convert to Christianity—an indication that East Anglian dominance had come to an end).

[11] S 113.

[12] See Patrick Sims-Williams, 'Kings of the Hwicce (act. c.670–c.780)' *Oxford Dictionary of National Biography* (Oxford University Press, 2004; online edn, September 2011); <http://www.oxforddnb.com/view/article/52342> (accessed 7 February 2015).

[13] Pauline Stafford, 'Ealdorman', in Michael Lapidge et al., eds., *The Wiley-Blackwell Encyclopedia of Anglo-Saxon England* (2nd edn, Chichester, 2014), pp. 156–7, provides an excellent overview of the term.

kingdom of Wessex collapsed upon the death of King Cenwalh in 672, with *subreguli* ('under-rulers') dividing it up amongst themselves, only to be reassembled by King Cædwalla over a decade later.[14] Ninth-century Wessex was still made up of smaller regions with their own rulers, but these regions were shires rather than kingdoms and their rulers were ealdormen rather than *subreguli*. A relatively loose relationship of subordination—that between king and client king—had been replaced by the rather firmer expectations of loyalty and obedience that character-ized the relationship between king and ealdorman.[15] This shift mattered. It made ninth-century high politics a distinctly different game from what it had been in the seventh: still complex and dangerous, but more predictable and probably somewhat less lethal (though the arrival of large-scale Scandinavian armies in the last third of the century changed that dramatically). Nonetheless, continuity needs to be stressed as well. Kingdoms still tended to be ruled not just by one king but by a number of subordinate rulers, responsible for specific regions.

Understanding this is important because ealdormen are easily misinterpreted. The ealdorman was not an administrative official employed to collect the king's revenues in a region, but essentially a more controllable version of a client king.[16] He was a regional military leader. Apart from turning up at assemblies held by kings, and thus acknowledging their superiority, the one duty that can certainly be ascribed to the office of ealdorman in this period is military leadership. We frequently find ealdormen leading armies from particular regions in Anglo-Saxon Chronicle entries for the ninth century.[17] In 802, for example a West Saxon ealdorman leading the men of Wiltshire, died in the course of defeating a Mercian ealdorman leading a Hwiccian army.[18] Just as seventh-century overlord kings depended on their client kings for a large portion of their armies when they went to war, ninth-century kings relied on their ealdormen raising forces from the regions they ruled.

The way ealdormen did this is not revealed in any detail by our sources and has been the subject of historiographical debates which it would not be profitable to rehearse here.[19] The most plausible interpretation is that ealdormen, like kings and

---

[14] *Ecclesiastical History*, iv.12.

[15] This is not, of course, to say that later ealdorman invariably were loyal and obedient. They were not, but it is probably fair to say that they were generally expected to be more loyal than client kings. Nor is it to imply that geographical divisions remained constant. The areas ruled by later ealdormen could correspond to earlier kingdoms, but it was by no means necessary for them to do so.

[16] The economic ties between kings and ealdormen or client kings are obscure in our evidence. As has been noted, it is likely that kings initially had no direct economic interests in the regions ruled by their client kings, exploiting them economically (if they did so at all) by demanding tribute from these kings. Later on it is plain—most obviously in Domesday Book—that kings held their own lands within all the regions of their kingdom: they seem to have exploited them directly rather than relying on subordinate rulers. These two poles are reasonably well understood, but process by which kings moved from one to the other is not (and is complicated by confusion over the eleventh-century earl's 'third penny', on which see Chapter 7, pp. 337–42).

[17] *Anglo-Saxon Chronicle*, s.aa. 802, 840, 845, 851, 853, 860.

[18] *Anglo-Saxon Chronicle*, s.a. 802.

[19] The main debate is about whether all free men were under a universal obligation to do military service. A concise critical review is provided by Molyneaux, *Formation*, pp. 79–85, which resolves the issue in much the same way as is proposed here. For the two sides of the debate: C. Warren Hollister,

some other great magnates, had their own military retinues living within their households. In addition, they would have been able to call on the loyalty of aristocratic families who had benefited from their favour in some way. Some of these people would have been warriors who, after a period of service in the ealdorman's household, had been rewarded with grants of land (or, more accurately, rights over land) so they could marry and set up their own households. To this core of men with personal obligations to the ealdorman could be added recruits drawn from the free population of the region he ruled. Offensive warfare could be profitable, the necessity of defending one's home against a hostile raiding army would have been obvious to all, and warfare of either type was doubtless attractive to some as an exciting way to gain honour and the increased social status that went with it. It is plausible that armies in this period often included volunteers from the free population.

Beyond that, it is likely that there was a theoretical obligation on all free adult males to fight, at least in defensive warfare, regardless of their personal inclinations. Kings can commonly be found alienating their rights over land in this period, but from the mid-eighth century onwards they become increasingly careful to state explicitly that they retained three key military rights: bridge-work, fortification-work, and military service.[20] Ine's laws include several fines for neglect of military service, one of which applies to ordinary freemen.[21] It is unclear whether this apparently universal obligation to do military service was commonly exploited in any determined or organized way, with ealdormen dragooning reluctant free farmers into their armies. It is probable that for most scenarios the combination of an ealdorman's household, practised warriors from the regional aristocracy, and volunteers from among the free population was sufficient. It is difficult to imagine that any ealdorman would particularly wish to lead an army which in large part consisted of ill-equipped farmers, conscripted against their will, but it is possible this was necessary in dire emergencies.

Kings, then, drew their military power primarily through political networks. They were able to call on the loyalty of their own household warriors as well as on that of noblemen who had benefited from their favour—great ecclesiastical magnates with their own military retinues as well as secular aristocrats[22]—but it seems that the main figures through which armies were raised were subordinate rulers. In the seventh century these subordinate rulers were mainly client kings, whereas by the ninth they were mainly ealdormen; either way, these were the men who we find

---

Anglo-Saxon Military Institutions on the Eve of the Norman Conquest (Oxford, 1962); Richard P. Abels, *Lordship and Military Obligation in Anglo-Saxon England* (London, 1988).

[20] See below, p. 129. For a detailed discussion of the evolution of these rights, see Nicholas Brooks, 'The Development of Military Obligation in Eighth- and Ninth-Century England', in Peter Clemoes and Kathleen Hughes, eds., *England before the Conquest: Studies in Primary Sources Presented to Dorothy Whitelock* (Cambridge, 1971), pp. 69–84.

[21] Ine 51. The rather elaborate interpretations proposed by Abels (*Lordship and Military Obligation*, pp. 11–25) in order to avoid reading this law in the obvious way strike me as unconvincing and unnecessary.

[22] For bishops taking part in battles (albeit always alongside kings or ealdormen), see *Anglo-Saxon Chronicle*, s.a. 825, 836, 845, 871.

raising and leading armies from their regions. When kings from the mid-eighth century onwards reserve the rights to receive bridge-work, fortification-work and military service in their charters, granting all their other rights over the land in question to the beneficiary, they were ensuring that their military capabilities remained undiminished by their generosity. If he needed it, the relevant ealdorman could still demand military service from the people living on the land to which such grants pertained, and he was still entitled to have the local free population labour on military construction or maintenance projects. In Mercia and Wessex, at least, royal military rights were kept separate from all other royal rights; it seems that in the ninth century kings generally relied on their ealdormen to exploit these rights on their behalf, just as the most powerful seventh-century kings drew on their client kings for their military power.

The Extraction of Food and Labour

The celebrated military feats of kings and ealdormen were supported by the agricultural labour of the majority of the population. Farmers were in no way insulated from the elite's world of large-scale slave- and cattle-raiding, which could and occasionally did intrude into their lives with sudden and devastating brutality. Most of the time, however, they interacted with this world in much more mundane ways, supplying it with food and labour. Farmers were far from equal. The unfree were generally exploited much more fully than the free, but the most fortunate slaves' lives may have been better in some respects than those of the poorest free people, those who lacked the land necessary for economic independence.[23] The lives of dependent free families, much of them spent working for the benefit of others, were probably more similar to those of slaves than those of the richest free farmers, who would often have had their own free and unfree dependants.[24] There were also gradations of status among the unfree—the *þeow* is contrasted with the *esne* in Æthelberht's laws—though exactly what they signified is obscure.[25]

The free population of early English kingdoms lived mainly on land known in the historiography as 'warland'.[26] The landholdings of individual householders were assessed in units that were usually known as 'hides' (there were regional variations in terminology), by which liability for the various dues the free population owed to

---

[23] See Faith, *English Peasantry*, ch. 3. This point is made very effectively in a broader European context in Alice Rio, 'Self-Sale and Voluntary Entry into Unfreedom', *Journal of Social History* 45 (2012), pp. 661–85; Wickham, *Framing*, pp. 558–66.

[24] Faith, *English Peasantry*, ch. 5. As Thomas Charles-Edwards once put it, with reference to the freeman's portrayal in Æthelberht's laws, 'the Kentish *ceorl* is, in a small way, a lord in his own right': T. M. Charles-Edwards, 'Kinship, Status and the Origin of the Hide', *Past and Present* 56 (1972), pp. 3–33 at 12.

[25] Abt 85–90. A plausible guess is that the distinction is between the slave who serves in his or her owner's households (the *þeow*) and unfree dependants who live in their own households (Abt 85 shows that an *esne* could be married). Generally on slavery, see the encyclopedic David A. E. Pelteret, *Slavery in Early Medieval England: From Alfred the Great until the Twelfth Century* (Woodbridge, 1995).

[26] This is the term adopted by and clearly characterized in Faith, *English Peasantry*, ch. 4. It is one of several seemingly interchangeable terms used by Anglo-Saxon sources; alternatives include *utland* ('outland'—presumably in opposition to 'inland', on which more shortly) and *gafolland* ('tribute-land').

their rulers was apportioned.[27] The most important of these was the provision of food renders, but eighth-century charters imply that labour services were also common-place.[28] The early evidence is generalized, but references to established custom in sources from the late Anglo-Saxon period (and indeed beyond) give a flavour of what might have been involved: obligations to undertake building and repair work at specific centres, to transport goods and livestock, to run errands or provide escorts on horseback, and to provide agricultural labour (mainly haymaking, harvesting and ploughing) at specific times of year.[29] The early evidence on food renders is better. Our earliest reference may come in Æthelberht's laws, where it is stated that 20 shillings should be paid for the king's *fedesl*.[30] The meaning of this is not clear but if, as Lisi Oliver suggested, this can be translated 'the king's feeding', 20 shillings may be the sum payable in compensation for the offence of refusing to supply a customary food render.[31] Ine's laws are more certain on this point. They provide the following statement of the food render—*foster*—owed by every ten hides of land.

> 10 vats of honey, 300 loaves, 12 ambers of Welsh ale, 30 ambers of clear ale, 2 full-grown cows or 10 wethers, 10 geese, 20 hens, 10 cheeses, a full amber of butter, 5 salmon, 20 pounds of fodder and 100 eels shall be paid as *foster* from every ten hides.[32]

Clearly this is notional; not every ten hides of land can possibly have had access to eels and salmon. It does, however, provide an illustration of the types of resource that a king might routinely extract from his rural population in the late seventh century.[33]

It is generally accepted that kings exploited these food renders by travelling around their kingdoms, moving between various royal centres and consuming the food renders of the areas surrounding them.[34] Kings, then, had a network of collection points within their kingdoms to which the free population of associated

---

[27] The key discussion is Charles-Edwards, 'Kinship, Status'; for a succinct overview, see Rosamond Faith, 'Hide', in Lapidge et al., *Encyclopedia*, pp. 243–4.

[28] The evidence comes in the form of exemptions, for example 'from all work due to the king or ealdorman' (S 58: *a cunctis operibus vel regis vel principis*). See also S 106, 134, 1612.

[29] Faith, *English Peasantry*, pp. 107–14.　　　　[30] Abt 12.

[31] Lisi Oliver, '*Cyninges Fedesl*: The King's Feeding in Æthelberht, ch. 12', *Anglo-Saxon England* 27 (1998), pp. 31–40. However, an attractive alternative reading is proposed in Carole Hough, 'The Structure of English Society in the Seventh Century: A New Reading of Æthelberht 12', in Hough, *An Ald Recht*, pp. 74–86. For discussion, see Chapter 1, p. 58, n. 84.

[32] Ine 70:1.

[33] Several similar lists survive in charters of the late eighth and ninth centuries; see Wickham, *Framing*, p. 321 for a brief discussion and references. Wickham's argument that these renders were relatively light is challenged in Ryan Lavelle, 'Ine 70.1 and Royal Provision in Anglo-Saxon Wessex', in Gale R. Owen-Crocker, ed., *Kingship, Legislation and Power in Anglo-Saxon England* (Woodbridge, 2013), pp. 259–73 at 266–70.

[34] For an excellent recent textbook account, see Robin Fleming, *Britain After Rome: The Fall and Rise* (London, 2010), pp. 104–6. Part of the reason for doing this must have been that the food supply to which a king was entitled in any given area was limited, and large royal households ate their way through it quite rapidly, eventually exhausting it and compelling the household to move on. This is something of a simplification, however. If kings wished to stay in one place for prolonged periods it would not have been impossible to organize. Produce from neighbouring regions could be brought to them—the customary services demanded from free farmers in later periods often included transportation—and they may have been able to buy food once they exhausted their own supplies.

districts would bring their food renders. These collection points were very probably working farms, consisting of land belonging to the king farmed by a dependent free and unfree workforce. The land belonging to farms of this sort (whether held by the king or granted to others) is known as 'inland' in the literature.[35] When the surrounding free population of the warland rendered their livestock, it would probably have been added to the inland herds. When the warland population rendered their seasonal labour services—harvesting, ploughing and hay-making— they would have rendered it on inland fields.[36] Each of these royal farms would have needed someone in charge of it. This figure usually seems to have been known as a reeve (*gerefa*), this being a general term for someone with administrative responsibilities.[37] The reeve's job would have included the management of the dependent inland workforce, keeping track of the obligations of the local warland population, and ensuring that everything was ready when the king and his house-hold arrived and needed to be entertained. Quite possibly the earliest references we have to such a reeve is in the laws of Wihtred, which state that if an *esne* (an unfree dependant) belonging to the king is charged with an offence, the reeve must either clear him (perhaps by swearing an oath denying the charge on his behalf) or give him over to be flogged.[38]

It thus seems likely that kingdoms in this period were covered by a network of inland farms, supervised by reeves and worked by free and unfree dependants, to which the surrounding warland population rendered food and labour services. Because food renders seem to have been a universal obligation, it is likely that the reeve was a fairly universal figure as well. All heads of free households would have known where to take their food renders and that probably meant they knew the local reeve, part of whose job it was to keep track of these food renders. He would have been free, conceivably even a minor nobleman, but certainly not someone of the stature of an ealdorman or bishop, able to support a substantial warrior household.[39] His main duties were agricultural, not military.[40] There may have been some isolated free households which were fortunate enough not to be known to any reeve and could get away without making food renders, but there is no reason to think this was common.

---

[35] See Faith, *English Peasantry*, ch. 2.

[36] It should not, however, be imagined that inlands tended to form territorially contiguous blocks; outlying pockets of inland, known in the literature as 'berewicks', associated with larger central inlands and often featuring place-names suggestive of specialized production, seem to have been common. See Faith, *English Peasantry*, pp. 42–7.

[37] See Pauline Stafford, 'Reeve', in Lapidge et al., *Encyclopedia*, pp. 397–8. For further discussion: William Alfred Morris, *The Medieval English Sheriff to 1300* (Manchester, 1927), ch. 1; James Campbell, 'Some Agents and Agencies of the Late Anglo-Saxon State', repr. in and cited from James Campbell, *The Anglo-Saxon State* (London, 2000), pp. 201–25 at 207–11.

[38] Wi 22.   [39] See below, p. 154.

[40] Though we cannot, of course, assume it is relevant to our period, it is worth noting that the eleventh-century text known as *Gerefa*, which discusses the duties of a reeve in detail, makes this abundantly clear: for example, in emphasizing the need to know which agricultural tasks need to be performed at which times of year (Ger 8–12) and to understand and provide the tools needed by those under a reeve's authority (Ger 14–18:2).

It is clear, however, that not all reeves and inlands were the king's. Withred's law stating the reeve's responsibility to clear an *esne* of a charge or hand him over to be flogged in fact concerns not just the king's reeves and *esne*s, but also those of bishops.[41] Numerous charters from the period show kings granting land to ecclesiastical beneficiaries which explicitly free that land from all dues owed to the king (the only significant exclusions made are military service, bridge-work, and fortification-work).[42] The implication was not that all the families who lived on this land could now stop rendering their dues, but that henceforth they were to provide them to the charter's beneficiary: in practice to a reeve running an ecclesiastical inland. Royal charters in favour of secular beneficiaries are rarer— they tend to survive only when the privileged noble subsequently passed on the land to a church—but they prove secular lords were granted land on the same terms.[43] (There are in any case strong indications that it was normal practice for kings to grant such land rights to noblemen as rewards for service, though probably on a temporary basis.)[44] The charters clearly imply that the king had surrendered his right to received food renders and labour services to such men, which probably means that they had inlands and reeves of a sort, though perhaps on a smaller scale than kings and major churches. Indeed, one of Ine's laws states that noblemen are entitled to bring their reeve with them if they move (along with their smith and their children's nurse).[45] Ealdormen almost certainly gained rights over reeves and

---

[41] Wi 22.

[42] These reservations become more common across the period, with specific reference to bridge- and fortress-work appearing first in Mercian, then Kentish and only later in our West Saxon evidence. For a detailed review, see Brooks, 'Military Obligations', pp. 72–82.

[43] For example S 58, where the grantee is explicitly given the land to be possessed 'by ecclesiastical right' (*iure ecclesiastico possidendam*). Other eighth-century grants to laymen: S 57, 63, 114, 123, 128, 139, 148, 153, 264.

[44] This is the implication of Bede's letter to Bishop Ecgberht of York, which expresses concern that excessive generosity to monasteries had left Northumbrian kings with insufficient land to give to the sons of nobles or veteran warriors, who had reached a life-stage when they wished to marry and set up their own households (Bede, *Epistola*, ch. 11.) For discussion, see Patrick Wormald, 'Bede and the Conversion of England', repr. in and cited from Patrick Wormald, *The Times of Bede: Studies in Early English Christian Society and its Historian*, ed. Stephen Baxter (Oxford, 2006), pp. 135–86 at 153–7.

[45] Ine 63. The verb used is *faran*, 'to go'. It is not obvious where he is expected to be going but he must leave all but these three people behind him when he departs. The point is to stop men stripping inlands of their workforces when, for whatever reason, they relinquished them. It is possible that Ine 64–66 also imply the existence of small-scale inlands. They order that noblemen who depart from areas of land of 20, 10, and 3 hides show at the point of departure 12, 6, and 1½ hides of *gesett land*. It seems likely that this means occupants must ensure there are warland households paying the dues required from this number of hides when they leave, ready for the next nobleman granted the king's rights over the area. What sort of irresponsible aristocratic conduct this was intended to address is unclear. One possibility is that Ine was trying to limit the inland-warland ratio of his land grants to 4:6, allowing it to go up to 1:1 only for very small three-hide grants. (This is to follow Aston, 'Origins', pp. 65–7, except in his characterization of the occupants of this *gesett land* as 'tenants'.) In this reading the law is intended to stop lords unscrupulously seizing the land of free warland households so as to add it to the inland. However, this is at odds with the emphasis of Ine 63, where the aim is clearly to prevent lords from acting in a way that *reduced* the economic value of the inlands in their care. A possible alternative reading would involve postulating a significant labour shortage in the wake of the severe outbreak of bubonic plague which began in the 660s and culminated in the 680s, on which see John Maddicott, 'Plague in Seventh-Century England', *Past and Present* 156 (1997), pp. 7–54. There was more *gesett land* available to be farmed than there were farmers available, so the lords who were entitled to receive

inlands by virtue of their office. Later evidence suggests that the position of earl—the eleventh-century term for an ealdorman—was associated with possession of specific landed properties, properties of sufficient size to place men appointed as earls in a different league of wealth to the richest secular aristocrats below that rank.[46] Though it cannot be demonstrated, it is quite likely that ealdormen were supported in this way in the eighth and ninth centuries, with specific inlands—perhaps even specific reeves—passing to whoever held the office of ealdorman.

Kingdoms in this period must, in effect, have been divided into a number of districts, each focused on a location to which free farmers delivered their food renders. (Some of these districts may have coincided with districts from which men customarily assembled, but it is unlikely that this was universally the case.)[47] Each of these districts would have been supervised by a reeve of some sort, but these reeves would have served many different masters. This is a crucial point for our purposes. The king's reeves did not constitute, and probably never had constituted, a uniform tier of royal officials covering a kingdom's entire rural population. In many places, the local reeve must have working for some other lord—an ealdorman, bishop, monastery or lay aristocrat—and the people who lived in these areas could probably have gone for years on end without encountering anyone who could be described as a royal administrator. These people could still be called upon for military service or for labour on military projects, but if kings wanted to affect their lives in other ways they would have to work through these non-royal reeves and their lords.

Parallel Hierarchies

Kings, then, seem to have had two distinct hierarchies for exploiting their people in this period. For military purposes they relied on subordinate rulers: initially mainly client kings but, increasingly over the course of this period, ealdormen. These central figures in kings' military apparatus were war leaders and political patrons, not administrators in any very meaningful sense. The royal military rights ealdormen sometimes exploited were never included in grants to lords. This distinguished them from the king's rights to receive food renders and non-military labour services, which were routinely given away to favoured noblemen as a reward for loyal service. These royal rights, when they remained in the king's hands, were administered by his reeves: relatively lowly figures whose concerns were as

---

renders from *gesett land* had to compete for their labour; Ine's measures were thus intended to ensure that lords acted responsibly towards the warland population, not driving them away and depriving the inland with which they had been entrusted of important seasonal labour and valuable food renders. For further discussion of Ine 63–8, see T. M. Charles-Edwards, 'The Distinction between Land and Moveable Wealth in Anglo-Saxon England', in P. H. Sawyer, ed., *Medieval Settlement: Continuity and Change* (London, 1976), pp. 180–7 at 185–6; D. M. Hadley, *The Northern Danelaw: Its Social Structure, c. 800–1100* (London, 2000), pp. 76–7.

[46] See Stephen Baxter, *The Earls of Mercia: Lordship and Power in Late Anglo-Saxon England* (Oxford, 2007), pp. 141–5; Maitland, *Domesday Book and Beyond*, p. 168.

[47] See Chapter 6, pp. 243–4.

agricultural as ealdormen's were military. When these rights were granted to lords, they usually employed their own reeves. If the rural population were called upon to perform military activities, then, they would have dealt with ealdormen or their representatives, whereas for routine demands on their property and labour they had to deal with reeves, many of whom—perhaps even a majority—worked for secular or ecclesiastical aristocrats rather than the king.

It is important to stress that these systems were separate. The king's ealdormen massively outranked the king's reeves—in wealth and status they are not even vaguely comparable—but we should not think of them as their superiors in a single administrative hierarchy.[48] Ealdormen do not seem to have functioned as middle managers, supervising the work of royal reeves within their shires: both reported directly to the king. We can see this in tenth-century laws. When kings envisaged punishing reeves for misconduct the local ealdorman was not the figure they called upon.[49] Rather, kings asked their bishops to impose such punishments, which they surely would not have done had ealdormen been responsible for routine oversight of reeves' activities.[50] Tempting though it is to imagine ealdormen and reeves as parts of a unified royal administrative hierarchy, the evidence suggests that this was not in fact the case.

LEGAL REVENUES AND LOCAL ADMINISTRATORS

The next crucial question for us is how the king's legal rights fit into this picture. Ought we to imagine that, like royal military rights, they were carefully reserved to the king and exploited through ealdormen? Or should we understand them as a sub-category of non-military rights, administered through reeves but frequently granted to aristocrats? For once, the answer here is perfectly clear: the evidence overwhelmingly favours the latter interpretation. When the king retained the right to receive them, legal revenues were the responsibility of royal reeves, but it seems to have been universally accepted that these revenues, alongside food renders and labour services, were part of the standard package of royal rights transferred to lay and ecclesiastical lords. There are two principal reasons for accepting this interpretation. The first is the laws, which emphasize reeves and lords as recipients of fines. The second is charters: they never exclude legal revenues from grants of royal rights

---

[48] As, for example, they are presented in Morris, *Medieval English Sheriff*, p. 21.

[49] II As 25:1. See also III Eg 3.

[50] The reason bishops seemed a more natural choice than ealdormen for the disciplining of reeves may be related to the episcopal role in imposing penitential discipline on the laity, but it is also worth noting that Æthelstan's ordinance on tithes shows that royal reeves were responsible for rendering the king's ecclesiastical dues, and implies that they were expected to assist in the collection of dues from the free population (I As Prol, 1, 4, 5). Reeves (quite possibly including those of lords other than the king) may thus have answered directly to their local bishops in certain capacities as a matter of routine. It is possible that reeves were expected to help extract military service from their lands too, but if so this role was clearly not sufficient to make ealdormen seem like the natural people to discipline them. For penance, see Rob Meens, *Penance in Medieval Europe, 600–1200* (Cambridge, 2014), esp. pp. 88–100, 158–64.

over land, and occasionally they make it clear that they were included. This interpretation is also supported by later evidence in a number of ways. Although it makes sense to confine detailed discussion of this to its proper context—in Chapters 6 and 7—a brief review of the retrospective inferences that can reasonably be drawn from this later material is necessary here.

Laws

Although relatively limited by comparison with the more plentiful West Saxon legal tradition, late seventh-century Kentish laws provide some evidence for reeves acting as legal administrators and for lords possessing the right to receive fines. The laws of Hlothere and Eadric order that the process of 'vouching to warranty' take place in the king's hall (*sele*), which probably refers to a rural royal centre supervised by a reeve.[51] As has already been noted, Wihtred's laws envisage reeves working for the king or a bishop either clearing an *esne* who had been accused of an offence, or handing him over to be flogged.[52] Presumably the *esne* here is an unfree labourer working on an inland supervised by the reeve in question. They also seem to envisage lords as recipients of fines: if a nobleman takes up an unlawful union, Wihtred states that he should compensate his lord (*dryhten*) with 100 shillings.[53] Though rather limited, these references suggest that lords other than the king could receive fines, and that reeves overseeing royal and episcopal inlands could have important legal roles.

The late seventh-century West Saxon evidence is stronger. One of Ine's laws refers specifically to reeves as collectors of fines. People who captured thieves had a duty to keep them securely until they handed them over to the king. If, for whatever reason, the thief escaped, his former captor was liable to punishment. If he managed to recapture the thief on the same day he escaped he was to pay no more than the full fine, but if a night passed he was to come to whatever terms he could 'with the king and his reeve'.[54] In addition, the following passage shows that lords could be recipients of fines:

> If a nobleman comes to terms with the king, or with the king's ealdorman, or with his lord, on behalf of his household dependants (*inhiwan*), free or unfree, he, the nobleman, shall not have any portion of the fines (*witerædenne*), because he has not previously taken care at home to restrain them from evil-doing.[55]

Most importantly for present purposes, the passage shows that people might come to terms with the king, an ealdorman, or their lord for fines. This accords with the idea that the recipient of a fine was the same person who was entitled to an

---

[51] Hl 7. They also refer to the king's *wicgerefa*, 'town-reeve', witnessing transactions in London and again order that vouching to warranty associated with those transactions take place in the king's *sele* in that town (Hl 16–16:2). This is not in itself very significant for current purposes because it is quite likely that commercial centres such as London, where royal revenues would mostly have been paid in coin, were administered in a different way from rural areas, which primarily produced renders in kind. It does, however, seem to associate the *wicgerefan* with supervision of the king's *sele*.

[52] Wi 22.   [53] Wi 5:1.   [54] Ine 72–3.   [55] Ine 50.

offender's food renders. Like food renders and non-military labour services, punitive fines might be due to the king; they might be due to an ealdorman, who held the right to receive royal revenues from particular areas by virtue of his office; or they might belong to some other lord who had been granted these rights as a reward or, in the case of ecclesiastical lords, as an endowment. This passage's own concern, however, is to define lords' responsibilities for offences committed by *inhiwan*—dependants associated with households.[56] This aligns well with the way non-legal obligations worked. Because food renders and labour services were assessed on the basis of hides, formally they fell on heads of household. *Inhiwan* would have been the people who did most of the work involved in producing food renders or performing labour services, but they did so on behalf of their heads of household, who were the ones held responsible for payment. What this passage seems to imply is that fines worked the same way. Though *inhiwan* ultimately paid their own fines, it was assumed that they would do so through their lords, who would attend to whatever negotiations were necessary. Ine was asserting that lords were not entitled to profit from their roles as intermediaries by taking a cut of the fine paid.

It is clear, then, that lords who were entitled to receive fines were sufficiently common in Ine's Wessex to be taken into account when framing laws. Tenth-century laws are even more explicit about this, suggesting that the profits from all those offences punished by *wite* or by wergild-forfeiture were commonly held by lords. The code known as II Æthelstan, which contains the earliest clear references to this, stipulates that it is possible for someone to come to a financial agreement with his accuser to avoid an ordeal but adds that it is not possible to avoid the *wite* in this way 'unless he to whom it is due is willing to consent'.[57] The implication is that there were many possibilities for who this person could be. Earlier in the same code there is a regulation forbidding the defence of fleeing thieves on the penalty of payment of the thief's wergild 'either to the king or to him to whom it is legally (*mid ryhte*) due'.[58] It thus appears well understood in the early tenth century that the recipients of punitive fines were frequently people other than the king and his reeves. This is confirmed by later texts, which often allude to a class of lords who had the right to receive punitive fines, wergild forfeitures, and property forfeited by executed offenders. In addition to variations on 'he to whom it is due' the laws have a number of ways of referring to these lords: simply *hlaford* ('lord'); *landhlaford* ('land-lord'); *landrica* ('land-ruler'); or someone who is *wites wyrðe* ('worthy of *wite*') or *weres wyrðe* ('worthy of

---

[56] It is possible that dependants associated with a household did not have to live in the household. Unfree or dependent free labourers who worked for wealthy nobles on their land might well have been considered *inhiwan*, even if they lived in separate buildings (such a scenario is envisaged in Ine 67). Even if free, such households would not have paid their own food renders or labour services if they lacked even a fraction of a hide of land on which they could be assessed. They would have been regarded, for these purposes, as appurtenances of the landed households for which they worked. See Faith, *English Peasantry*, pp. 70–80; Charles-Edwards, 'Land and Moveable Wealth', pp. 184–7; ASD s.vv. 'inhiwan', 'hiwan'.

[57] II As 21.   [58] II As 1:5.

wergild').[59] The term thegn (*þegn*) also seems to be used to refer to these figures in certain contexts: we will come to this shortly.

Late ninth- and early tenth-century laws are equally explicit about reeves, repeatedly making it clear that they had responsibility for a variety of legal tasks on a local level. Alfred's laws envisage a king's reeve providing food to a kinless prisoner undergoing penance for perjury at a king's *tun* (the central farm within a royal inland), they allude to people making accusations at assemblies in the presence of a king's reeve, and they order that traders wishing to travel into the kingdom bring all the men they wish to take with them before the king's reeve at an assembly.[60] One of Edward the Elder's two law codes, most notably, is framed as an order issued to 'all reeves', and his other one, though generally addressed, assumes reeves had the authority to schedule local assemblies and exact fines.[61] Unlike Alfred's laws, which are careful to specify that the reeves in question are the king's, Edward's are directed to reeves generally; this would seem to imply that the king was trying to command not just his own reeves but those working for other lords as well. This is not stated explicitly, however. Fortunately, there are some texts which clearly show that men with local legal responsibilities in this period were not just the king's reeves. These occur in early tenth-century laws issued by Æthelstan and Edmund, which discuss the figure of the thegn (*þegn*) alongside that of the reeve, threatening each with punishment for negligence in their duties. Æthelstan's Exeter code, for example, threatens reeves who take bribes to obstruct justice with a severe fine, and adds that if a thegn (*þegn*) behaves in the same way he should receive the

---

[59] Variations on 'he to whom it is due': II Cn 24:1, 73a:1. *Hlaford*: Hu 2:1, 3; III Eg 7:1; Duns 6:2–6:3; I Atr 1:5, 1:9; II Cn 25:1. *Landhlaford*: II As 10; VI As 1:1; II Eg 3:1;IV Eg 11; I Cn 8:2. *Landrica*: IV Atr 8:1; I Cn 8:2. *Wites wyrðe* and *weres wyrðe*: I Atr 1:7; II Cn 30:3b, 30:6. Possible objections to the idea that this terminology refers to a *single* class of lords with the right to receive *all* punitive fines and forfeitures are its diversity—can we really assume that these phrases all mean the same thing?—and the fact that it is not used consistently: in fact, many laws refer to fines being paid to the king, making no reference whatsoever to lords. I am proposing here that it was generally understood that when laws referred to a payment 'to the king' they actually meant 'to the king [or to whomever has the right to receive the king's revenues]', and that when they referred to a payment 'to the *landhlaford*', they actually meant 'to the *landhlaford* [which is one of several well-known labels for the person entitled to receive the king's legal revenues, and in many cases this will of course be the king himself]'. An alternative starting assumption would be that the different wording reflects an attempt to differentiate between recipients. My reasons for proposing we accept the former assumption and reject the latter can be distilled to two key arguments. First and foremost, as shall be seen shortly, the language of charters implies that their beneficiaries received all the king's non-military rights as a single block. We should take this seriously and keep it in mind when reading the laws. Second, although analysis based on the assumption that the laws use this terminology precisely may produce clear results on a small scale (for example, Molyneaux, *Formation*, p. 176), the application of this logic across the entire legal corpus would result in incoherence. This is argued in Stephen Baxter, 'Lordship and Justice in Late Anglo-Saxon England: The Judicial Functions of Soke and Commendation Revisited', in Stephen Baxter et al., eds., *Early Medieval Studies in Memory of Patrick Wormald* (Farnham, 2009), pp. 383–419 at 405–6 (with references to scholarship that takes the opposite line). The impossibility of reconciling different terms on the assumption that they are being used precisely rather than loosely is particularly apparent in manuscript emendations to Cnut's laws discussed in Julius Goebel, *Felony and Misdemeanor: A Study in the History of English Criminal Procedure* (New York, 1937), pp. 371–3. The package of legal revenues traditionally granted to lords is analysed in depth in Chapter 7, in the context of an argument for significant change in the early eleventh century.

[60] Af 1:3, 22, 34.   [61] I Ew Prol; II Ew 2, 8.

same punishment.[62] The code known as III Edmund, which survives only in a post-Conquest Latin translation, threatens anyone who refuses to place their own men under surety with a fine, whether they be 'reeve or thegn, nobleman or commoner' (*praepositus vel tainus, comes vel villanus*), treating thegns as a category distinct from but related to reeves.[63]

Interpreting the term *þegn* in this period is not as simple as it might be. It originated as a word with a purely functional meaning—a thegn was someone who served a superior—but because of its use to denote men of high-status who served in royal households (and probably those of great magnates) it eventually became a general term for someone of noble status. This shift of meaning was in progress during the tenth century. Under Alfred, the term can be found referring to people ranging in status from bishops and ealdormen to the humblest free servants, whereas by the early eleventh thegns look more like a social class: men with wergilds of 1200 shillings.[64] In our early tenth-century legal references it is likely to denote a figure who had served in the household of the king or a great magnate, perhaps most commonly as a warrior but not necessarily, and been rewarded with a grant of the king's non-military rights over land. One of our texts, in fact, implies this, assuming legal responsibilities pertained specifically to thegns who were *gelandod*— 'landed' in the sense of having been given land—presumably distinguishing between thegns who had received such a reward and those still in the process of earning one.[65] These figures would usually have had much smaller landed endowments than those of great magnates. Whereas ealdormen and bishops would usually have sent their reeves to attend local assemblies on their behalf, many of these lesser figures could routinely have been present in person. In practice, then, the people with a direct interest in punitive fines at a local level would have been the king's reeves, reeves working for other lords, and thegns who had been granted the king's non-military rights over relatively small parcels of land as a reward for service. It thus makes sense for the laws to threaten reeves and thegns with punishment for dereliction of their legal duties.[66]

[62] V As 1:3–1:4. See also IV As 7; VI As 11.   [63] III Em 7:2.

[64] See H.R. Loyn, 'Gesiths and Thegns in Anglo-Saxon England from the Seventh to the Tenth Century', *English Historical Review* 70 (1955), pp. 529–49 at 540–9; George Molyneaux, 'The Ordinance concerning the Dunsæte and the Anglo-Welsh Frontier in the Late Tenth and Eleventh Centuries', *Anglo-Saxon England* 40 (2011), pp. 249–72 at 265–7.

[65] VI As 11. The same distinction is almost certainly visible in Ine 51, where noble (*gesiðcund*) men with and without land (*landagende* and *unlandagende*) are assigned different fines for neglect of military service (see also Ine 45). It is likely that all men described as thegns or as *gesiðcund* came from wealthy families and thus owned land. The distinction is therefore probably between types of land rights: a *gelandod* thegn was one who held the right to receive the king's non-military revenues from an area of land assessed in hides (food renders, labour services and fines) as opposed to one whose landholding obliged him to pay the various dues assessed on each hide. This distinction is discussed in more detail in Chapter 7, pp. 319–20.

[66] An alternative reading is that great magnates such as ealdormen and bishops were considered *gelandod* king's thegns, and that the term was not limited to relatively minor aristocrats such as former household warriors. In this reading, royal commands to reeves and thegns refer to the king's own reeves on the one hand and privileged aristocrats on the other, the latter being responsible for performing legal functions either personally or through their own reeves.

Charters

The second principal reason for believing that the king's punitive legal rights were administered by reeves together with rights to food renders and non-military labour services, and that all these rights were commonly conveyed to aristocrats as a package, is that this is implied by the language of charters. The earliest charters—those of the seventh and early eighth centuries—tend to be vague about the rights they conveyed: they neither grant nor reserve any rights in specific terms, just make it clear that the king had given away the land fully and permanently, using such phrases as 'in free liberty of possession' (*in voluntariam possidendi libertatem*).[67] By the late eighth century, however, as has been noted, it had become common to begin with a general statement that the land granted was free from all secular burdens, but then to qualify this by stating that three specific rights were excluded: military service, bridge-work and fortification-work. In the literature these are sometimes termed the *trinoda necessitas* or the 'common burdens'.[68] As Nicholas Brooks has shown, the most plausible way of understanding their emergence is that when kings granted people large tracts of land they had always intended to convey their economic rights over those lands to the beneficiary— the food renders, primarily—but had assumed that they would continue to be able to call on the services of the people living on those lands for military purposes. The later reservation of these three rights should thus be understood as an attempt to formalize existing expectations, not to establish new obligations, though the specific emphasis on bridges and fortifications may reflect developing eighth- and ninth-century military realities.[69]

The important point here is that it became standard practice to reserve only these three military rights when granting land, and to state that it was free of all secular dues other than these. Logically, it is implied that the king's legal revenues are included in such grants, being secular burdens which are not specifically reserved. (It is perhaps worth reiterating that the intended effect was not to free the general population of their obligations to pay fines, make food renders or perform labour services, but rather to transfer the king's right to receive them to the beneficiary.) Without specific reference to fines, however, this interpretation could always be doubted. It might be argued that nobody ever dreamt that the right to receive fines was something kings could grant, and that they were therefore not implied by such phrases as 'all secular burdens'.[70] The laws, as we have seen, show this would be incorrect, but so too do some charters from the late eighth and ninth centuries.

---

[67] S 102.

[68] On terminology see Richard Abels, '*Trinoda Necessitas*', in Lapidge et al., *Encyclopedia*, p. 475 and the literature there cited.

[69] Brooks, 'Military Obligations', pp. 72–84. This effectively demolishes the opposing case, made in Eric John, *Land Tenure in Early England* (Leicester, 1960), pp. 64–79.

[70] Though this case has never been made for this period, an argument along precisely these lines is applied to the eleventh century in Naomi Hurnard, 'The Anglo-Norman Franchises', *English Historical Review* 64 (1949), pp. 289–327 and 433–60, at 292–310.

The earliest of these is a charter of 767 in which Uhtred, client king (*regulus*) of the Hwicce under King Offa of Mercia, conveys to his thegn (*minister*) Æthelmund five hides of land. His rights over that land are explained as follows:

> Let everyone know that this land is free from every tribute, small or great, of public matters, and from all services whether from king or ealdorman (*vel regis vel principis*) except for the building of bridges or the necessary defences of fortifications against enemies. Also in every way we forbid in the name of God Almighty that if anyone in this aforenamed land steals anything from outside it, anything be paid to anyone except specifically 'price for price' (*pretium pro pretio*) as settlement, nothing outside as fine (*ad penam nihil foras*).[71]

As well as the general statement that the land is free from all dues with the exception of the king's military rights, which would become standard features of charters in subsequent decades, this one includes a discussion of fines and compensation payments. The drafter's intention is to assert that, in spite of the king's grant, the people living on this land still have to pay compensation for harm they do to people living outside it. This is exceptionally pedantic. Very few people can ever have imagined that kings intended their grants to allow people living on the land concerned to be free of the duty to pay compensation when they committed offences. Nonetheless, payments from offenders resident on such land to victims resident elsewhere clearly could be understood, by the legalistically minded, to constitute secular dues being paid from land supposedly freed of them. The point of the passage is to explain that compensation still does have to be paid to victims: it is only punitive fines that belong to the beneficiary and are, in that sense, not permitted to leave the granted land.[72] This, then, is a particularly pedantic bit of charter drafting, highly valuable to us for making explicit a point which must usually have been considered so obvious as not to require discussion.

For the next century and a bit we sometimes find similar statements in charters. Indeed, this 767 charter is one of a series of sixteen identified by Frederic William Maitland which were issued between the 760s and the 880s and take the trouble to explain what this general freedom implied for royal legal revenues.[73] The emphasis on

---

[71] S 58. The translation here is based on Dorothy Whitelock, ed., *English Historical Documents*, vol. 1: *c.500–1042* (2nd edn, London, 1979), no. 74: a slightly later grant couched in almost identical language (S 59). For discussion see, Patrick Wormald, 'Charters, Law and the Settlement of Disputes in Anglo-Saxon England', repr. in and cited from Wormald, *Legal Culture*, pp. 289–310 at 297–8.

[72] See Maitland, *Domesday Book and Beyond*, pp. 274–6.

[73] Ibid., pp. 290–2. The relevant charters are: S 58, 106 (in the early ninth-century endorsement rather than the mid-eighth-century original), 154, 171, 183, 185, 186, 188, 199, 206, 218, 220, 278, 292, 294b, 1277. Three of these (S 183, 278, 294b), appear to be outright forgeries, but for each of these commentators have argued that they were formulated with reference to genuine ninth-century models. See S. E. Kelly, ed., *Charters of Abingdon Abbey*, 2 vols. (Oxford, 2000–2001), nos. 9 (S 183) and 11 (S 278); Simon Keynes, 'The West Saxon Charters of King Æthelwulf and His Sons', *English Historical Review* 109 (1994), 1109–49 at 1115–16 (for S 294b). There is also a potential problem with the date given in S 154—a reference to King Ecgberht of Wessex at a time before he began to reign—but this seems best explained as either a mistake in copying or a later interpolation; see H. P. R. Finberg, *The Early Charters of the West Midlands* (2nd edn, Leicester, 1972), no. 233 and Patrick Sims-Williams, *Religion and Literature in Western England, 600–800* (Cambridge, 1990), p. 171, n. 127. Goebel, *Felony and Misdemeanor*, p. 356, notes that S 121, which may have some

the fact that compensation ought to be paid to victims in spite of the beneficiary's right to receive fines, which attracted Maitland's attention, appears to be peculiar to Mercian charters, but we do occasionally find references to fines in ninth-century West Saxon texts. In addition to the two genuine West Saxon charters that Maitland noted,[74] we can add several that refer to freedom from 'penal matters' (*res penalia*),[75] 'penal cases' (*penalia cause*),[76] or 'all legal matters' (*omnes res legales*).[77] These are often associated with statements of freedom from *furis comprehensio*, which probably refer—as Julius Goebel argued—to the duty visible in the laws of Ine to hand captured thieves over to the king: they are making explicit the grantee's right to receive the thieves themselves, not just the fines they paid.[78]

Comparable phrases do not, to the best of my knowledge, appear in charters from the tenth century and later,[79] and they were only ever present in a minority of charters in the eighth and ninth centuries, but it should not be understood that these particular grants were unusual. Rather, these phrases should be taken as an indication that charter-drafting fashions in certain periods and places tended

authentic basis, also belongs in this group, though rather than legal revenues generally the punitive revenues it mentions are those relating to thieves (neither their fines nor their persons, should they be enslaved, are to leave the liberated land).

[74] S 292, 1277. The latter is a charter issued by a bishop rather than the king, but this is not a problem for the argument presented here: it only shows that the bishop already had the privilege and was able to delegate it. S 294b, though a forgery, uses the same language as S 1277 (the former grants immunity *ab . . . taxationibus quod nos dicimus Uuitereden*, the latter *a taxationibus quod dicimus wite redenne*) which may indicate that this terminology was more widespread in ninth-century Wessex. The similar grant of freedom from *tribulatione que witereden nominatur* in the dubious charter of King Ecgberht of Wessex in favour of Abingdon (S 278) supports this interpretation, especially as this language is absent from the forged charter of King Cœnwulf of Mercia (S 171) with which it shares other important passages (see Maitland *Domesday Book and Beyond*, p. 292).

[75] S 328, 288.   [76] S 290, 331, 298.   [77] S 326, 329.

[78] Goebel, *Felony and Misdemeanor*, pp. 356–8; Ine 28. The charters are: S 288, 290 (of which Goebel was unaware), 292, 298, 300, 326, 328, 334. As Goebel notes, the 'cum furis comprehensione' clauses tacked onto quittances in two rather dubious Rochester charters (S 271, 321) 'seem a curious defiance of grammar' (p. 356, n. 63). Maitland, *Domesday Book and Beyond*, p. 282, supposed that 'The highest criminal jurisdiction was probably excepted from the grant. Being a grant of wites it will not extend to the "bootless" the "unemendable" crimes.' These charters show otherwise. Given that we have no charters which explicitly exclude *furis comprehensio* from the rights granted (and several charters showing that scribes in this period could be very pedantic about listing things which were excluded), we should understand the few references to its inclusion as clarifications of the content of the standard grant rather than as unusual additions to it. S 180, 1861 stipulate that malefactors be handed over to a royal *vicus* (presumably an inland centre supervised by a reeve), but only when they had been caught in the act for the third time. This suggests a desire to ensure that privileged lords saw to it that wrongdoers (almost certainly thieves) were properly punished: under normal circumstances privileged lords were to be left to deal with such people as they judged best, but if they were so unduly lenient that offenders could be caught in the act twice and survive to be caught for a third time, the king reserved the right to intervene.

[79] This comment applies to traditional 'diplomas'. 'Writ-charters'—a format of grant that emerges in the eleventh century—offer much more legal detail. For discussion, see Chapter 7, esp. pp. 308–9. A possible exception is S 1031, a single-sheet grant from Edward the Confessor to Westminster Abbey in 1060, written in a contemporary hand, which—perhaps somewhat suspiciously—also exempts the abbey from the three common burdens. Julia Crick, 'St Albans, Westminster, and Some Twelfth-Century Views of the Anglo-Saxon Past', *Anglo-Norman Studies* 25 (2003), pp. 65–83 esp. at 81–3, has shown that this clause underlies the similar statements in a number of forged or interpolated charters supposedly from the late Anglo-Saxon period: S 774, 912, 1040, 1450.

towards fuller explanations of what was meant by freeing land from all secular burdens. Some charter drafters felt it was helpful to explain that the general exemption from secular dues included punitive revenues (both ordinary fines and the profits associated with enslaving or ransoming captured thieves) but most thought it unnecessary. At no point, absolutely crucially, do we find such punitive revenues listed with the king's military rights as exceptions to the general grant of the king's rights. Given the deep pedantry which was sometimes applied to explaining the limits of the standard general grant, this must be significant. If legal revenues were customarily excluded from royal grants, there would have been at least one charter draftsman in this period who thought it important to say so explicitly. The correct reading of charter immunity clauses from this period, then, is that they customarily conveyed to the beneficiary not only the king's rights to food renders and labour services, but also his right to receive the profits of punitive justice. This, as we have seen, is consistent with the laws.[80]

Retrospective Inferences

The early evidence just discussed is quite sufficient to show that legal revenues were integral to a bundle of non-military rights which were routinely held by lords other than the king. When the king retained these rights, royal reeves exploited them on his behalf; when they belonged to lords, they usually employed their own reeves. This interpretation does not rely on retrospective inferences drawn from later evidence in any significant way; nonetheless, it is worth noting that some such inferences can reasonably be drawn and that these tend to confirm this picture. Three later developments need to be considered: the tenth-century administrative reforms which culminated in the establishment of the hundredal system; the emergence of the language of 'soke' in eleventh-century sources; and mid-eleventh-century earls' right to receive a 'third penny' of certain royal revenues.

[80] This used to be regarded as straightforward—see F. M. Stenton, *Anglo-Saxon England* (3rd edn, Oxford, 1973), pp. 306, 492–3—but recent scholarship is more troubled by the relative silence of the charters, seemingly taking the view that the evidence is insufficient to disprove the possibility that many legal revenues were reserved to the king in the period before the tenth century. Wickham, for example, does not include legal revenues in his discussion of rights over land in the period, justifying this in a footnote with the observation that 'justice' was reserved to kings (*Framing*, p. 315, n. 30). Molyneaux is non-committal on the issue, but takes seriously the possibility that tenth- and eleventh-century evidence of lords' entitlement to legal revenues reflects a shift in which kings endowed aristocrats with substantially greater legal privileges than they had hitherto possessed (*Formation*, pp. 175–7). This may in part reflect the influence of the argument in Hurnard, 'Anglo-Norman Franchises', pp. 292–310, that some royal legal revenues—those associated with 'the major crimes'—had traditionally been so closely associated with the king that nobody ever imagined they could be delegated to lords (this argument is discussed in Chapter 4, p. 188, n. 106). However, it should be noted that although this is not clear from his published work, it seems from a lecture draft that Wormald broadly accepted the interpretation proposed here. See Patrick Wormald, *Papers Preparatory to the Making of English Law: King Alfred to the Twelfth Century*, vol. 2: *From God's Law to Common Law*, ed. Stephen Baxter and John Hudson (University of London, 2014) <http://www.earlyenglishlaws.ac.uk/reference/wormald/>, pp. 207–8 ('from the late eighth and early ninth centuries, grants of bookland bequeathed rights to the fines of the incriminated within an estate'). This interpretation is also implicit in Brooks, 'Military Obligations', p. 71.

The first of these is the most telling. The administrative reforms made by successive tenth-century kings suggest dissatisfaction with a system which allowed them to exert direct influence over areas in which they had retained their non-military rights, but not over people living on land where they had granted their rights to others. This interpretation, which derives in large part from the arguments of George Molyneaux, is set out in Chapter 6.[81] In brief, the progression of late Anglo-Saxon laws suggests that kings initially tried to direct local legal practice through rural reeves (perhaps those of other lords as well as those working for the king directly): this is particularly clear in evidence from the reigns of Alfred and Edward the Elder (which will be discussed later in this chapter).[82] There is then a period, beginning in the reign of Edward the Elder and intensifying in that of Æthelstan, in which kings appear to be trying to implement their legislation through their network of *burh*s: fortifications which these kings' laws also envisage functioning as centres of commerce, many of which would eventually develop into urban centres.[83] At this stage laws exhibit a marked tendency to associate important activities, such as the pursuit of wrongdoers and the witnessing of transactions, with *burh*s rather than with rural reeves and their associated local assemblies. This could be read as an attempt to bypass the network of royal and non-royal rural reeves: an indication that kings were not confident in their ability to effect change through orders issued to these figures.

However, the experiment with relying on *burh*s proved temporary. In laws from the mid-tenth century onwards, especially those associated with King Edgar (957–975), the focus of royal legal commands concerning legal practice shifts to a reformed network of rural assemblies known as 'hundreds'. There was doubtless considerable continuity between hundreds and earlier rural assemblies but in this context there is one key difference: whereas kings had tried to direct the activities of earlier assemblies through a patchwork of royal and non-royal reeves, they dealt with hundreds directly. Laws on hundreds are notable for not expecting the participation of reeves; rather, they create an increasingly elaborate template for how local communities, led by the most senior members of hundred assemblies, ought to run their affairs. Hundreds thus makes sense interpreted as a more effective way of bypassing an unreliable network of rural reeves than the earlier experiment with *burh*s, which perhaps had proven too remote for most of the rural population to interact with on a routine basis. The whole trajectory of tenth-century administrative reform, in other words, suggests dissatisfaction with the network of rural reeves inherited from the period we are concerned with here, which would make sense if—as the early evidence suggests—a large proportion of these reeves worked for lords other than the king.

---

[81] The next two paragraphs summarize Chapter 6, pp. 243–50.
[82] See below, pp. 143–6.
[83] On this development: Richard Holt, 'The Urban Transformation in England, 900–1100', *Anglo-Norman Studies* 32 (2010), pp. 57–78.

The second later development to consider is the emergence of the language of 'soke' in the eleventh century.[84] A standard way of referring to the right to receive legal revenues in this period was with the term 'sake and soke' (*sac 7 socn*), or often just 'soke'; this is discussed in detail in Chapter 7.[85] The important point is here is simple: as well as meaning the right to receive punitive fines, soke could also mean the right to receive labour services and food renders owed by the free farming households of the warland. A 'sokeman' was a freeman; his performance of relatively light labour services and his payment of relatively light food renders functioned as a badge of his free status. A lord could hold a soke—an area of land—within which, as well as a central inland and some outlying pockets, there would be 'sokeland' inhabited by sokemen who owed him soke. From them he would receive food renders, seasonal labour services and those fines covered by sake and soke. This language is very late, of course, and not all of it can be found everywhere—soke is ubiquitous as a shorthand for the right to receive fines but its other uses are regionally specific—nevertheless it hints that royal legal revenues, food renders and non-military labour services had at some point been understood as constituent parts of a standard bundle of royal rights, commonly held by lords, even if their various aspects were becoming more distinct by the eleventh century.[86] This, of course, is exactly what our earlier evidence—especially the generalized grants of freedom from secular burdens in charters—would lead us to expect.

Finally, we need to touch on the eleventh-century earl's right to receive the 'third penny' of certain royal revenues, though only very briefly as the key point here is that this is not in fact relevant to the period with which we are concerned. Although the later existence of the earl's third penny has sometimes led to the assumption that ealdormen (the forerunners of earls) were traditionally entitled to a third of royal revenues, there is no evidence that can demonstrate this; Chapter 7 argues that the third penny is most plausibly understood as an eleventh-century innovation.[87] One piece of evidence that is sometimes cited in support of the idea of an early origin for the earl's third penny is pertinent here, however. Alfred's laws state that if a man wished to go from one district (*boldgetale*) to another to seek a lord, he was to do so with the permission of the ealdorman in whose shire (*scir*) he had previously lived, and if he moved without permission he was to pay a fine of

---

[84] The term, in fact, first appears in two charters of the late 950s associated with Yorkshire (S 659, 681), but does not recur in any charters or writs until the reign of Cnut—for which, see Florence E. Harmer, ed., *Anglo-Saxon Writs* (1989), p. 171 (and no. 28, which is S 986).

[85] Chapter 7, pp. 323–5.

[86] The literature on soke in its various guises is extensive. See John Hudson, *The Oxford History of the Laws of England*, vol. 2: *871–1216* (Oxford, 2012), pp. 59–60, 114, 209–10; Baxter, *Earls of Mercia*, pp. 210–13; Hadley, *Northern Danelaw*, chs. 3–4; Faith, *English Peasantry*, pp. 90, 118–19, 121–5; C. A. Joy, 'Sokeright' (University of Leeds PhD thesis, 1972); R. H. C. Davis, ed., *The Kalendar of Abbot Samson of Bury St. Edmunds and Related Documents* (Camden Society Third Series 84, London, 1954), pp. xxxii–xlvii; F. M. Stenton, *Types of Manorial Structure in the Northern Danelaw* (Oxford, 1910); Paul Vinogradoff, *English Society in the Eleventh Century: Essays in English Mediaeval History* (Oxford, 1908), pp. 115–39, 320–32, 431–46; Maitland, *Domesday Book and Beyond*, pp. 66–107, 258–90. When published, Purkiss, 'Early Royal Rights' will become essential reading here (see above, p. 112, n. 1).

[87] Chapter 7, pp. 337–42.

120 shillings to the king. This fine, however, was to be paid in two halves, one in the shire which the man left, the other in the one into which he moved.[88] The conventional interpretation is that the fine paid 'to the king' was split in this way because it was paid via that shire's ealdorman, who was entitled to keep an unspecified cut for himself.[89] This need not, however, imply that the existence of an early equivalent to the later earl's third penny. It is important to recognize that the fine under discussion is for what should probably be regarded as a military offence: the point of the law seems to be that men seeking service with a lord in a different shire would be depriving their current ealdorman—the military leader of a shire—of their services as warriors. They therefore had to ask for this ealdorman's permission to leave, and if they neglected to do so they incurred a fine. This passage thus suggests that legal revenues relating to military activity (just like labour services relating to military activity, and military service itself) may have been kept separate from the rights customarily granted to lords. Rather than showing the existence of a right to keep a cut of *all* royal revenues, then, it seems likely to be another hint of the ealdorman's responsibility for military matters within his shire.

The Distribution of Legal Revenues

The systems by which royal legal revenues were collected in this period are difficult to understand if studied in isolation. It is all too easy to assume that the profits of punitive justice naturally require their own administrative system, separate from systems which managed revenues which look more like taxation or rental income to modern eyes, but this was not the case between the seventh and early tenth centuries. The pertinent division in this period was between military and non-military rights. Kings were careful to preserve their military rights. We never find them making grants which would later prevent their demanding people serve in armies or contribute their labour to military construction projects. It seems that ealdormen had a key role in exploiting these military rights: we find them raising armies, at least, and there are hints that they may have been responsible for imposing fines on people who neglected their military duties.

By contrast, kings seem to have been content to give away all their other rights. Especially as their kingdoms increased in size, they had the right to receive far more food renders and non-military labour services than they needed to support their own households.[90] It made sense to use those rights as gifts, rewarding men for loyal service and thereby encouraging loyal service in others. The king's legal revenues (probably excepting those relating to military offences) clearly fell into this category. Where the king held the right to receive punitive fines, they were

---

[88] Af 37–37:1.   [89] For example, Baxter, *Earls of Mercia*, p. 90.

[90] It is not, it should be noted, safe to assume that kings would have been able to sell surplus agricultural produce on the open market. To make that assumption we would need a plausible answer to the question of who would buy them, and such an answer is difficult to come up with before the growth of towns in the late tenth and eleventh centuries.

collected by the same king's reeves who collected food renders and oversaw labour services. In areas where they were given away, they were given away together with the right to these food renders and labour services. When great magnates and monasteries held these rights they exploited them through reeves in just the same way that kings did, but they were often also held by lesser figures: perhaps former members of the households of kings, bishops and ealdormen. These men were more likely to be present at local assemblies, looking after some of their legal interests in person and delegating fewer responsibilities to their reeves.

The right to receive legal revenues thus seems to have been widely dispersed in this period. Quite how widely is impossible to tell. It may be that in the smaller kingdoms of the late seventh century, kings held the rights to receive non-military revenues from the majority of the population; however, it is perhaps likely that in larger kingdoms such as mid-ninth-century Wessex or Mercia the majority of people, if they had to pay a fine, would have paid it to a reeve working for a lord other than the king. In the much larger English kingdom of the late tenth century we sometimes even find laws that treat lords as the natural recipients of legal revenues, making no reference to the king whatsoever.[91] Larger, later kingdoms were almost certainly more decentralized in this sense than were earlier, smaller ones.

Late Anglo-Saxon kings seem to have found this decentralization troubling and, as we have already noted, we can find them enacting reforms. This is not the place to discuss why these kings were less satisfied with existing arrangements than their predecessors: the increasing size of the kingdom may have made the limited network of royal reeves seem ever more inadequate, but it is also likely that ideological factors had a role—a sign of the influence of Carolingian examples, perhaps.[92] The important point here is that this later dissatisfaction seems to have been new. There is nothing to suggest that kings of the eighth and ninth centuries were worried by the alienation of their legal revenues with their other non-military rights, or by the resulting incompleteness of their networks of royal reeves. Tempting though it is to infer earlier dysfunction from later dissatisfaction, we should resist this. We should assume, rather, that the legal worlds of the seventh, eighth and ninth centuries functioned well enough on their own terms, and try to understand how.

LOCAL JUDGEMENTS AND ROYAL LEGISLATION

Now we have a broad understanding of who was responsible for the extraction of royal legal revenues, and of who ultimately profited from them, we can start to think through what this meant in practical terms. The primary focus of legal practice in this period, as it very probably had been in the fifth and sixth centuries and would continue to be in the tenth and eleventh, was the local assembly. A great deal of important legal activity took place outside assemblies, of course, and we will

---

[91] For example, Hu 2:1, 3; I Atr 1:7.　　[92] See Introduction, p. 23, n. 61.

come to that in the final section of this chapter, but assemblies were particularly significant because they were where judgements were made. Assemblies had authority. Many people would have had opinions about what a just outcome would be in any given case, but the only opinions that were meant to be acted upon were those of assemblies, formally expressed in judgements. Ensuring that assemblies issued judgements in accordance with royal legislation was crucial for royal legal ambitions. If local assemblies refused to recognize that the king was entitled to receive the punitive fines he claimed in his legislation, these punitive fines would have no meaningful existence. For it to be worth legislating at all, kings needed to have some means of ensuring their new laws were transmitted to local assemblies and were subsequently applied in their judgements.

This is not to say, however, that scrupulous obedience to every aspect of royal legislation was necessary. The level of recognition kings would have deemed acceptable from assemblies is open to debate, but we should be wary of assuming that they intended to impose a uniform legal system which did away with all differences of local custom. This is unlikely to have been a realistic goal at this point: it was only in the late twelfth century, with the advent of a system of itinerant royal justices who travelled from county to county judging cases according to a centralized set of rules, that it seems to have become feasible.[93] Earlier kings may not always have been happy about local customary variations—one of the most plausible interpretations of early law-making is as an attempt to make practices that existed in some locations standard across entire kingdoms—but for the most part they probably had to be satisfied if local judgements adhered to the broad thrust of their legislation. In practice what mattered to kings was probably a generalized sense that their wishes were being respected. They could afford to be relaxed about minor differences on points of detail, as these must have been inevitable, but flagrant disregard for royal orders would be humiliating, particularly if it were widespread.[94] Few kings could afford obvious displays of ineffectuality.

To understand what kings needed to do to ensure that assemblies applied their laws, we first need to think through what assemblies were and how they worked. The little we know about pre-Christian law from Æthelberht's code suggests that assemblies were well-established parts of the legal landscape long before the explosion of royal punitive claims in the late seventh century. Assemblies are assumed to exist—they had their own 'peace'—and the very existence of formalized laws is suggestive of judgements in a formal context.[95] We need not imagine a clearly defined system of evenly sized districts, each with its own assembly, but we should, I think, be prepared to accept that the vast majority of free men—perhaps all of them—would have known of a local assembly to which they could bring a legal case

---

[93] See Paul Brand, '"Multis Vigiliis Excogitatam et Inventam": Henry II and the Creation of the English Common Law', repr. in and cited from Paul Brand, *The Making of the Common Law* (London, 1992), pp. 77–102.

[94] On this theme, see Levi Roach, 'Law Codes and Legal Norms in Later Anglo-Saxon England', *Historical Research* 86 (2013), pp. 465–86.

[95] See Chapter 1, pp. 44–5 and especially p. 33, n. 21 for the implications of the verb *mathelian*.

if they needed to do so. Although it is tempting to imagine that the districts from which assemblies drew their members coincided with the districts which owed their food renders to particular inlands, this need not always have been so. It may have been the case in some locations, but we cannot safely assume that in general things were so neatly arranged. They were not in later periods: the assembly districts we know about—hundreds—sometimes owed their revenues to a single collection point, but this was not the norm.[96] There is some later evidence which suggests that the districts which customarily assembled in this period could vary widely in size, with some being significantly larger than later hundreds.[97]

These early assemblies, we must surely presume, traditionally ran their own affairs: we can reasonably label them 'communal'. This does not mean that we should assume that all those who attended were equally capable of influencing the judgements they made. Accepting that all free men were entitled to participate in assemblies, and that the decisions made were understood to represent the community's collective will, does not require us to accept any particular view of how those decisions were reached. It would be naive to assume local assemblies were bastions of primitive democracy, of course, but it would be no less naive to assume that the powerful invariably found them easy to manipulate. The important point is that contemporaries throughout the period tended to think about assembly decisions as collective decisions. The strongest evidence for this lies in the accounts of assembly decisions sometimes found in charters and chronicle narratives of ecclesiastical land disputes. Patrick Wormald, in a study of these sources, noted that 'in nearly every text the judging, decreeing or settling verb is in the plural: the rhetoric of Anglo-Saxon process remained participatory and communal.'[98] This communal and participatory rhetoric is important insofar as it reveals broad assumptions about what assemblies were and where their authority lay, but—as Wormald was hinting—if we want to understand who controlled their decisions in practice we need to dig deeper into how they functioned.

Presidents and Legal Authorities

It is likely that most, perhaps all, assemblies had someone who was formally in charge of proceedings: a president (in the sense of a figure who presides). Rank almost certainly determined who filled this role. This principle is rarely articulated explicitly, but it does appear in one early twelfth-century treatise in a discussion of

---

[96] See Chapter 6, pp. 243–4.

[97] See Helen M. Cam, 'Early Groups of Hundreds', repr. in and cited from Helen M. Cam, *Liberties and Communities in Medieval England* (London, 1963), pp. 91–106; Molyneaux, *Formation*, pp. 102–3.

[98] Wormald, 'Charters, Law', pp. 305–6. Indeed, Wickham has recently argued that in a comparative European context England is particularly notable in this respect: 'English evidence . . . is overall considerably more collective in character, both at the level of the kingdom and at that of the county, than in either Francia or Italy'. Chris Wickham, 'Consensus and Assemblies in the Romano-Germanic Kingdoms: A Comparative Approach', in Verena Epp and Christoph H. F. Meyer, eds., *Recht und Konsens im frühen Mittelalter* (Vorträge und Forschungen 82; Konstanz, 2016), pp. 387–424 at 416.

how hundreds—local assemblies—ought to run their affairs: 'one of the most substantial men (*unus de melioribus*) shall preside over the whole hundred and be known as the alderman'.[99] Whenever a king was present at an assembly he would naturally fill this role: Æthelberht's laws envisage kings calling great assemblies at which all those present benefited from his protection.[100] The same, presumably, was true for other great magnates: as long as the king was not present an ealdorman or bishop would take precedence over all others, and in the absence of such figures whoever was most senior. Alfred's laws imagine assemblies being presided over not just by an ealdorman but by an ealdorman's deputy (*gingra*) or a king's priest, with the penalties payable for violence at these assemblies dependent on the rank of the president.[101] A key practical reason for having such a figure, presumably, was that without someone directing proceedings they were likely to descend into chaos, or at least deep inefficiency. It made sense for the most senior man present to preside, because the president's job involved keeping discussion under control: the personal authority that came from outranking all others present must have made it easier to do this effectively.

Presidents could doubtless exercise a degree of influence over an assembly's decisions, both because their position as president gave them some control of proceedings and because their superior status meant their opinions carried weight. This need not, however, mean that they were legal authorities: the people upon whom assemblies relied for authoritative statements of law and how it should be applied. We know that in the pre-Christian period there existed legal experts of some sort: bearers of prestigious oral traditions of *æ* like that which Æthelberht had committed to script. These men must have functioned as legal authorities in assemblies, their purpose being to provide indisputably correct information as to the proper compensation payable for the affronts which came before them.[102] The laws of Hlothere and Eadric may include a reference to precisely this happening: they order that when accused of an offence 'the person [charged] is always to give surety to the other and carry out that justice (*riht*) which the judges of the Kentish people (*cantwara deman*) may appoint for them'.[103] It is possible *cantwara deman* simply means the people of Kent, judging collectively in an assembly, but it is more naturally read as a reference to a particular group, and the legal experts who had memorized the Kentish *æ* recorded in Æthelberht's code are the obvious choice.[104] It is possible that such legal experts presided over assemblies as well as functioning as legal authorities—their expertise presumably would have increased their status— but there is no reason to assume that the two roles invariably went together. A high-ranking president could easily have directed an assembly's business generally, calling

[99] Hn 8:1.
[100] Abt 2. Though note the absence of any reference to a protector figure in Abt 1.
[101] Af 38–38:2.   [102] See Chapters 1 and 2, pp. 34, 69–76.   [103] Hl 8.
[104] Ine 8 refers to someone called a *dema* in similar circumstances, penalizing those who refused to give surety when accused 'in the presence of any *scirman* or other *dema*'. The *dema*, at least, could plausibly be interpreted as a legal expert who had memorized *æ*. See Chapter 2, p. 72. On the *scirman*, see below, p. 143.

on men with acknowledged legal expertise only when technical issues arose which required elucidation.

The obscure groups of 'lawmen' (*lahmen* or *lagemanni*) or 'judges' (*iudices*) which appear in later evidence associated with various areas outside Wessex, particularly but not exclusively in the Danelaw, probably had a similar function.[105] The six Welsh and six English *lahmen* which the *Ordinance concerning the Dunsæte* shows operating somewhere on the southern end of the Anglo-Welsh frontier sometime in the late tenth or eleventh century, appear to have been a panel responsible for agreeing on and expounding the proper application of law. The verb used for this activity is *tæcan*—'to show' in the sense of showing the way, 'to direct', sometimes even 'to teach'—which suggests authoritative guidance. The subject on which they offered this guidance was *riht*, which is probably best translated 'justice' or 'what is right', with the sense being that *riht* would result from the judicious application of law to the facts of particular cases.[106] An early twelfth-century text from York, similarly, explains that although *iudex* was one possible Latin rendering of the term *lagaman*, an alternative was *legis lator*, perhaps simply 'law-giver' but most literally 'bearer' or 'carrier' of law.[107] It seems, then, that these terms allude to legal experts whose role was to offer authoritative guidance to assemblies on the correct application of law to the cases which came before them. The York text also mentions that the position of *lagaman* was hereditary, which would accord well with the idea that these figures were the bearers of a formal oral legal tradition that was passed from generation to generation, but this is speculation. Lawmen and judges were clearly legal experts of some sort but the nature of their expertise is obscure.

Legal knowledge, however, came in different forms. Someone who had learnt a formal compensation tariff from his father, and was able to recite it, may well have been able to inherit his father's position as an authority on *æ* while still a young man. We should not assume, however, that the authority to pronounce on other forms of law would come with this. The natural repositories for knowledge of an assembly's customary practices—its *þeawas*—would have been its members, particularly the older ones: those who could most accurately recall how similar cases had been handled in the past. Providing they were well respected, such men were probably able to act as legal authorities, resolving issues of interpretation on which younger men were unable to agree. Appealing to customary practice as remembered by the older men of an assembly may well have been the most common way of invoking legal authority in this period, but it is difficult to detect in our sources. We sometimes find examples of it in later practice, however. The most famous and clear-cut of these is an account of the Penenden Heath trial in the 1070s, which at one point called on the expertise of Æthelric II, the former bishop of Chichester, 'a very old man, very learned in the laws of the land, who had been brought in a cart at the king's demand in order to discuss and expound these same old legal

---

[105] See Chapter 2, pp. 74–5.   [106] Duns 3:2. ASD s.vv. 'tæcan', 'riht'.
[107] R. C. Van Caenegem, *English Lawsuits From William I to Richard I*, 2 vols. (Selden Society 106–7, London, 1990–1), no. 172A. DML, s.vv. 'legislator', 'lator'.

customs'.[108] A late tenth-century case from Ely, similarly, called upon the knowledge of the 'wise and old men' of Cambridgeshire, though in this case our record focuses only on what they had to say about the facts of the case, rather than their knowledge of legal customs.[109]

Communal assemblies, then, could be reliant on specific individuals or groups for statements of what the law was and how it applied to specific cases. Although the final decisions made by assemblies were clearly understood as expressions of collective will, these decisions resulted from a process which had been shaped, in part, by the guidance of men with recognized legal expertise. Although the influence they were able to exert through their role is heavily emphasized in the historiography, the presidents of assemblies were not necessarily the figures who controlled the laws they applied.[110] The president was a chairman: his key role was to maintain order and see to it that his assembly dealt with its business as efficiently as possible. The main quality necessary for this was rank: this was not a society in which inferiors decided when and for how long their superiors were allowed speak. Legal authority had different roots. People were recognized as legal authorities because of their knowledge of legal matters, which might be acquired through lengthy experience or through focused efforts of learning.[111] In order for their legislation to be implemented in local assemblies, then, kings needed to ensure two things: first, that there were people at local assemblies with knowledge of royal laws; and second, that these figures were recognized as having the authority to pronounce on these laws and to guide their assemblies in applying them to particular cases. As long as this was achieved the king's laws would be implemented in judgements: it did not matter much who these figures were or whether they also presided in their assemblies.

The Transmission of Royal Legal Authority

The promulgation of legislation in large royal assemblies is the most obvious way in which early kings tried to ensure their legal demands were known and accepted by their people. The laws of both Ine and Wihtred include prologues which talk about great gatherings which included not only their bishops and ealdormen but also large numbers of laymen and the clergy. This was probably normal practice. Part of the

[108] Van Caenegem, *Lawsuits*, 5B.
[109] E. O. Blake, ed., *Liber Eliensis* (Camden Society Third Series 92, London, 1962), ii. 25. On forms of legal expertise, see John Hudson, 'From the *Leges* to *Glanvill*: Legal Expertise and Legal Reasoning', in Stefan Jurasinski, Lisi Oliver, and Andrew Rabin, eds., *English Law Before Magna Carta: Felix Liebermann and Die Gesetze der Angelsachsen* (Leiden, 2010), pp. 221–49.
[110] For example, Wormald, 'Charters, Law', p. 306; Hudson, *Oxford History*, pp. 88–9. It should be noted that the examples cited by historians emphasizing the decisive role of assembly presidents tend to be land cases, for which we have good reason to think technical legal judgements were both less certain and more decisive. See Chapter 6, pp. 267–8.
[111] People of high rank could also have legal expertise, of course, and powerful people are usually well placed to insist on having things their own way when they think they know best. Power and authority could very easily coincide, but they need not always have done and it would be unwise to start from the assumption that they did.

point, presumably, was to make new legal pronouncements known to prominent people from around the kingdom so that they could go back to their home districts and implement them. If all went well, these men would have had little trouble exerting the authority necessary to have the king's legal claims respected, by virtue both of their local prominence and of their having been personally present when the king's *domas* received the collective endorsement of the kingdom's elite. Alternatively, we might imagine a more indirect form of transmission: ealdormen expounding the laws made in a royal assembly at assemblies in their own regions.[112] If the king's new laws related to reasonably common occurrences they would soon have occasion to be put into practice, and once established as practice they would become embedded as the assembly's customs, to be remembered by the old and wise members of the assembly. It is possible that written copies of laws helped in this process, at least during and after Alfred's reign, but the extent to which they were used is uncertain.[113] It is unlikely that every reeve was expected to have his own reference library of laws—many may have been illiterate—but it may have been hoped they would sometimes consult copies kept by monasteries, bishops, or ealdormen.[114]

This initial dissemination of laws would have been backed up to some extent by the king's own role as an appellate judge. This royal judicial role, as was noted in the last chapter, is strongly implied by some of Ine's laws, which look like attempts to express judgements from specific cases in general terms, and by our earliest description of the West Saxon inauguration ritual, which states that 'in all judgements [the king] should order justice and mercy so that through that the kind and merciful God may grant us his mercy.'[115] Royal judgement seems to have been an even more central feature of Alfred's perception of his role. His law code—known as the *Domboc*, or 'judgement-book'—contains far more laws that look like judgements from difficult cases than the laws of any of his predecessors or successors.[116] The king's attention to his judicial duties is celebrated by his biographer, Asser, who explains that he 'would carefully look into nearly all the judgements which were passed in his absence anywhere in his realm', and that many

---

[112] IV Eg 15–15:1 imagines ealdormen as vectors for the transmission of laws to the regions they ruled. The many 'official' and 'unofficial' legal texts of Æthelstan's reign (discussed in Chapter 4, pp. 174–7) have prompted fruitful investigation of these issues. See Roach, 'Legal Norms'; Patrick Wormald, *The Making of English Law: King Alfred to the Twelfth Century. Volume I: Legislation and Its Limits* (Oxford, 1999), pp. 291–300; Simon Keynes, 'Royal Government and the Written Word in Late Anglo-Saxon England', in Rosamond McKitterick, ed., *The Uses of Literacy in Early Mediaeval Europe* (Cambridge, 1990), pp. 226–57; David Pratt, 'Written Law and the Communication of Authority in Tenth-Century England', in David Rollason, Conrad Leyser and Hannah Williams, eds., *England and the Continent in the Tenth Century: Studies in Honour of Wilhelm Levison (1876–1947)* (Turnhout, 2010), pp. 331–50.

[113] Alfred's *Domboc* is unusual in that it was certainly composed primarily as a written text, though it does mention that the king took the trouble to show it to all his *witan* and get their approval (Af Int. 49:10). The relevant literature is cited in Chapter 1, p. 31, n. 14.

[114] I Ew Prol may imply that reeves were expected to consult Alfred's *Domboc* in written form.

[115] Nicholas Orchard, ed., *The Leofric Missal*, 2 vols., (London, 2002), ii, p. 432 (no. 2466); translated in Mary Clayton, 'The Old English *Promissio Regis*', *Anglo-Saxon England* 37 (2008), pp. 91–150, at 108, n. 98. See Chapters 2 and 5, pp. 76–7, 205–6.

[116] See Chapter 6, p. 265, n. 99, and Wormald, *Making*, p. 282.

disappointed litigants were very eager for him to do so.[117] If anyone felt that a local assembly judgement had failed to award them what they deserved, Asser states, they would bring the matter to the king's attention so it could be rectified.[118]

Where fines were concerned the natural people to bring such appeals would be the men whose duty it was to collect them: the king's reeves in areas where he retained the right to receive fines, and the beneficiaries of royal grants, either in person or through their own reeves, in areas where he did not. These figures would in any case have needed to monitor local assemblies so they knew what fines they were entitled to collect from whom. If they noted that an assembly was failing to take the king's punitive rights into account they were presumably expected to speak up and insist that the law be followed properly. It was only if they failed to carry their argument that an appeal to the king would be necessary. The possibility of such appeals, perhaps to be followed by punishments for false judgement,[119] would have encouraged local assemblies to do their best to judge in accordance with royal legislation—to acquiesce when a reeve (royal or otherwise) or thegn asserted that a fine was owed unless there was good reason not to. By simply monitoring local assemblies and asserting their rights, reeves and privileged lords were acting as legal authorities. Just as there were old men who knew their assembly's customs, and men who were able to recite *æ*, these figures were meant to know what fines they, or their masters, were entitled to receive for what offence, and their authority was ultimately underwritten by the possibility of an appeal to the king.

There are hints that kings had always wanted reeves to behave in this way. The most convincing reading of Ine's reference to a charge being made in the presence of a *scirman* or other *dema* ('judge'), is that *scirman* is here (as it is in some later texts) being used to denote a reeve.[120] If this is so, it may well indicate that Ine expected reeves to function as legal authorities, like other 'judges'—possibly a reference to men learned in *æ*.[121] We cannot be sure of this on the basis of this one rather opaque passage in Ine's laws, but it is wholly clear in a number of texts from the late ninth and early tenth centuries. Alfred's law code, the *Domboc*, envisages people making accusations at assemblies in the presence of a king's reeve. Edward the Elder, Alfred's son, began one of his codes with this statement: 'King Edward

---

[117] W. H. Stevenson, *Asser's Life of King Alfred Together With the Annals of St Neot's Erroneously Ascribed to Asser* (2nd edn, Oxford, 1959), ch. 106.

[118] An example of this happening in practice is provided by the case of Helmstan recorded in the Fonthill Letter (S 1445), discussed in Chapters 6 and 7, pp. 258–9, 266, 269–70, 317–18.

[119] These are implied by Asser (Stevenson, *Asser's Life*, ch. 106) and by tenth-century laws (esp. III Eg 3 but probably also, for example, II Ew 8; V As 1:3–1:4); we cannot know how frequently they were applied in practice. We should remember, too, that, if carried too far, local defiance of royal wishes could draw a military response: see the evidence for kings ravaging particular areas of their own kingdoms assembled in Molyneaux, *Formation*, pp. 78–9.

[120] Ine 8. See the discussion in Molyneaux, *Formation*, p. 111, where it is pointed out that *scirman* is used as a synonym for *gerefa* in the late Anglo-Saxon text known as *Gerefa* (Ger 5, 12) and to translate *praepositus*—the Latin term usually used to denote a reeve—in the Old English version of Gregory's *Pastoral Care*.

[121] That is, West Saxon equivalents to the *cantwara deman* in the laws of Hlothere and Eadric noted above (p. 139). See Chapter 2, pp. 71–2.

commands all the reeves that you give such just judgements as you know to be most right and as it stands in the judgement-books (*dombec*).'[122] Asser's *Life of King Alfred*, similarly, assumes that judgements were the responsibility of reeves (*praepositi*), but he also mentions ealdormen (*comites*) and thegns (*ministri*) in this capacity.[123] The reference to ealdormen probably alludes to shire assemblies at which major land disputes were judged.[124] The reference to thegns is probably an allusion, like those in the early tenth-century laws discussed above, to former royal servants grand enough to be rewarded with the right to receive the king's non-military dues, but not so grand that they were above turning up at local assemblies in person and advocating their own interests.[125]

These references to reeves and other powerful figures making judgements have caused considerable historiographical difficulty. They contrast with the bulk of our evidence for law in practice in which, as has been noted, the judgements issued by assemblies are represented as collective decisions.[126] The apparent contradiction is probably something of an illusion: it may simply be that our texts are referring to different sorts of judgement. Kings expected their reeves and thegns to be legal authorities, capable of making judgements about how the law applied in the circumstances of any given case. That is, offering authoritative guidance on technical decisions, such as how many oaths were needed to deny a given charge or, when dealing with multiple competing claims, which party should be allowed to prove its claim with an oath. These are sometimes termed 'mesne judgements' by legal historians.[127] The final judgements made by assemblies—their orders about who should now pay what to whom—were still understood as expressions of the community's collective will. Providing the analogy is treated with due caution, it might be helpful to think of the judgements given by legal authorities as rough equivalents to modern judges' rulings on 'points of law', and the judgements for which assemblies were collectively responsible as approximating modern 'court orders'. Thegns and reeves, acting as legal authorities, were held personally responsible for the judgements they issued (on points of law) because it was their duty to know the law and ensure it was properly applied in their local assemblies. If ignorance led them to fail in this duty they needed to be rebuked and sternly admonished to educate themselves appropriately. But if they tried to abuse their authority, issuing corrupt mesne judgements (on points of law) in an attempt to

[122] I Ew Prol.   [123] Stevenson, *Asser's Life*, ch. 106.
[124] On shire assemblies, see Molyneaux, *Formation*, pp. 165–72; Hudson, *Oxford History*, pp. 48–50 (though note that there is little foundation for the speculation that more 'serious' offences were reserved to shire assemblies: see Chapter 7, p. 322).
[125] See above, pp. 127–8 and Chapter 6, p. 249, n. 41.
[126] Solutions to this apparent contradiction have ranged from W. H. Stevenson's rejecting the authenticity of Asser's final chapter to Wormald's harbouring doubts about how far the communal rhetoric surrounding judgements corresponded to reality. See Stevenson, *Asser's Life*, pp. 342–3; Wormald, 'Charters, Law', pp. 304–6.
[127] Hudson, *Oxford History*, pp. 78–9. 'Medial judgement' is adopted in Frederick Pollock and Frederic William Maitland, *The History of English Law Before the Time of Edward I*, 2 vols. (2nd edn, Cambridge, 1898), ii, p. 698.

ensure that the final judgements (court orders) issued collectively by assemblies served their own interests, they deserved severe punishment.[128]

Kings thus seem to have expected their reeves and thegns to have had the authority to tell local assemblies what the law was and how it should be applied. (Note that this need not imply that they were expected to preside, though they sometimes may have done.)[129] They seem to have expected the same function of ealdormen from at least Alfred's time, though the assemblies at which they presided were much grander, more obviously political affairs than the local ones at which relatively routine forms of wrongdoing were judged. We should imagine these figures' legal authority in the same context as that exercised by the other legal authorities surveyed above: the obscure figures who memorized *æ*; the old and wise men who knew their assembly's customs; and the legal experts known as 'lawmen' or 'iudices'. Indeed, their duties can even be found described in the same terms. Just as the *Ordinance concerning the Dunsæte* uses the phrase *riht tæcan* to describe the duties of its twelve *lahmen*, Edgar's laws at one point describe the duties of the bishop and ealdorman in a shire assembly as *tæcan Godes riht ge worldriht*.[130] That is, they have the authority 'to show' (*tæcan*), in the sense of directing or showing the way, 'justice' or 'what is right' (*riht*) with respect to both God and the world.[131] Their functions are essentially the same as the *lahmen* of the *Dunsæte*: they are to expound the law to their assemblies, guiding them on its right application.

It is important to acknowledge that this authority was not limitless. A reeve could not simply make up the law to suit his own interests: assemblies would not accept this. Asser, in effect, tells us this directly, explaining that Alfred's intervention in judgements was necessary because nobles and commoners (*nobiles* and *ignobiles*)

---

[128] These are the two options set out in Stevenson, *Asser's Life*, ch. 106, and implied by III Eg 3. A useful brief discussion of the key distinction here is provided in Roger D. Groot, 'Proto-Juries and Public Criminal Law in England', in Dietmar Willoweit, ed., *Die Entstehung des öffentlichen Strafrechts: Bestandsaufnahme eines europäischen Forschungsproblems* (Cologne, 1999), pp. 23–39 at 29–30.

[129] Both Asser and Edward the Elder's laws assume that reeves were in some senses in charge of the assemblies they attended—with the authority to make judgements and to control both when assemblies took place and when particular cases would be resolved—and this has led historians to assume that they presided (Stevenson, *Asser's Life*, ch. 106; I Ew Prol; II Ew 8; Hudson, *Oxford History*, pp. 47–8). This may be accurate, but there are three reasons to suspect otherwise. First, these texts should probably be read as products of an Alfredian intellectual environment in which the king's role as judge for his people was of considerable ideological significance; they may, therefore, be prone to exaggerate the role of reeves as conduits for royal judicial authority. See David Pratt, *The Political Thought of Alfred the Great* (Cambridge, 2007), ch. 11. Second, none of these texts explicitly states that reeves presided at assemblies (indeed, as we shall see shortly, Asser undercuts his own emphasis on reeves' importance by noting that they had had trouble getting assemblies to accept their authority). And third, later laws do not expect reeves to preside in hundreds, as is shown in Chapter 6, pp. 247–50. Ultimately, however, for the reasons outlined earlier in this chapter (pp. 138–41) the issue of who presided at assemblies is something of a distraction, which is perhaps accorded more weight in the historiography than it warrants. See, for example, Patrick Wormald, 'Lordship and Justice in the Earliest English Kingdom: Oswaldslow Revisited', repr. in and cited from Wormald, *Legal Culture*, pp. 313–32 esp. at 326, 331–2; and the emphasis on who presided in Hudson, *Oxford History*, pp. 56–8 and (even while raising some important doubts) 61–2.

[130] Duns 3:2; III Eg 5:2. The verb *gereccan* used in I Ew Prol has similar associations: ASD s.v. 'gereccan'.

[131] ASD s.vv. 'tæcan', 'riht'.

'frequently disagreed violently among themselves at assemblies of ealdormen or reeves, to the point where virtually none of them could agree that any judgement reached by the ealdormen or reeves in question was just'.[132] They would therefore appeal to the king, who demanded that not only reeves (*praepositi*) and ealdormen (*comites*) but also thegns (*ministri*) apply themselves to attaining the wisdom required to perform their duties properly, or forfeit their positions. The possibility of an appeal to the king, then, may well have worked to reinforce a reeve's authority to expound royal law on a local level, making assemblies more likely to listen, but it probably also deterred them, to some extent, from blatant attempts at creative corruption.[133]

If reeves and thegns were to act as legal authorities successfully, it therefore seems likely that they actually did need to have good working knowledge of the law. They needed to earn the respect of their local assemblies. Kings clearly hoped that they would achieve this, and Alfred seems to have worked hard in admonishing them to educate themselves, but it would be rather optimistic to assume that all of them did.[134] We cannot reasonably assume that their authority was such that assemblies accepted their guidance unquestioningly even when prominent members thought it was incorrect. We should probably imagine that reeves and thegns needed to ensure that there was a consensus within their assemblies which regarded any given technical legal judgement as just—that if they wanted to twist the law to suit their own agendas they would, at the very least, have needed to persuade the most influential local political players to back them.[135]

It is perhaps likely that the dissemination of royal legislation through grand assemblies combined with the monitoring of local assemblies by reeves and thegns did manage to get most royal legislation implemented in some form on a local level. What that meant may well have varied considerably from locality to locality, but the possibility of appeals to the king (from both reeves or thegns complaining about obstructive locals and from locals complaining about corrupt reeves and thegns) would have ensured at least some degree of consistency. The increasing dissatisfaction with this state of affairs in the tenth century, implicit in the attempts at administrative reform noted above, is readily comprehensible from a modern perspective. There are no signs, however, that any of Alfred's predecessors were frustrated in the same way. They may well have regarded the obedience of local

---

[132] Stevenson, *Asser's Life*, ch. 106; translation from Simon Keynes and Michael Lapidge, eds., *Alfred the Great: Asser's Life of King Alfred and Other Contemporary Sources* (London, 1983), p. 109.

[133] See Chapter 6, pp. 265–6.

[134] It could be read as an indictment of reeves' and thegns' legal knowledge that the standard defence for men accused of making corrupt judgements seems to have been to claim that they knew no better—ignorance of the law must have been fairly common for it to be a valid excuse (Stevenson, *Asser's Life*, ch. 106; III Eg 3). On the other hand, it may be that the points of law in question were particularly abstruse: assessing the relative merits of complex inheritance claims so as to rule on who should swear an oath in a land case, for instance, may well have involved a higher level of expertise than ruling on how many oath helpers were necessary to deny a theft charge. See Chapter 6, pp. 266–7.

[135] See Chapter 6, pp. 264–5.

assemblies to the broad thrust of royal legal pronouncements as good enough, perhaps even the best that could reasonably be hoped for.

Historiographical Implications

To sum up, from the late seventh century, kings were faced with an existing network of communal assemblies with established sources of legal authority, and they needed to find a way of ensuring their legislation was implemented. Some things they could attend to personally: by promulgating their legislation at major assemblies they could instil in prominent figures from various localities a sense of responsibility for their new laws, and by hearing appeals they could keep themselves informed of potentially deviant local practices. Beyond that they had to rely on others. The obvious figures were the reeves who were responsible for collecting kings' non-military dues, including legal fines. This, however, posed a problem because there were plenty of areas in which kings had given away the right to receive those dues. In those areas they had to rely on privileged lords, either acting in person or through their own reeves. These figures had a financial interest in monitoring local assembly proceedings and, if they seemed to be in danger of neglecting to impose punitive fines, to speak up and assert that they were required by royal legislation. They were natural legal authorities of a sort, not necessarily the only legal authorities available to assemblies—many people probably felt they understood the law—but the people on whom kings relied to ensure that their laws were implemented. The education of reeves (not just the king's) and privileged lords was therefore important: if they were ignorant their assemblies would not respect them and royal legislation would not be implemented properly. Reeves and thegns needed to know the king's laws to be able guide assemblies in their application. They probably succeeded in broad terms—we have no reason to suspect the existence of areas that entirely ignored royal legal pronouncements—but it is likely that there were still substantial variations in local assembly customs. This was probably good enough for kings throughout most of the period we are concerned with here, but from Alfred's reign onwards there are increasing signs of discontent and the tenth century witnessed serious attempts at reform.

This, I would contend, is the important process to understand here: that by which kings influenced the laws which assemblies applied. However, we have strayed onto historiographically charged territory, and readers familiar with it will inevitably be trying to interpret this argument in the framework of the long-standing debate about the existence of 'private jurisdiction' in the Anglo-Saxon period.[136] The issue of

---

[136] See Henry Adams, 'The Anglo-Saxon Courts of Law', in Henry Adams et al., *Essays in Anglo-Saxon Law* (Boston, 1876), pp. 1–54; Maitland, *Domesday Book and Beyond*, pp. 259–92; Goebel, *Felony and Misdemeanor*, ch. 6; Hurnard, 'Anglo-Norman Franchises', pp. 289–327; Helen M. Cam, 'The Evolution of the Mediaeval English Franchise', *Speculum* 32 (1957), pp. 427–42; Wormald, 'Lordship and Justice'; T. B. Lambert, 'Royal Protections and Private Justice: A Reassessment of Cnut's "Reserved Pleas"' in Stefan Jurasinski, Lisi Oliver, and Andrew Rabin, eds., *English Law Before Magna Carta: Felix Liebermann and Die Gesetze der Angelsachsen* (Leiden, 2010), pp. 157–75; Hudson, *Oxford History*, pp. 56–63.

jurisdiction is discussed in detail in Chapter 7, so I will not dwell on it unduly here. However, it may be helpful to make a few points explicitly so as to avoid misunderstandings.

In the context of the existing literature, an assembly at which legal authority is wielded by a king's reeve, who may also preside, could easily be taken to fit the category of 'royal court'. One in which a thegn—interpreted as a lord who has been granted the right to receive the king's non-military revenues—or a non-royal reeve is expected to exercise legal authority, and perhaps also preside, could likewise be seen as a 'private court'.[137] This is not what I am arguing. A problem with the historiographical debate about 'private courts' and 'royal courts' is the rather crude assumption that assemblies (i.e. 'courts') must have been under the control of either the king or a privileged lord. This leaves no room to interpret assemblies' judicial functions as a manifestation of communities' collective authority to discipline delinquent individuals, which was clearly central to how they had been understood in England since the pre-Christian period. This communal tradition needs to be taken into account, and for that we need to stop thinking about 'control' in absolute terms, as though powerful men could either control an assembly entirely or exert no influence in it at all. Rather than trying to place assemblies into 'royal' or 'private' categories, then, we should try to be as precise as possible the nature of the influence wielded in them by various parties.

The analysis of the transmission of the king's legal authority here is part of this agenda (as is the more detailed examination of later material in Chapter 6).[138] What I have tried to emphasize is that reeves generally (not just the king's) and thegns seem to have had an important role in assemblies as legal authorities on punitive matters. That they could be threatened with punishment for false judgements implies this: if assemblies deviated from royal legislation as a result of their faulty guidance, kings held them personally responsible. It does not, however, imply that assemblies were under their absolute control, even in matters of legal interpretation. No modern court could refuse to accept its judge's rulings on points of law but Asser's account is predicated on the assumption that assemblies in this period were different. Reeves and thegns were legal authorities but their authority was far from absolute: they were probably often influential,

---

[137] Wormald, 'Lordship and Justice', pp. 318, 326; Baxter, 'Lordship and Justice', p. 417. More broadly, Hudson, *Oxford History*, pp. 56–62; Wormald, 'Charters, Law', p. 304. The lack of attention to passages which explicitly place thegns alongside reeves as figures held responsible for the implementation of royal law in the localities (IV As 7; V As 1:2–1:4; VI As 11; III Em 7:2; above, pp. 127–8) is thus rather puzzling in the context of this debate, especially in conjunction with the later reference to a 'judge' (*dema*) forfeiting his 'thegnship' (*þegenscipe*) for false judgement (III Eg 3). In the terms of the established debate, these could easily be interpreted as strong evidence in favour of 'private courts'. The clear association of these thegnly duties with land grants in VI As 11 (i.e. the reference to *gelandod* thegns discussed above, p. 128) is particularly striking. My main point here, however, is not that privileged lords had more involvement in local justice than the established literature allows (though I do think this), but that the way the debate has been framed is problematic—on which, see Chapter 7, pp. 301–6.

[138] Chapter 6, pp. 253–68, where other ways of influencing assemblies' final decisions (for example, through manipulation of proof procedures) are discussed in detail.

but if someone else with recognized expertise in legal matters happened to be a member of their assembly, he would probably have been influential as well. As will be discussed in more detail in Chapter 6, that influence in any event would probably have been most apparent in specific cases—probably mostly about the inheritance of land—where the legal issues involved were so complex or unusual that it was unclear what to do. Such cases may have presented opportunities for profitable corruption, but the majority may well not have done.[139] To argue for the existence of assemblies that, within reason, recognized reeves' and thegns' authority to expound the law is not to argue for the existence of 'royal courts' and 'private courts'. These were communal assemblies that, as communal assemblies must have done for centuries, relied on people with legal expertise to guide them on both the substance of law and its proper application.

DETECTION, ACCUSATION, AND ENFORCEMENT

Ensuring that assemblies applied royal legislation in their judgements was not the whole battle, of course. If the new royal punishments visible in late seventh-century law were to have a practical reality, people who committed relevant offences would have to be brought to assemblies for judgement in the first place. Their offences would have to be detected and someone would have to bring accusations against them. If they were convicted, there then had to be some mechanism of enforcement. How did kings ensure these things took place? The obvious answer is partially right: as with assemblies, they relied not just on their reeves but on lords who held the right to receive the king's legal revenues, often working through reeves of their own. Because they profited from the revenues generated by fines, these privileged figures had good reason to attend to these matters, or to instruct their reeves to do so. This is only part of the answer, however, and in some senses misleading. It conjures up a vision of the reeve as an all-purpose agent of law-enforcement, someone whose job routinely involved detecting offenders, bringing them to trial in an assembly (where he also acted as a kind of judge), and then enforcing the sentence. It is a very different image from that of the manager of an inland farm, primarily responsible for supervising its dependent workforce. There is a real danger here that we assume reeves and thegns had a much bigger job to do than they really did. We need to think carefully about how the king's needs for detection, accusation, and enforcement in relation to punitive justice would have fitted in with existing legal practices.

---

[139] Chapter 6, pp. 264–8 This is not to say that reeves and thegns lacked discretionary power in other cases, just that this power did not arise from their ability to influence technical legal decisions. For the argument that they would have been able to exercise considerable discretion over the sums they accepted as fines, see Chapter 6, pp. 283–9.

Detection and Accusation

Let us turn first to detection and accusation. These processes would have required little intervention from reeves and thegns because a lot of offences kings wished to punish would have been brought to the attention of assemblies by the dynamics of existing legal practice. The crucial point to appreciate is that matters touching on personal honour needed to be conducted in public. To resurrect our fictional example from Chapter 1, if Ælfstan has been affronted by Berhtred, whatever the nature of the affront, his honour has been challenged and there is social pressure on him to take action.[140] If he does not wish to gain a reputation as a man who meekly accepts ill-treatment he must prove to his neighbours that he is not such a man, either by taking vengeance against Berhtred or by forcing him to pay appropriate compensation. Doing either of these privately would be pointless. For the damage to Ælfstan's honour to be rectified, everyone who knew he had been affronted needed to know about the action he had taken to address that affront. Feuding was an inherently public activity; all offences that either generated feuds or occurred during them were likely to come to the attention of an assembly sooner or later.

This is most obvious for offences that constituted affronts. If Berhtred killed Ælfstan, Ælfstan's kinsmen had a good reason to bring a case against him for homicide in an assembly. That assembly could then issue a judgement including not just the wergild for Ælfstan's family but the sums due to his lord and to the king. Theft is similar. Its secrecy made detection more difficult, of course, but victims had every reason to try their utmost to seek out and recover their stolen property, and this process generated formal accusations. Some procedural offences involved affronts—seizing property, for instance, without first seeking a judgement authorizing it—and would have worked in the same way, but most did not. They would usually, however, have occurred in the context of existing cases. Refusal to submit to the judgement of an assembly, for example, could only arise if an accusation had already been made: no additional effort would be needed to bring the offence to an assembly's attention. Harbouring a fugitive represents a deliberate attempt to obstruct an existing case. If Berhtred fled rather than paying Ælfstan the compensation he had been awarded in an assembly judgement, Ælfstan would have a strong incentive to hunt him down. If it turned out that he was being harboured by a friend or relative within the same kingdom, the proper course of action for Ælfstan would presumably be to demand that this person surrender Berhtred, compelling him to do so by bringing a case against him if needs be. Again, the offence could come before an assembly without the need for a third party concerned with its detection and prosecution.

Some offences punished in late seventh-century law, however, seem much less likely to have come up naturally as men pursued their own claims for compensation. Religious offences are the obvious examples here. Failing to observe the Sabbath harmed nobody, so honour would not demand that anyone made an accusation, nor was this an offence that would come up in the course of another

---

[140] See Chapter 1, pp. 41–4.

case. People might inform on their neighbours out of spite, of course, or pious concern, but Wihtred's laws suggest anxiety that such motives would prove insufficient: they offer men who accused their neighbours of working on Sunday half of any fine that resulted from their prosecution.[141] The same problem presumably applied to offences such as neglect of baptism or making offerings to devils, although we have no evidence of similar schemes for them. We might suspect that churchmen could act as prosecutors here because of their pastoral concerns, which could also have had a financial element, for example in terms of fees charged for baptisms. This certainly would have been the case for the offence of refusing to pay ecclesiastical dues. It may well be that kings were largely content to leave ecclesiastical authorities to sniff out impieties beyond those which came to the attention of assemblies through alarmed or spiteful neighbours; there is, at any rate, little to suggest they wanted their reeves to perform this role.

There were, however, some offences which would have required reeves' and thegns' attention. Without the intervention of such a third party it is hard to imagine how a case in which someone caught a thief but subsequently let him go (rather than handing him to the king) would come before an assembly for judgement. The promises of rewards for men who did hand thieves over, made by both Ine and Wihtred, may well reflect the difficulty of detecting failures to do so: the impracticality of punishing misconduct meant that, though expensive, it made sense to try rewarding good conduct instead.[142] A similar sort of situation may be envisaged by Ine's law penalizing men who made secret agreements.[143] This makes most sense as a reference to attempts to suppress knowledge of offences for which the king would have been entitled to a fine. It may have been tempting to try to extort money from offenders by threatening to reveal their misdeeds, or to accept bribes in return for not doing so. Because it served the interests of all the parties involved to keep such deals secret there were no natural prosecutors for this behaviour. If kings were serious about wanting to punish it, they would need to ensure that they made specific efforts to detect it and bring accusations against offenders. That this was indeed a particular duty of reeves is implied by a law of Æthelstan which, alongside injunctions not to neglect punitive justice in general terms, singles out permitting secret agreements as an offence for which reeves (and implicitly thegns) could themselves be punished.[144] Presumably it was hoped that reeves and thegns would be alert to rumours that illicit deals had been made, investigating any such rumours in the hope of prosecuting the offenders. The need for specific threats on this point, however, suggests concern that this was not happening often enough.

There are some exceptions, then, but for the most part there was probably little need for reeves and thegns to make special efforts to detect punishable offences and prosecute those responsible. Most offences could come to the attention of assemblies by other means, so all that was strictly necessary was for these figures to attend

---

[141] Wi 11.   [142] Ine 28; Wi 26:1.   [143] Ine 52.
[144] VI As 11. Ine 73 contains a much vaguer hint of reeves' responsibility in these situations: men who allow thieves to escape must come to whatever terms they can 'with the king and his reeve'.

assemblies and make certain the law was properly applied. They needed to monitor other people's accusations for indications that punishable offences had been committed and ensure that punishments for these offences were included in judgements. It was also hoped that they would take the initiative and bring accusations when a secret deal to conceal an offence came to light. There was nothing to stop them doing more than this, of course, but we should not assume that they routinely did so.[145]

Enforcement

Different considerations apply to the enforcement of punitive fines and forfeitures.[146] It is important first to note the obvious point that in most cases enforcement action was probably unnecessary. It is likely that in normal circumstances, when an assembly judgement ordered someone to pay a fine they usually paid the fine (if they had the resources to do so). They would have done so largely because they expected that, while they might resist temporarily, they would eventually be forced to pay what they owed, along with additional penalties for refusing to cooperate.[147] It would be unwise, however, to assume that defiance was never a problem. One remarkable charter from the reign of Æthelred II contains a narrative of a case in which, for a long time, it was a successful strategy:

> These are the crimes which Wulfbald committed against his lord [i.e. the king]. First, when his father died he went to the land of his stepmother, and took there everything that he found, within and without, the lesser and the greater. When the king sent to him and commanded that he return his plunder, then he ignored that, [and] then his wergild was assigned to the king. And the king at once sent to him again and commanded him likewise, [and] he ignored it, and his wergild was a second time assigned to the king. Then besides he went forth and over-ran the land of his kinsman, Byrhtmær æt Burnan [presumably "of Brabourne" (Kent)]. When the king sent to him and commanded that he vacate that land, he ignored it, and his wergild was assigned to the king for the third time. And yet again the king sent to him and commanded him to leave, and he ignored it, and his wergild was assigned to the king a fourth time. Then there was the great meeting at London with Ealdorman Æthelwine and all the king's council. Then all the counsellors, clerical and secular, assigned to the king all of Wulfbald's possessions and his very self, just as the king wished, either for life or for death. And he held all this, uncorrected, until he died. And on top of all this, when he died, his widow and her child went and slew Eadmær, king's thegn and Wulfbald's

---

[145] For example, Lantfred's Translatio et Miracula S. Swithuni, ch. 25, has a king's reeve apprehending a slave for an unspecified misdeed: see Michael Lapidge, ed., The Cult of St Swithun (Winchester Studies 4.ii, Oxford, 2003), p. 308. VI As 8:4 shows that the men of London wanted surrounding reeves to accept responsibility for tracking stolen cattle across their districts.

[146] For an incisive discussion along similar lines to those adopted here, see Alice Taylor, 'Lex Scripta and the Problem of Enforcement: Anglo-Saxon, Scottish and Welsh Law Compared', in Judith Scheele and Fernanda Pirie, eds., Legalism: Community and Justice (Oxford, 2014), pp. 47–75.

[147] This consideration would, of course, have weighed more heavily on the poor than the rich, who would often have been in a better position to resist payment if they wished. For a more detailed discussion of these dynamics, see Chapter 6, pp. 283–9.

paternal uncle's son, and his fifteen companions, who were on the land at Brabourne which he had held as plunder in opposition to the king.[148]

Clearly nobody had dared to confront Wulfbald while he was alive. Indeed, the grisly fate of Eadmær and his fifteen companions, who were probably attempting to wrest possession of Brabourne from Wulfbald's widow, suggests that there was good reason to be afraid. Nonetheless, the charter implies that Wulfbald's widow was eventually dispossessed, as its purpose is to grant the land in question to the king's mother. Wulfbald did not suffer for his defiance, then, but eventually his family did.

Cases like Wulfbald's cannot have been the norm, but when they did occur they presented a threat. If it became clear that outright defiance of assembly judgements was a viable strategy, others would be tempted to adopt it rather than submit to punishment. A number of tenth-century laws suggest that this was regarded as a problem.[149] Their solution heavily emphasizes communal involvement. The earliest passage is from laws issued by Æthelstan at an assembly in Grately, Hampshire:

20:1. If, however, he [a man who has failed to attend an assembly three times and therefore owes a fine] will not do justice nor pay the fine for disobedience, the leading men are to ride thither, all who belong to the *burh*, and take all that he owns and put him under surety.

20:2. If, however, anyone will not ride with his fellows, he is to pay the fine for disobedience to the king.

20:3. And it is to be announced in the assembly that everyone is to be at peace with everything with which the king will be at peace, and to refrain from theft on pain of losing his life and all that he owns.

20:4. And he who will not cease for these penalties—the leading men are to ride thither, all who belong to the *burh*, and take all that he owns. The king is to succeed to half, to half the men who are on that expedition. And they are to put him under surety.

20:5. If he knows no-one to stand surety for him, they are to take him prisoner.

20:6. If he will not permit it, he is to be killed, unless he escapes.

20:7. If anyone wishes to avenge him or carry on a feud against any of them, he is to be at enmity with the king and all the king's friends.[150]

Æthelstan, then, requires local leading men (*yldestan men*) to undertake the risky business of riding against defiant wrongdoers. He attempts both to coerce them, threatening a fine for those who refuse, and to entice them with the promise of half the profits that come from the expedition. The rhetoric is assertive, but the point of

---

[148] S 877; translation from Sean Miller, *The Charters of New Minster, Winchester* (Anglo-Saxon Charters 9, Oxford, 2001), no. 31, p. 150, which also provides extensive discussion. See also, Simon Keynes, 'Crime and Punishment in the Reign of King Æthelred the Unready', in Ian Wood and Niels Lund, eds., *People and Places in Northern Europe, 500–1600: Essays in Honour of Peter Hayes Sawyer* (Woodbridge, 1991), pp. 67–81 at 78–81.

[149] II As 20–20:7; VI As 1:1, 8:2–8:3; III Em 2; Hu 2–3:1; III Eg 7–7:2; II Cn 25–25:2.

[150] II As 20:1–20:7.

the law is to persuade people to participate and the effort devoted to doing so suggests it was not easy. There were real dangers for those who rode on such expeditions, from both immediate resistance and later vengeance.

The implication of these tenth-century laws is that enforcement expeditions against the defiant were expected to be communal operations. The standard rule seems to have been that those who participated were entitled to half of any goods seized, the other half going to whoever had the right to receive the king's legal revenues.[151] We might have expected to find reeves or thegns bearing responsibility for leading such collective expeditions, but in fact this is not the case in any of our evidence. It appears from the regulations of the London 'peace-guild' (*friðgyld*), a detailed set of anti-theft rules instituted for London during in Æthelstan's reign, that it was possible to send word to reeves of neighbouring districts to ask them to raise men to help in enforcement expeditions (in order that 'wrongdoers may be the more afraid of us because of our numbers'), but kings never even come close to demanding that reeves command these expeditions.[152] Indeed, except for in this London text they are not mentioned at all. This is probably an indication that the wealthiest notables at local assemblies were often much more substantial figures than reeves, and more natural leaders for their communities. Rural reeves' primary duties probably always remained agricultural, managing inland farms and their dependent workforces, and there is no reason to suspect that they had armed retinues of their own which would allow them to coerce people independently.[153] When Alfred's laws imagine a scenario in which someone involved in a feud needed armed assistance, they state that he must first ride to the ealdorman and ask for help and then, if he refuses, ride to the king himself: the idea that a local reeve might have been able to assist is not even contemplated.[154]

We should, therefore, be wary of imagining the rural reeves who collected legal fines as powerful law-enforcement officers. They do not seem to have had significant independent powers of coercion, nor do they seem to have had the stature to be the normal leaders of communal enforcement expeditions. Thegns who had been granted the right to receive legal revenues must have been a different matter. They were likely to be among the most senior men present at any local assembly and therefore well suited to a leadership role, but beyond that there is little we can say because our evidence does not discuss their duties as enforcers. On reeves, we probably ought to conclude that their interest in collecting fines gave them a role in enforcement, but not a dominant one. The London peace-guild regulations treat the reeves of neighbouring districts as men who could be threatened with

---

[151] VI As 1:1 is slightly different. It is discussed in Chapter 7, pp. 331–2.

[152] VI As 8:3.

[153] This reading requires us to understand the rich and prominent reeves which occasionally appear in our sources as reeves with more significant responsibilities than ordinary rural reeves. The early ninth-century Kentish reeve named Abba, whose will (S 1482) shows him to have been very wealthy, is much more likely to have been of a similar status to Beornwulf, the *wicgerefa* of Winchester, whose death is recorded in the *Anglo-Saxon Chronicle* (s.a. 897) than the rural reeves with whom we are concerned here.

[154] Af 42:3.

punishment if they did not cooperate in the way that was demanded: the local reeve is to accompany the Londoners when their expeditions enter his district; neighbouring reeves are to send reinforcements when the Londoners ask for them; should the Londoners track stolen cattle into a reeve's district, he is to follow the tracks until they leave again or he is to pay over the value of the cattle (on the understanding that the Londoners will then work with him to ensure the thief is punished).[155] This last demand in particular suggests that once the prominent men of an area decided to mount an enforcement expedition, rural reeves were far from in control of proceedings. They were expected to be present because they were entitled to receive half the expedition's profits and they were expected to help with getting reinforcements from their districts organized, but their role was clearly a subordinate one.

A subordinate role could still be an important role, however. Because they were the ones who needed to collect fines we should probably imagine that reeves were important in recruiting the participants for enforcement expeditions. The very fact that tenth-century laws repeatedly try to exhort, threaten, and bribe people to take part in expeditions suggests that communal enforcement was an ideal which proved difficult to realize. The spontaneous displays of communal solidarity envisaged by the laws may have occurred on occasion, but we should probably regard them as the best outcome a reeve could possibly hope for when he set about trying to assemble a party of armed men to ride to an offender's farm. It is likely that most of the time this was a matter of persuasion. The most desirable targets for such persuasion were local elites: the 'leading men' who would naturally assume a leading role in any expedition and have the best chance of persuading others to join in. In some cases a sense of communal duty and the prospect of profiting from the seizure of moveable goods may well have outweighed concerns about the dangers involved, but if this was always the case our laws on the subject would scarcely have been necessary.

The people most motivated to join enforcement expeditions organized by reeves would have been men with engaged in feuds with the offender: men who needed to extract compensation or take vengeance for the sake of their own honour. Let us resurrect the fictional Ælfstan and Berhtred one final time. If Ælfstan accuses Berhtred of theft in an assembly and he is duly convicted, the judgement will include two orders: Berhtred must pay compensation to Ælfstan and a fine to the local reeve. When Berhtred, characteristically, defaults on both payments, the natural thing for Ælfstan and the reeve to do is to work together. Ælfstan is a member of a free kindred and well liked by his neighbours: he can assemble a party of men willing to ride to Berhtred's property and forcibly extract payment. The reeve may not be able to persuade the entire community to help him, but his is an influential position and some men will be willing to gain his favour by doing their communal duty, especially as there is the potential to profit from doing so. Separately neither Ælfstan's party nor the reeve's may be large enough to confront a dangerous man like Berhtred on his home turf, but together they have a much

---

[155] VI As 8:2–8:4.

better chance of doing so successfully. In practice it must often have made sense for the people enforcing fines and those enforcing compensation claims to form one large group and do both simultaneously.[156]

This final point aligns well with our conclusions on detection and accusation: the interests of reeves and thegns trying to implement punitive fines were remarkably well served by the dynamics of feuding. Men who had been affronted needed to restore their wounded honour in front of all their peers. Formal accusations made by such men would have brought most of the offences royal law was concerned to punish to the attention of assemblies. Similarly, when it came to enforcing the punitive sentences passed by assemblies, reeves and thegns must frequently have found natural allies in men involved in feuds, whether they were trying to extract compensation payments or seeking violent vengeance. In practice, the prosecution of punishable offences and the enforcement of the punishments ordered in assembly judgements—what might be thought of as distinctly 'vertical' aspects of legal practice—must frequently have been inextricably linked with, perhaps even dependent upon, the 'horizontal' dynamics of affront and compensation. We saw in the last chapter that royal punishment was largely complementary to feuding in in terms of its theoretical aims; here it seems that the imposition of punishment was complemented by feuding in practical terms as well. Indeed, assistance from men involved in feuds must sometimes have been necessary for punishments to take place at all.

CONCLUSION

When late seventh-century kings began to assert a substantially larger role in the punishment of wrongdoing within their kingdoms, the administrative challenge they faced was not as formidable as we might assume. Kings did not suddenly need to impose something resembling 'the state' on a 'stateless' environment; indeed, there is no reason to think that they created any new institutions at all, let alone an entirely new administrative apparatus dedicated to law. Rather, they relied on existing structures. Specifically, kings relied on the local administrators responsible for extracting food and labour from their people.

In areas where the king retained his non-military rights—that is, his rights to food renders, labour services and legal revenues—these local administrators would have been the king's own rural reeves. These figures' main duties were agricultural: they supervised dependent workforces on royal inlands, directed the seasonal labour of the local warland population, and ensured that food renders were collected and properly looked after. They do not seem to have been independently powerful figures with their own military households, but they did not need to be in order to

---

[156] In the Wulfbald case (see above, pp. 152–3), it should be noted, the only possible reference to an enforcement party is that to Eadmær, the king's thegn who was killed with his fifteen companions. Given that he was the son of Wulfbald's uncle it is almost certain that he and his followers were killed whilst attempting to take possession of land to which he had a direct claim (or shortly after doing so).

perform either their agricultural duties or the legal ones kings increasingly asked of them. There were, however, many areas where kings did not retain their non-military rights. In those areas the right to receive food renders, labour services and legal revenues was held by secular and ecclesiastical aristocrats. Kings were entitled to no revenues from such places and their reeves would have had little reason to venture into them. From a modern or later medieval perspective this situation may smack of 'reckless liberality' on the part of early medieval kings, so it is important to stress that they were neither weak nor short-sighted in alienating their revenues in this way.[157] Legal fines were probably mostly paid in kind throughout this period, and beyond what they needed to sustain their own households kings had little need for agricultural produce. It made much more sense to give away these rights as patronage, rewarding and thus encouraging political loyalty, than to hang onto them uselessly. The situation meant that kings had to rely not just on their own reeves but also on those of other lords, or on these lords themselves—thegns—if they were locally involved enough to see to such affairs personally, but until the tenth century there is little evidence that they regarded this arrangement as unsatisfactory (nor in an age of privatization do we have any reason to regard it as shocking).

These figures were in turn able to rely on two well-established patterns of legal practice: the communal traditions associated with assemblies and the honour-driven dynamic of feuding. These existing practices were comprehensive enough to mean that, except for attending assemblies to represent their employers' interests, reeves had no essential roles to play in legal practice. Accusations relating to punishable offences would have been brought to assemblies by men whose honour had been affronted, either because the original offence required both punishment and compensation or because a punishable procedural offence was committed in the course of a case originally brought before an assembly as a compensation claim. There is nothing to suggest that reeves were expected to spend their time trying to detect wrongdoing so they could make accusations themselves, although they clearly were meant to bring cases in assemblies if they gained knowledge of conspiracies to conceal offences. Once assemblies made judgements involving fines, most of the time they probably did not need to be enforced. If offenders could pay fines, they probably paid them, albeit almost certainly after a process of negotiation.[158] Their main alternative was flight, in which case a reeve's duty would be to seize any goods left behind; beyond that there was little that could be done.[159]

It was only when offenders refused to acquiesce in their own punishment and did not leave the area that enforcement became an issue. In such circumstances reeves could appeal to communal solidarity. Defiant offenders had challenged their local assembly's authority, so reeves could exhort the members of that assembly to do

---

[157] The phrase is from Frederic William Maitland, *Domesday Book and Beyond: Three Essays in the Early History of England* (Cambridge, 1897), p. 282.

[158] See Chapter 6, pp. 283–9.

[159] Unless there were sureties to be pursued, which probably was not common until the late tenth century: see Chapter 6, pp. 279–82.

their communal duty and mount an enforcement expedition, with the prospect of sharing in any goods seized serving as an additional incentive. They could also work in conjunction with men who were feuding with the offender: those who had accused him in the assembly in the first place and needed to be seen to take action, either to avenge his original affront or to force him to pay compensation for it. Reeves may not have been well suited to taking enforcement action independently, then, but they did not need to be in order either to mobilize established traditions of communal solidarity or to enlist help from men involved in feuds.[160] As long as enforcement took place occasionally, so as to demonstrate that defying punishment only increased its severity in the end, people probably tended to comply with assembly judgements.

A crucial point to grasp here is that the network of royal and non-royal reeves, and of privileged lords, on which kings relied was not a coercive apparatus intended to project centralized royal *power* into the localities. The coercive force behind legal practice in this period was supplied by local networks of obligation rooted in all manner of concepts—most obviously kinship, lordship, and community—not by a system of royal or aristocratic officials. Rural reeves and thegns can, however, be understood as an apparatus for the projection of royal *authority*, albeit perhaps a rather ramshackle one. These figures' primary legal function was to attend assemblies and ensure the law generally, and the punitive demands articulated in royal legislation in particular, were being properly applied. Reeves and thegns were expected to monitor assemblies, and if it appeared that a punitive fine was being neglected in any given case their duty was to assert the authority of royal legislation and demand the assembly included the fine in its judgement. In guiding assemblies on the proper application of law these figures behaved in the same way as other forms of legal expert. They were not employing coercive force on behalf of the king, and though royal reeves were concerned with the king's revenues this was obviously not the case for non-royal reeves and thegns. Nevertheless, all these figures were acting as conduits for royal legal authority: the authority initially constructed in great assemblies where the king's *domas* were proclaimed and endorsed.

This role in the transmission of royal authority to assemblies was important, no doubt, but we should bear in mind that assemblies could almost certainly have managed without it: there were other sources of legal authority available. In truth, all these figures—royal reeves, non-royal reeves, thegns—seem to have been fairly peripheral to legal practice. Their routine legal administrative responsibilities did not amount to very much: monitoring local assemblies and overseeing the payment of fines. This ought not to be surprising. As the last chapter argued, the new royal punishments of the late seventh century were 'new' mainly in the sense of being newly royal. Kings were filling a space in Anglo-Saxon legal culture where punishment already made sense; indeed, punishment on an essentially communitarian logic may well have been an established element of legal practice, in some places at

---

[160] And if this did not work they could always hope the king would send his own household warriors to enforce the fine when he came to consume his food renders, or ask the regional ealdorman for military assistance.

least. Reeves and thegns did not have to do much because they were working with the grain of a legal system which existed independently of them. Communities had their own reasons to assemble and discipline their delinquent members, and honourable men had little option but to pursue those who had affronted them, both within assemblies and outside them. This had all been going on long before kings became interested in punishing wrongdoing. To say that royal reeves, non-royal reeves and thegns were responsible for administering, running, or directing local justice would therefore be a substantial overstatement of their role. Local justice largely ran itself; these figures were expected to monitor it, to guide it when necessary, and to collect its profits.

PART II

ORDER AND 'THE STATE' IN LATE ANGLO-SAXON ENGLAND

4

Substantive Legal Change

INTRODUCTION

It was during the late Anglo-Saxon period, a label often applied to the two centuries separating the accession of King Alfred in 871 and the Norman Conquest of 1066, that 'England' came into being as political unit. The advent of the Scandinavian armies which overcame the kingdoms of Mercia, Northumbria, and East Anglia in the 860s and 870s, although a major threat to Wessex at the time, ultimately left West Saxon kings by far the richest and most powerful men in Britain. The period up to 954 saw them expand their rule by diplomatic and military means, to the point where it encompassed most (but not all) of the territory which had been covered by those kingdoms, and indeed some areas which had not.[1] The century that followed witnessed significant political consolidation and economic growth, on which another period of Scandinavian invasion and, from 1016 to 1042, rule seems to have had no significant negative impact.[2] It was during this late Anglo-Saxon period that England's system of shires and their subdivisions, 'hundreds' or 'wapentakes', first crystallized, and kings established the network of powerful officials known as sheriffs ('shire-reeves'), which would be central to the projection of royal influence in the localities for centuries to come. Late Anglo-Saxon kings can be found not only raising an annual land tax but also maintaining a uniform coinage across the kingdom, ensuring consistency across dozens of mints and successfully insisting that every few years a large proportion of the coins in circulation were recalled and exchanged for the current issue.[3] This period thus witnessed a major shift in England's political and administrative structures. Collectively, this chapter and the three that follow assess whether this was accompanied by a comparable transformation in its legal order.

---

[1] The essential discussion is now George Molyneaux, *The Formation of the English Kingdom in the Tenth Century* (Oxford, 2015), ch. 1, which provides a concise political narrative, a clear analysis of both how and why it took place, and comprehensive references to earlier literature on the subject. For more detailed narratives: Pauline Stafford, *Unification and Conquest: A Political and Social History of England in the Tenth and Eleventh Centuries* (London, 1989), esp. ch. 2; Simon Keynes, 'England, c.900–1016', in Timothy Reuter, ed., *The New Cambridge Medieval History*, vol. 3: *c. 900–c.1024* (Cambridge, 1999), pp. 456–84.

[2] Molyneaux, Formation, chs. 4–5; Robin Fleming, Britain After Rome: The Fall and Rise, 400 to 1070 (London, 2010), chs. 9–11; Stafford, *Unification and Conquest*, chs. 3–5, 8, 12; Richard Holt, 'The Urban Transformation in England, 900–1100' *Anglo-Norman Studies* 32 (2010), pp. 57–78; Chris Wickham, *The Inheritance of Rome: A History of Europe from 400–1000* (London, 2009), ch. 19.

[3] Molyneaux, Formation, ch. 4.

The details and periodization of many of the administrative innovations just summarized are of crucial importance for the understanding late Anglo-Saxon legal developments, but it is not with them that we must begin. The purpose of this chapter is to assess the extent and nature of substantive legal change in the period. That is, its concerns are essentially the same as those of Chapter 2: it draws out the laws' differing approaches to different categories of wrongdoing, and attempts to define and assess changes in those approaches across the period. It is important to start here because a clear understanding of what late Anglo-Saxon law was (and was not) attempting to do is essential background for the chapters that follow. Chapter 5 turns to the question of why the laws take the shape they do. It uses the greater detail provided by late Anglo-Saxon evidence to expand on the discussion of the same issue in Chapter 2, examining the ideals—both implicit assumptions and explicit ideology—which underlay kings' efforts to bring about societal change by legislative means. It is in the final two chapters that late Anglo-Saxon administrative developments come into focus. Chapter 6 asks how kings sought to control local legal practice, which involves assessing the implications of both new legal structures and the new procedural regulations that kings sought to implement through them. Chapter 7, finally, analyses the financial implications of legal practice, examining the shifting evidence for the destination of legal revenues and drawing out their implications for the relative importance of royal officials, privileged lords, and local communities in the practical administration of justice. The present chapter's analysis of substantive legal change is thus intended to double up as something of an introduction to those that follow.

The Evidence

Before we can turn to any of this, however, it is important to consider the available evidence. Relative to the earlier periods which have been our focus thus far, late Anglo-Saxon evidence for law is plentiful. The most important sources we have are texts associated with the tradition of royal legislation that thrived between the great law codes produced under Alfred (871–99) and Cnut (1016–35). (Almost all these texts are known only through later manuscripts, most of them made after 1066, and for some we have to rely on Latin versions produced by Anglo-Norman translators.)[4] The distinction between *æ* and *domas* explicit in the prologues of seventh-century laws is not a feature of late Anglo-Saxon legislative discourse, but this is not to say that we should understand all the texts associated with this legislative tradition as belonging to a single genre of 'law'.[5] Alfred's *Domboc*, for instance, a text evidently composed with profoundly ideological intent, has no close analogues. Its unusual features include a long prologue based on the Old Testament, the addition of Ine's laws as an appendix, a proliferation of what could be read as laws arising from royal judgements in specific cases, and a personal injury

---

[4] Patrick Wormald, *The Making of English Law: King Alfred to the Twelfth Century*, vol. 1: *Legislation and Its Limits* (Oxford, 1999), provides comprehensive discussion of the corpus.

[5] See Chapter 2, pp. 67–82.

tariff (a particularly striking feature given how earlier royal *domas* appear to have avoided making direct statements of *æ*).[6] At the other end of the period, we have a series of laws composed by Archbishop Wulfstan II of York (1002–23) for both Æthelred and Cnut which seem similarly ideological in intent but share none of these features. Rather, they have a more homiletic style in line with the archbishop's other writings, high in moralizing rhetoric and low in attempts to enact substantive legal change.[7] Cnut's great law code, also a Wulfstan product, has a more practical air, but is distinct from the other royal law texts of this period in that it seems to have been intended primarily as a compendium of earlier legislation; it often does little more than restate established law.[8]

These late ninth- and early eleventh-century texts are noteworthy, however, because they stand in contrast to the corpus of royal legislation that lies between them.[9] Most tenth-century kings are known to have issued two or more sets of laws, and these are broadly similar in character to the royal *domas* of the late seventh century.[10] These texts, like their predecessors, almost invariably proclaim themselves as the products of royal assemblies, and this conciliar context is reflected in the word they most commonly use to describe themselves: *gerædnes*.[11] The conventional translation of this term as 'decree' or 'ordinance' obscures its intimate connection with the terminology of counsel: the noun *ræd* ('counsel') and the verb *rædan*, key senses of which are 'to give counsel' and 'to consult'.[12] The late Anglo-Saxon laws, as this chapter will show, clearly inherited their central legislative agenda from the earlier period, but they were perhaps also bequeathed a certain seriousness of purpose: most seem to reflect practically minded attempts to grapple with perceived societal problems and solve them through the establishment of new legal rules.[13] The fact that these texts frequently recapitulate measures promulgated

---

[6] Wormald, *Making*, pp. 265–85, 416–29; Chapter 2, pp. 71, 73–4.

[7] Wormald, *Making*, pp. 330–49, 449–65; A. G. Kennedy, 'Cnut's Law-Code of 1018', *Anglo-Saxon England* 11 (1982), pp. 57–81.

[8] Mary P. Richards, 'I-II Cnut: Wulfstan's Summa?', in Stefan Jurasinski, Lisi Oliver and Andrew Rabin, eds., *English Law Before Magna Carta: Felix Liebermann and Die Gesetze der Angelsachsen* (Leiden, 2010), pp. 137–56; Wormald, *Making*, pp. 349–66. In this respect the code's closest analogues are the later Anglo-Norman legal compilations, which attempt the same thing without formal royal endorsement. However, the high-political context here is important; see Pauline Stafford, 'The Laws of Cnut and the History of Anglo-Saxon Royal Promises', *Anglo-Saxon England* 43 (1981), pp. 173–90.

[9] Wormald, *Making*, pp. 430–49.

[10] Eadred (946–55) is the longest-reigning tenth-century king who cannot be shown to have engaged in legislation.

[11] When late Anglo-Saxon laws give themselves a label this is usually the term they choose, but it should be noted that this is only common from Edgar's reign onwards. Especially in the early tenth century, the laws often just state that the rules they contain are what the king had decided, making some allusion to the involvement of as assembly but not referring to themselves explicitly (e.g. II Ew Prol; V As Prol; II Em Prol). An exception to this is I Edward, which is framed as a royal command to 'all reeves'.

[12] ASD s.vv. 'gerædnes', 'gerædan', 'rædan', 'ræd'; Felix Liebermann, ed., *Die Gesetze der Angelsachsen*, 3 vols. (Halle, 1898–1916), ii. p. 96.

[13] This focus on problem-solving is clearly visible in Æthelstan's anti-theft campaign, discussed below (pp. 174–7), and is a central theme of Chapter 6. Though the later laws are frequently much more elaborate, in this respect they are often reminiscent of late seventh-century texts' repeated

in earlier laws should not be taken as a sign that they lacked originality; most tenth-century legislation, examined carefully, reveals some innovative measure.[14] They also tend to be relatively coherent. It is usually possible to identify a single theme which legislators were attempting to tackle (good examples include I and II Edmund, II, III and IV Edgar, and I Æthelred), but there are others, such as II Æthelstan, which include material seemingly unrelated to their primary concerns. Again, the overall picture is not too unlike that for the late seventh century *domas*, if we bear in mind that our chaotic text of Ine's laws probably results from the stringing together of several slightly more coherent but still fairly disparate, sets of laws.[15]

Alongside this body of laws in the names of kings we have a less cohesive set of law texts that do not characterize themselves as such, many of which are shorter than the surviving royal codes (sometimes mere fragments), anonymous, and thus often difficult to date.[16] This, combined with the uncertainty about the contexts that underlie their production, can make them harder to use for a lot of purposes. But the lack of uniformity here means such generalizing statements are inevitably misleading to some extent: some of these texts can be tied reasonably securely to particular periods and some explicitly discuss the legal arrangements of specific localities.[17] Indeed, some pose fewer interpretative difficulties than royal codes, and even those which cannot be pinned to a context narrower than 'late Anglo-Saxon England' can still be useful for some questions. This material, like the royal codes, has been comprehensively reviewed in Patrick Wormald's monumental *Making of English Law*, and it would be unnecessary and unhelpful to attempt to reproduce his conclusions about individual texts here. Instead, I have aimed to clarify their status (and cite scholarship specific to them) whenever they have a significant role to play in the arguments pursued.

I have adopted a similar policy for the range of post-Conquest materials, most of which are also reviewed by Wormald. Domesday Book, a grand survey of the English kingdom conducted in 1086, is not primarily concerned with the kingdom's legal arrangements but contains valuable material nonetheless, not least in its brief summaries of the legal customs of several shires.[18] There are several Anglo-Norman legal compilations and treatises, which draw extensively on Anglo-Saxon law and

---

attempts to create threats and incentives that would result in men confronting and capturing thieves, then handing them over to the king for punishment (see Chapter 2, pp. 99–102). Note that, if its underlying premise is accepted, even VII Æthelred, which orders that the entire kingdom collectively undergo penance so as to regain God's favour, can be read as an eminently practical piece of legislation.

[14] This is another underlying message of Chapter 6.　　　[15] Chapter 2, p. 68.

[16] The anonymous texts are discussed in detail in Wormald, *Making*, 366–97.

[17] Key locally specific texts are III and VI Æthelstan, IV Æthelred 1–4:2 and the *Ordinance Concerning the Dunsæte*. On these, see Wormald, *Making*, pp. 290–308, 371, 381–2 and the earlier literature there cited, but also now George Molyneaux, 'The Ordinance Concerning the Dunsæte and the Anglo-Welsh Frontier in the Late Tenth and Eleventh Centuries', *Anglo-Saxon England* 40 (2012), pp. 249–72 and the more recent articles cited below, p. 174, n. 46 and p. 187, n. 102.

[18] The essential guide to this material is Robin Fleming, *Domesday Book and the Law* (Cambridge, 1998), which collects, numbers, translates and comprehensively indexes all the law-related passages in the text.

sometimes seek to explain its terminology to an audience presumed unfamiliar with it. This can be a very helpful interpretative aid for the Anglo-Saxon texts but the hazards of anachronism are obvious and I have tried to limit my use of this body of material as much as possible, drawing on it only when it adds something of substance and alerting the reader to the uncertainties introduced by doing so.

In addition to the greatly expanded range of normative sources available for the late Anglo-Saxon period we have much more evidence for law in practice. Of the 178 cases listed in Wormald's invaluable 'Handlist of Anglo-Saxon Lawsuits', 169 are from Alfred's reign or later.[19] This material is disparate. The majority of cases are reported in charters, some of them (particularly during the reign of Æthelred) in considerable detail, but most in terse allusions to how the land rights being transferred had earlier been forfeited to the king for some form of wrongdoing (often unspecified). Other cases derive from monastic cartulary chronicles, which record the legal endeavours of the abbots of the houses that produced them: their attempts (often successful) to defend their lands by legal means against lay and clerical aggressors. Beyond this, the narratives of high-political conflicts that appear in various chronicles, histories, and hagiographies sometimes touch upon legal proceedings in which the defeated parties end up executed or outlawed, and a few miracle stories involve saints rescuing relatively low-status people from gruesome punishments for wrongdoing. Domesday Book also contains a handful of incidental references to pre-Conquest disputes. The interpretative difficulties posed by these diverse materials are many and varied, but in the present context the most fundamental are their tendency to be terse and their overwhelming focus on land disputes between lay and ecclesiastical aristocrats (as opposed to the routine local legal practice relating to wrongdoing that is the main subject of this book, and the focus of the laws).

At its best, this evidence can provide detailed narratives in which relatively minor aristocrats forfeit their landed property as a result of engaging in some form of wrongdoing other than the unjust occupation of land. This can be extremely valuable in enriching analysis based primarily on other sources. (The case of Wulfbald, discussed in the last chapter, is an excellent example.)[20] But material of this quality is not common and we should not delude ourselves about its potential to elucidate legal practice beyond aristocratic disputes over title to land, for which charters and cartulary chronicles are of course our richest seam of evidence. One cannot gain a holistic understanding of law in the late Anglo-Saxon period by working through a series of case narratives and resorting to the laws only to clarify points of uncertainty. To this written material we can add the archaeological evidence for execution and mutilation assembled and discussed in Andrew Reynolds's *Anglo-Saxon Deviant Burial Customs*.[21] This provides valuable

[19] Patrick Wormald, 'A Handlist of Anglo-Saxon Lawsuits', repr.in and cited from Wormald, *Legal Culture*, pp. 254–87, nos. 20–178.
[20] Chapter 3, pp. 152–3.
[21] Andrew Reynolds, *Anglo-Saxon Deviant Burial Customs* (Oxford, 2009). It should be noted that an incisive critical reassessment of this body of evidence is currently being prepared by Alyxandra Mattison as part of her University of Sheffield doctoral thesis ('The Execution and Burial of Criminals

confirmation that afflictive penalties were in practice imposed in this period (and indeed much earlier), and for the burial of at least some executed corpses in cemeteries separate from those in ordinary use.[22] Obviously enough, however, this evidence rarely if ever allows us to deduce why or by whom these people were killed, or to know much at all about their identities, although associated place-name evidence can sometimes provide useful hints.

Broadly, then, our best evidence for late Anglo-Saxon law comes in the tenth century, when there developed a tradition of kings, in conjunction with their secular and ecclesiastical elites, attempting to use legislation to engage in detail with local legal practice and solve problems they discerned there. In the early eleventh century this legislative activism gave way to the period of Wulfstan's dominance, which lasted until early in Cnut's reign, when the emphasis shifted away from the establishment of new substantive rules towards hortatory and condemnatory rhetoric, and towards the compilation of legislative wisdom found in earlier texts.[23] The greater detachment of these texts from contemporary legal practice makes them less useful for many of the questions addressed in this and later chapters, though by no means for all of them.[24] We must then confront a dearth of evidence for the forty to fifty years preceding the Norman Conquest. This void is problematic. The post-Conquest texts suggest that this was not a period of dramatic change—the basic shape of the legal system as it appears in both Domesday Book and texts such as the *Leges Henrici Primi* is roughly the same as that visible in earlier evidence—but where a shift of some sort can be discerned it is usually impossible to tell whether it took place in this period or after 1066. The case material does not help here, as our most useful narratives cluster in the reign of Æthelred.

For the most part we simply have to acknowledge the chronological patchiness as an interpretative difficulty; Anglo-Saxon legal culture and practice is much more obscure to us in the ninth century, and (particularly after the 1020s) in the eleventh, than it is in the tenth. But we should also consider the possibility that these shifts in the nature of the source material may in themselves be evidence of important changes in the period: the waxing and waning of kings' interest in the project of changing their societies for the better by making intelligent adjustments to substantive and procedural law. The sudden appearance of this type of legislation in the wake of Alfred's reign attests to tenth-century kings' investment in this effort—significantly greater, it is probably safe to infer, than any of their eighth- and ninth-century predecessors—and the lack of new laws in this mould in the

in Early Medieval England, *c*.850–1150: an Examination of Changes in Judicial Punishment across the Norman Conquest'). I am grateful to her for allowing me access to a draft of her third chapter, in which she raises significant objections to several aspects of Reynolds's interpretation. It is to be hoped that her analysis will find published form soon; it will be essential reading when it does. (Regrettably, her work came to my attention only in the final stages of revising this book so I have not been able to make full use of it here.)

[22] See Chapter 5, pp. 220–3.

[23] This is a feature not just of Cnut's great code but of other texts associated with Wulfstan: *Grið, Geþyncðo, Norðleoda Laga, Mircna Laga*. See Wormald, *Making*, pp. 391–5.

[24] Their value for the analysis of legal ideals described in Chapter 5 is unsurprising, but the distinctive approach to legal revenues in certain passages is also crucial in Chapter 7.

eleventh century must reflect some shift in the extent, or at least the nature, of royal engagement with legal matters in the period. This issue is reflected upon in more depth in Chapter 7, which considers the changing source-base around the millennium and explores the implications of writs: new royal grants that emerge in the eleventh century, with a distinctive vocabulary for the description of legal privilege.

Likewise, the overwhelmingly West Saxon focus of our main source material probably also reflects something important about the nature and extent of royal engagement with law in the area that came to be known as the Danelaw. Edgar's rather tentative approach, affirming the Danes' right to decide their own customs at the same time as trying to impose measures of his own, is most naturally read as a halfway stage between his predecessors' apparent non-engagement and Æthelred's seemingly confident production of a code for the area known as the Five Boroughs.[25] The fact that his successors did not legislate in a comparable way almost certainly reflects the general cessation of royal legislative activism, not any reversal in this trend of growing royal confidence regarding the Danelaw.

The Literature

The established literature on late Anglo-Saxon law is intimately bound up with broader assessments of English government in the period. Modern historians now more or less accept James Campbell's vision of a late Anglo-Saxon 'state'.[26] There is a debate about the appropriateness of this term in a medieval context but scholarly preferences as to the acceptance or rejection of the language of statehood have had little impact on matters of substance.[27] The picture of a centralized administrative system that meant royal government could routinely affect the lives of even relatively ordinary people is widely accepted.[28] George Molyneaux has established

---

[25] IV Eg 2–2:2, 12–15; III Atr Prol., 1–1:1. I suspect that the available source material provides scope for the profitable exploration of this and other aspects of the differing legal arrangements that characterized the north and east of the English kingdom. The few law texts that discuss what was understood to be Danish law share most of the basic assumptions of the main body of English law—the same concern about theft, for instance—but there are some interesting contrasts in specifics (notably the size of penalties for breach of protection: III Atr 1–1:2) and emphasis (for instance a preference for financial securities over suretyship: III Atr 1:2; cf. I Atr 4) that may reflect important societal differences. The customs of those Danelaw shires that are discussed in Domesday present a similar picture. I have touched upon some of these points of contrast as and when they have arisen in the context of my broader analysis, but make no pretence that this results in an adequate treatment. The very specific questions the handful of relevant texts prompt and the focused analysis (and detailed engagement with other forms of evidence for regional difference) they really require unfortunately precluded their being fully explored in the context of these four chapters. On the Five Boroughs (Lincoln, Stamford, Nottingham, Derby, and Leicester) see N. J. Higham, 'The Five Boroughs', in Michael Lapidge et al., eds., *The Wiley-Blackwell Encyclopedia of Anglo-Saxon England* (2nd edn, Chichester, 2014), pp. 191–2.

[26] This vision is most clearly accessed through the introduction to, and essays collected in, James Campbell, *The Anglo-Saxon State* (London, 2000). Also, James Campbell, 'Observations on English Government from the Tenth to the Twelfth Century' (1975) repr. in and cited from Campbell, *Essays in Anglo-Saxon History* (London, 1986), pp. 155–70.

[27] See the literature cited in the Introduction, p. 2, n. 3.

[28] The widespread acceptance of this interpretation is clear in modern textbooks. See, for example, Robin Fleming, *Britain After Rome: The Fall and Rise 400 to 1070* (London, 2010), pp. 269–76;

that it is misleading to apply this interpretation to the entire period from Alfred to 1066 but even his critique—easily the most ambitious and well-reasoned one to date—does not challenge the idea of late Anglo-Saxon governmental sophistication in its essentials, so much as postpone its emergence until the third quarter of the tenth century.[29] There is little disagreement about the capacity of Anglo-Saxon kings from Edgar's reign onwards to direct local activities through the system of shires and hundreds, to operate a sophisticated system for the regulation of coinage, and from at least 1012 to tax the population annually, perhaps to extraordinarily high levels.[30]

This dominant vision of a centralized and powerful late Anglo-Saxon 'state' has (as the Introduction argued) affected the way historians think about law in the period. The states with which modern historians are most familiar—their own—deal with wrongdoing within their borders by issuing legislation that defines and prohibits wrongful acts, and by punishing people who commit those acts. It has generally been assumed, though only occasionally explicitly argued, that this was how the late Anglo-Saxon kingdom approached the problem of maintaining order, and that this marked a significant shift away from the feud-based legal culture which defined the earlier Anglo-Saxon period. As Wormald put it, giving force and clarity to assumptions more hazily visible in the historiography since at least the 1940s, 'we have moved from a polity where injury is redressed to one with a developed notion of crime and punishment. And such a polity performs at least one of the functions of a "state".'[31] The core idea here, visible throughout much of the modern literature on the subject, is that the late Anglo-Saxon period witnessed an important shift; a legal order which since the seventh century had incorporated elements of both 'horizontal' and 'vertical' justice is thought in this period to have become much more impressively vertical, with royal punishment displacing traditional compensation-based justice as increasingly sophisticated governmental structures gave kings the administrative capacity they needed to intervene more routinely and forcefully in the lives of their people.[32]

This chapter reassesses this position. It does not seek to question the idea that late Anglo-Saxon kings were enthusiastic about punishment, as this is beyond question: the law codes that survive can at times be horrific in the punishments they prescribe.[33] Indeed, the fact—attested in late Anglo-Saxon laws, charters and

Charles Insley, 'Southumbria', in Pauline Stafford, ed., *A Companion to the Early Middle Ages: Britain and Ireland, c.500–c.1100* (Oxford, 2009), pp. 322–40.

29 Molyneaux, Formation, esp. chs. 3–4.
30 For a convenient review of the literature see Molyneaux, Formation, pp. 195–9.
31 Patrick Wormald, 'Giving God and King Their Due: Conflict and Its Regulation in the Early English State', repr.in and cited from Wormald, *Legal Culture in the Early Medieval West* (London, 1999), pp. 333–57, at 342. See the discussion in the Introduction, pp. 1–7.
32 Carole Hough, 'Legal and Documentary Writings', repr.in and cited from Carole Hough, *An Ald Recht: Essays on Anglo-Saxon Law* (Newcastle upon Tyne, 2014), pp. 2–24 at 13; Daniela Fruscione, 'Beginnings and Legitimation of Punishment in Early Anglo-Saxon Legislation from the Seventh to the Ninth Century', in Jay Paul Gates and Nicole Marafioti, eds., *Capital and Corporal Punishment in Anglo-Saxon England* (Woodbridge, 2014), pp. 34–47.
33 The unmistakable enthusiasm of the elaborate discussion of execution methods in IV As 6:3–6:7 is particularly chilling, as is the implication of EGu 10 that mutilated offenders had to be left for three days before it was permissible for others to tend to their wounds. The range of late Anglo-Saxon

archaeology—that at least some offenders were denied Christian burial makes the Anglo-Saxons appear a peculiarly unforgiving people, intent not only on inflicting unbearable suffering on wrongdoers in this life but also on removing all hope of salvation in what lay beyond.[34] The key contention here is that punishment remained in this period, as it had been in the late seventh century, a remedy used for three main categories of wrongdoing: theft, religious misconduct, and procedural offences. It is readily apparent that kings intensified their efforts to deter these forms of wrongdoing in this period, and that the establishment of new or increased punishments was a central means by which they did this. However, for violent offences we find the same pattern in this period as we did in the seventh century. Kings did not prohibit and punish; instead they attempted to deter wrongful violence primarily by extending their protection to those who might be harmed. If we recognize this and examine the evidence closely, it become apparent that this period saw a major intensification of royal efforts in this sphere, with the king's protection extended in innovative and far-reaching ways.

It is worth emphasizing that the argument pursued here is *not* the inverse of the current consensus—far from it. I am not attempting to replace a picture of late Anglo-Saxon state-like sophistication with a vision of primitive and ineffective rulership. The established picture of powerful late Anglo-Saxon kings, whose increasingly well-organized governmental structures enabled them able to project their influence into the localities with great effect, is not in question here (providing Molyneaux's revisions are accepted). This chapter's central argument is not that these kings were weak but that they had no intention of revolutionizing the legal order they inherited from the seventh century. The project they were engaged in was not the creation of a 'developed notion of crime and punishment' comparable to that of modern states, but the improvement of English society within a framework of legitimate royal activity shaped by long-established ideas about good order and its proper maintenance. The continuing importance of this framework, manifested in the characteristically Anglo-Saxon differentiation of forms of wrongful conduct associated with punishment and protection, is the subject of this chapter. This is such a fundamental feature of late Anglo-Saxon law—and a feature so easily misunderstood by those coming to the period with modern preconceptions about the nature and purpose of law—that it is crucial to be clear about it before embarking on more the detailed discussions in the remaining chapters of this book.

The present chapter's argument is made in two sections: the first examines the intensification of punishment within its traditional sphere (with a particular focus on the rich evidence for theft), then the second turns to an examination of late Anglo-Saxon laws' approach to violence. No aspect of the first section's argument is particularly controversial. Theft is without doubt the primary theme of late Anglo-Saxon legislation, and the fact that the laws made many and varied attempts to

---

punishments, brutal and otherwise, is reviewed in John Hudson, *The Oxford History of the Laws of England*, vol. 2: *871–1216* (Oxford, 2012), pp. 180–98.

[34] The evidence of laws and charters is reviewed, and the interpretation of this custom discussed, in Chapter 5, pp. 220–3. For the archaeological evidence: Reynolds, *Deviant Burial*, ch. 4.

ensure that thieves met with appropriate punishment is well understood (and always has been).[35] The second section, however, is a different matter. Violence is a much more marginal concern in the laws, rarely addressed directly or in detail, and the central features of their approach to it are thus less immediately apparent. The interpretation offered here is that, as had been the case in the seventh century, late Anglo-Saxon kings accepted violent feuding as an element of traditional legal practice and made no significant efforts to establish new royal punishments for violent offences; instead, they engaged with violent forms of wrongdoing by extending their protection in a number of different ways, which cumulatively are likely to have had a significant practical impact on those pursuing feuds against their enemies. Several aspects of this case are in direct contradiction to established readings, but rather than allow the analysis to become embroiled in negative arguments—the point-by-point refutation of established ideas—I have focused on setting out a positive case for my own interpretation. Brief discussions of the key points of contention and of their broader significance are provided towards the end of the chapter, but remarks on divergences from earlier scholarship are generally confined to the footnotes.

THEFT AND THE INTENSIFICATION OF PUNISHMENT

It was argued in Chapter 2 that the new royal punishments which emerged in the seventh century applied to three categories of wrongdoing: religious misconduct, procedural offences, and theft. By the reign of Alfred, then, royal punishment for these types of offence had been established for roughly two centuries. The principle that kings had a right and duty to punish wrongdoing that fell within these three categories was, we can reasonably assume, traditional and uncontroversial. The late Anglo-Saxon evidence suggests an intensification of royal efforts to impose punishments for all three types of offence, but it is for theft that this is most clearly visible and theft will be the main focus here.

Nonetheless, let us begin with religious offences. Our seventh-century sources provided evidence for royal punishment of illicit marriages, failures to observe the Sabbath, making offerings to devils, failing to baptize children, and refusing to pay church dues.[36] Royal laws of the later period do not include penalties for pagan worship or refusal to undertake baptism, probably because these were problems of the conversion period that were not major causes for concern in the areas applying English law in the tenth and eleventh centuries.[37] On the other subjects, however,

---

[35] The threefold categorization adopted here obscures the laws' overwhelming focus on theft to some extent; it should be noted that most royal legislation on procedural matters is either explicitly or implicitly targeted at theft, as its analysis in Chapter 6 makes clear.

[36] Wi 5–5:1, 11–15; Ine 2–4.

[37] The Northumbrian Priests' Law does contain examples of such prohibitions, however: Northu 10–10:1, 48–54:1. Even in the West Saxon tradition there was a general concern that the population observe Christianity properly, visible primarily in Wulfstan texts which stress the importance of

late Anglo-Saxon laws are more elaborate. Punished offences relating to marriage include the abduction and marriage of nuns, adultery, incest, the refusal of foreigners to regularize their marriages, and the over-hasty remarriage of widows.[38] Punishments for failure to observe the Sabbath form part of a wider category of punishments for refusal to observe Christian fasts and festivals, notably Lent.[39] Probably the most prominent religious theme in late Anglo-Saxon legislation, however, is the payment of various ecclesiastical dues, with secular punishments specified for non-payment in the laws of Æthelstan, Edgar, Æthelred, and Cnut.[40] There is thus some shifting of punitive priorities but the main impression is of an intensified concern to maintain minimum standards of Christian observance among the laity, and possibly a more rigorous interpretation of what these standards were.

We get a similar picture for procedural punishments, albeit on a somewhat grander scale: easily the most significant theme in late Anglo-Saxon legislation is the establishment or regularization of specific legal procedures (this aspect of late Anglo-Saxon change is discussed in depth in Chapter 6), and punishments for breach of these procedures are an important part of this. Indeed, the number and variety of these punishments is striking. Those relating directly to formal judicial process include punishments for various types of perjury, unjust judgements, failure to hold and attend assemblies, and errors in the administration of ordeals.[41] Another major strand of late Anglo-Saxon legislation concerns procedures designed to make people and their property legally accountable, so punishments here touch on matters such as failure to find various forms of surety, failure to provide surety, failure to ensure that significant purchases were witnessed, and failure to notify neighbours of one's acquisition or slaughter of livestock.[42] Perhaps the most significant theme, however, is that of people's duty to participate in the suppression of wrongdoing (primarily theft). There are punishments for those who neglect their duties to track or pursue thieves and to participate in enforcement actions, as well as punishments for the more active offences of obstructing such activities or shielding

---

shunning pagan practices and undertaking the sacraments (albeit without setting down punishments for those who fail to live up to these ideals). See VI Atr 6, 27; VIII Atr 44; I Cn 16–28.

[38] Af 8; I Em 4 (though note that the penalty here is ecclesiastical); Cn 1020 16–17; II Cn 50, 53, 54, 55, 73. See also the text known as *Ymb Æwbricas* (text: Robin Flower, 'The Text of the Burghal Hidage', *London Medieval Studies* 1 (1937), pp. 60–4 at 62. Commentary and translation: Wormald, *Making*, pp. 175–6, 372–3). For further rules and exhortations on this theme that do not involve specific punishments see Af 18; V Atr 10; VI Atr 11–12; I Cn 6:3–7.

[39] Af 40:2; II As 24:1; II Eg 5; VIII Atr 16–17; II Cn 46. There are also numerous non-specific exhortations on this subject: Af 43, V Atr 12:3–20; VI Atr 22–25, 43–44; Cn 1020 18; I Cn 14:1–17.

[40] I As 4–5; II Eg 1–4; IV Eg 1–1:6; VIII Atr 6–15; Cn 1027 16–17; I Cn 8–14; II Cn 48. See also I Em 2, for the threat of excommunication for non-payment. For other statements on this theme see I As Prol-1; III As 1; II Eg 5:2; IV Eg Prol; V Atr 11–12:2; VI Atr 16–21, 43; VIII Atr 43; Cn 1018 11–12:4.

[41] Various types of perjury: Af 32; II As 10:1, 11; III Eg 4; III Atr 7; II Cn 16, 36–7. Unjust judgements: III Eg 3; III Atr 13:2; II Cn 15:1. Holding and attending assemblies: II Ew 8; II As 20; Hu 7:1; II Cn 17–18. Ordeal procedure: Ordal 1:6; III Atr 6:2.

[42] Failure to find surety: II As 2–2:1; III As 7; III Em 7; III Eg 7–7:1; I Atr 3, 4; III Atr 5; II Cn 20, 33. Failure to provide surety: III As 7; III Em 7. Failing to buy goods with witnesses: I Ew 1–1:1; II As 10; IV Eg 11; I Atr 3. Informing neighbours about property: IV Eg 7–10; III Atr 9.

wrongdoers.[43] The most striking contrast with seventh-century precedents here is the focus on routine matters. The earlier laws penalized people who refused to submit to judgements, resorted to violence before seeking a judgement, made secret settlements, or harboured fugitives—they focused on people actively doing wrong.[44] The late Anglo-Saxon laws do this as well, but as the preceding lists make clear they focus much more strongly on omissions—on people who fail to do what they ought. Again, then, we have a shift in punitive priorities as part of a significant intensification of royal interest in the punishment of procedural violations.

The evidence for theft permits us to go into more detail. Ine's laws, as was noted in Chapter 2, range quite widely in their approach to thieves: the various punishments imagined include flogging (for slaves), the payment of a fine, wergild forfeiture, property forfeiture, enslavement, mutilation, and execution. It is clear that theft was the main target of royal punitive ambitions in this early period, prompting a range of different measures that seem likely largely to have aligned with existing ideas about the social harm cause by the secrecy of theft and the need for disproportionate punishment to be inflicted when thieves were caught in the act.[45] In our late Anglo-Saxon evidence, however, we have a series of texts that allow us to construct a much more detailed picture of a determined king creating and attempting to implement rules that increased the severity of punishment for theft. These texts are associated with assemblies that took place during the reign of King Æthelstan (924–39), and although none can be dated to specific years the order in which they took place can be established. Our first text is from an assembly at Grately (Hampshire), and there followed assemblies in Exeter, Faversham (Kent), Thunderfield (Surrey), London, and Whittlebury (Northamptonshire).[46]

Æthelstan's first known pronouncements on theft, those in the Grately code, begin with the statement 'first, no thief shall be spared, who is seized in the act, if he

[43] Refusal to participate: II Ew 2; II As 20:2, 22:2; VI As 8:5; Hu 3, 5:1; III Eg 7:2; I Atr 1:8–1:9; II Cn 25:2, 29, 29:1, 30:7–30:9, 33:2. Obstruction and protection of wrongdoers: II Ew 5:2, 7; II As 3–3:2, 7, 20:7, 20:8; IV As 3:1, 4; V As Prol:3, 1; VI As 8:3; III Em 3, 6:3; Hu 6; IV Eg 13–14; I Atr 1:12–1:13; III Atr 13; II Cn 13:2, 15a, 31:1a–31:2; 33:1a; 66:1.

[44] Hl 8–9; Ine 8, 9, 13, 30, 52. Ine 51, the fine for failure to perform military service is an exception.

[45] Ine 7–7:1, 10, 12, 18, 35–7, 43–4, 48, 57, 72–3. See Chapter 2, pp. 99–102.

[46] VI As Prol; VI As 10. II Æthelstan is a record of the assembly at Grately; V Æthelstan that in Exeter; III Æthelstan either the assembly at Faversham or another closely associated Kentish assembly; IV Æthelstan the Thunderfield assembly. VI Æthelstan is a long text from London with several smaller texts, including that associated with Whittlebury, appended to it. There is debate about which texts are 'official' records of assemblies and which are 'private' (a distinction of no significance here) and about whether the Kentish assembly from which III Æthelstan emerged was in fact the assembly at Faversham or separate from it (again, insignificant in the present context). For detailed discussion, see Wormald, *Making of English Law*, pp. 291–308; Simon Keynes, 'Royal Government and the Written Word in Late Anglo-Saxon England', in Rosamond McKitterick, ed., *The Uses of Literacy in Medieval Europe* (Cambridge, 1990), pp. 226–57, at 235–41; Levi Roach, 'Law Codes and Legal Norms in Later Anglo-Saxon England', *Historical Research* 86 (2013), pp. 465–86, at 468–79; Sarah Foot, *Æthelstan: the First King of England* (New Haven, 2011), pp. 136–48; David Pratt, 'Written Law and the Communication of Authority in Tenth-Century England', in David Rollason, Conrad Leyser and Hannah Williams, eds., *England and the Continent in the Tenth Century: Studies in Honour of Wilhelm Levison (1876–1947)* (Turnhout, 2010), pp. 331–50.

is over twelve years old and [if the value of the stolen goods] is more than eight pence'.[47] The idea that thieves caught in the act could legitimately be killed must have been well established—it is evident in both seventh-century and tenth-century laws, and there is no reason to think it had been forgotten in intervening centuries—but this need not imply that such executions routinely took place. The most plausible interpretation of this statement is that it is insisting on a stricter implementation of existing punishments and trying to establish, perhaps for the first time, clear criteria governing when merciful treatment of thieves caught in the act was permitted.[48]

Æthelstan's later legislation, however, represents a significant break from punitive tradition. The second (Exeter) text begins with an expression of frustration: 'I, King Æthelstan, declare that I have learned that our peace (*frið*) has not been kept to the extent either of my wishes, or of the provisions laid down at Grately. And my counsellors say that I have suffered this too long.' It seems that the king and his advisers decided they wished to increase the severity of punishment for theft radically, and that they thought carefully about how they could most effectively bring this about. The solution they arrived at was to proclaim an amnesty for thieves, such that those who committed theft could for a specified period compensate their victims without suffering any punishment, thus giving everyone ample opportunity painlessly to rid themselves of all taint of theft before the dawn of a new, distinctly merciless order. Both our second and third texts (the Exeter code and the Kentish text associated with Faversham) contain proclamations of such amnesties, whereas our record of the fourth (Thunderfield) assembly formally announces their end, issuing new laws that applied only to thefts that took place after that assembly.[49] Unfortunately, most of this last text survives only in the twelfth-century Latin of the *Quadripartitus*, though we do have a small fragment of a somewhat less flowery Old English version. It is worth quoting at length (this is from the *Quadripartitus* version):

> And if there is a thief who has committed theft since the council was held at Thunderfield, and is still engaged in thieving, he shall in no way be judged worthy of life, neither by claiming protection nor by making monetary payment, if the charge is truly substantiated against him – whether it is a freeman or a slave, a noble or a commoner, or, if it is a woman, whether she is a mistress or a maid – whosoever it may be, whether taken in the act or not taken in the act, if it is known for certainty – that is

---

[47] II As 1.

[48] That this rule was perceived as strict by contemporaries is evident from the fact that the king was later pressured into greater leniency: the Whittlebury text declares that the king now 'thinks it cruel to put to death such young people and for such slight offences' and raises the relevant thresholds to twelve pence and fifteen years (VI As 12:1, 12:3). However, it did not fundamentally depart from older ideas about appropriate punishment. In their essentials Æthelstan's initial statements on theft accord with established assumptions that thieves caught red-handed should be killed (visible in the laws of Wihtred and Ine: Wi 25–26:1; Ine 12, 35) and that thieves proven guilty by other means should pay a fine (visible in Alfred's laws: Af 9:1–9:2—though note that the threshold used here to distinguish between thefts that warrant higher and lower fines equates to 150 pence).

[49] III As 3; IV As 6; V As 3:1.

if he shall not make a statement of denial – or if the charge is proved in the ordeal, or if his guilt becomes known in any other way.[50]

The Old English fragment begins at this point, and both versions explain that thieves can if they wish seek a variety of powerful protectors (king, archbishop, church buildings, bishops, abbots, ealdormen, and thegns, with some slight discrepancies in detail between the two texts) but that they would only be entitled to protection for a period of either nine or three days (depending on the rank of the protector) after which they would inevitably face execution.[51] As the Old English text puts it: 'but let him seek whatever protection (*socn*) he may, his life shall be spared only for as many days as we have declared above'.[52]

The thrust of Æthelstan's attempt to change the punishment of theft was thus that thieves were to die, not only if they were caught in the act but also if they were accused and proven guilty by other means.[53] This shift had a discernible impact in later legislation, but this need not imply it was a long-term success. Edmund, Æthelstan's successor, explicitly thanks his *witan* for the *frið* (peace) they now enjoy from theft in one of his laws, and in another he orders that all men unite to seize anyone who had been proven a thief.[54] Both Edgar and Cnut likewise issued laws including analogous orders that thieves be executed no matter what protection (*socn*) they sought; however, it is notable that these passages' language may well indicate that they applied only to thieves caught in the act.[55] A passage in one of Æthelred's laws, which asserts that people who had never failed in ordeal, nor broken an oath, nor paid *ðeofgyld*, ought to be entitled to deny a charge on oath, is also rather telling.[56] The possibility of paying something termed 'thief-payment' and living to be treated with suspicion by one's neighbours implies that some thieves were not executed in the way that Æthelstan appears to have wished. Indeed, we should probably question whether it was ever a realistic aspiration to impose capital punishment on all thieves, however their guilt was proven, in defiance of centuries of engrained tradition.

Nevertheless, the seriousness with which Æthelstan appears to have taken the task of instituting legal change is striking. Rather than simply announce the new and merciless regime, the ground was prepared carefully with an amnesty that was presumably intended to pre-empt attempts to challenge the legitimacy of the initiative with complaints about unfairness. It seems likely, moreover, that local

---

[50] IV As 6.   [51] IV As 6:1–6:2.   [52] IV As 6:2c.

[53] It is potentially problematic that we rely so heavily on the *Quadripartitus* text for this conclusion, but it is probably safe. Æthelstan's amnesty on thieves (discussed above), which we know about from other texts, implies an attempt to prepare for a very significant reform. This measure fits its context perfectly.

[54] II Em 5; III Em 2.

[55] III Eg 7:3; II Cn 26. The thieves are specifically described as *æbære*, 'manifest', which should almost certainly be taken to mean that their guilt was undeniable (DOE s.v. 'æbære'). The most common circumstance in which thieves' guilt could be established undeniably was, of course, capture in the act (however, see Chapter 6, pp. 268–74). I did not properly appreciate this when I wrote T. B. Lambert, 'Theft, Homicide and Crime in Late Anglo-Saxon Law', *Past and Present* 214 (2012), pp. 3–43, and would now express the argument on pp. 17–18 rather more cautiously.

[56] I Atr 1:2. This passage is reiterated in II Cn 30:1. See also III Atr 4.

elites were ordered to hold large-scale assemblies to implement the king's scheme in their regions, and that at least some were monitored to ensure that they did so. The fact that the Kentish text begins by protesting that the assembly had undertaken their task 'with all the zeal of which we were capable, and with the help of the councillors whom you have sent us', and ends with a plea for the king's mercy, suggests a central determination to ensure that these measures really were implemented in the localities.[57] Moreover, we might reasonably suspect that the written responses that survive from this Kentish assembly and from the similar one representing London are unusual mainly in their having been written down and preserved: there may well have been other local and regional assemblies which left no written record. The overriding impression is of a concerted and carefully planned effort by the king and his immediate circle to ensure that the changes being made were regarded as legitimate and properly implemented by local elites. We can even see the king reacting to objections about excessive cruelty, using the final council at Whittlebury to make changes to the thresholds for compulsory capital punishment established in the first assembly at Grately: thieves were now only to be executed if they were over fifteen and their stolen goods worth more than twelve pence.[58] That it was necessary to go to such lengths to conciliate local goodwill tells us something important about kings' ability to introduce new punishments in the first half of the tenth century: it was far from easy, and even concerted efforts could not hope to be fully effective.

For present purposes, however, the key significance of Æthelstan's campaign against theft is that it allows us to see the increased punitive ambition of tenth-century kings in much greater definition than was the case for either religious or procedural offences. The picture is essentially the same—intensification within an established sphere of royal punitive activity—but this example also allows us some insight into the seriousness of purpose that lay behind this intensification. The cruelty of these reforms should not distract us from their powerful idealism. It is hard to read these texts and doubt either that Æthelstan genuinely cared about theft or that his concerns resonated with his aristocracy.[59] This, like the regulation of legal practice and the enforcement of minimum standards of Christian observance among the laity, was precisely what good Anglo-Saxon kings had been meant to do for at least two centuries. The late Anglo-Saxon period, it seems, saw kings taking their traditional punitive role more seriously than their predecessors, with at least some devoting considerable energy and political capital to its rigorous fulfilment.

---

[57] III As 1, epilogue.   [58] See above, p. 175, n. 48.

[59] The rhetoric of royal frustration and even some of the penalties that characterize this legislation ('the enmity of the king and all his friends'—II As 20:7, and also later: II Em 1:3; III Em 2) are suggestive of personal involvement by the king, though it is possible that this is misleading. Stronger evidence for Æthelstan's personal commitment to the issue is the frequency with which it is addressed: we know of several royal assemblies on the subject and two local ones organized to implement royal decrees. It seems unlikely that this level of activity could have been prompted without the king's personal commitment (if the process were being driven by an ecclesiastical adviser, for instance). For an attempt to access Æthelstan's personal motivations through his laws, see Foot, *Æthelstan*, pp. 145–8.

The laws' evidence of intensified punishment within these three traditional fields of royal punitive activity is consistent with evidence derived from other sources, although it should be noted that on their own these other sources are rather ambiguous. If we first examine the evidence of aristocratic land forfeitures for wrongdoing derived (primarily) from charters, we find patterns suggestive of both intensification and a focus on theft.[60] As was noted above, this sort of evidence is virtually absent before the tenth century. Forfeitures with no obvious political dimensions start to appear at the very beginning of the tenth century and become relatively frequent occurrences by its second half. Although this could simply reflect changes in the nature of the source-base—both the larger number of documents that survive from the later period and evolutions in their form—it is certainly possible that the emergence of evidence for punitive land-forfeiture among the aristocracy is a manifestation of a more general intensification of royal punitive efforts. Many of these forfeitures are non-specific—we learn only that land has been forfeited for some form of wrongdoing—but where offences are detailed theft is the most common, and there are a few examples of forfeitures for marital irregularities, also a notable punitive focus in legislation.[61] Procedural punishments are harder to gauge. In some of these cases we should probably imagine that forfeiture of land was a result of a refusal or failure to pay a fine rather than a direct result of the initial offence: this is explicitly stated in one unusually thoroughly described case but it is precisely the sort of detail likely to be omitted from most of our records, which tend to mention the causes of forfeitures only in passing.[62] This material, at any rate, gives us no reason to doubt the laws' impression of intensified punitive efforts relating to theft, religious offences, and procedural violations.

The archaeology of execution is also broadly consistent with the picture outlined here. Wormald was one of the first to notice the implications of this growing corpus of evidence, and argued that it was likely to reflect the generalized intensification of royal punishment in the late Anglo-Saxon period.[63] It is true that Andrew Reynolds's re-evaluation of the corpus, including a survey of all relevant radiocarbon dated skeletons from 'execution cemeteries', suggests a much broader chronology than had previously been recognized, beginning in the seventh century and persisting into the twelfth, with no clear indication of a late Anglo-Saxon

---

[60] Wormald, 'Handlist' pp. 284–6. For discussion of land forfeiture as a punishment for both aristocratic and non-elite wrongdoers, see Chapter 7, pp. 317–21.

[61] Forfeitures for which the specific offence is unknown: Wormald, 'Handlist', nos. 33, 36, 44, 48, 63, 72, 73, 81, 88, 97, 99, 101, 107, 118, 131. Forfeitures for theft: nos. 25, 37, 41, 45, 56, 100, 129. Forfeitures for marital or sexual offences: nos. 29, 53, 68.

[62] The detailed case is from the 950s: S 1447; Wormald, 'Handlist', nos. 38–9; A. J. Robertson, ed., *Anglo-Saxon Charters* (2nd edn; Cambridge, 1956), no. 44. A certain Æthelstan was found guilty of stealing a woman (presumably a slave); he gave her up and paid compensation for her but did not have the money to pay his forfeited wergild and refused to allow his brother to do so on his behalf. In the absence of payment his land was forfeited to the king and regranted to an ealdorman.

[63] Patrick Wormald, 'Frederic William Maitland and the Earliest English Law', repr.in and cited from Wormald, *Legal Culture*, p. 45–69, at 61; Patrick Wormald, *Papers Preparatory to the Making of English Law: King Alfred to the Twelfth Century*, vol. 2: *From God's Law to Common Law*, ed. Stephen Baxter and John Hudson (University of London, 2014) <http://www.earlyenglishlaws.ac.uk/reference/wormald/>, pp. 129–38.

intensification.[64] However, this does not disprove that there was a late Anglo-Saxon shift towards more severe punishment, or even executions, as the body of evidence under analysis—a total of nineteen radiocarbon date-ranges from only seven cemeteries—is small and possibly unrepresentative. It gives a sense of the period in which this tradition of burying executed corpses in separate cemeteries was to some degree active, not of when it reached its height. The late Anglo-Saxon period remains the most plausible time to imagine this happening, but we should remember that such assessments of plausibility rest on inferences drawn from the written source material much more than firm archaeological dating evidence. Reynolds's assembly of associated evidence from charter boundary clauses is perhaps more directly revealing, in that it includes two references to places which unambiguously associate locations of execution and burial with theft ('where the thieves lie' and 'where the thieves hang'); he found no toponyms which explicitly associate execution with other forms of wrongdoing.[65] The only possible exception to this—'the place where the *ceorl* [was] slain because of the goat'—could be read as a reference to execution for either theft or sexual misconduct.[66] Again, this evidence is consistent with the picture drawn from the laws but it can only independently attest to the basic point that execution for wrongdoing, especially theft, was a part of contemporary socio-legal practice.

It is important to contextualize the apparent increase in intensity of royal punishment that is observable in this period. A conventional historiographical reading of this greater emphasis on the punishment of wrongdoing would be that it represented a significant step in the growth of the state, and in the establishment of what Wormald termed a 'developed notion of crime and punishment'.[67] We need to remember, however, that contemporaries would not have understood it in these terms. Punishment was not an end in itself for late Anglo-Saxon kings. Rather, it was a tool they could use in support of specific aims. For instance, when we think about kings prescribing punishments for laymen who failed to observe minimum standards of Christian observance, we should remember that these punishments form part of a broader royal concern about religious matters that found expression in law. Notably, they sit alongside royal protections of ecclesiastical personnel and ecclesiastical space—significant themes in late Anglo-Saxon legislation which are discussed below.[68] They also fit with laws concerned with the proper behaviour of churchmen, covering clerical celibacy and various forms of secular misconduct, as well as outlining more positive requirements (specifically, that psalms be sung and masses said for the king).[69]

---

[64] Reynolds, *Deviant Burial*, pp. 153–5.   [65] Ibid., pp. 277–8.
[66] Ibid., p. 281. A context of bestiality may also be implied by the skeletal evidence assembled at p. 172.
[67] Wormald, 'God and King', p. 342.
[68] Below, pp. 186, 189. Specific offences include the molestation of nuns, theft from churches, attacking priests in various ways, and breaches of ecclesiastical sanctuary: Af 2, 5, 6, 8, 18; II As 5; II Eg 5:3; VI Atr 13–14; VIII Atr 1–5, 33–4; I Cn 2–3; II Cn 40, 42, 49.
[69] Celibacy: I Em 1; IV Eg 1:6–7; V Atr 9; VI Atr 5, 41; I Cn 6a-6:2a. Secular misconduct: VIII Atr 18–30; I Cn 5; II Cn 41, 43. Psalms and masses: V As 3; VII Atr 6.

These wider ecclesiastical concerns, however, are notable precisely for their lack of secular penalties: misbehaving clerics are threatened with unconsecrated burial and the loss of their ecclesiastical office, and, they are warned that bishops have whatever secular assistance they need in the enforcement of ecclesiastical discipline, unless they refuse to cooperate once defrocked they are not subject to royal punishment.[70] Secular punishment thus sits alongside royal protections and ecclesiastical discipline as one of several tools used in royal legislation on religious matters, a tool appropriate for some tasks but evidently not others.

A similar case can be made for theft. The specification of punishments is in fact a surprisingly small element of late Anglo-Saxon legislation on theft. Æthelstan's attempts to increase the severity of punishment for thieves are not representative; in general much more attention is given to measures intended to ensure that thieves were identified and prosecuted than to specifying what punishments they ought to suffer. Indeed, most late Anglo-Saxon procedural regulations are targeted at theft. This is the case not only for those concerned with thieves directly—failing to participate in or actively obstructing their apprehension—but all those procedures associated with property. The point of ordering that all sales be witnessed and that neighbours be notified whenever livestock were acquired or consumed was to make it harder for thieves to keep or sell stolen property.[71] Even the requirement for all men to be under surety was directly associated with theft.[72] Late Anglo-Saxon anti-theft measures were mostly focused on the establishment of communal procedures and only indirectly concerned with punishment.[73] Though the threat of punishment underpins these procedural structures in important ways, it was only one part of a multi-layered legislative effort primarily targeted at theft.

While punishment is a central theme of this chapter, then, it is crucial that we keep it in perspective. As historians it is legitimate for us to be interested specifically in royal punishment and to isolate the punitive trends in our evidence for the purpose of analysis, but we should not fall into the trap of supposing that our concerns were shared by contemporaries. The intensification of punishment discernible in this period is just one part of a larger picture, and not necessarily the

---

[70] Unconsecrated burial: V As 3. Loss of ecclesiastical office: VIII Atr 26–7; I Cn 5: 3; II Cn 41. Secular enforcement of episcopal authority: IV Eg 1:8; II Cn 43.

[71] This is most obvious in IV Eg 3–14:2.   [72] III Eg 6–6:2.

[73] These procedures are discussed in detail in Chapter 6. And while many of the legal procedures that appear in late Anglo-Saxon laws were associated with punishments for those who failed to comply, we should recognize that these punishments were often several removes away from the laws' overall aims. These usually focused on making life difficult for thieves in various ways; the observance of the procedures themselves was a secondary contribution to that primary goal. The punishments for breaching those procedures might thus be thought of as tertiary elements of the legislative enterprise. Indeed, some measures involve even more elaborate chains. For instance, there are several laws designed to force people to find sureties, penalizing those who fail to do so. Among these are laws that envisage enforcement expeditions against often-accused men, which would either force such men to find sureties or kill them. All men were expected to take part in these expeditions, and penalties are specified for those who refused. These penalties are thus punishments designed to enforce the observance of a legal obligation to help punish the breach of (and thus enforce the observance of) a different legal obligation (to have surety), which itself seems primarily designed to help suppress theft. See I Atr 4–4:3; II Cn 25–25:2.

most prominent. It would be wrong to imagine that kings in this period understood their establishment of new punishments as part of a general effort to make royal punishment a more important part of law and thus to make the late Anglo-Saxon kingdom more impressively state-like. Increasing the number and severity of royal punishments was not a strategic aim; the promulgation of new rules specifying punishments, rather, was one of the tools kings used in pursuit of their legal ambitions, and perhaps not even the most important. To understand the role of punishment in the late Anglo-Saxon period, the simple conclusion that its use intensified is thus inadequate. We need to understand *why* punishment mattered to contemporaries, the ideals in pursuit of which punishments were imposed. This issue is addressed in detail in Chapter 5.

VIOLENCE AND ITS REGULATION

Here, however, the priority is to establish how much the shape of the early medieval legal order changed in the late Anglo-Saxon period. Do we find kings extending their punitive role beyond its traditional spheres, so that it covered violent offences in a way that previously it had not? Or was the late Anglo-Saxon legal landscape essentially similar to that of the late seventh century, kings engaging with violence primarily through the extension of protection, while punishment remained confined to theft, procedural offences and religious misconduct? The evidence strongly favours the latter position, with only a few minor and explicable exceptions. The most salient fact to keep in focus is the lack of punishments for violence in the laws. They contain no indication of any significant new royal punishment for homicide, non-lethal violence or rape, and this absence cannot reasonably be ignored. As the preceding analysis amply demonstrates, our evidence for late Anglo-Saxon law is extensive and provides plentiful material on royal punishment within its traditional spheres; it is hard to imagine how or why significant new punishments for violent offences could have existed without leaving a trace in this evidence.[74]

In part this is an argument from silence: it relies on the notion that a legal change as significant as the extension of royal punishment to violent offences would appear in our copious legislative evidence. It is more than just this, however. It is important to note that the laws can frequently be found positively recognizing the legitimacy of feuding, which of course involved the threat and occasional use of violence by affronted parties. In part we can see this in the consistent assumption that seventh-century arrangements for dealing with homicide remained current. Ine's laws outline three payments for homicide: the wergild to the slain man's family, a sum known as *manbot* to his lord, and the apparently punitive (though perhaps originally protective) *wite* to the king.[75] These three payments appear in both

---

[74] Wormald's central justification for dismissing this consideration—that the laws represent an intellectual genre out of step with legal practice—is discussed below (p. 197, n. 148) and challenged directly in the Introduction (p. 21, n. 58).

[75] Ine 6:4, 70.

Edmund's and Cnut's laws.[76] Indeed, they recur again in the post-Conquest treatises, most notably in this passage from the *Leges Henrici Primi* that purports to describe contemporary law:

> If any Englishman is slain without fault on his part, compensation shall be paid to his relatives according to the amount of his wergild and the custom of the district relating to wergild. *Wite* and *manbot* shall be paid to the appropriate lords as justice requires, in accordance with the amount of the deceased's wergild.[77]

Other references, moreover, suggest that feuding remained a legitimate practice. It can scarcely be ignored that early eleventh-century laws written by Archbishop Wulfstan explicitly acknowledge that priests accused of homicide were, along with their families, legitimate targets for vengeance in feud.[78] In Wulfstan's mind, at least, it seems that monks were the only ones who were exempt from paying and receiving feud compensations (*fæhðbote*), because they had left their 'kin-law' (*mægðlage*) when they accepted 'rule-law' (*regollage*).[79] This implies that feuding remained a legitimate element of legal practice for everyone else. The regulations of the Cambridge Thegns' Guild, also probably dating from around the turn of the millennium, are likewise explicit on the legitimacy of violent vengeance in certain circumstances, ordering that slain guild-brothers be avenged by the guild should adequate compensation not be paid.[80]

The broad picture, then, is clear enough. There is no evidence for any significant new royal punishments for violence, but there are repeated indications both that feud continued to be understood as a legitimate element of legal practice and that the legal framework surrounding homicide, at least, remained essentially as it had been in the seventh century. The most striking feature of late Anglo-Saxon legislation here is this essential continuity with the traditional model for resolving cases of wrongdoing involving violence, a model which was evidently inherited from late seventh-century law and which the late seventh century in turn had largely inherited from the pre-Christian period.

The only evidence that directly opposes this impression appears in Cnut's laws, which prescribe penitential pilgrimage and the payment of compensation as the proper course of action for both killers of priests and priests who killed.[81] Again, these two passages tell against the idea that kings had any interest in prohibiting feuding outright; if it was possible to kill a priest without incurring punishment the same must surely have been true of laymen. However, this is not their most

---

[76] II Em 3–4, 7–7:3; I Cn 2:5 (for *manbot* and with *mægbot* representing wergild); II Cn 15 (*fihtwite*, albeit in a Danelaw context).

[77] Hn 69:1. For the other post-Conquest treatises: ECf 12:3–12:6; Leis Wl 7–11:2. I emphasize the *Leges Henrici* here because that text's representation of homicide law is central to Naomi Hurnard's argument for royal punishment, discussed below: pp. 197–9.

[78] VIII Atr 23; I Cn 5:2b.

[79] That is, when they vowed to follow a monastic rule. VIII Atr 25; I Cn 5:2d.

[80] Benjamin Thorpe, ed., *Diplomatarium Anglicum Ævi Saxonicum: A Collection of English Charters from the Reign of King Æthelberht of Kent to That of William the Conqueror* (London, 1864), pp. 611–12.

[81] II Cn 39–39:1, 41–41:2.

significant element: both passages make clear that penitential pilgrimage and compensation to the dead man's kin are to be imposed on the killer under threat of severe royal punishment. Unless the killers began to make amends to both God and men within thirty days they would either forfeit all their property (if they were killers of priests) or be outlawed (if they were priests who killed).[82] This is the first solid sign we have that English kings wished to enforce the payment of compensation for homicide.[83] If this had been generalized to all killings and consistently enforced its effects could have been momentous: homicide would no longer need to be a matter for feud, because the compensation it required would be imposed by the state rather than the dead man's family. However, except in the specific circumstances described in Cnut's laws, to argue that the payment of wergild for homicide was enforced under threat of royal penalties in eleventh-century England would be to engage in unwarranted speculation. Indeed, as has just been noted, the ecclesiastical section of this same code contradicts one of these laws, presenting the payment of compensation as optional in the case of homicidal priests. No royal involvement is imagined in cases of non-payment; instead, the priest and his kinsmen are expected to 'bear the feud', accepting whatever the consequences of the killing proved to be.[84] As there is no evidence to suggest that English kings ever tried to enforce compensation settlements in feuds between laymen these passages are something of an analytical dead end, but it is important to keep them in mind. They make it clear that contemporaries regarded the ideal solution to homicide cases to be compensation and penance, and they show that in the early eleventh century it was thinkable that kings might wish to enforce adherence to this ideal in cases involving clergymen.

Core Royal Protections

Violent feuding thus appears to have remained part of legitimate legal practice in the late Anglo-Saxon period, and there is no sign that kings ever contemplated challenging this in principle except in cases involving clergymen. This does not mean that they were unconcerned by violence, however. Rather, it reflects the fact that the main thrust of laws relating to violence in this period was not outright prohibition but more stringent regulation, primarily through the inventive use of royal protections. Most notably, by the end of the Anglo-Saxon period the king's protection extended to all churches, all houses and all major roads; it was also available on a personal basis through local royal officials (albeit probably at a price). The cumulative effect of these protections must have been significant. For those trying to kill someone, the impossibility of doing so in any of these protected locations without offending the king must have presented a major obstacle,

---

[82] II Cn 39:1; 41:2. These seem likely to be different ways of referring to the same punishment.

[83] This is essentially the approach that Carolingian kings took to feuding. See Alfred Boretius, ed., *Capitularia Regum Francorum*, 2 vols. (Monumenta Germaniae Historica, Legum sectio II, Hanover, 1883–97), i, 51 (no. 20, ch. 22); i, 97 (no. 33, ch. 32); i, 123 (no. 44, ch. 5); i, 284 (no. 139, ch. 13).

[84] I Cn 5:2b.

especially as in the context of feud potential victims were likely to be alert to the danger and consciously taking advantage of the protections available to them. If a vengeance target felt threatened enough to procure the king's personal protection from a local royal agent there was no way of harming him at all without incurring major liabilities to the king. Some killings, and presumably a lot of non-lethal violence, would have resulted from unanticipated confrontations in contexts where legal protections were far from the protagonists' minds. Doubtless these royal protections would have caught some of these simply because they covered some of the main locations where people met one another and spent their time, but their effect on behaviour would certainly have been greatest in the context of enmities, informing the decisions of those calculating how best to kill or avoid being killed.

Many of these royal protections seem to have been late Anglo-Saxon innovations and, insofar as the limited evidence available allows us to reconstruct their emergence with any reliability, it appears that the law code known as II Edmund was a watershed moment. This is most obvious for the offence of *hamsocn*: attacking someone in a house.[85] The first known use of the term is in this code, where it is ordered that people committing *hamsocn* are to forfeit their property and lives to the king.[86] As far as can be gathered from post-Conquest Latin sources (our Old English texts clearly assumed that it needed no elucidation) the term was associated specifically with violence committed in houses by external attackers, not by those already within the house. (However, we should be wary of accepting this exclusion, like other fine distinctions visible only in later sources, as accurate for the Anglo-Saxon period.)[87] This would make the scenario envisaged for the offence of *hamsocn* essentially that treated in this passage from Alfred's law code:

> Moreover we command: that the man who knows his opponent to be dwelling at home is not to fight before he asks justice for himself. If he has sufficient power to surround his opponent and besiege him there in his house, he is to keep him seven days inside and not fight against him, if he will remain inside; and then after seven days, if

---

[85] A great deal of useful material on this offence is assembled in Rebecca V. Colman, 'Hamsocn: Its Meaning and Significance in Early English Law', *American Journal of Legal History* 95 (1981), pp. 95–110.

[86] II Em 6.

[87] The most extensive discussion is in the *Leges Henrici Primi*, which begins with the statement 'Hamsocn which in Latin means attack on a house (*quod domus inuasionem Latine sonat*) occurs in several ways as a result of both external and internal circumstances' (Hn 80:10). This agrees with our other Latin texts from the period, which tend to translate *hamsocn* as some variation on *domus invasio* (In Cn II, 12, 15; Cons Cn II, 12, 15; Quadr II Cn 12, 15). The *Leges Henrici* go on to provide a series of not entirely consistent statements about *hamsocn* which nevertheless are united by the understanding that the offence involved an attack on someone within any house (indeed, any building) by someone coming from outside. It is implied that if a fight starts among those within a house it only becomes *hamsocn* if one of those involved flees to another building (with a separate roof) and is attacked within (Hn 80:11c). A different and otherwise unattested offence of *insocna* or *infiht* is said to cover violence within houses that resulted from internal strife rather than external attack (80:12). Whether this distinction existed in the Anglo-Saxon period is unclear, however. Indeed, the *Leges Henrici*'s initial statement that *hamsocn* could occur in several ways as a result of both external and internal circumstances (*extrinsecis et intrinsecis accidentis*) is, if not a reference to violence arising from both external attackers and internal conflict, very obscure indeed.

he will surrender and give up his weapons, he is to keep him unharmed for thirty days, and send notice to his kinsmen and his friends.[88]

Importantly, there is no sign in Alfred's legislation of a penalty for failing to respect the protection of the house. If, after the anticipated surrender, someone attacked the man who was meant to remain unharmed, Alfred envisaged nothing beyond the payment of the fine and compensation appropriate to the offence (except that the attacking kindred should forfeit the claim they were prosecuting in this way, which is assumed to be for the death of a kinsman).[89] Edmund's insistence on total forfeiture for attacking an enemy in a house half a century later thus appears to have been an innovation.

Edmund's code is also significant for containing the first reference to the offence of *mundbryce* ('protection-breach'), which appears in the same clause as *hamsocn* with the same penalty of full forfeiture of life and property. Kings had long been able to place specific people under their personal protection, with the standard value of that protection being the king's *mundbyrd* ('protection-value'): £5 from Alfred's laws onwards.[90] The novel terminology of *mundbryce* may simply reflect Edmund's insistence that compensation by payment of *mundbyrd* should no longer be possible—some new language was necessary—but it could be that in it we can detect a sign of a more significant shift, which saw the king's protection go from being something dependent on a personal grant by the king himself to being available locally from royal agents. That this shift took place is made explicit by the *Leges Henrici Primi*, which state that breach of the protection conferred by the king's own hand would result in mutilation, whereas breach of the king's protection as granted by royal officials rendered the offender liable to the king for £5.[91] This two-tier understanding of the king's protection is also visible in Cnut's laws, where we can see both protection granted by the king's own hand (*handgrið*), breaches of which would result in the forfeiture of life and property to the king, and the offences of *mundbryce* and *griðbryce* for which £5 is appropriate compensation.[92] (*Grið* is a term with Scandinavian roots meaning both 'peace' and 'protection' that first entered Anglo-Saxon legal vocabulary in the late tenth century and seems to have displaced *mund* as the primary means of referring to the king's protection in the eleventh.)[93]

Edmund does not outline a two-tier system—all breaches of his *mund* are to result in forfeiture—but there are some hints that he might have envisaged it as being available from his agents as well as from him personally. It is in this code that we find our first reference to the king's *mund* being established independently of the king, in a passage (discussed further below) allowing the parties settling a feud to perform a ceremony placing all of them under royal protection.[94] It is also notable that the offence is simply called *mundbryce*, not *cyninges mundbryce*; indeed, there is nothing in the text that explicitly links the protection under discussion to the king's person. This is hardly conclusive, of course, but we know that at some

[88] Af 42–42:1.   [89] Af 42:4.   [90] Af 3.   [91] Hn 79:3–79:4.
[92] I Cn 2:2, 2:5, 3:1; II Cn 12, 15.   [93] DOE s.v. 'grið'.   [94] II Em 7:3.

point royal protection became something royal agents could grant, and Edmund's legislation shows both a clear interest in reforming and extending protections, and some signs that the king's *mund* was coming to be regarded as less personal. At any rate, there are no indications that royal officials were granting the king's protection on his behalf before this point, so again this looks to have been a late Anglo-Saxon innovation.

II Edmund also marks a departure in terms of royal protection of churches, placing them on a par with the king's own residence and threatening full forfeiture of life and property for anyone who attacked someone sheltering in one.[95] This definitely represents an increase in severity but it was perhaps not as significant a departure as the protection of houses represented by *hamsocn*. Alfred's code contains a passage detailing the treatment of men who flee to churches in exactly the same terms as for those sheltering in their own homes: the same scheme of seven days unmolested within followed by surrender and thirty days in the custody of enemies. For churches, however, there is a penalty for breach: anyone attacking the man in the church would owe the king his *mundbyrd* of £5 and the church an unspecified sum for its peace (*frið*).[96] Other statements on violence in churches before Edmund's reign are less clear about royal involvement. Ine's laws demand a 120-shilling payment to a monastery for fighting within it, a figure reiterated in a different section of Alfred's law, whereas Æthelstan implies that the cost of attacking someone in a church was the church's own *mundbyrd*. None of these laws makes any reference to a royal protection.[97] It may be, then, that Alfred attempted to introduce a royal protection for all churches which had not previously existed, and that Edmund's law represents an attempt to reinforce it with harsher penalties. Indeed, it is possible Alfred's extension of royal protection was more theoretical than real—it is associated with what we must suspect is an unrealistically elaborate scheme for both church- and house-protection, and Æthelstan's laws show no awareness of its existence—and that Edmund was the one who established the idea firmly. At any rate, the notion that killing people in churches should result in full forfeiture of life and property seems to have been a consistent feature of Anglo-Saxon law from Edmund's time onwards.[98]

Edmund's reign thus emerges as a possible turning point in royal use of protections. This could be a trick of the evidence; it is perfectly possible that his laws, the only ones we have specifically concerned with the problem of violence, were recapitulating and reinforcing innovations made under earlier kings. However, Edmund certainly does seem to have introduced a new level of severity in treatment for breaches of royal protection: offenders were to forfeit all they owned and their lives were to be at the king's mercy. There is no sign of the king's protection being valued at £5 here. Later on, however, this sum re-emerges as the

---

[95] II Em 2.
[96] Af 5. Note that the use of the term *frið* here differs from the usage discussed in Chapter 5, pp. 207–10.
[97] Ine 6:1; Af 2; IV As 6:1.
[98] VIII Atr 1:1; I Cn 2:2. Though note it is not explicit in II Eg 5:3.

appropriate penalty for *hamsocn* and for *mundbryce* (or its later equivalent *griðbryce*) when that *mund* had been granted by an official rather than the king himself: there is some relaxation of Edmund's harshness. This can be seen to an extent in the protection of churches. In Wulfstan's legislation, Edmund's insistence on complete forfeiture remains for killings within churches but not for lesser acts of violence.[99] Edmund was thus at least responsible for an attempt to increase the effectiveness of royal protections by making the penalties for their breach more severe, and it is plausible that he was also responsible for the introduction of the new royal protection covering houses, the widening of the availability of the king's personal protection, and perhaps even the establishment of comprehensive royal protection for churches. But whether or not it is correct to link them to Edmund, it seems that these were all late Anglo-Saxon developments; we cannot find royal protections working in this way in seventh-century texts.

Edmund, however, does not appear to have established the king's protection of roads. Again, this is an offence attested in late Anglo-Saxon law but subject to clear exposition only in the *Leges Henrici Primi*, which state that 'if an assault is made on anyone on a royal road (*in uia regia*), this is the offence of *forsteal*, and compensation amounting to 100 shillings shall be paid to the king.'[100] (The shillings here are Norman shillings, making this sum equivalent to £5.) The text goes on to explain that a road 'which leads into a city or fortress or castle or royal town' was called a royal road, and that no penalty applied if two people met on a road and freely decided to fight one another: *forsteal* was only considered to have taken place when an attack was made on someone who wished to proceed peacefully.[101] We can perhaps see some of this in the Latin legal text known as IV Æthelred (traditionally but somewhat problematically dated to the late tenth-century) where the offence of 'attacking an innocent person *in uia regia*' is penalized with £5.[102] The picture is complicated by the fact that in some Anglo-Saxon laws the term *forsteal* is used to mean obstruction, of either the pursuit of thieves or the law generally, but in these cases the word seems to be being used loosely, to describe people being obstructive, rather than technically, to designate a particular offence called *forsteal*.[103] We first see it used in this more technical sense in the laws of

---

[99] VIII Atr 1–5:2; I Cn 2–3:2.   [100] Hn 80:2.

[101] Hn 80:3a, 80:4–80:4a. Various, and presumably unequal, specifications as to a royal road's proper width are given in Hn 80:3. A different tradition, that the king had only four named roads, can be found in ECf 12c, 12:7, 12:9. This, however, is dismissed as a literary fiction in Alan Cooper, 'The King's Four Highways: Legal Fiction Meets Fictional Law', *Journal of Medieval History* 26 (2000), pp. 351–70.

[102] IV Atr 4. For a discussion and revised translation of this passage see Alan Cooper, 'The Rise and Fall of the Anglo-Saxon Law of the Highway', *Haskins Society Journal* 12 (2002), pp. 39–69, at 53–5. The critique of this document's validity as a tenth-century source presented in Derek Keene, 'Text, Visualisation and Politics: London, 1150–1250', *Transactions of the Royal Historical Society* 18 (2008), pp. 66–99, at 93–4, applies only to the material on tolls in IV Atr 1–3. There is no reason to doubt that the passage in question here is Anglo-Saxon in origin, though Keene's arguments suggest that we should be cautious with the attribution to Æthelred. M.K. Lawson, *Cnut: England's Viking King* (2nd edn, Stroud, 2004), pp. 186–8, tentatively attributes the text to Cnut's reign.

[103] III Em 6; V Atr 31; VI Atr 38. The appearance of *forsteal* in III Em 6 could be read as a more technical usage: it appears as *foristeallum* in the Latin of the *Quadripartitus*, the only text we have for

Cnut, and it is thus probably reasonable to assume that royal protection of major roads was established at some point between the reigns of Edmund and Cnut, it being highly unlikely that it would have failed to appear in II Edmund had it existed at that time, given its obvious relevance to that code's themes. There is no solid evidence that any such protection existed in earlier legislation.[104]

The four protections just described are major themes in late Anglo-Saxon law. *Hamsocn, mundbryce* and *forsteal* are identified in Cnut's laws as three of four royal rights (the other being the fine for neglect of military service) which belonged solely to the king, unless he chose specifically to honour someone with their grant.[105] That is, no lord had the right to collect payment for these offences unless he could show a specific royal grant. They appear in this capacity in eleventh-century grants to a handful of major ecclesiastical institutions, and also in Domesday Book, again usually to list them among the rights reserved to the king. These were clearly regarded as important rights and, significantly, they were understood to be related. Not only do they tend to appear together, they all came to share the same £5 penalty associated with the king's protection since at least Alfred's reign.[106] The protection of churches does not fit quite so closely with this group because it was not a right kings were willing to grant to others in the same way, but its discussion in the laws is characterized by the language of *grið* and *mund* to the extent that the

---

this code. This should probably be taken to mean that the translator thought the word *forsteal* in the original was being used in a technical sense, but this would be an understandable error for a translator working at a time when *forsteal* clearly *was* understood as a technical legal term. The text makes most sense when it is translated in a non-technical way as 'obstruction' and it seems likely that this was how it was used in the original. For discussions that treat *forsteal* as a technical term the meaning of which shifted in the late tenth century—a scenario I now regards as unnecessarily elaborate—see Lambert, 'Protection, Feud and Royal Power', pp. 97–102; Lambert, 'Theft, Homicide and Crime', pp. 29–30; Cooper, 'Rise and Fall', p. 50.

[104] Though note that this does not mean the idea of royal responsibility for roads was unheard of. See Chapter 2, p. 65, n. 7, and Chapter 5, pp. 233–4.

[105] II Cn 12.

[106] For a fuller discussion, see Chapter 7, pp. 332–6, and T.B. Lambert, 'Royal Protections and Private Justice: A reassessment of Cnut's "Reserved Pleas"', in Jurasinski, Oliver and Rabin, eds., *English Law Before Magna Carta*, pp. 157–75. In historiographical terms, the notion that these protections were important royal rights is in direct opposition to the argument made in Naomi Hurnard, 'The Anglo-Norman Franchises', *English Historical Review* 64 (1949), pp. 289–327 and 433–60, at 302–10. Hurnard correctly perceived that *hamsocn, mundbryce* and *forsteal* were offences which aggravated other offences, but she argued that the only offences to which they could possibly have applied were very minor. This argument stems almost entirely from her belief that homicide was something the king already punished in its own right. As she put it, discussing what a grant of these three rights would have conveyed: 'It is absurd to assume that they were held to cover the more serious crimes, that any and every matter which could be alleged to be aggravated by such circumstances was conveyed by their grant. The lesser cannot be taken to cover the greater, the emendable to include the capital cause, the vaguer grant to override the specific reservation' (p. 303). Because she saw homicide as an offence subject to severe royal punishment in its own right, in other words, she thought these protective rights were superfluous to royal needs in homicide cases: they would only be of use to the king (and hence to any aristocrat granted them) in matters so minor as normally to be beneath royal attention. This characterization of royal protections as insignificant relies so fundamentally on the premise that homicide was a 'major crime' that it collapses—indeed, is essentially inverted—if we accept that this premise is false, as is argued here. Hurnard's reasons for considering homicide a 'major crime' are discussed below, pp. 197–9.

conceptual links are unmistakeable. These four major protections should be understood as a coherent and important group.

We can add some outliers to this group. Most notably, Cnut's laws tell us that there was a peace (*grið*) covering the army, a breach of which would result in either loss of life or wergild forfeiture, and that all those going to and from an assembly (*gemot*) were to enjoy protection (*grið*) unless they were notorious thieves.[107] Beyond this there are repeated but somewhat vaguer statements in Wulfstan's laws that kings should protect the clergy and foreigners, acting as protectors to them if they had no others, to the extent of avenging injuries to them.[108] We are also told that widows of a respectable life are to enjoy 'God's *grið* and the king's' and, more concretely, that anyone doing violence to a widow or virgin must forfeit his wergild.[109]

Whether there were royal protections for specific times before the Norman Conquest is less clear. The early twelfth-century text known as the *Leges Edwardi Confessoris*, which claims (albeit rather unconvincingly) to represent late Anglo-Saxon practice, includes temporally defined protections notionally covering everyone for periods of eight days at Easter, Pentecost and Christmas, as well as for eight days after the coronation of a king. A breach of any of these would, we are told, incur the same penalty as a violation of the protection given by the king's hand.[110] The *Leges Henrici*, too, appear to imply that royal protections applied during religious festivals.[111] Domesday passages for Chester and Dover refer to particular periods in which the sums owed to the king or his officials for wrongdoing increased dramatically.[112] It is certainly plausible that these represent late Anglo-Saxon practice in some way, but it is also possible that they reflect the enhanced post-Conquest influence of the continental Truce of God movement.[113] Anglo-Saxon laws do not envisage the protection of specific times as a royal function. Alfred's code states that all compensations for wrongdoing committed during Lent and whilst the army was away were to be doubled.[114] II Cnut calls the former offence *lencgtenbryce*, and explains that it can be committed by fighting (*fihtlac*), sexual activity with women (*wiflac*) or robbery (*reaflac*) 'or by any great misdeed' and that it also applied on high festivals.[115] This shows that the idea of periods of time during which everyone had additional legal protection, and in which wrongdoing was particular heinous, was familiar to the Anglo-Saxons; however, the notion that kings could legitimately extend *their* protection to everyone at these

---

[107] II Cn 61, 82.
[108] II Cn 42; VIII Atr 33–4. See also EGu 12, which mentions earls and bishop as protectors.
[109] V Atr 21; VI Atr 26; II Cn 52–52:1. See also Hn 13:6.   [110] ECf 12, 27.
[111] Hn 68:1–68:2.   [112] DB i., 1r, 262v.
[113] See in particular, Julius Goebel, *Felony and Misdemeanor: A Study in the History of English Criminal Procedure* (New York, 1937), esp. ch. 5. More generally: H. E. J. Cowdrey, 'The Peace and Truce of God in the Eleventh Century', *Past and Present* 46 (1970), pp. 42–67; Thomas Head, 'Peace and Power in France Around the Year 1000', *Essays in Medieval Studies* 23 (2006), pp. 1–17; Ernst-Dieter Hehl, 'War, Peace and the Christian Order', in David Luscombe and Jonathan Riley-Smith, eds., *The New Cambridge Medieval History, Volume 4, c. 1024—c. 1198, Part I* (Cambridge, 2004), pp. 185–228, at 189–94.
[114] Af 40:1.   [115] II Cn 47.

times so that they would have a claim for its breach against anyone who committed an offence is not firmly attested before 1066.

Restricted Protections

In addition to this tradition of extending generally applicable royal protections to places, people and perhaps even times, such that anyone who harmed a protected individual was understood to have affronted the king, late Anglo-Saxon laws contain a handful of more restricted forms of protection. These protections' effects were limited to specific groups: members of such a group were to be heavily penalized if they harmed a protected individual, but these penalties would not apply if anyone else committed the same act against the same victim. These restricted protections were thus suitable for targeting violence that occurred in very specific scenarios; their benefit was that they were precise in their effects, but this meant that their implications were much less extensive than the general protections just surveyed. Late Anglo-Saxon law contains four of these protections, targeted at men who sought to avenge thieves, those who plotted against their lords' lives, those who reignited feuds by taking vengeance after a compensation settlement had been agreed, and those who took vengeance on families who had disclaimed responsibility for a killing by formally disowning the killer.[116]

These measures are structurally similar in that they designate both protected individuals and a restricted group against whom they are to be protected. In the case of plotting against lords' lives, the protected individual is the lord and the restricted group his own men. In the other scenarios the aim is to prevent illicit forms of vengeance, so the protected individuals are those who might be targeted for such vengeance (the families of the original killer and, except in the scenario where he has been disowned, the killer himself) and the associates of the original slain man are the restricted group. It should, however, be noted that this structural similarity is largely not reflected in the language used to describe these measures, which are framed in rather disparate ways in the laws.[117] Although their structural similarities

---

[116] Avenging thieves: II As 6:2–6:3, 20:7; VI As 1:5; III Em 2. Plotting against lords: Af 4:2; II As 4; II Cn 57, 64. Reigniting feuds: II Em 7:3; Wer 4. Vengeance against families who had disclaimed responsibility for a killing: II Em 1:1–1:3.

[117] The restricted protection intended to stop feuds being reignited is explicitly linked to the king's personal protection, or *mund*, which our two law texts explain is to be invoked at the stage in compensation negotiations at which sureties have been found to guarantee payment (II Em 7:3; Wer 4). The implication is that violence after this point will constitute a breach of the royal *mund*: a personal affront to the king that justifies severe retribution. (On the form of this retribution, see II Em 6; cf. DB i, 269v, 270r.) The passages which discuss plotting against lords (Af 4:2; II As 4; II Cn 57, 64), by contrast, make no reference to royal protection at all, the logic underlying them evidently being that men owe a duty of loyalty to lords which made plotting to kill them a truly heinous act. Indeed, the passage in Alfred's laws does not even envisage the king playing a role in the execution and forfeiture of offenders, seemingly taking the view that lords themselves were the ones entitled to retribution for such egregious disloyalty. The other two scenarios—vengeance against either killers of thieves or families who had disowned killers—clearly were understood to be linked, as the penalty for violation in both is expressed in the same way: those who take illicit vengeance are to incur 'the enmity of the king and all his friends' (II As 20:7; II Em 1:3; III Em 2). Royal involvement is thus central to

warrant grouping them together for analysis it is doubtful that contemporaries would have recognized them as a coherent category. They are perhaps best understood as a series of carefully targeted measures, each designed to deal with a specific type of illegitimate violence essentially as a one-off.

The practical significance of these measures is hard to assess. The prohibition on avenging thieves was probably the most important of them: an integral part of Æthelstan's sustained anti-theft campaign based on long-standing communitarian logic (visible in the late seventh century but probably much more deeply rooted) which demanded that honest men be able to confront thieves without fear of reprisals.[118] The anxiety that men might refrain from killing thieves because of such fears permeates these texts in a way that suggests the threat of vengeance was a genuine concern, in Æthelstan's time at least. The severe penalties for plotting against a lord's life may have found practical significance in the context of essentially political conflicts between lords and their men: they could have been invoked as a threat, strengthening lords' hands in such disputes. But we might doubt that cases in which men really did go so far as to plot to kill their lords arose with any great frequency, so it is perhaps reasonable to speculate that these laws owe their repetition in different texts primarily to their significance as ideological statements.[119] The practice of establishing the king's protection over peace-making parties at the point when a feud was settled is obscure in the laws, appearing only in two closely related texts, but there is a strong indication that these passages reflect some practical reality in the Domesday Book section covering the lands between the Ribble and the Mersey, where among the payments reserved to the king alone is listed one for 'a fight after an oath has been made'.[120] It is hard to guess how frequent such post-settlement violence may have been, but given that these settlements were consensual we should probably assume it was rarer than violence against killers who declared their victims to be thieves, a characterization which the slain man's relatives may often have disputed.

The attempt in II Edmund to create a procedure that allowed kindreds to disown kinsmen who had killed, and thereby to evade liability in feud is perhaps least likely to have had a practical reality. (It is important to emphasize this negative point because Patrick Wormald represented this measure as a fundamental assault on the principle of kin-responsibility that underpinned feuding, attributing such decisive influence to it as to state that with it Edmund had 'prohibited feud outright'.)[121]

---

both these measures in a way that it is not for lord-betrayal, but there is no explicit reference to royal protection as there is for the measure designed to prevent feuds being reignited.

[118] Ine 16, 28, 35. See Chapter 2, pp. 100–1.   [119] See Chapter 5, pp. 210–13.

[120] DB i, 269v, 270r. This, to my mind, is very likely to be a reference to the 'common pledge on a single weapon' which established the king's *mund*. Otherwise it is difficult to explain why the king would be involved at all, the offence being simple perjury. See Wer 4 and II Em 7.

[121] II Em 1–1:3. Wormald, 'God and King', p. 337–9; *Making of English Law*, p. 311 (for quotation). This characterization is inaccurate. Edmund's procedure gave kindreds the *option* formally to disown a kinsman who had killed, thereby escaping liability for his actions and becoming *unfah*—beyond the scope of legitimate feuding. Anyone who disregarded this *unfah* status and took vengeance on one of those who had disowned the killer was threatened with forfeiture of property and 'the hostility of the king and all his friends'. However, it is clear throughout that unless

The actions this procedure required—disowning a kinsman at his time of greatest need—would surely under most circumstances have been viewed as cowardly and dishonourable; we should probably imagine that its intended targets were such notorious troublemakers that their relatives' decision to wash their hands of them would have been looked upon with sympathy.[122] Even in these circumstances, however, there is reason to suspect the measure may have lacked contemporary legitimacy. In direct contrast to Æthelstan's attempts to prohibit vengeance against the killers of thieves, which seem to have inspired it in some way, Edmund's measure represents a departure from deeply rooted tradition. As is discussed in Chapter 5, earlier laws which consider essentially the same scenario—killers who flee into exile and thereby relieve their families of liability for their actions—never attempt to erase this liability entirely, always insisting that whatever family remained pay some proportion of the compensation owed.[123] Edmund's measure leaves the families of slain men with nothing. Against this backdrop Edmund's innovation looks radical, potentially to the extent of being problematic, and unlike the other restricted protections discussed here this measure does not recur in later evidence.[124] Generally, then, this and the other three restricted protections were limited in their application, such that even collectively it would be difficult to think of them as having significantly reshaped the legal system in the late Anglo-Saxon period. Indeed, the most significant of the four—that covering the killers of thieves—has close seventh-century analogues.[125]

Punishments for Violence

Late Anglo-Saxon law's approach to violent wrongdoing is thus clear. Feuding remained a legitimate part of legal practice and though kings made important efforts to regulate it using their protections, they made no attempt to introduce significant new punishments for violent offences. This is not, however, to say that

unfah status was secured through this procedure, the kinsmen of a killer remained liable either to pay compensation or to suffer vengeance. Only if kindreds routinely made use of the procedure would this measure have had a significant impact on the principle of kin-responsibility, and there is little to suggest that they did. The underlying purpose of this measure is discussed in Chapter 5, pp. 225–7.

[122] A potentially helpful analogy is the Cambridge Thegns' Guild's explicit refusal to aid guild-brothers who killed 'foolishly and wantonly', which contrasts with their obligation to contribute money to help anyone who killed 'as an avenger by necessity and to remedy the insult to him': Thorpe, *Diplomatarium*, pp. 611–12. See Chapter 5, pp. 228–9.

[123] Chapter 5, p. 232; Abt 23; Af 27–27:1.

[124] This in itself is potentially significant, as later laws, especially Cnut's, have a pronounced tendency to recapitulate earlier legislation: it is quite unusual for early tenth-century laws not to be echoed in some way by subsequent kings. Edmund's kin-abandonment procedure does appear again in Hn 88:12–88:12d, but here the author takes the unique step of introducing it 'scriptum est in legibus regis Eadmundi', singling this one measure out in a text overwhelmingly based on material from Anglo-Saxon law codes. This could indicate many things but one plausible reading is that although the author found this written in Edmund's laws he did not recognize its role within legitimate legal practice. The author's immediate resort to the Frankish *Lex Salica* for a slightly contradictory law allowing kinsmen to disown their kindreds (Hn 88:13) could also be taken to indicate discomfort with Edmund's statement.

[125] Ine 28, 35.

there were no punishments for violence at all in this period. The point is that those punishments which did exist lacked either significance or novelty. Late Anglo-Saxon law did contain a handful of punishments for violent offences, and these need to be reviewed briefly and their characterization as either traditional or marginal justified. There are also two published arguments for the establishment of a new and severe practice of royal punishment for homicide in the late Anglo-Saxon period, and it is important to discuss these briefly so as to make clear why they have not been accepted.

The most obvious punishment for violence in the laws is the fine for fighting, sometimes referred to as *fihtwite* in late Anglo-Saxon texts, which appears frequently enough in the laws for us to be confident that it was a permanent fixture, though it is never discussed in detail.[126] The important point here is that this was not a new punishment but one inherited from the seventh century: the same *wite* for fighting we find in Ine's laws, which Chapter 2 argued was probably a relabelled royal protection.[127] Regardless of its origins this was clearly understood as a punitive fine in this period and thus constitutes an important exception to the general trend for kings not to punish violent offences. However, it is an exception derived from the seventh-century past and therefore cannot be understood to have formed part of an innovative extension of royal punishment in the late Anglo-Saxon period.

It is, however, in this period that we find the first specification of punishments for *morð*—that is, for murder as opposed to homicide. Three passages refer to these punishments, two from Æthelstan's reign and one from Cnut's, all specifying death as the appropriate punishment.[128] What precisely made a killing a case of *morð* is an issue that is difficult to resolve using Anglo-Saxon sources. Most of the legal references occur in codes written by Wulfstan, in passages where the archbishop was very much in his homiletic mode. *Morð*-works and *morð*-workers appear in lists of unrighteous deeds to be avoided and evil people to be shunned (usually alongside such figures as witches, perjurers and magicians), giving us little sense of what *morð* involved beyond its being very bad indeed.[129] One passage in Cnut's laws, however, offers us a hint, stating that in cases of *open morð*—that is, 'discovered' *morð*: situations where an offence of *morð* was brought to light—the body should be returned to the kindred.[130] We know from a passage in the post-Conquest treatise known as the *Leges Henrici Primi* that honourable killers were expected to lay out

[126] See II Em 3; Wer 6; II Cn 15 (on the Danelaw). Fuller treatment can be found in the *Leges Henrici Primi*: Hn 23:1, 70:4, 80:6–80:6a, 94–94:1b, 94:2d.

[127] Ine 6–6:4. Chapter 2, pp. 90–4.

[128] II As 6; II Cn 64; Blas. It is not wholly clear that *Be Blaserum* dates from Æthelstan's reign but this seems likely. See Wormald, *Making of English Law*, pp. 367–8.

[129] V Atr 25; VI Atr 7, 28:2, 36; EGu 11; Cn 1020, 15; II Cn 4. Bruce R. O'Brien, 'From Morðor to Murdrum: The Preconquest Origin and Norman Revival of the Murder Fine', *Speculum* 71 (1996), pp. 321–57, at 343–5, dismisses the idea that the association with supernatural activities in these texts reflected social reality.

[130] II Cn 56. The interpretation of this passage adopted here is essentially the radically revised one put forward in Stefan Jurasinski '*Reddatur Parentibus*: The Vengeance of the Family in Cnut's Homicide Legislation', *Law and History Review* 20 (2002), pp. 157–80, in conjunction with which all previous translations should now be read.

194   *Law and Order in Anglo-Saxon England*

their victims' bodies respectfully and to make public their responsibility for the killing at the earliest opportunity, which presumably involved making the location of the corpse known so that it could be recovered by its family.[131] The law on *open morð* thus refers to a situation in which this has not taken place: a hidden, or at least unannounced, body is discovered and returned to its family for proper burial.

A plausible interpretation of *morð*, then, is that it involved killing in secret, so that the affronted kindred would not know against whom they should pursue their grievance.[132] This makes it a direct analogue to theft, possessing exactly the same socially corrosive secrecy that (as was argued in Chapter 2) justified its harsh communal and royal punishment.[133] We would thus expect it to be among the offences communities and kings wished to punish severely. Indeed, perhaps the most puzzling thing about *morð* is why it is such an obscure element of Anglo-Saxon law, nowhere near as prominent as theft. The core of the explanation, I suspect, is that the two main reasons for killing people in this society were to avenge previous affronts or to steal their belongings: the logic of the former demanded publicity, whilst the latter—an aggravated sub-category of theft—was already covered by fiercely punitive legislation.[134] The prescription of the death penalty for *morð* is, therefore, an example of a new late Anglo-Saxon royal punishment for violence and thus an exception to the general rule. Nonetheless, it seems likely that the obscurity of *morð* reflects its rarity, and that the offence's secrecy was the feature that attracted punishment rather than its violence; its severe treatment is

---

[131] Hn 83:6–83:6a.

[132] This contrasts with O'Brien, 'From *Morðor* to *Murdrum*', pp. 343–9. O'Brien argues that *morð* had no association with secrecy but rather connoted lord-slaying and killings for which no compensation was possible. It seems to me that the evidence of poetic usage underlying this argument, which shows that the term *morðor* was used for killings that were particularly grievous for a number of reasons (including lord-slaying), aligns well with the more hortatory passages on *morð*-works and *morð*-workers noted above. However, it does not provide much help in making sense of those few passages of interest here, where *morð* is used as a technical term denoting a specific punishable offence. It strikes me as highly plausible that this was a word that in strict legal terms referred to a specific form of utterly reprehensible homicide, but which was employed much more loosely in poetic (and probably other) contexts to refer to killings that were judged reprehensible for all manner of reasons. The association of 'discovered' *morð* with the finding of a body—the discovery of a hitherto secret killing—in II Cn 56 aligns with the well-established association with secrecy of cognate words in other Germanic languages, which underpinned the long-standing historiographical consensus that *morð* meant 'secret killing' against which O'Brien argued (pp. 337 n. 75, 343–4 n. 101, 351–2). For a fuller discussion of *morð* see T. B. Lambert, 'Protection, Feud and Royal Power: Violence and Its Regulation in English Law, c.850-c.1250' (University of Durham PhD thesis, 2009), pp. 58–62.

[133] Chapter 2, p. 100.

[134] Moreover, in practical terms it must have been almost impossible to catch a murderer in a situation so compromising that there was no possibility of denial. For a thief this was simple: if he was caught soon after the theft with the stolen goods in his possession, denial was impossible. *Morð*, however, was not necessarily an act to which one had to commit; a killing only became *morð* if the killer tried to evade responsibility. A killer who had been intending to commit *morð* could easily change his mind if he were caught in a compromising position (e.g. fleeing the scene with a bloody weapon) as he would only have to announce his responsibility publicly and the killing would be a simple homicide. Unless he was caught in the process of actively hiding the body, how could anyone prove a killer was intending to conceal the deed? In practical terms, offences of *morð* which had been committed in such a way that they were impossible to deny with an oath—the criterion both Æthelstan and Cnut demand for the death penalty (II As 6; II Cn 64)— must have been very rare indeed. If this interpretation of the term's legal meaning is correct the obscurity of *morð* laws is much less surprising.

thus readily explicable by the logic that had underpinned the punishment of theft since at least the seventh century. Again, this hardly demonstrates late Anglo-Saxon kings making significant inroads into the punishment of violence.

Finally, there is one passage in Alfred's laws which specifies a fine of 60 shillings for raping a slave (or castration for slaves that rape slaves), in addition to a 5-shilling compensation payable to the slave's owner.[135] At first sight this does look like royal punishment for rape, but there is no sign of this in the much fuller discussion earlier in Alfred's code of rapes and other sexual assaults against free women, which specifies various levels of compensation payment but makes no reference to punishment.[136] This may appear contradictory but it need not be read as such. It should be remembered that this was a culture which saw no contradiction in setting the proper compensation for the loss of a middle fingernail at 2 shillings (10 pence) and demanding the death penalty for thefts of goods worth over 8 pence.[137] Repulsive as the notion is to us, it is not implausible that the Anglo-Saxons should have seen a fundamental difference between raping a slave (an offence against property) and raping a free woman (an offence against the person), as these two separate and at first sight seemingly irreconcilable passages imply. The fine for the rape of a slave should thus probably be understood as a fine for illicit interference with someone else's property, perhaps in some way akin to theft.[138]

Beyond the laws there is very little evidence bearing on the existence of royal punishment for violence. The archaeology, of course, can show that people were executed but it cannot reveal the reasons for their execution, and the associated place-name evidence, such as it is, contains nothing to link execution specifically to violent offences (or indeed, as was noted above, to any offences other than theft and some form of misconduct involving a goat).[139] The evidence of case narratives is only slightly less meagre. We have one account of a man who bludgeoned his own mother to death in a fit of rage, whose actions imply that fearsome royal

[135] Af 25–25:1.   [136] Af 11–11:5.   [137] Af 58; II As 1.
[138] For an alternative reading, see Carole Hough, 'Alfred's *Domboc* and the Language of Rape: A Reconsideration of Alfred, ch. 11', repr. in. and cited from Hough, *An Ald Recht*, pp. 169–202. Taking the view that it is 'inconceivable' (p. 185) that the financial implications of raping a slave should exceed those for raping a free woman, she argues that we should understand an earlier passage which discusses the levels of fines in apparently general terms to apply here. This passage (Af 9:1) states that for offences where the *angild* (single-fold compensation) was under 30 shillings the appropriate *wite* was 60 shillings, but that above this threshold the figure should be 120 shillings. However, the next clause explains that there had once been different fines for theft of gold, horses, bees and many other things, but that they were now all alike at 120 shillings (Af 9:2)—the most plausible reading is that these two consecutive clauses are linked by their concern to standardize fines for theft. Whether we can legitimately project the scheme of fines set out in this theft-focused passage onto a context of rape—and indeed onto any and all contexts in which we find compensation specified without mention of a fine—is questionable. As Hough notes, the rule supplied in Af 9:1 is contradicted by Af 12 (a *wite* of 30 shillings specified for damage to other people's trees). We have already taken into account the evidence for a 'fight-fine' (*fihtwite*) across this period, so adopting Hough's reading would not significantly affect the interpretation of the regulation of violence presented here. It would imply that a fine for rape, like the fine for fighting, was a traditional part of the legal landscape by Alfred's time, and one in which late Anglo-Saxon legislators had no interest whatsoever. But we should recognize that to do so would be to make a major interpretative leap on the basis of ambiguous evidence, in order to resolve apparent inconsistencies in the evidence that might be explained in less drastic ways.
[139] See above, p. 179.

punishments for homicide were not part of his legal environment: he consulted priests and wise men (*sapientes*) about what he should do, and they instructed him to make a penitential pilgrimage to Rome.[140] As Wormald noted, this is one of a cluster episcopal letters and chronicle narratives that reveal penance being imposed for killings of close relatives (for which feuding and compensation would usually be impossible) but make no reference to any form of secular punishment.[141]

Against this, we might think to set the seven case records which seem to show killings being punished. These were the core of Wormald's argument for the royal punishment of homicide. Although he drew attention to the passage in II Edmund which allows kindreds the option of disowning killers, arguing that this represented a major royal assault against the principle of kin-responsibility, the main thrust of his case was that the laws' apparent tolerance for feuding was deceptive. 'It is not because kings made rules for the control of feud, the holding of courts and the punishment of "crimes" . . . that I believe these things to have happened. It is because I *find* them happening, in ground-level conflicts'.[142] The seven relevant homicide cases appear in different contexts: four occur in land charters from the reign of Æthelred, one crops up in a late tenth-century list of sureties given to Peterborough Abbey, and two are found in narrative sources (the Anglo-Saxon Chronicle and the Chronicle of Ramsey).[143] However, five of these seven killings had victims whom we might expect to have had direct relationships with the king and thus to have benefited from special royal protection: two royal reeves, a king's thegn, an earl and an abbot.[144] As Wormald himself acknowledged, these cannot be used to demonstrate a general royal punishment for homicide. The remaining two cases are those which bear the weight of his argument.[145]

The problem is that these two cases are notable primarily for their lack of detail. The sum-total of what we learn from them is that someone called Wistan forfeited some land to King Æthelred for 'unjust killing' (*unriht monnslihte*) and that, also in the late tenth century, a certain Osgot gave some land to the abbot of Peterborough

---

[140] The pope then instructed him to make amends for his grievous sin by donating property to a worthy religious house and he chose Ely, where the story was duly recorded. E. O. Blake, ed., *Liber Eliensis* (Camden Society Third Series 92, London, 1962), ii. 60.

[141] Wormald, *Papers Preparatory*, p. 96 n. 249. He noted seven more beyond this Ely narrative, six of them occurring in a group of penitential letters possibly collected by Archbishop Wulfstan: see D. Whitelock, M. Brett and C. N. L. Brooke, eds., *Councils and Synods with other Documents Relating to the English Church I: A.D. 871–1204*, 2 vols. (Oxford, 1981), no. 43 (i. pp. 233–7). Three of these concern men who killed their own children (II, V, VIII), two fratricides (III, VII), and one parricide (I); two are said to have been accidental (V and VIII) and one committed in hot-blooded rage (III). The other is an account of a man who accidentally suffocated his own son while sleeping: W. T. Mellows, ed., *The Chronicle of Hugh Candidus, A Monk of Peterborough* (London, 1949), pp. 29–30. We should probably add to this group a chronicle account of a penitential grant of land resulting from the cold-blooded murder of a stepson: W. Dunn Macray, ed., *Chronicon Abbatiae Rameseiensis* (Rolls Series 83, London, 1886), ch. 74, p. 134; Wormald, 'Handlist', no. 145.

[142] Wormald, 'God and King', p. 352 (emphasis in original).

[143] Wormald, 'Handlist', nos. 58, 60, 61, 71 (charters); no. 50 (surety list); nos. 148, 161 (chronicles).

[144] Ibid., nos. 58, 60, 71, 148, 161.

[145] Wormald, 'God and King', p. 340. For an attempt to extract the full implications of these case records, see Lambert, 'Theft, Homicide and Crime', pp. 32–9.

to redeem the outlawry he had incurred by killing someone called Styrcyr.[146] The terseness of these two references to homicide is such that we cannot be confident they adequately describe the cases involved. As we have seen, late Anglo-Saxon law contains references to numerous possible aggravating factors that could increase a killer's liabilities beyond the standard wergild to the family, *wite* to the king (or privileged lord), and *manbot* to the victim's lord. It is entirely plausible that such aggravating circumstances would be omitted in this sort of brief allusion to an earlier land transaction. Indeed, as was noted above, it is common for charters from this period to state that someone had forfeited their land without giving any explanation as to why. Wormald's reading of these snippets was that they refer to cases of unaggravated homicide, devoid of complicating factors, but this is just one of dozens of plausible real-life scenarios that could lie behind them. It is equally possible, for instance, that the unidentified person Wistan killed enjoyed some form of royal protection, and that Osgot (a man with a distinctly non-aristocratic landholding of 40 acres) was originally outlawed because he struggled to pay a punitive fine we already know about, *fihtwite*.[147] In short, these cases are susceptible to numerous plausible alternative readings, most of which do not demand the rather extreme interpretative response that Wormald adopted: to infer the existence of an otherwise unattested practice of royal punishment for unaggravated homicide in direct contradiction to contemporary laws.[148]

Finally we can turn to post-Conquest sources. These have already been drawn upon for the general support they offer to the picture presented by our Anglo-Saxon texts; the only significant evidence that remains to be addressed is that which underpins Naomi Hurnard's argument for royal punishment of homicide. The

---

[146] See Wormald, 'Handlist', nos. 50 (Wistan), 61 (Styrcyr). These are, respectively, S 1448a: A. J. Robertson, ed., *Anglo-Saxon Charters* (Cambridge, 1956), no. 40; and S 892: A. S. Napier and W. H. Stevenson, eds., *The Crawford Collection of Early Charters and Documents* (Oxford, 1895), no. 8.

[147] Osgot's case is discussed further in another context in Chapter 7, p. 320.

[148] This rapid summary of the evidential basis of Wormald's case is accurate but perhaps in some ways misleading. It is important to appreciate that his argument was framed by the traditional dichotomy between horizontal and vertical justice: he was explicitly attempting to place the late Anglo-Saxon legal system somewhere on a 'spectrum' between the two ('God and King', p. 336). The question of punishment for homicide was thus elided with the question of the significance of royal punishment generally, for which, as we have seen, there is a wealth of late Anglo-Saxon evidence. Wormald's scholarship thus operated within an intellectual context where the rather sparse legal passages that touch directly on the treatment of violence could be taken as sporadic hints of the existence of horizontal justice and set against the generally punitive tenor of the great mass of laws which focus on other issues, particularly theft. With the central interpretative issue framed as a choice between these two models it was logical to attribute decisive significance to the overwhelmingly punitive emphasis of the evidence, especially as the idea that late Anglo-Saxon kings punished homicide in this period seems to have been in alignment with contemporary historiographical common sense. The flimsiness of Wormald's argument is only apparent once we jettison this much more widely held but rather unhelpful dichotomy and appreciate that compensatory and punitive elements could coexist without being in tension, playing distinct but complementary roles within a coherent legal order. The strand in Wormald's scholarship that sought to question the practical relevance of written law, instead emphasizing its ideological purposes, was also important here, as it allowed awkward aspects of the laws (their occasional explicit recognition of the legitimacy of feuding and their failure to mention punishment of homicide) to be dismissed as archaizing features in an inherently conservative intellectual tradition of written law, out of step with the meteoric rise of vertical justice under late Anglo-Saxon kings. See Introduction, p. 21, n. 58.

central pillar of this argument is a single phrase in the early twelfth-century *Leges Henrici Primi*: *homicidium wera soluatur uel werelada negetur*.[149] Literally, this means 'homicide may be compensated by wergild or denied by a wergild-oath'. Alone this could be taken to mean that killers had to pay their victims' wergilds to their bereaved families, or deny their liability with an oath of equivalent value: exactly what our Anglo-Saxon evidence would lead us to expect. However, this passage is part of a list of offences for which the offender's wergild is forfeited to the king, and it occurs in a section of the *Leges Henrici* that is followed by the statement 'the matters decided above are those which are assigned to the justice or mercy of the king and to his treasury.'[150] Hurnard, therefore, interpreted this as a rule that killers must forfeit their own wergilds to the king.[151]

While the strict logic of Hurnard's reading cannot faulted—the passage does indeed imply what she says it implies if one reads it in isolation—her position rapidly becomes untenable if the *Leges Henrici* are considered more holistically. The notion that the author of this text believed simple homicide was punished by the forfeiture of wergild to the king cannot be sustained. As was noted above, he makes his understanding of the law on simple homicide crystal clear elsewhere, setting out the traditional seventh-century model of wergild to the victim's family, *manbot* to the victim's lord, and a *wite* to whichever lord had the right to it.[152] At no point anywhere else in this very long text (which unlike its Anglo-Saxon predecessors repeatedly touches on issues related to violence) is the idea of killers forfeiting their own wergilds even hinted at. A more sensible explanation, I would suggest, is that the implication Hurnard discerned in this passage was accidental. The author was

---

[149] Hn 12:3.   [150] Hn 12:3, 19:1.

[151] Hurnard, 'Anglo-Norman Franchises', p. 300 n. 1. Although to my knowledge nobody has yet done so, it is worth noting that an argument could be constructed along similar lines for non-lethal violence and rape. In a list of royal rights near the beginning of the *Leges Henrici Primi* (Hn 10:1) we find reference to the offences of *premeditatus assultus* and *uiolentus concubitus*, which their modern translator quite reasonably renders 'premeditated assault' and 'rape'. It would be possible to argue from this that rape and non-lethal violence were punished by the king in the early twelfth century, and that this reflected Anglo-Saxon practice which contemporary law codes for some reason failed to mention. However, quite apart from the obvious objection that this might represent Norman innovation and thus be alien to Anglo-Saxon legal culture, we should note that these offences are deeply obscure even in an Anglo-Norman context. They are only mentioned once in the course of the *Leges Henrici*, a very long treatise which generally goes to considerable trouble to explain how the fines it mentions were applied in practice. That there is no further reference to either of these royal rights (or indeed to several others occurring in the same list) could potentially be a sign of later interpolation. This is a particular danger because, though most of its material is undoubtedly of early twelfth-century origin, we cannot be confident that the *Leges Henrici* existed as a unified text before it was incorporated within a more extensive legal compilation, known as the *Leges Anglorum*, in about 1200. (The essential discussion here is Nicholas Karn, 'Rethinking the *Leges Henrici Primi*', in Jurasinski, Oliver, and Rabin, eds., *English Law Before Magna Carta*, pp. 199–220, esp. at 204–10.) It is therefore much safer to rely on the *Leges Henrici*'s more substantial discussions and to treat references to legal terminology not otherwise considered in the text with caution. Unfortunately there is no more substantial treatment of rape—it is not a subject the text covers—but non-lethal violence is discussed in some detail, and it is notable that the only punitive fines involved are the familiar *fihtwite* and the previously unattested *blodwite* ('blood-fine'), which appears to have been an analogous fine applied to fights involving bloodshed (Hn 94–94:5; specifically on the similarity of the two fines, see Hn 94:1b). The absence of any reference to a royal punishment for premeditated assault in this discussion is, to my mind, telling.

[152] See above, p. 182.

listing offences which required wergild payments and it naturally occurred to him that the archetypal situation in which a wergild needed to be paid was homicide; he therefore included the statement *homicidium wera soluatur uel werelada negetur*, forgetting that in a section devoted to the definition of royal rights this could seem like a reference to royal punishment.[153]

CONCLUSION

The most striking impression conveyed by our late Anglo-Saxon evidence for law is that of considerable royal activism throughout the tenth century. Although the overwhelming focus was evidently on theft (as it had been in earlier centuries), royal concern about all forms of wrongdoing appears to have intensified, resulting in ambitious attempts to enact substantive legal change. Those changes, however, worked within a traditional framework. Punishment was a tool largely reserved for theft, religious misconduct and procedural offences, whereas violent wrongdoing was addressed primarily through the extension of royal protections. It is important to emphasize, however, that this brand of legislative activism was a tenth-century tradition rather than a late Anglo-Saxon one. The nature of royal legislation changes significantly under Wulfstan's influence in the early eleventh century—it shifts away from its traditional concern with local legal practice, placing much more emphasis on moralizing rhetoric, the definition of ecclesiastical rights, and the recapitulation of earlier legislation—then it dies out completely. This is not to say that the legal changes made by tenth-century kings were undone in the eleventh century, for there is little to suggest this was the case. The post-Conquest evidence certainly does not point in this direction generally, and in some cases there is positive evidence for the maintenance of tenth-century claims: both writs and Domesday Book offer powerful confirmation of the reality of the king's key

---

[153] Hurnard seems to have anticipated a counter-argument along these lines, noting the possibility of 'confusion between the victim's *wergeld*, paid as compensation to the kindred, with the culprit's, paid as a penalty to the king'. Her riposte to such an argument was to point to a Domesday Book entry for Kintbury (Berks) which listed *homicidium* among the king's customs, though again she anticipated the obvious objection: 'This also might possibly be thought to be a mistake, *homicidium* being confused with *murdrum*, the fine payable by the district. But unless both these instances are due to errors, it must be concluded that homicide was a reserved plea.' ('Anglo-Norman Franchises', p. 300 n. 1; see DB i, 61v). Her implication that it is extremely unlikely that both these passages could contain 'errors', of course, only makes sense if we restrict the scope of our analysis to these two passages. If we consider them as part of the much more extensive corpus of statements relating to homicide in the Anglo-Saxon laws, Domesday Book and Anglo-Norman legal treatises, on the other hand, it hardly seems surprising that among the many passages available Hurnard was able to find two which were ambiguous enough to be interpreted in a way that aligned with her interpretation. It should be noted, however, that Hurnard's argument on homicide was incidental to the main thrust of the article in which it appeared. Indeed, the existence of royal punishment for homicide was evidently an assumption she believed her peers shared; she does not treat it as a controversial aspect of her case but as something she could safely postulate with only a cursory attempt at justification. The flimsiness of her case thus reflects the fact that she did not believe a more robust case needed to be made; she was merely articulating and, to her credit, trying to provide some evidential foundations for the common-sense assumptions of her generation.

protective rights.[154] The fact that eleventh-century kings do not seem to have been interested in improving their societies through the establishment of new laws should not be taken to mean that their interest in the practical implementation of laws which already existed also reduced. Indeed, Chapter 7 argues the exact opposite.

In a historiographical context the most significant conclusion of this chapter, however, is not its vision of a tenth-century intensification in royal efforts against wrongdoing, which was then sustained in the eleventh; it is the argument that these efforts continued to be conducted within a traditional legal framework, which determined the categories of wrongdoing for which royal protection and punishment were appropriate. This is a point of considerable importance for our understanding of the place of the late Anglo-Saxon period in England's long-term legal development. In this rather fundamental respect, the tenth and eleventh centuries align very closely with the seventh century and much less well with the common law's approach to wrongdoing in the later medieval period. While this clearly should matter to us, we should also remember that this observation would have been meaningless in a late Anglo-Saxon context.[155] Contemporaries must have noticed the increasing range and severity of royal punishments and protections as they were established, and the more reflective among them probably would have understood this as a symptom of the growing strength and ambition of kings. The notion that the approach to wrongdoing underlying them was somehow old-fashioned or primitive—that it in some way reflected royal weakness or lack of determination in the legal sphere—is unlikely to have made sense to English observers until later legal and cultural changes established a different set of assumptions about the nature and purpose of law.

The conclusion that, in its approach to wrongdoing, late Anglo-Saxon law resembled early Anglo-Saxon law much more than it did the common law of the late twelfth and thirteenth centuries would not have been surprising to historians writing a century ago. Frederic William Maitland famously wrote of the system of *bot* and *wite*—the distinctive combination of compensation payments and punitive fines that characterized Anglo-Saxon law—disappearing 'with marvellous suddenness' in the twelfth century.[156] That this idea is more surprising now reflects, as the

---

[154] A similar point can be made about the post-Conquest institution of 'frankpledge', which strongly implies tenth-century suretyship regulations were effectively implemented. See Chapter 6, pp. 276–82. It may be that some of the harsher demands made by tenth-century kings proved impractical—it has been noted that later laws imply an amelioration of Æthelstan's insistence on the death penalty for all convicted thieves and Edmund's prescription of full forfeiture for *hamsocn* and *mundbryce*—but it would be unwise to assume that problems with such measures' over-ambition only manifested themselves in the eleventh century.

[155] Indeed, even from a modern perspective it is debateable how helpful it is to interpret the Anglo-Saxon legal order, with its recognition of the legitimacy of feud violence, as a developmental stage preceding the monopolization of legitimate violence by the state. However widely applicable such developmental models may prove to be, the anachronistic value-judgements that so readily attach themselves to this sort of normative teleology—the categorization of certain places and periods as advanced and others as primitive—have the potential to distort and obscure much more than they reveal.

[156] Frederick Pollock and Frederic William Maitland, *The History of English Law Before the Time of Edward I*, 2 vols. (2nd edn, Cambridge, 1898), ii, p. 481.

Introduction noted, the broader rehabilitation of late Anglo-Saxon government from the mid-twentieth century, which reached its apogee with Campbell's pointed insistence on the appropriateness of the term 'state' for the tenth- and eleventh-century kingdom. The extent to which Anglo-Norman kings relied on structures and institutions inherited from the Anglo-Saxon past is now much more fully appreciated, and a central thrust of Wormald's scholarship was that the late Anglo-Saxon legal inheritance was similarly crucial.[157] Although this book is deliberately framed in such a way as to avoid viewing Anglo-Saxon law through this sort of retrospective lens, in broad terms I suspect this idea has considerable merit. Specifically on the issue of the different spheres associated with punishment and protection, however, the evidence surveyed in this chapter strongly suggests modern perceptions of the late Anglo-Saxon source material have been distorted by historians' instinctive expectation that so impressively state-like a kingdom must have had a correspondingly state-like legal system.

This, at any rate, strikes me as the best explanation for the lack of scrutiny given to the idea that late Anglo-Saxon kings established new and powerful punishments for violence. As has been seen, on close inspection both the published arguments for this proposition are sufficiently tenuous that it is highly doubtful either would have survived a serious critical review, had it occurred to any of their authors' peers to attempt one. In historiographical terms, there is of course no denying that the arguments of this chapter represent a direct critique of arguments made by both Hurnard and Wormald. However, it would be unfair and inaccurate to frame it thus, with the focus on these specific historians and their flawed arguments. What is really at issue is the collectively constructed historiographical 'common sense' which was both context for these arguments and left them unscrutinized. That 'common sense' enshrines an assumption that it is the natural desire of every ruler or government to create a legal order similar to our own, in which the state claims a monopoly of legitimate violence and takes it upon itself to punish all significant forms of wrongdoing.[158] This makes it seem implausible that kings might develop a sophisticated governmental apparatus and not use their increased power to outlaw feuding, because the only conceivable reason for their failing to replace a horizontal legal order with a vertical one is that they lacked the power to do so. This widespread assumption should be understood as the target of this chapter's historiographical critique. But its key point is substantive. The late Anglo-Saxon period saw kings intensify their efforts against wrongdoing, and they did so in accordance with and in pursuit of well-established ideals. It is to the more detailed scrutiny of those ideals that we must now turn.

5

Ideals of Kingship and Order

INTRODUCTION

This chapter examines the role which late Anglo-Saxon kings were expected to perform in the field of law and order. This is an important subject in its own right, but it is also crucial context in which to interpret the findings of the previous chapter and indeed those of the next two: late Anglo-Saxon kings' legal achievements can only properly be assessed in the context of contemporary expectations. Fortunately, this is the sort of analysis for which our late Anglo-Saxon source-material is well suited: the laws provide a very useful window onto the terms in which kings, and the elites who participated in the legislative process, discussed and understood their own legal systems. They provide excellent evidence for the ideas that shaped royal and aristocratic understandings of proper legal order and the king's role in its maintenance.[1] Interrogated carefully they can reveal not only ideological concepts of which contemporaries would have been conscious—the language used to explain, to justify and to exhort—but also generally held assumptions about the ordering of society which no one needed to state explicitly but nevertheless shaped legislation in profound ways. The line between such implicit assumptions and explicit ideological concepts is a difficult and blurry one, but that is not a problem in this context: we are interested in legal culture in broad terms and have no pressing need to draw any sharp distinction.

It is important, though, to emphasize that what are at stake here are ideals of kingship and order not just in legal ideology but in legal culture more broadly conceived. Indeed, the most fundamental elements of contemporary understandings of good order are almost certainly those which were so obvious to all concerned that they did not need to be stated at all, let alone explained or justified with language we might identify as ideological. If our aim is to uncover widely shared

---

[1] Whether this elite discourse offers a good approximation of broader social assumptions about the role of the king in the maintenance of order is, of course, open to debate. The fact that our few sources for local legal arrangements—notably the regulations of the London 'peace-guild' (VI As 1–8:9) and the borough and shire customs recorded in Domesday Book (e.g. D.B. i, 56v, 87v, 172r, 262v)—tend to align reasonably well with the concerns of codes originating in royal assemblies is an encouraging sign, suggesting that there was no major disparity between local and kingdom-wide elites in terms of their understanding of the overall shape (if not the exact detail) of the legal system. That much legislation focuses on theft of livestock and the various mechanisms which local communities of farmers ought to adopt to deter and punish it could also be read this way. Laws may have been produced by an elite, but this elite seems to have had relatively earthy concerns; the world imagined by their legislation was populated primarily by free farmers.

ideals about kingship and order, an exclusive focus on the ideological concepts consciously articulated by lawmakers could prove problematic, focusing attention on what was novel and potentially contentious whilst marginalizing the traditional and uncontroversial. This chapter does not assume the existence of a single, coherently articulated ideology defining the role of kings in the maintenance of order. Rather, it tries to elucidate a range of ideas bearing on both the role of kings and the maintenance of order, taking particular note of where the two overlap but acknowledging that in some respects they do not. Royal punishment of religious misconduct by the laity, for example, should be understood not in isolation but as the legal tip of a much larger ideological iceberg: a broad royal duty to protect the Church and help maintain the kingdom's favourable relationship with God. To explain a particular legal phenomenon we may need to think much more broadly about the role of kings, lifting our gaze to ideas that extend well beyond law and the maintenance of order. Nor should we assume that the maintenance of order was a purely royal enterprise. Rather, it makes sense to think in broad terms about what constituted good order and then to consider what role the king and others were expected to play in bringing it about.

This broad focus means that the chapter incorporates several topics that are prominent in the literature but places them alongside hitherto rather more obscure ideas, arranging and weighting these ideas in a way that readers familiar with the existing historiography may find surprising. There are not, in fact, very many points in what follows where established arguments are directly contradicted, but together the nuances suggested and the less familiar ideas introduced nevertheless result in a distinctly different overall picture. Once again, this is a subject on which the most influential existing work is that of Patrick Wormald, who, as was noted in the last chapter, detected the emergence of 'a developed notion of crime and punishment' under late Anglo-Saxon kings.[2] To be specific, it was central to Wormald's assessment of the period's significance that the roots of the later notion of 'felony'—the label applied to all serious forms of wrongdoing under the common law from the late twelfth century onwards—could be found well before the Conquest. Wormald summarized his interpretation most clearly in the context of a tribute to Frederic William Maitland:

> All this bears on the question of the origins of the concept of felony. Like everyone since, Maitland was uncertain how a word whose basic meaning is "broken faith with a lord" became a term for "crime of any considerable gravity". He hesitantly thought the link lay in "the rule that the felon's fee should escheat to his lord". But this fails to explain why larceny should be treated as severely as treason itself. An explanation is to hand in a feature of Old English jurisprudence mentioned above: the twelve-year-old's "oath and pledge" whereby loyalty entailed disavowal of theft. A "king's enemy" is thus one who plots conventional offences against his people as well as treason against his person. Crime is indeed a breach of faith, so punished like any other form of infidelity.

---

[2] Patrick Wormald, 'Giving God and King Their Due: Conflict and Its Regulation in the Early English State', repr. in and cited from Wormald, *Legal Culture in the Early Medieval West* (London, 1999), pp. 333–57, at 342.

By Angevin times this theory could well have infiltrated the mind-set and vocabulary of a post-Conquest Establishment that had first crossed the Channel with more straight-forward notions of disloyalty.[3]

The argument here was one that Wormald made in much greater detail in the materials for the second volume of his *Making of English Law*, which have recently been published online. The passage above is a fair summary of the argument's main thrust—Anglo-Saxon kings punished crime as disloyalty—but understates its breadth. The legal ideology that underpinned the pursuit of crime also encompassed ideas about *frið* ('peace'), obedience, and what was pleasing to God.[4]

Wormald's view of the ideology of late Anglo-Saxon law was, nonetheless, that it revealed the thinking behind the punishment of 'crime' generally, a category within which he explicitly included violent offences. In the light of the preceding chapters this element of his analysis clearly cannot be accepted: like their seventh-century predecessors, late Anglo-Saxon kings prohibited and punished religious misconduct, procedural offences, and theft, but tended to approach violence using protections. They did not, then, need an ideology of crime and punishment which covered all forms of wrongdoing—indeed, such an ideology would hardly have made sense—and it would therefore be surprising if we found one. This book, particularly in Chapters 2 and 4, has repeatedly emphasized that we need to be alert to the possibility that the Anglo-Saxons thought about different types of wrongdoing in different ways, whereas Wormald's work in some important respects proceeded from an assumption that they could all be grouped together. No doubt many readers will already have noted the way that he, in the passage above, moved from an oath associated specifically with theft, through 'conventional offences', to a theory about 'crime' in general. Although this chapter accepts most of Wormald's observations on specific points, it endeavours to respect contemporary categorizations, resisting the temptation to map early medieval ideas onto modern concepts in this manner.[5]

The purpose of this chapter, then, is not to replace Wormald's coherent royal ideology of crime and punishment with an equally coherent ideology that underpins all aspects of late Anglo-Saxon justice; nor, however, is it to argue for baffling complexity and variety. The aim is to show that the characteristically Anglo-Saxon amalgam of legitimate feuding and harsh royal punishment described in the last

---

[3] Patrick Wormald, 'Frederic William Maitland and the Earliest English Law', repr. in and cited from Wormald, *Legal Culture*, p. 45–69, at 62. For early twelfth-century uses of the term felony see Hn 43:7, 46:3, 53:4, 88:14.

[4] Patrick Wormald, *Papers Preparatory to the Making of English Law: King Alfred to the Twelfth Century. Volume II: From God's Law to Common Law*, ed. Stephen Baxter and John Hudson (University of London, 2014), <http://www.earlyenglishlaws.ac.uk/reference/wormald/>, chs. 8 and 9. This chapter was drafted at a time when I had access to these papers but was unaware of their impending online publication.

[5] Although I have tried my utmost to do this I am sure I must have failed in many respects, unconsciously imposing conceptual frameworks derived from my own environment on the evidence and thereby distorting it. I hope readers will appreciate that the critique presented here does not stem from the hubristic notion that I have overcome this most fundamental of problems in historical methodology, or indeed any belief that it ever can be more than partially mitigated.

chapter makes good sense when understood in its own cultural context. The various ideas that made up this cultural context were not a unified ideology, but they did overlap and interlock to some extent and they did not produce any very strong tensions or contradictions: they cohere. This is important because one could all too readily assume the opposite. As was noted in both the Introduction and Chapter 4, it is very easy unthinkingly to slip into the belief that the benefits of top-down, punitive justice systems which outlaw feuding practices—that is, justice systems like our own—are so universally apparent to those in power across human cultures that that we can safely assume any ruler with a genuine interest in the improvement of law and order would wish to implement one. If we do this, we can end up interpreting Anglo-Saxon law as an uneasy compromise arising from the natural conflict between the (vertical) punitive agenda of royal justice and an engrained (horizontal) culture of violent feuding that was gradually being eradicated. Indeed, despite its longevity, it is all too easy to dismiss the Anglo-Saxons' legal order as a mere transitional phase: a half-civilized staging point between a barbarous past, characterized if not by unrestrained bloodshed then at least by endemic feuding, and a later medieval world readily recognizable as a precursor to our own. Under-standing the broad coherence of contemporary ideals of kingship and order allows us to escape this trap.

This agenda is rather similar to that pursued by Chapter 2 for seventh-century law.[6] Given that essentially the same framework seems to have defined legitimate royal activity in this earlier period, it is possible—perhaps even probable—that many of this earlier chapter's conclusions remain valid for the tenth and eleventh centuries. We have good reason to suspect that free Anglo-Saxon men remained weapon-bearing men, at least in theory, expected to be able to use violence in defence of their own honour in feud, and that responsible feuding continued to be viewed positively, as a good method of addressing the communal threat posed by violent wrongdoing. The fundamental logic underpinning royal punishment of theft, religious misconduct and procedural offences may still have been that punishment was necessary because such offences could not adequately be addressed through feuding. We cannot, however, simply assume these things. It is possible, after all, that the logic which governed the establishment of royal punishment in the seventh century had been forgotten and the pattern it formed had simply become customary, a state of affairs to be explained with new and different ideas. Moreover, our body of sources for the late Anglo-Saxon period is so much richer than that of the earlier era that it allows us to form a much more detailed picture of later legal culture, a valuable exercise regardless of whether it suggests fundamental continuity or change.

Before we turn to the detail of late Anglo-Saxon evidence, however, it is important to consider a vital piece of evidence for the ideology of kingship this period inherited from earlier centuries: the West Saxon royal inauguration ritual. Our first description of this ritual—a Latin text known as the 'first *ordo*'—appears

---

[6] Chapter 2, pp. 106–9.

in a text which must have existed in its present form by at least 856, but which cannot be placed with any certainty in the two preceding centuries.[7] It could, then, date from the period covered in Chapter 2, but all we know for certain is that the ideas about kingship displayed here were traditional by the time of Alfred and his successors.[8] The text envisions a newly inaugurated king issuing three commands to his people, to each of which the assembled notables respond 'Amen':

> First, that the Church of God and all Christian people preserve true peace, in God the omnipotent. [Response: Amen]. The second is that he should forbid robbery and all injustices (*rapacitates et omnes iniquitates*) to all ranks. [Response: Amen]. The third is that in all judgements he should order justice and mercy so that through that the kind and merciful God may grant us his mercy. [Response: Amen].[9]

By the late tenth century this ritual had been modified so that kings swore an oath to perform these three duties *before* they were consecrated. The effect of this was to make the three duties seem less customary and more compulsory, but aside from this shift in emphasis this threefold conception of the duties of kingship remained identical from its establishment at some unknown point in the seventh, eighth, or early ninth century until 1066.[10]

These three royal commands, later promises, thus represent a formulation of the legal duties of kings which was both traditional and current throughout the late Anglo-Saxon period, and as such their importance is obvious. Their interpretation, however, is difficult because of their brevity. What did *omnes iniquitates* convey to contemporaries? What did it mean for all Christian people to preserve 'true peace'? Was the command that all judgements be just and merciful literally about judgements alone, or did it stand for a broader duty to ensure justice and mercy through a variety of means? It would be possible to read each of these commands in a number of different ways, and this range of plausible interpretations renders the ritual ambiguous. It is only with reference to other sources—particularly the later laws—that we can come to grips with how contemporaries understood the legal duties of kingship being referred to here. Nonetheless, there can be no doubt that in broad terms the three commands within the inauguration ritual were meant in some sense to define the king's role in the maintenance of order: precisely the central concern of this chapter. This threefold structuring of royal responsibilities should therefore be kept in mind throughout what follows.

---

[7] Janet L. Nelson, 'The Earliest Royal *Ordo*: Some Liturgical and Historical Aspects', repr. in and cited from Nelson, *Politics and Ritual in Early Medieval Europe* (London, 1986), pp. 341–60, at 343–53.

[8] Hence its only being mentioned in passing in Chapter 2, p. 76.

[9] Text: Nicholas Orchard, ed., *The Leofric Missal*, 2 vols. (London, 2002), ii, p. 432 (no. 2466). Translation: Mary Clayton, 'The Old English *Promissio Regis*', *Anglo-Saxon England* 37 (2008), pp. 91–150, at 108, n. 98.

[10] For debate about the inauguration rituals used in 1066, see George Garnett, 'The Third Recension of the English Coronation *Ordo*: The Manuscripts', *Haskins Society Journal* 11 (2003), pp. 43–71; Janet L. Nelson, 'The Rites of the Conqueror', repr. in and cited from Nelson, *Politics and Ritual*, pp. 375–401.

The chapter has three sections. The first addresses the ideas surrounding royal punishment of secular wrongdoing. This is precisely the ground covered by Wormald in his analysis of royal legal ideology and the themes that emerge here are essentially the same, though the precise significance attributed to each is not. The second section examines the king's responsibility for ensuring his kingdom retained God's favour, a well-trodden historiographical theme in broad terms, though less prominent in specifically legal scholarship. The final section considers late Anglo-Saxon ideals relating to violence: the effects, positive and negative, which violence was understood to have on order, the contexts in which violence was and was not legitimate, and the rationale underlying royal attempts to engage with violent wrongdoing through legislation.

KINGSHIP AND SECULAR ORDER

We begin, then, with the king's responsibility for maintaining order, as conceived in more or less secular terms. This is essentially the same conceptual territory covered by Wormald's discussions of royal ideology and the key landmarks are the same: ideas of peace, loyalty and obedience. In historiographical terms the primary significance of what follows lies in variations in emphasis: the contours of this landscape are mapped out differently.[11]

Peace (*Frið*)

The most prominent of the ideological concepts that emerge in late Anglo-Saxon law is *frið*, or 'peace'.[12] It is usually used in a very general way as a means of remarking on the condition of the kingdom; when kings referred to *frið* they often did so in the context of identifying defects in it that could then be remedied.[13] Edward the Elder's second code, for instance, explains how in Exeter the king exhorted his *witan* to consider 'how their *frið* might be made better than it had been', and Æthelstan's Exeter code similarly complains that 'our *frið*' had

---

[11] The underlying reasons for these differences are twofold. First, and most obviously, a central aim here is to think critically about the conceptual range of the ideas we find in the laws: whereas Wormald assumed that peace, loyalty and obedience were concepts deployed in support of royal punishment of 'crime', Chapter 4 showed that in practice kings took radically different approaches to some of the types of wrongdoing he placed within this umbrella category. The second difference is prioritization. For Wormald the loyalty oath and its implications were central, but this was because he was consciously engaging in a retrospective search for the origins of late twelfth-century ideas about felony. From such a perspective the oath of loyalty is indeed central—the seed from which great things would eventually grow—but for understanding the late Anglo-Saxon period we need to look at evidence for ideas' contemporary significance, not their future trajectories.

[12] See DOE, s.v. 'frið'. On early medieval ideas about peace more generally, see Paul J. E. Kershaw, *Peaceful Kings: Peace, Power, and the Early Medieval Political Imagination* (Oxford, 2011); Thomas Renna, 'The Idea of Peace in the West', *Journal of Medieval History* 6 (1980), pp. 143–67; Roger Bonnaud Delamare, *L'Idée de Paix à l'Époque Carolingienne* (Paris, 1939).

[13] The term could be used differently, however, for instance the use in Alfred's laws noted in Chapter 4, p. 186.

not previously been kept as well as the king would have liked.[14] Edmund's second code, however, shows that it was possible for *frið* to be remarked upon in a more positive light:

> I thank God and all of you who have well supported me, for the *frið* that we now have from thefts; I now trust to you, that you will support this measure [i.e. Edmund's new legislation concerned with feuding] so much the better as the need is greater for us all that it shall be observed.[15]

These references are far from isolated; Æthelred's legislation in particular makes frequent use of the idea that its purpose was *friðes bot*, the 'improvement' or 'amendment' of *frið*.[16] *Frið*, then, was a concept that was often used to explain legislation. Kings and their assembled notables were clearly meant to be concerned about *frið*, and *frið* was therefore cited both to justify legislative initiatives and to exhort people to assist in their implementation. Used in this sense, it should be noted, *frið* seems to have been a communal matter: it is not the king's peace that excites concern, but 'our peace' (*ure frið*)—everybody's. We might think of it as the peace of the kingdom or of its people.

The idea that certain acts could be harmful to this peace is clearly present in the laws, if often only implicitly, but there is no sign that this notion underpinned a theory of royal punishment in any direct way. Whereas from the late twelfth century it is clear that certain offences qualified for royal punishment because of their status as breaches of the 'king's peace'—plaintiffs had to make this accusation in explicit terms for their prosecutions to be valid[17]—there is no evidence that late Anglo-Saxon *frið* had this sort of technical significance. Kings and other notables worried about the kingdom's peace, and they made laws to improve it, but there is no sign that royal punishment came to rely explicitly on the concept. There was no chain of reasoning that said 'X qualifies as an offence against *frið*, therefore the king has the right to punish it'. (Indeed, since *frið* seems not to have been a royal possession but a communal one, that logic may not have made sense in any case.) Seventh-century kings asserted their right to punish a range of offences without a theory of peace; late Anglo-Saxon kings were clearly concerned about a general *frið* but there is nothing to indicate that they came to see their right to impose punishments as dependent upon it. In other words, though scholars approaching this period from the later Middle Ages may find it tempting to see parallels between common law ideas about the king's peace and late Anglo-Saxon notions of *frið*, the two are not as similar as they may at first seem.[18]

---

[14] II Ew 1; V As Prol.   [15] II Em 5.

[16] I Atr Prol; III Atr Prol; VI As 11, 12:3; V Atr 26:1; VI Atr 32; II Cn 8.

[17] G. D. G. Hall, ed., *The Treatise on the Laws and Customs of the Realm of England Commonly Called Glanvill* (Oxford, 1965), i. 2.

[18] Julius Goebel, *Felony and Misdemeanor: A Study in the History of English Criminal Procedure* (New York, 1937), pp. 423–40; Frederick Pollock, 'The King's Peace', in Pollock, *Oxford Lectures and Other Discourses* (London, 1890), pp. 65–90. For a more detailed review of the historiography on this point, see T. B. Lambert, 'Protection, Feud and Royal Power: Violence and Its Regulation in English Law, c.850-c.1250' (University of Durham PhD thesis, 2009), pp. 164–71.

For present purposes it is important to note that *frið* is often associated specifically with theft. We have already seen Edmund thanking his *witan* for the *frið* they had come to enjoy from theft, and this is not an isolated case. Most strikingly, in the text known as VI Æthelstan we find the leading men of London forming what they term a *friðgyld*—a 'peace guild'—for the purpose of suppressing theft. In this text the leading men of the guild collectively command that all the surrounding reeves should help one another in the tracking of stolen livestock so as to maintain 'our *frið*', condemn men who are so complacent about *frið* that they fail to monitor where their livestock wander, and warn that were Londoners to be negligent about *frið* in future they would be tyrannized by thieves.[19] We also find Archbishop Wulfstan, writing in both Æthelred's and Cnut's codes, explaining that *friðes bot* should be promoted in such a way 'as shall be best for the householder and worst for the thief', and Edgar singling out a law concerning the investigation of stolen livestock as so important to *frið* that it was, unusually, to be observed by the Danes as well as the English.[20]

Other uses of *frið* are less specific. They tend to come in the prefaces of law codes and thus could be read as associating all the laws within those codes with the concept. The codes that can be viewed in this way are II Edward, II Æthelstan (and the subsequent elaborations on this code recorded in III, IV, V, and VI Æthelstan), III Edmund, IV Edgar, I Æthelred, and III Æthelred.[21] Theft and the security of property more generally are a major theme in these laws: there is a great deal of material on such issues as suretyship (often clearly envisaged in the context of theft), tracking stolen livestock and the witnessing of sales (so that all men can prove that their property is not stolen).[22] Other issues are discussed too, however. Theft, then, is the only offence which is ever explicitly linked with *frið*, and even its more general uses tend to be associated with theft laws to some extent. We cannot say that *frið* was associated solely with theft, but it would be fair to state that when late Anglo-Saxon lawmakers worried about threats to their people's *frið* it was usually theft that

[19] VI As Prol, 8:4, 8:7, 8:9. A brief account of an assembly at Whittlebury is appended to the end of this code, which records that the king and his councillors made some adjustments to anti-theft legislation, also concludes with a statement that if these measures are observed 'ure frið' will be better kept than it had been previously (VI As 12:4). On the idea of thieves tyrannizing the men of London, see Chapter 2, p. 100 n. 125.

[20] VI Atr 32; II Cn 8; IV Eg 12:1–14:2. It is also worth noting that II As 20:3 uses the verb *friðian* (maybe best rendered 'to be at peace with') in association with a command to refrain from theft on pain of death: 'And it is to be announced in the meeting that everyone is to be at peace with everything with which the king will be at peace, and to refrain from theft on pain of losing his life and everything he owns'.

[21] See II Ew 1; III Em Prol; IV Eg 2, 15, 16; I Atr Prol. Our text of II Æthelstan has no preface in its surviving form, so we cannot be sure that the code as a whole was framed with reference to *frið*. However, references in other codes make it clear that it was strongly associated with the concept (V As Prol; III As Prol, 2, 2:5; VI As 10, perhaps also II Em 5). Excluded from this list are the two codes attributed to Æthelred which give prominent place to Wulfstan's uses of the coupling *frið* and *freondscipe*, as this seems to represent a somewhat different concept (V Atr 1:1; VI Atr 8:2).

[22] For example, on suretyship and theft, see II Ew 3 and I Atr 1; on tracing livestock see II Ew 4, III Em 6; on witnessing sales, III Em 5, IV Eg 3:1–11. It is noteworthy that the concerns of III Æthelred, a code for part of the Danelaw, do not align as clearly with what is otherwise a fairly coherent group of laws. These themes are discussed in detail in Chapter 6.

leapt first to their minds. This description of the conceptual range of *frið* aligns closely with the second command in the royal inauguration ritual discussed above, which also specifically picks out *rapacitates*—which could be a Latin rendering of thefts—in a concept that could also seemingly apply more vaguely to wrongdoing generally (*omnes iniquitates*).

It is worth emphasizing, finally, that the legislation these worries seem to have prompted did not tend solely or even mainly to be about punishment, at least not directly. It seems to have been understood that *frið* could best be improved not only by threatening ever more frightening punishments to deter thieves, but also by imposing tighter communal legal procedures (such as those requiring purchases to be witnessed) which ensured legitimate and illegitimate transfers of property could readily be distinguished. Indeed, though concern about *frið* mainly occurs in the context of kings and their legislation, we should also note that it does not appear to be exclusively royal. Kings were clearly meant to worry about *frið* but it is equally plain that others were meant to share their concerns, and that the improvement of the kingdom's *frið* was held to be a communal enterprise for the collective benefit of all. *Frið* should not be understood as the sort of peace that kings imposed with fearsome punishments, then, or at least not exclusively. Rather, the achievement and improvement of peace was a collective endeavour which kings were expected to lead—a mandate which encompassed, but was not limited to, the imposition of severe punishments.

Oaths and Loyalty

We can now turn to the central plank of Wormald's ideology of crime and punishment: the notion that wrongdoing was punished on the theory that it constituted a violation of the oath of loyalty that every Anglo-Saxon male over the age of twelve had to swear to the king. A significant part of the attraction of this idea lies beyond the chronological and geographical boundaries of Anglo-Saxon England. By the thirteenth century we know that the concept of 'felony' under-pinned the royal punishment of serious wrongdoing: plaintiffs in such cases had to make a formal accusation that the accused had acted 'feloniously as a felon'.[23] Because the language of felony seems to have been rooted in ideas about lord-betrayal it is probably accurate to say that by this point the most serious offences were indeed punished on the theory that they constituted disloyalty—violations of an oath which all men had to take.[24] There is also strong evidence that this idea was important in Carolingian Francia. This is from Charlemagne's *Capitulare missorum generale* of 802:

---

[23] Samuel E. Thorne, ed., *Bracton: De Legibus et Consuetudinibus Anglie*, 4 vols. (Cambridge, Mass., 1968–77), ii, p. 388. On the emergence of felony as a category, see John Hudson, *The Oxford History of the Laws of England, Volume II, 871–1216* (Oxford, 2012), p. 711; Frederick Pollock and Frederic William Maitland, *The History of English Law Before the Time of Edward I*, 2 vols. (2nd edn, Cambridge, 1898), ii, pp. 487–90.

[24] For the oath: Ass Nor 6.

[The oath of loyalty to be taken by all men over the age of twelve] is to be expounded publicly to all, in such a way that everyone can understand, how important and how many are the matters which that oath comprehends—not only, as many have hitherto thought, fidelity to the lord emperor as regards his life and not bringing an enemy into his realm for hostile purposes and not consenting to, or remaining silent about, another's infidelity towards him, but that all should know that the oath has the following meaning within it . . . [25]

The text then goes on to stipulate first that all should maintain themselves in God's holy service and then that nobody should do any of the following: steal anything that in any way belongs to the emperor; steal from or in any way harm churches, widows, orphans, or pilgrims; allow a benefice from the emperor to go to ruin; disregard military service; thwart the emperor's commands; or contrive to pervert the course of justice in the courts.[26] There is clear evidence, then, for the idea that the oath of loyalty had wider duties associated with it under the Carolingians, and that something rather similar to this theory underpinned the punishment of crime in England from the late twelfth century onwards.

In this context, as Wormald rightly observed, the late Anglo-Saxon evidence is highly suggestive. The nature of the loyalty oath is first spelled out in III Edmund, which survives only in a Latin translation:

In the first place, all shall swear in the name of the lord, before whom that holy thing is holy, that they will be faithful to King Edmund, even as it behoves a man to be faithful to his lord, without any dispute or dissension, openly or in secret, favouring what he favours and discountenancing what he discountenances. And from the day on which this oath shall be rendered, let no-one conceal the breach of it in a brother or relation of his, any more than in a stranger.[27]

That this general oath predated Edmund's reign is made clear in a reference in Edward the Elder's second code to the oath and pledge 'which all the people have given'.[28] This code is introduced with Edward's concern to improve *frið*, but rather suggestively moves on to explain that the king had asked which of his councillors were willing to devote themselves to the implementation of his initiatives, 'favouring what he favoured and discountenancing what he discountenanced', seemingly implying that they were bound to do so by the terms of the oath they had sworn.[29] The loyalty oath is also, perhaps, visible in Alfred's laws, which begin by emphasizing the importance of every man abiding carefully by his oath and pledge and then go on to state that it is better to break than to keep an oath to conceal wrongdoing or to betray a lord. It is possible that these statements allude to a general oath of loyalty, the central elements of which were loyalty to a lord (i.e. the king) and the foreswearing of all association with wrongdoing, and that the point of the passage is to assert the priority of this oath over other

[25] Alfred Boretius, ed., *Capitularia regum Francorum*, 2 vols. (Monumenta Germaniae Historica, Legum sectio II, Hanover, 1883–97), i, p. 92 (no. 33, ch. 2). Translation: P. D. King, *Charlemagne: Translated Sources* (Kendal, 1987), 234.

[26] Boretius, *Capitularia*, i, pp. 92–3 (no. 33, chs. 3–9).   [27] III Em 1.

[28] II Ew 5.   [29] II Ew 1:1.

less virtuous oaths people might be induced to swear. But if this is so, the reference is oddly oblique: it is possible (and rather more natural) to read this passage as a general injunction to be faithful to all oaths except those to perform wrongful acts.[30]

The issue of whether Alfred can be credited with the creation of a general oath, however, is something of a distraction; Edward the Elder's code makes it clear that a general oath of some sort did exist shortly after his reign and—crucially—it implies that it could be breached by certain types of wrongdoing. The nature of this wrongdoing is the central issue, and just as for *frið* we find that theft is firmly centre-stage. Edward's reference to the oath all the people had sworn comes in the context of theft law: everyone was to have ready on his land men who would guide others wishing to track their own stolen livestock, and on no account was anyone to hinder the pursuers nor in any way protect or harbour the wrongdoer. The next clause states, 'if anyone neglects this and breaks his oath and pledge which the whole nation has given he shall pay compensation as the *domboc* [Alfred's law code] orders.'[31] In this instance, at least, the oath is closely associated with theft.[32] This is even more explicit in Cnut's laws, which state that 'it is our desire that everyone, over twelve years of age, shall take an oath that he will not be a thief or a thief's accomplice'.[33] Whether this is a way of referring to the same loyalty oath that makes its legal significance clear or simply evidence for an additional anti-theft oath is uncertain, but either way it is plain that the punishment of theft had come to be justified, at least in part, by reference to a general oath not to participate in theft in any way.

The Carolingian evidence, incidentally, is remarkably similar in this regard. The duties specified in Charlemagne's capitulary text are not, in fact, particularly broad: they concern acts that either harmed the emperor's interests directly (and thus could easily be termed infidelity) or reflected royal duties (familiar to us from seventh-century Anglo-Saxon legislation) to protect the church and to ensure the proper functioning of legal mechanisms. One early ninth-century capitulary explicitly labels the thief as *infidelis*, which suggests that theft had somehow also come to be categorized as disloyalty,[34] and this is confirmed by a capitulary text from 853 that—rather like Edward the Elder's code—explicitly links the oath of fidelity with the duty not to hide thieves but to assist in their apprehension.[35] We even have associated texts from the mid-ninth century which, like Cnut's code, describe oaths specifically targeted at theft.[36] Using the breach of a general oath as a justification

---

[30] Af 1–1:2. See Wormald, 'Frederic William Maitland', p. 62; Matthias Ammon, ' "Ge mid wedde ge mid aðe": The Functions of Oath and Pledge in Anglo-Saxon Legal Culture', *Historical Research* 86 (2013), pp. 515–35, at 519–20; John Hudson, '*The Making of English Law* and Varieties of Legal History', in Stephen Baxter et al., eds., *Early Medieval Studies in Memory of Patrick Wormald* (Farnham, Surrey, 2009), pp. 421–32, at 424–5; Paul R. Hyams, *Rancour and Reconciliation in Medieval England* (Ithaca, 2003), p. 100; David Pratt, *The Political Thought of Alfred the Great* (Cambridge, 2007), pp. 233–8.

[31] II Ew 4–5.   [32] Cf. Ammon, 'Functions of Oath and Pledge', p. 533.   [33] II Cn 21.

[34] Boretius, *Capitularia*, i. p. 156 (no. 67, ch. 2); Goebel, *Felony and Misdemeanor*, pp. 120–1.

[35] Boretius, *Capitularia*, ii. pp. 272–3 (no. 260, chs. 4–8).

[36] Boretius, *Capitularia*, ii. p. 274.

for royal punishment was clearly significant both in Carolingian Francia and late Anglo-Saxon England, but in neither case did that justification extend to a category of offences as broad as the later concept of felony.

In a late Anglo-Saxon context it is particularly striking how closely aligned *frið* and the oath of loyalty are. It is not just that both were significant primarily in the context of measures against theft, but also that on two of the three occasions in our late Anglo-Saxon evidence when the oath is discussed it seems closely associated with *frið*. III Edmund, at any rate, is introduced as *de pace et iuramento faciendo* ('concerning peace and the oath which is to be made')—*pax* here is highly likely to be a Latin rendering of *frið*—while II Edward, as was noted, reveals the king citing what looks like the same oath formula in a bid to persuade his audience to devote themselves to the collective effort to improve *frið*.[37] The oath, then, makes most sense conceived as part of a wider enterprise for the establishment of peace; indeed, we should probably see it as subordinate to *frið* in that the oath was not an end in itself but a means by which kings secured the cooperation of their people in their efforts to ensure peace. The oath powerfully reinforced every man's duty to cooperate with the king against thieves; it did not explain or justify royal action against thieves in the way that the rhetoric of *frið* clearly did.

Disobedience (*Oferhyrnesse*)

Another ideological concept worthy of note in this context is the fine for *oferhyrnesse*, meaning disobedience, which is a frequent presence in laws of Edward the Elder and Æthelstan. It seems to imply a royal right to issue commands not to engage in certain types of wrongdoing and to punish those who disobeyed.[38] A brief survey of the types of wrongdoing explicitly associated with the term *oferhyrnesse* in the laws is revealing, in that unlike general oaths and *frið* there is no strong association with theft. Rather, the term is most frequently mentioned as a penalty for disobedient or uncooperative reeves,[39] and is otherwise associated almost exclusively with offences that could be characterized as breaches of legal procedure: refusal to accept an assembly's judgement in land cases,[40] receiving another lord's man when he is not free of all charges of wrongdoing (and thus helping him to evade prosecution),[41] refusal to attend assemblies,[42] refusal to ride on enforcement expeditions,[43] abandoning the tracking of stolen livestock early,[44] and buying goods outside a *port* (a recognized commercial centre) and thus failing to ensure title to the purchased goods was properly established before trustworthy

---

[37] III Em Prol; II Ew 1–1:1.

[38] For a thorough recent discussion of the term, see Alice Taylor, '*Lex scripta* and the Problem of Enforcement: Anglo-Saxon, Welsh, and Scottish Law Compared', in Fernanda Pirie and Judith Scheele, eds., *Legalism: Community and Justice* (Oxford, 2014), pp. 47–75 at 54–60. See also, Hudson, *Laws of England*, pp. 189–90.

[39] II Ew 2; I As 5; II As 25; V As 1:2, 1:3; VI As 8:4.   [40] I Ew 2–2:1. See also II Ew 1:2–1:3.
[41] II Ew 7; II As 22:1; V As 1–1:2.   [42] II As 20.   [43] II As 20:2.   [44] VI As 7.

witnesses.[45] The types of wrongdoing that are punished as disobedience to royal commands, then, are all related to the proper functioning of legal structures.[46]

This limitation in scope should be taken seriously. Though with a little imagination it would be possible to build the royal right of command into a general constitutional principle (much as an earlier generation of historians did for a small number of Carolingian references to the royal *bannum*),[47] implying that kings had a general right to command their subjects and to punish disobedience, this would not be accurate. The commands involved are specific to legal procedure, and there is no sign of any right to command beyond this field of activity. We certainly have no grounds for thinking that kings felt it appropriate to issue more sweeping commands encompassing forms of serious wrongdoing—commands that nobody commit theft or homicide, for example—and then to justify royal punishment of those acts with the theory that they constituted disobedience. Indeed, if we were to understand *oferhyrnesse* in more general terms, we might be tempted to view it as a originating in the individual's duty to participate fully in communal legal practices. This would, at least, fit with the London *frið*-guild demanding payment of 'our *oferhyrnesse*' from men who abandoned the search for their stolen livestock too early (a passage which also demonstrates that the right to issue commands relating to legal procedure and to punish disobedience was not exclusive to the king).[48]

An Ideology of Crime and Punishment?

The ideas reviewed here could be argued to form a unified whole. A general concern about the kingdom's *frið* explains royal action against theft, very much in line with the second command visible in the inauguration ritual, while the oath explains and reinforces the free population's duty to cooperate with their king in these matters. It would perhaps be logical to assume that the oath also created a duty to obey the king, and that the fine for disobedience was understood specifically in the context of that duty of obedience. Moreover, the thought that these ideas were connected gains some support from chronology: the first incontrovertible instances of all three concepts occur in the laws of Edward the Elder.[49] We should not, however, get carried away. Kings clearly expected cooperation against theft and obedience to their commands on legal procedure long before we find this rhetoric of peace, loyalty and obedience: it would be unwise to assume that their emergence signals the creation of any radically new understanding of the duties of either kings or their people. A more sensible reading would be that this was a new set of concepts which

---

[45] I Ew 1:1.

[46] The slight exceptions to this rule are from the later tenth century, when *oferhyrnesse* had ceased to be a common term: IV Atr 6 threatens the penalty for those who refuse to accept properly minted coinage and IV Eg 1 characterizes plague as punishment for *oferhyrnesse* to God.

[47] See Francois Louis Ganshof, *Frankish Institutions under Charlemagne* (Providence, 1968), pp. 11–12. Cf. Matthew Innes, *State and Society in the Early Middle Ages: The Middle Rhine Valley, 400–1000* (Cambridge, 2000), pp. 5–6 for a more limited view.

[48] VI As 7.   [49] I Ew 1:1, 2:1; II Ew 1, 1:1, 2, 5, 7.

served to explain and to reinforce traditional ideas about both what kings ought to be trying to achieve and the duty of their people to cooperate with their efforts.

We also need to be careful to acknowledge that though these ideas do seem to fit together, the fit is not perfect. The oath of loyalty may have had implications for theft, but we should not forget that until we are informed about an oath specific to theft in Cnut's reign these implications seem to have been bound up in an oath that made no direct reference to wrongdoing at all. The oath of loyalty which all free men swore to the king was, we must surely presume, primarily about loyalty in politics and warfare, the legal significance attributed to it being a secondary matter. The duty to obey implicit in the fine for *oferhyrnesse*, we should also note, need not be closely bound up with the loyalty oath. Kings were thought to have the right to command their people long before Alfred's reign—note the three commands in the inauguration ritual—so while such an interpretation seems natural it is hardly necessary, and the range of offences associated with the oath and *oferhyrnesse* do not align very closely. Indeed, an alternative reading of *oferhyrnesse* would be that the disobedience related more to the third element of the inauguration ritual: the command that justice and mercy be observed in all judgements. Interpreted broadly, this could be taken to imply that the king had overall responsibility for seeing that justice was done properly, and this included commanding his reeves to perform their functions correctly, but also ordering that people engage as they ought with the legal process: attending assemblies, accepting their judgements, helping to enforce them, and so on.

The third element of the inauguration ritual just mentioned has not received much attention here as yet, primarily because the core questions about what just judgements meant to contemporaries and what role the king played in providing them are treated in detail in the next chapter, which covers legal practice. However, it is important to note here that the image of king as judge is absolutely central to Alfred's code, which was known as the *Domboc*: 'judgement-book'. The code was evidently intended both as a symbolic demonstration of royal legal wisdom and as a means of disseminating that wisdom: it was presumably one means by which Alfred was attempting to fulfil his inauguration ritual's requirement that 'in all judgements he should order justice and mercy'.[50] Edward the Elder explicitly continues this theme, ordering that reeves make just judgements in accordance with the *Domboc,* that they should on no account fail to interpret *folcriht* (perhaps in this context best rendered 'the law of the people'), and that they ensure all cases had days fixed on which they would be decided.[51] Our examples of *oferhyrnesse* would make sense in this context, as disobedience to the commands which kings issued as part of their duty to oversee a properly functioning judicial system. It thus seems sensible to think not of a unified royal ideology, but rather of separate but complementary strands of thought, capable of overlapping and interlocking so as to reinforce one another.

---

[50] See Chapter 6, p. 265.
[51] I Ew Prol. On *folcriht* see Hudson, *Laws of England*, pp. 247–8.

KINGSHIP AND GOD'S FAVOUR

Kings did not just have a duty to maintain worldly social order, however, they also had explicitly religious responsibilities. The broadest of these relates to the maintenance of their kingdom's place in God's favour. That God dealt with peoples as moral units, rewarding those who pleased him with everything from victory in war to good weather and punishing those who did not with various forms of calamity, was an idea with a long and illustrious pedigree by the late Anglo-Saxon period. It drew, of course, on the model of God's relationship with the Israelites in the Old Testament, and is visible, as we saw in Chapter 2, in the way Bede, writing in the early eighth century and drawing in part on the earlier British writer Gildas, represented the misfortunes that befell the Britons in the fifth and sixth centuries.[52] The idea that kings had a particular responsibility for maintaining this relationship was old too. The extent to which pre-Christian Anglo-Saxon kingship—and Germanic kingship more generally—entailed a duty to maintain a people's 'luck' is still debated,[53] but it is clear that Irish kingship was understood in this way by at least the seventh century, as it is represented as such in a number of contemporary texts including *On the Twelve Abuses of the World*.[54] The ninth abuse listed in this highly influential text is that of an 'unjust king', the results of which included not just the shattering of the kingdom's earthly peace but a variety of dire cosmological consequences.[55]

This understanding of kingship proved popular in both insular and continental contexts in the succeeding centuries, most conspicuously in the politicization of royal sinfulness and penance under Louis the Pious, in what has been termed the Carolingian 'penitential state'.[56] There are signs of it in an English context from a relatively early stage—it is clear that the ninth abuse was known to English churchmen from at least the mid-eighth century—but this pattern of thought is most visible in the late tenth and early eleventh centuries. Bishop Æthelwold of Winchester is known to have given a Latin copy of the *Twelve Abuses* to Peterborough, and the text's influence is visible in the writings of both Archbishop

---

[52] See Chapter 2, pp. 96–7.

[53] William A. Chaney, *The Cult of Kingship in Anglo-Saxon England: The Transition from Paganism to Christianity* (Manchester, 1970), esp. ch. 1; Marita Blattman, ' "Ein Unglück für sein Volk": Der Zusammenhang zwischen Fehlverhalten des Königs und Volkswohl in Quellen des 7.–12. Jahrhunderts', *Frühmittelalterliche Studien* 30 (1996), pp. 80–102.

[54] For the text, see Siegmund Hellmann, *Pseudo-Cyprianus De XII Abusivis Saeculi* (Leipzig, 1909); Aidan Breen, 'Towards a Critical Edition of *De XII Abusivis*: Introductory Essays with a Provisional Edition of the Text Accompanied by an English Translation' (Trinity College Dublin PhD thesis, 1988). On the wider currency of these ideas in early medieval Ireland see Rob Meens, 'Politics, Mirrors of Princes and the Bible: Sins, Kings and the Well-Being of the Realm', *Early Medieval Europe* 7 (1998), pp. 345–57, at 351–3.

[55] Hellmann, *Pseudo-Cyprianus*, pp. 51–3; Breen, 'Towards a Critical Edition', pp. 400–9; For a convenient summary and general discussion see Meens, 'Politics, Mirrors of Princes and the Bible', pp. 350–1.

[56] Mayke de Jong, *The Penitential State: Authority and Atonement in the Age of Louis the Pious, 814–840* (Cambridge, 2009).

Wulfstan and Ælfric of Eynsham, who produced an abridged Old English translation.[57] The Old English version of the royal inauguration ritual (which translates
the B version of the second *ordo*, in which the king's three commands have become
three promises) appends a brief sermon, quite possibly written by Archbishop
Wulfstan, which borrows directly from the *Twelve Abuses* and makes the importance of good kingship clear:

> The Christian king who observes these things will earn for himself worldly honour and
> eternal God will have mercy on him both in this present life and also in the eternal
> which will never come to an end. If he fails to fulfil that which was promised to God,
> then within a very short time after that things will grow worse among his people, and in
> the end it will all turn out for the worst, unless he previously make amends for it in his
> lifetime.[58]

Here we see that, by Wulfstan's time at the latest, fulfilment of all a king's inaugural
promises could be seen as essential not just to the king's personal salvation but to
the earthly condition of his people. Moreover, we also see here a link between the
king's personal virtue and the well-being of his kingdom: he must make amends for
his sins or it will all turn out for the worst. Recent work has drawn attention to a
series of charters framed as part of Æthelred's penance for his youthful sins,
interpreting them in precisely this light.[59]

The king's duty to ensure his kingdom as a whole retained God's favour, then,
was hardly novel in the late Anglo-Saxon period but it does seem to have become a
point of particularly pressing concern by the end of the tenth century. In the laws
this comes across forcefully in the texts written by Wulfstan, substantial sections of
which are best interpreted as a programme by which the English people might
regain their place in God's esteem. Within this broader concern there are two
particular strands I would like to draw attention to here. The first is that these
ideas are central whenever we find the laws justifying their concern to uphold
among the laity (and to an extent also among the clergy) what seem to have been
regarded as minimum acceptable standards of Christian observance. Though hardly
surprising—this is probably the rationale on which kings had punished ecclesiastical offences for centuries—it is important to establish this clearly. The second
strand of thought involves concern about the pollutant properties of sin, specifically
sin which had not been expiated through penance, the taint of which needed to be

[57] Mary Clayton, '*De Duodecim Abusiuis*, Lordship and Kingship in Anglo-Saxon England', in
Hugh Magennis and Stuart McWilliams, eds., *Saints and Scholars: New Perspectives on Anglo-Saxon
Literature and Culture* (Cambridge, 2012), pp. 141–63 at 149–63. For Ælfric's translation: Mary
Clayton, *Two Ælfric Texts: 'The Twelve Abuses' and 'The Vices and Virtues': An Edition and Translation
of Ælfric's Old English Versions of 'De duodecim abusiuis' and 'De octo uitiis et de duodecim abusiuis'*
(Cambridge, 2013).
[58] Clayton, 'Old English *Promissio Regis*', pp. 131–45 (the case for Wulfstan's authorship), 148–9
(quotation).
[59] Levi Roach, 'Penitential Discourse in the Diplomas of King Æthelred "the Unready"', *Journal of
Ecclesiastical History* 64 (2013), pp. 258–76, at 270; Catherine Cubitt, 'The Politics of Remorse:
Penance and Royal Piety in the Reign of Æthelred the Unready', *Historical Research* 85 (2012),
pp. 179–92, at 185–91.

kept away from the king and cast out of the community in order to maintain the kingdom's place in God's favour.

Minimum Standards of Christian Observance

Kings in this period, as we have seen, used both protections and punishments to target laymen who failed to maintain certain minimum standards of Christian observance, focusing on sexual (particularly marital) misconduct, on respect for sacred times (particularly the Sabbath) and places, and most frequently of all on the payment of various church dues.[60] Some part of the rationale for this is made explicit in two texts which address the reasons for disasters befalling the kingdom. One of Edgar's codes begins by explaining that the king 'has been considering what remedy could be found for the plague which has greatly afflicted and reduced his people throughout the length and breadth of his dominion', and that he and his councillors concluded that their misery arose 'because of sin and disregard of God's commands, and especially through the withholding of the tribute which Christian people should render to God by their tithes.' Edgar therefore commanded that these be paid, and ordered his reeves (under threat of punishment themselves) rigorously to impose the existing punishments for non-payment.[61] Interestingly, this is connected with prescriptions about the conduct of priests—'it is my will that . . . the servants of God who receive the dues which we render to Him shall live a pure life, so that, by virtue of their purity, they may intercede for us with God'— which are themselves backed up with the promise of secular assistance for bishops attempting to discipline wayward clergymen.[62]

A very similar message is visible in the second text, which emerged from an assembly held in Bath in 1009, 'when the great army came to the country', and which prescribes various means by which 'we may obtain the mercy and compassion of God and through his help withstand our foes.'[63] The remedies envisaged hinged on mass penitence by the people as a whole: all were to fast for three days before Michaelmas, then proceed barefoot to church to make confession, and from every hide of land a penny was to be paid to the church (under threat of punishment). All *hiredmen* (perhaps 'members of a household') were to give an additional penny as alms, with lords giving on behalf of those who could not afford to do so, and all *heafodmen* (perhaps 'heads of household') were to render tithes. Slaves, meanwhile, were to be excused work so as to encourage them to fast. Throughout these three days all monks were to sing psalms, and every priest was to say mass 'for our lord and for all his people'. Moreover, until some improvement came about, each monastery was to have a daily mass said specifically on the subject of the country's current distress, with all brothers prostrating themselves before the altar and singing the psalm 'Oh Lord, how are they multiplied'. And from that

---

[60] Chapter 4, pp. 172–3, 186, 189. For a broader view of minimum standards focusing on a later period, see Norman Tanner and Sethina Watson, 'Least of the Laity: the Minimum Requirements for a Medieval Christian', *Journal of Medieval History* 32 (2006), pp. 395–423.

[61] IV Eg Prol-1:5.   [62] IV Eg 1:6–1:8.   [63] VII Atr Prol.

point forward all men were to turn earnestly to God, and pay church dues in full and on time.[64]

The idea that the people as a whole needed to undergo penance in order to redeem themselves before God clearly shows what was at stake here. Kings were partly responsible—in conjunction with the Church, of course—for ensuring that their people maintained a good relationship with God, and in the extreme circumstances that inspired both these texts this responsibility came to be particularly sharply defined. These were points at which divine favour seemed to have deserted the kingdom, prompting reflection on what had gone so horribly wrong and how it might be fixed. The centrality of payment of church dues in these urgent analyses is very striking—it was clearly identified as major problem—but it should be noted that marital misconduct and respect for holy times, the other main themes of royal legislation on minimum standards of lay piety, come up frequently in Wulfstan's more extended legislative sermonizing, in a context which makes plain that the central purpose was to secure a favourable place in God's esteem for the kingdom and its people.[65]

The insistence on a more demanding set of moral standards for the clergy—focusing on their celibacy in particular—fits with this nicely, both because this was what God expected of his servants and, as Edgar's code makes clear, because the purity of their lives was an essential precondition for effective intercessory prayer on behalf of both the king and his people.[66] But here we tend not to find kings imposing secular punishments as they do for lay religious misconduct. Edmund does prescribe forfeiture of worldly possessions alongside forfeiture of consecrated burial for sexually active priests who did not undergo penance but, given the lack of secular penalties in any of our other texts this appears exceptional. Edgar's promise of secular support for episcopal discipline seems more likely to be representative of late Anglo-Saxon practice.[67]

---

[64] VII Atr 1–8.

[65] On marriage: V Atr 10; VI Atr 11–12; I Cn 6:3–7:3. On respect for sacred time: V Atr 13–20; VI Atr 22–25:2; I Cn 15–17:3. On maintaining God's favour for the people as a whole: V Atr 25; VI Atr 30; I Cn 19:3. This is, of course, both a major feature of Wulfstan's homiletic works—most famously his 'Sermon of the Wolf to the English'—and a well-established historiographical theme. See Simon Keynes, 'An Abbot, an Archbishop, and the Viking Raids of 1006–7 and 1009–12', *Anglo-Saxon England* 36 (2007), pp. 151–220, esp. at 170–89; Patrick Wormald, *The Making of English Law: King Alfred to the Twelfth Century* (Oxford, 1999), pp. 330–45, 449–65; Patrick Wormald, 'Archbishop Wulfstan and the Holiness of Society', repr. in and cited from Wormald, *Legal Culture*, pp. 225–51; Malcolm Godden, 'Apocalypse and Invasion in Late Anglo-Saxon England', in Godden, D. Gray and T. Hoad, eds., *From Anglo-Saxon to Early Middle English: Studies Presented to E.G. Stanley* (Oxford, 1994), pp. 130–62; George Molyneaux, 'Did the English really think they were God's elect in the Anglo-Saxon period?', *Journal of Ecclesiastical History* 65 (2014), pp. 721–37; Levi Roach, 'Apocalypse and Atonement in the Politics of Æthelredian England', *English Studies* 95 (2014), pp. 733–57; George Molyneaux, 'The Formation of the English Kingdom, c.871–c.1016' (Oxford University DPhil thesis, 2009), pp. 43–61. For the 'Sermon of the Wolf' see Dorothy Whitelock, ed., *Sermo Lupi ad Anglos* (rev. edn, Exeter, 1976).

[66] IV Eg 1:7–1:8. See also, I Em 1; V Atr 9; VI Atr 5, 41; I Cn 6a-6:2a.

[67] I Em I; IV Eg 1:7–1:8.

Sin, Penance, and Pollution

There was, of course, no way kings could legislate to prevent their people committing all sinful acts. Sin was an inevitable part of the human condition and its complete elimination was beyond the scope of the king's responsibilities; the main responsibility for dealing with sin fell to the Church, and to the mechanisms of confession and penance by which sinners could reconcile themselves with God.[68] If sinners availed themselves of the opportunity for salvation that confession and penance afforded them, sin was not in itself something for kings to worry about. When sinners refused to undergo penance, however, there was a problem: not only would obdurately sinful individuals surely fail to find salvation, those who harboured them could be tainted by association in the eyes of God, and thus lose his favour. We can again see this line of thought quite clearly for homicide. Most explicitly, Wulfstan's legislative campaign to maintain God's favour through the purification the kingdom incorporates repeated exhortations that unrepentant killers be cast out of the land.[69] Even more interestingly, we find King Edmund forbidding killers who had not begun penance from coming into his presence, perhaps suggesting that it was particularly important that kings—with their special role in maintaining God's goodwill towards the kingdom—remain innocent of any charge of consorting with the resolutely sinful.[70]

Though to modern eyes it is particularly striking that the Anglo-Saxons should have taken this attitude to homicide—viewing what we would see as the most serious of crimes as something which could be addressed adequately through penitential means—we should bear in mind that in both these contexts unrepentant killers form part of a wider category of unrepentant sinners. As people to be kept out of the king's presence, they are grouped with similarly impenitent excommunicants, murderers, and perjurers.[71] As people to be cast out of the land, unrepentant killers were associated with unrepentant murderers, perjurers, injurers of the clergy, witches, sorcerers, and 'foul, polluted, notorious prostitutes'.[72] The concern here was not specifically about killers, it was about the spiritual dangers of association with those who refused to atone for grievous sin.

This logic may be that which underpinned one of the most striking themes of Anglo-Saxon legal practice: the denial of Christian burial to certain types of wrongdoer. Our earliest reference to this is Æthelstan's Grately code, which orders

[68] On penance see Rob Meens, *Penance in Medieval Europe, 600–1200* (Cambridge, 2014); Catherine Cubitt, 'Bishops, Priests and Penance in Late Saxon England', *Early Medieval Europe* 14 (2006), pp. 41–63; Brad Bedingfield, 'Public Penance in Anglo-Saxon England', *Anglo-Saxon England* 31 (2002), pp. 223–55; Sarah Hamilton, 'Rites for Public Penance in Late Anglo-Saxon England', in Helen Gittos and M. Bradford Bedingfield, eds., *The Liturgy of the Late Anglo-Saxon Church* (London, 2005), pp. 65–103; Allen J. Frantzen, *The Literature of Penance in Anglo-Saxon England* (New Brunswick, 1983). Now also: Stefan Jurasinski, *The Old English Penitentials and Anglo-Saxon Law* (New York, 2015).
[69] V Atr 23–25; VI Atr 28:2, 36; VIII Atr 26; II Cn 6.   [70] I Em 3; II Em 4.
[71] I Em 3; II Em 4; V Atr 29; VI Atr 36. For the distinction between killers and murderers, see Chapter 4, pp. 193–5.
[72] Cn 1018 7–10:1; II Cn 6; EGu 11 (for quotation). See also I Em 6.

that proven perjurers be excluded from consecrated cemeteries when they die unless a bishop can attest to their having done the penance prescribed to them by their confessor.[73] Edmund's laws add to this theme, ordering that consecrated burial be denied to killers as well as to a variety of sexual offenders (adulterers, men who lay with nuns, and any clergy who failed to observe celibacy) unless, of course, they made amends.[74] The pattern here is strikingly similar: these offenders are not to lose their lives for their offences, but unless they make amends for their sins they are to be excluded from Christian cemeteries when they die. To view this as a manifestation of the extremely punitive spirit of late Anglo-Saxon law (the framework within which denial of Christian burial is usually understood)[75] is not entirely satisfactory, as there is no sign of secular punishment here. The point of excluding these people from Christian cemeteries, rather, seems twofold: as a threat to encourage sinners to submit to ecclesiastical discipline, and as a means of keeping the good Christians buried in those cemeteries safe from the taint of pollution that was associated with unrepented sin. Just as burial in proximity to those of prodigious virtue—saints—was held to confer spiritual advantage, burial alongside the prodigiously sinful seems to have been understood as spiritually dangerous.[76]

Impenitent sinners thus had to be segregated from the Christian community for its own safety, and this idea manifested itself in three different forms: expulsion from the community during life, separation from good Christians after death, and the prevention of contact with the king, who as symbolic head of the community had special responsibility for ensuring its good relations with God. That these three types of exclusion formed a coherent agenda is particularly clear in I Edmund, a short text devoted almost entirely to them: two of its six clauses deal with exclusion from Christian burial, two mention exclusion from the community of living Christians, and one exclusion from the presence of the king.[77] It was introduced as the result of Edmund's archbishops and bishops 'taking counsel for the welfare of their [own] souls and [the souls] of those who have been placed under their charge'.

---

[73] II As 26.   [74] I Em 1, 4.

[75] See Victoria Thompson, *Dying and Death in Later Anglo-Saxon England* (Woodbridge, 2004), pp. 170–80; Wormald, *Papers Preparatory*, pp. 129–38; Andrew Reynolds, *Anglo-Saxon Deviant Burial Customs* (Oxford, 2009), pp. 248–9. Also Nicole Marafioti, 'Punishing Bodies and Saving Souls: Capital and Corporal Punishment in Late Anglo-Saxon England', *Haskins Society Journal* 20 (2008), pp. 39–57 at 41, albeit in the context of a subtle dissection of the difficulties of reconciling this notion with ecclesiastical thought on the subject.

[76] John Blair, 'The Dangerous Dead in Early Medieval England', in Baxter et al., *Early Medieval Studies in Memory of Patrick Wormald*, pp. 539–59, esp. at 552–3. John Blair, *The Church in Anglo-Saxon Society* (Oxford, 2005), pp. 228–45, 463–6. Note also the isolated and peripheral burial location of the sinful and impenitent monk discussed in *Ecclesiastical History*, v. 14, and the possible rationale for such concerns about spiritual pollution—the presence of demons—implicit in the admittedly much later *De Nugis Curialum* of Walter Map (d. 1209/10): 'they say that people shudder in dread when there are thieves or deer close by at night. I have no idea why that should be the case with the deer; but with thieves, it is not they who cause the goosebumps, but the demons that go along with them.' See Walter Map, *De Nugis Curialium: Courtiers' Trifles*, ed. and trans. M. R. James, C. N. L. Brooke, and R. A. B. Mynors (Oxford, 1983), iv. 6. I am grateful to Rick Sowerby (whose translation of Map I have borrowed here) for both these references.

[77] I Em 1–4, 6.

The context of pastoral concern for the welfare of the community at large is thus explicit.[78]

This context is less obvious in some of our later evidence for denial of Christian burial. The text of uncertain but possibly eleventh-century date known as IV Æthelred prescribes unconsecrated burial for those killed in the course of committing (what are clearly Latin renderings of) *hamsocn* and *forsteal,* and perhaps also *mundbryce.*[79] One of Æthelred's laws, repeated in Cnut's code, orders that any men generally regarded as *ungetreow* (literally 'untrue' or 'unfaithful') by their local communities be placed under surety, and that if no surety could be found they be killed and buried in unconsecrated ground along with all who dared defend them.[80] Æthelred's Wantage code, intended for the Danelaw, also implies that Christian burial was normally denied to slain thieves: it explains that the relatives of such a slain man could undertake an ordeal to clear him of the charge, thus gaining the right to exhume their kinsman and bury him properly.[81] We also have two records of cases which make it plain that Christian burial was meant to be denied to those who, in one case, died in the course of defending a thief, and in the other, much more obscurely, forfeited his property 'by the sword that hung on his hip when he drowned'—perhaps a reference to the treasonous bearing of arms against the king.[82] There is nothing in any of these passages about penance, but this is hardly surprising: the offender's opportunity to undertake it was cut short by death in each of these cases. All were killed, or prescribed to be killed, in the act of sinning (except perhaps the *ungetreow* man, whose *ungetreow* status should probably be taken to imply that he was an inveterate and unrepentant wrongdoer) and therefore by definition went to the grave polluted by unrepented sin. The expectation that such offenders be denied Christian burial is consistent with the logic that emerges from the earlier texts; it is only that the earlier texts concern sinners who lived out their lives without taking the opportunity to undergo penance, whereas for these later ones the emphasis on immediate execution meant the possibility of undergoing penance did not exist.[83]

---

[78] I Em Prol. It is even more prominent in those later laws written by Wulfstan, where this is the central theme. Denial of Christian burial is not a major concern here, but it does occur in a passage in the ecclesiastical section of Cnut's laws, which argues that people who disdain to learn the Pater Noster and the Creed, and do not truly believe in God in their hearts, are not true Christians and should be entitled to receive neither the sacrament nor consecrated burial (I Cn 22–22:6). In this passage Wulfstan is in full homiletic mode, so we probably ought to regard this as ideological rhetoric rather than a serious attempt to enforce lay piety with the threat of unconsecrated burial, but the context within which it occurs is telling. It is part of a long passage in which Wulfstan exhorts the laity to observe Christianity diligently and to purify the land by casting out wrongdoing, both for the sake of their own souls and so that 'the mercy of God will be granted the more readily to us all' (I Cn 19:3). Here again, then, we find the denial of Christian burial appearing as part of a broader effort to keep the community as a whole pure and in God's favour.

[79] IV Atr 4. On the date of this text, see Chapter 4, p. 187, n. 102.

[80] I At 4–4:2; II Cn 33–33:1a. On the *ungetreow,* see Chapter 6, pp. 261–4.

[81] III Atr 7–7:1.

[82] Death in defence of thief: S 883. Drowning forfeiture: S 1447.

[83] It should be noted that executed wrongdoers were denied access to Christian funerary rites alongside suicides by the Council of Braga in 560, and that this text was known to Archbishop Wulfstan who included it in his collection of canon law (see J. E. Cross and Andrew Hamer, eds.,

It thus seems likely that the exclusion of executed corpses from Christian cemeteries was part of a broader concern about excluding the pollution of unrepented sin from Christian society, thereby retaining God's favour. This line of thought seems to go back to the seventh century. We have, at any rate, seemingly incontrovertible radiocarbon-dating evidence for the burial of executed corpses in places with pagan associations as far back as the late seventh or eighth century.[84] Moreover, we can see a similar logic visible in seventh-century texts; Wihtred of Kent's laws on unlawful unions seem to reveal a familiar thought process:

> Men in an unlawful union shall take up a just life with repentance of sins, or be separated from the community of the church. Foreign men, if they will not set their union to right, must depart from the land with their possessions and with [their] sins. Our own men among the [Kentish] people shall suffer the loss of the community of the church without forfeiture of goods.[85]

The idea that foreign men, at least, should be made to depart the land 'with their sins' and the exclusion of those who do not repent seem to prefigure clearly the late Anglo-Saxon patterns just outlined. Concern about the pollutant properties of sin, though particularly prominent in the laws of Edmund and at the turn of the millennium, way well be a tradition inherited from the early days of Anglo-Saxon Christian kingship.

God, Church, and King

Maintaining God's favour was a broader programme of activity than the two themes which have been emphasized here. Indeed, it is possible to read the ecclesiastical section of Cnut's great code—the culmination of Wulfstan's legislative endeavours—as essentially a programme for the restoration and maintenance of God's favour. As well as material on the payment of church dues, respect for holy times, the regulation of sexual conduct, and the exclusion of sin, it touches on proper respect for holy places (including the protection of churches), the proper conduct of male and female ecclesiastics, and—at some length—on how important it was for everyone to be a good Christian. It was essential for the laity to attend carefully to Christian teaching, to undertake confession and communion regularly, and 'day and night to be in terror of sin, dreading the Day of Judgement and shuddering at the thought of hell, and ever expecting their last day to be close at hand.'[86] The message here is as much about the duty of the Church to shepherd the

---

Wulfstan's Canon Law Collection (Cambridge, 1999), pp. 112–13). The text itself offers no explanation for their exclusion, but it would have fitted well with the ideas discussed here: suicides by definition die in a state of unrepented sin. On suicide, see Mary Clayton, 'Suicide in the Works of Ælfric', *Review of English Studies* 60 (2009), pp. 339–70; Alexander Murray, *Suicide in the Middle Ages*, vol. 2: *The Curse on Self-Murder* (Oxford, 2000), esp. 181–8; 270–6.

[84] Reynolds, *Deviant Burial*, pp. 153–5. For a discussion that usefully situates execution cemeteries as just one element in a diverse overall picture of mortuary practice, see Dawn M. Hadley and Jo Buckberry, 'Caring for the Dead in Late Anglo-Saxon England', in Francesca Tinti, ed., *Pastoral Care in Late Anglo-Saxon England* (Woodbridge, 2005), pp. 121–47.

[85] Wi 3–4:1.   [86] I Cn 25.

laity and to intercede with God on their behalf as it is about kingship. In its broadest form royal responsibility for maintaining God's favour thus boils down to royal oversight, support and protection of the Church. In this form it aligns well with the similarly broad first element of the royal inauguration ritual: 'that the Church of God and all Christian people preserve true peace, in God the omnipotent.'[87]

The strands of thought picked out here, however, suggest particular areas of royal attention. Kings seem to have been so fundamentally responsible for project of maintaining God's favour that their personal sinfulness could jeopardize not only their own salvation but the earthly fortunes of their people. Kings were not capable of subjecting an entire population to damnation in the afterlife—salvation was a matter for individuals under the pastoral guidance of the Church—but their office made them personally responsible for ensuring that God treated their people well in worldly terms. As such it was important that they remained personally untainted by grievous sins, both by addressing their own failings through penance and by ensuring that they were not polluted by association with those who refused to atone for their enormities. They also needed to ensure that their people did not offend God through flagrant impiety. Churchmen could undertake the task of inculcating the finer points of Christian morality in their flocks and they could help the repentant atone for even the most grievous of sins, but those who refused either to meet basic standards of Christian observance or to submit to penitential discipline demanded secular intervention. Such figures needed either to be forced to conform to communal moral standards or excluded from the community whose place in God's esteem they threatened. Whether the rhetoric of exclusion had any effect on the living we cannot tell—it may just have been rhetoric—but it is clear that the dead were in practice segregated, with potentially dangerous spiritual pollutants buried in separate cemeteries which often had pagan rather than Christian associations.

VIOLENCE AND SOCIETY

The place of violence in late Anglo-Saxon law may seem something of a puzzle. We have seen that the laws' more explicitly religious rhetoric touches on violence on occasion, but thus far only incidentally and in ways that make it clear violence was not the main issue. Killers could be dangerous spiritual pollutants, but only if they failed to do appropriate penance. The practical measures in the laws, moreover, do not tend to address violence in its own right but rather focus on violence in particular circumstances, using specific protections. Case material supports this, showing that killings within the family seem to have been dealt with not through the imposition of punishment but by penance, whereas those few records of land forfeiture for violence where we have sufficient detail suggest a context of royal

---

[87] See above, p. 206.

protection.[88] The only royal punishment visible in late Anglo-Saxon law for violence in its own right was the fine for fighting (*fihtwite*) but this was inherited from a seventh-century measure that may have originally been a protection and it remained isolated in late Anglo-Saxon law, which otherwise seems to work on the assumption that violent feuding was a legitimate element of legal practice. This all begs the question of how the Anglo-Saxons thought about violence: to what extent was violence—even killing—regarded an offence against the community as a whole, a threat to order?

There can be no doubt that violence, particularly lethal violence, was taken very seriously in Anglo-Saxon law. This is most easily demonstrated in crude financial terms. The principal deterrent to homicide was the requirement to pay wergild: 200 shillings for a freeman in the West Saxon legal tradition, and 1200 shillings for a nobleman. These are very large sums. The king's *mundbyrd* of £5—the penalty settled upon for breaching the crucially important protections represented by *hamsocn*, *mundbryce*, and *forsteal*—equates to only 240 shillings, whilst the standard fine for *oferhyrnesse* appears to have been 120 shillings.[89] We should also remember that, although this is not the ideal outcome they prioritize, the laws make it clear that killers who could or would not pay for their acts financially should expect to be made to pay for them physically: they faced legitimately being killed themselves in vengeance for their actions.[90] The penalties faced by killers in Anglo-Saxon law, then, meet or exceed the highest standards of severity set by royal demands. The issue we are addressing here is not whether violence was regarded as a 'serious' matter by Anglo-Saxon law and society, but whether violence was taken to be damaging to the community as well as to its immediate victims.

Peace and Concord

The most obviously pertinent ideas here come in the prologue to II Edmund, which begins by stating that Edmund and his advisers had been considering 'how I could best promote Christianity' and that they had concluded it seemed 'first of all especially needful that we steadfastly maintain peace (*gesibsumnesse*) and concord (*gepwærnesse*) among ourselves throughout all my dominion'.[91] The word for 'peace' used here, we should note, is *gesibsumnesse*, which derives from the same word, *sib*, used in the late Anglo-Saxon translation of the inauguration ritual to refer to the 'true peace' to be preserved by the Church of God and all Christian people.[92] This is a term for peace which, unlike *frið*, is rooted in ideas of shared kinship (the modern English 'sibling' derives from the same concept) and friendship.[93] The ideal being referenced is that Christians, all being members of one fictive family, ought to live in a state of mutual charity with one another.[94]

---

[88] Chapter 4, pp. 195–7; Lambert, 'Theft, Homicide and Crime', pp. 34–6.
[89] I Ew 2:1; IV Atr 4–4:1; II Cn 58, 63.
[90] II Em 1; VIII Atr 23; I Cn 5:2b. Chapter 4, pp. 181–2.   [91] II Em Prol–Prol 1.
[92] Clayton, 'The Old English *Promissio Regis*', p. 148.
[93] ASD s.vv. 'ge-sib', 'ge-sibbsum', 'ge-sibbsumnys', 'ge-sibsum', 'ge-sibsumnes', 'sibsum', 'sibsumness'.
[94] Kershaw, *Peaceful Kings*, ch. 3, esp. 140–1, 152; Bonnaud Delamare, *L'Idée de Paix*, esp. ch. 9.

Edmund's concern was that this ideal state of harmonious Christian coexistence was being disrupted; specifically, he declared that 'the wrongful and manifold fights that take place among us distress me and all of us greatly'.[95]

It would be easy to read this as ideological opposition to violence in principle but we need to be careful on this point. The issue was not violence itself but the effect that violent enmities had on communal cohesion, understood here in emphatically Christian terms—it was the disruption of Christian peace and concord by violent acts that was problematic, not necessarily violence in its own right. This is, in fact, underlined by the main body of the code, which begins with this statement: 'If henceforth anyone slay a man, he is himself to bear the feud, unless he can with the aid of his friends within twelve months pay compensation at the full wergild.'[96] This was an idealized vision of responsible feuding rather than a measure Edmund intended to enforce: no penalties for violation are given, and the clauses that follow presume that kindreds needed to disown their homicidal members in order to gain exemption from the threat of vengeance. This makes it all the more useful for current purposes, as it demonstrates that the ideal for which Edmund was aiming was hardly non-violent. The primary hope, presumably, was that a compensation settlement would be reached and the disruptive state of enmity created by the original killing brought to an end, with Christian peace and concord thus re-established. But the primary emphasis here is on what should happen if this was not possible: the original killer himself should 'bear the feud'. That is, he alone should be targeted for vengeance killing. The point here, it seems, is that taking vengeance on the original killer keeps the enmity contained: with the original killer himself killed, it was presumably hoped that the symmetry of the situation would be recognized and a peace settlement would be possible. If someone essentially innocent of the original killing had been chosen for vengeance, on the other hand, the killer's cousin, for instance, the obvious injustice of the act would only have provoked bitter feelings that would have made a peace settlement more difficult to achieve, and it could potentially have drawn a wider set of relatives—the cousin's own cousins—into a long-lasting enmity that fundamentally ruptured communal peace and concord.

Edmund's target, then, was not violence in principle but violence which caused or exacerbated enmity; it was the enmity that worried him more than the violence. The concrete measure he tried to take—the establishment of a procedure allowing kindreds to disown killers and gain legal protection from vengeance in feud—demonstrates the point even more clearly.[97] The idea was not to prevent vengeance killing. Disowning a killer involved abandoning him to his enemies: it was an explicit declaration that he could be killed without incurring any legal liability with respect to his erstwhile kindred. It ensured, in fact, that the only way the affronted kindred could gain satisfaction for the original killing was through violence: few killers could have hoped to meet the liabilities incurred by a homicide without drawing on the wider resources of their kin. The point presumably was that once

---

[95] II Em Prol 2.   [96] II Em 1.   [97] II Em 1:1–1:3. See Chapter 4, pp. 191–2.

the killer was abandoned to a violent death, peace could be restored between the two kindreds involved. Christian peace and concord would not then be endangered even if the disowned killer later met a gruesome end at the hands of his victim's relatives. Edmund was not trying to prevent violence, he was trying to prevent enmity and, contrary to what one might expect, that involved encouraging properly targeted vengeance killings.

The royal protections which are prominent in the rest of Edmund's code align well with this agenda, in that (as was discussed in Chapter 4) their intention seems to be to prevent the rapid escalation of conflicts by strengthening the refuges traditionally available to those in fear. Their feud context is often explicit. *Hamsocn*, if we believe the *Leges Henrici*, was targeted specifically at people who sought out their enemies in houses (quarrels that flared up among people in a house together not being covered), whilst *forsteal* was envisaged in the context of men ambushing their enemies while they travelled on roads. Indeed, the only plausible context for someone actively seeking out the personal *mund* (or *grið*) of the king by petitioning a local royal agent is one of established enmity.[98] These protections, in short, should be understood as attempts to encourage the peaceful settlement of feuds, and the re-establishment of peace and concord, by targeting the specific types of vengeful violence that tended to lead their escalation. The practical measures envisaged in Edmund's code, and indeed in those of his successors, thus match up well with his broader ideological opening: the issue of concern was not violence in its own right but the presence of conflict and enmity dividing a theoretically united Christian society. Concern for peace and concord required and justified the tighter regulation of feuding so as to ensure it was carried out responsibly; it did not involve the condemnation of homicide as intrinsically threatening to order.

Freedom and Order

This conclusion leaves our original question even more urgently in need of an answer. We have seen that killing posed a threat to society in that it involved sins which might not then be repented, and also in that it could lead to enmities which ruptured the state of peace and concord which ought to characterize Christian society, but in none of these discussions was violence—even lethal violence—treated as a threat to communal wellbeing in its own right. Violence was a great personal wrong, of course, but it does not in principle seem to have been held to cause great social harm. It was only when violence had particular consequences—the prevalence of enmity or unrepented sin—that it became a matter of concern demanding royal attention, which was invariably expressed in terms of emphatically Christian ideals. Why should this have been?

Probably the best explanation is cultural: feuding was rooted in identity. It was understood as important that free men be weapon-bearing men, willing and able to use violence in the defence of their own honour and in the maintenance of order.

---

[98] Chapter 4, pp. 183–90.

This capacity for legitimate violence seems likely to have been an integral part of what made a free man both free and male. Indeed, it is notable that late Anglo-Saxon laws often refer to the free, both noble and common, in terms of their wergilds—as two-hundred-men and twelve-hundred-men—suggesting a conceptual link between free status and potential involvement in feuding.[99] We find something similar in Cnut's threat that men who failed to join a tithing would not be entitled to any of the rights of a freeman, of which the right to wergild if slain and the right to make a oaths of denial were mentioned specifically.[100] The symbolic importance of weapon-bearing for free status is also suggested by Cnut's specification of relatively steep compensations for disarming other men or tying them up: a tenth and a half of their wergilds respectively.[101] These were attacks on symbols of personal status: what better way to humiliate a free, weapon-bearing man than to bind or disarm him?[102]

The ideal free man was meant to carry weaponry and be able to use it. Moreover, though violence (and killing in particular) may have been sinful in principle from an ecclesiastical standpoint, from a secular perspective killing could be not just a necessary evil but highly commendable. This passage from the London *frið*-guild, set up in response to Æthelstan's anti-theft campaign, makes a good example:

> We have pronounced that, no matter who did the deeds which avenged the injury of us all, we were all in one friendship and in one enmity, whichever should result; and he who was before others in killing a thief, should be the better off by 12 pence from the money of us all for the deed and for the enterprise.[103]

When it came to the enforcement of justice and order, then, violence was not only necessary but to be praised and rewarded. This passage from the late tenth- or early eleventh-century text known as the Regulations of the Cambridge Thegns' Guild is in many respects similar:

> And if anyone kill a guild-brother, nothing other than £8 is to be accepted as compensation. If the slayer scorns to pay the compensation, all the guildship is to avenge the guild-brother and all bear the feud. If then one avenges him, all are to bear the feud alike. And if any guild-brother slays a man and does it as an avenger by necessity and to remedy the insult to him, and the slain man's wergild is 1200 [shillings], each guild brother is to supply half a mark to his aid; if the man is a ceorl, 2 ores; if he is servile [or Welsh?] (*wylisc*), 1 ore. If, however, the guild-brother

---

[99] Ine 70; Af 10, 39:2, 40; VI As 8:2; III Em 2; Að 1; Wer 1–1:1, 7.   [100] II Cn 20.

[101] II Cn 60. This represents a tenfold increase on Alfred's specification of 10 shillings as the appropriate compensation for tying up a ceorl (Af 35).

[102] Af 35:1–35:6 suggest that whipping and forcibly cutting the hair or beard of a freeman were understood as belonging to the same category of humiliating affronts as forcible binding. Whipping was certainly associated with unfreedom in Anglo-Saxon law (e.g. Ine 48, 54:28; VII Atr 3; II Cn 45:1–45:2, 46–46:2) and it is plausible that hair- and beard-styles were also markers of status (see Robert Bartlett, 'Symbolic Meanings of Hair in the Middle Ages', *Transactions of the Royal Historical Society*, sixth series, 4 (1994), pp. 43–60, esp. at 44–5). For earlier analogues, see Chapter 1, pp. 35–6.

[103] VI As 7.

kill anyone foolishly and wantonly, he is himself to be responsible for what he has done.[104]

Violence here is implicitly praiseworthy in the case of avenging another guild member, just as it was praiseworthy to avenge the injury done to the London *frið*-guild by being ahead of others in killing a thief. Moreover, we can also see here that homicide was regarded as justified when avenging a personal affront—the guild brothers will not share such a killer's feud, but they will help him pay a wergild. Indeed, killing was blameworthy only when undertaken 'foolishly and wantonly'.

The strong message of these texts is that killing can be not only legitimate but positively commendable. Killing is something that honourable men do in response to affronts that they or their associates had received. It takes skill and courage, entailing considerable personal risk both immediately and in the long term because of the threat of vengeance, so those who undertake it are worthy of admiration. We might instinctively wish to draw a distinction between the first text, which can be interpreted as the execution of a thief in accordance with royal law, and the second, which seems to revolve solely around personal and collective honour, but the language used gives us no grounds for doing so. Both represent killing in terms of vengeance for a previous offence against the collective, and state that this collective will stand together in any feud that results. These two texts both represent guilds, of course, but this sort of language is visible in unimpeachably royal law too: Æthelstan and Edmund both invoke communal solidarity with those brave enough to kill thieves, threatening 'the enmity of the king and all his friends' for anyone who dared to try to avenge one.[105]

Indeed, as was noted in Chapter 3, the laws often encourage men to participate in violence, using bribes and threats to persuade the men of the locality to band together in expeditions against thieves and other offenders.[106] The text known as the Hundred Ordinance, which probably dates from the reign of Edgar, for instance, orders that all the men of the hundred go without delay in pursuit of thieves, killing them when they are found. They are rewarded for their efforts with the promise of half the thief's goods, and threatened with fines—30 pence for the first offence—if they refuse to participate.[107] Such laws not only presuppose the existence of weapon-bearing freemen, they rely utterly on their willingness to come together and kill their enemies. Without their participation the vision of order underlying much of late Anglo-Saxon law would not have been practical: violence was not just a positive force for order and against wrongdoing but an essential element of it.[108] The laws had no need to encourage people to kill their own personal enemies, of course, but, as Edmund's laws make clear, they accepted that

---

[104] Benjamin Thorpe, ed., *Diplomatarium Anglicum Ævi Saxonicum: A Collection of English Charters from the Reign of King Æthelberht of Kent to That of William the Conqueror* (London, 1864), pp. 611–12; translation from Dorothy Whitelock, ed., *English Historical Documents*, vol. 1: *c.500–1087* (2nd edn, London, 1979), no. 136.

[105] II As 20:7; III Em 2. See also II Em 1:3.   [106] Chapter 4, pp. 190–1.

[107] Hu 2–3.   [108] This is discussed further in Chapter 6, pp. 268–83.

violent vengeance for major affronts to honour such as homicide was legitimate, especially if the target for vengeance was the original offender.

The freeman's right to use violence is certainly not a prominent aspect of the ideological rhetoric of late Anglo-Saxon law, but this does not make it unimportant. It is relatively difficult to uncover because it was an ever-present assumption, something that did not need to be stated directly because it was traditional and unchallenged. Its fundamental importance is demonstrated most forcefully by the way explicit ideological rhetoric had to accommodate it: it is only when we take it into account that kings' apparent lack of concern about violence in principle, as opposed to its negative social effects, is explicable. Violence itself was sinful and it constituted a major affront to those who suffered it; however, it was also necessary for the maintenance of order, and the right to bear weapons and to use them was an important element of what it meant to be a free male. Crucially, it had always been like this. This was not a society which had ever had a police force separate from the free population; order had always depended on free men being willing to use violence to avenge affronts, and probably also to stand together when one of their number caught a thief and killed him, avenging the harm done to the community by thieves in general.[109] It was not the business of lawmakers to impinge on something so fundamental to both good order and personal liberty. Indeed, the maintenance of such rights, expressed in very general terms, was on occasion part of legal rhetoric, as, for example, when Edgar proclaimed that it was his will that *woruldgerihta*—secular rights—be maintained throughout his realm.[110] Good kings were meant to uphold their people's freedoms, not to abrogate their immemorial right to carry and use weaponry. Nor is there any sign that kings in this period would have wished to do this. It seems, rather, that those who enthusiastically engaged in the tenth-century royal project of improving society through legislation were invested in a vision of order that was underpinned by the freeman's capacity and duty to use violence.

Defining Illegitimate Violence

This is not to say that kings were unconcerned about all types of violence. All free men had a right to bear and use weapons, but they could not legitimately use them wherever, whenever, and against whomsoever they pleased. There was a difference between feuding in a responsible way—using violence constructively, in a positive contribution to social order—and doing so recklessly, in a way that tended to spread enmity, needlessly disrupting the state of peace that should have existed among Christians. As the passages from the London *frið*-guild and the Cambridge Thegns' Guild quoted above make clear, it was possible to kill honourably and to be commended for being ahead of other men in so doing, but it was also possible to

---

[109] See Chapters 2 and 3, pp. 99–102, 152–6.

[110] IV Eg 2. Some references to *folcriht* may have had connotations of this sort—it was the king's job to ensure that just judgements were given in which all men's rights were respected: II Ew 8; III Eg 1:1; VI Atr 8:1; II Cn 1:1. Cf. II Cn 20 for a more negative use of *freoriht*.

kill foolishly and to deserve no aid from anyone. Late Anglo-Saxon law contains a lot of ideas about the circumstances in which violence was or was not legitimate, which taken together allow us to infer a fairly detailed but largely implicit set of ideals demarcating the limits of legitimate feuding.

Establishing what these ideas were is relatively easy, as these mainly follow the contours of the late Anglo-Saxon measures against violence—primarily protections— discussed in the last chapter. In terms of legitimate targets for violence, there was clearly an ideal that vengeance should be taken against the person responsible for the original affront if this was at all possible, that vengeance was wholly wrong in the case of slain thieves, that priests could be part of feuds whereas monks could not, and that attacking the weak—specifically foreigners and widows—was not right. In terms of place, it seems that churches, houses, and major roads were thought to be spaces where men should be safe from their enemies—as indeed was the king's presence—and that they should similarly be able to attend assemblies and serve in the army without fear of attack. In temporal terms, we find laws which make it clear that violence during Lent and on major festivals was regarded as particularly heinous.[111] We can get this much by simple inference from what royal legislation tried to achieve, resting on what seems the fairly safe assumption that kings protected people in, say, houses because there was a strand in contemporary thought which said that people in houses ought to be safe from attack. A more complicated issue is tracking cultural and ideological change. Were these ideas about when, where, and against whom it was legitimate to use violence current even in the seventh century, but only given firm royal backing in the late Anglo-Saxon period? Or did they themselves develop over time? Would a seventh-century West Saxon freeman have recognized the idea that, for example, it was deeply wrong to attack someone in their own home? These questions are both important and difficult to answer.

Let us turn first to the issue of the collective liability of the kindred for feuds provoked by individual members. As has been noted, the ideal set out by Edmund was that vengeance should be targeted only at the man personally responsible for the original affront, and even then only if he had failed to pay compensation within twelve months.[112] Nevertheless, his laws go on to assume that the existing consensus was otherwise, treating a killer's kinsmen as legitimate targets for vengeance unless they formally disowned him.[113] This contradiction suggests that we should read the initial statement that killers ought to bear the feuds they provoked alone rather more loosely: though it was technically legitimate to target other members of a killer's family for vengeance, as the rest of Edmund's laws imply, it was right and proper for vengeance to fall on the killer himself if that could be arranged: he was the most honourable and socially responsible target that could be chosen.[114] What

---

[111] Af 40:1; II Cn 47.   [112] II Em 1.   [113] II Em 1:1–1:3.

[114] This fits with earlier statements on the relative liability of killers and their families. In Æthelberht's laws, for instance, it is said that if a killer departs from the land his kinsmen still have to pay half the wergild, and presumably remain legitimate targets for vengeance until they agree to do so (Abt 23). Alfred is less generous to the kinsmen, but follows a similar logic when discussing killers without paternal relatives. In such a situation the killer's maternal relatives are to pay their third and his

we seem to find here, then, is Edmund attempting to reinforce an old ideal that vengeance should be directed at the person responsible for the original affront if possible, but treating its corollary—that if this was not possible his family remained liable at least to some extent—as potentially dangerous to peace and concord. As was discussed in Chapter 4, he tried to address this threat with a procedure that allowed kindreds to escape liability entirely by disavowing their kinsman, but there is little to suggest this innovation proved effective.[115]

Both killers and their kinsmen thus remained legitimate targets for vengeance except in specific circumstances. Among the most deeply rooted of these is the prohibition on vengeance for a slain thief. This is visible in seventh-century law, but it is probably significant that it takes a somewhat weaker form than in its late Anglo-Saxon manifestations. Wihtred's laws state that no wergild is to be paid for a slain thief, which implies that vengeance was not permitted, whilst Ine twice orders that the kindred of a slain thief swear oaths not to pursue an enmity against the killer.[116] The idea that it is wrong to avenge slain thieves is clearly present, then, but there are no explicit references to punishments for doing so. Indeed, the attempt to procure oaths from thieves' kinsmen to guarantee they would not take vengeance perhaps suggests that the illegitimacy of vengeance was not as well established then as in the early tenth century, when Æthelstan and Edmund could prescribe the severest penalties for avengers without relying on their having earlier bound themselves in this way.[117] It may be, therefore, that the illegitimacy of vengeance against killers of thieves was better established in early tenth- than late seventh-century culture.

Perhaps the most significant circumstances in which late Anglo-Saxon laws treat violence as illegitimate are spatially defined. As Chapter 4 showed, the idea seems to have emerged that people ought to be entirely safe from their enemies in specific locations: primarily houses, churches, and major roads. For houses there is a particularly notable shift in emphasis between the seventh-century and late Anglo-Saxon laws. The early texts make it clear that all free men were understood to protect their own homes and those within them, and they even show kings trying to reinforce these protections with their own, but when they envisage a context it is always that of quarrels erupting among drunken house-guests.[118] These are protected spaces in the sense that guests within them are expected to behave peacefully towards one another, with open displays of aggression constituting affronts to the host requiring compensation. They are not envisaged, explicitly at any rate, as places where people ought to be safe from their enemies. This is not to say that

---

gegildan another third; for the final third he must flee—go into exile (Af 27). If the killer also lacks maternal kin his *gegildan* must pay half but for the rest he must flee (Af 27:1). (Who the *gegildan* are here is deeply obscure, but for present purposes unimportant; see Chapter 6, p. 278, n. 143.) In all these passages we find that the killer can flee into exile and relieve his relatives of some of the liability for his actions, but only for some of it. This general assumption that a killer's kinsmen retained some degree of responsibility is also visible in a later Wulfstan law on clergymen charged with homicide, which states that the killer 'is to clear himself with his kinsmen, who must bear the feud with him or pay compensation for it' (VIII Atr 23; I Cn 5:2b).

[115] Chapter 4, pp. 191–2.   [116] Wi 25; Ine 28, 35.
[117] II As 6–6:2, 20:7; III Em 2.   [118] Abt 5, 8, 13, 15; Hl 11–14; Ine 6–6:5.

houses were not used as refuges—it would be surprising if people under threat did not seek the protection of their more powerful connections, especially as they had an established right to protect guests in their homes—just that they are not discussed in these terms.[119] As we saw in Chapter 4, however, the emphasis changes in the late Anglo-Saxon evidence. Alfred's code articulates a scheme in which people targeted for vengeance in feud could safely remain in their own homes for seven days, though no penalties for violation are prescribed. A penalty first becomes visible in Edmund's laws, with their reference to *hamsocn*, which various post-Conquest texts understand as the offence of an attack on a house; that is, as something committed by external enemies as opposed to misbehaving house-guests.[120]

It is possible that this reflects shifting ideas about the limits of legitimate violence: whereas there is no sign that attacking someone in their own home was reprehensible in the seventh century, we find Alfred effectively defining it as such in the late ninth century, and respect for the inviolability of homes as refuges in feud being enforced by royal protection from the mid-tenth century. Were this an isolated development we might be tempted to imagine that it is an illusion of our imperfect sources: that the inviolability of houses was traditional and that Alfred's scheme would have been recognized even in the seventh century as the way that socially responsible men dealt with enemies who sheltered in their own homes. It is not an isolated example, however. The transition from seventh-century discussions of protection in the context of ensuring peaceful behaviour to late Anglo-Saxon discussions of protection in the context of feud is a more general trend. Tenth-century laws invariably present protection as being from external enemies in feud, whether it is the protection of houses, churches or that which applied to the presence of high-ranking figures, whereas seventh-century laws never do this, hospitality being the context envisaged whenever a context is clear.[121] The first clear reference to churches as inviolable refuges in feud is a passage in Alfred's code essentially identical to the one for houses just discussed.[122]

The development fits well, moreover, with the protection of roads that lies behind the late Anglo-Saxon offence of *forsteal*. The only clear early precedent we have for this is Bede's description of Edwin of Northumbria as a king who ensured a

---

[119] Ine 5–5:1 does envisage people fleeing to monasteries to escape corporal and capital punishment.

[120] Af 42–42:1; II Em 6. Hn 80:10–80:11b is particularly explicit on this last point but the other glosses on the term have similar implications. See Chapter 4, pp. 184–5.

[121] A good example of the tenth-century emphasis on the deliberate seeking of protection from attack is the list of time-limited protections offered by churches and various ranks of secular and ecclesiastical aristocrats in IV As 6–6:3. Seventh-century discussions of protection apart from those already discussed (Hl 11–14; Ine 6–6:5) tend not to offer a clear context. Ine 5, interestingly, though it states that those who flee to churches should not suffer afflictive punishments (execution or whipping) but should pay compensation, does not consider the possibility of such a supplicant being attacked by an outsider. Eleventh-century laws authored by Archbishop Wulfstan start to show concern for general good behaviour in churches once again (VIII Atr 4; I Cn 3), but this seems to reflect a specific concern to define churches' rights to legal revenues against those of the king. For a full discussion see Lambert, 'Protection, Feud and Royal Power', pp. 71–92.

[122] Af 5–5:3. See Chapter 4, p. 186.

peace throughout Britain such that that 'a woman with a newborn child could walk about the island from sea to sea and take no harm'.[123] This suggests that it was thought that men and women ought to be able to travel in safety, and that their ability to do so was a measure of a king's success in the maintenance of order. (It is possible but far from certain that Æthelberht's laws hint at ideas similar to this in the pre-Christian period.)[124] By at least the reign of Cnut, as was discussed the last chapter, this notion had become a lot more solid.[125] Kings ensured that travellers were as safe as they were meant to be by extending their protection to major roads, which became 'royal roads'. It seems probable that the ideal of good kingship presented by Bede is in some sense the ancestor of the late Anglo-Saxon notion that the king should guarantee his people's ability to travel on major roads without hindrance, but again here there is a considerable jump between a loosely stated ideal in the early period and a much more clearly defined, feud-related expectation visible in our later texts.[126]

The important point here is that it would be wrong to consider the late Anglo-Saxon royal protections whose significance was emphasized in Chapter 4 in an ideological and cultural vacuum. Kings did not simply protect houses, churches, roads, and those men who killed thieves; they did so because there were influential strands of contemporary thought which said that these places and people were beyond the boundaries of legitimate violence. This is not to say that those strands of thought were universally accepted, or that they remained stable across the centuries. We have to accept that although our evidence can show us the existence of ideas about the proper scope of legitimate violence, it can only give us the vaguest of hints about how widely held they were or about how they waxed and waned over time.[127] Nor can we assume the laws afford us anything like a complete picture, something apparent in the fact that, though it would be surprising were this not the general expectation, they never clearly imply that vengeance ought to be taken against men rather than women or children. The sources could be misleading, then, but it is nonetheless worth noting that they do tend to point in the same direction: ideas about the circumstances in which people ought to be immune from violent

---

[123] *Ecclesiastical History*, ii. 16. This passage is quoted and discussed in Chapter 2, p. 65.

[124] See Chapters 1 and 2, p. 60, n. 93 and p. 65, n. 7.

[125] IV Atr 4–4:1; II Cn 12; Chapter 4, pp. 187–8.

[126] Another notion that seems to become stronger across our evidence is that there were times of year when it was particularly wrong to attack an enemy. As was noted in Chapter 4, our earliest reference to this is Alfred's statement that during Lent or whilst the army was in the field all compensations were to be doubled, to which Cnut's laws add that this also applied on major religious festivals, but it is only after 1066 that we can find evidence that at such times people were legally under royal protection. Here, then, we have a similar pattern to that observed for places and people. A relatively loose set of ideas about respect for significant times develops so as to become much more clearly defined, first gaining legal recognition, then becoming the focus of royal protection. See Chapter 4, pp. 189–90.

[127] A good illustration of this is the protection of foreigners and widows. This only appears in legislation associated with Wulfstan (V Atr 21; VI Atr 26; VIII Atr 33–4; II Cn 42, 52–52:1; EGu 12) but the implications of this are not clear: these passages could be establishing a new idea, giving greater force to an old one, or restating principles that were entirely traditional and obscure in earlier texts simply because they were uncontroversial.

attack which leave a relatively light imprint in our earliest sources are articulated with greater force and clarity in the later Anglo-Saxon period, and gain new or more powerful legal reinforcement in the form of royal protections or punishments. This may reveal the conscious promotion of such ideas by kings. Alfred's attempt to define what should be done by attackers who pursued their enemy to a house can certainly be read in this way: an attempt to engender respect for the inviolability of houses, drawing on but also transforming older ideas about protected space, without attempting to enforce this with any new measures.

A rather crude schematic model for the developments visible in our imperfect evidence, then, might be as follows. At various points in our period men with authority (sometimes kings, perhaps, but probably others too) took what had previously been relatively vague ideas—under a good king people can travel safely, houses are places where additional protections apply, killers of thieves should not have to fear vengeance—and worked out their implications for feuding practice. They then used their authority to set up the conclusions they reached as the standard of good feuding conduct to which honourable and socially responsible men should aspire. Over time it was increasingly widely accepted that it was wrong to attack enemies in their houses, to ambush them on roads, or to avenge thieves. At a later stage, kings and their advisers noted that these now-traditional standards of good conduct were not being observed rigorously enough and tried to enforce them using royal protections. The royal protections examined in Chapter 4, then, may have been the culmination of a broader cultural and ideological shift, only sporadically visible in our sources. Driven by increasingly established ideas that certain places and people—perhaps even times—ought to be immune from violence, the boundaries of legitimate violence gradually narrowed so that aspects of acceptable seventh-century feuding practice would have seemed extreme to eleventh-century observers.

CONCLUSION

The picture which emerges from this survey of the explicit ideology and more implicit assumptions in late Anglo-Saxon law is not particularly tidy. Unlike the satisfyingly neat vision of a late Anglo-Saxon ideology of crime and punishment offered by Wormald, the ideas picked out here are probably best understood as separate strands of thought, though they could certainly overlap and interact. With respect to kings, at least, there are three central concerns, which fit reasonably well with the three commands of the royal inauguration ritual. The most straightforward is the king's duty to forbid *rapacitates et omnes iniquitates*, which aligns well with the conceptual associations of both *frið* and the duties associated with the oath of loyalty. That is, we find in the laws' statements on these subjects the same combination of a strong focus on theft (presumably at least part of what was meant by *rapacitates*) and a much vaguer sense that other types of wrongdoing (*omnes iniquitates*) are also included.

The king's duty, articulated in the second element of the inauguration ritual, to see that the Church and all Christian people preserve 'true peace' is rather vague, and in this respect it aligns well with the very broad religious duties of kingship that seem to be implied by the laws. The broadest of these extends well beyond the merely legal: kings, in conjunction with the Church, were responsible for maintaining their people's favourable relationship with God, and this involved supporting the Church in its pastoral role (including by pressuring grievous sinners to undergo penance) as well as working to maintain the 'peace and concord' which so concerned Edmund—a state of Christian friendship and charity within the kingdom. The extension of royal protections that was identified in Chapter 4 as one of the more significant innovations in substantive law in the late Anglo-Saxon period should probably be understood within the context of this ideological agenda: kings made particular efforts to target those forms of violence through which feuds tended to escalate. The king's third duty, to ensure just judgements, is slightly more difficult. We can see it being addressed directly in Alfred's production and, presumably, dissemination of his *Domboc*, and in his successors' measures designed to ensure that the agents who were to implement the king's legal wisdom on his behalf did so properly. If we accept that this duty implied a more general oversight of the processes by which justice was done in English society, fines for disobedience (*oferhyrnesse*) also align well this concern.

Law in this period was not solely about the king, however. The final sections of this chapter attempted the rather more difficult business of analysing attitudes towards violence generally and the specific circumstances which bore on its perceived legitimacy. These are issues central to understanding contemporary ideas about good legal order, but the connection between them and the duties of kingship is indirect. Nonetheless, the conclusions that emerge here—that order was understood to be dependent on freemen being willing to use violence, and that the limits of legitimate violence seem often to have become rather more precisely defined before they acquired royal sanction—are helpful in understanding why kings understood their duties in the way that they did. Indeed, if we were not to appreciate that within certain parameters vengeful violence was perceived by contemporaries as a positive and necessary contribution to good order, it would be very hard to comprehend why kings (who we can see expressing concern about the maintenance of peace and concord) did not seek to prohibit it outright.[128]

---

[128] It is worth emphasizing that my point is about contemporary *perceptions* of the contribution of violence to good order. It is no part of my argument that violence in feud did in fact contribute to the maintenance of order rather than undermine it. We know so little about the reality of violence in this period that we cannot possibly draw conclusions as to what it did or did not achieve. I would stress that this is not an argument that the Anglo-Saxons in fact managed to maintain peace through feud in the way that Max Gluckman famously suggested was possible, though it is one which implies that they *thought* they were doing something along roughly those lines. For a deeply sensible and erudite review of the historiography of feuding and violence, which draws out the scholarly fault-line running through precisely this issue and reflects upon Gluckman's influence, see Stephen D. White, 'The "Peace in the Feud" Revisited: Feuds in the Peace in Medieval European Feuds', in Kate Cooper and Conrad Leyser, eds., *Making Early Medieval Societies: Conflict and Belonging in the Latin West* (Oxford, 2016), pp. 220–43.

This is not, then, a unified ideology but it is a broadly coherent landscape of ideals and assumptions. Within this landscape, I would suggest, the legislative priorities of late Anglo-Saxon kings make sense. Crucially, it is a landscape that would have been relatively familiar to seventh-century Anglo-Saxons. Specific features are much more prominent in our later evidence, but they can usually be discerned in some form in earlier thought. Rhetoric about *frið* is a tenth-century phenomenon, for instance, but the central royal duty to which it referred—the suppression of theft—had been a major feature of royal legislation in the seventh century. The general pattern is that earlier ideas are articulated much more clearly and precisely in the late Anglo-Saxon period. These ideas may not align with our expectations of state-like authority—there is little sign that late Anglo-Saxon elites regarded 'horizontal' forms of justice as a threat in themselves and wished to eradicate them—but then, why should they have? It makes sense that late Anglo-Saxon kings wished to improve their society in line with ideals that were essentially traditional, albeit often expressed in newer, more precise and forceful language. The fact that in the same period they developed governmental structures which in many respects look impressively state-like is consistent with that aim. Indeed, as Chapter 6 will argue, there is good reason to think that kings' sincerely held ambitions to improve society through legislation were part of what drove some of the more fundamental administrative reforms of the tenth century.

6

Local Legal Practice and Royal Control

INTRODUCTION

The late Anglo-Saxon period witnessed major legal change. Chapters 4 and 5 have highlighted the increased priority which kings from Alfred's reign onwards accorded to their legal responsibilities. We have not only seen their attempts to change substantive law through the establishment of new or more powerful forms of punishment and protection, but also examined the cultural and ideological framework that drove them to act in this way. Most prominently, the surviving legislation is littered with declarations of concern about the state of the kingdom's *frið* ('peace') and with measures framed as attempts to bring about improvements in it—measures usually explicitly targeted at theft. The laws leave little room for doubt that kings wished to exercise control over local legal practice: not only do they repeatedly assert this desire in broad ideological terms, they also (at least in the tenth century) reveal a constant stream of royal commands on matters of local legal procedure. This chapter attempts to make sense of these commands, reconstructing and analysing the effort to project royal influence into the localities that they represent.

To some extent this agenda meshes well with that of much of the recent literature on this subject, which tends to emphasize how unusually impressive English kings were in this period, enacting structural reforms which enabled them to exert much more control over local justice than rulers elsewhere in Europe (in practice, comparisons tend to focus primarily on West Francia).[1] This may be an accurate assessment.[2] My concern here, however, is neither to contest the idea that English kings did in fact succeed in increasing their control of local legal practice in the period, nor to challenge this conventional assessment of comparative governmental strength; the aim is to work through what enhanced royal control meant in terms of legal practice. 'Royal control', we should bear in mind, is an imprecise concept, potentially so vague as to be unhelpful. It would certainly be analytically lazy (and very probably simply wrong) for us to assume that 'control' in

---

[1] See in particular Patrick Wormald, 'Lordship and Justice in the Earliest English Kingdom: Oswaldslow Revisited', repr. in and cited from Wormald, *Legal Culture*, pp. 313–32 and the long-running debate about 'private jurisdiction' to which this contributed (for references, see Chapter 3, p. 147, n. 136).

[2] Though for a cautionary note on taking West Francia as representative of wider European trends, see George Molyneaux, *The Formation of the English Kingdom in the Tenth Century* (Oxford, 2015), pp. 233–48.

the abstract was the goal towards which kings were aiming in this period: that they were determined to direct people's actions on a local level simply for the sake of being 'in control'. Kings wanted their orders to be obeyed, of course, but they issued their orders for specific reasons.

This chapter looks in detail at the rationale underlying various procedural innovations, arguing that they are best explained as attempts to address the practical legal problems perceived by elite law-makers. They make most sense, that is, if we take the ideological framing of the laws examined in Chapter 5 seriously, and accept that the central legislative aim of tenth-century kings was the one they openly declared: improvement of the kingdom's *frið* through the suppression of theft. There is every reason to suppose that the laws represent genuine attempts to do this, and that this either reflects the fact that kings' commitment to this ideological project was sincere, or at least demonstrates that the kingdom's elite were collectively invested in it to the extent that it was politically expedient for kings to feign a significant personal interest. (It should be noted that, although we might cynically assume that the true motivation underlying royal legislation was the extraction of revenue, there is, as Chapter 7 will argue, little evidence to suggest this was the case before the eleventh century.)[3] That is to say, we should almost certainly understand the establishment of tighter royal control over local legal practice not as a project in its own right—part of a self-conscious state-building agenda—but as a by-product of an ideologically inspired drive to improve *frið*.

We also need to be alert to the possibility that control can be exercised in different ways. An important conclusion of Chapter 3 was that kings in the seventh, eighth and ninth centuries largely managed to get what they wanted from local legal practice—and thus in some sense exercised control over it—with a distinctly limited administrative apparatus. They relied on a network of local reeves, many of whom were employed by lords other than the king, whose main duties were to monitor local assemblies, to guide them on matters of legal interpretation when necessary, and to collect any fines or forfeitures those assemblies awarded to their lords. It would be easy to assume that the extension of royal control over local legal practice in the late Anglo-Saxon period meant the creation of a more extensive network of royal administrative officials, 'royal control' here being the control such local officials wielded over local institutions. Much of the literature on this issue adopts this essentially institutional model, focusing on the supposedly crucial question of whether royal representatives or those of privileged aristocrats presided at local assemblies—the underlying assumption being that assemblies' presidents controlled their decisions.[4] Chapter 3 argued that this framework was unhelpful for

---

[3] See Chapter 7 and Molyneaux, *Formation*, pp. 182–93.

[4] Wormald, 'Lordship and Justice', p. 332; Stephen Baxter, 'Lordship and Justice in Late Anglo-Saxon England: The Judicial Functions of Soke and Commendation Revisited', in Stephen Baxter et al., eds., *Early Medieval Studies in Memory of Patrick Wormald* (Farnham, 2009), pp. 383–419 at 417. John Hudson, *The Oxford History of the Laws of England*, vol. 2: *871–1216* (Oxford, 2012), ch. 3 is more nuanced but essentially similar: he broadly accepts Wormald's interpretation but notes points at which the evidence could conceivably be read in other ways. Nonetheless, despite highlighting (p. 62) the fundamental problem with focusing on presidents—that the extent to which these figures

understanding royal involvement in local legal practice in the earlier period: instead of treating assemblies as administrative institutions under the control of officials it took them to be distinctly political gatherings and focused on thinking through how their decisions were made and who would have been able to influence them. (Chapter 7 provides a full critique of the concept of 'jurisdiction', which underlies this traditional historiographical concern with assembly presidents.)[5] This same approach is adopted here. Direct administrative control exercised by local officials is taken seriously as a possible model for 'royal control' (hence the considerable significance attributed to the emergence of sheriffs), but it is not assumed to be the only one available. Indeed, it is argued that some of the most important structural reforms of the tenth century represent a deliberate attempt to bypass problematic local officials and shape local legal practice by other methods.[6]

Thus, while it rejects assumptions about the importance of assembly presidents that have been embedded in the historiography since the nineteenth century, this chapter draws heavily on the sometimes very astute insights more modern scholarship has provided into the dynamics of local legal practice.[7] Stephen Baxter, most notably, drawing mainly on Domesday evidence, has done a great deal to illuminate the importance of personal or 'commendatory' lordship in a legal context.[8] Local justice, as Baxter and others have repeatedly and conclusively shown, was inextricably linked with local patronage networks, networks which connected to political patrons on a much grander scale who could be drawn into local disputes if the stakes were high enough to warrant it. We need to take this insight seriously and conceptualize royal control of local justice in a way that takes it into account, considering local assemblies as key arenas for local patronage politics and situating kings' ability to influence the outcomes of legal cases in that context. Our first priority must be to understand how formal legal structures worked and the ways it

were able to manipulate judicial outcomes is uncertain—this insight is absent from the discussion that surrounds it. It is assumed throughout that the key analytical issue is who presides over or 'holds' an assembly (pp. 52, 56, 58, 61–2), and this culminates in speculation that lords who possessed the right to receive legal revenues from an entire hundred may in practice have been able to appoint their own hundred reeves and 'therefore in a sense exercise jurisdiction over the hundred' (p. 62). On 'hundred reeves' see below, pp. 247–8, esp. n. 34.

  5 Chapter 7, pp. 301–6.
  6 It thus follows leads given by Alice Taylor, '*Lex Scripta* and the Problem of Enforcement: Anglo-Saxon, Scottish and Welsh Law Compared', in Judith Scheele and Fernanda Pirie, eds., *Legalism: Community and Justice* (Oxford, 2014), pp. 47–75; and Alice Taylor, 'Crime Without Punishment: Medieval Scottish Law in Comparative Perspective', *Anglo-Norman Studies* 35 (2013), pp. 287–304.
  7 See, in particular, Patrick Wormald, 'Charters, Law and the Settlement of Disputes in Anglo-Saxon England', repr. in and cited from Wormald, *Legal Culture*, pp. 289–310; Paul R. Hyams, *Rancor and Reconciliation in Medieval England* (Ithaca, 2003), ch. 3; Simon Keynes, 'Crime and Punishment in the Reign of King Æthelred the Unready', in Ian Wood and Niels Lund, eds., *People and Places in Northern Europe, 500–1600: Essays in Honour of Peter Hayes Sawyer* (Woodbridge, 1991), pp. 67–81; John Hudson, 'Feud, Vengeance and Violence in England from the Tenth to the Twelfth Centuries', in Belle S. Tuten and Tracey A. Billado, eds., *Feud, Violence and Practice: Essays in Medieval Studies in Honour of Stephen D. White* (Farnham, 2010), pp. 29–53. For a particularly incisive comparative discussion of the extent to which the nature of our sources is likely to obscure legal practice in this period, see Pauline Stafford, 'Kings, Kingships and Kingdoms', in Wendy Davies, ed., *From the Vikings to the Normans* (Oxford, 2003) pp. 11–39 at 27–33.
  8 Baxter, 'Lordship and Justice'.

may have been possible for interested parties—kings, royal and non-royal reeves, lords with and without rights to receive legal revenues, even relatively ordinary people—to influence the outcomes of cases that came before them. It is only in this context, I would suggest, that we can meaningfully consider the extent to which assemblies were under royal control. And because calculations about the likely outcome of formal assembly procedures must have been crucial context for any informal negotiations outside them, it makes sense to begin with these core institutional mechanisms and work gradually outwards from there to a broader understanding of legal practice.

That, at least, is how this chapter proceeds. It has six sections. The first examines the key structural changes of the late Anglo-Saxon period, assessing the significance of the emergence of both the hundredal system and sheriffs. (Other innovations, including the emergence of shires—a standard part of narratives of administrative development in this period—have little direct relevance to the local non-elite legal practice with which we are concerned here.)[9] This provides a broad overview of how kings were able to increase their control of local legal practice in this period. The second, third, and fourth sections focus on assemblies, and specifically on the obstacles their procedures presented to those seeking to secure convictions for wrongdoing. The second section looks at the dynamics of accusation and denial, arguing that the standard form of proof, the collective oath of denial, put free defendants in a very strong position to resist prosecution for wrongdoing (providing they had no record of dishonesty and had not been caught in the act). The third assesses the likelihood that locally powerful figures, such as privileged lords and royal officials, had sufficient discretionary control over assembly procedure that they were able to impose disadvantageous forms of proof on people they regarded as probable malefactors, negating the theoretical procedural advantage enjoyed by free defendants. It concludes that this is unlikely. The fourth section examines an alternative way of getting around free defendants' right to deny charges levied against them: the creation of (sometimes highly elaborate) procedural obligations designed in such a way as to catch wrongdoers—primarily thieves—in situations where denial was impossible. This was the focus of some of the most ingenious late Anglo-Saxon legislation.

The fifth section turns from the problem of ensuring wrongdoers were convicted in assemblies to that of ensuring these offenders were, in practice, punished. The principal challenges to this were open defiance, which clearly needed to be over-come by force, and attempts to escape punishment by fleeing. This latter problem called for a subtler approach, and found it in the form of legislation demanding all men find and permanently maintain sureties to guarantee their punitive liabilities: probably the most far-reaching of all late Anglo-Saxon legal reforms. In its sixth and final section the chapter considers negotiated settlements. It argues that throughout this period it was common for cases to be settled and punishments imposed following negotiations between the parties involved: formal proof procedures

---

[9] For shires, see Molyneaux, *Formation*, pp. 155–72.

were probably relatively rare, and the need for enforcement action rarer still. Nonetheless, these negotiations must have been shaped by the dynamics of formal proof and enforcement, and the changes of this period cannot but have had a significant effect on the negotiating positions of the parties involved. The structural and procedural legal reforms of this period, it is argued, were intended to result—and quite probably did result—in an appreciable shift in the balance of power between prosecution and defence.

STRUCTURAL CHANGE

The implementation of royal legislation on a local level in the period leading up to the tenth century was discussed in detail in Chapter 3, and the conclusions drawn there form the background to the analysis which follows. It would be superfluous to rehearse these conclusions in detail here, but three basic points are worth reiterating before we turn specifically to hundreds and sheriffs. Firstly, kings commonly, and with good reason, gave away their rights to receive legal revenues to a range of lay and ecclesiastical aristocrats; this meant that although in some localities legal administration fell to the king's own reeves, in many others it did not. In these places local legal matters were the province either of reeves working for privileged lords or of the privileged lords themselves if they were based locally and chose to attend to their affairs in person—these are the 'thegns' of early tenth-century laws.[10] Secondly, all these figures had a role in ensuring the king's legislation was implemented by local assemblies. Kings did their best to publicize their legislation widely, beginning by promulgating it in great assemblies of their kingdoms' most influential people, and they made efforts to monitor its local application by hearing appeals. Beyond this, however, kings relied on their reeves, the reeves of great magnates, and lesser lords representing their own interests to monitor local assemblies and, if necessary, to guide them on the proper application of the king's laws. This monitoring and guidance should not be confused with absolute 'control': everyone who attended an assembly was monitoring its proceedings, and there is good evidence that reeves and privileged lords were not the only figures in assemblies capable of claiming the authority to pronounce on the proper application of law.[11]

Thirdly, local legal administration did not extend much beyond monitoring local assemblies in this way and collecting fines. Accusations could largely be left to people who had been affronted, and enforcement—when it was needed—relied on the participation of the local community, often working in conjunction with affronted parties pursuing the offender for vengeance or compensation. Local rural reeves and privileged lords might organize such enforcement expeditions but reeves, at least, were not well suited to coercing people independently. Their primary responsibilities were agricultural: they supervised dependent workforces on

---

[10] Chapter 3, pp. 127–8.   [11] Chapter 3, pp. 136–49.

inland farms, they organized seasonal labour services from the warland population, and they ensured that the payments in kind they rendered—primarily livestock and food products—were properly tended and stored. It may be pertinent to note here that the late tenth- or early eleventh-century text known as *Gerefa* expresses concern that reeves, if they lacked personal authority, might be dominated by the labourers they were meant to be directing.[12] These figures are unlikely to have had their own armed retainers, so when enforcement was necessary their only option, apart from ignoring the problem, was to appeal to others for help. Locally based privileged lords may have been able to act more independently, but rural reeves (as opposed to the grander reeves in charge of important military and commercial centres) were probably incapable of using force against an offender except with the assistance of local men.[13]

Hundreds

At the turn of the tenth century there were two distinct ways of dividing up the legal landscape: the kingdom was made up of two structures of rural districts, which overlaid one another.[14] On the one hand, there were what might be termed 'assembly districts': the districts from which assemblies drew their members. On the other, there were what we might think of as 'revenue-collection districts': the districts from which rural reeves, who supervised inlands on their lords' behalf, were entitled to extract food renders, labour services, and punitive fines. When kings granted lands to aristocrats as rewards for loyal service, then, they were granting rights over specific revenue-collection districts (presumably with associated inlands).[15] A key point which is easy to overlook is the lack of any necessary

---

[12] Ger 7.   [13] Chapter 3, pp. 152–6.

[14] The analysis in Molyneaux, *Formation*, ch. 4, provides the foundation for what follows. The interpretation of hundreds proposed here should be understood as an attempt to build on Molyneaux's conclusions.

[15] One possible label for these districts is 'estates', but calling them this here would be problematic. Although we might think of some of the land within them as being 'owned' or even just 'held' by whichever lord had been granted the king's rights in them—the areas known as inland—they must usually (in the ninth century, at least) have had warland areas, and the free farmers who lived in these areas are likely to have been understood to own their own land. It therefore seems something of a misrepresentation to speak of these people as living on 'estates' which belonged to kings or lords. One way of avoiding this would be to adopt the language of 'extensive lordship', which is used in the literature to denote the rights to receive relatively light dues and labour services from warland households. This, however, is equally problematic, because it is almost certainly the case that the late Anglo-Saxon period saw a shift in which these districts became more like 'estates': an increase in the size of inlands and a corresponding decline in the number of warland households, perhaps accompanied by a growing sense that the free farmers of the warland were tenants rather than landowners. The extent of this shift is uncertain and contentious. It is impossible to assess reliably with Anglo-Saxon evidence: we have a few snapshots of conditions in particular locations but no way of ascertaining how representative they are of society as a whole. Domesday Book is more promising but also problematic: the existence of substantial numbers of 'sokemen' suggests that free warland households were a prominent feature of certain Scandinavian-influenced areas (which is not to say that they should be understood as a 'Scandinavian' phenomenon); see D. M. Hadley, *The Northern Danelaw: Its Social Structure, c. 800–1100* (London, 2000), ch. 3. Elsewhere, however, we are prevented from reaching certain conclusions by the ambiguity of the Latin term *villanus*, which may

relationship between assembly districts and revenue-collection districts. It was possible for the men who assembled in a particular place all to owe their food renders to a particular inland, but there is little reason to think the world was usually so tidy. It certainly was not later on: it was possible for all the men of a hundred to owe their legal revenues to the same royal estate or to the same lord, but it was equally possible for that not to be the case.[16] Some revenue-collection districts may have straddled the borders of two assembly districts; the lords or reeves in charge of such revenue-collection districts would have had to attend both assemblies to assert their rights. Likewise, some assembly districts would have spanned multiple revenue-collection districts; these assemblies could be attended by several reeves or lords with the right to receive fines.[17] It need not have been at all normal for all the fines imposed by a single local assembly to be paid to the same recipient.

We saw in Chapter 3 that late ninth- and early tenth-century sources often emphasize the duties of the men who supervised revenue-collection districts. Reeves (royal and otherwise) and privileged lords are expected to function as local legal authorities, and threatened with punishment if they abuse their power. Molyneaux, however, has shown that—beginning in the reign of Edward the Elder and continuing under Æthelstan—we can see kings attempting to rely on a different administrative network to implement their legal commands. Functions such as the

well have been used as a catch-all term for 'rustics' from a variety of household types. On this, see Rosamond Faith, *The English Peasantry and the Growth of Lordship* (London, 1997), esp. pp. 123–5, where the possibility of numerous free warland households surviving until 1066 is emphasized. Chris Wickham, *Framing the Early Middle Ages: Europe and the Mediterranean, 400–800* (Oxford, 2005), pp. 347–50 (esp. n. 112), also emphasizes the ambiguity of the evidence but argues for a significant shift beginning in the late ninth century, such that by the tenth century it is appropriate to use the word estate and to think in terms of exclusive ownership. The analysis here does not depend on any particular reading of late Anglo-Saxon changes in rural social structure, and the term 'revenue-collection district' is intended to reflect this. Inelegant though it is, it has the virtue of being equally appropriate however one envisions the late Anglo-Saxon rural landscape, accurately describing both 'zones of extensive lordship' and 'estates'. (Whatever else these areas of lands were, they were certainly districts from which their holders collected revenue.) All I would observe on this point is that kings continue to produce new laws for the better regulation of the communal legal practices of non-noble free farmers throughout the tenth century, which suggests their continued significance within areas under English law during that period (though it should be noted that legal freedom need not imply economic independence).

[16] For a detailed dissection of a single hundred with multiple lords, see Stephen Baxter and John Blair, 'Land Tenure and Royal Patronage in the Early English Kingdom: A Model and a Case Study', *Anglo-Norman Studies* 28 (2006), pp. 19–46. The index to Robin Fleming, *Domesday Book and the Law: Society and Legal Custom in Early Medieval England* (Cambridge, 1998), p. 522, assembles Domesday references to entire hundreds and wapentakes belonging to particular individuals. For hundreds which owed all their revenues to lords other than the king, see Helen M. Cam, 'The Private Hundred in England Before the Norman Conquest', repr. in and cited from Helen M. Cam, *Law-Finders and Law-Makers in Medieval England* (London, 1962), pp. 59–70.

[17] Later evidence for groups of several hundreds sharing a single assembly suggest that it was possible for assembly districts to cover relatively large areas before the establishment of the hundredal system; if this inference is correct, these assembly districts would almost certainly have encompassed multiple revenue-collection districts. See Helen M. Cam, 'Early Groups of Hundreds', repr. in and cited from Helen M. Cam, *Liberties and Communities in Medieval England* (London, 1963), pp. 91–106.

witnessing of transactions and the pursuit of thieves are associated not with reeves or thegns but with *burh*s.[18] (*Burh*s were fortifications, but they were also often assumed to be commercial centres and many would eventually become centres of population.)[19] One possible explanation for this is that the experiment with *burh*s was prompted by frustration with the fact that there were many rural areas where there were no royal reeves. *Burh*s' key attraction may have been that they formed a network that covered the regions of the kingdom which applied English law reasonably evenly: all free men were meant to have a duty to maintain their local *burh*, and perhaps even to garrison it when necessary.[20] In theory, everyone ought to have had some contact with their *burh*- or *port*-reeve, and these men worked for the king, whereas many local rural reeves worked for other lords. Another attraction of *burh*s may well have been that their reeves were men of greater stature. These figures were responsible for strategically important fortifications so it is probable that they were noblemen with their own military retainers. It may be that kings were frustrated by their rural reeves' lack of clout, and that they chose to rely on *burh*s in part because the reeves there were more capable of enforcing their will independently of local opinion.

Whatever logic underlay it, this experiment with relying on *burh*s seems to have been a failure. There are two main reasons for thinking this. One is that, although Edward the Elder and Æthelstan both issued laws attempting to confine trade to *burh*s, where transactions could be witnessed by their reeves, Æthelstan later repealed these laws.[21] This suggests that it proved impractical to demand that people travel to *burh*s to buy and sell things, and that the attempt to insist on this therefore had to be abandoned. The second reason is that later kings stop relying exclusively on *burh*s for this and other functions which had been associated with them in earlier laws. Whereas Æthelstan relied on *burh*s not only for the witnessing of transactions but also for mounting communal enforcement expeditions, in laws issued by later kings *burh*s no longer have a central role. Rather, kings start demanding that the same functions take place in a reformed system of rural districts: hundreds and wapentakes.[22] It seems likely that the attempt to rely on *burh*s as an administrative network failed because in practice *burh*-reeves' primary non-military responsibilities were the collection of revenues associated with their *burh*s, and they had little reason to venture far into the countryside. Although they

[18] Molyneaux, *Formation*, pp. 106–9.

[19] As Molyneaux, *Formation*, pp. 106–7, notes the term *burh* is often used interchangeably with the word *port*, which has clear commercial associations. For *burh*s as military centres which only gradually acquired urban characteristics: Richard Holt, 'The Urban Transformation in England, 900–1100', *Anglo-Norman Studies* 32 (2010), pp. 57–78.

[20] Molyneaux, *Formation*, pp. 89–91, challenges the well-established idea that the *burh*s listed in the Burghal Hidage were permanently garrisoned, and casts doubt on the assumption that they were garrisoned by the general population at all. See N. P. Brooks, 'England in the Ninth Century: The Crucible of Defeat', *Transactions of the Royal Historical Society* 29 (1979), pp. 1–20 at 17–20.

[21] The ban on trading outside *burh*s: I Ew 1–1:1; II As 12, 13:1. Its repeal: IV As 2; VI As 10.

[22] II As 12, 13:1, 20–20:6; III Em 2; Hu 2–3:1; III Eg 7–7:3; IV Eg 3:1–6:2. III Em 5 suggests that witnessing of transactions, though no longer limited to *burh*s was not yet associated with hundreds. See Molyneaux, *Formation*, pp. 153–4.

occasionally needed to call on the surrounding population to help with repair work, perhaps even with garrison duties in times of danger, they probably had no routine interaction with the rural population and little interest in attending the local rural assemblies where most legal judgements were made.

Our first hint of hundreds' existence comes in one of Edmund's laws, where the people taking enforcement action against thieves are assumed to constitute a hundred.[23] Our best information on the hundred comes from a text known as the *Hundred Ordinance*, which seems to refer back to Edmund's law.[24] Because this text is anonymous it is difficult to date: most commentators have thought it likely to come from Edgar's reign but it is possible that it was written under one of his predecessors.[25] Edgar's legislation, at any rate, confirms that the hundred had become the primary focus of local legal practice by the time of its issue, and this remains the case under all subsequent kings.[26] The wapentake is also first attested in Edgar's legislation.[27] (Although from here on I will refer only to hundreds my arguments should be understood to apply to wapentakes as well.) Hundreds were in some senses direct successors to earlier assembly districts. How they relate to those earlier districts in topographical terms is obscure: some rationalization is plausible (and more probable in areas where we later find hundreds assessed at precisely 100 hides), but it is conceivable that many of them had the same boundaries as the assembly districts which preceded them.[28] Hundreds, however, were a significant innovation not because of their geography but because they formed a uniform system. Previously, it is probable that there had been a mishmash of different assemblies and associated districts, separated by a range of qualitative and quantitative distinctions. The advent of the hundredal system, however, meant that all local assembly districts were now hundreds: they were all supposed to order their affairs in exactly the same way. Kings could now create and adjust a template for how a single hundred should operate, and all local assemblies—because they were hundred assemblies—were expected to implement this template.

For our purposes it is crucial to recognize that the establishment of the hundredal system entailed a fundamental shift in kings' approach to legal administration. The hundred was an assembly district, whereas previously legislation had focused on men with responsibility for revenue-collection districts. Late ninth- and early tenth-century laws focused on royal reeves, non-royal reeves, and 'landed' thegns, but the subsequent experiment with *burh*s may well imply that kings were dissatisfied with their ability to implement their commands through this variegated and largely non-royal network of revenue-collectors: they were searching for a means of achieving their legal goals without relying on these figures. The attempt to use *burh*s failed,

[23] III Em 2.   [24] Hu 2.

[25] Patrick Wormald, *The Making of English Law: King Alfred to the Twelfth Century*, vol. 1: *Legislation and Its Limits* (Oxford, 1999), pp. 378–9.

[26] III Eg 5, 7:1; IV Eg 3:1, 5, 8:1; 10. For general discussion, see Hudson, *Oxford History*, pp. 50–5.

[27] IV Eg 6.

[28] For a succinct overview of the limits of what can be known, with references to the extensive earlier literature, see Molyneaux, *Formation*, pp. 146–7.

probably because they were too remote for most of the rural population to interact with on a routine basis, but the establishment of hundreds allowed kings to achieve the same goal—bypassing the figures in charge of rural revenue-collection districts—much more effectively. They could now issue orders directly to hundreds: to assembly districts. Absolutely vitally, it is clear that the people in charge of these assembly districts were *not* the reeves and lords who supervised revenue-collection districts. Rather, they seem to have been expected to be prominent members of the local community: equivalents to the 'most senior men' (*yldestan men*) discussed in Chapter 3, who were expected to lead enforcement expeditions in Æthelstan's legislation.[29]

The hundred's leading figure was known as the 'hundredman' (*hundredes man*, 'man of the hundred' or *hundredes ealdor*, 'leader of the hundred').[30] He was assisted by figures known as 'tithingmen' (*teoðingmen*).[31] The terms occur in the *Hundred Ordinance* and in one of Edgar's law codes, but their meaning is not explained. We can get some help in understanding them from arrangements made by the London *frið*-guild in Æthelstan's reign. There too we find administrative divisions called hundreds subdivided into units called tithings. These divisions do not seem to represent assembly districts in this context but the way the terms are used is suggestive. A tithing (*teoðung*, literally 'tenth') was a group of ten men, and our text explains that the most senior man (*yldestan*) of each such group 'shall have charge of the [other] nine in all those dues which we have all agreed upon'.[32] Just as tithings are treated as subdivisions of hundreds, the text treats hundreds as subdivisions of a greater whole—the London *frið*-guild—so it is probably implicit here that hundredmen were likewise the most senior members of their hundreds. The most plausible reading of the late Anglo-Saxon evidence alone, then, is that the hundredmen in Edgar's laws and the *Hundred Ordinance* were expected to be senior members of hundred assemblies.[33] Post-Conquest evidence generally confirms this. The early twelfth-century legal treatise known as *Leges Henrici Primi* is explicit: 'a tenth man shall preside over the nine others of the tithing, and similarly one of the most substantial men (*unus de melioribus*) shall preside over the whole hundred and be known as the alderman'.[34]

---

[29] II As 20:1. See Chapter 3, p. 153.   [30] Hu 2; IV Eg 8:1.
[31] Hu 2, 4. See also II Cn 20.   [32] VI As 3. See also VI As 8:1.
[33] III Atr 3:1 associates a reeve with wapentake assemblies. The reeve here, however—quite possibly a sheriff at this date—is acting as a prosecutor, not directing the activities of the wapentake. This is a role we would expect to find reeves filling, as they were the ones responsible for extracting fines for their lords.
[34] Hn 8:1a. I emphasize the *Leges Henrici* here because this passage's meaning is unambiguous, unlike allusions to the figures in charge of hundreds in other post-Conquest Latin texts. Elsewhere, Latin terms that we might translate as 'reeve' are used, but seemingly rather loosely. For example, the *Inquisitio Eliensis*, a survey of the lands of the abbey of Ely connected with the Domesday inquest, lists *prepositi* and *prefecti* of specific hundreds among those who gave sworn testimony, but it also assumes that every vill had a *prepositus* and this suggests that the term is being used in a way that could encompass communal head-men as well as revenue-collectors employed by lords. (See N. E. S. A. Hamilton, ed., *Inquisitio Comitatus Cantabrigiensis* (1876), pp. 97–101; James Campbell, 'Some Agents and Agencies of the Late Anglo-Saxon State', repr. in and cited from James Campbell, *The Anglo-Saxon State* (London, 2000), pp. 201–25 at 207–8.) Similarly, the *Leges Edwardi Confessoris*, a twelfth-century text which may

The establishment of hundreds, then, represents a major shift in late Anglo-Saxon kings' approach to local justice. Rather than relying on the people responsible for local revenue collection to supervise local assemblies, kings now dealt with local assemblies directly. The local figures upon whom they relied became hundredmen, the most senior members of local assemblies. A local nobleman with the right to receive legal revenues might well have been a suitable person to fill this role, but he would have done so by virtue of his rank, not because of his legal privileges. Although it cannot be ruled out that it happened occasionally, there is nothing to suggest that it was normal for a hundredman to be a reeve working for the king, or for any other lord. Hundredmen were local leaders and not normally revenue collectors; reeves were revenue collectors and not normally local leaders. These are very different roles and it is important to keep them separate.[35]

---

date from the reign of Stephen—see Bruce R. O'Brien, *God's Peace and King's Peace: The Laws of Edward the Confessor* (Philadelphia, 1999), pp. 44–61—explains that it was possible to be a *greve* (i.e. *gerefa*, 'reeve') of a shire, wapentake, hundred, borough, or vill (ECf 32). However, the Latin term it associates with *greve* is *prefectus*, which denotes an official only once elsewhere in the text, where it is stated that men who find stray livestock are to show them to the *prefectus hundredi* (ECf 24:2–24:3). This is very close to the role attributed to the *hundredes ealdor* in IV Eg 8:1, and indeed it is noted in ECf 32 that the people now termed *greves* had earlier been called *aldermanni*. This is perhaps significant because the term consistently used for officials performing revenue-collection and prosecutorial functions in this text is different—*iusticia*, 'justice'—which suggests that the terms *greve* and *prefectus* may denote figures with other characteristics. (See ECf 3, 6a–6:1, 8:2, 9–9:2, 10:2, 15, 20:1a–20:6, 23a–23:4, 36:4–36:5, 38:2–38:3a; I am grateful to Thomas Hemming for drawing this to my attention in his Oxford MSt dissertation.) By contrast, Robin Fleming's study of the legal content of Domesday Book found just three explicit references to hundred reeves: two *prepositi* and a *prefectus* (Fleming, *Domesday Book and the Law*, nos. 65, 2053, 2192; DB i. 218v, ii. 99r, 120r). This makes them very rare, and each example comes from a hundred that was in the hands of the king, so a potential explanation might be that these are cases in which the district supervised by the local royal reeve happened to coincide with a hundred. In short, the issues of what Latin terms such as *prefectus* and *prepositus* signified, how they related to Old English terms such as *gerefa*, and how their meanings shifted over time are far from straightforward and would probably reward in-depth analysis. By the late thirteenth century the men in charge of hundreds—now known as bailiffs—were officials who might pay an annual farm for their office: see Helen M. Cam, *The Hundred and the Hundred Rolls* (London, 1930), pp. 145–53. However, William Stubbs, *The Constitutional History of England in its Origin and Development*, 3 vols. (6th edn, Oxford, 1903–6), p. 113, n. 6, cites two passages which suggest that faint echoes of a hundred alderman who represented the local community remained even then.

[35] The widespread assumption that hundredmen were just royal reeves by another name is thus unhelpful. See, for example, Wormald, 'Lordship and Justice', p. 332; Baxter, 'Lordship and Justice', p. 417; Hudson, *Oxford History*, p. 52; Campbell, 'Agents and Agencies', pp. 210–11; and, for that matter, T. B. Lambert, 'Protection, Feud and Royal Power: Violence and Its Regulation in English Law, *c*.850–*c*.1250' (University of Durham PhD thesis, 2009), p. 131. Most notably, Frederic William Maitland, *Domesday Book and Beyond: Three Essays in the Early History of England* (Cambridge, 1897), p. 277, built a far-reaching argument on the assumption that assemblies would not have taken place without a powerful figure directing them (see quotation in Chapter 7, p. 302, n. 21). Pauline Stafford, 'Reeve', in Michael Lapidge et al., eds., *The Wiley-Blackwell Encyclopedia of Anglo-Saxon England* (2nd edn, Chichester, 2014), pp. 397–8, is exceptional in tacitly acknowledging the fragility of the case for hundred reeves: 'there were royal reeves, bishops' reeves, nobles' reeves; reeves on royal estates, in towns and boroughs; shire reeves, reeves over wapentakes and probably hundreds.' H. M. Chadwick, *Studies on Anglo-Saxon Institutions* (Cambridge, 1905), pp. 234–5, noted that hundredmen are not said to be reeves, but concluded that they actually were because their duties correspond to those of reeves in earlier legislation. He did not consider the possibility that the purpose of establishing the hundredal system was to reduce the extent to which kings relied on reeves for these functions.

The rhetoric of our Anglo-Saxon evidence for hundreds is notably communal. When the *Hundred Ordinance* discusses meetings of the hundred, it does not imagine a powerful figure playing an instrumental role in 'holding' or 'calling' them; rather, it is the people of the hundred who are commanded to *gegaderian* ('to gather together' or 'to assemble').³⁶ In both this text and in Edgar's laws the hundred, as a collective entity, appears as a recipient of fines.³⁷ In Cnut's laws it is the hundred's collective opinion that decides whether an individual should be forced to have his lord prove his trustworthiness with an oath.³⁸ Indeed, those same laws imply that it is the hundred, not any individual, which will make the technical legal decision as to how a man should answer accusations brought against him.³⁹

This rhetorical emphasis on communality need not imply that hundreds were in reality any more communal than previous assemblies had been. Hundredmen probably presided at hundreds but it is likely that the people responsible for collecting fines—royal reeves, non-royal reeves, and privileged lords—continued to act as legal authorities, monitoring hundreds and guiding them in the proper application of the law. Edgar's laws, at any rate, are clear that fines for false judgements need to be collected by bishops.⁴⁰ This implies that the people who normally collected fines were unsuitable for the job, which suggests that—as had been the case before—they were the people the laws envisaged being punished for false judgement.⁴¹ It is likely that assemblies throughout the Anglo-Saxon period were expressions of collective authority, but that in practice communities relied on guidance on the application of the law provided by individuals or small groups. Hundreds probably did not differ much in this respect from earlier assemblies; the difference in rhetorical emphasis in the later texts is more likely to be a product of those texts' aims. Earlier laws emphasized the importance of reeves and privileged lords ('thegns') because kings were issuing commands to reeves and privileged lords, who were then to try to implement them in communal assemblies; laws about hundreds emphasize communality because kings were bypassing reeves and privileged lords, issuing commands directly to communal assemblies.

The establishment of the hundredal system is significant because it allowed this change to happen. Forcing all local assembly districts into a uniform framework

---

³⁶ Hu 1. DOE s.v. 'ge-gadrian'. It is also noteworthy that Edgar's laws do not associate hundred assemblies with anyone identifiable as a royal agent. This is significant because when same passage moves on to shire assemblies it is at pains to insist on the presence of the relevant ealdorman and bishop. III Eg 5–5:2.

³⁷ Hu 2:1–3:1; IV Eg 8:1. See Chapter 7, pp. 315–17.   ³⁸ II Cn 30.

³⁹ II Cn 27. When Domesday Book talks about judgements given by hundreds, it assumes that these judgements were made collectively. See Fleming, *Domesday Book and the Law*, nos. 545, 724, 1096, 1776, 2057, 3105; DB i. 165v, 182v, 373v, 376r, ii. 99r, 423v–424r.

⁴⁰ III Eg 3.

⁴¹ The term used for the potentially corrupt judge in this passage (III Eg 3) is, perhaps deliberately, vague and functional: *dema* (judge). As well as a fine, the law threatens this *dema* with loss of his 'thegnship' (*þegenscipe*). This obviously fits well with privileged lords acting as judges in person, as figures doing precisely this are referred to as thegns in early tenth-century laws (see Chapter 3, pp. 143–6). The term thegn, however, could mean 'someone who serves another', so losing one's thegnship could just mean losing one's position as a royal servant in this context. A reeve would lose his office, a privileged lord the grant which entitled him to the king's legal revenues.

enabled kings to engage with assemblies directly. Though they were still expected to act as legal authorities and collect fines, for all other purposes reeves were bypassed entirely. Instead, kings relied on men who naturally assumed a dominant role in their local assemblies by virtue of their wealth and status. This, of course, meant that kings could issue orders to every local communal assembly in the kingdom, even those where they had no local reeve and were entitled to no revenue. Kings now, for the first time, had a universal and more-or-less uniform network of local legal and governmental institutions to which they could issue commands. In theory it allowed them to exercise tight control over local legal practice, using their legislation to elaborate a finely detailed template of how every hundred should be organized.

An important point to appreciate, then, is that there were not people who could meaningfully be described as 'royal agents' or 'royal officials' running each hundred.[42] The hundredal system was meant to make it possible to control local legal practice, but through legislation rather than through a network of royal administrators.[43] Kings relied on communities to organize themselves, implementing the king's commands under local leadership. Hundreds may have constituted a 'royal' administrative system, in the sense that assembly districts were moulded into a coherent system at a king's behest, but it was an administrative system run by local communal leaders. Indeed, one of the reform's fundamental purposes seems to have been to allow kings to shape local legal practice to their liking *without* relying on their all-too-patchy network of reeves. To assume that hundred assemblies were directly supervised and controlled by people who can properly be termed royal officials is thus a major misunderstanding.

---

[42] These terms are problematic because they are vague. Indeed, it is possible that their frequent use in modern scholarship underlies the conflation of hundredmen and reeves (see the references cited above, p. 248, n. 35). A royal reeve and a hundredman might both be termed 'officials', in the sense that they both occupied an office, but though it is fair to term the reeve a 'royal official' because he is clearly a royal employee, it is only in the loosest sense that the hundredman works for the king. If he is an official he is surely more of a communal official: the fact that his communal office is shaped by royal legislation should not obscure that. Although both royal reeves and hundredmen might be termed 'royal agents', in the sense that they both performed functions demanded of them by the king, this is far too wide a definition of 'royal agent' to be useful. Royal legislation frequently demands that all free men perform specific functions: they must join tithings, swear oaths of loyalty, pursue thieves, perform military service, attend assemblies. Are all free men thus 'royal agents'? Unless we are careful to define this sort of terminology precisely it will hinder our understanding of the period, obscuring more than it reveals.

[43] Although this chapter had been drafted before it came to my attention, it should be noted that its arguments align closely with those in Taylor, 'Crime Without Punishment'. Taylor argues a very similar point in slightly different terms, for example: 'the legitimacy of law depended not on monopolizing *practice* but on monopolizing the capacity to create rules when the need arose' (p. 303, emphasis in original) and 'once it is acknowledged that control over crime can be independent from control over punishment, then we may go some way to understand how the ideological force of law regulated society even without an institutional means of enforcement' (p. 304). In an Anglo-Saxon context I would be reluctant to assert that kings 'monopolized' the capacity to create rules (see Chapter 7, pp. 300–1), or to imply that hundreds were not in some sense 'institutions', but such minor modifications have no effect on the thrust of her argument, which is utterly convincing.

Sheriffs

The introduction of sheriffs can be dealt with more swiftly here because it is less liable to be misunderstood. With hundreds, kings gained a universal network of administrative districts which they could command directly, but they did not gain a universal network of royal reeves. The local reeve in many places was still the reeve of some lord other than the king. Kings also had *burh* reeves but their concerns may well have been confined to *burh*s. In the late tenth century, however, a new type of reeve emerges in our evidence: the sheriff (*scirgerefa*, 'shire-reeve'). Though an older generation of scholarship tended to place the origins of the sheriff earlier, firm evidence of the existence of reeves responsible for full shires (as opposed to smaller districts to which the term *scir* was sometimes applied) does not emerge until the late tenth century.[44]

The earliest known figure likely to have held this role is a priest called Wulfsige, referred to as a *scirigman*, who can be detected acting on the king's behalf in Kent at some point between 964 and 988.[45] We also know of someone called Leofric, described as 'the *sciresman*', playing a prominent role in a Kentish shire assembly sometime between 995 and 1005.[46] These are our two earliest references to specific sheriffs (or perhaps 'proto-sheriffs'—it is only in the eleventh century that term *scirgerefa* starts to occur). Molyneaux has noted that both charters and *Anglo-Saxon Chronicle* annals from the years around the millennium abound with references to reeves and high-reeves, and has speculated that at least some of these may well be references to sheriffs.[47] One charter from the 990s, for instance, refers to 'Æthelwig, my reeve in Buckingham, and Wynsige, the reeve in Oxford'.[48] These figures have sometimes been assumed to be sheriffs of Buckinghamshire and Oxfordshire, and given that we find them exercising authority together in the countryside some way from both Buckingham and Oxford, this seems plausible.[49] The evidence is far from ideal, then, but it suggests that sheriffs began to appear towards the end of the tenth century: there is evidence for their existence in some places under Æthelred, much stronger evidence under Cnut,[50] and under Edward the Confessor it is clear that it was normal for each shire to have a sheriff.[51]

This aligns with the evidence of the laws in an interesting way. Throughout the tenth-century, as was noted in Chapter 3, it was assumed that when a potentially dangerous and defiant individual needed to be confronted, the proper response was for the community to band together and mount an enforcement

---

[44] For a review of the evidence which firmly establishes the sheriff's late tenth-century origins (and for references to older scholarship arguing for earlier origins), see Molyneaux, *Formation*, pp. 179–82. The following paragraph draws heavily on this discussion.

[45] S 1458.   [46] S 1454.   [47] Molyneaux, *Formation*, p. 181.   [48] S 883.

[49] See John Blair, *Anglo-Saxon Oxfordshire* (Stroud, 1994), pp. 103–4; Hudson, *Oxford History*, p. 39.

[50] See Molyneaux, *Formation*, p. 180, n. 297 for evidence showing sheriffs of Herefordshire, Kent, Staffordshire, and Worcestershire under Cnut.

[51] See Stephen Baxter, *The Earls of Mercia: Lordship and Power in Late Anglo-Saxon England* (Oxford, 2007), pp. 121–3; Hudson, *Oxford History*, pp. 38–40; William Alfred Morris, *The Medieval English Sheriff to 1300* (Manchester, 1927), pp. 23–39.

expedition.[52] In Æthelred's legislation, however, we find a departure. Essentially the same situation is envisaged—someone needs to ride to an untrustworthy man's home and either place him under surety or kill him—but the party doing the enforcement is now 'the king's reeve': there is no mention of a communal expedition.[53] This is a significant shift: no earlier text assumes that the king's reeves have this sort of coercive role. A possible explanation is that the type of king's reeve being envisaged here is a sheriff. There can be little doubt that sheriffs were much more substantial figures than rural reeves, quite possibly possessing their own military households. In counties close to the border, at any rate, the Domesday sheriff's duties included leading military expeditions into Wales.[54] Their capacity for independent coercion must have been much greater than that of the rural reeves they supervised; it therefore fits well that our first evidence for kings expecting their reeves to act as enforcers coincides with our first evidence for sheriffs.

The possibility that the emergence of a network of sheriffs had a significant effect on local legal practice should, then, be obvious. Before the sheriff, kings had a network of rural reeves, but this network only covered revenue-collection districts held by the king, and these reeves were relatively insignificant figures. (They had a network of *burh*-reeves too, but this had proven unsuitable for the routine regulation of rural legal practice.) The king's rural reeves had no local superiors. When one of them needed to be disciplined, the king had to rely on the bishop to implement the fine. With the emergence of the sheriff, however, this changed. The king's rural reeves now had a local superior (as did *burh*-reeves), a figure responsible for the collection of royal revenues across an entire shire. He, presumably, would now be the natural figure to discipline the royal reeves he supervised—it is probably significant that when Cnut's laws recapitulate earlier measures on this point they leave out the bishop's role in exacting fines[55]—and also the natural person upon whom they could call if a fine needed to be enforced.

The sheriff also gave kings an official capable of exercising authority in lands where the king's non-military rights had been granted to lords. They could, presumably, take action to ensure the workings of hundreds accorded with royal commands, even in hundreds where the king had the right to no legal revenues at all. Before the sheriff, kings not only lacked the right to any income from revenue-collection districts supervised by privileged lords or non-royal reeves, they lacked the means to extract payments. Even if they had claimed the right to receive revenues from these areas they would have struggled to collect them. With the establishment of sheriffs, however, it became much more practical to intrude into these supposedly liberated lands, and potentially to start claiming new rights in them. It may be no coincidence that the first solid evidence for a regular kingdom-wide system of taxation—the *heregeld*—comes in 1012, a point by which sheriffs

[52] Chapter 3, pp. 152–6.
[53] I Atr 4. The text in question cannot be dated with any certainty within Æthelred's reign, but there are a few problematic hints suggestive of a date in the 990s. See Wormald, *Making*, pp. 328–9.
[54] DB i. 179r, 252r. See Baxter, *Earls of Mercia*, p. 121, n. 303, for references to sheriffs killed in battle.
[55] II Cn 15:1. Cf. III Eg 3.

are likely to have been firmly established.[56] As Chapter 7 will show, there is good reason to think that kings were unable to resist this temptation with legal revenues as well, asserting the existence of a stratum of royal rights above those commonly granted to lords. For now, however, our concern is not with the distribution of legal rights but with kings and their capacity to control legal practice.

ACCUSATION AND DENIAL

Now the outlines and broad significance of the most pertinent changes in late Anglo-Saxon legal structures are clear, we can turn to the detail of local assembly practice, and specifically to the operation of formal proof procedures. Our starting point here must be the strong ideal of openness that runs throughout our corpus of Anglo-Saxon law. Honourable people do not hide their actions: if they cause harm to another person either through violence or by taking their property, they make their responsibility public. This is a large part of why thieves appear to have been so hated: their key characteristic was that they tried to hide their responsibility.[57] If someone openly admits having taken someone else's possessions he cannot be a thief: he will usually be a man who claims (justifiably or otherwise) that he has a right to whatever he has taken. Killing was the same. The clearest illustration of this comes in the early twelfth century in the *Leges Henrici Primi*, which are perhaps most likely to be drawing on an otherwise unknown Anglo-Saxon text here. They state that a man who had killed someone was to lay out his victim's body respectfully, taking none of his property, and 'make this known at the nearest village and to the first person he meets, and also to the lord that has soke, so that it may be possible for a case to be established or denied as against the slain man's relatives or associates.'[58] The ideal, at least, was that there be no dispute whatsoever about the facts of the killing, because the killer publicly declared his responsibility. There is no sign that the victim's family might need to prove a charge against the killer: his declaration renders this unnecessary. The legal issues that arise, rather, are the validity of the killer's actions. He is the one who may have to establish a case— perhaps so as to demonstrate that he was not liable for the man's wergild, or even for a punitive fine[59]—and the victim's relatives are the expected defendants.

---

[56] See Chapter 7, pp. 307–8.   [57] Chapter 2, pp. 89, n. 93, 100–1.

[58] Hn 83:6–83:6a. The idea that this passage is based on an existing text is mainly speculation and could be mistaken. However, much of the *Leges Henrici* is based on identifiable texts and it is hardly unlikely that some other texts were used which have since been lost. This passage is not at all like other passages in the text where the author seems to be speaking from personal experience. (On this, see Nicholas Karn, 'Rethinking the *Leges Henrici Primi*', in Stefan Jurasinski, Lisi Oliver, and Andrew Rabin, eds., *English Law Before Magna Carta: Felix Liebermann and Die Gesetze der Angelsachsen* (Leiden, 2010), pp. 199–220 at 215–20.) It has a flavour rather more like Anglo-Saxon texts such as *Wergeld*, II Edmund, and the Regulations of the Cambridge Thegns' Guild than anything else we know of from the early twelfth century. The reference to the lord with soke, if we could be sure it derived from an earlier text (which we cannot), would prove that the original was Anglo-Saxon (rather than Scandinavian, for instance) and probably eleventh-century.

[59] He might assert, for example, that this was rightful vengeance for an earlier killing for which no compensation had been paid, or that he had acted in self-defence. Either of these possibilities (both of

The ideal, then, was that there be no dispute over the facts of any case. When people were accused of offences which they had in fact committed, they were not meant to perjure themselves with oaths of denial. Rather, they were expected to explain why they had acted as they had so that, once everything had been taken into account, a fair compensation settlement and any necessary punitive fines could be implemented. However, people did not always live up to these ideals, and thieves posed a particularly difficult challenge: assemblies needed to have ways of ascertaining who was telling the truth when one man denied another's accusation. There were some circumstances in which defendants were not permitted to make a formal denial; when a thief was caught in the act of theft, for instance, his guilt was taken as self-evident and it was well established that he had no right to deny it. However, when the undisputable facts of a case left room for doubt some mechanism for resolving that doubt was needed. This was the purpose of formal proof procedures: various forms of (usually collective) oath-swearing and the procedure known as 'trial by ordeal'.

In the most basic sense it was these proof procedures that decided cases. If a defendant successfully denied the charges made against him using a formal means of proof, he won his case and paid neither compensation nor a fine. If he failed to make a formal denial at the proof stage, however, his guilt was established and it was then up to the assembly to decide what, if any, compensations and punishments were appropriate. Proof procedures were decisive, then, and we must understand how they worked if we are to assess the extent to which their results were open to manipulation.

Before examining formal proof procedures in detail, however, we should note that there are strong indications contemporaries found them worrying. The ideal was that there be no dispute over the facts of a case. When facts were disputed, formal proof was a necessary evil: the only way of resolving an impasse. The theory underlying both types of formal proof—oaths and ordeals—was that the truths they revealed came with divine guarantees: God would not allow an innocent man to fail an ordeal, and anyone who knowingly swore a false oath was damning his soul for all eternity.[60] Although it seems the Anglo-Saxons accepted this logic in principle, in practice they treated both forms of proof as necessary expedients; their results had to be respected, but seemingly not to the extent of allowing them to condemn a defendant to death. This is evident from the standard treatment of

which are envisaged by the text) would be relevant to a final judgement as to what compensation, if any, one party owed to the other. On the possibility that punitive fines applied to killings committed in some circumstances but not others, see Chapter 2, p. 93, n. 106, and more broadly Chapters 4 and 5, pp. 181–99, 224–35.

[60] See Robert Bartlett, *Trial by Fire and Water: The Medieval Judicial Ordeal* (Oxford, 1986), ch. 4. As Hudson, *Oxford History*, p. 84, notes (with an example and a number of further references) miracle stories suggest some people believed that, at least some of the time, God was just as unwilling to permit false oaths to be made. Even an unwitting false oath could be dangerous. We have one story in which a certain Thorkel unwisely swore an oath to the innocence of his wife. Fortunately he called on no more powerful divine authority than his own beard, which he tugged as he swore, and God's punishment for this blasphemous perjury was limited to the beard coming away in his hand. See W. Dunn Macray, ed., *Chronicon Abbatiae Rameseiensis* (Rolls Series 83, London, 1886), ch. 74, pp. 133–4.

thieves who were not caught in the act, and whose guilt therefore had to be established using proof procedures (or by negotiation in the shadow of such procedures). The traditional rule was that thieves who were proven guilty in this way should be fined but not executed. However, when they were caught in positions where their guilt was beyond dispute—when they were taken in the act or immediately afterwards with their stolen goods in hand—it was proper for them to be killed. As we have seen, seventh-century laws declare that thieves caught in such circumstances could legitimately be slain by the men who caught them, and they demand that any captured thieves be given to the king, who had the option of executing or enslaving them.[61]

As we saw in Chapter 4, in the early tenth century Æthelstan made an attempt to overturn this tradition, ordering that thieves be killed regardless of the means by which they were proven guilty, with oaths and ordeals specifically mentioned among those means.[62] However, later laws suggest that he failed in this. The laws of Æthelred and Cnut assume that people could be convicted of theft and pay *ðeofgyld* ('thief-payment'), surviving to be accused again and forced to undergo trial by ordeal.[63] Moreover, when laws issued under Edgar and Cnut recapitulate Æthelstan's measures demanding death for all thieves, the language used suggests that thieves in question were specifically those whose guilt was self-evident—those for whom denial by formal proof would have been impossible.[64] It seems, then, that Æthelstan attempted to persuade his people to kill thieves on the basis of oaths and ordeals, but was unable to overcome the traditional reluctance to allow matters of life and death to hang on formal proof procedures.[65]

Forms of Proof

For present purposes, the most important point to note about proof procedures is that in normal circumstances they seem to have been weighted in favour of the defendant. For free men and women in good standing, formal denial of a charge involved an oath of exculpation. As Cnut's laws explain, 'every trustworthy man, who has not been frequently accused, and has failed neither at oath nor at ordeal, is to be entitled to the simple process of exculpation within his hundred'.[66] This oath involved the defendant swearing an oath in conjunction with a number of other

---

[61] See Chapter 2, pp. 84–5, 90.

[62] The key text is IV As 6 (quoted in Chapter 4, pp. 175–6), which is problematic because it only survives in a post-Conquest Latin translation. An Old English fragment survives for immediately following passages (IV As 6:1–6:3) and is slightly different from and somewhat less elaborate than the Latin version. We cannot, therefore, be wholly confident that the original law really did specify that thieves convicted by oath and ordeal should invariably die. Nor, however, can we safely assume otherwise.

[63] I Atr 1:2; II Cn 30:1, and below pp. 262–4.   [64] III Eg 7:3; II Cn 26–26:1.

[65] As was just noted (above, n. 62) it is possible that Æthelstan did not, in fact, make this attempt and that the impression that he did so is the result of a later interpolation. The main point here—that the Anglo-Saxons were unwilling to entrust matters of life and death to formal proof—would only be strengthened if this were so.

[66] II Cn 22.

free adults acting as oath-helpers. (The evidence bearing on female oath-helpers is limited but sufficient to prove that they could be called upon, at least in support of female principals.)[67] We have one text which provides appropriate oath formulas for this, and it suggests that nothing very elaborate was involved. The accused would have to swear 'by the lord, I am guiltless, both in deed and counsel, of the charge of which N. accuses me'; his oath-helpers would have to assert that this was true, saying 'by the lord, the oath that N. swore is clean and unperjured'.[68] The main obstacle to making an exculpatory oath, then, was finding the requisite number of people willing to act as oath-helpers, which could vary but may most often have been eleven.[69] (The laws sometimes ask for oaths of equivalent value to the property in dispute but how this was calculated is not entirely clear.)[70] If the defendant successfully managed to assemble this collective oath the case was over: he had proven himself innocent of the charge.

It thus seems denying a charge was a relatively easy thing to do in this period, at least for free people of good reputation. Making a formal accusation, by contrast, may have been a risky business. The laws of Edgar and Cnut both specify that men who brought charges which the defendants were able to disprove should lose their tongues or redeem them by paying their wergilds.[71] The implication here seems to be that whenever a charge was successfully denied the accuser would be punished in this way, but it may not have been quite that simple. The verb used in these passages— *geunsoðian*, 'to disprove'—is rare, so we cannot be confident it means the same thing as the verbs usually used of oaths of denial (for example, *ætsacan* or *oðsacan*); it is possible that to disprove a charge to the point where an accuser would face punishment for making a malicious prosecution was a more onerous undertaking than the normal procedures for formal denial.[72] This is speculation, however, and even if it is accurate the main point still stands: it was relatively easy for a free defendant in good standing to deny a charge, and people who made accusations were in danger of being punished themselves if their accusations were proven to be false.

---

[67] See Carole Hough, 'Alfred's *Domboc* and the Language of Rape: A Reconsideration of Alfred, ch. 11', repr. in and cited from Carole Hough, *An Ald Recht: Essays on Anglo-Saxon Law* (Newcastle upon Tyne, 2014), pp.169–202 at 179–81. The key text is S 1454, a dispute narrative from the early 990s which lists eleven men and thirteen women as the most prominent members of a group of oath-helpers which offered their support to a noblewoman named Wynflæd in a land dispute. It is notable that the female oath-helpers include inter-generational family groups: 'Eadgifu of Lewknor and her sister and her daughter' as well as 'Ælfgifu and her daughter'. This could perhaps be taken as a hint that the list includes not only widows and abbesses, whom we might expect to find conducting their own legal affairs as heads of their households, but also noble wives or daughters resident in households headed by men (their husbands or fathers) but seemingly swearing independently of them.

[68] Swer 5–6. N. refers to different people in these two examples.

[69] Hudson, *Oxford History*, pp. 81–2.

[70] Ine's laws provide a lot of information on this point (Ine 14, 15, 19, 25:1, 28:2, 30, 35:1, 45, 46, 48, 52, 53, 54, 54:2), valuing oaths both in hides and in shillings, and seemingly equating the two (Ine 52), in a way that suggests the value of people's oaths at this point usually corresponded to the amount of land they owned. See Hudson, *Oxford History*, pp. 82–3; Chadwick, *Anglo-Saxon Institutions*, pp. 134–53.

[71] III Eg 4; II Cn 16. Af 32 is similar. II Cn 36 specifies loss of a hand for perjury, but not in the context of false accusation.

[72] DOE s.v. 'æt-sacan'; ASD s.v. 'ge-unsoþian', 'oþ-sacan'.

Denial was much more difficult for men of bad reputation. Laws issued under Æthelred and recapitulated under Cnut make it clear that different rules entirely applied to people who were classified as *tihtbysig* (literally, 'charge-laden'). If the defendant was unable to deny his *tihtbysig* status, he was not permitted to make an oath of denial regarding whatever charge had been brought against him. Instead, he had to undergo the triple ordeal.[73] What this meant is spelled out in earlier texts. For a single ordeal the accused would either have to carry a red hot piece of iron weighing one pound over a distance of nine feet, or have to plunge his hand wrist-deep into a vessel of boiling water and pick out a stone. For the triple ordeal, however, the iron would weigh three pounds or the water would be so deep he needed to submerge his arm up to the elbow. If, after three days, the resulting burn was judged to be clean the accused had successfully denied the charge, but if it was judged to have festered he was guilty.[74] It scarcely need be pointed out that the ordeal was to all intents and purposes a punishment in itself, or that, unless those responsible for assessing the burn were minded to stretch the definition of 'clean' in the accused's favour, the chances of conviction in even a single ordeal must have been considerable.

Prosecuting someone who qualified as *tihtbysig* was thus a great deal easier than if the accused had the full legal capacity of a freeman. There was a world of difference between denying a charge by a simple oath and undergoing the threefold ordeal. However, between these two extremes a number of shades of grey were possible. Not only could different accusations require different sizes of oath—there was a threefold oath to correspond to the threefold ordeal, for instance—but it was also possible for restrictions to be placed on the pool of potential oath-helpers. Our clearest example of such a 'selected' oath is a statement in Cnut's laws that when someone was accused of failing to perform one of the three common burdens (bridge-work, *burh*-work, and military service) and wished to deny it, fourteen possible oath-helpers would be nominated for him and he would have to persuade eleven of these to swear in his support.[75] With the pool of people from which the

---

[73] I Atr 1:1–1:4; II Cn 30–30:3. For detailed discussions of Anglo-Saxon ordeals, see Sarah Larratt Keefer, '*Ðonne se Cirlisca Man Ordales Weddigeð*: The Anglo-Saxon Lay Ordeal', in Baxter et al., *Early Medieval Studies in Memory of Patrick Wormald*, pp. 353–67; Patrick Wormald, *Papers Preparatory to the Making of English Law: King Alfred to the Twelfth Century*, vol. 2: *From God's Law to Common Law*, ed. Stephen Baxter and John Hudson (University of London, 2014) <http://www.earlyenglishlaws.ac.uk/reference/wormald/>, pp. 72–90.

[74] II As 23; Blas; Ordal 1–5; Hu 9. The ordeal of cold water was much less terrifying. The outcome depended on whether the blessed water accepted the accused when lowered into it—if he sank he was innocent, if he floated he was guilty. However, there is no indication that this was an option for the triple ordeal.

[75] II Cn 65. The similarities with later trial by jury are worth remarking upon. In normal collective oaths there was probably a great deal of pressure on a defendant's relatives and close associates to act as oath-helpers, but it seems likely that most others could simply refuse to participate on the grounds that it was not incumbent upon them to do so. Oaths were serious matters, potentially imperilling the soul, so it was probably not expected that people would swear in support of people to whom they had no obligation. If the fourteen people empanelled as potential oath-helpers in the context of this law could legitimately adopt this attitude, however, the procedure would have been extremely unfair. Presumably the idea was that the fourteen thus nominated would look into the matter diligently and be willing to support the defendant's oath if they believed it to be truthful, on the basis of their assessment of the

accused had to find his oath-helpers so limited, denying a charge was probably significantly more difficult. Most references to selected oaths do not give details as to the numbers involved, but it may be that the requirement to find eleven oath-helpers from a pool of fourteen was unusually stringent: Edward the Elder's legislation seems to allow a man to prove his ownership of a single cow with one oath-helper chosen from a pool of six.[76] One of Æthelstan's laws, by contrast, seems to forbid this practice, stating that oaths should be in proportion to the value of the goods concerned and sworn 'without selection'.[77]

Oaths and Local Politics

Perhaps the most important point to take from this is that the outcome of most prosecutions must have rested on the accused's ability to make an oath of denial, and that this depended on his ability to find oath-helpers among the local free population. Under unrestricted conditions this presumably meant soliciting support from personal contacts: a man's relatives, personal lord, friends, fellow guild members—anyone who could be persuaded to help. Personal popularity was important. But we should remember that a lot rode on these oaths, and the party bringing the prosecution had good reason to apply pressure to such people in a bid to dissuade them from agreeing to swear. These situations also offered opportunities to lords whose patronage networks were such that they could reliably assemble the requisite number of oath-helpers. Such lords had the power to rescue men who faced ruin because they lacked sufficient oath-helpers, and could exact a high price for their assistance.

The most famous of Anglo-Saxon legal cases, that of Helmstan narrated in the text known as the Fonthill Letter, illustrates this well.[78] We are told that Helmstan stole a belt and that as a result of this a certain Æthelm Higa immediately brought a seemingly unconnected claim against him for his land at Fonthill. Presumably this was because, now he was a known thief, Helmstan's ability to defend himself against accusations was reduced. Even on unrelated matters he could no longer resort to a simple oath. (The text appears to imply that Higa was not the only one to seize the opportunity to bring a claim against Helmstan at this time.) There

---

available evidence and their prior knowledge of the characters involved. The dynamics of 'selected' collective oaths may thus have been rather more akin to later juries than to normal, 'unselected' collective oaths.

[76] I Ew 1:4. Other references to selected oaths: IV Atr 7:3; II Cn 22–22:1; Hn 31:8a, 64:9a; Leis Wl 14:1; 14:3, 15–15:1.

[77] V As 1:5.

[78] S 1445. See the edition, translation, discussion, and references to earlier scholarship initially published as Nicholas P. Brooks, 'The Fonthill Letter, Ealdorman Ordlaf and Anglo-Saxon Law in Practice', in Baxter et al., *Early Medieval Studies in Memory of Patrick Wormald*, pp. 301–17, and later, updated to take more recent work into account, in S. E. Kelly and N. P. Brooks, eds., *The Charters of Christ Church Canterbury*, 2 vols. (Oxford, 2013), no. 104 (at p. 857 for comprehensive references to earlier scholarship). In fact, the letter narrates two separate cases involving Helmstan but here we are concerned only with the first (on which also see below, p. 266); the second is discussed below, pp. 269–70 and in Chapter 7, pp. 317–18.

followed some argument about whether in the circumstances Helmstan should be allowed to defend his land with an oath at all, which was eventually resolved by King Alfred in his favour, probably because Helmstan held a charter which proved his title (and had a powerful patron able to press his claim). Helmstan was still in trouble, however, because he was unable to make the oath required, perhaps because the number of oath-helpers required had been set high because of his reputation as a thief.[79] His only way out was to make a deal with his godfather, the letter's author, an ealdorman named Ordlaf.[80] As Ordlaf put it, 'he begged me that I should support him and said that he would rather give [the land to me] than that the oath should fail or it ever [be allowed to Higa]'. The deal that was done, then, involved Helmstan handing his land over to Ordlaf on the condition that he be allowed to retain possession of it for the rest of his life; in return, Ordlaf used his influence to ensure Helmstan had enough oath-helpers to win his case.

The swearing of oaths, then, did not take place in a political vacuum. The ideal may have been for men to make objective assessments of the issue at hand and on that basis decide whether or not to take part in a collective oath. As we have no reason to think Anglo-Saxons generally took oath-swearing lightly, we must assume that such assessments often did play a role in these decisions. If a potential oath-helper did not, in fact, trust that his principal was telling the truth he would be committing a terrible sin by swearing in his support, gambling with his eternal salvation. But there were other factors too. Refusing to support a friend in need was an implicit declaration of distrust, an insult only a small step down from openly calling him a perjurer, liable to ruin a friendship permanently. Beyond these immediate considerations all manner of obligations could come into play and pull in different directions. If, for instance, the accused had once participated in an oath of denial on your behalf he would probably expect you to reciprocate. But what if your lord demanded the opposite because the accusation had been made by one of his own men and he was supporting it? There must have been cases where it was clear that offering support to the accused would mean incurring the wrath of a powerful local lord, but that failing to do so would have dire consequences for a friend, leaving potential oath-helpers in very uncomfortable positions. We must be careful not reduce these matters to pure political calculation: we know that Anglo-Saxons cared about honour, and honour must sometimes have led men to come to the aid of their friends even if this meant making a powerful enemy. Nonetheless, whether or not any individual was able to assemble the oath he required must have been heavily influenced by local social networks and patronage politics.

Although contemporaries would have understood these social and political networks well, it is generally impossible for us to reconstruct them in detail.

---

[79] Perhaps also because his opponents had been exercising political pressure. Æthelm Higa is said to have ridden to the final oath-swearing with someone called Byrhthelm, just as Helmstan rode with his godfather, which may indicate that he too had a powerful patron. If so, he is unlikely to have been idle in the case.

[80] Mark Boynton and Susan Reynolds, 'The Author of the Fonthill Letter', *Anglo-Saxon England* 25 (1996), pp. 91–5, argue that Ordlaf was not in fact the letter's author, but Brooks, 'Fonthill Letter', pp. 313–14, demonstrates that he was.

Hints of their operation are visible in most studies of charters, and Baxter has shown that networks of personal lordship can be studied on a larger scale using the unusually detailed information contained in Domesday Book for the counties of Norfolk, Suffolk, and Essex, but even this can only give us a small part of the complete picture.[81] What does seem clear is that the people who made practical decisions about the collection of fines—royal reeves, non-royal reeves, privileged lords who attended their local interests in person—could punch above their weight in terms of local political influence. An example of such a figure, excavated from Domesday Book by Baxter, is Ulfkell of Framingham (Norfolk). In spite of his rather small landholdings Ulfkell was clearly highly influential: approximately 120 free men had commended themselves to him as their personal lord. The reason for this is almost certainly because Ulfkell was a king's reeve (*praepositus regis*), and most likely, as Baxter has speculated, the reeve with responsibility for Norwich: what the laws would call a *burh*- or *port*-reeve.[82] It is likely that a lot of people who were responsible for the collection of punitive fines were a bit like Ulfkell, in that their duties allowed them to exert more political influence than people of equivalent wealth and status. This is probably in large part because they could exercise some discretion in the fines they imposed: their favour was worth securing because it was within their power to let an offender off with a relatively light punishment, or perhaps even to drop the charges against him entirely. This capacity for discretion is discussed below.[83]

Yet while such figures may normally have had an enhanced capacity to exercise influence on formal proof procedures, this is not to say that they would always have found it easy to control their outcomes. It is unlikely that they were ever the only political patrons operating in an assembly, and it must in any case have been a lot easier to use one's influence to help someone assemble a collective oath than to prevent them doing so. Indeed, we must surely suspect that it would often have been impossible to prevent defendants from finding the oath-helpers they needed to deny a charge: the numbers required do not seem to have been that high. These considerations apply both before and after the establishment of hundreds; there is no reason to think the hundredal system changed the dynamics of local patronage in any fundamental way.[84] The introduction of sheriffs, however, probably had a significant impact on local political networks. These were powerful and influential men who had good reason to try to use their influence to extract more punitive fines from areas where the king was entitled to receive them. The same basic consideration applies, even so: if all a free man needed to deny a charge was support from eleven other free men, it must have been very difficult to convict him if his neighbours genuinely thought he was innocent.

---

[81] Baxter, 'Lordship and Justice'; Baxter, *Earls of Mercia*, pp. 215–25.

[82] Baxter, *Earls of Mercia*, pp. 217–19.   [83] Below, pp. 283–9.

[84] If there was a clear rule that oath-helpers had to be drawn from within assembly districts, any redrawing of the boundaries of those districts that took place in the establishment of the hundredal system would naturally have changed the dynamics of local patronage politics. However, we have no way of identifying the effects of this, if there were any.

The Problem of Deniability

It appears, then, that free Anglo-Saxons in good legal standing were in a much better position to resist prosecution than the citizens of any modern liberal democracy. This must have constituted a major obstacle to the imposition of punishment for wrongdoing. Kings needed local assemblies to convict people of offences. If they were unable to do so, the offences they wished to see punished would go unpunished, and their legislative efforts might appear ineffectual, even ridiculous. Æthelstan seems to have been particularly worried about this problem. A significant theme in his legislation is the existence of men who were protected from prosecution, particularly for theft, because they belonged to powerful kindreds. As Æthelstan presents it, these men were known thieves who simply could not be convicted because of their kindreds. Presumably this was mainly because their families were willing to act as oath-helpers, enabling them to deny any charges brought against them, but the implication may also be that these kindreds had no respect for the prohibition on avenging slain thieves, to the extent that their neighbours were afraid to confront them even if they caught them in the act of thieving. The only possible way to deal with this problem of notorious thieves who were untouchable because of their powerful families, Æthelstan implies, was for him to intervene in person and order them (on pain of death) to move to another area of the kingdom where, separated from their kindreds, they would be vulnerable to prosecution if they dared continue to steal.[85]

Æthelstan's solution to this problem is thus presented a last resort prompted by extreme frustration, a radical measure justified by the deplorable faithlessness of such thieving kindreds. In normal circumstances it was clearly not acceptable for kings to smash through the legal defences of free defendants, imposing punishments on them even when it had not been possible to prove them guilty on any charge. Most free men were men of honour: when there was some doubt about an accusation it was right that they had the opportunity to deny it on oath. The trustworthy majority would not perjure themselves by denying charges of which they were guilty and kings had no business eroding the rights of the upstanding free population; indeed, we sometimes find them presenting themselves as the staunch upholders of these rights, in this matter and in others.[86] The problem was that incorrigibly sinful and dishonest people, mainly thieves, took advantage of the free defendant's right to deny charges on oath. They flagrantly perjured themselves—displaying an alarming indifference both to their own honour and the fate of their souls—simply so as to avoid punishment and continue their outrageous behaviour with impunity. The conduct of this utterly reprehensible few was a serious problem, but in the long run it was not a problem that could legitimately be solved by making all free men more vulnerable to prosecution. Any solution needed to be carefully targeted.

[85] III As 6; IV As 3; V As Prol. 1- Prol. 3. See also VI As 8:2–8:3. The context of theft is explicit in all the texts except V Æthelstan, where the same measure is framed in more general terms.

[86] In general terms: III Eg 1:1; V Atr 1:1; VI Atr 8–8:1; II Cn 1:1. Specifically on this point: II Cn 20, 22, perhaps also V As 1:1–1:5.

THE LIMITS OF JUDICIAL DISCRETION

One possible way of overcoming this problem with deniability has already been noted: it was an established aspect of procedure that some defendants were not entitled to deny charges on oath, their only way of defending themselves against accusations being to undergo an ordeal. If it were possible to ensure that thieves and other dishonest men were subjected to procedural disqualifications in this way, there would be an excellent chance of convicting them. We need, then, to understand how decisions about procedural disqualifications were made, and the extent to which various powerful figures—assembly presidents, privileged lords, royal and non-royal reeves—may have been able to influence them. Should we imagine that local authority figures, whoever they were, were capable of exercising some degree of discretion when it came to procedure, such that they could impose more onerous proof requirements on men they regarded as notorious malefactors?

Imposing Procedural Disqualifications

Fortunately, this topic is discussed at length in the laws on *tihtbysig* ('charge-laden') status first issued under Æthelred and then recapitulated under Cnut. Exactly how *tihtbysig* status was initially asserted is not entirely clear, but Cnut's laws appear to imply that it required three people to make accusations and the general opinion of the hundred to be that the accused was *ungetreow* ('untrue' or 'unfaithful').[87] Once asserted, however, both texts explicitly state that *tihtbysig* status could only be refuted by the accused's lord who, either in person or through his reeve, had to swear alongside two trustworthy (*getreow*) local men that the accused had never failed in oath or ordeal, nor paid ðeofgyld ('thief-payment'). Æthelred's laws state that these two oath-helpers had to be thegns—which by this point probably meant anyone of noble status—but Cnut's do not insist on this.[88]

No earlier laws offer this level of detail, but the principles underlying them accord well with these later texts. There seem to have been two main ways in which a free man might lose his right to defend himself on oath and qualify for *tihtbysig* status. One was to undertake to deny an accusation and then fail to do so, either on oath or in an ordeal, presumably because this constituted a proven incident of dishonesty, of being 'unfaithful' or 'untrue' (*ungetreow*). This principle is visible in the laws on perjury

---

[87] II Cn 30. The equivalent passage in Æthelred's laws (I Atr 1:1) does not discuss this.

[88] I Atr 1:2; II Cn 30:1. Both passages say that if the lord asserts his man has neither failed in oath or ordeal since a specific assembly (at *Bromdune* for Æthelred, Winchester for Cnut) he can then go on to swear an oath that the accused has *never* failed in oath or ordeal, nor paid ðeofgyld. The passage thus seems goes to some lengths to make clear that lord's initial assertion, which is limited to the period since the assembly, does not align with the more comprehensive oath he has to swear. Why this should be is obscure. The inconsistency between this passage and II Cn 22:1, which allows *ungetreow* men to clear themselves with a threefold oath, probably reflects Cnut's laws' status as a compendium of earlier legislation (see Chapter 4, p. 165): II Cn 22–22:3 is probably recapitulating an otherwise unknown earlier text in which the priority was the protection of free defendants' right to exculpate themselves, whereas I Atr 1–1:13 (which underlies II Cn 30–31:2) seems to be an attempt to crack down on lords who shielded their men from punishment.

in Edward the Elder's legislation, which order that men who once failed to deny a charge on oath should never thereafter be allowed to swear an oath, always having to undergo the ordeal.[89] Importantly, however, previous convictions for offences where there had been no attempt at denial were generally not a problem. A man could openly admit most offences, paying the fines and compensations associated with them, and suffer no loss of reputation: he had never been shown to be dishonest. The exception to this rule, according to Æthelred and Cnut, was theft. Being convicted of theft and thus paying *ðeofgyld* was the second way of losing the right to swear an oath: it did not matter whether a denial was attempted or not.[90] People who paid *ðeofgyld* had either failed in an attempt to deny a charge, thus proving themselves dishonest, or they had admitted to being thieves, and admitting to being a thief constituted an admission of dishonesty, of being *ungetreow*. This accords with Æthelstan's laws on ordeal, which state that they were for people who, as well as being often accused, had been found guilty of an offence that is likely to be theft.[91] A past record of dishonesty, then, whether acquired through failed attempts at formal proof or through convictions for theft, laid a defendant open to procedural disqualifications.

These rules about procedural disqualifications show that law-makers assumed their imposition to be governed by established facts. If a man had previously been convicted of theft or failed to make an oath of denial, this would usually have been well known. His lord had the option of perjuring himself and denying this, persuading two others to join him, but it is unlikely that noblemen (or freemen) often took their oaths or their reputations so lightly as to be willing to swear to something generally regarded as a falsehood. On the other hand, if a man did have an unblemished record it is unlikely that his lord would refuse to support him. He would have the option of doing so, of course, but lords were meant to support their men in such situations: few can have been willing to betray their men's trust in so public a fashion unless they very clearly had good reason to do so.[92] In theory, there was little room for manoeuvre in procedural decisions such as this.

We need, however, to think through the possibility that in practice this was not the case. Is it possible that powerful figures were able to impose procedural disqualifications even on men with unblemished legal records, and thus ensure they faced the ordeal and were convicted? The only hint that this was possible is that Cnut's laws explicitly guarantee the right of free men in good standing to deny charges by simple oath: this could be taken as an indication that sometimes they

---

[89] I Ew 3. II As 26 probably means the same thing but its language is less explicit.

[90] I Atr 1:2; II Cn 30:1.

[91] II As 7. Two of the three manuscripts leave the offence unspecified, but one states it is theft: see Felix Liebermann, ed., *Die Gesetze der Angelsachsen*, 3 vols. (Halle, 1898–1916), i. p. 154, iii. p. 103. The immediately preceding passages (II As 6:2–6:3) are concerned with people who avenge thieves, which may indicate that a context of theft is implicit even in the manuscripts where the offence is left unspecified.

[92] It should be remembered that lords were in competition with one another for commendations; letting a commended man down in so visible a way would surely, except in the most exceptional of circumstances, have severely undermined a lord's efforts to attract others. See Baxter, 'Lordship and Justice'.

were not being allowed this right.[93] It need not be read in this way, however. It is part of a longer discussion of formal proof procedures in which even *ungetreow* men are allowed to defend themselves against charges using collective oaths, albeit of a more stringent variety than those used by men of good reputation.[94] This suggests that there were competing norms on this issue, and that when we find kings ordering that *ungetreow* men entirely lose their right to defend themselves on oath, we should probably infer that they were attempting to impose unusually rigorous rules, and perhaps cutting against the more merciful grain of local custom.

This could explain why Cnut's passage on *tihtbysig* status seems to imply that such people could only be forced to undergo the ordeal if they were regarded as *ungetreow* 'by the hundred': in practice, it was not possible to force people to undergo the ordeal at all if local opinion was against it.[95] The laws, of course, imply that even when local opinion was against a defendant he could still be rescued from the ordeal by his lord swearing an oath on his behalf, and there is little reason to doubt this. There may have been cases where, with local opinion onside and with the tacit approval of his lord, a defendant with no formally proven record of dishonesty could be forced to undergo the ordeal, but it is difficult to imagine that such circumstances arose very often. The laws, at least, assume that dishonest men were treated as dishonest because their records showed them to be dishonest, not simply because they were regarded with suspicion. More importantly, they imply that there were important structural checks in place—both local opinion and a defendant's own lord—which would have made it difficult for powerful figures to impose procedural disqualifications on people who did not deserve them.

The Rigidity of Procedure

Most of these observations on the imposition of procedural disqualifications apply just as fully to procedural decisions more generally: there was not meant to be room for discretion. Questions of procedure were technical legal questions to which there was meant to be only one right answer. Differing local legal customs might mean the one right answer in an assembly in Devon differed from the one right answer in an assembly in Surrey, but custom dictated a single correct way of doing things within each assembly. In general, there is good reason to suppose that legal practice lived up to this ideal, and that even the royal reeves, non-royal reeves and privileged lords responsible for exercising legal authority in hundreds would mostly have struggled to mould procedural decisions to their liking in specific cases. They were not meant to do this—it was corrupt by contemporary standards as well as our own—but there were also important practical checks which must have made it difficult to achieve.

The most important of these checks was that such figures' decisions were open to the scrutiny of all the other members of the assemblies in which they were operating. For all relatively run-of-the-mill cases this would have been a knowledgeable audience:

[93] II Cn 22.   [94] II Cn 22:1.   [95] II Cn 30.

the proper procedures would have been familiar to the members of assemblies from repeated use. The number of oath-helpers necessary to deny an accusation of theft, for example, would surely have been common knowledge, especially among the more senior members of an assembly. As Robin Fleming has demonstrated, Domesday Book makes clear that such men were the repositories of a great deal of knowledge about the recent legal history of their hundreds.[96] It may well have been possible for a powerful figure to bend the law if the members of his assembly were just as keen to see a notorious figure convicted, but it seems unlikely that there was much scope for well-known rules to be distorted in their application except by general consent.

Beyond this, it is important to note that appeals against defective legal decisions were possible, certainly to the king and perhaps also to the shire assembly.[97] It may be that relatively humble defendants were in no position to make such appeals but their personal lords would have been. There is good evidence that appeals were common in this period. Asser states that the demand for Alfred's services as an appellate judge was very high.[98] Alfred's law code, as has been noted, is filled with what look very like royal judgements issued to resolve legal quandaries, which could well have come to the king's attention as appeals.[99] The fact that Alfred seems to have heard Helmstan's case in an informal setting, while washing his hands, may well offer some slight confirmation of this: it perhaps hints that demand for royal judgement was so high that litigants had to seize upon spare moments such as these if they wanted to secure the king's attention.[100] Most tellingly of all, both Edgar

[96] Fleming, *Domesday Book and the Law*, pp. 36–45.

[97] II Cn 19 demands that people seek justice three times in the hundred and once in the shire assembly before taking enforcement action to seize property to which they had established a claim. This might suggest that the shire could serve as a venue for appeals against decisions taken in hundreds, but this is not mentioned in the earlier passage (II Cn 17) discussing appeals specifically. The *Leges Henrici Primi* state that different shires had different customs (Hn 6:3a) but do not say the same for hundreds, which could be a hint that—at least by the early twelfth century—shire assemblies routinely oversaw hundredal justice, maintaining some degree of uniformity by hearing appeals. Hn 7:6 implies that 'disordered' cases from hundreds came before shires (maybe also Hn 9:4a). On the procedure of *wemming*, which seems to have been that used for challenging a judgement, see Hn 33:2, 67:2.

[98] Chapter 3, pp. 142–3.

[99] For example: Af 9 (what wergild should be paid for an unborn child?); Af 13 (when a man is accidentally killed by a felled tree, who gets the tree?); Af 14 (who is responsible for people born deaf and dumb, and thus unable to deny or confess to wrongdoing?); Af 16 (if someone steals a cow or mare but leaves her calf or foal, which dies for want of milk, what compensation does he owe for the calf or foal?); Af 20 (if someone lends property to a monk without the monk's lord's permission and the monk loses it, who is liable for the loss?); Af 23–5 (who is liable for harm done by animals?); Af 26 (what compensation is appropriate for raping an underage girl?); Af 27–27:1 (if a man who lacks maternal or paternal kinsmen kills someone, who is liable to pay the wergild?). Although the uncertainties with which Alfred's laws tend to be concerned revolve around the extent and distribution of liability for compensation rather than procedural issues, they may imply that kings heard appeals on difficult legal questions unrelated to major land cases. (Note also the hopelessly elaborate passage, Ine 62, quoted in Chapter 2, p. 77, which seems to show the king resolving a complicated procedural quandary relating to suretyship and ordeal). It cannot, however, be assumed that all these laws represent actual cases: presenting Alfred as a judge was part of the text's rhetorical intent, and some of these examples of abstruse legal wisdom could have been concocted for this purpose. Wormald, *Making*, p. 282, suggests that some represent judgements from actual cases but notes the possibility that others reflect the influence of Old Testament exemplars.

[100] S 1445.

and Cnut issued laws prohibiting appeals to the king before all local avenues had been exhausted, which suggests that such appeals were commonplace enough to be irritating.[101] Even if local opinion was against them, then, defendants had a good chance of resisting attempts at judicial corruption as long as they managed to maintain a good relationship with a personal lord. The presence of such a lord speaking up for his man's rights at a hundred assembly would probably have been sufficient to deter anyone else from making a flagrant attempt to convict the defendant through the corrupt misapplication of the law.

However, not all rules were unambiguous and widely understood. There must have been occasions when the supposed single right answer to a technical question was far from readily apparent, even the subject of dispute. Conditions of legal uncertainty—when there was either no clear precedent available for how a case should be treated, or more than one seemingly legitimate course of action—may well have provided powerful figures with the opportunity to exert influence, perhaps even to the extent of deciding cases. There are perhaps three principal scenarios in which uncertainty of this sort was likely to arise. First, doubts about the proper application of law could be caused by discrepancies between royal legislation and local custom. As we saw in Chapter 3, kings held reeves and privileged lords responsible for ensuring that their legal pronouncements won out in such conflicts, but the degree of precision that was expected of them is not clear. There may been scope for discretion. There must have been cases where applying new royal legislation to the letter would favour one party, while taking a slightly more relaxed view of the king's demands in line with local custom favoured the other.[102] Presumably, though, these uncertainties tended to arise out of new legislation, and once they were resolved they were unlikely to recur because the decisions taken would establish precedents that restricted future practice.

The second scenario in which legal uncertainty was likely to arise was in unusual cases: those which raised complex or obscure legal questions for which established custom could provide no authoritative answer. In the Helmstan dispute, for instance, it is clear that there was disagreement and uncertainty over whether Helmstan should be entitled to defend his title to Fonthill with an oath. We might guess that the difficult legal issue here was balancing the procedural disadvantages resulting from Helmstan's conviction for theft against the procedural advantages that normally accompanied the possession of charters in land cases. King Alfred deputized a number of senior figures to look into the detail of the case and resolve these issues, bringing the parties to a just settlement, but it proved impossible to find an interpretation of the law which both sides would accept. The case could therefore only be settled by the personal judgement of the king. Alfred (while washing his hands) endorsed Ealdorman Ordlaf's argument that—in part because of the evidence of the charters—Helmstan was 'nearer to the oath' and should be allowed to swear in defence of his land.[103] It may be that similarly tricky but less economically significant cases were resolved at local assemblies, and that the

---

[101] III Eg 2; II Cn 17.   [102] See Chapter 3, pp. 141–7.   [103] S 1445.

reeves and privileged lords who acted as legal authorities in them could therefore choose a way of resolving the uncertainties that suited their own interests. This is possible, but the temptation to abuse this power must often have been tempered by the possibility of an appeal.

Finally, and relatedly, there is good reason to think that procedural uncertainty was a much greater feature in the resolution of disputes over title to land (and to property more generally) than it was in resolving accusations of wrongdoing. This is because disputes over title did not have a clear structure of accusation and denial. All accusations of wrongdoing involved one party accusing the other of having committed a wrongful act; the key procedural issue to resolve was what form of proof the accused party needed to undertake to deny the charge. In disputes over title, however, the key issue was not the commission of a specific act: the party bringing the case was claiming the right to the property in question and his opponent was claiming the same right.[104] The main procedural question that needed to be resolved was not the appropriate form of proof, but which of the two parties should be allowed to undertake it (thus proving his title and winning the case). This seems to have involved the assessment of their competing claims, which could consist of convoluted arguments about inheritance of landed property stretching back over generations.[105] It often seems that both parties' cases had some merit, and that the decision as to who should be allowed to swear was a marginal one: both parties might be 'near' the oath in some sense, but priority had to be awarded to the side which was 'nearer'. (We find this language not just in Helmstan's case but also in a late tenth-century dispute over land in Huntingdonshire.)[106] The people who made these marginal, possibly even subjective, decisions about the relative merits of competing inheritance claims may often have been, in effect, the people who decided the outcomes of these cases.[107]

---

[104] The distinction here is essentially that noted by Hudson, *Oxford History*, p. 70: 'Cases can be fitted within a broad categorization. The party bringing the plea was claiming that a wrong had been done to him, or that the other party was in possession of something that belonged to the claimant.' This distinction was clearly important in shaping procedures but it was rather fuzzier with respect to consequences. Patrick Wormald, 'Giving God and King Their Due: Conflict and Its Regulation in the Early English State', repr. in and cited from Wormald, *Legal Culture in the Early Medieval West: Law as Text, Image and Experience* (London, 1999), pp. 333–57 at 351–2, presents evidence which shows that defeat in a land dispute could, at least sometimes, lead to punishment for robbery (*reaflac*—on which see Chapter 2, pp. 89–90). For disputes over ownership of movable goods conducted through 'vouching to warranty' procedures, see below, pp. 270–3 and Hudson, *Oxford History*, pp. 155–60. Though Hudson (p. 155) speculates that this procedure could be used to recover property without giving rise to an accusation of theft, he does so on the basis of twelfth- and thirteenth-century analogies. Both the relevant Anglo-Saxon oath formulas are explicit about the property having been stolen, though only one alleges that the current possessor was the thief (Swer 2, 4).

[105] See Julie Mumby, 'The Descent of Family Land in Later Anglo-Saxon England' *Historical Research* 84 (2011), pp. 399–415; Hudson, *Oxford History*, pp. 122–36.

[106] S 1445; E. O. Blake, ed., *Liber Eliensis* (Camden Society Third Series 92, London, 1962), ii. 25.

[107] Macray, *Chronicon Abbatiae Rameseiensis*, ch. 103, pp. 169–71, allows us to see the discretionary power of judges in these situations in crude financial terms: the abbot of Ramsey gave twenty marks of gold to the king in return for his goodwill and five marks to the queen for her intercession, thereby securing a contested bequest.

It was probably sometimes possible, then, for powerful local figures to exert influence on the outcomes of cases by manipulating technical legal decisions about procedure, but it seems likely that the potential for this was limited. Assembly customs, bound by well-known precedents, were probably more rigid than flexible in most routine matters. The one major exception to this is likely to have been disputes over inheritance, particularly of land. The rules on this were probably clear enough when competing claims were simple—between a dead man's son and brother, say—but it was possible for cases to be much more complicated. Interpreting how the law applied to them may well have been difficult, and this may given reeves and privileged lords significant discretionary power in their roles as legal authorities, permitting them to decide which party would be allowed to swear (and therefore win their case). There is good reason to think that high-status disputes were likely to be more complex and thus provide more scope for judicial discretion—the involvement of charters could add an extra layer of complication—but it may be that disagreements over relatively petty pieces of land could be just as fraught.[108] Disputes over title to landed property are not really our concern here, however. They are important for our purposes primarily because they provide a plausible explanation of why late Anglo-Saxon laws often threaten punishment for corrupt judgements: the judgements law-makers were worried about may well have been those involving land.

In the cases in which we are interested here—those involving accusations of wrongdoing—it seems unlikely that the scope of judicial discretion was sufficient to allow powerful people to make decisive interventions in procedural rulings. Marginal adjustments may have been possible, especially if they accorded with the mood of local assemblies, but this was probably not a method by which a great many additional convictions for wrongdoing could be obtained on the king's behalf. Kings could not hope to solve the problem of dishonest men abusing their right to deny charges by relying on their local representatives' ability to vary how law was applied. And from what little we can tell it seems there were structural checks—first and foremost the existence of commendatory lordship—which would have made it practically difficult for reeves or local privileged lords to go beyond the boundaries of legitimate discretion and engage in judicial corruption, however just the cause.

CIRCUMVENTING DENIABILITY

One of the main issues that worried kings in this period, then, was the existence of dishonest men who had never been caught out in their dishonesty. If they were caught and convicted, even once, these men could (in theory) be shackled with procedural disqualifications for the rest of their lives, perhaps even forced to undergo an ordeal if they ever wanted to deny another accusation. We find kings

---

[108] See Chapter 7, pp. 317–19.

trying to ensure this happened with their legislation—they seem to have been concerned that local assemblies were rather more forgiving of such men than was right—but really this was a side issue. We have just seen that local reeves' and privileged lords' discretionary control over the judicial process is unlikely to have been sufficient to allow them to impose procedural disqualifications on men with no proven record of dishonesty. The wall of deniability that made it extraordinarily difficult to secure a first conviction could not be finessed out of existence by local authority figures, or at least not as a matter of routine.

Nor could this wall legitimately be battered down. The only contemporary attempt at a solution that has been discussed thus far illustrates this well: Æthelstan's expedient of personally commanding notorious offenders to move away from their home areas, thereby disconnecting them from the local networks which supplied them with oath-helpers. This was obviously and worryingly extra-legal—the use of arbitrary administrative decrees to deny basic freedoms to people who had never been convicted of wrongdoing—and had to be framed as an emergency measure in response to a crisis. In general terms the wall of deniability that protected the upstanding free population from malicious accusations was evidently regarded as a good thing: a core aspect of personal liberty which legislators could not legitimately ignore in this way, or attack directly. Instead, they had to accept the wall's existence and work around it, finding ways to prevent thieves and other malefactors being given the opportunity to make use of it. That is, rather than seeking ways of convicting free men in good legal standing once a deniable accusation had been made against them, we find law-makers exercising considerable ingenuity so as to ensure that dishonest men were caught in situations where their guilt was manifest and therefore undeniable. The establishment of the hundredal system seems to have been the key development here: it seems to have given kings much greater confidence that they could issue detailed instructions on how local communities should run their legal affairs. All the major innovations seem to have taken place in the second half of the tenth century in the context of the hundred.

The Pursuit of Thieves

The most obvious way of ensuring that dishonest men were caught in situations where their guilt was undeniable was to insist on the pursuit of thieves: if they could be apprehended in possession of the stolen goods they could be executed, either on the spot or at a later juncture. This seems to be precisely what happened in the second case we know of involving Helmstan, also reported in the Fonthill Letter. Even after his initial theft of a belt had caused such trouble, forcing him to hand over his land to his godfather, Helmstan did not mend his ways. He went on to steal some oxen. Their tracks were followed and Helmstan was found in possession, and thus 'utterly ruined'. (In fact, he managed to avoid capture and later wished to deny his involvement, but he had scratched his face on some brambles while escaping and the marks on his face seem to have made his identity as the fleeing thief undeniable.) He presumably ought to have been executed at this point, but he managed to escape, was declared a fugitive by the king (now Edward the Elder), and ultimately avoided punishment by fleeing to King Alfred's grave in Winchester and persuading Ealdorman Ordlaf to intercede for him once again.[109]

Early tenth-century laws assume that a man who had lost his livestock might want to assemble a party of friends and neighbours and follow their tracks until he came upon a thief. They demand that lords and reeves make provisions for following the tracks of stolen livestock once they enter their districts, but they do not seek to punish men who fail to pursue their own stolen property.[110] It is only with the establishment of hundreds that we find the following of tracks made compulsory. This, in fact, is the context in which our first evidence for the hundred emerges: III Edmund orders that people who refuse to participate in the pursuit of thieves pay 120 shillings to the king and 30 shillings to the hundred.[111] The most complete articulation of these rules comes in the *Hundred Ordinance*, which orders that the men of the hundred band together and go in pursuit of thieves, killing those they came upon, and instructs the hundredmen of neighbouring hundreds to join in the search when it passed into their districts.[112] The punishments threatened here for non-compliance are more lenient, and perhaps more realistic: 30 pence for a first offence, 60 for a second, 120 for the third and full forfeiture and outlawry on the fourth occasion.[113] The aim was to ensure that as many thieves as possible were, like Helmstan, caught in circumstances where their guilt was undeniable.

Witnessing Transactions

Many thieves, however, would inevitably escape immediate detection. Before Edgar's reign it seems that these figures, if they were identified, would always have faced deniable charges. The most reliable way of finding a thief once his immediate trail had gone cold was to find the stolen goods themselves. If this was possible, their owner could then try to claim them by the process known to legal historians as 'vouching to warranty'. The person in possession of allegedly stolen goods had two options if he wished to avoid being convicted as a thief. The simpler course was to claim that the allegedly stolen goods were not stolen at all: they belonged to him and had always belonged to him. He could do this with an oath, providing he had sufficient oath-helpers. His other option was to claim that he had bought

---

[109] S 1445. For another case illustrating the fate of thieves caught in undeniable circumstances, see S 883.

[110] II Ew 4; V As 2; VI As 8:4. (Note that the communal expeditions against thieves envisaged in II As 20:3–20:8 do not suppose a context of immediate pursuit.) The London *frið*-guild's response to Æthelstan's legislation, however, was much more assertive, insisting that its members band together to track down stolen cattle and that neighbouring reeves pick up the trail themselves when it entered their districts (VI As 4–5, 7, 8:8).

[111] III Em 2. Punishments for obstruction of cattle tracking also appear clearly for the first time in this code: III Em 6. VI As 8:4 is roughly analogous, but this London text is notable for being considerably more ambitious than the legislation issued by Æthelstan himself.

[112] Hu 2–2:1, 5.

[113] Hu 3–3:1. Hu 5:1 threatens neighbouring hundredmen who fail to assist in searches with a 30 shilling fine. On a similar theme, see IV Eg 13–14.

the allegedly stolen goods from someone else, naming the seller and ideally also some witnesses who could verify that the transaction had taken place. (This is 'vouching' the seller 'to warranty'.) If he could do this, the seller was faced with the same problem: he had either to prove he owned the goods with a collective oath, or he had to vouch someone else to warranty. Long chains of vouching were possible, but eventually the process would stop, either with an oath asserting ownership—in which case the theft-victim's identification of the stolen goods is shown to be faulty and he loses his case—or in someone failing either to produce this oath or to vouch someone else to warranty. The person who fails to continue the process is thus, in theory, identified as the thief and duly convicted.[114]

The process of vouching to warranty, then, gave alleged thieves plenty of opportunities to deny involvement. It could also lead to conditions of great uncertainty. The ideal was that everything would be established beyond doubt: people would always be careful to buy goods—particularly livestock—before witnesses. If the goods they bought were subsequently claimed as stolen property, the buyer would then be able to prove that he had bought them from the seller. However, if there were no witnesses the seller would be able to deny the sale with an oath, leaving the buyer in trouble but the identity of the actual thief unclear. The buyer might be the thief, his claim to have bought the goods in an unwitnessed sale a ruse to avoid punishment, or he might simply have been incautious in buying goods from a dishonest man without trustworthy witnesses. He should certainly give up the stolen goods to their owner, but once this was done was it really right to punish the buyer as a thief? As we have seen, doing so was a serious matter: it meant not only a fine but the establishment of a formal record of dishonesty, and thus potentially the loss of the right to swear oaths of denial in the future. Local assemblies may well have been reluctant on this point.

The way that law-makers traditionally tried to address this problem was through laws demanding that transactions take place before witnesses. In the seventh century it seems that buying in the presence of witnesses was not always compulsory. One Kentish law demands that people buying in London do so before witnesses, but it does not penalize men who fail to do so beyond giving up the purchased property, and there is no mention of such a requirement for transactions taking place elsewhere.[115] Ine's laws envisage merchants wishing to travel into Wessex to trade, and demand that they do so in front of trustworthy witnesses, but again there is no sign that exchanges with other parties were expected be witnessed.[116] Indeed, even in a situation where the merchant is caught in possession of stolen goods with no witnesses to verify their legitimate purchase, he forfeits the goods but is not automatically treated as a thief. Rather, he is given the opportunity to deny complicity in the theft with an oath.[117]

The approach of late Anglo-Saxon law was different: from the laws of Edward the Elder it is consistently asserted that all significant purchases had to be witnessed. This seems to have proven difficult to implement. Edward begins by insisting that

[114] For a more detailed overview of these procedures, see Hudson, *Oxford History*, pp. 155–60.
[115] Hl 7, 16–16:3.   [116] Ine 25–25:1, 75.   [117] Ine 25:1.

all purchases be made in a *port* (a term used interchangeably with *burh*), and be witnessed by the *port*-reeve or other trustworthy men, threatening those who fail to do so with a severe fine.[118] However, as has been noted, this ban on trading outside a *port* seems to have proven unworkable and was abandoned under Æthelstan, although the insistence on trustworthy witnesses remained.[119]

It was only under Edgar, after the establishment of the hundred, that law-makers seem to have felt capable of creating structures which made it realistic to impose severe punishments for violations of witnessing procedure. Every hundred was to nominate a standing group of at least twelve witnesses, each of whom was to swear to testify truthfully about what he witnessed regardless of money, fear, or favour. Two such men were to be present at every transaction within the hundred.[120] Moreover, the hundred was to be kept informed of transactions that took place elsewhere. Men were expected to inform their neighbours of their purchases on their return from journeys where they bought livestock, making the names of the men who had witnessed the transaction known within five days.[121] Those who failed to do so would forfeit their livestock even if it transpired they had bought them legitimately.[122] The point, in effect, was to force everyone who acquired new livestock to vouch their seller to warranty in advance. If, in fact, the livestock were stolen, the thief would be forced to tell a bare-faced lie, naming witnesses to a transaction that never took place. If anyone thought to check, the lie would easily be revealed: the named witnesses would be able to swear that they knew of no such transaction. The thief would thus be caught in an impossible position: the only explanation for his having lied about the witnesses was that the livestock were stolen. Edgar's laws state that in this situation the livestock were to be seized and kept by the lord with the right to receive the thief's fines until the rightful owner came to claim them with witnesses. The thief was to be executed and to forfeit his property. Denial in these circumstances was impossible.[123]

The key point here is that thieves no longer needed to be accused of theft, a charge which they could still deny. Instead, these laws aimed to create conditions in which thieves had no option but to commit a procedural offence: making a false statement about the witnesses to a purchase. If they were caught out doing so there was nothing they could do to deny it: their guilt was a matter of record and they could be executed without the need for formal proof procedures of any sort. In theory, at least, the hundredal system had allowed Edgar to use his legislation to shape local legal practice in an ingenious way, creating a situation in which all the doubt and deniability that had previously been associated with vouching to

---

[118] I Ew 1.   [119] II As 10, 12; IV As 2; III Em 5.   [120] IV Eg 3:1–6:2.
[121] IV Eg 7–8:1.   [122] IV Eg 8:1–10.
[123] IV Eg 11. For a less detailed precursor, insisting that the hundred be informed of the provenance of all livestock brought in from elsewhere, see Hu 4–4:1. Æthelred's code for part of the Danelaw even orders that livestock must be slaughtered before witnesses, and the hide and head kept for three days afterwards, presumably so that the slain animal could be identified and any claims relating to it made. Failure to do so, however, was not sufficient cause to be punished as a thief: the fine was 20 shillings (III Atr 9).

warranty procedures was eliminated and thieves would be easily convicted on undeniable charges.

Compulsory Suretyship

We can see a similar solution for the problem of men with poor local reputations. These figures appear as a problem in various Anglo-Saxon laws, referred to in different ways. We have seen that Æthelstan's laws talk about men who belong to such powerful kindreds that they cannot be restrained from theft, but they also show concern about lordless men from whom no justice can be obtained.[124] These are probably the same sort of people who, in the laws from Edgar's reign onwards, are labelled 'untrue' or 'unfaithful' (*ungetreow*).[125] However represented, the main problem with such figures was that although the local population thought ill of them it was not possible to prove them guilty of a specific offence for which they could then receive a fitting punishment. These were probably the men who got the blame, rightly or wrongly, for unsolved thefts in their neighbourhoods. They were believed to be responsible for a string of offences, but in each case sufficient doubt about their responsibility existed for them to evade punishment.

Late Anglo-Saxon laws can often be found trying to deal with these people by punishing them not for any specific act of wrongdoing, but for neglect of a general legal duty to have surety. Under Æthelstan it was insisted that the lordless man attend an assembly at which his relatives would find him a lord willing to accept responsibility for him: if this failed to occur for whatever reason the man's life was forfeit—he could be slain as a thief by whoever met him.[126] From Edgar's reign onwards, as is discussed in detail below, all men had a legal duty not just to have a lord but to have sureties who were liable for any punitive fines they incurred (not just compensations, as seems to have been the case before). Suretyship of this sort was a much more serious commitment, with potentially ruinous financial consequences for those who gave guarantees to the wrong men.[127] Moreover, it was to be rigorously enforced. Expeditions were to be mounted against untrustworthy men: they were to be given a final chance to find sureties if they could, but they were to be killed if they proved unwilling or unable to do so.[128] Such men may well have been able to deny any specific charge brought against them, even if most people firmly believed they were guilty. The absence of proper sureties, however, was an undeniable and—if we believe the laws—potentially lethal fact.

Securing Convictions

The crucial point here is that kings seem to have tried to get around the strong position occupied by free defendants in formal assembly procedures by using their power to legislate. They did not rely on powerful local representatives influencing the outcomes of formal proof procedures, or on their discretionary imposition of

---

[124] II As 2; III As 7:1.   [125] III Eg 7; I Atr 4; II Cn 30, 33.   [126] II As 2–2:2.
[127] See below, pp. 277–82.   [128] III Eg 7–7:2; I Atr 4–4:2.

procedural disadvantages on defendants they regarded with suspicion. It is likely that neither of these were practical options. Rather, the new hundredal system allowed kings to elaborate an increasingly detailed template for local communal legal practice and they tried to use this ability to circumvent offenders' entitlement, as free defendants with no proven record of dishonesty, to deny charges through collective oaths. The compulsory pursuit of thieves ought to have resulted in more thieves being caught in circumstances where their guilt was undeniable, while the legal requirements that the witnesses to all purchases be announced publicly and that all men be able to find surety could likewise be lethal to thieves (and indeed to other forms of dishonest free man). Thieves' activities meant that they would at times be in possession of goods for which they could not provide sufficient proof of purchase and, once suretyship came to entail liability for punitive fines, anyone widely regarded as untrustworthy would have found it much more difficult to persuade their neighbours to act as sureties for them. Kings did try to ensure local assemblies convicted more thieves and other notorious malefactors in this period, then, but their main tool for doing so was their ability to shape local legal practice through legislation. Rather than relying on their own (or anyone else's) reeves' agency within the judicial process, they established new procedural rules in the expectation that they would be implemented under local communal leadership.

ENFORCEMENT, DEFIANCE, AND FLIGHT

Securing more convictions for wrongdoing in local assemblies was important, of course, but it was just as crucial to ensure that the people who were convicted subsequently paid what they owed or suffered an appropriate physical punishment. Chapter 3 argued that early tenth-century kings inherited a situation in which their main local representatives were rural reeves, men who are unlikely to have been capable of taking enforcement action independently. This did not make them entirely toothless because it was possible for them to work with their local communities, and in alliance with men involved in feuds, in order to coerce offenders when necessary.[129] In the seventh, eighth, and ninth centuries this situation seems to have been understood to be adequate. In the tenth, however, there are signs of royal discontent. The laws make efforts to deal with two distinct problems of enforcement: that posed by offenders who defied punishment, and that posed by offenders who fled rather than face it.

The Problem of Defiance

We can deal with defiance relatively quickly here because the issues involved are simple and, to an extent, have already been discussed. It is, unfortunately, impossible to measure how big a problem defiance of punishment was during this period.

---

[129] Chapter 3, pp. 155–6.

However, the case of Wulfbald, discussed in Chapter 3, should stand as a warning that the king was not always able to ensure he was paid what he was owed. At some point relatively early in the reign of King Æthelred, Wulfbald is said to have seized land and goods that did not belong to him, and then to have ignored no fewer than five judgements against him. Eventually, probably in the late 980s, he died of natural causes having lived out his life in untroubled enjoyment of the land and goods he had seized. After his death there was an attempt to dispossess his family of the land he had taken but it ended catastrophically, with Wulfbald's widow and child (presumably commanding an armed band) killing sixteen men on one of the disputed properties. In 996 the land in question was granted to the king's mother, so its forfeiture must eventually have been enforced, but the narrative shows that even the personal involvement of the king was no guarantee that the law would be enforced on a defiant offender in this period.[130] Wulfbald's case was clearly unusual but just how unusual is difficult to assess. It would be possible to list numerous cases in which kings seem to have gained what they were owed with minimal difficulty, which could then be set against this example of royal impotence.[131] Doing so, however, would bring us no closer to a reliable assessment of how frequently judgements favouring the king were enforced. The problems with attempting to assess the efficacy of royal law-enforcement through quantitative analysis of case records are too numerous to be worth listing here, but chief among them must be that our records are almost invariably associated with lands that were eventually forfeited to the king. It is only because Wulfbald's widow was eventually dispossessed that we know about this case at all. Complete failures of enforcement did not produce charters.

As was discussed in Chapter 3, laws from the early tenth century onwards treat defiant individuals as a problem. Up to and including Edgar's reign they are consistent in trying to solve this problem by ordering local communities to organize enforcement expeditions, threatening those who refuse to take part in such expeditions with punishment, and rewarding those who did their communal duty with a cut of any property seized.[132] However, Æthelred's laws mark a turning point. When I Æthelred envisages a near-identical situation to one discussed in Edgar's laws—an *ungetreow* ('untrue') man who needs to be forced to find sureties or slain if he cannot—they assume that the 'king's reeve' would be the appropriate person to do this, and make no mention of a communal expedition.[133] The most plausible interpretation of this, as was suggested above, is that this reflects the emergence of a

---

[130] S 877. Quoted Chapter 3, pp. 152–3. The key reference point for dating is the assembly called by Archbishop Æthelgar, seemingly shortly after the final massacre, which must have taken place during his archiepiscopate (November 988 to February 990); see Sean Miller, *The Charters of New Minster, Winchester* (Anglo-Saxon Charters 9, Oxford, 2001), p. 152.

[131] Such a list would include the majority of the numerous forfeitures among the 178 cases catalogued in Patrick Wormald, 'A Handlist of Anglo-Saxon Lawsuits', repr. in and cited from Patrick Wormald, *Legal Culture in the Early Medieval West: Law as Text, Image and Experience* (London, 1999), pp. 253–87.

[132] II As 20–20:7; VI As 1:1, 8:2–8:3; III Em 2; Hu 2–3:1; III Eg 7–7:2. See Chapter 3, pp. 153–4.

[133] I Atr 4.

new and more powerful type of king's reeve—the sheriff—who very probably had his own military retainers and was thus much better suited to undertaking enforcement independently. The text is not explicit so this reading could be disputed, but regardless of what we make of this specific passage it is highly likely that the introduction of the sheriff changed the dynamics of local enforcement significantly. With armed support available from a nearby sheriff, rural reeves were much less dependent on the cooperation of the communities they worked with. Whereas resistance or even just apathy from the men of the local assembly would previously have made enforcement impossible, with the establishment of sheriffs this probably became less of a problem. The threat of a sheriff's intervention almost certainly made people less likely to resist punishment than they would have been before sheriffs existed.[134]

The Problem of Flight

Defiance, however, had probably always been relatively rare. A much more prevalent problem facing the men responsible for imposing punishments on offenders must have been the likelihood that some would rather flee than submit. The fines specified by the laws are so large that many people would surely have been unable to pay them in full, using only their own resources. Alfred's laws state that the standard penalty for offences (presumably thefts) of up to 30 shillings in value was a fine of 60 shillings, increasing to 120 shillings once that threshold was passed.[135] The London *frið*-guild, which in Æthelstan's reign established a collective insurance scheme to compensate individuals for stolen property, valued sheep at a shilling each, pigs at two shillings, and cows at four.[136] A 60-shilling fine, by this reckoning, would have required sixty sheep, thirty pigs or fifteen cows: richer free farmers may have been able to pay this from their own resources, but many others surely would not. If for whatever reason an offender was unable to pay, and was unwilling to submit to penal enslavement instead, he could try to do what Wulfbald did and defy punishment entirely. That, however, could end disastrously: a much safer option was probably just to leave the area. (Another option, attempting to negotiate a reduced fine, is discussed below.) Fleeing probably had its risks, but with a bit of good fortune it may well have been possible to start a new life in another region, and for many this must have seemed a much more enticing prospect than penal servitude. That this was regarded as a problem in the first half of the tenth century is demonstrated by the constant repetition of laws concerned about people leaving localities in which they had incurred charges and seeking new lords elsewhere.[137]

---

[134] Though see below, p. 291.   [135] Af 9:1.   [136] VI As 6:2.

[137] II Ew 7; II As 22; IV As 4–5; V As 1–1:1; III Em 3. II Cn 28:1 suggests that legislators' concerns had changed since Edmund's reign: the problem is not lords receiving men from elsewhere but lords sending their men away so they could avoid punishment (an issue that is addressed in different terms in I Atr 1:12 and II Cn 31:1a). This change is consistent with the shift under Edgar that is about to be discussed in detail. Whereas in early tenth-century laws the main worry was that if men moved to different regions no-one would meet the punitive liabilities they owed to whichever lord was entitled to

Apart from threatening men who harboured fugitives with punishment, the main way late Anglo-Saxon laws tried to deal with the problem of flight was through suretyship arrangements. Suretyship was a traditional element of Anglo-Saxon law, almost certainly dating back to the pre-Christian period. A surety guaranteed that his principal would pay particular debts, becoming liable for them himself should the principal default. The sureties of interest here are those relating to compensations and punishments for wrongdoing, but suretyship was not limited to this context and could form a part of all manner of agreements (we have laws associating sureties with betrothals and livestock purchases, for instance).[138] In the context of wrongdoing, suretyship arrangements can broadly be divided into two classes: the standing suretyship arrangements which all members of a community were expected to have in place at all times, and one-off arrangements which were demanded as guarantees for particular transactions. After the establishment of the hundredal system, late Anglo-Saxon laws show a particular concern to strengthen standing suretyship arrangements so as to deal with the problem of offenders who fled rather than submit to punishment. To understand the significance of these later reforms we need briefly to survey the evidence for how standing suretyship arrangements had traditionally functioned.

Standing suretyship arrangements are assumed even in seventh-century texts. Ine's laws, for instance, order that in the absence of other arrangements householders must stand surety for their dependants in cases of theft, to the extent of paying the full value of the stolen goods.[139] Hlothere and Eadric, similarly, order that if anyone has a foreigner as a guest in his home for three nights, feeding him his own food, he will be liable to pay compensation for any harm his guest does.[140] In normal circumstances, however, it seems to have been expected that kindreds would act as suretyship groups. This is at its clearest in cases of homicide, where several laws make it clear that even if the killer fled the area, his relatives to some extent remained liable for the wergild that he had incurred. Æthelberht's laws state that in such circumstances the kindred still had to pay half the wergild.[141] Alfred's

them, in our evidence from after Edgar's reign the concern is not about the financial implications but the possibility that personal lords might be so committed to protecting their men as to help them escape afflictive punishment. This would make sense if Edgar's establishment of compulsory suretyship for punitive liabilities meant the financial aspects of punishment were now effectively guaranteed: the problem that remained would be that personal lords might be so committed to protecting their men as to help them escape, calculating that it was better to absorb the considerable financial costs of doing so than to allow a loyal man to suffer execution or mutilation. That legislators' concerns seem to have changed in this way by Cnut's reign could be taken as an indication that Edgar's legislation on compulsory suretyship had been effectively implemented.

[138] Af 18:1; I Atr 3–3:1.

[139] Ine 22. The term being rendered 'household dependant' here is *geneat*. See Carole Hough, 'The Structure of English Society in the Seventh Century: A New Reading of Æthelberht 12', in Hough, *An Ald Recht*, pp. 74–86, at 83–6; Dorothy Whitelock, ed., *English Historical Documents*, vol. 1: *c.500–1042* (2nd edn, London, 1979), p. 401, n. 1; Liebermann, *Gesetze*, iii. p. 71. Af 34, similarly, seems to imply that travelling merchants formally had to stand surety for the men they brought with them.

[140] Hl 15. II Cn 28 imposes the same three-night limit on hospitality, after which the host has to assume the obligations of lordship.

[141] Abt 23.

laws, on the other hand, envisage a killer who lacks paternal relatives fleeing, leaving his maternal relatives liable for a third of the wergild and his *gegildan* another third, whilst if he lacked kinsmen on either side his *gegildan* would be liable for half the wergild.[142] The *gegildan* are obscure but they are clearly acting as sureties here.[143]

The evidence suggests, however, that such standing suretyship arrangements were limited in scope before the late tenth century: they covered compensation payments but not punitive fines. Most clearly, Ine's laws state that lords are liable to pay *angild*, 'single-compensation', for any property their household men steal, but explain that the lord's having paid this does not exempt the thief himself from punishment.[144] There is no suggestion that the lord was liable for any fine or wergild forfeiture the thief incurred, only the compensation he owed to his victim. The kindred's liability for wergild is analogous: while they remain liable for at least some of the compensation owed to the slain man's kindred even when the killer fled, there is no mention of liability for the *wite* in such circumstances.[145] Anglo-Saxon law seems to have begun from the principle that a man's lord, relatives, or other associates should share responsibility for rectifying the harm that he caused, but that they could refuse to contribute to punitive fines if they wished. This principle is probably what is being articulated in some rather difficult passages in III Edmund and the *Hundred Ordinance*, in which people who had in some sense 'maintained' a man are held liable for *angild*.[146] It is clear that by virtue of their relationship with the wrongdoer these men were functioning as sureties for any compensations he incurred, but not for punitive fines.[147]

---

[142] Af 27–27:1.

[143] They also had the right to receive part of the dead man's wergild in the event of his being killed (Af 28), and are the people Ine's laws assume would wish to swear oaths on behalf of men slain as thieves (Ine 16, 20). The term usually means 'guild members' (DOE, s.v. 'ge-gylda'), so it is possible that we should look to models such as London's *frið*-guild (VI As 1–8:9), as is suggested by Liebermann (*Gesetze*, ii, s.v. 'Genossenschaft', pp. 445–6). There we can see groups of ten men, which later would be termed tithings, with legal responsibilities for one another's behaviour (VI As 3). However, it should be noted that the main aim of the *frið*-guild seems to have been the suppression of theft, there being no mention at all of liability for others' violent deeds, so it is possible that the Cambridge Thegns' Guild, coming a century or more later than Alfred's laws but addressing this subject directly, offers a better model in some respects (see Chapter 5, pp. 228–9). For a good account of the difficulties of interpretation here, see William Alfred Morris, *The Frankpledge System* (London, 1910), pp. 8–9.

[144] Ine 22. DOE s.v. 'an-gylde (noun)'. The distinction between punitive and compensatory liabilities is also evident in the charter evidence: see Chapter 3, p. 130.

[145] Abt 23; Af 27–27:1.

[146] III Em 3; Hu 6. *Angild* is the term used in the *Hundred Ordinance*; III Edmund survives only in a Latin translation where the relevant verbs (*emendare* and *componere*) imply compensation rather than punishment.

[147] In the *Hundred Ordinance* the difficult phrase suggesting some form of 'maintenance' is *se ðe hine to ðam hearme geheold*; the Latin equivalent in III Edmund is *qui aliquem manutenebit et firmabit ad dampnum faciendum*, which is probably an attempt to render a very similar Old English original. Dorothy Whitelock suggested that the meaning was probably 'he who by maintaining him made it possible for him to commit that injury' (*English Historical Documents I*, p. 433, n. 2). The ambiguity about the nature of this 'maintenance' is probably deliberate: it was intended as an all-encompassing reference to all those whose relationship with the wrongdoer meant they were obliged to act as his sureties: that is, kinsmen, lords, and any other associates (such as Alfred's *gegildan*).

Early tenth-century laws are quite firm that everyone must have such sureties. In particular, personal lords (not, usually, the same lord who was entitled to receive a man's fines) are to stand surety for all their own men and to be fined if they refuse to do so.[148] If a man has no lord, his kinsmen have a duty to find him one, or he can be killed as a thief.[149] If no lord is willing to trust him, the kinsmen have to persuade him to do so by acting as sureties themselves, presumably guaranteeing that they will meet any liabilities the lord incurs by accepting him.[150] Everyone was to have these sureties so that if anyone committed an offence and ran away his victims would still be compensated for the harm that he did. Punitive fines, however, were not covered by these standing arrangements. This meant that if a man was accused of a punishable offence he needed to find additional sureties to guarantee that he would meet his punitive liabilities. Edward the Elder's laws, for instance, envisage a man who has already been found a lord needing to persuade his kinsmen and friends to stand surety for him after an accusation of theft.[151] The implication appears to be that though the man's lord (and probably his kinsmen) were automatically his sureties for the compensation he owed, additional sureties were required to guarantee payment of a potential punitive fine. If nobody was willing, goods could be taken from his property as security, but if he lacked sufficient goods his only option was to submit to imprisonment until his case came to judgement.[152] Similarly, III Edmund demands that lords stand surety for all their men, but immediately adds that men of ill repute shall be placed under surety.[153] It is probable that the suretyship all lords were expected to provide for their men was for compensation payments, whereas the sureties demanded from the untrustworthy were to guarantee the punitive liabilities such men were thought likely to incur.

Edgar's laws, however, offer a different vision of standing suretyship arrangements. They order not just the untrustworthy but all free men to provide themselves with surety (*borh*) whose duty was 'to produce and hold him to every legal duty', such that if anyone did wrong and escaped the surety would 'incur what he [the wrongdoer] would incur'.[154] That this does indeed imply punitive liabilities as well as compensations is strongly suggested by the discussion of the case of theft that follows: if the surety can capture the thief within twelve months he is to surrender him to justice (*to rihte*) and get back what he previously had paid.[155] The

---

[148] III As 7–7:3; III Em 7–7:2. For a clear discussion of different types of lordship, see Baxter, 'Lordship and Justice'; Baxter, *Earls of Mercia*, pp. 204–15.

[149] II As 2–2:2.

[150] III As 7:2. Having a lord functioning as a middleman in this way makes more sense than is immediately apparent. Having one lord—a man of wealth and honour—guaranteeing compensation payments would mean that those seeking compensation could secure what they needed from a single figure. It would then be the lord rather than the victim who had to pursue the individual members of a suretyship group, each of whom might dispute the extent of or otherwise attempt to evade his personal share of the group's collective liability.

[151] II Ew 3.   [152] II Ew 3:1–3:2.   [153] III Em 7–7:1.

[154] III Eg 6–6:1. The verb rendered 'incur' here is *beran*—to bear, perhaps in the sense of 'to produce' (as in to bear children), given that there is no sign sureties were expected to undergo afflictive sanctions (DOE, s.v. 'beran'). More broadly, see also IV Eg 3.

[155] III Eg 6:2.

natural reading here is that the surety paid a punitive fine, most likely the thief's wergild, to the lord with the right to receive it, and was reclaiming it by handing over the thief.[156] This is certainly the case in discussions of the surety which appear in both Æthelred and Cnut's legislation, in which the surety of a fugitive thief is ordered to pay both the *ceapgyld* (the value of the stolen goods) and the thief's wergild to the appropriate lord.[157] (It is probably no coincidence that these rules first appear alongside a statement of the limitation of a man's liability to punitive fines: on no account is he to forfeit more than his own wergild.)[158]

What exactly it meant to provide oneself with surety under Edgar and his successors has been disputed. We are told that lords had to have the men of their household within their own surety, but this is contrasted with normal practice which suggests that they did not have to perform this function for men who were bound to them but not part of their households.[159] The type of surety men who were not attached to lords' households were expected to find is not clear in Anglo-Saxon sources. After the Norman Conquest, however, it is apparent that standing suretyship arrangements were collective in nature: unless they were part of lords' households, men had to be members of groups known as tithings, who stood surety for one another, as part of the system known as 'frankpledge'. Whether this system was a Norman innovation or something inherited from the Anglo-Saxon past has long been the subject of debate, as the evidence is inconclusive. Groups called tithings are attested as subdivisions of hundreds under Edgar, but it is not clear they had any suretyship functions at this point. Cnut's laws state that all free men over the age of twelve must be 'brought within hundred and tithing (*on teoðunge*)' if they are to be entitled to the rights of a freeman, then add that 'everyone shall be brought within hundred and under surety (*on borh*)'.[160] Scholars have disagreed over whether the requirement to be *on borh* was a reiteration of the requirement to be *on teoðunge*, as would be the case under the frankpledge system, or whether this passage shows that the two at this stage remained separate, with mutual surety groups only merging with tithings after 1066. Current opinion inclines towards the former but the issue can never be definitively resolved.[161]

This uncertainty about whether frankpledge existed in its precise post-Conquest form before 1066 is not significant for current purposes (its significance in the

---

[156] The other possibility is that all the surety had initially paid was the value of the stolen goods, the *angild*, but if this were the case the scenario we have to envisage is rather odd: the surety handing the thief over to the party from whom he stole in return for a refund.

[157] I Atr 1:7, 1:10–1:11; II Cn 30:6, 31–31:1. This requirement that all men have comprehensive surety is not significantly undercut by passages which require men in particular situations to find sureties. Such passages do exist but the situations they envisage can be interpreted as either those in which a man's surety arrangements had lapsed and needed renewal (such as after a conviction for theft or perjury—I Atr 1:5; II Cn 30:3b, 36:1) or those concerning men whose suretyship arrangements were uncertain and were therefore regarded as untrustworthy by their neighbours (we find them given a final chance to find surety before being killed—III Eg 7; I Atr 4:1; II Cn 25, 33).

[158] III Eg 2:2.   [159] I Atr 1:10–1:11; II Cn 31–31:1.   [160] II Cn 20.

[161] See Morris, *Frankpledge*, ch. 1; W. L. Warren, *The Governance of Norman and Angevin England, 1086–272* (London, 1987), pp. 39–42; Patrick Wormald, 'Frankpledge', in Lapidge et al., *Encyclopedia*, pp. 197–8; Wormald, *Papers Preparatory*, pp. 175–81; Hudson, *Oxford History*, pp. 74–5, 391–2; Molyneaux, *Formation*, pp. 195–6; O'Brien, *God's Peace*, pp. 85–8.

literature derives from legal historians' retrospective preoccupation with the origins of later institutions). The important point is clear: from Edgar's reign onwards kings tried to impose much more onerous standing suretyship arrangements on their people. Whereas previously the signs are that all men were expected to have sureties for compensation payments, the sureties that Edgar and his successors demanded from all free Anglo-Saxon men were also liable for any fines and wergild forfeitures. It is difficult to overstate the significance of this innovation. The idea, clearly, was to make the enforcement of punitive legal claims easier than had hitherto been the case. Those with a right to profit from the punitive fines paid by thieves and other offenders could no longer be thwarted by their flight, as they could now claim these payments from the relevant sureties.[162] The effect was to shift the full burden of enforcement onto sureties: having been compelled to pay for an offender's wrongdoing, these men could only recoup their potentially ruinous loss by hunting down the offender within twelve months and handing him over so he could be punished in person. The hope, presumably, was that this would give sureties a strong incentive to prevent offenders from fleeing if they possibly could, or even to restrain them from committing offences in the first place.[163]

We should not underestimate how radical this reform was. The notion that every man must have standing suretyship arrangements guaranteeing all future punitive liabilities up to the value of his own wergild must be regarded as an extraordinary departure from tradition and a major economic imposition. Although they probably understood the good intentions behind the scheme, few people can have appreciated being forced to accept such potentially crippling liability for their neighbours' misdeeds. Edgar seems, in effect, to have been forcing the entire population to find sureties of a sort that were previously required only from the

---

[162] Indeed, it would often have been more profitable if an offender fled. If he was produced for punishment in person his sureties were not liable to pay his fine on his behalf, and if he was then unable to pay his fine in full there was little a lord or reeve could do about it. He could seize the offender's property and put him to work as a penal slave, or he could negotiate a reduced fine with the offender's kinsmen. In financial terms claiming full payment from sureties would almost always have been preferable, and indeed we have laws (I Atr 1:8, reprised in II Cn 30:7) which identify this as a problem, envisaging lords encouraging offenders to flee so they could claim their wergilds from their sureties.

[163] In identifying Edgar's reforms as the most significant innovation, the account of the development of suretyship obligations presented here diverges significantly from Patrick Wormald's arguments about the origins of frankpledge, which strongly emphasize Alfred's reign. Most stridently, see Patrick Wormald, 'Engla Lond: the Making of an Allegiance', repr. in and cited from Wormald, *Legal Culture*, pp. 359–82 at 366–7: 'In the first place, swearing of the oath [of loyalty] was associated, from very early on and quite possibly from Alfred's time, with simultaneous enrolment in a tithing or frankpledge, which meant taking responsibility (including financial responsibility) for lawful behaviour by one's community as a condition of one's legal rights as a free man.' His other works are more measured. Wormald, 'Frankpledge', p. 198: 'there were no doubt a series of refinements of detail throughout the tenth century before the medieval system became fully recognisable'; Wormald, *Papers Preparatory*, pp. 181: 'It is reasonable, may well seem responsible, to hold that this powerful engine of social control took time to construct, each scion of Alfred's dynasty fitting further cogs into place . . . But there is a good case, here as elsewhere, that the basics go back to Alfred.' Though I would of course accept that Edgar's suretyship reforms built on earlier ideas and practices, it seems to me that the central ingredient of frankpledge is compulsory standing suretyship for punitive liabilities, and there is no sign of this in the legislation of any of Edgar's predecessors.

notoriously untrustworthy, or from people with specific charges to answer. This was no small request, and we might well doubt that people complied with it willingly. After 1066 it becomes apparent that the system of frankpledge, the direct descendant of Edgar's reforms, needed careful maintenance. Twice a year there was a special meeting of the hundred assembly which everyone had a duty to attend, and where it was ensured that everyone had the proper suretyship arrangements in place. This process came to be known as 'view of frankpledge', and it eventually becomes clear that the biannual hundred assemblies at which it took place were supervised by the sheriff: they became known as 'the sheriff's tourn'.[164] We thus cannot rule out the possibility that while compulsory standing suretyship was mandated under Edgar, it was not implemented with full effect until the introduction of sheriffs gave kings the means to coerce hundreds into compliance with this drastic royal demand. But this is speculation: we should certainly not discount the possibility that many local hundredal leaders were willing and able to impose these suretyship obligations independently, or that ealdormen and bishops in conjunction with shire-level elites were able to force non-compliant hundreds into line.[165] We have to acknowledge that our evidence cannot resolve this issue.

The Dynamics of Enforcement

Our evidence, then, suggests that late Anglo-Saxon kings made significant efforts to ensure punishments were more effectively enforced. They did so initially using the same distinctively tenth-century methods by which they sought to obtain convictions in local assemblies: they tried to shape local legal practice through their legislation. Not only were there repeated attempts to exhort, entice, and intimidate local figures into participating in enforcement expeditions against offenders who refused to cooperate with assemblies and their judgements, under Edgar there was a truly fundamental reform of compulsory suretyship. The point of these reforms was to create structures of obligation that forced local communities to police themselves, without the need for any forceful intervention from reeves, privileged lords, or anyone else. Again, then, we see kings relying on legislation as their primary tool for controlling local legal practice, rather than attempting to impose order through their uneven and problematic network of reeves and privileged lords. It is difficult to assess just how effective these measures were before the advent of sheriffs. We would be unwise to suppose that the communal model on which the hundred was based was ineffectual, but even if we were to assume that it was highly effective we would still have to accept that the establishment of a kingdom-wide network of sheriffs is likely to have changed the dynamics of local law-enforcement significantly. It is certainly notable that the laws stop relying on

---

[164] The earliest reference to a special biannual session of the hundred is from Henry I's reign (Hn 8:1); the first reference to the sheriff's role is in 1166 (Ass Clar 9), by which point it was clearly well established. See Hudson, *Oxford History*, pp. 391–5, 555–6; Morris, *Frankpledge*, ch. 4.

[165] There is some contemporary evidence that bears on this question, albeit not decisively: see above, p. 276, n. 137.

the communal enforcement model under Æthelred, and the later functioning of the frankpledge system suggests that oversight by sheriffs was essential to the maintenance of effective compulsory suretyship for punitive liabilities. However things had stood before its establishment, it is probable that the network of sheriffs dramatically enhanced kings' ability to project coercive power into the localities on a routine basis, and made it less important for them to secure the willing cooperation of local elites.

NEGOTIATION IN THE SHADOW OF THE LAW

Thus far this chapter has focused on processes of formal proof and on mechanisms of enforcement. There is good reason for this: kings needed to be able to obtain convictions through assembly judgements and to be able to enforce them. Much of the time, however, the processes themselves were not necessary. The knowledge that both conviction and enforcement were highly likely must often have been enough to persuade offenders who had been caught out to submit, admitting their guilt and complying with their own punishment. Conversely, the knowledge that either conviction or enforcement was unlikely must often have been enough to stop people bringing charges in the first place, potentially risking punishment for false accusation. As Patrick Wormald observed in his study of legal cases drawn from charters and chronicles, actual instances of oaths being sworn or ordeals taking place are rare.[166] The cases we know about from these sources are major land disputes, and their dynamics may well have been distinctive, but it would not be very surprising if the same were true for ordinary accusations of wrongdoing.

It seems to have been possible to abandon cases at any point before the proof stage with the mutual consent of the parties involved. Formal accusations could thus be used to apply pressure, as a form of brinkmanship: many may have been made not with the intention of pursuing a case to proof, but rather to improve the accuser's negotiating position in the hope of extracting a more advantageous settlement. One remarkable, albeit somewhat obscure, account of a land dispute from 990 seems to show this happening. When one party was about to make an oath, the other was persuaded to set aside the need for formal proof and accept a settlement (in which he gave up the land in return for a substantial sum in gold and silver), 'because afterwards there would be no friendship' and because he apparently risked forfeiting his wergild for having unjustly seized the land if he lost.[167] There is evidence that deals were just as possible when it came to the punishment of wrongdoing. A Domesday Book entry from Suffolk provides a clear example. A certain Brungar was found in possession of some stolen horses and the case came to the hundred assembly, which was attended both by the lord who had the right to receive Brungar's punitive fines (the Abbot of Bury St Edmunds) and

---

[166] Wormald, 'Charters, Law', pp. 294–5, 301–2.
[167] S 1454. This case is discussed in detail in Wormald, 'God and King', pp. 343–53, with a full translation at pp. 356–7.

by Brungar's personal lord (Robert fitzWimarc), who had a duty to help defend his man. The Domesday entry states that these two lords 'went away amicably without a verdict that the hundred has seen'. The implication seems to be that they resolved the matter between themselves.[168]

The laws suggest that there was nothing improper about such deals. Æthelred's code for part of the Danelaw asserts that such extra-judicial agreements ought to have equal status to those arrived at in assemblies: 'and where a thegn has two alternatives before him – love or law – and he chooses love, that is to be as binding as a judgement (*dom*)'.[169] That this consideration applied to punitive matters as well as compensation payments is suggested by a number of passages. Edgar orders that in all judgements there be such mercy (*forgifnes*) 'as shall be justifiable in the sight of God and acceptable in the sight of men', a theme which is taken up at length in Archbishop Wulfstan's legislation for Æthelred.[170] Earlier, the language used in seventh-century laws suggests the possibility of negotiations: the verbs *þingian* and *geþingian*—'to make terms', 'to come to agreement'—are used in relation to fines.[171] In the early tenth century Æthelstan ordered that people could come to a settlement to avoid an ordeal, making what terms they could, presumably with their accuser, but that this should not allow them to avoid payment of the fine 'unless he to whom it is due is willing to consent'.[172] This seems to imply that it was up to the people who were entitled to collect fines to use their discretion, mercifully accepting less than they were entitled to receive if they thought it right to do so. On the opposite tack, Edmund explicitly ordered that in cases of homicide no *manbot* or *fihtwite* be forgiven, which suggests both that it had been legitimate to accept lesser sums beforehand and that for other offences there was still room for discretion.[173] Many of Edmund's harsher demands are ameliorated in later legislation, and given his successors' emphasis on mercy it is perhaps likely that even if this stricture was initially observed (which it may not have been) its effects did not last long.[174]

There are thus strong indications that it was a common and legitimate part of legal practice for deals to be made regarding the imposition of punishment. This makes sense given what we know about the size of fines and expectations about who would actually pay them. Many offences required men to pay a fine equivalent to

[168] DB ii. 401v–402r; see Baxter, 'Lordship and Justice', pp. 410–11, for speculation as to the nature of the deal done.

[169] III Atr 13:3. On this theme: Michael Clanchy, 'Law and Love in the Middle Ages', in John Bossy, ed., *Disputes and Settlements: Law and Human Relations in the West* (Cambridge, 1983), pp. 47–68.

[170] III Eg 1:2; VI Atr 10:2, 52–3; Cn 1018 4–6; Cn 1020 11; II Cn 2–2:1. Edgar uses the term *bot*, 'compensation', which could be taken to imply that he was not referring to punishments in his injunction to be merciful. The term *bot*, however, is often used to encompass both punitive fines and compensations to individuals. That this is certainly the case here is demonstrated by the next passage, which defines offences for which punitive fines were payable as *botwyrðe*: 'compensation-worthy' (III Eg 2:2). Later laws define offences only punishable by death or outlawry, not by a punitive fine, as *botleas*: most literally, 'compensation-less' (III Atr 1; VIII Atr 1:1; I Cn 2:3; II Cn 64). Chapter 2 (at p. 109) argued that this usage may well have arisen from punishments being understood as compensation payable to an affronted community as opposed to that owed to affronted individuals (for Wormald's views on this see the works cited at p. 88, n. 84).

[171] Ine 50, 73.   [172] II As 21.   [173] II Em 3.   [174] Chapter 4, pp. 186–7.

their own wergild—200 shillings for an ordinary freeman—and fines of 120 shillings are not uncommon. Even a fine of 60 shillings, as was discussed above, was very probably beyond what a lot of free men could afford to pay using their own resources. In practice, people who paid fines probably relied on their families and friends for help.[175] The alternative was penal slavery.[176] The laws, at least, seem to expect kinsmen to help offenders pay their fines rather than face enslavement, but they equally make it clear that they were under no formal obligation to do so. If they chose, they could let their kinsman be enslaved, but they would lose the right to be paid wergild in the event of his being killed.[177] The people from whom reeves and privileged lords needed to extract fines, then, would often not really have been the offenders themselves but their families and other close associates. Because these figures could abandon the offender to penal slavery if they wished, paying nothing at all, they were in a strong position to negotiate. Because reeves and lords may well have preferred to receive a payment than to have to find work for a penal slave, they would often have had a good reason to try to come to a compromise. These are circumstances in which negotiated deals would have made sense.[178]

The dynamics of these negotiations were not solely about penal enslavement, however. All parties involved needed to take into account their prospects of success in formal proof procedures and the likelihood of any enforcement action taking place after a judgement. We should remember that there were risks involved in attempting to deny a charge: if a defendant undertook to do so but failed to produce the necessary oath on the appointed day, he had not only lost his case but proven himself to be dishonest. He would not thereafter, according to some laws, be entitled to defend himself against accusations except by ordeal. This catastrophic outcome seems to have accompanied conviction for theft in any case, but for all other accusations it could be avoided by admitting the offence. Defendants who thought they had a chance of denying a charge other than theft, but had concerns about the reliability of their oath-helpers might well be tempted to negotiate a deal with a reeve or lord. The reeve or lord, on the other hand, realizing

[175] We have one case record (S 1447) in which a man forfeited his wergild for theft but was unable to pay; his brother then offered to do so on his behalf. In this case the brother's assistance came at too high a price and was rejected, but not all families can have been as dysfunctional as this one.

[176] On which, see Alice Rio, 'Penal Enslavement in the Early Middle Ages', in Christian Giuseppe de Vito and Alex Lichtenstein, eds., *Global Convict Labour* (Leiden, 2015), pp. 79–107. An early version of this paper presented to an Oxford seminar in April 2013 inspired much of the following analysis.

[177] Ine 24:1; II Ew 6. The right to wergild only lapsed after the space of a year according to Ine; II Edward seems to imply the effect was immediate.

[178] The enslavement of the offender need not have marked the end of negotiations, or even their failure. The laws imply that he could be liberated at any time if his debts were paid, so refusing to make a deal could have been employed as a form of brinkmanship by both parties. An offender's kinsmen might allow him to be enslaved so as to pressure a reeve or lord to accept a more reasonable fine (and perhaps also to make the offender suffer a bit for the trouble he had caused). Alternatively, a reeve might enslave an offender so as to pressure a kindred into making a better offer, in the hope that they would not long tolerate the indignity of having a slave as a relative, or wish to be known as a family so lacking in honour as to prioritize wealth over a kinsman in need.

that there was a good chance the defendant would be able to deny the charge if it did come to proof, had a solid reason to offer a relatively lenient punishment.

Concerns about enforcement may have had a similar influence on negotiations. We might imagine a reeve or privileged lord being able to press his advantage in an assembly and gain a formal conviction—perhaps because the offender's guilt was undeniable—but then being unable to force the defiant offender to submit to punishment. In particular, before the advent of sheriffs, reeves seem to have been reliant on local assistance for communal enforcement expeditions. If the defendant in question happened to be well liked by his neighbours, a lord or reeve might well not have felt confident of his ability to assemble a suitably large enforcement expedition. Rather than insist on the full fine and fail collect it (as repeatedly happened in the case of Wulfbald), lords and reeves may often have calculated that it made sense to come to a negotiated agreement: a merciful fine in return for acquiescence in its payment. Concerns about flight might have had similar effects. A lord or reeve with an established reputation for the strict imposition of punishments could simply end up driving all offenders in his district to flee, failing to extract much by way of useful revenue and in the process poisoning his relationship with the families of those forced into hiding or exile. In fact, we have one document which seems to show a late tenth-century abbot of Peterborough making two separate deals, receiving payment in return for allowing men who had fled and been outlawed to return home; presumably these deals were made in negotiations with the families of the offenders.[179] At least before the advent of strict rules on suretyship it may often have been prudent for those charged with collecting fines to be willing to remit some portion of them: doing so not only maintained good community relations, it maximized revenue.

We should, then, probably look at the fines set out in the laws not as the equivalents of modern 'mandatory minimum sentences' but as statements of an offender's maximum possible liability for a given offence. This is common enough in the modern world too: the maximum fine for breaking the speed limit on a British motorway, for example, is £2500, but in practice most offenders agree to pay a fixed penalty of £100 in return for not contesting the charge in court.[180] There is some evidence which may suggest that the large fines set out in royal legislation were rarely imposed in practice. The *Hundred Ordinance*, for example, is an anonymous and probably therefore a less 'official' legal text, and is notable for containing much more lenient punishments for people who fail to participate in enforcement expeditions. A first offender is fined 30 pence (6 West Saxon shillings): twenty times less than the 120-shilling fine Edmund and Edgar specify for a near-identical offence.[181] We sometimes find a similar situation in accounts of local legal customs in Domesday Book: the men of Lewes (Sussex), for instance, were

[179] Or indeed with any other interested parties: a lord for instance, or fellow guild members. See the discussion in Chapter 7, p. 320 and p. 335, n. 141. The document is S 1448a.
[180] http://www.speedingfinesuk.co.uk/speeding_fines_penalties.htm— accessed 17 February 2015.
[181] Hu 2–3; III Em 2; III Eg 7–7:2.

privileged to the extent that they paid a maximum fine equivalent to 20 West Saxon shillings for several offences which in royal law might well have rendered the offender liable for 120 shillings.[182] We should probably take these texts as indications that normal practice involved threatening offenders with a crushingly large fine if they dared to contest charges brought against them, but routinely allowing those who admitted their guilt to pay much less than the full penalty. Whereas royal laws naturally threaten devastating maximum fines, other texts sometimes give figures that aligned more closely with what offenders paid in practice.

It seems likely, then, that there was considerable room for negotiation over the payment of fines in this period. We can only speculate as to what these negotiations might have looked like. A plausible possibility is that, although deals were negotiated in advance of assemblies, they were not presented as such. Rather, it may have been necessary for the offender to admit the charges against him and humbly beseech the relevant reeve or privileged lord to be merciful in the punishment he imposed. Other members of the assembly could then, if they wished, add their backing to this appeal, and the reeve or lord would then be able to make a show of his magnanimity, wisely and kindly bowing to the will of the community and imposing a relatively light sentence. This sort of stage-managed theatricality was commonplace in high-political assemblies at this time, so it is far from fanciful to imagine something similar took place in hundred assemblies.[183] It need not always have been stage-managed, of course. Defendants may well have attempted spontaneous pleas for mercy after unexpected defeats, and if prominent members of an assembly were minded to reinforce these pleas with their own, they may well have been able to pressure a reeve or lord into a light sentence. We should remember that before the advent of sheriffs, at least, reeves were heavily reliant on communal support and would probably have found it difficult to make decisions which went against the clearly expressed will of an assembly.

The acceptance of negotiation and compromise in punitive matters does not in itself constitute evidence of weakness of the part of those doing the punishing or strength on the part of the punished.[184] 'Plea bargains' have for some time been the standard way of resolving criminal cases in the United States, with jury trials

---

[182] DB i. 26r. The fines mentioned are for bloodshed, rape, adultery, and fleeing justice. Other examples of Domesday customs with at least some low fines include Chester (DB i. 262v), Hereford (DB i. 179r, at least for French inhabitants), Archenfield (DB i. 179r), and West Derby (DB 269v). Domesday can only be a very rough guide here: the legal customs recorded there tend to be those which belonged specifically to the king (on which see Chapter 7, pp. 322–42), which presumably were those least prone to variation. Chapter 7, p. 336, n. 144 sets out the Domesday evidence for the size of the fine for neglect of military service.

[183] See Levi Roach, *Kingship and Consent in Anglo-Saxon England, 871–978* (Cambridge, 2013), esp. ch. 8 and pp. 14–20; Levi Roach, 'Public Rites and Public Wrongs: Ritual Aspects of Diplomas in Tenth- and Eleventh-Century England' *Early Medieval Europe* 19 (2011), pp. 182–203; Levi Roach, 'Penance, Submission and *Deditio*: Religious Influences on Dispute Settlement in Later Anglo-Saxon England' *Anglo-Saxon England* 41 (2012), pp. 243–71; Julia Barrow 'Demonstrative Behaviour and Political Communication in Later Anglo-Saxon England' *Anglo-Saxon England* 36 (2007), pp. 127–50.

[184] An opposition between a culture of negotiated settlements and powerful state-directed justice does seem to be implied by Wormald, 'Charters, Law', pp. 306–8.

becoming rarer as the frequency and severity of punishments increases.[185] The number of possible scenarios in which the Anglo-Saxon equivalents of plea bargains may have occurred is almost limitless: in some the prosecutor would have had the upper hand, in others the defendant. The important point to grasp here is that, overall, the negotiating positions of those involved must have been affected by the changes of the late Anglo-Saxon period. With the establishment of hundreds came much more ambitious attempts to define local communal legal duties. Assuming they had some effect on reality, the new laws issued—on the compulsory tracking of stolen livestock, the compulsory witnessing of transactions and informing of neighbours, and on compulsory standing sureties covering punitive liabilities— would have greatly strengthened the negotiating positions of those trying to impose punishments in certain cases. The pursuit of stolen livestock would have produced more thieves caught in possession, and unable to deny their guilt; the laws requiring neighbours to be informed of purchases would have forced thieves into making false statements about witnesses, which they would be unable to deny when caught; and the fact that surety was compulsory would have meant that people could be punished simply for failing to find them, again not something that could be denied in an assembly. When faced with deniable charges, defendants could use the possibility that they might be able to succeed in formal proof as a bargaining chip in an attempt to secure a lighter sentence. When caught in such undeniable circumstances, this was no longer an option. They could still try to negotiate a deal but they had much less hope of securing a good one.[186]

Outside assemblies, too, we find kings trying to make enforcement more reliable, in part by encouraging and threatening local communities into mounting their own expeditions against defiant individuals. It may be that the establishment of hundreds meant their wishes on this were respected more frequently. Sheriffs, however, may well have changed local calculations dramatically once they were firmly established. The king's reeves, at least, because they had a powerful local ally, would no longer have had to worry so much about securing local cooperation in enforcement: they and the offenders with whom they negotiated would have known that defiance could relatively easily be met with an armed response, and that local sympathies mattered much less than they once had. With enforcement more certain, although probably still not quite inevitable, royal reeves—though perhaps not privileged lords and their reeves—had much less need to give ground, less need to heed local opinion on the application of mercy. The establishment of compulsory suretyship covering punitive liabilities was an even more fundamental change. Once this was in place (and the later institution of frankpledge implies that

---

[185] William J. Stuntz, *The Collapse of American Criminal Justice* (Cambridge, Mass., 2011), esp. pp. 257–60. Over 95 percent of criminal convictions now result from guilty pleas, most of which arise from plea bargains (p. 7).

[186] Stuntz, *Collapse*, pp. 260–2 on 'criminal intent' provides a loose parallel here: defences which had been possible in the early twentieth century being circumvented by laws deliberately framed with reference to a definition of intent so all-encompassing as that 'in most cases, findings of criminal intent are automatic' (p. 262).

it had been for some time by 1066)[187] reeves and lords would have known that they could extract fines—probably in full—from the sureties of men who had fled rather than face justice. They no longer needed to fear driving offenders into flight with excessive severity, so they could afford to take a tougher line when negotiating punishments.

The uncertainties of attaining convictions in assemblies, then, and the problems of flight and defiance, had probably all contributed to a general tendency towards the merciful application of punishments towards the beginning of the tenth century. The various measures that kings tried to implement in the wake of the establishment of the hundredal system, however, seem likely to have changed the dynamics of local justice, as does the later introduction of sheriffs. Just how effectively the laws which underpin this analysis were implemented will always remain a point of uncertainty, but the direction of travel in this period is clear: it is probable that by the early eleventh century defendants were more often faced with undeniable charges in assemblies, and less able to defy enforcement outside them, than they had been in the early tenth, and that suretyship rules had made it much more difficult to flee from punishment. As a result, people who were likely to be convicted of offences must often have found it more difficult to negotiate merciful sentences.

CONCLUSION

There were significant changes in kings' ability to get the outcomes they wanted from local justice in this period, and the establishment of hundreds seems to underlie most of them. The hundredal system was significant for forming local assemblies and their associated districts into a uniform structure. This did not change their nature in any fundamental way—assemblies had always been expressions of communities' authority to discipline delinquent individuals and hundreds were clearly no different in this respect—but it did allow kings to use their legislation to set out an increasingly elaborate template for local legal practice and expect it to be implemented throughout the kingdom. For most local assemblies this probably meant doing more: where previously there had been communal ideals undermined by various forms of apathy, there was now to be communal activism on a single royally defined model. For kings it meant there was less need to rely so heavily on the problematically uneven network of royal reeves, privileged lords, and reeves employed by privileged lords; laws issued after the establishment of the hundredal system largely bypassed these figures, relying on local communal leaders—hundredmen and tithingmen—for their practical implementation.

It is hard not to be impressed by the legal innovations that tenth-century kings attempted to enact through this reformed legal structure. The intelligence and seriousness of purpose underlying law-making in this period is evident even before the hundredal system's emergence in the care taken to ensure that legislative

[187] See below, p. 291, n. 190.

innovations were accepted as legitimate. We saw this in Chapter 4 in the way Æthelstan's anti-theft campaign prepared the ground for harsher punishment with an amnesty, reacted to objections about excessive cruelty by adjusting the min- imum age and value thresholds for execution, and generally aimed to secure the willing cooperation of local elites (with staggering success visible in the enthusiastic response from London's *frið*-guild).[188] The same spirit is in evidence in later tenth- century legislation. A major preoccupation in this chapter has been the right of free defendants in good standing to deny accusations through collective oath, a right clearly regarded as a core feature of personal liberty but one which made it very difficult indeed for those involved in the prosecution of wrongdoing to secure convictions. The way late Anglo-Saxon legislators sought to maintain this vital aspect of legal freedom for the honest majority, while cracking down on dishonest men's persistent abuse of it through shameless acts perjury, invites respect. It demonstrates clear-sighted understanding of the limits of legitimate legislative innovation, as well as considerable imagination and ingenuity in the design of procedures—Edgar's elaborate laws on witnessing are the prime example—that managed to address the problem while respecting those limits. And indeed, in terms of sheer ambition there is little that can match the establishment of compulsory standing suretyship arrangements for punitive liabilities, a reform which must have drastically increased the effectiveness of punishment for wrongdoing on a local level, and presumably thereby multiplied its deterrent effects.

For all of that, however, it is important to acknowledge the extent of uncertainty about when and how rapidly any of these reforms took effect, perhaps even whether they were effectively implemented at all. A key interpretative problem is what significance we ought to attribute to the establishment of the network of sheriffs. This is an important and largely unanswerable question. There is very little evidence bearing on the effectiveness of the hundredal model before the advent of sheriffs. The laws' detailed and sensitive engagement with local legal practice shows that law-makers were in touch with practical realities, so we probably ought to attribute some significance to their evident confidence in their capacity to micro- manage local legal procedure through legislation focused on the hundred. It is also worth noting that in spheres where there is independent evidence bearing on Edgar's administrative reforms it verifies their contemporary effectiveness. Most notably, his reform of the coinage demonstrates his ability to exercise control over all the moneyers in his kingdom and to ensure the general population cooperated with periodic re-coinages, which is a clear warning that it would be unwise to assume his other attempts at reform were unrealistic fantasies; but suggestive as this is we cannot securely infer from it that his reforms of suretyship and witnessing were successful.[189]

---

[188] Chapter 4, pp. 174–7.

[189] On coinage and its implications, see Molyneaux, *Formation*, pp. 116–41. The apparent success of late tenth-century kings in establishing hundreds, shires, and sheriffs could also be called upon in support of a general argument for royal effectiveness in this period. As Molyneaux later (p. 196) sums up, 'How far the decrees of these kings took effect is largely unknowable, but we should be very wary of any suspicion that their legislation was a dead letter'.

Our other evidence for the effectiveness of late Anglo-Saxon legal reforms is retrospective, and thus cannot safely be brought to bear on their practical implementation before the establishment of sheriffs. The post-Conquest existence of frankpledge, for instance, implies that some form of compulsory standing suretyship for punitive liabilities was a practical reality by 1066: it confirms that Edgar's legislation was effectively implemented but it cannot tell us when or by what means.[190] It could be that hundreds were responsible, acting under communal leadership at a time when sheriffs had barely been imagined, or it could be that local communities generally resisted these novel and onerous suretyship obligations until sheriffs were able to coerce them into compliance. There can, of course, be no doubt that this kingdom-wide network of powerful royal officials significantly increased kings' ability to employ coercion on a local level. The problem, in general terms, is that without a secure understanding of how effectively legislation was being implemented before sheriffs appeared on the scene we have no reliable means of gauging their significance. We should be careful, though, not assume any effects were immediate or revolutionary: the advent of the sheriff was not the advent of inevitable and overwhelming coercive state power. It is worth noting that our best evidence for defiance of royal punishment—the case of Wulfbald—took place in Kent at a time when Kent probably had a sheriff.[191] There is no sign of a sheriff attempting to seize Wulfbald's repeatedly forfeited wergild in our narrative; indeed, the first (albeit disastrous) attempt at enforcement seems to come from Wulfbald's cousin Eadmær, who was almost certainly attempting to wrest back land which Wulfbald had unjustly seized from his father.[192] We have some evidence, then, which hints that the first sheriffs did not immediately and radically alter existing dynamics in matters of law enforcement, but this need not imply that their impact was limited in the longer term.

---

[190] A particularly telling consideration here is geography: frankpledge did not exist north of the Humber, nor in most of Cheshire, Shropshire, and Herefordshire, and this seems much more likely to reflect late Anglo-Saxon than post-Conquest geopolitical realities. See Morris, *Frankpledge*, ch. 2; Hudson, *Oxford History*, p. 392. It is also worth noting that Anglo-Saxon laws which aimed to combat theft by insisting that transactions be witnessed have good analogues in some Anglo-Norman texts (Leis Wl 21–21:3, 45–6; ECf 38–38:2) and there is even some hint of a requirement to show newly acquired livestock to neighbours (ECf 24–24:3). These could be taken as indications that the intricate scheme set out in IV Eg 3:1–11 had some sort of impact on practice. The requirement to have witnesses for all transactions seems to have died out in the twelfth century, however (see Hudson, *Oxford History* pp. 687–9), which could perhaps be read as a sign of increasing urbanization and economic growth: ECf 39–39:2 records urban butchers (and others) objecting to the requirement on the grounds that the number of transactions they had to make every day made it impractical. This should caution us against the assumption that the absence of later evidence for procedures visible in tenth-century law has a bearing on how effectively they were implemented in the first place. We need to bear in mind the possibility that Anglo-Saxon rulers successfully imposed administrative measures which their successors, for whatever reason, did not maintain. Broadly on this theme, see W. L. Warren, 'The Myth of Norman Administrative Efficiency', *Transactions of the Royal Historical Society* 34 (1984), pp. 113–32.

[191] Wulfbald's defiance of royal authority took place in the 980s (S 877; see above, p. 275 and Chapter 3, pp. 152–3). Wulfsige, *scirigman*, appears as a high-ranking member of a Kentish shire assembly in a charter (S 1458) issued sometime between 964 and 988.

[192] This reading relies on the supposition that Eadmær was the son of the Brihtmær from whom Wulfbald seized the land. On this, see Miller, *Charters of New Minster*, p. 152.

However, to focus on the limits of our knowledge here is to miss the more fundamental point. The possibility that royal legislation proved ineffectual is, in fact, irrelevant to many of the more important conclusions about legal practice drawn here. Tenth-century kings had a strong tradition of identifying specific legal problems and trying to solve them through their legislation, and doing so in conjunction with their senior magnates in major assemblies. The laws we have seem to reflect considered analysis of social problems by well-informed contemporaries with a sincere desire to bring about improvements. Even if their schemes generally did not work out as they intended we can infer a lot about contemporary legal practice from the problems they identified and from their assumptions about how they could (and could not) plausibly go about solving them. The key conclusions of this chapter are about what problems existed and what methods kings tried to use to address them: whether they succeeded or not is a relatively peripheral issue.

For example, my best guess (and it is no more than that) is that Edgar's laws on witnessing were overambitious: it proved impossible to establish a positive duty to make public declarations about the witnesses for all purchases in the way they specified, and therefore relatively few thieves were executed after having been caught out making false statements in the way the laws imagined. But this possibility has no impact on the inferences we can draw from the scheme about its practical context: even if it was a complete failure it still implies that free defendants' right to deny accusations of theft using oaths was identified as a problem, that law-makers understood that they could not challenge this right in principle, and that tighter laws on witnessing seemed like a promising way of working around the issue. In short, the value of laws as a source for legal practice does not rest on whether or not they were effectively implemented. Even if we were to assume that most legislation in this period was ineffectual (which would be unwise), the central conclusions of this chapter would not be significantly affected.

There is, however, one problematic feature of our evidence that does deserve emphasis. We can infer a great deal about legal practice in the tenth century because we have laws showing kings and their advisers trying to solve particular socio-legal problems by creating new procedures for local communal assemblies to implement. As was noted in Chapter 4, we are not so fortunate in the eleventh century.[193] Some of Wulfstan's legislation for Æthelred and Cnut is bears similarities to what came before—VII Æthelred, written in 1009, should be understood as a sincere attempt to use legislation to address God's displeasure, the root cause of Scandinavian invasion—but more generally there is a clear shift in approach. Rather than focusing on establishing a detailed procedural template for hundredal legal practice, Wulfstan's laws often read more like sermons: exhortations to turn from sin. They do not afford us the same sort of insight into the assumptions underpinning local legal practice (though they are, of course, very useful in other ways). Cnut's great law code is superficially more promising—Wulfstan's more homiletic material is

---

[193] For the remainder of this paragraph, see Chapter 4, pp. 164–6.

present but not dominant—yet this is because it recapitulates earlier legislation, almost certainly including some which does not survive elsewhere. This makes it impossible to be sure that any given passage represents Cnut (or anyone else) engaging with contemporary legal problems in the same way as his predecessors. And Cnut's code marks the end of the Anglo-Saxon legislative tradition: Edward the Confessor certainly did not make laws in the same way—there was such interest in 'the law of Edward' after 1066 that it is almost inconceivable he issued laws which were subsequently lost—and there is no evidence that any other eleventh-century king did.[194]

This eleventh-century shift is significant for two reasons. Most obviously, it is an obstacle to our understanding: eleventh-century assumptions about non-elite legal practice relating to wrongdoing are much more obscure to us than those of the tenth-century. (Aristocratic disputes over title to land are a different matter, of course, but they are not our principal concern here.)[195] We can get an impression of broad continuity from Anglo-Norman compilations and treatises, and to some extent from the customs recorded in Domesday Book, but the potentially anti-quarian nature of much of this evidence makes it difficult to assess how far this is illusory.[196] However, the cessation of the tradition of close royal legislative engage-ment with local communal procedural rules should also be considered as a signifi-cant phenomenon in its own right. We can ask why it took place, and this chapter's analysis suggests a hypothesis we can test. As we have seen, the key to tenth-century kings' legal ambitions was their ability to control these communal structures through their legislation, *not* through a network of officials: hundreds make most sense as a way of bypassing a problematic network of administrators (royal reeves, non-royal reeves and privileged lords). The introduction of the sheriff, however, eventually gave eleventh-century kings a much more potent network of adminis-trators through which they might implement their will. It may well be that the apparent decline of royal legislative activism in the eleventh century is related to the increasing power they were able to wield through this administrative hierarchy. That is, kings now tried to achieve their legal ambitions by issuing specific orders to their sheriffs, rather than applying their ingenuity to the construction of an increasingly elaborate template for local communal legal practice.[197] This possibil-ity is explored in Chapter 7, which makes the case for a shift in royal and aristocratic attitudes to punitive justice around the turn of the eleventh century.

---

[194] Wormald, *Making*, pp. 407–11, 415; Hudson, *Oxford History*, p. 258.

[195] See above pp. 267–8 and Introduction, p. 21.

[196] For discussions emphasizing the difficulties of using these texts, see Hudson, *Oxford History*, pp. 869–71; John Hudson, *The Formation of the English Common Law: Law and Society in England from the Norman Conquest to Magna Carta* (London, 1996), pp. 57, 249–50. For a more optimistic approach, see Karn, 'Rethinking the *Leges Henrici Primi*', esp. pp. 218–20.

[197] See Wormald, *Making*, pp. 347–8, 414–15, for the suggestion that kings in this period were moving away from solemn law codes and increasingly reliant on less formal means of communication, akin to the legislative writs of the Anglo-Norman kings.

7

Rights and Revenues

INTRODUCTION

Since the nineteenth century historians have debated the extent to which Anglo-Saxon kings delegated legal rights to their aristocracies, allowing privileged lords to control the administration of justice in specific areas and to take the profits that arose.[1] The issue is clearly of some importance. Assessments of the extent of aristocratic legal privilege significantly affect our understanding of the way kings attempted to achieve their legal ambitions, of the administrative capabilities of the early medieval 'state', and of the nature of lords' relationships with their men. In the late Anglo-Saxon period these issues become particularly pressing because there is evidence of major change. This is most obvious in the period after the Norman Conquest. The ambiguous evidence bearing on what exactly was new in post-Conquest arrangements and what had been inherited from before 1066 has led to disagreement among legal historians, and the debates which have resulted from this—in spite of their inaccessibility to non-specialists—have shaped modern understandings of the Anglo-Saxon period in fundamental ways.

This chapter is concerned exclusively with changes that took place before 1066, and like the rest of this book it tries as much as possible to work forward from earlier to later evidence. On this subject more than any other this approach represents a major departure from historiographical orthodoxy. It involves the rejection of a series of myths and misconceptions which have shaped the way historians have thought about legal rights and privileges for well over a century. Such a significant break from tradition requires explicit explanation and justification if it is not to cause confusion, and this is what the first section of this chapter sets out to provide.

These historiographical issues clarified, the chapter turns to an analysis of the late Anglo-Saxon period. The approach adopted is straightforward. The second section investigates the way legal rights and revenues were distributed using tenth-century (and earlier) evidence, then the third section turns to eleventh-century sources and asks the same questions. The specific differences between tenth- and eleventh- century material are highlighted and analysed in detail, and a case is made for a period of change in the decades around the year 1000. It is suggested that this was a period which witnessed intense competition over legal revenues,

---

[1] References to the main contributions to this debate are assembled in Chapter 3, p. 147, n. 136.

from which kings emerged in a much stronger position than ever before. Many legal rights which had previously been understood to pertain automatically to privileged lords were, by Cnut's reign, formally reserved to the king. The chapter argues, in other words, that significant centralization took place in these decades, and it attempts to work through how we might most plausibly imagine this playing out in practice. Before we can turn to this analysis, however, it is necessary to explain how and why certain assumptions underlying it diverge from those discernible in much of the existing literature.

MYTHS AND MISCONCEPTIONS

When, in the 1990s, Patrick Wormald lectured to undergraduates in advance of the publication of *The Making of English Law*, he introduced his lecture on the themes covered by this chapter with this splendid sentence: 'Now this, I'm afraid, is a real *snorter*, which has given me as many hours of agony as the minutes you're about to experience.'[2] He was quite right: the historiography on this subject is convoluted and self-referential, readily accessible only to specialists who have learnt to think in its terms.[3] Yet much of the agony Wormald and many others (myself included) have experienced in coming to grips with this scholarly tradition arguably arises not from the difficulty of the sources themselves, or from any baffling complexity in the world that produced them, but primarily from the interpretative framework which has been constructed around these sources and this world. I hope to demonstrate in this chapter that if we abandon this established interpretative framework the landscape of late Anglo-Saxon legal privilege is much more readily comprehensible. Questions about legal privilege need not be 'snorters' at all if reframed in a way that is sensitive to contemporaries' understanding of their own world.[4]

[2] Patrick Wormald, *Papers Preparatory to the Making of English Law: King Alfred to the Twelfth Century*, vol. 2: *From God's Law to Common Law*, ed. Stephen Baxter and John Hudson (University of London, 2014) <http://www.earlyenglishlaws.ac.uk/reference/wormald/>, p. 201 (emphasis in original).

[3] John Hudson, *The Oxford History of the Laws of England*, vol. 2: *871–1216* (Oxford, 2012), pp. 56–62, does an excellent job of summarizing it for a lay reader, but (as was noted in Chapter 6, p. 239, n. 4) he achieves this by observing the existence of numerous possible interpretations, not attempting to resolve the contradictions he highlights.

[4] That, at least, is the conclusion I have reached after about a decade of struggling with this subject. The historiographical critique presented here represents a distillation of an instinctive discomfort that I initially found hard to articulate, but which I managed to express in increasingly coherent forms as I repeatedly came back to the same fundamental questions. I experienced this as the frustratingly gradual realization that several basic assumptions embedded in my thinking, and in the literature, were distorting my understanding of the period. Ironing out these issues to my own satisfaction involved more rewriting than I care to contemplate—years of apparently wasted work at a time when rapid publication was an urgent priority. This section is an attempt to make a direct case for the abandonment of these unhelpful assumptions; it argues that they are incorrect, and attempts to do this forcefully and quickly so that the chapter can return to its primary task of analysing late Anglo-Saxon legal privilege. I hope readers will appreciate that in characterizing these assumptions as myths and misconceptions, and in trying to make their status as such readily apparent, I do not mean to imply that this ought to have been obvious all along. It was not to me. Nor do I wish to give the impression that the historians whose work I cite to illustrate the prevalence of these myths and misconceptions are somehow blameworthy for blindly wandering into error.

Three problems in particular need to be highlighted here. First, when historians discuss the legal privileges of the aristocracy in this period they usually implicitly assume a legal environment where all significant legal rights derived from the king, and could only ever come into the possession of other parties through delegation or usurpation. When confronted with the idea directly few today would deny that such an assumption is questionable, yet it is inextricably entwined with long-term narratives that still subtly but significantly inform modern perspectives on the late Anglo-Saxon period. Second, specialist literature on the subject traditionally assumes that the gold-standard of medieval legal privilege was the possession of 'jurisdictional' rights: the existence or otherwise of jurisdictional privileges serves in as a key barometer of the balance of power between the king and the aristocracy. However, the appropriateness of applying this concept to the Anglo-Saxon period is questionable, as there is little explicit evidence that contemporaries thought in jurisdictional terms at all. (The meaning of the term 'jurisdiction' in this context is discussed in detail below.) Third, for law as for other matters, the entire late Anglo-Saxon period, from Alfred to 1066, has tended to be understood as a single block. This has profoundly influenced scholarship on legal privilege, promoting the assumption that evidence from across the period ought to combine to create a coherent picture of the way legal rights were distributed, subtly restricting the range of 'plausible' readings available for individual texts. Contradictions between tenth- and eleventh-century evidence have perhaps not always been fully appreciated, and have sometimes even been smoothed over in attempts to reconcile seemingly isolated earlier sources with better-documented later realities. These three issues will be addressed in turn here.

The Origin of Legal Rights

The historiographical debate about the extent of aristocratic legal privilege in late Anglo-Saxon England has always been framed in a wider context: with reference both to contemporary West Francia and to England in the centuries after 1066. In the literature, at least, the interpretation of the key issues here is bound up with contested narratives about the significance of the Norman Conquest and the rise of English feudalism. Was mid-eleventh-century England a kingdom in which kings had grievously weakened their own positions by giving away their legal rights to over-mighty aristocrats, a kingdom thus ripe for conquest by vigorous Norman dukes capable of reasserting the crown's dominance? Or was it an impressively centralized 'state', in which kings held onto their legal rights much more fully than their continental contemporaries, allowing them to avoid the political disintegration that afflicted West Francia in this period and thereby to postpone the emergence of significant aristocratic legal privileges until the imposition of continental realities after the Norman Conquest? The twentieth century saw a major historiographical shift, essentially from the first of these positions to the second. It is useful, very briefly, to sketch the outlines of that shift here.

Frederic William Maitland, writing at the end of the nineteenth century, identified a significant process of decentralization in the half century before 1066:

Cnut himself and the Confessor – the latter with reckless liberality – expressly grant to the churches . . . [the] reserved pleas of the crown. The result is that the well-endowed immunist of St Edward's day has jurisdiction as high as that which any palatine earl of after ages enjoyed. No crime, except possibly some direct attack upon the king's person, property or retainers, was too high for him.[5]

Maitland thought that the legal privileges which we find kings granting to lords in eleventh-century writs were the highest of royal rights, and he was also convinced that these rights were 'jurisdictional': that lords who possessed them were entitled to hold their own 'private courts'. During the next century, however, this interpretation was overturned. In 1949 Naomi Hurnard argued that the legal rights conveyed in eleventh-century writs were not as important as Maitland had thought; in fact, they were of negligible significance.[6] As was noted in Chapter 4, this characterization is unsustainable, being underpinned by her assumption that homicide was a 'major crime'.[7] Nevertheless, her argument was influential and it came to be accepted that with very few exceptions the legal rights held by privileged pre-Conquest lords were minor, entitling their courts to deal only with petty offences.

Next, in 1995 Patrick Wormald made a strong case against the existence of any 'private courts' at all before 1066, at the root of which is the very sensible logic that the lack of any reliable positive evidence to suggest their presence ought to be taken as an indication of their absence.[8] Wormald's conclusion gives a good indication of the intellectual framework within which this debate about the nature and distribution of legal rights in pre-Conquest England has traditionally been understood.

> Landed property (other than the king's) was not in its own right a basis for the exercise of judicial power in early England. . . . [It] matters to the historian whether . . . [great magnates exerted their] ascendancy by manipulation of political patronage as opposed to the assertion of jurisdictional rights, because it matters whether we think that relations between property and power in eleventh-century England had more in common with what early modern historians study than with patterns in the Carolingian empire's twilight. It affects our view of more history than England's alone to know that . . . [magnates] guarded their legal interests not by means of mechanisms to be expected of the "feudal" epoch but by virtue of the sort of power-brokerage associated with the functioning of states in much more recent times.[9]

Wormald's argument, building on Hurnard's, was in effect that the process Maitland identified—kings alienating their most important legal rights to their aristocracy—did not get underway in England until after 1066. Pre-Conquest England was as yet untainted by the 'feudal revolution' which had overtaken much of Europe. Characteristically feudal aristocratic legal privileges would only

---

[5] Frederic William Maitland, *Domesday Book and Beyond: Three Essays in the Early History of England* (Cambridge, 1897), pp. 282–3.
[6] Naomi Hurnard, 'The Anglo-Norman Franchises', *English Historical Review* 64 (1949), pp. 289–327 and 433–60, at 292–310.
[7] Chapter 4, p. 188, n. 106.
[8] Patrick Wormald, 'Lordship and Justice in the Earliest English Kingdom: Oswaldslow Revisited', repr. in and cited from Wormald, *Legal Culture*, pp. 313–32.
[9] Ibid., p. 332.

arrive with the Norman conquerors, and they would remain in place for the remainder of the Middle Ages, only to be eradicated in the early modern period. Late Anglo-Saxon aristocrats were able to influence judicial processes, of course, but they influenced them through political patronage in the same way that early modern aristocrats did, not through their possession of significant formal legal privileges.

The important point to grasp here is that this influential historiographical tradition interprets conclusions about the distribution of late Anglo-Saxon legal rights with reference to an established master narrative. In spite of their differences, Maitland and Wormald—and indeed virtually all those who came in between—subscribed to the same set of basic assumptions: kings began with a monopoly of important legal rights; at some point, either before or after the Norman Conquest, there was a process of feudalization in which those rights were delegated to or usurped by the aristocracy; eventually early modern rulers managed to suppress these feudal legal privileges and restore the state's monopoly of the administration and profits of justice. The fundamental problem with this narrative is its starting point: it assumes that there was an initial royal monopoly of important legal rights.[10] Aristocratic legal privileges are thus understood as resulting from a period of feudalization in which this monopoly was broken.[11]

The basic objection to this is that, as previous chapters have argued, there is no reason to think that this royal monopoly of important legal rights ever existed in a meaningful form.[12] Kings asserted their right to receive punitive legal revenues in the seventh century and seem to have collected them, along with their food renders, through their reeves. The tradition of rewarding household warriors with grants of the king's non-military rights (primarily but not exclusively food renders) over specific areas was probably established before this point, so it is likely that when kings began to assert their more punitive legal role there were significant parts of their kingdoms where characteristically royal rights belonged to privileged lords. It is certainly the case that privileged lords already existed when Ine of Wessex and Wihtred of Kent legislated in the late seventh century: their laws refer to these

[10] An important exception here is Helen M. Cam, 'The Evolution of the Mediaeval English Franchise', *Speculum* 32 (1957), pp. 427–42 esp. at 429, where she makes the crucially important point that 'the character of a privilege must depend on the system from which exemption is granted, and the Frankish immunity implied a system of comprehensive and centralized control, however decadent, for which there is no parallel in England.' Julius Goebel, *Felony and Misdemeanor: A Study in the History of English Criminal Procedure* (New York, 1937), ch. 6, is also careful to place the rights kings gave away in the context of what they had to give in the first place. Neither Cam nor Goebel, however, rigorously followed up the implications of this insight for 'jurisdiction' in general terms, as this chapter attempts to do.

[11] Chris Wickham, *Framing the Early Middle Ages: Europe and the Mediterranean, 400–800* (Oxford, 2005), p. 315, n. 30, provides a good illustration: 'Justice was also reserved to kings [in the pre-800 period]; even in the late Saxon period, there was little private justice in England, and the judicial aspects of Continental-style immunities were also absent'. The logic here is that the absence of private justice before 800, though somewhat surprising, might be expected to some extent, but that kings' ability to protect their judicial rights from aristocratic encroachment *even in the late Saxon period* is a sure sign that there was something unusual about England.

[12] For this paragraph see, primarily, Chapter 3, pp. 125–6.

figures. A plausible interpretation is that, from the very start, whenever kings asserted new legal rights they did so in the knowledge that there were areas of their kingdom which pertained to privileged lords, and that these lords would naturally receive whatever new revenues they claimed. Even in the earliest period, then, we need not imagine that kings first asserted rights which were exclusively royal and subsequently alienated them. Royal legal rights and aristocratic legal privileges may well have emerged simultaneously.

The proliferation of aristocratic legal privileges between the seventh and tenth centuries, moreover, need not be understood in terms of kings alienating rights they already possessed. It makes rather more sense to understand it as a side-effect of the expansion of kingdoms. As kings extended their domination over wider areas of land, absorbing lesser kingdoms, they also absorbed the landscapes of legal privilege within those kingdoms. It is unlikely that any such expansion involved a victorious king eliminating all existing privileged lordships within a defeated kingdom and claiming the right to receive all legal revenues for himself—asserting a royal monopoly which was subsequently to be alienated.[13] Far more plausible is that established landscapes of privileged lordships were inherited by these dominant kings, who gradually stepped into the role that had been played by the kings they displaced, becoming the arbiters of who was entitled to hold those lordships. The ultimate victors in this process, of course, were West Saxon kings: it surely cannot be doubted that, as a result of it, they gained the right to receive legal revenues from large tracts of land in what had been Surrey, Sussex, Kent, Essex, Mercia, East Anglia, and Northumbria. But West Saxon kings cannot have been the only ones to profit; the more fortunate members of their aristocracy—those lucky enough to receive the king's favour—must have done so as well. This process of expansion cannot but have resulted in there being more privileged lords in the early tenth-century kingdom of Wessex than there had been in its late seventh-century predecessor, but it would be inaccurate to understand it as one in which West Saxon kings weakened themselves by alienating their most fundamental rights. It makes much more sense to think of royal legal rights and aristocratic legal privileges growing in tandem, with West Saxon kings and nobles together profiting from the gradual and partial dispossession of kings and nobles from other kingdoms.[14]

The idea that widespread aristocratic legal privilege, identified in the eleventh century or beyond, needs to be explained as the result of a period in which a royal monopoly of important legal rights was privatized is therefore ahistorical.

---

[13] George Molyneaux, *The Formation of the English Kingdom in the Tenth Century* (Oxford, 2015), pp. 40–5, provides a detailed discussion of what is essentially this point: though his focus is on rights over land generally rather than the right to legal revenues specifically, we have seen that there is no reason to think that the two were separable in this period (Chapter 3, pp. 124–36).

[14] It is important to note that the process of expansion involved the incorporation of many nobles and churches from absorbed kingdoms, and even some former royal families (as in the case of the Hwicce, discussed in Chapter 3, p. 116), into the dominant kingdom's elite. We should not imagine that West Saxon aristocrats were the only winners in this process; as Molyneaux, *Formation*, pp. 43–5, shows, there is good evidence for West Saxon kings bestowing valuable patronage on certain members of the existing elites of regions over which they extended their domination, in the hope of securing their loyalty.

Aristocratic legal privileges, rather, are likely to have emerged alongside royal legal rights, and the process by which dominant kingdoms absorbed their neighbours must have resulted in both growing together. This was not a period in which kings and aristocrats were competing for a limited pool of legal rights. Rather, the pool was growing quite rapidly—both through the assertion of new punitive rights by kings and the expansion of kingdoms—and kings and aristocrats were together sharing the benefits of this growth. The long-running debate over whether the feudalization process in which major royal rights were alienated took place before or after 1066 is thus unnecessary: there is no reason to assume it took place at all.

Later in the Middle Ages it became an established legal fiction that all significant legal rights held by people other than the king had been either legitimately delegated or illegitimately usurped. The *Quo Warranto* proceedings of Edward I's reign, most strikingly, show that this myth about the royal origins of legal rights was an important part of contemporary thought.[15] Analysing this later period whilst accepting this legal fiction is therefore not as problematic as it might be; the late medieval legal landscape makes sense when interpreted within this basically mythical narrative because it was a narrative which shaped the way contemporaries understood their own world. This was only the case to a much more limited extent in the late Anglo-Saxon period. There can be no doubt of the simple fact that many aristocrats held legal rights by virtue of grants which, directly or indirectly, were understood to derive from the king. This does not, however, mean that *all* significant legal rights were understood in this way. It is important for us to bear in mind that some people in this period possessed important legal rights simply by virtue of being who they were: we need to be alert to the potential significance of the rights that pertained to all free men, all householders, all nobles, all churches, all local communal assemblies. Many of these rights were rights to compensation for breach of protection, some of which could be just as significant in financial terms as any punitive fine: in cases of homicide, we should remember, the value of the kindred's right to wergild was much greater than the value of the *wite* payable to the king or a privileged lord. Communities' legal rights, however, could be more punitive: we have clear tenth-century evidence for a communal share of certain fines and property forfeitures. There is no reason to think that any of these rights were understood as arising from royal grants.

We also have a few hints from this period that it was possible for powerful bodies to assert significant legal rights that went beyond the standard rights associated with particular ranks. We find towns asserting both punitive and protective rights,[16]

---

[15] Donald W. Sutherland, *Quo Warranto Proceedings in the Reign of Edward I, 1278–1294* (Oxford, 1963), ch. 1.

[16] The composite text known as IV Æthelred includes a passage from London detailing the king's right to £5 compensation for what seem to be Latin renderings of the three most important royal protections (definitely *hamsocn* and *forsteal*, maybe also a garbled version of *mundbryce*). This is followed by a statement 'if he [who has committed one of these offences] values the friendship of the town itself, he shall pay us 30 shillings as compensation, if the king will grant this to us' (IV Atr 4:2). What this seems to represent, then, is the men of London collectively adding their protection over (at least) houses and roads to that of the king. Though they thought it wise to present this as a request to the king rather than as a unilateral demand, it seems probable that they anticipated royal approval

churches asserting unusually extensive sanctuary rights,[17] and one secular guild asserting the right to be compensated whenever a member was killed.[18] It is clear that royal approval was sought for some of these locally specific legally privileges, but not for all of them; the members of the Cambridge Thegns' Guild, at least, appear to have thought they could legitimately assert their rights without reference to any external authority. Even where we do find royal approval being sought it is plausible that this was essentially a matter of kings acquiescing to customs which were already understood to be legitimate on a local level. This chapter is primarily concerned with the legal privileges of aristocrats, which were understood to have been delegated by kings in one way or another. However, we need to remember that these delegated privileges were part of a wider landscape of legal rights, many of which had nothing to do with kings at all.

The assumption that all significant legal privileges were delegated royal rights is thus problematic for two principal reasons: first, because it has shaped an influential and inaccurate long-term narrative of the development of legal privilege which has distorted historians' interpretations of this period; and second, because it can leave us blind to the existence of important legal rights that owed nothing to royal grants. It is therefore important to make a conscious effort to avoid this assumption.

The Nature of Legal Rights

What exactly were 'legal rights' in this period? The specialist literature on the subject starts from the assumption that they could fall into two categories: rights to receive legal revenues and rights to perform legal functions. The former are sometimes labelled 'fiscal' rights, the latter 'jurisdictional' rights. It is now accepted that kings did not grant jurisdictional rights to aristocrats and the conventional and influential interpretation of this fact is that it reveals unusual royal strength: it is taken to imply that kings retained possession of the right to perform all important

---

rather than outraged rejection. (On this text: Chapter 4, p. 187, n. 102.) Hn 68:2 appears to imply that towns more generally were places in which people were likely to enjoy additional protections. For the punitive legal revenues claimed by the London *frið*-guild in Æthelstan's reign, see below, p. 315, n. 59 (though note the request for royal approval at VI As 8:9).

[17] See, in particular, R. C. Van Caenegem, *English Lawsuits From William I to Richard I*, 2 vols. (Selden Society 106–7, London, 1990–1), no. 172A. According to this composite text, which incorporates genuine material from an inquiry into the privileges of the Archbishop of York held in 1106, the churches of Ripon and Beverley in Yorkshire could offer protection within an area described as circle of a mile radius around the churches, with the penalties for breach becoming increasingly severe as they approached the centre. York Minster claimed the right to offer supplicants safe-conduct to and from any point within thirty leagues of the church on up to three occasions; anyone who dared to attack the protected person would owe the church eight pounds compensation. For discussion, see T. B. Lambert, 'Spiritual Protection and Secular Power: The Evolution of Sanctuary and Legal Privilege in Ripon and Beverley, 900–1300', in T. B. Lambert and David Rollason, eds., *Peace and Protection in the Middle Ages* (Toronto, 2009), pp. 121–40; T. B. Lambert, 'Protection, Feud and Royal Power: Violence and Its Regulation in English Law, c.850–c.1250' (University of Durham PhD thesis, 2009), pp. 136–41.

[18] Benjamin Thorpe, ed., *Diplomatarium Anglicum Ævi Saxonicum: A Collection of English Charters from the Reign of King Æthelberht of Kent to That of William the Conqueror* (London, 1864), pp. 611–12. See Chapter 5, pp. 228–9.

legal functions and that the legal privileges held by the aristocracy were therefore relatively insignificant. Kings may have granted away their fiscal rights, in other words, but they maintained something very close to a monopoly on jurisdiction.[19] All this is based on a premise that, if stated in general terms outside this historiographical context, few modern commentators would be prepared to accept without reservation: that kings claimed an exclusive right to exercise administrative control over legal practice through their officials.[20] This supposed royal right to administer justice is the 'jurisdiction' of the literature, its alienation or retention by kings the focus of debate since the nineteenth century. The assumption that, whether held by kings or lords, such a right must have existed in some form—even if it is not clearly visible and might be questioned in certain contexts—underlies our readiness to believe that local assemblies can reasonably be treated as 'royal courts', controlled by royal agents.[21] It also underlies the idea that royal officials were central to the enforcement of the law—the notion that they alone could legitimately inflict

[19] This is the message of Wormald, 'Lordship and Justice'. It is accepted by Stephen Baxter, 'Lordship and Justice in Late Anglo-Saxon England: The Judicial Functions of Soke and Commendation Revisited', in Stephen Baxter et al., eds., *Early Medieval Studies in Memory of Patrick Wormald* (Farnham, 2009), pp. 383–419, and in broad terms by Hudson, *Oxford History*, pp. 60–2, though he notes the silence of pre-Conquest sources on 'many important issues' (p. 62). The argument that Anglo-Saxon legal privileges were fiscal rather than jurisdictional has deeper roots than this, however. The fullest statement of the case is Goebel, *Felony and Misdemeanor*, ch. 6, but it was first essayed in Henry Adams, 'The Anglo-Saxon Courts of Law', in Henry Adams et al., *Essays in Anglo-Saxon Law* (Boston, 1876), pp. 1–54. One partial exception to the modern consensus on this point is the right of *infangenþeof*. Goebel, *Felony and Misdemeanor*, pp. 367–8, presented a strong argument for regarding it as a fiscal right. Hudson, *Oxford History*, p. 59, however, defines it as a jurisdictional right (though without explaining why, which may suggest he overlooked Goebel's argument). Wormald appears never to have adopted a position on this issue. *Infangenþeof* is discussed in detail below, pp. 329–32.
[20] This premise has recently been challenged directly: Alice Taylor, '*Lex Scripta* and the Problem of Enforcement: Anglo-Saxon, Scottish and Welsh Law Compared', in Judith Scheele and Fernanda Pirie, eds., *Legalism: Community and Justice* (Oxford, 2014), pp. 47–75. My ideas on jurisdiction were not yet fully developed in December 2012 when this paper first came to my attention at a workshop in Oxford; it undoubtedly contributed to their crystallization in the argument that follows here. For earlier expressions of discomfort with jurisdictional assumptions see, for example, Hudson, *Oxford History*, p. 65 ('the distinction between lords' courts, if they existed in this period, and royal courts . . . may have been less important to contemporaries than it has been to some historians') and A. G. Kennedy, 'Disputes about *Bocland*: The Forum for their Adjudication' *Anglo-Saxon England* 14 (1985), pp. 175–95 at 194 ('The Anglo-Saxons had no single word for jurisdiction, and it may be that in using abstract notions of this sort we are attempting to describe an order of a kind that did not exist', 'the sources yield no sound jurisdictional rules about the conduct of suits').
[21] It may be helpful to note that this premise is the fundamental underpinning for the argument in favour of the existence of aristocratic jurisdictional privileges, which in the absence of explicit evidence boils down to an appeal to what is clearly supposed to be basic common sense. See Maitland, *Domesday Book and Beyond*, p. 277: 'As a general rule, the person in whose name the court is held, be he king or lord, gets the profits of the court. No one in the middle ages does justice for nothing, and in the ninth century the days when national officers would be paid by salary were far distant. . . . When [a church held the right to receive legal revenues from an entire hundred] . . . it was almost of necessity the lord of the court as well as the lord of the land. Why should the sheriff hold that court, why should he appoint a bailiff for that hundred, if never thereout he could get one penny for his own or for the king's use?' The notion that local assemblies had to be 'held' by an agent of a specific authority-figure—either the king or a lord—and simply would not take place otherwise, is an assumption we cannot safely accept.

physical punishments on wrongdoers, performing executions or mutilations.[22] As we have seen in earlier chapters, neither of these assumptions fits well with the evidence from the period.

As Chapters 3 and 6 argued, local assemblies seem to have remained fundamentally communal throughout this period.[23] The authority underpinning their judgements was not an expression of delegated royal jurisdiction, but rather the authority of the assembled community over the individual. Two facts, in particular, make this plain. First, that the verbs used to refer to final assembly judgements are usually in the plural suggests the authority behind those judgements was collective.[24] Second, that the presiding figure in hundred assemblies was expected to be a senior local man rather than an official of any sort suggests that local assemblies remained expressions of the authority of the communities that gathered in them in the late tenth century, just as they must have been in the pre-Christian period. This is not to say that kings had no influence in these gatherings. From the point when they began to legislate in the seventh century, kings needed to ensure that their legislation was respected by local communal assemblies. This meant relying on their own reeves to act as legal authorities, attending assemblies and guiding them on the proper application of the law. Because kings did not have local reeves for every local assembly they also demanded that lords who had been granted the right to receive legal revenues performed this function, or sent their own reeves to do so in their stead. If these figures—royal reeves, non-royal reeves, and privileged lords acting in person—could be understood to wield absolute legal authority within local assemblies, we might be justified in thinking of them as possessing jurisdiction of a sort: they had an exclusive right to perform the specific legal function of stating and interpreting the law. An assembly in which a royal reeve wielded legal authority would thus be a 'royal court', whereas one in which a privileged lord or his reeve performed this role would be a 'private court'.

However, as we have seen in Chapters 3 and 6, there is no reason to think that these figures' authority was absolute. Indeed, Asser's *Life of King Alfred* implies that it derived from the extent of their legal knowledge, and that when this was lacking other members of assemblies who believed they knew better could and did argue with them.[25] Kings wanted reeves and privileged lords to act as local legal experts—conduits for their legislation—and they held them responsible for performing this function, threatening to punish them for corruption: this suggests that they had real legal authority to abuse, but it does not show that they were the *only* people who had such authority. Other members of local assemblies, particularly

---

[22] Goebel, *Felony and Misdemeanor*, p. 368, points out that this is mistaken in the case of thieves caught in the act, but he takes the insight no further and it has had little impact on the modern literature (see above, p. 302, n. 19).

[23] The next two paragraphs summarize arguments made in Chapters 3 and 6, pp. 136–49, 243–50, 262–8.

[24] Patrick Wormald, 'Charters, Law and the Settlement of Disputes in Anglo-Saxon England', repr. in and cited from Wormald, *Legal Culture*, pp. 289–310 at 305–6.

[25] W. H. Stevenson, *Asser's Life of King Alfred Together With the Annals of St Neot's Erroneously Ascribed to Asser* (2nd edn, Oxford, 1959), ch. 106.

their more senior and well-respected members, must often have had considerable legal expertise. The *Leges Henrici Primi*, indeed, seem to assume that technical legal judgements in hundred assemblies were made collectively, with all but the poorest participating in the process and sharing liability for any fines for defective judgement that resulted.[26] The notion that royal reeves or privileged lords were in any position to assert a monopoly of authoritative legal knowledge in local assemblies is not sustainable. We would be making a major mistake if we were to imagine them as the equivalents of modern judges, with absolute authority within their own courts on matters of legal interpretation.

The right to enforce the law, likewise, was held communally. The legitimacy of violent vengeance in feuds is assumed throughout the late Anglo-Saxon legal corpus: even priests, Cnut's laws explicitly state, are appropriate targets for vengeance if they will not pay compensation for the harm they do.[27] Men who caught thieves in circumstances where their guilt was undeniable were entitled to kill them; indeed, they were to be commended and rewarded for daring to do so.[28] Before the emergence of the sheriff, at least, when enforcement action needed to be taken against a defiant offender it was assumed that it would be taken by a communal expedition, and when we are told about the leaders of such expeditions they are invariably senior local men, not reeves.[29] Kings gained a reliable source of local coercive power with the establishment of sheriffs: this must have meant they were less reliant on communal enforcement expeditions led by local notables, but there is no reason to think that such expeditions ceased to be legitimate.

The broader point here is that the right to perform legal functions appears not to have been formally restricted in this society. Any member of an assembly was entitled to try to guide it in the proper application of the law, and everyone was entitled to attempt to kill a thief caught in the act. Having the right to try to influence a debate about an obscure legal point, of course, is not the same thing as being capable of winning that debate. Having the right to slay a thief, similarly, is not the same thing as being able (or indeed willing) to fight and kill him. In practice the rich and powerful were much better placed to make use of their rights; they were more likely to speak and be listened to in legal debates and had less reason to fear reprisals from the families of executed or mutilated offenders. But this in no way detracts from the central point: this was a society in which there were few rules governing who was entitled to perform legal functions. Nobody had an exclusive right to make a judgement or enforce the law in any given area.[30] If we were to

---

[26] Hn 29–29:1b, 29:4.

[27] I Cn 5:2b (also VIII Atr 23). See Chapters 4 and 5, pp. 181–3, 224–35.

[28] Chapter 5, pp. 227–30. Note that the king's assertion of his right to punish wrongdoers caught in the act for the third time in S 180 and 1861 does not imply an exclusive right: rather, the king is reserving the right to intervene if—for whatever reason—wrongdoers are not being properly punished.

[29] Chapters 3 and 6, pp. 152–6, 274–6.

[30] Insofar as the right to participate in these processes was implicitly limited, it was limited to the category of free adult males, but even this does not represent a rigid rule. Free women were probably understood to have a right to participate in assemblies, at least when they were heads of their own households or when they were victims of offences, and there is incontrovertible evidence that they could act as oath-helpers in formal proof procedures (see Chapter 6, p. 256, n. 67). Laws on

think about this period in terms of jurisdictional rights, we would have to think of those rights as widely dispersed, vaguely defined and unevenly exploited. Jurisdiction could not be owned by an individual: it could not be bought, sold, stolen, inherited, or given as a gift. If jurisdiction was property at all, it was the communally held, inalienable property of the free population. It is likely, however, that it never occurred to contemporaries to think about their legal world in terms of jurisdiction at all, let alone to theorize about who might have owned it.[31]

We should thus recognize that jurisdiction is a cultural construct, not a universally applicable legal concept. Rather than assuming its existence throughout English legal history we ought to be asking when, how and why it emerged. These are big questions which extend well beyond the Norman Conquest, well beyond England, and therefore well beyond the scope of this book. I will not attempt to answer them here, though at the end of the chapter I will briefly consider the possibility that people were beginning to think about legal privilege in jurisdictional terms in the decades leading up to 1066. (The Conclusion will also sketch out some of the evidence for the emergence of jurisdiction after the Norman Conquest.) The main focus here has to be on legal rights as they were understood by contemporaries. These rights were not rights to perform legal functions—rights to *do* things—but rights to receive payments. Some of these rights were 'fiscal' in the sense that they were rights to receive legal revenues that in normal circumstances

---

enforcement almost certainly imagine free adult males as the enforcers—they had a duty to participate—but this need not imply that it was considered illegitimate for others to do so. If an unfree man stumbled upon a thief, for instance, and ended up fighting and killing him, would that have been regarded as illicit conduct? There is no reason to think so. The same point could be made for women and children. However, it should be noted that post-Conquest evidence suggests some formalization of wealthier members of hundred assemblies' dominant role in judgements. Various categories of poor people are excluded from judgement in the early twelfth-century *Leges Henrici Primi*, seemingly on the logic that they lacked the resources to contribute to fines for defective judgements (Hn 29–29:1b). Similarly, S 1109 (a forged writ of Edward the Confessor which had assumed its current form in time to be incorporated into the Ramsey Chronicle in the late twelfth century) assigns the soke of all the 'assembly-worthy' (*motwurði*) men of the hundred-and-a-half of Clacklose to Ramsey Abbey, no matter whose men they might be. The apparent implication that only an elite of the free population was assembly-worthy aligns suggestively with Domesday's explanation that in the manor of Fersfield (Norfolk) it was only those men with more than 30 acres whose sake and soke lay 'in the hundred' (DB ii. 130v). I owe these last two references to a draft chapter of a University of Oxford doctoral thesis currently being prepared by Richard Purkiss ('Royal Lordship and Regional Government: East Anglia, c. 869–1086'), which contains detailed and astute analysis of this issue in the context of East Anglian hundreds and addresses the intricacies of the operation of soke in much greater depth than has been possible in this book. I am grateful to the author for allowing me early access to this work. The piece of Anglo-Saxon evidence that bears most directly on the question of whether there were formalized barriers preventing poor freemen from participating in tenth-century communal legal practice is the statement that only those with property worth more than 30 pence were expected to pay the annual dues of the London *frið*-guild (VI As 2). It is not clear that this meant the poor were excluded from participation in the guild's activities, however. Indeed, the passage may imply nothing more than that only the property-owning members of the guild needed to contribute to its collective insurance scheme, the main purpose of which was to compensate the owners of stolen property (see below, p. 315, n. 59).

[31] Note that my argument here is that people generally did not think about legal rights in jurisdictional terms; I do not mean to rule out the possibility that the notion was current in some form in intellectual circles.

were owed to the king's treasury (the 'fisc') but, as has just been discussed, it would be wrong to restrict our analysis of legal rights in this period to delegated royal rights alone. It is probably better to think of legal rights in this period more neutrally: as 'financial' or 'economic'.

The Case against Continuity

The literature on the subject of aristocratic legal privilege traditionally operates on the basis of an assumption of continuity throughout the period from Alfred's reign to the Norman Conquest. It is firmly established that complexities which emerge for the first time in new eleventh-century forms of evidence ought to be understood as long-standing features of the legal landscape which had not been recorded in earlier sources. When they are remarked upon, it tends to be assumed that discrepancies between tenth- and eleventh-century evidence are illusory, the historian's job being to reconcile any apparent contradictions and create a coherent account of way legal rights were distributed throughout the period.[32] This chapter questions this assumption of continuity. The methodology it adopts is simple: it examines tenth- and eleventh-century evidence separately, drawing out differences and analysing them as potential indications that a change took place. Ultimately it will argue that these differences collectively constitute strong evidence that a major shift took place, perhaps beginning in the final years of the tenth century but becoming clearly visible only in the first quarter of the eleventh.

---

[32] This is most clearly illustrated by Goebel, *Felony and Misdemeanor*, p. 367–8, esp. n. 108, which proposes and goes to some lengths to justify a rather strained reading of tenth-century evidence relating to the forfeited property of slain thieves in order to reconcile it with the implications of eleventh-century writs (see below, p. 330, n. 119). Maitland, *Domesday Book and Beyond*, pp. 282–3, as we saw above, argued that the 'highest criminal jurisdiction' had traditionally been excluded from grants, but that Cnut's 'predecessors' were guilty of losing them, and that Edward the Confessor was guilty of 'reckless liberality' in this regard. In that he acknowledged changing patterns of privilege Maitland is an exception, but he assumed (as Goebel would later) that the system from which exemptions were granted remained stable: the later grants are understood as kings giving away rights they had previously monopolized, not as signs that the king had asserted new rights. The slipperiness of Maitland's argument here is discussed at great length in Hurnard, 'Anglo-Norman Franchises', pp. 289–302, but Hurnard makes essentially the same assumption: as we have seen (Chapter 4, pp. 188, n. 106, 197–9), she uses (distinctly shaky) post-Conquest evidence for royal punishment of homicide to argue that tenth-century royal protections (*hamsocn* and *mundbryce*) could only possibly have applied to very minor offences. More recently, Wormald's scholarship has emphasized the extent to which late Anglo-Saxon law can be traced back to Alfred's reign, arguing that ambiguous passages in Alfred's laws and those of his early tenth-century successors need to be interpreted in the light of more detailed later laws. This tendency is most visible in his published arguments on frankpledge and the oath of loyalty (on which see Chapters 5 and 6, pp. 203–4, 210–13, p. 281, n. 163) but his chapter drafts show that this was fundamental to the methodology of his second volume: discussions of specific themes begin with long series of quotations from laws relevant to those themes, often spanning over two centuries. Again, he is clearest about his thinking in the context of the oath of loyalty; Wormald, *Papers Preparatory*, pp. 122–3: 'it is in the nature of Anglo-Saxon legislation . . . to leave even basic principles to be reconstructed from a set of glimpses . . . just as it is typical of a twelfth-century culture . . . to clarify what was hitherto obscure. The defects of the evidence do not of course give a free run to historians' imagination. But they do allow them to take a hint. Legislation on the oath from Alfred to Cnut offers a series of suggestive hints.' On the tendency of retrogressive analyses to produce assumptions of broad continuity, see Introduction, pp. 8–9.

Working forwards from early to later evidence is not intrinsically a methodo-logically controversial thing to do. However, the assumption of continuity between the tenth and eleventh centuries is so deeply engrained in the historiography that abandoning it represents a radical step. Some readers may well feel that a picture of the tenth century that fails to incorporate eleventh-century evidence is simply incomplete; others may suspect that the shift identified in fact arises from changes in the production and transmission of texts rather than any real change to the distribution of legal rights. In this context it is not enough to point out that, respect for scholarly tradition aside, there is no positive reason to assume continuity between the tenth and eleventh centuries on this issue. A prima facie case for understanding the decades around the year 1000 as a period of change in areas relevant to the distribution of legal revenues needs to be established. This case has two main pillars: first, that this was a period that witnessed crucial structural changes which increased the kings' capacity to extract revenues generally; and second, it is also one in which we find a shift in our evidence for specifically legal revenues, with our sources suddenly showing much more concern to define precisely which revenues belonged to whom.

The clearest sign that kings' capacity to extract revenue increased significantly in this period is the emergence of a kingdom-wide system of taxation. From 1012 it seems that a tax known as the *heregeld* ('army-payment') was levied annually, until it was (temporarily) abolished in 1051.[33] The previous two decades may have seen one-off taxes levied to fund the tribute paid to Scandinavian raiders. The *Anglo-Saxon Chronicle* gives figures for such tributes in 991, 994, 1002, 1007, and 1009, totalling £89,000: we cannot be sure that a forerunner to the *heregeld* was involved in raising any one of these payments but it is plausible.[34] The *heregeld* is significant because it shows that kings were capable of asserting the right to receive new forms of revenue in this period, and not just from their own lands but from all the land in the kingdom. This second point is crucial: the *heregeld* demonstrates, for the first time, that kings had the administrative capacity to collect revenues even from land where they had granted away their non-military rights and where the local rural reeve worked for a privileged lord.

This is very probably closely related to the establishment of a network of sheriffs, which also took place in this period. As we saw in Chapter 6, the first clear evidence for sheriffs appears in the final quarter of the tenth century in two charters relating to Kent, though by what point it was normal for every shire to have a sheriff is not clear (this certainly was the case by 1066). Later sources show that sheriffs were

---

[33] See M. K. Lawson, 'The Collection of Danegeld and Heregeld in the Reigns of Æthelred II and Cnut' *English Historical Review* 99 (1984), pp. 721–38. The *heregeld* was certainly imposed after 1066; for discussion, see Sally Harvey, *Domesday: Book of Judgement* (Oxford, 2014), pp. 212–14. This may imply that at the time of the Conquest it had been collected more recently than 1051 (this is the conclusion of an unpublished paper by John Maddicott—I would like to thank him for his kindness in allowing me to read it).

[34] See Lawson, 'Collection', p. 725–6 (for discussion), 736 (for figures). Different views exist as to the accuracy of these figures but the issue is of little consequence here. For recent observations on their plausibility and references to earlier debate, see Harvey, *Domesday*, p. 211.

instrumental in the collection of the *heregeld*.[35] It seems likely that the emergence of the two at roughly the same time is not a coincidence: the presence of sheriffs may well have been essential prerequisite for making the collection of *heregeld* practicable as a matter of routine, and the need to collect *heregeld* may well have made the need for sheriffs more urgent, accelerating their establishment as a kingdom-wide tier of administrators. The advent of the sheriff, as was observed in Chapter 6, gave kings a powerful administrative official capable (as the *heregeld* more or less proves) of intervening in and collecting revenues even from lands where the king's non-military rights and the local rural reeve pertained to a lord other than the king.[36] If sheriffs at this early point, as they often did later on, made large up-front cash payments (known as farms) in return for their offices, in effect buying the right collect and keep the majority of the king's revenues from their shires, they would have had a strong incentive to try to maximize their legal revenues at the expense of local privileged lords.[37] There is evidence that privileged churches regarded this as a problem by Cnut's reign.[38] The emergence of sheriffs, then, was a significant development which—even if we lacked specific evidence that changes took place—we might well expect to have resulted in increased conflict between the king and privileged lords over legal revenues.

The idea that the period around the year 1000 witnessed intensified conflict over legal revenues finds support in legal sources, in both records of royal grants and the laws themselves. The most obvious sign of change is the emergence of a new format of royal grant, the writ. Up until the eleventh century there was basically one type of charter in Anglo-Saxon England, known as the diploma. As we have seen, when diplomas discuss the rights conveyed to their beneficiaries they define them negatively: they begin with a statement that the beneficiary received all royal rights and then list exceptions, usually just the three 'common burdens' (the key military rights of fortification-work, bridge-work and military service). In the early eleventh century a new type of written grant emerges, the writ.[39] (Our first undoubtedly genuine writs survive from Cnut's reign though there are clear signs that writs had existed in some form under Æthelred.)[40] Though diplomas continued to be issued there is a marked decline in their numbers before the format finally becomes extinct

---

[35] Lawson, 'Collection', pp. 723–4; Harvey, *Domesday*, p. 214–15.

[36] Chapter 6, pp. 251–3.

[37] The evidence is surveyed in Morris, *Medieval English Sheriff*, pp. 28–34. See also, Harvey, *Domesday*, pp. 239–59.

[38] A writ of Cnut dating 1017–20 (S 985), which includes 'Æthelwine *scirman*' in its address, illustrates this particularly clearly: 'And I [Cnut] inform you that the archbishop spoke to me about the freedom of Christ Church – that it now has less protection (*mund*) than it once had. Then I gave him permission to draw up a new charter of freedom (*freols*) in my name. Then he told me that he had charters of freedom in plenty, if only they were good for anything'. Translation from Florence E. Harmer, ed., *Anglo-Saxon Writs* (Manchester, 1952), p. 182.

[39] For discussion, see Simon Keynes, *The Diplomas of Æthelred 'the Unready', 978–1016: A Study in their Use as Historical Evidence* (Cambridge, 1980), pp. 140–5; Richard Sharpe, 'The Use of Writs in the Eleventh-Century', *Anglo-Saxon England* 32 (2003), pp. 247–91.

[40] Two writs in the name of Æthelred survive (S 945, 946), and though both are suspect in their current form it has been argued (Sharpe, 'Use of Writs', p. 251, n. 6.) that the address clause in S 946 derives from a genuine writ of Æthelred. More broadly, see the conclusions of Keynes, *Diplomas*, p. 145.

around 1100.[41] Writs had radically different conventions for the description of legal privilege. Rather than defining the rights delegated negatively as the diploma had, they do so positively, working on the principle that if a legal right is not specifically listed it is not part of the grant. There is still a standard package of legal privileges, usually termed 'sake and soke', but now there are various additional rights: *toll* and *team*, *infangenþeof*, the three main royal protections of *hamsocn*, *mundbryce*, and *forsteal*, and a few others. A writ that granted sake and soke alone, then, implicitly excluded not just the king's military rights, as had been traditional, but all these additional rights as well.

The assumption in writs that a number of specific legal privileges existed above and beyond the standard grant of sake and soke is unprecedented. Each of these additional rights is analysed in detail below, and a case is made for regarding their emergence as evidence of change. The pertinent inference at this stage, however, is a more general one: the emergence of the writ must, at the very least, be taken as evidence for an increased concern in this period to define the legal privileges held by lords with precision. This concern surely arose as a result of conflict. The point of listing individual legal rights by name must have been to enable their beneficiaries to prove they had these specific rights when someone (a sheriff would be the most plausible candidate) claimed otherwise. A similar—and similarly novel—concern to define the destination of legal revenues with precision is visible in eleventh-century laws. Most significantly, Cnut's laws offer a list of 'the rights which the king possesses over all men in Wessex . . . unless he wishes to honour anyone further', followed by passages specifying the king's rights in Mercia and the Danelaw. The rights in question are the three main royal protections (*hamsocn*, *mundbryce* and *forsteal*), the fine for neglect of military service (*fyrdwite*), and rights over fugitives including the fine for harbouring them (*flymenafyrmþ*).[42] (All of these appear in writs, though none is particularly common.) Slightly earlier, under Æthelred, we find an assertion of the king's right to receive fines paid by all men who held *bocland*.[43] We ought to recognize that these laws represent a break in continuity: no earlier royal laws show this sort of explicit concern to establish the king's right to legal revenues against the claims of other lords.[44]

Eleventh-century laws are also noteworthy for very carefully dividing the rights of the king and the Church. This is particularly visible in cases where a church's protection (*ciricgrið*) was breached. Killing someone 'within church walls' involved forfeiture of land and life unless the king was willing to grant the killer his life back

---

[41] The obvious inference—that the rise of writs prompted a decline in diplomas—is challenged in Keynes, *Diplomas*, pp. 140–5. It is now accepted that although the functions of writs and diplomas overlapped to an extent, they were distinct. One of the most notable distinctions (drawn out clearly in Sharpe, 'Use of Writs') is that diplomas granted rights in perpetuity whereas writs made no such claim and seem to have required relatively frequent renewal.

[42] II Cn 12–15a. These are the king's rights in Wessex. In Mercia they are identical. In the Danelaw there are some differences: *forsteal* is omitted, the term *griðbryce* is used instead of *mundbryce*, and *fihtwite* is included.

[43] I Atr 1:14.

[44] The one exception to this, VI As 1:1, is not strictly a royal law. It is discussed in detail below, pp. 331–2.

in return for his wergild. If the king did this, however, or if the *ciricgrið* was violated in some other way (various offences short of homicide are mentioned, and it is possible that killings within ecclesiastical precincts but outside 'church walls' are implicitly included) the church itself was to be compensated, in proportion to its rank (four ranks are specified) and the severity of the offence. The detail of this scheme, which appears in laws written by Archbishop Wulfstan for both Æthelred and Cnut, is extraordinary.[45] Its determination to define with precision which revenues belong to the king and which to the church is unlike anything in earlier laws. Another of Wulfstan's passages may be relevant here too. It explains that previously *worldwitan* (perhaps 'wise laymen'—a reference to kings and their great assemblies) had established secular laws (*woroldlaga*) to uphold the just laws of God (*to godcundan rihtlagan*), with the revenues shared between Christ and the king, but complains that since Edgar's day these revenues had been separated and that this had caused much woe in matters both spiritual and secular.[46] Like the passages in Cnut's laws defining the king's rights, and like the newly detailed language used in writs, these passages on ecclesiastical rights suggest that the distribution of legal revenues had become an issue of contention in the early eleventh century, and that interested parties sought to protect their revenues by defining their established rights in precise terms.

In short, it would be unwise to begin our analysis of the late Anglo-Saxon period with the assumption that no significant shifts in the distribution of legal revenues took place. The decades around the year 1000 saw a significant structural change, the introduction of sheriffs, which gave kings the capacity to collect revenues throughout their kingdoms in an unprecedented way, including from within lands granted to privileged lords. Writs emerge which describe legal privileges with unprecedented precision, presumably so as to allow their beneficiaries to defend their revenues against challenges from sheriffs, and an equally unprecedented concern to define the proper recipients of legal revenues appears in the laws. The first decades of the eleventh century in particular, then, are associated with major breaks in continuity both in general structures of royal revenue-extraction and in the way our sources discuss specifically legal revenues. On this basis, it seems sensible to abandon the traditional assumption of continuity between the tenth and eleventh centuries and, with our minds open to the possibility that a significant change may have taken place, to look afresh and in detail at the tenth- and eleventh-century evidence.

THE TENTH-CENTURY EVIDENCE

If we focus solely on sources from the tenth century and earlier, the picture of the distribution of legal revenues that emerges is fairly straightforward. As we saw

[45] VIII Atr 1–5:2; I Cn 2–3:2. For more Wulfstan texts which perhaps show concern to limit the king's interest in breaches of church protection to those which take place within church walls, see Grið 2; EGu 1; VI Atr 14.
[46] VIII Atr 36–8.

in Chapter 3, when kings gave away their legal rights, they gave them away wholesale. There is no sign that there were different classes of privileged lords, some of whom were entitled to receive more royal revenues than others. All our evidence suggests that there was one standard grant. In charters from the eighth century onwards the content of such grants was defined negatively: everything was included except the king's key military rights, the three 'common burdens' of bridge-work, fortification-work, and military service. Occasionally we find charters which try to make the legal rights included in these grants more explicit. Some Mercian charters are at pains to stress that the compensation due to victims of affronts still needed to be paid, but as we never find a charter that specifically includes these in the grant we can be confident that this was nothing unusual. Likewise, some charters explicitly mention that *wites* and rights over captured thieves were included in their grants, but as there are no examples of their exclusion (and as the language of the charters is quite explicit about the land being freed from *all* royal rights barring only those mentioned) we can be confident that these are simply more elaborate descriptions of the rights conventionally granted. The implication is clear: there was one standard package of royal rights and it was comprehensive.[47]

The only exceptions to this rule are provided by a handful of charters in which kings vary the standard grant by reserving certain non-legal rights for themselves. Offa of Mercia, for example, reserved a portion of the food renders due to him at Westbury-on-Trym (Gloucestershire) in the course of granting all his other rights over 60 hides of land there to the church of Worcester.[48] There is nothing, however, to suggest that kings ever chose to retain specific *legal* revenues when they granted their rights to aristocrats (beyond any associated with the three common burdens).[49] This makes sense. Revenues from the punishment of wrong-doing must have been unpredictable, varying from year to year not just in the amount collected but also in the form taken by payments, which would presumably frequently have been in kind rather than in coin. Welcome though these occasional windfalls may well have been to privileged lords, for kings their irregularity was a problem. Kings are likely to have reserved food renders with specific practical purposes in mind: it probably indicates that they intended to continue visiting the land concerned annually and wished to ensure that when they did so they had a reliable supply of ale, meat, cheese, and grain to feed their households. It makes

[47] See Chapter 3, pp. 129–32.

[48] S 146. Patrick Wormald, 'How Do We Know So Much About Anglo-Saxon Deerhurst?', repr. in and cited from Patrick Wormald, *The Times of Bede: Studies in Early English Christian Society and its Historian*, ed. Stephen Baxter (Oxford, 2006), pp. 229–48 at 243–4, argues that this charter is an early ninth-century forgery, based on some lost exemplar. Given that (as Wormald, 'Charters, Law', p. 296 points out) the list of food renders reserved to the king is an unlikely thing for a forger to manufacture, it is probable that (if the charter is indeed a forgery) the relevant section here derives from a genuine exemplar. For other examples, see S 1188, 1861. S 1263 shows a bishop making a (seemingly somewhat uneven) exchange of lands with a certain Brihthelm, but retaining the right to limited food renders from the lands given away.

[49] S 180 and 1861 show kings reserving the right to punish wrongdoers caught in the act, but only if lords twice fail to do so: the agenda here is the maintenance of order, not the reservation of revenues. See Chapter 3, p. 131, n. 78.

sense that kings prioritized reliable non-legal revenues which could systematically be exploited by their itinerant households. It would be understandable if they wished to avoid alienating these useful streams of income—though the evidence suggests they did so only very occasionally—but they had no reason to want to retain unpredictable and administratively awkward revenues from the punishment of wrongdoing. We should not, then, be surprised to find that they routinely gave these rights to lords. (This seems odd to modern audiences only because of our tendency to assume, wholly anachronistically, that legal revenues *ought* to pertain to the sovereign, whereas food renders and labour services have fewer royal associations.)

The laws complement the evidence of charters nicely, frequently assuming that legal revenues of various types belonged to lords other than the king. There is nothing in the laws to suggest that such privileged lords were entitled to receive some types of royal legal revenue and not others: we find them receiving not only punitive fines (*wite*s and wergild forfeitures) but also the goods seized from executed offenders. Though they are far from scrupulous about these matters—they are generally frustratingly casual about the issue of precisely who they expect to receive fines—we can fairly frequently find them operating on the assumption that the countryside was divided into parcels of land, each of which had a figure known as a *landhlaford* ('land-lord') or *landrica* ('land-ruler'). They do not always use these technical terms—the most common term, in fact, is simply *hlaford* ('lord'), and circumlocutions such as 'he to whom it is due' or 'he who is worthy of *wite*' are common—but there is no reason to think these variations in vocabulary are significant. Rather, the laws seem to be alluding to a single category of lords with the right to receive royal legal revenues using a number of interchangeable terms.[50] Again, the impression conveyed is of a standard, comprehensive grant of the king's legal rights.

The implications of this for different forms of landholding need spelling out explicitly. The standard package of rights conveyed by charters included all the king's rights except the three common burdens. This means that every holder of a charter—the Old English term is *boc* ('book')—was entitled to receive all the king's revenues from the land covered by the grant, including legal revenues. Such land was often referred to as *bocland*. Every holder of *bocland* was thus a *landhlaford*. This does not imply, however, that all *landhlaford*s held *bocland*. The key feature of the *boc* was that it conveyed *perpetual* enjoyment of this standard grant of royal rights, allowing the beneficiary to bequeath it to his heirs on whatever terms he wished. Other forms of grant were possible, and it is probable that these allowed their recipients to enjoy the same standard bundle of rights on a less permanent basis. It is highly likely that ealdormen and bishops enjoyed the standard set of non-military royal rights over large areas of land by virtue of their positions: these rights were not theirs to give away as they wished or to bequeath to their heirs (this was not *bocland*), but for the duration of their time in office they were the *landhlaford*s

[50] See Chapter 3, p. 127. n. 59.

of the people who lived on this land.[51] Kings and major magnates could also make temporary gifts of their rights over land to minor nobles: land held on this basis was known as *lænland* ('loan-land'). It is likely that many minor aristocrats became *landhlafords* by virtue of holding *lænland*.[52]

Landhlafords, then, were far from equal. The king was a major *landhlaford*, of course, and a wide range of aristocrats, from immensely wealthy ealdormen to relatively insignificant king's thegns, owed their positions as *landhlafords* to the king's generosity. Others had no direct relationship with the king, however. Well-endowed *landhlafords*—bishops, ealdormen, monasteries—could afford to use their rights over land as patronage, rewarding those who had shown loyalty with grants that made them *landhlafords* on a small scale. The webs of patronage that defined who possessed the rights of a *landhlaford* and on what terms could be complex, but the tenth-century evidence suggests that on a local level this did not matter: regardless of who the *landhlaford* was or how he came to occupy his position, for the duration of his tenure he was the figure entitled to receive the king's non-military revenues.[53] Where the king was not himself the local *landhlaford* he was entitled to receive no legal revenues apart from those associated with the common burdens. This one explicit exception aside, kings gave to *landhlafords* everything it was possible for them to give. We do need to be aware, however, that there were important legal rights which it was impossible for kings to grant to *landhlafords*, either because they were not the king's to give in the first place or because it would have been absurd for *landhlafords* to hold them. There are four points worth mentioning in this context.

---

[51] VI As 1:1 imagines *landhlafords* as holding either *bocland* or bishop-land (*bisceopa land*).

[52] For a useful discussion of *lænland*, see Hudson, *Oxford History*, pp. 98–102. Though the focus here is very much on the relationship between the lessor and lessee, and on issues of heritability which gave rise to disputes, rather than on the basic question of what rights were conveyed to lessees with which we are concerned here, the passage from the Old English version of St Augustine's *Soliloquies* quoted at the outset (p. 98) is pertinent. It envisages a man being granted land on a temporary basis by his lord as a *læn* ('loan'), but hoping that in time his lord would look upon him kindly and convert that grant into *bocland* to be held in perpetuity. This suggests that *lænland* tended to involve the same rights as *bocland*, just held for a limited period. For this passage, see Thomas A. Carnicelli, ed., *King Alfred's Version of St. Augustine's Soliloquies* (Cambridge, Mass., 1969), p. 48. On life-grants of land as a reward for service in a great household being part of a standard noble male life-cycle, see T. M. Charles-Edwards, 'The Distinction between Land and Moveable Wealth in Anglo-Saxon England', in P. H. Sawyer, ed., *Medieval Settlement: Continuity and Change* (London, 1976), pp. 180–7 at 181–4; Patrick Wormald, 'Bede and the Conversion of England', repr. in and cited from Patrick Wormald, *The Times of Bede: Studies in Early English Christian Society and its Historian*, ed. Stephen Baxter (Oxford, 2006), pp. 135–66 at 153–7.

[53] Before the eleventh century our written records of leases of *lænland*, like grants of *bocland*, never make a point of reserving legal revenues, though they occasionally specify non-legal renders and services which the leased land must continue to provide. The explanation for this is probably the same as that discussed above for royal grants: when lords reserved particular rights to themselves in such documents they had specific practical requirements in mind, and they therefore prioritized predictable sources of goods and labour. For discussion, see Vanessa King, 'St Oswald's Tenants', in Nicholas Brooks and Catherine Cubitt, eds., *St Oswald of Worcester: Life and Influence* (London, 1996), pp. 100–16 at 113–15; Ann Williams, *The World Before Domesday: The Anglo-Saxon Aristocracy 900–1066* (London, 2008), pp. 77–80. (In eleventh-century leases it is possible to find reservations of legal rights in the same terms as contemporary writs; see S 1423.)

Affront and Compensation

First of all, it ought to come as no surprise that kings were unable to grant to *landhlafords* the right to receive compensation payments for affronts. Such compensations represent legal revenues of a sort, but it is clear that *landhlafords* generally had no right to them unless they happened to be the affronted parties. As was noted in Chapter 3, the fact that royal grants had no effect on affronted parties' right to compensation is explicitly discussed in a number of late eighth- and ninth-century Mercian charters.[54] For the most part the principle here is obvious: the right to be compensated for an affront belonged to the person who was affronted, not to the king, so the king was in no position to grant that right to someone else. But what about the king's own right to compensation if he was affronted? There are two possible ways of understanding this right. We might interpret affronts as deeply personal matters, with compensation necessarily paid to the victim himself because its purpose was to recompense him for the harm done and, crucially, to demonstrate that his wounded honour had been restored. On this logic it would not make sense for any man's right to compensation, let alone the king's, to be held by someone else. The other reading would be that the king's rights to compensation belonged to him, and he could do what he pleased with them, granting them to others if he felt that was appropriate.

This point is significant for present purposes because we need to be alert to the possibility that some significant royal legal rights in this period were rights to compensation for affront, and may therefore have been kept separate from the rights granted to *landhlafords*. We saw in Chapter 4 that some of the most important late Anglo-Saxon legal innovations relating to violent offences were the new royal protections, at least two of which seem to have been established under Edmund. By the time of Cnut's laws, it is clear that kings protected all churches, houses, and major roads, and that they allowed sheriffs to extend their personal protection to individuals on their behalf. If any of these protections was breached, the king was entitled to £5, which since Alfred's time had been the traditional value of the compensation due to the king for breaching his protection (the king's *mundbyrd*).[55] Was it possible for these rights to be transferred to privileged lords? In the eleventh century, as we shall see, they were treated this way, albeit relatively rarely.

If we work solely on the basis of tenth-century evidence, however, there is no sign that this was a possibility. This is because the issue does not arise: although breaches of royal protection are fundamental to one tenth-century law code, II Edmund, the possibility of *compensation* being paid for such breaches is never explicitly discussed. In that text, men who breach royal protection by attacking either those within in houses or churches, or those who had been placed under the king's *mund* by some other arrangement, are not permitted to pay compensation. Rather, they are to lose all they possess and the king is to decide whether they live

---

[54] Chapter 3, pp. 130–1.
[55] This paragraph summarizes Chapter 4, pp. 183–90. Chapter 5, pp. 230–5, is also relevant.

or die.[56] Edmund, in essence, is demanding that breaches of his protection be avenged, allowing for compensation only if the offender somehow persuaded him to be merciful. The king did not make any explicit claim to the possessions forfeited by such offenders. This may well be because they were not understood as compensation: someone who is killed for his offence can hardly be expected to pay compensation for it as well. There is therefore little reason to suspect that these forfeited goods were treated differently from other punitive goods forfeitures: *landhlafords* may have received them in the same way that they received the possessions forfeited by other executed offenders—slain thieves, for example.[57] In the 940s the king could not rely on a network of sheriffs to extract payments from lands where he had granted his non-military revenues to other people. It may therefore have made sense to treat breaches of protection in a way that did not create obligations to pay compensation which the king lacked the means to enforce.[58] Far more practical, perhaps, to demand the death penalty and allow *landhlafords* to collect the resulting goods forfeitures, thereby securing their assistance in the enforcement of these new protective rules.

Communal Revenues

The second point of which we need to be aware is that communities were entitled to receive legal revenues in certain circumstances.[59] These rights are particularly prominent when communal enforcement expeditions are discussed in tenth-century laws. The *Hundred Ordinance*, for instance, envisages an entire hundred going in pursuit of a thief, catching him in a position where his guilt was

---

[56] II Em 2, 6.   [57] See below, pp. 315–17.

[58] A possible sign that it was impractical to demand compensation for breaches of protection from non-royal lands is provided by the contrasting approach to violence in churches in the laws of Alfred and Æthelstan. Alfred's demand for payment of his own *mundbyrd* (Af 5) is not reflected in Æthelstan's discussion of protection for fugitives (IV As 6:1–6:2b), which orders anyone who harms the fugitive within the time-limits specified to compensate by paying the protector his *mundbyrd*; churches are mentioned as possible protectors but there is no indication that kings had special rights in them.

[59] There is nothing implausible about the idea that the hundred, as a communal entity, could be the recipient of a payment. The regulations of the London *frið*-guild give a striking example of the arrangements that communities could make for holding property in common in this period, with no sign of external prompting. The guild was divided into groups called hundreds, each consisting of ten subgroups, called tithings. The head of each hundred, together with the ten heads of the tithings, were responsible for holding the money of the hundred and keeping an account of what was disbursed and received (VI As 3). All members of the guild with property worth thirty pence paid an annual four pence into this communal fund, into which were also paid revenues from legal cases pursued in common and, presumably, the proceeds of expeditions against thieves which accrued to 'the fellowship' (VI As 1:1, 2). The guild also asserted the right to fine its members: 30 pence (or an ox) for non-payment of dues (VI As 2), and 'our *oferhyrnesse*' for failing to pursue a theft case (VI As 7). It disbursed money to cover expenses incurred in the prosecution of cases against thieves (VI As 7), to reward the killers of thieves (VI As 7), to allow the heads of the hundreds and tithings to feast together every month (VI As 8:1), and to compensate victims of theft at agreed rates (VI As 6:1–6:4, 8:8). The text even envisages a special scheme by which slave owners paid higher premiums, seemingly to cover the greater risk they posed to the guild's collective finances by their propensity to run away (VI As 6:3). We do not know what the late tenth-century hundreds discussed below did with the goods that accrued to them. They may have just sold them and distributed the proceeds, but it is plausible that some chose to hold them in common.

undeniable, and killing him. The thief's goods are then to be seized: 'and the value of the stolen property is to be given to him who owns the cattle, and the rest is to be divided in two, half for the hundred, half for the *hlaford*—except for the men; and the *hlaford* is to succeed to the men.'[60] This is representative of tenth-century rules about enforcement expeditions: the general expectation seems to have been that the profits should be halved and split between the *landhlaford* and whoever participated in the expedition.[61] The hundred is also occasionally represented as the recipient of fines paid by people who refused to participate in enforcement expeditions. In III Edmund these people are ordered to pay 120 shillings to the king and 30 shillings to the hundred.[62] The *Hundred Ordinance*, much more leniently, allows first offenders to pay 30 pence solely to the hundred, but orders that fines for subsequent offences (60 pence for the second, 120 pence for the third) be split between the hundred and the *landhlaford*.[63] Communal legal revenues do appear in one other context. In Edgar's laws on the witnessing of transactions anyone who bought new livestock had to give his neighbours details of the purchase: specifically, the identity of both the seller and the witnesses to the sale. If he failed to do this within five days he forfeited the livestock, half to the *landhlaford* and half to the hundred.[64]

The laws are clear that these revenues belonged to communities, not to *landhlafords*. One way of reading this might be that they had once unambiguously belonged to kings, before at some point a wise ruler chose to divert royal revenues so as to encourage communal participation in legal practice. A rather more plausible reading, to my mind at least, is that they never belonged to kings in the first place. *Landhlafords* were not entitled to them because formally their revenues were those which kings had granted, and communal revenues had never really been the king's to give. Chapter 2 suggested that communities may well have had traditions of imposing punishments on delinquent individuals long before kings claimed the right to receive punitive fines. The communal rights which appear in tenth-century laws may be recognizing and regularizing a traditional expectation that communities should receive profits that arose from punishing people who committed offences against the community as a whole (as opposed to offences that affected specific individuals but did not threaten communal cohesion).[65]

However, the circumstances in which we find evidence for this expectation of communal profit are suggestive. The right to half the goods forfeited by executed offenders comes up only in the context of communal enforcement expeditions, and the first references to this in Æthelstan's reign make it fairly clear that this was understood as a reward for those involved.[66] The fines for people who refused to join such expeditions could be understood in the same way: as profits deriving from those expeditions which the men who went on them were entitled to share. The community's claim in relation to Edgar's highly ambitious scheme of rules for the monitoring of purchases could well be explained by the fact that this system relied

[60] Hu 2:1.
[61] See III Eg 7:1; II As 20:4. VI As 1:1 is slightly different; it is discussed below, pp. 331–2.
[62] III Em 2.   [63] Hu 3–3:1.   [64] IV Eg 8:1.   [65] Chapter 2, pp. 102–4.
[66] II As 20:4; VI As 1:1.

entirely on the vigilance of local communities: without their involvement it would not have worked.[67] The principle involved, in other words, may well be that people who played an important role in extracting legal revenues were entitled to share in those revenues. It is argued below that this principle was significant in the developments of the eleventh century, so it is important to take note of its presence here.

The Punishment of *Landhlafords*

The third point to note is that different rules applied when people who were themselves *landhlafords* committed offences. Although they unquestionably had these rights available to give, it would have been absurd for them to grant any *landhlaford* the right to receive revenues deriving from his own punishment. That is, it would be wrong to imagine a *landhlaford* committing an offence and then paying the relevant fine to himself. This point is less facile than it appears. We need to appreciate that *landhlafords* were not just a small minority, distinguished from the rest of the population primarily by their greater wealth and power, but that legal revenues arising from their punishment necessarily followed different routes to other people's fines and forfeitures. Precisely because of their anomalous position, however, the punishment of *landhlafords* is over-represented in our source material. This is because our most important evidence for real-life legal cases relates to land. Charters and monastic chronicles reasonably frequently relate how a holder of *bocland* committed an offence and forfeited that *bocland* to the king; they then explain how this land ended up being granted to an ecclesiastical institution of some sort (usually the institution which preserved the record of the transaction). The information our case evidence provides about the destination of legal revenues is thus highly unrepresentative, and we need to be very careful not to over-generalize when using this material to draw conclusions on this topic.

For our purposes, the issue of who received fines and forfeitures from people who in normal circumstances collected fines and forfeitures is not particularly central. It does not really help us understand wider patterns. But this is not to say we should ignore it entirely; a brief outline may still be helpful. The destination of revenues from the punishment of *landhlafords* seems to have varied depending on the basis on which the punished *landhlaford* enjoyed his rights. The case of Helmstan, reported in the document known as the Fonthill Letter, several aspects of which were discussed in Chapter 6, yet again provides a particularly instructive example.[68] Helmstan was a *landhlaford* by virtue of two distinct grants; he was eventually caught in the act of theft and forfeited both of them. The inherited land (*yrfe*) he held at Tisbury was forfeited to the king, 'because he was the king's man'—this may imply that Tisbury was *bocland* granted by an earlier king to one of Helmstan's forefathers, which Helmstan had inherited along with a duty to reciprocate royal generosity through service. The land he held at Fonthill, however, he forfeited to

---

[67] This scheme is discussed in detail in Chapter 6, pp. 270–3.
[68] S 1445. Chapter 6, pp. 258–9, 266–7, 269–70.

Ealdorman Ordlaf, because (as a result of earlier events narrated in the letter) Ordlaf held it as *bocland* and had leased it to Helmstan for the duration of his life. Helmstan's forfeiture thus resulted in his losing his position as *landhlaford* in both Tisbury and Fonthill, with that role reverting to the figure who had made the initial grant in both cases: the king became the *landhlaford* in Tisbury (the letter explains that the king's reeve, Eanulf Penearding, seized possession) and Ordlaf became the *landhlaford* in Fonthill.[69] The operating principle here seems to be that when a *landhlaford* committed an offence serious enough to lead to his forfeiting that role, it should revert to whoever had granted it to him: either the king or some great magnate. Even in the eleventh century, it is worth noting, we do not find kings claiming the right to land forfeitures in general terms, but only when the offender held *bocland*: indeed, II Cnut explicitly protects lords' right to receive forfeitures of land that they granted to their men.[70]

When a *landhlaford*, rather than forfeiting his position entirely, had to pay a fine, who received it? Laws up to and including Edgar's reign consistently imply that when a *landhlaford* was found guilty of issuing a false judgement, it was the bishop's duty to collect the fine on the king's behalf.[71] It is possible that bishops were expected to collect fines for other types of offence in the same way, but this is not stated explicitly. In fact, we have one example from the reign of Eadred which seems to show the local ealdorman filling this role: trying to collect a wergild forfeiture on the king's behalf from a thief who held *bocland*.[72] Under Æthelred there is a shift in emphasis: we have a law declaring that all fines paid by men who held *bocland* belonged to the king, which also orders that whenever such figures paid compensation for an offence they do so with the knowledge of the king's reeve,

---

[69] S 1445.

[70] II Cn 13:1; 77–77:1. These passages are suggestive of some tension: II Cn 77 is part of the section of Cnut's code in which the king promises to restrain his own exactions, so the protection of lords' rights to forfeitures here is probably a sign that they had hitherto been under threat. II Cn 13:1 is, in fact, rather pointed: it asserts that the king is entitled to forfeitures of *bocland* no matter whose man its erstwhile holder had been. This suggests that other lords may well have felt they had a claim to *bocland* forfeitures, and that Cnut was explicitly denying such claims' validity. To make sense of this, we might imagine a scenario in which a great magnate initially leases some land to a favoured subordinate, making him a *landhlaford*; at a later point, as a reward for further faithful service, this magnate then wishes to make that grant permanent, transforming it from *lænland* to *bocland*, and secures a royal charter in favour of his subordinate. (This is the scenario considered in the Old English version of St Augustine's *Soliloquies*: see above, p. 313, n. 52.) If this subordinate then commits an offence, to whom does his position as *landhlaford* revert? The magnate had been *landhlaford* before granting the land to his subordinate, and he may well believe himself entitled to receive it back after the forfeiture. Transforming the land into *bocland*, however, did not just give this subordinate the right to perpetual possession, it formally severed the magnate's ties to it, placing the holder in a direct relationship with the king with respect to the *bocland*—hence the king's claim to receive the forfeiture—even though it had no effect on the personal relationship between the magnate and his subordinate. It is likely that Cnut's assertion of his rights against those of other lords had this sort of context in mind. Some leases show a similar concern, carefully asserting that the lessee could not forfeit the land, or that it was to return to the lessor unforfeited: they are making clear that the land was not held as *bocland* and that the king therefore had no claim to it, should its holder commit an offence which required forfeiture of property (see Hudson, *Oxford History*, p. 121).

[71] II As 25:1; III Eg 3.   [72] S 1447.

probably an early reference to the sheriff.[73] The point is that this reeve's job was to collect any fines owed to the king; it was essential that he knew about all offences for which compensation was paid so he could claim any fines associated with them. It seems, then, that the king claimed the right to receive fines paid by all *landhlafords* who held *bocland* and presumably the same applied to *landhlafords* who held *lænland* from the king himself. *Landhlafords* who held *lænland* from another lord, however, may have been different: it could be that these figures owed their fines, like their land forfeitures, to the lords who had leased them their land. The fact that the laws only ever assert a royal monopoly on fines paid by men holding *bocland*, at any rate, suggests that different rules could apply to *landhlafords* who held their positions on different terms.

Land Forfeitures

The fourth and final point to be aware of here is rather less certain: it is possible that kings had no entitlement to receive land forfeitures from free householders and were therefore unable to grant them to other *landhlafords*. To comprehend the uncertainty surrounding land forfeitures in this period it is necessary first to understand that there were two distinct levels of rights over land. Ordinary free households lived on what is known as warland and held land assessed in hides: they had the right to farm that land for their own benefit, but they had to pay certain customary dues in proportion to the number of hides they possessed. *Landhlafords* were the recipients of grants which were also measured in hides, but these grants did not entitle them to farm those lands themselves: rather, they were the men who received the dues paid by the free households which lived on the warland they had been granted. There is, as we have seen, plenty of evidence for *landhlafords* forfeiting their rights over land for wrongdoing. However, there is surprisingly little to suggest that it was possible for ordinary free households to do the same. Tenth-century laws do not discuss land forfeiture as a punishment, or at least not explicitly: they often speak of offenders forfeiting all that they possess, but whenever we are supplied with more detail it is clear that forfeiture of goods is what is implied.[74]

---

[73] I Atr 1:14. Note that the translation in A. J. Robertson, ed., *The Laws of the Kings of England from Edmund to Henry I* (Cambridge, 1925), p. 55, which states that no compensation must be paid 'unless in the presence of the king's reeve', is too strong a reading. The key term here, *gewitnes*, need mean no more than 'knowledge' or 'cognisance' (ASD s.v. 'gewitnes').

[74] All the passages in which thieves and untrustworthy men are slain by communal expedition, most notably, assume that the forfeited property was readily divided into fractions, which makes it unlikely that land was included. Particularly telling are Hu 1:2 (all the thief's property except his men are to be divided, but all the men are to go to the *landhlaford*) and VI As 1:1 (a circumstantial discussion of the destination of forfeited property that makes no allusion to land at all). Note that all the evidence for land forfeiture surveyed in Hudson, *Oxford History*, pp. 192–4, concerns land held by *landhlafords*. The smallest portions of land recorded as forfeited in charters amount to a hide and a half: a very large holding for an ordinary farmer. They could plausibly be understood as elements of scattered landed endowments held by *landhlafords*, which—after forfeiture to the king—could be re-granted individually. The relevant charters (neither of which is free of suspicion) are S 753, 792.

We do have one text from Peterborough Abbey which shows a late tenth-century abbot coming into possession of land from free households in two separate cases, but in neither does it seem that the land was forfeited.[75] Rather, the offenders were initially outlawed for their offences and the land was handed over later in return for the outlawry being lifted. In these cases, at least, there is no sign that the offender forfeited his land when he was outlawed. Instead, the text seems to indicate that a deal was struck between the abbot and the kinsmen of the outlawed offender (who presumably could not safely be present to negotiate in person), in which the abbot agreed to accept land as full payment of the offender's debt. It seems that land, here, is functioning as one of the many possible forms of wealth in which a punitive fine a might be paid. An attractive interpretation is that free householders were not understood hold their land in absolute ownership; rather, they were only ever the custodians of land which in an important sense belonged to their families. If such a householder were to commit an offence and flee from justice, rightful possession of his land would thus revert back to his wider family, who would then be in a position (if they so wished) to negotiate a deal with the *landhlaford* that allowed for the offender's safe return.[76]

An Ely text supports this interpretation to an extent, by showing that at least some land was considered immune to forfeiture. It relates how, in the context of a land dispute shortly after the death of King Edgar, the wise and old men of the district had testified 'that there was no land so free in the whole of Huntingdonshire that it could not be lost through forfeiture, apart from two hides at Bluntisham which Ælfsige *Cild* held, and another two near Spaldwick.'[77] (Domesday Huntingdonshire contained over 800 hides.)[78] The type of landholding being discussed here is almost certainly that of *landhlafords* rather than that of ordinary free householders. We would expect to find that all landholdings at this level were forfeitable to someone, so this pair of two-hide holdings warrants explanation. A possible interpretation is that a few noble families, like that of Ælfsige *Cild*, retained a memory of a period before they had been made into *landhlafords*, when they were rich free householders with large two-hide farms. These family lands could not be forfeited (except to other family members), but any rights as *landhlafords* they subsequently acquired could be. This is not a lot of evidence—and it should be noted that both the examples just cited come from the Danelaw which may have had both a greater number of free farmers and different rules on outlawry[79]—but it provides an elegant explanation of the otherwise puzzling absence of explicit reference to land forfeiture in laws from this period.

---

[75] S 1448a.

[76] This interpretation takes its lead from the arguments presented in T. M. Charles-Edwards, 'Kinship, Status and the Origin of the Hide', *Past and Present* 56 (1972), pp. 3–33 at 19–33.

[77] E. O. Blake, ed., *Liber Eliensis* (Camden Society Third Series 92, London, 1962), ii. 25; translation from Janet Fairweather, *Liber Eliensis: A History of the Isle of Ely from the Seventh Century to the Twelfth* (Woodbridge, 2005), p. 121.

[78] H. C. Darby, *The Domesday Geography of Eastern England* (3rd edn, Cambridge, 1972), p. 325.

[79] II Cn 13–15a. On free farmers, see D. M. Hadley, *The Northern Danelaw: Its Social Structure, c. 800–1100* (London, 2000), ch. 3.

If this theory is incorrect and it was, in fact, possible for free householders to forfeit their land outside their kindred in this period, the only possible recipients for such forfeitures are *landhlafords*. If there was a general royal right to receive such forfeitures, we would surely have expected it to be mentioned in Cnut's laws alongside his assertion of the king's entitlement to forfeited *bocland*.[80] Moreover, the idea that kings had the right to receive land forfeitures from within areas where they had explicitly granted their non-military rights to lords is not plausible: seizing such land would be a clear violation of the terms of these grants and it is in any case difficult to imagine upon whom kings would have relied to take possession in areas where there was no local royal reeve. Land forfeitures from non-*landhlafords*, in short, are notably obscure in the tenth century, so obscure that it is possible they were not a feature of legal practice.

Whether the eleventh century saw any significant change here is just as difficult an issue. Cnut's code states that people who breach the king's *handgrið* or breach *circigrið* within church walls should lose both land and life, which may indicate some sort of change, but we cannot rule out that 'land' here refers to the sort of land held by *landhlafords*.[81] One thing, at least, seems clear: there is no indisputable evidence that non-*landhlafords* could forfeit their land for wrongdoing at any point before 1066, and even if we were to make a leap of faith and accept this was possible we would have no grounds on which to assume kings had any special claim to them. If it was possible for free households to forfeit their lands for wrongdoing in this period, they must have forfeited them to their *landhlafords*.

The Tenth-Century *Landhlaford*

These four points are important because we need to be aware of the limits of what kings could grant to privileged lords. The king, obviously enough, could not grant to lords rights he did not himself possess: he could not give away rights to compensation which belonged to free individuals, nor could he give away rights to punitive revenues which belonged to communities, and it is possible that he was unable to give away rights to land forfeitures from free householders because this land in fact belonged in some sense to their wider kindreds. It may be that kings were unable to give away their own rights to be compensated for affronts for a different reason: these rights were understood as so personal as to be inalienable. We can see that this changed in the eleventh century, with relatively rare grants of the king's more impersonal rights to compensation for breach of protection, but this possibility is not apparent in any earlier evidence. Other rights could not be

---

[80] II Cn 13:1, 77–77:1.

[81] I Cn 2:2. It is striking that land is not mentioned in the passage from which this is drawn (VIII Atr 1:1), nor in any of the other Wulfstan laws that make the same point (VI Atr 14; Grið 2; EGu 1), but what this signifies is obscure. Domesday Book provides some very strong evidence that forfeitures of land and goods were understood as separate rights: we hear of St Mary's, Stow, having two thirds of the soke relating to forfeitures in several places, but this is separate from their rights to a third of forfeitures of land, the only examples of which noted relate to lords who held soke over others—*landhlafords* (DB i. 376r). It would not be safe to extrapolate from the situation in Lincolnshire, however.

given to *landhlafords* simply because it would be absurd for them to hold them: privileged lords obviously could not be allowed to receive punitive fines they themselves paid. All of these considerations, however, are just explanatory glosses to the basic rule that kings gave to *landhlafords* all the legal revenues that it was possible for them to give, saving only those legal fines relating to the three common burdens of bridge-work, fortification-work, and military service. The significant point here is that kings really did hold only these military revenues back; they otherwise gave privileged lords everything that was theirs to give.

This is not what historians usually assume. The literature tends to begin from the principle that more 'serious' offences were more important, and therefore more exclusively royal. This leads to an assumption that revenues resulting from different types of punishment ought to be treated differently: 'minor' offences for which it was possible to pay fines being distinguished from 'major' offences for which the offenders necessarily faced land forfeiture and either execution, mutilation, or outlawry.[82] This assumption must derive from later periods. From tenth-century and earlier sources it seems clear that—except for the local community's right to a share in certain circumstances—*landhlafords* received all punitive fines and wergild forfeitures, and there is nothing to suggest that the goods forfeited by offenders who fled or suffered execution were treated differently. If free householders could forfeit their land for wrongdoing, similarly, the only plausible recipient for such forfeitures is the local *landhlaford*. Our tenth-century evidence thus seems to imply the existence of a clear rule: *landhlafords* were entitled to receive *all* royal revenues arising from the punishment of non-military offences committed by people who were not *landhlafords* themselves. The division between 'major' and 'minor' offences is an anachronism.

THE ELEVENTH-CENTURY EVIDENCE

Eleventh-century evidence suggests a rather different picture of the distribution of legal revenues in Anglo-Saxon society. We find kings asserting the right to receive many more legal revenues from people living within areas pertaining to other *landhlafords*. Indeed, rather than all privileged lords being *landhlafords*, and being entitled to receive a standard and comprehensive package of legal revenues, we are faced with a more complicated world in which different lords were entitled to receive different revenues. The established interpretation here, as has been noted, is that this appearance of greater complexity is an illusion: new eleventh-century sources—first writs and later Domesday Book—are revealing a well-established legal reality (a division between 'major' and 'minor' offences) which had previously lain hidden behind more laconic forms of evidence. For the reasons outlined earlier, it seems to me that this is not something we can safely assume. We need to take

---

[82] This assumption can be tracked from Maitland (*Domesday Book and Beyond*, p. 282) through Hurnard ('Anglo-Norman Franchises', pp. 296–7) to Wormald ('Lordship and Justice', p. 317) and Hudson (*Oxford History*, pp. 58–9).

seriously the possibility that the differences between tenth- and eleventh-century evidence reflect a significant period of change in the treatment of legal revenues, perhaps associated with the parallel shift in the king's general revenue-collection capabilities suggested by the appearance of sheriffs and the *heregeld*. In order to do this we need to look in detail at the new terminology used to describe legal rights in eleventh-century sources, which for the most part first emerges in writs.

Sake and Soke

The most important and most common of eleventh-century rights to receive legal revenues is that known as 'sake and soke'. It is reasonably clear which legal revenues were conveyed by grants of sake and soke: it included the right to receive any *wites* paid by the people resident in the relevant area, and any wergild forfeitures. This is clearly expressed in the early twelfth-century legal treatise known as the *Leges Henrici Primi*, which contains a mass of information on sake and soke—Maitland, indeed, described it as 'a treatise on "soke"'[83]—but is at its most succinct in a clause dealing with the rights of 'vavassors' (vassals of vassals; presumably lords who had been granted their lands by lords other than the king):

> Vavassors who hold free lands shall have the pleas where the punishment is payment of the *wite* or of the wergild in respect of their own men and on their own land, and in respect of the men of other lords if they are seized in the act of committing the offence and are charged with it.[84]

Though dealing with a particular case, this is in essence the basic right of sake and soke according to the *Leges Henrici*.[85] The rule that a soke-holding lord usually had rights over his men, regardless of where their offences took place, but that this did not apply when offenders were caught in the act, is interesting. This rule is prominent in the highly soke-conscious *Leges Henrici*, and passages with similar implications can be found in other Anglo-Norman treatises, but it is not visible in any earlier texts so we cannot rely on it for the early eleventh century.[86] These passages may, however, be further hints at the existence of an important principle which we met in the context of communal legal revenues in tenth-century sources: that people who played an instrumental role in catching an offender could, by so doing, become entitled to receive a portion of the associated revenues.[87]

---

[83] Maitland, *Domesday Book and Beyond*, p. 80.   [84] Hn 27.

[85] Hn 80:6. By this point it seems clear that the right of sake and soke was understood to convey the right to hold a *hallmoot*—a hall-assembly—in which all cases involving revenues that pertained to the privileged lord were judged, but there is no evidence to demonstrate that this was common or even possible before 1066.

[86] Leis Wl 2:4; ECf 22:4.

[87] This is also visible in Domesday entries which explain that the recipient of fines paid by offenders depended on whether they were caught and charged at the time, or managed to escape and were charged later: Guildford and (DB i. 30r), Southwark (DB i. 32r), Wallingford (DB i. 56v). One passage for Oxfordshire (DB i. 154v) shows that anyone who managed to kill an outlaw was entitled to keep some or all of his goods, and a passage dealing with the forfeitures of executed thieves in Dunwich, Suffolk (DB ii. 312r-v, discussed below, pp. 346–7) suggests that the location where the thief was captured was a crucial issue. A passage for Dover (DB i. 1r) may be trying to deny the applicability of

Pre-Conquest evidence on the nature of sake and soke is less explicit. It is clear from the way these words are used that they represent the basic standard package of legal revenues: we find writs granting other rights along with sake and soke, but these extra privileges are never granted on their own. If a lord was to have any legal privileges at all, he had to have sake and soke.[88] There is some good evidence for the range of sake and soke in a manuscript of Cnut's laws dating from just after, or possibly just before, 1066.[89] This manuscript contains revisions to three passages in II Cnut which explain that the proper recipient of the revenues was the lord with sake and soke.[90] Most significantly, the passage ordering that men who commit robbery (*reaflac*) forfeit their wergild to the king is amended so that the recipient of the wergild is either the king or 'he who has soke'.[91] As Julius Goebel was the first to note, these three examples—all of which concern offences which appear for the first time in Cnut's code—seem to demonstrate that the right of soke-holding lords to receive all *wite*s and wergild forfeitures was so well entrenched that they could legitimately claim revenues even from newly established offences that were punished in these ways.[92]

Legal historians usually assume that sake and soke amounted to the right to receive the revenues from all cases within the 'jurisdiction of the hundred', as distinct from those cases which were judged in shire assemblies.[93] Underlying this assumption is the seemingly common-sense notion that the most serious offences, particularly those punishable by death, naturally require weightier consideration than more trifling matters and are therefore very unlikely to have been within the competence of the lowliest local assemblies. There is a problem, however: there is no evidence whatsoever that this was a contemporary assumption. In fact, our texts show no concern to define which assembly was the appropriate venue for any given offence, which in itself is strong evidence that this was not an important part of the way contemporaries thought.[94] Indeed, the apparent association between the archaeology of execution and hundredal geography would seem to prove that cases involving execution were not restricted to shire assemblies.[95] There are

---

this principle in a specific case: it states that even if offenders against the king's protection of major roads fled without being apprehended, the king's *minister* would pursue him and extract the appropriate fine.

[88] See Goebel, *Felony and Misdemeanor*, pp. 371–2; Hudson, *Oxford History*, p. 59; Harmer, *Writs*, pp. 74–6.

[89] The manuscript is that labelled 'G', in Felix Liebermann, ed., *Die Gesetze der Angelsachsen*, 3 vols. (Halle, 1898–916), i. pp. 278–370. It is discussed in detail in Patrick Wormald, *The Making of English Law: King Alfred to the Twelfth Century*, vol. 1: *Legislation and Its Limits* (Oxford, 1999), pp. 224–8.

[90] II Cn 37, 63, 73:1 (G only).   [91] II Cn 63 (G only).

[92] Goebel, *Felony and Misdemeanor*, pp. 371–2.

[93] Hudson, *Oxford History*, pp. 49, 59, 64–5; Wormald, *Lordship and Justice*, p. 318.

[94] The very limited information we have on relations between assemblies is discussed in Hudson, *Oxford History*, pp. 64–5.

[95] Andrew Reynolds, *Anglo-Saxon Deviant Burial Customs* (Oxford, 2009), pp. 155–6, 240–4. It is, of course, possible that offenders were sentenced by shire assemblies and then sent back to their hundreds for execution, but it seems far more sensible to accept the more obvious explanation—hundred assemblies did sometimes sentence people to death—than to resort to this sort of elaborate speculation. Hudson, *Oxford History*, p. 49, n. 47, suggests that the execution of thieves may have been part of the jurisdiction of the hundred because grants of 'sake and soke, *toll* and *team*, and *infangenþeof*'

other ways of defining the business of an assembly than through rules governing which types of offence they are allowed to judge. A possible scenario is that the cases which came to a shire assembly were those relevant to the community of aristocrats who attended it, most of whom were probably *landhlafords* themselves. The different assemblies may, in other words, have dealt with different social strata rather than with different offences. Given that there is no evidence that particular offences were associated with particular assemblies, and given that there are other ways we might imagine the business of assemblies being divided, it is safest to avoid assuming that specific types of legal revenue were clearly linked to hundred or shire assemblies in this period.[96]

The rights of lords entitled to sake and soke thus look very similar in many respects to the rights of *landhlafords* in the tenth century. Indeed, there can be little doubt that sake and soke is the direct successor to the standard grants of royal rights conveyed to privileged lords since the seventh century. We can even, as was noted in Chapter 3, see this in the other ways that the term soke is used in this period, which reveal associations with food renders and labour services that are most plausibly understood as the direct descendants of earlier non-legal royal rights.[97] The extent to which legal and non-legal royal revenues continued to be understood as part of a single package in the eleventh century is difficult to assess: the broader language of 'soke' is more prominent in some regions than others, and 'sake and soke' seems mostly to be used to refer to legal revenues alone. But in the present context these are side issues. The crucial point here is that sake and soke represents the standard package of legal revenues enjoyed by eleventh-century lords, and that it differs from the standard package of legal revenues enjoyed by their tenth-century and earlier predecessors in the number of rights excluded from it. That is, our eleventh-century evidence shows that there were several important legal revenues that were understood to be separate from sake and soke, whereas our earlier evidence suggests nothing of the sort. This is an important shift: we need to ask what these exclusions meant and how they arose. All the same, this should not be allowed to create the impression that sake and soke was a mere rump of the privileges which *landhlafords* of earlier centuries enjoyed. The right to receive all *wites* and wergild forfeitures from an area was no small thing, especially if it was accompanied by valuable economic rights encompassing annual dues and labour services. Sake and soke tends to be written off in modern scholarship as a set of minor rights, which even collectively amounted to nothing of any great consequence.[98] This is misleading.

---

may have represented the jurisdiction of the hundred, while other offences punished by the death penalty belonged to the shire. This argument is circular, however, and predicated on the assumption that different assemblies dealt with distinct bodies of offences, which Hudson subsequently shows to be ill-founded (pp. 64–5).

[96] Kennedy, 'Disputes about *bocland*', draws essentially this conclusion from an examination of case narratives relating to land held by charter.

[97] See Chapter 3, p. 134.

[98] See, in particular, Hurnard, 'Anglo-Norman Franchises', p. 290 ('[sake and soke, even in conjunction with several other rights] did not convey any high criminal jurisdiction, but only the

Toll and *Team*

The most common addition to sake and soke in eleventh-century writs is '*toll* and *team*'. Like sake and soke, these two terms come as a pair, but *toll* and *team* are different in that they are distinct rights. The right of *toll*, though doubtless highly valued by its recipients, is not of great concern to us because it is an economic privilege with no direct link to the punishment of wrongdoing: the right to receive tolls associated with trade, probably mainly at markets.[99] *Team*, however, is important. It seems to convey the right to take the profits associated with the procedure of 'vouching to warranty', which was discussed in detail in Chapter 6. Someone charged with possessing stolen goods could clear himself of liability by swearing that he bought them in good faith from someone else, a process known to legal historians as 'vouching' this third party 'to warranty'. This procedure, if successfully completed, transferred the charge to the seller, who then either had to prove he owned the goods in question or to vouch another person to warranty.[100] The profits that arose from vouching to warranty were most probably the fines paid when the process reached its conclusion: that is, primarily, fines paid for theft, but perhaps also fines paid by men who falsely accused others of possessing stolen property.[101]

The revenues conveyed by *team* may well have been significant. The procedure could not be used by thieves caught in the act but any later accusation of theft or of possessing stolen property could result in the defendant attempting to vouch someone else to warranty. In any case where the accused genuinely had bought the allegedly stolen goods the procedure would naturally have been used. But it may well also have been common in situations where the person accused of possessing stolen goods was in fact the thief. As was discussed in Chapter 6, thieves had good reason to try to deflect accusations by falsely vouching someone else to warranty, claiming to have bought the stolen goods in an unwitnessed transaction and thus casting as much doubt as possible on their own guilt. Edgar's laws on witnessing transactions and informing neighbours of purchases were probably an attempt to address this problem.[102] We have no statistics, of course, but it seems likely that the *team* procedure was commonplace in theft cases. Indeed, it may even be that the

---

right to deal with minor offences, such as medleys, assaults and wounding'), 310 ('the modest jurisdiction conveyed by *sac* and *soc*'); Wormald, 'Lordship and Justice', p. 318 ('minor pleas which alone could be heard at this level', 'the lowest hundredal level of jurisdiction'). Hudson, *Oxford History*, follows Hurnard and Wormald but adopts more cautious language (e.g., p. 59: 'Most probably, the offences covered simply by sake and soke were those within the jurisdiction of the hundred').

[99] Goebel, *Felony and Misdemeanor*, pp. 369–70; Hudson, *Oxford History*, p. 59; Harmer, *Writs*, pp. 76–7.

[100] Chapter 6, pp. 270–1. Hudson, *Oxford History*, pp. 155–9, provides a very useful discussion.

[101] Hudson, *Oxford History*, p. 59; Goebel, *Felony and Misdemeanor*, pp. 370–1. This definition is essentially that provided in ECf 22:3. Harmer, *Writs*, p. 77, speculates that *team* conveyed the right to receive the fees paid for the warranty procedure, but it should be noted that there is no evidence for the existence of such fees (the absence in ECf 22:3 is particularly telling). Fines for false accusation seem to be implied by II Atr 9:1. The reference to *æftergild* in II Cn 24 is obscure, but seems most likely to refer to compensation to the owner of the goods (see Hudson, *Oxford History*, pp. 158–9).

[102] Chapter 6, pp. 272–3.

majority of thieves who were fined rather than executed were convicted as a result of failing in it (either after being vouched to warranty themselves, or after trying unsuccessfully to transfer an accusation to someone else). A lord who had sake and soke but not *team* probably lacked the right to receive quite significant and relatively frequently occurring revenues: perhaps the majority of fines for theft paid by people who lived on their land.

The most important point to note about the revenues arising from vouching to warranty is that before our first references to *team* in writs from Cnut's reign there is nothing to indicate that they were in any way special. There is no reason to suspect that fines for theft which arose as a result of *team* procedures were treated any differently to fines for theft that arose when accused thieves made no attempt to defend themselves in this way. (Such cases must have taken place but it is possible that they were relatively rare.) The general rule for fines for theft was that they belonged to *landhlafords* just as all other fines did: Æthelred's laws explain that when a thief forfeited his wergild it belonged to the lord who was 'worthy of his fines'.[103] Our one discussion of vouching to warranty which mentions the fate of the fines associated with it appears in Cnut's laws, which may here (as elsewhere) be reproducing a tenth-century text. All it says, however, is that the fine for theft is to go to 'he who has the right to it'.[104] This is unhelpfully ambiguous. In a tenth-century context this would be a perfectly normal way of referring to the *landhlaford* and it is likely that these were originally tenth-century words, but given they appear under Cnut we cannot be wholly confident in such a reading.

In short, the laws provide several circumstantial discussions of *team* procedure, none of which provide any reason to suspect that it was anything more than a method for claiming stolen property and identifying thieves. On the basis of these texts alone one could only reasonably conclude that when vouching to warranty resulted in a fine being imposed, the offender paid this fine to his *landhlaford* just as he paid all other fines to his *landhlaford*. It may be significant that none of the laws' discussions of *team* procedure can securely be dated any later than Edgar's reign: the relatively brief passage in Cnut's laws is probably a version of an earlier text, as was

---

[103] I Atr 1:5–1:7.

[104] II Cn 24:1. It is well established that Cnut's code is a compendium of earlier legislative enactments, and that it is likely that some passages whose sources cannot be identified derived from lost earlier texts (see Chapter 4, p. 165). There are two reasons for thinking this is one such passage. First, the lack of reference to hundreds seems odd in the context of a law concerned with witnessing transactions, as hundreds were central to the laws on this subject issued under Edgar. Second, it includes a rather obscure statement that the process of vouching can take place three times but that on the fourth occasion 'he shall own it or give it to he who owns it'. It is difficult to be sure what this means, but the discussion of vouching to warranty appended to the peace treaty known as II Æthelred may be relevant. It states that the old rule used to be that the vouching to warranty took place on three occasions in the location where the initial accusation was made, but transferred to a new location on its fourth iteration. Recently, however, this had been abolished: the process was now always to take place where the original accusation was made (II Atr 9). The passage in Cnut may, albeit very obscurely, be an allusion to this original rule which had subsequently been abolished. Unfortunately the passage appended to II Æthelred is no easier to date, but it is probable that it too was composed before the establishment of the hundredal system (see below, p. 328, n. 105). If Cnut's laws are reproducing a lost earlier text on vouching to warranty, then, it is most likely to date from before Edgar's reign.

just noted, and the same can be said for the detailed discussion appended to the peace treaty known as II Æthelred.[105] Our first evidence for revenues associated with vouching to warranty belonging to a distinct category appears in Cnut's reign, in writ and lease references to *toll* and *team*.[106] I would suggest that we take this discrepancy between mid tenth- and early eleventh-century evidence seriously, and accept that it could indicate a significant change in the way these revenues were treated in the decades either side of the millennium.

This raises an important question: if revenues from *team* procedures had not been accorded any special treatment in the tenth century, why would this suddenly have changed? To answer this question we need to think through what that procedure involved. Two points in particular need to be noted. First, vouching to warranty could be a complex and arduous process, involving long chains tracing the passage of potentially stolen goods through multiple transactions. One law expresses concern about the demands placed on innocent parties by a procedure which could require them to traverse not just several hundreds but multiple shires in search of warrantors.[107] Reclaiming stolen goods and bringing thieves to justice through this procedure was not necessarily an easy business for a litigant. Second, it must be significant that the privilege of *team* always appears in writs in combination with *toll*. This suggests that the process of vouching to warranty came to be so closely associated with the right to hold a market that the two were rarely, if ever, separated. As Frank Stenton astutely observed, warranty chains were likely to involve transactions where tolls were taken, and the person who took the toll for any given transaction was its ideal witness.[108] It is perhaps likely that sales at markets involving tolls became more and more the norm as urbanization took off in the late tenth and eleventh centuries. This, however, is only to say that *team* procedures were increasingly likely to involve transactions in urban centres: it does not explain why the association with the privilege of *toll* should have become so strong.

A plausible hypothesis that brings together these two considerations is that *team* procedures had a strong tendency to bring claimants into urban or commercial centres, as they sought to track down witnesses to transactions that had supposedly

---

[105] II Atr 8–9:4. This discussion's lack of any allusion to the elaborate rules on witnessing in IV Edgar may imply it was composed before that text, and the lack of any reference to hundreds in spite of many good opportunities to mention them would fit with a date, at the latest, at the beginning of Edgar's reign. Wormald suggests this passage may originally have been a counterpart to IV Edgar, but the lack of any reference to the rules declared in that code to pertain to the entirety of England suggests otherwise, and the similarities of vocabulary he identifies are far from conclusive. See Wormald, *Making*, p. 321, 369–70.

[106] *Toll* and *team* are notably absent from S 986, a writ from Cnut to Christ Church, Canterbury, of 1020 which is otherwise comprehensive in the rights it grants (sake and soke, *hamsocn*, *griðbryce*, *forsteal*, *infangenþeof*, *flymenafyrmþ*). They are, however, present in S 1423, a Worcester lease dating 1016–1023. According to Harmer, *Writs*, p. 78, the earliest datable writ containing *toll* and *team* is S 992, which (if genuine) comes from 1033–5; its authenticity is uncertain, however.

[107] II Atr 8:3–9.

[108] F. M. Stenton, *Anglo-Saxon England* (3rd edn, Oxford, 1971), p. 498 (but note that Stenton's implicit assumption that all cattle sales were subject to tolls, wherever they took place, would be impossible to prove).

taken place at markets. This would have brought men who needed help in the difficult business of recovering their stolen property into contact with the key subordinates of sheriffs: *burh-* or *port-*reeves. It is possible that such reeves were prone to taking over *team* procedures which came to their attention, using their own resources (or those at the disposal of their sheriffs) to help track down warrantors. Their main reason for doing this would have been so that they could claim the fine that was paid when the process came to an end. As we have seen, tenth-century laws on communal rights to receive revenues suggest a basic principle that people who played an instrumental role in catching offenders be entitled to half the revenues associated with punishing them. We could perhaps speculate that sheriffs and their subordinates attempted to claim revenues from *team* cases on this basis, perhaps even initially confining their demands to half the fine and only later moving up to insistence on full payment. Æthelred's Wantage code—a set of laws probably issued in 997 intended for the area of the Danelaw known as 'the Five Boroughs'[109]—orders that *team* take place in the king's *burhs*.[110] This is a clear attempt to force *team* procedures into locations controlled by royal reeves, and could be taken as a sign that the process suggested here was already well underway, at least in some places, by the end of the tenth century. However, the fact that the privilege of *toll* and *team* was relatively widely held suggests that many lords were able to resist this process, successfully asserting their traditional right to receive fines paid by thieves. This working hypothesis for the privilege of *team*, then, involves only relatively minor *landhlafords* falling victim to predatory royal reeves.

Infangenþeof

The next most common legal right conveyed by eleventh-century writs is *infangenþeof*. The term literally means something like 'in-seized-thief', and post-Conquest evidence confirms what would, in any case, have been the most plausible reading: that it relates specifically to thieves captured in circumstances where their guilt was undeniable.[111] Modern historians have usually interpreted this right in jurisdictional terms. The most recent, and most authoritative, attempt at a defin-ition is John Hudson's: 'the right to summary trial and execution of thieves taken in the act or very soon after'.[112] This may well be how the term was interpreted in the twelfth century but, as Goebel pointed out, it makes little sense when set alongside Anglo-Saxon evidence.[113] If it were accurate, it would imply that the only people entitled to execute thieves were royal officials and those lords privileged with a grant of *infangenþeof*; anyone else who killed a thief who had been caught in the act would presumably be committing an offence. Such an interpretation is not con-sistent with the laws, which provide no evidence for any restriction on the right to

---

[109] On the date, see Keynes, *Diplomas*, pp. 196–7; Wormald, *Making*, pp. 328–9.
[110] III Atr 6:1.
[111] ASD s.v. 'infangenþeof'; DOE s.vv. 'ge-fangen', 'fon'. See ECf 22:4.
[112] Hudson, *Oxford History*, p. 59. See also Hurnard, 'Anglo-Norman Franchises', p. 292, n. 1; Stenton, *Anglo-Saxon England*, p. 498.
[113] Goebel, *Felony and Misdemeanor*, pp. 367–8.

kill thieves in these circumstances. On the contrary, they consistently urge men who came upon thieves in such compromising positions to kill them on the spot. Æthelstan's Grately code, for instance, threatens with wergild forfeiture anyone who failed in this duty by sparing a thief.[114] The London *friŏ*-guild's response to this royal initiative makes the situation even clearer: 'he who was before others in killing a thief should be the better off by 12 pence from the money of us all for the deed and for the enterprise.'[115] As Goebel put it, 'the right to hang is still a common right, now indeed a common duty.'[116] Moreover, it was potentially a rather dangerous duty, both because the thief might fight and because his family might seek vengeance. Those brave enough to undertake it were worthy of praise and financial reward. The notion that someone might solicit a royal grant entitling him to kill all the thieves caught in a given area, and expressly prohibiting others from doing so, would almost certainly not have made sense to the men of the London *friŏ*-guild. They may even have found it amusing.

They would, however, have had no difficulty understanding the value of the right to receive the possessions forfeited by thieves killed in this way, and this is clearly what was conveyed by *infangenþeof*. (This element of the right has never been disputed: the disagreement has been about whether *infangenþeof* conveyed both jurisdiction and the right to receive forfeited goods, or just the right to receive forfeited goods.) Fortunately, the fate of the goods forfeited by slain thieves is a subject on which tenth-century laws are perfectly explicit, as we have seen. The *Hundred Ordinance* provides the most detail. The men who pursue and slay a thief caught in the act are to seize all he has, and once the thief's victim has been recompensed for his loss the remaining property (saving any slaves) is to be divided: half to the hundred, half to the *hlaford* (who also gets the slaves).[117] The clear implication here, supported by a number of parallel texts, is that the king has no right to receive such forfeitures except in areas where he happens to be the *landhlaford*.[118] The emergence of *infangenþeof* in writs from Cnut's reign must, therefore, reflect a significant alteration to tenth-century realities: kings had somehow asserted that the goods forfeited by slain thieves belonged to them, and were only to be enjoyed by lords if they could show evidence that they legitimately held the right of *infangenþeof*.[119]

---

[114] II As 1:1.   [115] VI As 7.

[116] Goebel, *Felony and Misdemeanor*, p. 368. Hurnard, Anglo-Norman Franchises', p. 292, n. 1, briskly dismisses Goebel's argument: 'it does not appear that anyone could hang a handhaving thief: probably only the man who took him in the act could do so, and then only if he resisted arrest'. This is no more than Hurnard's opinion of what is plausible; she makes no reference to any evidence in support of her claim, and it is difficult to imagine to what pre-1066 source she might have resorted had she tried.

[117] Hu 2:1.   [118] II As 20:4; III Eg 7:1 (repeated in II Cn 25:1).

[119] Cf. Goebel, *Felony and Misdemeanor*, p. 368, n. 108. Because it did not occur to Goebel that the tenth-century realities represented by the laws might differ from the eleventh-century realities implicit in writs, he was forced to hypothesize that the hundred's half of the slain thief's goods specified in Hu 2:1 was not, in fact, due to the men of the hundred but actually belonged to the king. (This reading is unsustainable, as the analogy with II As 20:4 puts beyond doubt: see Wormald, 'Lordship and Justice', p. 329.) On this basis he argued that *infangenþeof* conveyed the right to only half the goods forfeited by slain thieves, the other half belonging to the *landhlaford*. One Domesday passage offers superficial

The existence of a major shift between the tenth and eleventh centuries with respect to this particular type of legal revenue—the forfeited property of slain thieves—is thus beyond doubt. A plausible explanation for this shift might be that, rather like vouching to warranty, killing thieves was a task which most people were not enthusiastic about undertaking themselves. (We can infer as much from the lengths to which the laws go to threaten, bribe, and cajole them into undertaking it.)[120] It would be understandable if most men did not find the grisly and sinful business of taking someone else's life appealing in the first place, and the prospect of incurring the enmity of a thief's family probably also provided a strong disincentive in some cases.[121] When people did stumble upon thieves they may well have preferred not to kill them but, if possible, to capture them and hand them over to someone powerful enough not to be concerned about possible reprisals. The task of executing people may thus often have fallen to powerful figures by default rather than by right. Sheriffs and their subordinates had good reason to step into this role, taking responsibility for the execution of thieves on the understanding that doing so would allow them to claim some of the revenues associated with these cases. As with *team*, we might even imagine that sheriffs' claims started off reasonable—perhaps as a demand for the half of the forfeited goods that would have gone to the community if they had collectively undertaken the work of enforcement—and grew from there.[122] *Infangenþeof* is less common a privilege than *toll* and *team*, but still fairly widespread: the *Leges Henrici Primi* assume that all archbishops, bishops, earls, and 'other powerful men' (*alia potestates*) held all three rights over their own lands.[123] This suggests that more powerful privileged lords found it relatively easy to resist this sort of royal encroachment on their traditional rights.

An early tenth-century source may even offer some insight into this process: the regulations of the London *frið*-guild, which were composed in Æthelstan's reign.

support to this idea: in Dover (DB i. 1r), it is stated, the king received half the forfeited goods of executed thieves; the recipient of the other half is left unclear. Analogous passages, however, suggest that the intended recipient is the thief's family; in Nottinghamshire and Derbyshire, for instance, we are told that when thegns who have sake and soke forfeit their land and goods, one half of each is split between king and earl, the other half belonging to the thegn's wife and heirs (DB. i. 280v). The only feature that ever recommended Goebel's interpretation on this issue—the reason for his alighting upon it in the first place—was the fact that it reconciles tenth- and eleventh-century evidence for the treatment of the forfeitures of slain thieves. If we accept that the differences in the evidence may indicate change between the two periods this feature loses its only claim to merit.

[120] See Chapter 3, pp. 153–6.

[121] Prohibitions on avenging slain thieves show that law-makers identified this as a problem: Ine 28, 35; II As 6:2–6:3, 20:7; VI As 1:5; III Em 2.

[122] The fate of goods forfeited by executed offenders other than thieves is not very clear. It is possible that the right of *infangenþeof* applied by analogy to, for instance, forfeitures of men slain because they were untrustworthy, would not attend assemblies and could not find sureties: they may not have been caught in the act and slain for it but these men were probably killed, in effect, because they were thought to be thieves. For earlier laws on this, see II As 20–20:6; III Eg 7–7:1. I Atr 4–4:1 may imply that the sheriffs were increasingly taking responsibility for enforcement action against these figures. The lack of any explanation of what happens to the slain man's goods in this passage would be consistent with the notion that the right to these revenues was not wholly clear: the old rules still had some validity, perhaps, but so too did the claims of sheriffs.

[123] Hn 20:2. ECf 21:1 also treats these rights as a common package.

This text provides an explicit discussion of the differing fate of the goods forfeited by thieves slain in communal enforcement expeditions depending on whether their *landhlaford* was the king or some other lord. On land where the king is *landhlaford* the standard rule, familiar from other tenth-century sources, applies: the king receives half the property forfeited by the thief, the other half belonging to the fellowship (*ferscipe*) which had pursued and killed him. When the pursuit involves a thief who lives in an area belonging to another *landhlaford*, however, the king's half does not transfer to the *landhlaford* as we would expect; rather, he retains it and the fellowship's half is subdivided so that they and the *landhlaford* each receive a quarter of the forfeited property.[124] At first sight this is puzzling: this London text contradicts what seems to be the standard rule, freely acknowledged by kings themselves in their legislation, that *landhlaford*s were entitled to whatever forfeitures the king was entitled to receive in such cases.[125] The London *frið*-guild's regulations seem to be claiming on the king's behalf revenues which in normal circumstances would have belonged to the *landhlaford* and the communal enforcement party. A plausible way of explaining this is to attribute it to the influence of the king's *burh*-reeve for London, perhaps the most powerful royal reeve of his day and probably, therefore, the figure from this period who most closely resembled an early eleventh-century sheriff. He, certainly, would have been the one who collected the king's share of the slain thief's goods in this scenario, and he therefore had a clear motive for trying to maximize it. He also had the opportunity; we have good reason to think that he was involved in producing the *frið*-guild's regulations: the text identifies itself with 'the bishops and reeves who belong to London'.[126] This may, then, be early and localized evidence of exactly the sort of process that, it is here suggested, occurred on a larger scale in the decades around the year 1000, driven by revenue-hungry sheriffs.

The *Gerihta*

Writs conveying rights beyond sake and soke, *toll* and *team*, and *infangenþeof* are relatively rare.[127] When they do occur, the rights they mention are precisely those which are listed in Cnut's laws as 'the rights (*gerihta*) which the king possesses over all men . . . unless he wishes to honour anyone further'.[128] In the literature they are often termed the 'reserved pleas', but here I will follow Goebel in adopting the contemporary label and refer to them as the *gerihta*.[129] Chief among these in areas under English law are the three major royal protections of *hamsocn*, *mundbryce*, and

---

[124] VI As 1:1.   [125] Hu 2:1; III Eg 7:1; II Cn 25:1.   [126] VI As 1.

[127] See T. B. Lambert, 'Royal Protections and Private Justice: A reassessment of Cnut's "Reserved Pleas"', in Jurasinski, Oliver, and Rabin, eds., *English Law Before Magna Carta*, pp. 157–75 at 172.

[128] II Cn 12–15.

[129] Goebel, *Felony and Misdemeanor*, p. 365. 'Reserved pleas' ultimately derives from Maitland, *Domesday Book and Beyond*, p. 283, but as the term reflects his assumption that jurisdiction over certain offences had always been reserved to the king, and only began to be ceded to aristocrats under Cnut's immediate predecessors, it seems best to abandon it.

forsteal.[130] (In the Danelaw there is no sign of *forsteal* and the term *griðbryce* is substituted for *mundbryce*.)[131] The king's protections, as we have seen, seem to have been tenth-century innovations: Edmund, in particular, may have played a significant role in their establishment. As was noted above, our only tenth-century evidence for their treatment comes in his laws, which demand that people who commit *mundbryce* and *hamsocn* forfeit their lives and all they possess, but do not make it clear who was meant to receive the forfeited goods. Eleventh-century texts reveal a change in the way these offences were penalized. Anyone who commits *hamsocn*, *mundbryce*, or *forsteal* is to pay the king £5.[132] This shift would make sense as part of an attempt to assert the king's particular ownership of these rights. £5 was not a sum associated with any of the legal revenues traditionally collected by *landhlafords*.[133] It did, however, have strong royal associations: it was understood as the traditional compensation payable for breaching the king's protection.[134] The point of changing the penalty for these offences may have been to characterize the revenues associated with them as compensations for breach of protection. That is, the change could be read as a conscious attempt to assert their status as

---

[130] II Cn 12, 14.   [131] II Cn 15.

[132] Latin renderings of *hamsocn*, *forsteal*, and probably *mundbryce* are associated with £5 in IV Atr 4–4:1, though on this text see Chapter 4, p. 187, n. 102. *Hamsocn* is explicitly linked to £5 in II Cn 62, *mundbryce* in VIII Atr 5:1 and I Cn 3:2. That *forsteal* is grouped with these two in II Cn 12 would suggest that their penalties were the same (even if we were to discount IV Atr 4–4:1), and post-Conquest sources tend to confirm this. The *Leges Henrici Primi* are perfectly explicit: Hn 12:2, 35:2, 79:4, 80:2. Earlier, Domesday Book repeatedly makes reference to these three offences. Throughout most of the area under English law the association with £5 is reasonably consistent: records of customs for Hereford (DB i. 179r), Shrewsbury (DB i. 252r), Worcester (DB i. 172r), and parts of Kent (DB i. 1r) specify £5 (100 Norman shillings) as the appropriate penalty for all three. (In Kent it is stated that the penalty for *griðbryce* is £8, but this Kentish anomaly is what we would anticipate on the basis of I Cn 3:2: £5 for the king and £3 for the archbishop.) Some entries order forfeiture of life and property in certain circumstances, but these can probably be reconciled with Anglo-Saxon pronouncements. Customs for Wallingford (DB i. 56v) and Oxfordshire (DB i. 154v) order that those who kill in breach of the king's peace forfeit their lives, but this is exactly what we would expect for those who committed homicide in breach the peace granted by the king's own hand (see I Cn 2:1; Hn 79:3–79:4) and the Oxfordshire entry is careful to make clear that this is indeed the type of royal protection under discussion. The Wallingford passage is more ambiguous on the source of protection but it is clear about the type of breach being a killing. The same Oxfordshire passage distinguishes between killing someone in their own house (forfeiture of life and limb) and killing or otherwise harming people in houses generally (£5). This could correspond to the otherwise obscure distinction between the *hamsocn* (£5) and *husbryce* (unemendable) in II Cn 62 and 64. The only clear exceptions to the general association of royal protections with £5 appear in the customs listed for Chester (DB i. 262v) and the area between the Ribble and the Mersey (DB i. 269v): figures of 20 and 40 shillings (£1 and £2) are cited (though £5 also appears in the Chester entry). In Danelaw areas, specifically York (DB i. 298v), Nottingham (DB i. 280v), and Lincoln (DB i. 336v), the only prominent protection is breach of the king's peace. There the sums payable are much larger: £144 divided between eighteen 'hundreds' of £8 (see Lambert, 'Protection Feud and Royal Power', pp. 85–6, 137–9).

[133] The fines which *landhlafords* had the right to collect were *wites*—to a maximum value of 120 shillings—and wergild forfeitures, presumably usually the standard non-noble wergild of 200 shillings. £5 was the equivalent of 240 West Saxon shillings. Edgar's law that nobody should forfeit more than his own wergild as a fine for an amendable offence suggests that this sum was not commonly extracted in this period, or at least not from non-noble offenders. In practice all these sums must have been negotiable (see Chapter 6, pp. 238–9); the values probably tell us more about how offences were categorized than how much was actually paid.

[134] See Chapters 2 and 4, pp. 86–7, 183–90.

revenues pertaining personally to the king, clearly distinct from the punitive fines and forfeitures to which *landhlafords* were traditionally entitled.

A similar case can be made for *flymenafyrmþ*, the fine for harbouring fugitives, another of the *gerihta* in Wessex and Mercia (though perhaps not in the Danelaw).[135] The offence itself had been part of West Saxon law since the seventh century: Ine orders those accused of *flymenafyrmþ* to clear themselves by an oath equivalent to their own wergild or to forfeit that wergild.[136] The same penalty seems to have been standard in tenth-century laws. Æthelstan, for instance, in the context of a law insisting that all men be found lords, threatens with wergild forfeiture those who harbour men who flee rather than submit to this.[137] When discussing fugitives with whom kings wished to deal particularly severely, we sometimes find laws demanding those who harboured them share their fate, forfeiting their lives and all their possessions.[138] We do not, however, find any solid indication that these revenues were specifically reserved to the king in the tenth century. The first sign of any specific royal interest in fugitives is the passage in Cnut's laws on the *gerihta*, in which the reservation of *flymenafyrmþ* is accompanied by a statement that only the king could grant fugitives *frið* ('peace'), and a change in the sum demanded from offenders to £5.[139] The novel use of this figure should probably be interpreted in the same way here as for the protections just discussed: as part of an attempt to imbue revenues associated with fugitives with a particularly royal character.

In Cnut's laws, then, we find two simultaneous departures: not only does the king for the first time explicitly lay claim to revenues from the three main protections and from *flymenafyrmþ*, the sums demanded from offenders are also adjusted in such a way as to differentiate them—again, for the first time—from the legal revenues to which *landhlafords* were entitled.[140] This is highly suggestive: there is no solid

---

[135] II Cn 12–14. The parallel passage for the Danelaw (II Cn 15a) is vague: those who harbour fugitives are to make amends 'as the law was before'. The term comes from *flyma*, meaning 'fugitive', and *fyrmþ* which derives from the verb *feormian*, 'to maintain' particularly in the sense of providing with food. See DOE s.vv. 'flyma', 'fyrmþ, feormþ', 'feormian'.

[136] Ine 30.   [137] II As 2–2:2. II As 20:8 is the same. II Ew 4 is likely to refer back to Ine 30.

[138] Af 4–4:1 probably relates specifically to the offence of harbouring the king's political enemies. The various rules on the offence of harbouring people banished from their native districts by the king's personal order are presented as an unusually severe measure justified by a particularly serious problem (IV As 3–3:2; V As Prol 1- Prol 3.). IV As 6:3, on those who harbour thieves, is likewise clearly an attempt to increase the standard punishment. II Em 1:2 threatens men who harbour kinsmen they had formally abandoned with the king's enmity and forfeiture of all property.

[139] II Cn 13–13:2. The term used for fugitive here is *utlaga*, 'outlaw', a Scandinavianism that seems to have been understood as an equivalent to the earlier *flyma*. II Cn 66–66:1, which discusses fugitives in conjunction with excommunicates, seems to imply the old penalties remained in force, but this is probably because it is based on earlier laws: II Cn 66:1 seems to represent VIII Atr 42, and the fact that it seems to contradict the passage immediately preceding it (II Cn 66) may indicate that this other passage derived from a different earlier text which is now lost.

[140] On the significance of a different departure, the adoption of the Scandinavian loan-word *utlah* (outlaw) and its eventual displacement of *flyma*, a process which began in the late tenth century, see Elisabeth van Houts, 'The Vocabulary of Exile and Outlawry in the North Sea Area around the First Millennium', in Laura Napran and Elisabeth van Houts, eds., *Exile in the Middle Ages: Selected Proceedings from the International Medieval Congress, University of Leeds, 8–11 July 2002* (Turnhout, 2004), pp. 13–28.

evidence that kings had ever stressed their right to these revenues before this point, yet here we find a concerted effort to claim exclusive ownership.[141] A plausible interpretation is that it had previously been normal for *landhlafords* to collect the fines and forfeitures of those who harboured fugitives as well as the forfeited goods of those who committed *hamsocn*, *mundbryce*, and *forsteal* (if this last offence existed before the eleventh). In the absence of sheriffs, kings lacked the means to collect these revenues from within the land granted to *landhlafords* on a routine basis, so even if they had been inclined to claim them (which we have no reason to suspect) it may not have been practical for them to do so.[142] The advent of the sheriff presented kings with new opportunities: there was now a network of royal reeves capable of collecting such revenues. It thus made sense for kings to assert their ownership of any revenues that could plausibly be presented as royal prerogatives, and Cnut's laws on the *gerihta* show a king doing precisely that. There was presumably little that privileged lords could do to resist the king's claims when they were asserted in so authoritative a fashion. They could petition him directly in the hope of obtaining a writ specifically granting them these rights, but the relative scarcity of surviving writs of this type probably indicates that this course of action was practical only for those with the king's personal favour.

Why claim these rights in particular? The basis of the royal claim to revenues from *hamsocn*, *mundbryce*, and *forsteal* is obvious enough: they represented breaches of the king's personal protection and the king, who was personally affronted by these offences, had a personal right to be compensated for them. The king's interest in fugitives is less direct: in theory at least, fugitives from one place had always been meant to be fugitives everywhere in the kingdom, their status was meant to be the same in all the areas ruled by the king and they therefore, in some sense, may have been understood to be connected to the king himself.[143] Here, however, we also need to take into account the practical similarities between cases involving fugitives

---

[141] The main reason for thinking that the stress laid on the king's exclusive right to offer peace to fugitives in II Cn 13 represents a novel claim, rather than the reiteration of an established one, is that there is no evidence of it before Cnut's code. There are, however, some limited positive hints that this right did not exist. Æthelstan's laws (IV As 6:1–6:2c), notably, had recognized the rights of thegns (perhaps implicitly thegns who were also *landhlafords*) and various magnates to offer protection to fugitive thieves, albeit only for limited periods, so the principle that the king alone could offer them *frið* could be read as a departure. As was noted above, p. 320, we have two examples of a late tenth-century abbot accepting payments from fugitives or their families, allowing them to return, but these are from Peterborough (S 1448a), and Cnut's laws are clear that rules about fugitives were different in the Danelaw (II Cn 15–15a). The Fonthill Letter (S 1445) seems to imply that the king had a central role both in declaring Helmstan a fugitive (*flyma*) and allowing him to return, but this need not be taken as an indication that all fugitives were treated this way. Helmstan was a *landhlaford* and the king's man; his status could account for the king's personal involvement in decisions about his fate.

[142] This reasoning, I would emphasise, applies only to cases in which kings took no direct interest. There is no reason to think kings would have struggled to extract compensation from anyone in their kingdom if they were sufficiently determined.

[143] This principle is explicitly asserted in III Atr 10 but implicit in the treatment of fugitives in all laws. For a wide-ranging discussion, see Paul Dresch, 'Outlawry, Exile and Banishment: Reflections on Community and Justice', in Fernanda Pirie and Judith Scheele, eds., *Legalism: Community and Justice* (Oxford, 2014), pp. 97–124.

and those involving vouching to warranty or the execution of thieves caught in the act. All these cases placed significant and unwelcome burdens on the men directly involved in them. The people involved in tracing fugitives, and therefore those bringing cases against people who harboured them, must frequently have had to travel significant distances to areas where they were outsiders. After the implementation of Edgar's suretyship reforms, in particular, we should probably envisage offenders' former sureties trying to hunt them down and claim back the money they had forfeited. These men must often have lacked local connections in the areas they needed to search; it would therefore make sense for them to request help from powerful local figures, and sheriffs would be the natural choice once they became commonplace. As with the execution of thieves, then, and the tracing of thieves through *team* procedures, the tracking down of fugitives (and thus the bringing of accusations of *flymenafyrmþ*) was a potentially onerous responsibility which sheriffs may well have accepted in the expectation that they could claim the revenues it generated.

There are two other fines which are mentioned as *gerihta* in Cnut's laws: *fyrdwite* and *fihtwite*, the latter of which is mentioned only for the Danelaw. *Fyrdwite*, of course, is the fine for neglect of military service, which the language of charters since the eighth century strongly suggests had traditionally been kept separate from the rights of *landhlafords*. There is therefore no mystery about its reservation here. However, its appearance in this context and its subsequent association, in some places at least, with the figure of £5 (which, again, is not previously attested for this offence) could suggest some attempt to reinforce the king's claim to it.[144] The reservation of the right to *fihtwite*—the 'fight-fine'—in the Danelaw is interesting.[145] It was argued in Chapter 2 that the king's right to receive a payment in cases of homicide originated as a right to receive compensation for breaches of the protection kings were understood to extend to their free populations, but also that Ine's laws show that right was reinterpreted in Wessex as a punitive *wite* for fighting.[146] In West Saxon law, at least, it seems that this old protection was so firmly converted into a *wite* that the right to receive it ceased to be personal to the king and became just like any other *wite*, a standard part of the package of legal revenues enjoyed by *landhlafords*. The appearance of *fihtwite* alongside two royal protections (*griðbryce* and *hamsocn*) in a list of legal revenues understood to be particularly personal to the king in the Danelaw, however, may indicate that in areas not heavily influenced by West Saxon law this transformation was less complete: that the payment demanded by kings for homicide continued to be understood as in some sense compensation for breach of royal protection and was therefore susceptible to being claimed by sheriffs.

---

[144] The £5 figure is attested in Domesday Book for Oxfordshire (DB i. 154v) and Warwick (DB i. 238r). However, customs for Worcester (DB i. 172r), Shrewsbury (DB i. 252r) and Hereford (DB i, 179r) all give a figure of 40 shillings (£2); those for Wallingford (DB i. 56v) mention land forfeiture and 50 shillings, depending on whether the man summoned made an attempt to send someone to serve in his stead. The figures given in Ine 51 are 30, 60, and 120 shillings, depending on rank.
[145] II Cn 15.   [146] Chapter 2, pp. 90–4.

The Earl's 'Third Penny'

All the legal rights discussed thus far in this section emerge into our evidence for the first time in the early years of Cnut's reign, in writs—which start to survive from that point—and in the case of the *gerihta* also in his great law code issued at Winchester in the winter of 1020–21.[147] By contrast, the final set of legal revenues we need to consider is solidly attested only in post-Conquest sources. In Domesday Book in particular there are multiple references to a tradition of dividing certain forms of revenue into thirds, with two of those thirds belonging to the king and the other to the regional earl; this earl's third is often referred to as the 'third penny'. (The term 'earl' appears to have displaced 'ealdorman' following Cnut's conquest without changing the nature of the underlying office in a discernible way.)[148] The picture presented by the Domesday evidence is not tidy but the underlying pattern is clear enough: there are two principal categories of revenue to which this customary division applied. The first is revenues from urban centres: it seems to have been the case that in many towns all revenues, whatever their nature (rents, tolls, legal fines), were divided between the king and earl in this way. The second category, which is of greater interest in this context, is a tier of rural legal revenues which Domesday sometimes refers to as 'the pleas of the shire' or 'the customs of the king and earl'.[149]

Only one explicit attempt to define the earl's third survives from the period. The text known as the *Instituta Cnuti*, composed at some point between the Norman Conquest and 1123, explains that earls are entitled to the third penny 'in vills where a market meets and in the punishment of thieves'.[150] This is so close an approximation of *toll* (customary dues associated with trade), *team* (fines paid by thieves as a result of vouching to warranty procedures), and *infangenþeof* (the right to receive the property forfeited by executed thieves) that it seems certain that these rights—wherever they were not held by a privileged lord—were included in the earl's third penny.[151] The fact that the *Instituta Cnuti* refers specifically to the punishment of theft tells against the inclusion of the more varied revenues, mostly unrelated to theft, included in both the standard package of sake and soke and the more exclusive *gerihta*. Domesday Book does seem to show that there were areas where

---

[147] On the date: Wormald, *Making*, p. 345 n. 382.

[148] Pauline Stafford, 'Ealdorman', in Michael Lapidge et al., eds., *The Wiley-Blackwell Encyclopedia of Anglo-Saxon England* (2nd edn, Chichester, 2014), pp. 156–7.

[149] Stephen Baxter, *The Earls of Mercia: Lordship and Power in Late Anglo-Saxon England* (Oxford, 2007), pp. 89–97, provides a clear recent discussion, which accepts the basic distinction between urban revenues and the pleas of the shire but draws attention to blurring of the boundaries between the two. For the terms quoted, see DB i. 238r, 336v. Much of the time, it should be noted, Domesday simply refers to people holding rights to the third pennies from particular geographical areas, presumably leaving the reader to infer that revenues being divided into thirds were those which belonged to the category of revenues customarily divided in this way.

[150] In Cn iii. 55. On dating, see Bruce O'Brien, 'The *Instituta Cnuti* and the Translation of English Law', *Anglo-Norman Studies* 25 (2003), pp. 177–98 at 184–6.

[151] Near-perfect rather than perfect because it does not take into account the possibility that some incomes from *team* derived from fines levied on parties who brought vexatious accusations (implied by II Atr 9:1), but this is a pedantic point unlikely to be of any significance.

the king shared his right to sake and soke with an earl—and it is possible that these arrangements reveal something interesting about the way ealdormen were supported in earlier centuries—but this was not the general pattern.[152] Moreover, the detailed discussion of sake and soke in the *Leges Henrici Primi* shows that these revenues were usually the exclusive property of whoever held them.[153] On the *gerihta*, Domesday shows that earls were sometimes entitled to receive thirds of specific rights but these passages only occur in the context of towns and should perhaps be understood as manifestations of the basic rule that all revenues arising within them were divided, whatever their nature.[154] Except in towns there is little reason not to take Cnut's reservation of these revenues to the king alone literally. Indeed, we might speculate that *toll*, *team*, and *infangenþeof* are absent from his list of *gerihta* precisely because they were shared with earls, the point being that the *gerihta* (all associated with the specifically royal sum of £5) belonged to the king alone, to be shared with nobody.

The origins of the earl's third penny are obscure. The plentiful Domesday evidence demonstrates that it was a well-established tradition by 1066; it is therefore safe to infer that it had existed for some years previously, but how many years is debatable. There can be no doubt of the third penny's existence in the early 1060s, of course, but on the basis of this post-Conquest evidence we cannot safely rule out an origin in the 1040s or perhaps even the early 1050s. It is often thought that the third penny's origins were much earlier than this, dating back at least to Alfred's reign and possibly beyond, but solid evidence is elusive.[155] For the urban third penny we have a number of texts which show that it was possible for the revenues of urban or commercial centres to be divided between multiple recipients; these have been cited as evidence suggestive of early roots for the third penny system but none of them mentions an earl's or ealdorman's share, or even implies its existence.[156] Nor is there any evidence for the custom of dividing

---

[152] Baxter, *Earls of Mercia*, p. 95 assembles evidence for earls taking third pennies of 'pleas of the hundred'; Williams, *World Before Domesday*, pp. 22–3, provides another helpful discussion. Because of the conventional wisdom that the rights conveyed by sake and soke represent 'the jurisdiction of the hundred', writers have tended to assume that references to third pennies from the pleas of particular hundreds refer to thirds of the revenues that would otherwise be covered by sake and soke. It is important to bear in mind a possible alternative reading. In many (but probably not all) cases it could plausibly be argued that the references to hundreds are geographical: they mean that third-penny revenues—those elsewhere referred to as the pleas of the shire or the customs of the king and earl—from these particular hundreds pertain to a particular lord or location. The Domesday evidence is complex, however, especially in the counties covered by Little Domesday (Norfolk, Suffolk, and Essex), and this is not the place to explore the viability of this interpretation in depth.

[153] For example, Hn 9:11, 19:2–19:3, 24:4.

[154] DB i. 280v shows that payments for breach of the king's peace throughout Nottinghamshire and Derbyshire were divided between the king and earl. It may well be correct to extrapolate from this to Lincolnshire and Yorkshire, where customs on this look very similar, but we cannot safely do this for the areas applying English law. For an explicit example of all urban revenues being divided, even the *gerihta*, see Chester (DB i. 262v). More usual are general statements that all customs from a particular town were split, such as that for Stafford (DB i. 246r).

[155] See Baxter, *Earls of Mercia*, pp. 89–90; Hudson, *Oxford History*, pp. 35–6.

[156] See Baxter, *Earls of Mercia*, p. 90. The earliest, S 223, issued in the late ninth century (or very early in the tenth), shows Ealdorman Æthelred of Mercia granting half the revenues of the *burh* of Worcester to the bishopric of Worcester. There is nothing in it to suggest that these revenues were

revenues specifically into thirds before the eleventh century. We find urban revenues divided into halves (under Alfred or Edward the Elder)[157] and quarters (under Edgar)[158] but our earliest reliable evidence for thirds comes from the reign of Harold Harefoot: an account of a dispute between St Augustine's and Christ Church, Canterbury, over a third of the tolls from Sandwich.[159] It is plausible that this disputed third had at one point belonged to an earl and subsequently been granted to one of the two houses, so this is our first potential hint of the existence of an urban third penny, but this speculative interpretation cannot be made to bear much weight.

The rural third penny is almost as obscure. As was noted in Chapter 3, there is one passage in Alfred's code that appears to show ealdormen collecting a fine on the king's behalf and keeping a cut for themselves. The fine in question makes most sense understood as a military offence—leaving an ealdorman's shire without his knowledge and thus denying him service as a warrior—so this may be a hint of a general expectation that ealdormen would collect military revenues on the king's behalf and be allowed to keep a portion of them.[160] We know from the terms of charters, of course, that the king's military revenues were explicitly excluded from grants to *landhlafords*. We also have one tenth-century case narrative in which an ealdorman appears to be claiming a wergild forfeiture from a convicted thief on the king's behalf. However, this thief was a holder of *bocland* and thus a *landhlaford* himself, so this too is a fine which we would not expect to find a *landhlaford* collecting.[161] A possible interpretation, then, would be that ealdormen sometimes collected on the king's behalf fines which fell outside those revenues to which *landhlafords* were entitled, and kept a cut of those fines as a reward for doing so.[162] The 'sometimes' in this sentence is important, however. We could perhaps extrapolate from Alfred's law to a general expectation that ealdormen, as regional military leaders, would oversee the collection of the king's military revenues, but such an interpretation is not viable for the punishment of *landhlafords*. When tenth-century laws envisage the king fining disobedient reeves or *landhlafords* who neglected their legal duties, the figure they expect to collect these fines is not the ealdorman but the bishop.[163] On the basis of this distinctly thin evidence it is probably safest to conclude there were not, in fact, clear rules about who should

customarily divided between king and ealdorman. The others are S 779 (Edgar grants Ely Abbey a quarter of his revenues in Cambridge), S 982 (Cnut grants two parts of tolls at Winchelsea, Sussex, to Fécamp), S 1467 (a dispute between St Augustine's and Christchurch, Canterbury, over third penny of tolls in Sandwich), and S 1158 (Edward the Confessor grants third part of tolls in Worcester to Bishop Wulfstan). The Winchelsea grant (S 982) is the most promising of these, in that Cnut's granting two parts of these revenues would be consistent with the third part belonging to the earl; however, the document is of doubtful authenticity. The royal grants of fractions of revenues from Worcester (S 1158) and Cambridge (S 779) have no obvious relevance to the question of whether the earl's third penny existed or not.

[157] S 223.   [158] S 779.   [159] S 1467.
[160] Af 37–37:1; Chapter 3, pp. 134–5.   [161] S 1447.
[162] We could perhaps speculate that the same happened for land forfeitures. It could, for example, have been the case that Ealdorman Leofwine, the beneficiary of S 892, played some part in the dispossession of Wistan recorded in it, the lands he received representing his share of the proceeds.
[163] See above, pp. 318–19; Chapter 3, p. 124, n. 50.

collect fines from *landhlafords*. Rather, we might speculate that whichever great magnate was willing to go to the effort of doing so could reasonably expect to be rewarded for his diligence with a cut of the proceeds.[164] The main conclusion to draw here, indeed, is that hints of the existence of anything resembling the late eleventh-century rural third penny are so sparse in the tenth and earlier centuries as to be virtually non-existent.

On the other hand, tenth-century laws provide a few clear indications the third penny's absence. As the *Instituta Cnuti* make clear, outside 'vills where a market meets' earls were entitled to the third penny 'in the punishment of theft'. The fate of revenues from the punishment of theft is already familiar to us from our examination of *team* and *infangenþeof*. The case for thinking that revenues from *team* began to be treated differently around the year 1000 is based primarily on silence: although vouching to warranty is discussed in detail several times in laws composed up to and including Edgar's reign, none of these discussions offers the slightest suggestion that the revenues involved were special. Our first indication of the procedure's unusual status comes in 997 (Æthelred's order in his code for the Five Boroughs that vouching to warranty take place in royal *burhs*), and the earliest direct evidence for its revenues belonging to a separate category appears under Cnut.[165] The case for *infangenþeof* is similar, except here the argument from silence is much more compelling. The division of the goods forfeited by executed thieves is far from an obscure issue in our tenth-century evidence. Several laws composed between the reigns of Æthelstan and Edgar provide explicit and sometimes highly detailed explanations of how such forfeited goods are to be divided up and shared between multiple recipients. At no point is an ealdorman mentioned. If ealdormen in fact had the right to a third of these goods, as later earls clearly did, these texts' failure even to hint at the existence of this right is extraordinary. In the context of these detailed discussions, the absence of anything resembling an earl's third constitutes strong evidence that until Edgar's reign, at least, ealdormen had no specific entitlement to the forfeitures of slain thieves.[166]

---

[164] S 883 may provide some support for this interpretation. At some point in the early 990s, the king's reeves in Buckingham and Oxford—quite possibly the sheriffs of their respective shires at this date—permitted two men who had died fighting in defence of a thief to be buried 'among the Christians'. Ealdorman Leofsige interfered, accusing the reeves of acting illegally. Why he did so is unclear but he may have been hoping to profit from the punishment of the reeves. If so, it is striking to note that there is little to suggest that the events in question took place within Leofsige's ealdordom; we cannot rule out the possibility but it is clear that Leofsige's primary responsibility was Essex. For a brief overview of Leofsige's career see Ann Williams, *Æthelred the Unready: The Ill-Counselled King* (London, 2003), pp. 62–3, 188; also, Wormald, *Papers Preparatory*, p. 161, n. 159.

[165] III Atr 6:1; S 992. See above, p. 328, n. 106.

[166] Particularly circumstantial discussions are VI As 1:1; Hu 2:1. See also III Eg 7:1; IV Eg 8:1. Because II Cn 25:1 is a restatement of III Eg 7:1 it cannot safely be taken as an indication of current practice in 1020. The absence of *toll* and *team* from S 986 (a writ in favour of Christ Church, Canterbury, which dates from the same year) is more striking in this regard. Later writs show that the same community claiming *toll* and *team*, but all the relevant writs of Edward the Confessor's reign have been tampered with, so we cannot be at all certain when this claim emerged. See Harmer, *Writs*, pp. 166–7, 172–80.

Limited though it is, our evidence thus suggests that the rural third penny 'in the punishment of thieves' described by the *Instituta Cnuti* developed at some point between Edgar's reign and, perhaps, the 1040s. This is a large window, but it centres suggestively on the period around the year 1000 which, this chapter has argued, witnessed intense competition over legal revenues. Could the third penny have emerged as a result of the same processes involving sheriffs posited here? It is certainly possible. We might speculate that when sheriffs and their subordinates were claiming revenues from the punishment of thieves—both those associated with vouching to warranty procedures and those arising from executions—they drew support from ealdormen (and later earls). Such high-powered political support could have been important in allowing sheriffs to emerge victorious from conflicts with privileged lords concerning these revenues. It would not be surprising if, in return for their support, ealdormen demanded a share of the revenues they helped secure. We do have some earlier evidence for ealdormen enforcing fines on behalf of kings and taking a cut, after all. Initially this may have been a matter of ad hoc negotiation but it would be natural if over time, and in some places, customary arrangements established themselves.

Unguided, however, this sort of process would not be likely to produce a kingdom-wide scheme as coherent as the one implied by our post-Conquest evidence. The fact that the earl's share of these revenues was standardized at a third suggests that some force was at work which led contemporaries to interpret ealdormen's and earls' exactions as part of a uniform system. Why might this have been? One possibility is that ealdormen had a long-established right to a third of the king's military revenues, so when they helped to claim new revenues their share of them was set at a third by analogy. This would neatly explain the earl's right to a third of revenues from drawn from *burh*s: because these had been military centres before they became centres of population and commerce we have some grounds on which to speculate that ealdormen had always had the right to a third of the revenues drawn from them. We might hypothesize that when ealdormen collected other revenues on their kings' behalf—such as fines owed by *landhlafords*—it was well understood that the appropriate reward for doing so was a third of those revenues. This is possible, but the fact that we only have evidence for divisions into halves and quarters in such contexts before the eleventh century poses a significant problem for the notion that thirds were the well-established fraction of choice in Anglo-Saxon administrative tradition.[167] We should not forget that this theory amounts to little more than plausible speculation.

Another possibility is that the figure of a third was inspired by non-English administrative practice. Recent writers have enthusiastically embraced the idea that the third penny reflects Frankish influence, citing parallels from the fifth- or sixth-century *Lex Salica*, the seventh-century *Lex Ribuaria*, and from Carolingian

---

[167] The lack of any obvious later association between third-penny and military revenues may also tell against this interpretation to some extent, but it need not be fatal: one could speculate that military revenues had been divided between kings and ealdormen in the tenth century, thus serving as a model, but that II Cn 12 shows the king asserting a new right to keep for himself all payments of *fyrdwite*.

capitularies of the late eighth and early ninth centuries.[168] However, the chronological gulf between these Frankish examples and the first explicit evidence that English ealdormen or earls were entitled to a third of anything is huge. It must thus be acknowledged that a francocentric explanation requires a significant leap of faith.[169] A possible alternative is Scandinavian influence. This has the benefit of aligning well with the chronology: the third penny is first solidly attested directly after a period in which England had been ruled by Scandinavian kings (and indeed several Scandinavian earls).[170] However, the evidence here is late: a thirteenth-century Icelandic text recounts the establishment in tenth-century Norway of a system that granted earls a third of all royal revenues.[171] If this is accurate it suggests a much more direct explanation of the appearance of the earl's third in England: incoming Scandinavian earls, familiar with this Norwegian system, asserted that wherever they were entitled to a share of royal revenues that share naturally ought to be a third. But we cannot be confident in the account's accuracy, so again we have to acknowledge that the theory of Scandinavian influence requires a leap of faith.[172]

Indeed, it is perhaps most important to keep the obvious point in view here: dividing revenues into fractions is not a particularly unusual or difficult thing to do, nor need the choice of thirds for such a division have any cultural significance.[173] There must have been some reason for the standardization of the earl's share of royal revenues at one third in the eleventh century but we need to accept that this reason is obscure to us. It is probably wisest to avoid exaggerating the explanatory potential of poorly substantiated theories about cultural influence, for all their superficial allure.

CONCLUSION

The differences between tenth- and eleventh-century evidence for the distribution of legal revenues are significant. Tenth-century and earlier evidence suggests a world in which legal revenues were neither a financial priority for kings, nor an issue

---

[168] See Baxter, *Earls of Mercia*, pp. 89–90. Hudson, *Oxford History*, pp. 35–6, follows suit.

[169] For an extended critique of the historiographical tendency towards francocentric readings of English developments, see Molyneaux, *Formation*, pp. 233–48.

[170] For the political context, see Pauline Stafford, *Unification and Conquest: A Political and Social History of England in the Tenth and Eleventh Centuries* (London, 1989), ch. 4.

[171] Harald Fairhair's Saga, ch. 6. Text: Bjarni Aðalbjarnarson, ed., *Heimskringla*, 3 vols. (Reykjavik, 1941–51), i. p. 98. Translation: Alison Finlay and Anthony Faulkes, trans., *Heimskringla*, 3 vols. (London, 2011-), i. p. 56.

[172] H. G. Richardson and G. O. Sayles, *The Governance of Medieval England from the Conquest to Magna Carta* (Edinburgh, 1963), p. 26, n. 1, takes the possibility of Scandinavian roots seriously, and argues that the third penny can hardly be older than the late tenth century (though for different reasons from those cited here). Baxter, *Earls of Mercia*, pp. 89–90, argues that the most plausible explanation for the Norwegian earl's third penny is that Frankish ideas were first imported into England and that English practice subsequently influenced Scandinavia. This is possible, but it should be remembered that Scandinavians had ample contact with the Frankish world; it is just as possible that the Scandinavian third penny was directly inspired by Frankish practices.

[173] See Molyneaux, *Formation*, p. 111, n. 113.

of contention for aristocrats.[174] The fact that *landhlafords* were entitled to receive them was a significant part of the legal landscape and because of this the laws occasionally mention them, but they are not particularly scrupulous about doing so. It is only rarely that they make a point of being precise about who received which revenues. In fact, this seems to occur only when defining the legal revenues to which communities were entitled, in situations where the intention is to encourage communal participation by setting out the potential profits involved. Though they are clearly implied by their language, charters tend not to mention legal revenues at all. We find kings reserving their military rights as a matter of form, and very occasionally we can see them carefully retaining the rights to specific annual dues, but they never treat legal revenues in this way. In the few charters where they are mentioned it is to confirm that they pass to the beneficiary. There are, in short, no signs of significant competition for the right to receive legal revenues. This could be because they were sporadic and unreliable, and presumably often paid in kind. It may well have been impossible to predict either how much the legal revenues from an area would be worth in any given year, or in what form they would end up being paid. Compared to reliable sources of income—annual dues (in cash or in kind) and labour services—the right to receive legal revenues may well have seemed of peripheral importance: potentially valuable, but not something to be counted upon.

Eleventh-century evidence offers a completely different picture. Rights to receive legal revenues seem to be the subject of conflict. Nobles, probably at significant expense to themselves, were keen to secure writs which defined in precise terms their entitlement to legal revenues beyond the standard package of sake and soke. This suggests that they anticipated having to defend their right to these revenues. In laws, we find kings for the first time explicitly laying claim to specific rights and— presumably because these laws were written by Archbishop Wulfstan—we can find the rights of the Church defined in unusually precise terms as well. An examination of specific legal revenues supports this. There are solid cases for a shift in the treatment of revenues associated with vouching to warranty, executed thieves, and the offences of *hamsocn*, *mundbryce*, and *flymenafyrmþ*. There are no signs that these revenues were unusual in tenth-century evidence—they were quite probably collected by *landhlafords* as a matter of routine—but in the eleventh we find them separated from the standard package of legal privileges, sake and soke, to be conveyed by specific grants. It seems likely that these changes represent the results of a period in which the king's right to receive legal revenues was aggressively extended, primarily through the agency of sheriffs, who start to appear in our evidence towards the end of the tenth century.

---

[174] Note that this is not what is often assumed. Patrick Wormald, ' "Inter Cetera Bona Genti Suae": Law-Making and Peace-Keeping in the Earliest English Kingdoms', repr. in and cited from Wormald, *Legal Culture*, pp. 179–98, at 194–5, implies that revenue-raising was a key priority for late seventh-century kings; Wormald, *Papers Preparatory*, p. 155, treats the 'intimate relation of government revenue and criminal law' as well established. For broader arguments against the assumption that concern for revenue motivated royal administrative innovation in the tenth century, see Molyneaux, *Formation*, pp. 182–93.

There are good reasons, however, for thinking that sheriffs received significant support in this from ealdorman and earls—who emerged from this period with a right to a third of some of these newly royal revenues—and we should not forget that the passage in Cnut's laws on the *gerihta* suggests that the king himself was involved in claiming ownership of a specific tier of legal revenues.

Why should this period have witnessed such intense competition for legal revenues? An attractive explanation is that these revenues had become more valuable. We might think of legal changes as a factor in this: Edgar's establishment of compulsory standing suretyship for punitive liabilities may well have made it significantly easier for lords and reeves to extract the revenues to which they had always, in theory, been entitled.[175] A more fundamental shift, however, might be the economic growth of the late tenth and eleventh centuries.[176] This was the period in which the process of urbanization seems first to have gained serious momentum.[177] In basic terms, larger urban populations must have significantly increased the market for the rural population's agricultural surpluses: there were now many more people with non-agricultural occupations and they needed to be supplied with food. The possibility of selling surpluses at markets in towns presumably made it easier for people entitled to revenues of various sorts to demand payments in coin. In general, profiting from land rights was now much less a matter of organizing an itinerary in which a household travelled from one centre to another consuming food renders; coins could be collected by a local reeve and sent to his lord wherever he happened to be.[178] Legal revenues were just as amenable to this treatment as revenues of any other sort, so their unpredictability was no longer a significant problem. It is thus possible that one underlying reason for the intensified competition over legal revenues visible around the millennium was that those revenues were increasingly paid in cash and were therefore worth fighting over in a way that they had not been previously.[179]

---

[175] Chapter 6, pp. 277–82 (suretyship), 283–9 (negotiation dynamics).

[176] See Peter Sawyer, *The Wealth of Anglo-Saxon England* (Oxford, 2013), chs. 2, 5; Robin Fleming, *Britain After Rome: The Fall and Rise* (London, 2010), chs. 9, 11; Christopher Dyer, *Making a Living in the Middle Ages: The People of Britain 850–1520* (New Haven, 2002), chs. 1–2; Rory Naismith, 'The English Monetary Economy, c.973–1100: The Contribution of Single-Finds' *Economic History Review* 66 (2013), pp. 198–225; S. R. H. Jones, 'Transaction Costs, Institutional Change, and the Emergence of a Market Economy in Later Anglo-Saxon England', *Economic History Review* 46 (1993), pp. 658–78.

[177] See Richard Holt, 'The Urban Transformation in England, 900–1100', *Anglo-Norman Studies* 32 (2010), pp. 57–78.

[178] This is implied by the use of the northern and western areas of Bampton Hundred in Oxfordshire as 'ministerial holdings'—rewards for royal officials, some of whom were expected to remain part of the king's household and must surely be understood as absentee landlords. See Stephen Baxter and John Blair, 'Land Tenure and Royal Patronage in the Early English Kingdom: A Model and a Case Study', *Anglo-Norman Studies* 28 (2006), pp. 19–46 at 41–4. Particularly telling, as Baxter and Blair point out (p. 41), is that Lew, which was held by the king's falconer in 1086, was granted along with some other lands, to a royal scribe in 984 (S 853). We should remember, however, that even in the early eleventh century (*Anglo-Saxon Chronicle*, s.a. 1006CDE) the king can be found travelling to Shropshire to consume his food renders (*feorm*).

[179] Although this observation applies to most of the area under English law in the late Anglo-Saxon period, there is good evidence that the east of the country—much of the Danelaw—had been more economically developed from an early period. See Wickham, *Framing*, pp. 810–13; John Blair, *The*

Legal revenues may also have been the subject of competition in this period because they were peculiarly vulnerable to usurpation. Discussions of communal legal revenues in tenth-century laws suggest a basic principle: those who put time and effort into catching and punishing an offender should have the right to receive some of the profits that arise. As was noted above, a similar principle is visible in both Domesday Book and the Anglo-Norman legal treatises, which could be reflecting late Anglo-Saxon ideas: lords with sake and soke were entitled to receive punitive fines from all their men *unless* they were caught in the act on someone else's land.[180] Sheriffs, in particular, may well have been employed on terms which gave them a financial incentive to claim as many revenues as possible for the king. There was no obvious basis on which they could claim the right to receive established annual renders—in cash, kind or labour—from lands which belonged to other lords, but they probably had good prospects of claiming legal revenues if they played an instrumental role in catching and punishing the offenders who paid them. Several of the new royal revenues that emerged in this period make sense in this context because they are associated with particularly onerous tasks: tracking down fugitives, tracing a series of warrantors and witnesses to transactions, executing offenders (usually thieves) and thereby risking incurring dangerous enmities. A plausible theory is that sheriffs focused on these revenues because these were the revenues which they could, by putting in some effort, wrest from *landhlafords* with at least a modicum of legitimacy. Dispossessing them of other forms of revenue was probably more of a challenge.

There is much more that could be written on the issue of how kings, earls, and sheriffs managed in the eleventh century to claim legal revenues which had belonged to *landhlafords* in the tenth. The writ itself is clearly an important part of this story: on the one hand it was the most reliable means by which privileged lords could defend themselves against sheriffs' encroachments, but on the other it may also have been the way that the traditional rights of *landhlafords* were reduced. If *landhlafords* had always, since time immemorial, been entitled to receive the forfeitures of men slain as thieves on their land, why is it that we can find lords in the eleventh century accepting writs which did not include *infangenþeof*? The answer to this question probably lies in the dynamics governing the acquisition of writs and the purposes to which they were put, issues which are too complex to be discussed in detail in this context.[181] We should also be alert to the possibility that

---

British Culture of Anglo-Saxon Settlement (H. M. Chadwick Memorial Lectures 24, Cambridge, 2013), pp. 3–14. A notable feature of our evidence for law in these historically richer (Danelaw) areas during in this period is the assumption that large sums of money were readily available, both in huge fines for breach of protection (III Atr 1:1–1:2) and in the insistence that people provide financial security in circumstances which in English law we would expect to see insistence on sureties (III Atr 7–7:1, 12).

[180] See above, p. 323, esp. n. 87.

[181] I intend to discuss these issues in more detail in a future article. In brief, I would suggest that lords' priorities in securing writs were usually to defend their possession of land against rival inheritance claims; in this context the specific privileges contained in those writs were of secondary importance. Kings (or the officials in charge of writ-production) may well have relied on sheriffs and earls for local information: it is possible that a cash payment and the local sheriff's or earl's good word was sufficient to procure a writ, in the absence of a known challenge. If this was so, minor nobles whose title was

some changes in this period did not involve sheriffs or earls at all. We might, for instance, imagine a shift in the terms on which great magnates made temporary grants of their land rights to minor nobles: given that legal revenues were no longer understood as a single block, it would make sense if magnates increasingly chose to retain certain rights for themselves—*toll* and *team*, for instance—when they transferred other revenues to favoured subordinates.[182] The eleventh century may, in short, have been a period in which the rights of magnates and their noble tenants were subject to more subtle distinctions than previously, helping to create the multiple tiers of legal rights visible in our post-Conquest sources.

Another possibility worth highlighting is that the methods by which sheriffs claimed legal revenues in this period could help explain the subsequent emergence of ideas about jurisdiction in English law. Claiming rights to specific legal revenues by performing specific legal functions stresses the link between functions and revenues, and this link is fundamental to a jurisdictional view of legal privilege. In a world where legal privilege is understood in terms of jurisdiction there are clear rules about who is entitled to perform particular legal functions, and the right to receive legal revenues is a necessary consequence of the right to perform the functions that produced them. It is easy to imagine how the processes proposed here could have contributed to the creation of such a world. Initially, taking responsibility for tasks such as executing thieves and hunting down potential warrantors or fugitives was probably just a means to an end: a way for sheriffs to claim the revenues arising from particular cases. From there, though, it is a small step to sheriffs or privileged lords making a public spectacle of these functions— particularly executions—as a way of asserting their right to the revenues associated with them. In time this could well have led sheriffs or lords to object to others engaging in such symbolic displays on their territory, in effect asserting a monopoly of the right to perform particular legal functions. Pushed to its logical conclusion, the process described here had the potential eventually to render rights to receive revenues indistinguishable from rights to perform functions, thus creating a legal landscape of the type modern historians have tended to assume was ever-present: one in which all significant legal rights were understood in jurisdictional terms.

How far this process had gone in England by 1066 is difficult to tell. We have no grounds for suspecting that ideas about jurisdiction were fully formed and dominant in the way that tends to be assumed, but that could in part be because our evidence is so limited. There are some signs that a transition was underway, and that jurisdictional traditions were emerging. A Domesday Book entry for Dunwich, Suffolk, is particularly telling here. It states that thieves captured in Dunwich were

---

subject to challenge by rival heirs may have found themselves negotiating with sheriffs and earls, and facing an unpalatable choice between securing a writ confirming their possession of a diminished set of legal rights, or securing no writ at all and potentially losing their inheritance entirely. In such a context the acceptance of writs which did not include every legal revenue that a lord's forefathers had enjoyed would be entirely comprehensible. This argument owes a great deal to the interpretation of writs offered in Sharpe, 'Use of Writs', although it does require some relatively minor modifications to Sharpe's position.

[182] S 1423 is a clear example of this.

to be judged there, and that though 'corporal justice' (*corporal iusticia*) was to be done in Blythburgh, the goods forfeited by the dead man were to remain with the lord of Dunwich.[183] This could be read as suggestive of precisely the process sketched out here. Blythburgh was a major royal centre with its own mint. The tradition of executing thieves there could have been initiated by a royal reeve based there eager to secure thieves' forfeited property (perhaps because of pressure from his sheriff) at some point in the early to mid eleventh century. The lord of Dunwich at this time (a possible candidate is Eadric of Laxfield, a major landholder and high-political actor who held the estate in 1066)[184] clearly managed to resist this to some extent, but without asserting his own right to perform executions. This shows that the connection between receiving legal revenues and performing legal functions was still relatively loose at that point, but Domesday's discussion of these arrangements probably implies that they were regarded as unusual by 1086: it was normal for the forfeitures to belong to the party responsible for the execution. This suggests that jurisdictional assumptions had been emerging in the period before 1066, most likely as a result of reeves seizing responsibility for legal functions, and that they were becoming the norm in 1086, but also that the process was untidy. People had started to think in terms of rights to perform specific functions, but the connection between performing these functions and receiving the revenues associated with them was still not absolute; and the right to receive revenues remained the right that really mattered.

If we want to understand significance of the shift in the distribution of legal rights in the decades around the year 1000, then, we still need to keep our eyes firmly focused on revenues. Economic growth must have made these revenues more valuable across this period. The introduction of sheriffs gave kings the administrative apparatus necessary to extract revenue from privileged lands as a matter of routine and, simultaneously, Scandinavian attacks placed huge pressure on kings to raise all the revenue possible for the defence of the kingdom. It seems likely that a combination of these factors led to the shift described in this chapter: to kings applying more and more pressure to sheriffs to raise as much money as possible, and thus to sheriffs—in conjunction with both their subordinates and ealdormen or earls—working hard to claim whatever legal revenues they could plausibly argue their administrative efforts entitled them to collect. Kings, earls, and sheriffs, at any rate, were the figures who emerged as winners from this period, the people we find profiting from legal revenues which had pertained to others in the tenth century.

The main losers were probably local communities. It seems likely that by taking responsibility for enforcement, sheriffs were first and foremost making a claim to the legal revenues that tenth-century laws from Æthelstan to Edgar treat as rewards for communal expeditions. We should not underestimate the significance of this. There is little to suggest that a communal right to profit from the punishment of

---

[183] DB ii. 312r-v.
[184] See Ann Williams, 'Eadric of Laxfield (d. in or after 1066?)', *Oxford Dictionary of National Biography* (Oxford, 2004), <http://www.oxforddnb.com/view/article/52350> (accessed 28 February 2015).

individuals survived this period; in post-Conquest texts, indeed, communities are frequently found paying fines collectively rather than receiving them.[185] Sheriffs also encroached on the rights of *landhlafords*, but not in an even way: the wealthy and influential were better able to resist this process than more minor lords. The assumption in the early twelfth-century *Leges Henrici* that all senior noblemen held *toll*, *team*, and *infangenþeof* may well reflect the simple reality that such figures were too powerful to be bullied by sheriffs.[186] Lesser nobles were more vulnerable, but even they tended to retain at least the right to sake and soke, and it would be a serious error to assume this was insignificant. Sheriffs did more than just nibble around the edges of minor *landhlafords'* privileges—*team* and *infangenþeof* together must represent the great majority of revenues from the punishment of theft—but they did not come close to swallowing them whole. Possession of sake and soke meant the right to almost all *wite*s and wergild forfeitures: this remained a society in which lords, even relatively minor ones, routinely enjoyed major legal privileges.

[185] See Conclusion, pp. 360–1.   [186] Hn 20:2.

Conclusion
Continuity, Change, and the Norman Conquest

This book spans almost five centuries, from the obscure decades which preceded Æthelberht of Kent's conversion to Christianity to the decades leading up to the Norman Conquest, which happen to be fairly obscure in legal terms as well. This was a period which witnessed significant legal developments, but the extent to which the basic assumptions underlying Anglo-Saxon law remained stable is perhaps more striking. Ideologically motivated kings made efforts to bring about legal change, and with some success, but these changes worked with the grain of the established legal order rather than against it. Though there can be no question that they were exposed to foreign influences, the ideas which most fundamentally shaped kings' legal ambitions were rooted in their own societies: traditional, deeply engrained, and largely secular assumptions about what good order was and how it ought to be maintained. Because Anglo-Saxon kings and aristocrats were immersed in native English legal culture, committed to its values, most of their reforms can be read as attempts to bring the legal system closer to its own ideals. There is little to suggest they were interested in instituting a new legal order founded on unfamiliar principles. (Though for most of the Anglo-Saxon period this would probably have been impossible, we should not discount the idea that in its final century kings had the capacity to bring about such a change had they wished to do so.) The effect of this was a coherent and stable legal order that endured for at least 400 years. In the century and a half after 1066, following the wholesale replacement of the English elite, that legal order disintegrated and was replaced by a new one: the common law, the direct ancestor of numerous modern legal systems. This complex and far-reaching process is not the subject of this book, but it involved the destruction of much that was distinctive about the Anglo-Saxon legal order, and this is crucial to one of its central contentions: that the legal historical tradition of studying the Anglo-Saxon period as a prelude to the common law, with an agenda informed by common law assumptions, is unhelpful.

Anglo-Saxon law focused on communities of free men. One of its defining features was the way it sought to balance the rights of free individuals, and the groups they formed, against the interests of free society as a whole. Laws through-out the period are careful to recognize free males' personal honour. They assumed that free men (and women though this is rarely emphasized) were generally honourable, accepting their oaths of denial as sufficient to prove their innocence unless they had a proven record of faithlessness, and providing sufficient supporting oaths could be found from other members of the free community.[1] Another basic assumption was that affronts committed against free males created legitimate grievances, which had the potential to justify violent revenge but were best dealt with through compensation settlements precisely calibrated to ensure that all sides emerged with their honour intact.[2] Such settlements served not only the interests of the affronted individual, salving their wounded honour and recompensing them for material losses, but those of the wider community: they put an end to potentially dangerous enmities.[3] The threat of vengeance was essential to bringing about these ideal outcomes and its legitimacy in principle seems to have been assumed throughout the period.[4] Hastily resorting to violence without allowing offenders the opportunity to come to a compensation settlement, however, escalated conflicts which could threaten the wider community, potentially dividing it against itself. Anglo-Saxon society, then, accepted the legitimacy of feuding in principle but this is not to say it accepted unrestrained violence. Feuds which were conducted in a socially responsible way, with due respect for established legal structures, were understood as positive contributions to order; but individuals who put satisfying their own honour above the needs of the community by indulging in precipitate, unnecessary, or disproportionate violence were regarded as a problem. Our sources are not particularly well-suited to this but it is possible to detect assumptions about when, where, and against whom violence was acceptable evolving and hardening across the Anglo-Saxon period.[5]

Not all forms of wrongdoing, however, could adequately be addressed by relying on affronted free men pursuing their own interests in feuds, however responsibly.[6] When people committed offences which were understood to be socially harmful yet did not affront the honour of any individual, feud and compensation was not an option. Religious offences might provoke divine wrath that endangered the community as a whole without affronting anyone in a way that required compensation; refusals to comply with communal legal processes, likewise, were not affronts against individuals. The possibility of provoking a feud could not deter people from these forms of wrongdoing. Secret forms of wrongdoing—in practice primarily theft, the one overriding concern of Anglo-Saxon legislation—were also problematic. Although the harm an individual thief did to his immediate victim could be addressed through compensation if he were caught, this was not much of a deterrent: secret offenders counted on not being identified. Moreover, thieves caused harm not just to victims but, through their secrecy, to entire communities, weakening communal solidarity by sowing suspicion among neighbours. Allowing thieves who were caught simply to compensate their victims in proportion to their loss was sufficient neither to deter future thefts nor to address the social harm theft caused. Feuding could deal effectively with the threat to society posed by some forms of wrongdoing, then, but not all of them. There were some forms of socially harmful behaviour which needed to be approached in some other way if they were

---

[1] Chapter 6, pp. 255–8.   [2] Chapter 1, pp. 35–9.   [3] Chapter 2, pp. 104–10.
[4] Chapters 4 and 5, pp. 181–3, 227–30.   [5] Chapter 5, pp. 230–5.
[6] For the next three paragraphs, see Chapter 2.

to be addressed at all. This was the role punishment played in Anglo-Saxon law: it filled this gap, dealing with types of wrongdoing that offended not just specific individuals but whole communities. Punishment, in short, complemented feuding. This was not a society which imagined 'horizontal' and 'vertical' justice as competitors.

The Anglo-Saxon legal order was thus characterized by the coexistence of two distinct approaches to wrongdoing, which applied to different categories of offence (though these overlapped to some extent—in theft, for example). Open offences which constituted affronts to individuals were matters for feud and compensation; punishment by contrast applied to religious misconduct, procedural offences, and theft (and thus by analogy to other secret offences such as *morð*, though these are not a significant theme in our evidence). The traditional division reflects the way law developed. The prestigious and formalized law of the pre-Christian period (*æ*), which probably had little to do with kings, was law about affront and compensation: law for men of honour engaged in feuding. The more punitive royal laws (*domas*) of the late seventh century explicitly represent themselves as complementary additions to this tradition. Even in the pre-Christian period, moreover, it is likely that prestigious rote-learnt compensation tariffs were complemented by legal customs (perhaps what a later text calls *þeawas*), which were rather more localized and not recorded with the same formality. Some of these early customs may have involved punishment. A plausible though entirely unprovable way of reading the reference to a punitive fine (*wite*) for theft payable to the king in the laws of Æthelberht is as an early indication that kings were keen to take responsibility for (and claim the profits from) established communal punitive practices. It makes sense, in other words, to think of punishments emerging to complement a legal order based primarily on compensation settlements and feuds, but we do not have to imagine that kings were instrumental in this process.

It is rather more convincing to envisage Anglo-Saxon society's basic assumptions about law and order shaping the role of kings than the other way around. Kings, in fact, had two distinct legal roles which correspond to the two approaches to wrongdoing visible in the laws. They were, of course, free and male, and this meant that the law recognized affronts to their honour just as it recognized affronts committed against other free males. The king's office made him the highest-ranking free man in his kingdom, which meant that affronts committed against him required more compensation than equivalent offences against lesser men, but it also gave him a particular relationship with his people and this seems to have allowed him to extend his protection to them in ways that had no parallels lower down the social scale. We find the king protecting all free men in Æthelberht's laws and, later on (perhaps reflecting hardening ideas about places in which violence was inappropriate) extending specific protections to houses, roads, and churches.[7] Such protections were unique to kings, but they were still protections and their breach

[7] Chapters 1 and 4, pp. 59, 183–90.

was still an affront which—like any other affront within this legal system—could either justify vengeance or warrant compensation.

As well as being powerful actors within the complex socio-legal web which the law sought to regulate, from the late seventh century kings in some senses stood above the fray, functioning as representatives, perhaps even embodiments, of their people.[8] They were the proper recipients of the sums paid by wrongdoers to atone for the harm they did to society as a whole (though they frequently delegated this right to others), and they had broad responsibility for maintaining law and order, establishing new laws and acting as their kingdoms' highest judges. As the three parts of the royal inauguration ritual make clear, kings were meant to lead the fight against theft and other socially threatening forms of wrongdoing, to uphold Christianity and the rights of the Church, and to ensure that the legal system functioned as it ought, providing justice to their people. Moreover, there are strong indications, especially in the tenth century, that kings had a special role in ensuring their people retained God's favour. The basic ideas here about the forms of wrongdoing which represented threats to society must, for the most part, have had pre-Christian roots: the secular ones are difficult to explain otherwise, and even the concern to maintain divine favour may well have had a pagan precursor. These notions of socially threatening conduct were not new, but it is possible that the seventh century saw kings (inspired by Romano-Christian models of kingship in the way Patrick Wormald argued)[9] enthusiastically embracing responsibility for their suppression creating a role which—though crafted from traditional ingredients—differed significantly from that of their pre-Christian ancestors.

It is vital to emphasize the limits of legitimate royal authority in this capacity, however. Seventh-century kings clearly asserted their right to make new laws on most matters, at least when acting in conjunction with great assemblies of their people, but they do not seem to have understood making changes to the basic rights of free men as part of their role. (We never find kings trying to make material adjustments to free men's rights to be compensated for affronts, to deny charges with collective oaths, or to inherit property from their families.)[10] Kings also asserted the right to receive the profits of punitive justice. They did not, however, assert the right to administer law in practice. Indeed, the idea of 'jurisdiction', familiar in later periods, was essentially absent: this was a society with few rigid rules dictating who was entitled to carry out legally significant acts. People did not assume that the authority to perform important legal procedures was the natural property of the king (or 'the state'), and that these procedures could therefore only legitimately take place under the direction of men nominated by the king. Rather, the Anglo-Saxons assumed that the right to perform legal functions naturally belonged to free adult males, individually and collectively, and this shaped their legal order in fundamental ways.[11]

---

[8] For this paragraph, see Chapters 2 and 5.
[9] Chapter 2, pp. 64–5.   [10] Chapter 2, pp. 76–80.
[11] Chapter 7, pp. 301–6.

On a broad level, the lack of rigid rules about who could perform which legal functions meant that what happened in practice depended heavily on local political factors: on who could persuade whom to do what. But the absence of rigid rules should not be taken to imply the absence of clear ideals and expectations. Affronted individuals were expected to take action to restore their own honour, and various forms of associate—kinsmen, lords, fellow guild members—were expected to help them. The system largely relied upon these people bringing formal accusations to assemblies and, indeed, bearing much of the burden of enforcement against defiant individuals.[12] Whether offended parties in fact chose to pursue cases, and whether they in fact received the support they needed from their associates, must have depended on circumstances. It would be naive to assume that people unthinkingly acted in predetermined groups or invariably prioritized personal honour over other considerations (personal safety, for instance). People who failed to pursue feuds or support their kinsmen probably usually paid a social price for their decisions—a diminished reputation—but in many circumstances this may well have been the prudent course.

The most prominent ideal in the laws, however, is not personal honour but communality.[13] (This is unsurprising given that legislators' primary concern was with offences that caused social harm; it need not imply that ideals of communality trumped those of personal honour in other contexts.) Communities were expected to assemble regularly to consider their members' legal cases, to come to agreement about how the law applied to such cases, to issue judgements that carried their collective authority, and (if individuals defied that authority) to band together in potentially violent enforcement expeditions.[14] They were also expected to participate in various procedures designed to isolate and identify thieves, which grew particularly elaborate in the tenth century: witnessing legitimate transactions, standing surety for trustworthy men, swearing to neighbours' ownership of property when vouched to warranty, collectively tracking stolen livestock.[15] The ideal was clearly one of great communal zeal in the performance of these functions, but the bribes and threats in the laws designed to persuade individuals to participate suggest that—as we would have been wise to suspect anyway—reality was often more apathetic. It was also almost certainly more hierarchical than the rhetoric of communality might suggest. We should imagine that communities routinely deferred to their richer, higher-ranking members—these must usually have been the people who decided whether a communal expedition in fact took place—and

---

[12] Chapter 3, pp. 150–2.

[13] This is perhaps an appropriate place to acknowledge the considerable debt this book owes to Susan Reynolds's wide-ranging scholarship on lay collective activity and legal change between the tenth and thirteenth centuries, which has been present in my mind throughout the writing process and influenced my thinking in a way that cannot really be reduced to footnotes on specific interpretative issues. The substantial agreement and overlap will, I think, be readily apparent to readers familiar with her work. See, in particular, Susan Reynolds, *Kingdoms and Communities in Western Europe, 900–1300* (2nd edn, Oxford, 1997); Susan Reynolds, 'Government and Community', in David Luscombe and Jonathan Riley-Smith, eds., *The New Cambridge Medieval History*, vol. 4: *c.1024–c.1198*, Part 1 (Cambridge, 2004), pp. 86–112.

[14] Chapter 3, pp. 136–56.   [15] Chapter 6, pp. 262–83.

also to people with acknowledged legal expertise when it came to decisions on technical matters (especially if they also happened to be wealthy and powerful).

Although there were few rigid rules about who did what, it was thus a fundamental assumption of the Anglo-Saxon legal order that free men—whether acting as affronted parties or as members of local communities—were responsible for the performance of all key legal functions. This situation is likely to have been deeply traditional, rooted in a pre-Christian period when kings may well not have been interested in legal matters (or even not have existed at all). Indeed, there is very little to suggest that kings and their agents had an integral role in the performance of routine legal functions for most of this period. Kings claimed the right to shape legal practice through their legislation, so they needed local men to monitor assemblies and ensure that the rules they set out were respected. They also claimed the revenues of punitive justice, so they needed local figures able to collect them. In some places the local figures kings relied upon were their rural reeves (whose main duties were overseeing the dependent workforces on royal 'inland' farms, collecting food renders from the free households of an associated area of 'warland', and organizing their labour services). In many other locations, however, kings had delegated their non-military rights to members of the aristocracy, and these figures—sometimes in person but probably more usually through rural reeves of their own—were responsible for monitoring legal judgements and collecting legal revenues.[16]

In both of these roles we should imagine reeves (royal and non-royal) within a wider context. Monitoring assembly judgements to ensure they accorded with royal law meant exerting legal authority, but in an environment where there were a lot of possible sources of legal expertise and thus the potential for arguments about technical legal issues. Reeves may well have been influential in such debates but they need not always have won, nor should we imagine they were always the best informed people present. Collecting legal revenues, on the other hand, need not mean enforcing their payment. Armed enforcement expeditions were, in any case, probably rarely necessary and when they were it is unlikely that reeves had a significant role to play beyond cajoling others into participation. Until the emergence of sheriffs around the turn of the millennium the laws never imply that reeves were expected to take a leading role in such expeditions.[17] After that point there are signs of change: indications, perhaps, that sheriffs were assuming responsibility for certain legal functions as a means of claiming the profits associated with them, and thus to some extent challenging the traditional assumption that the practical implementation of law was a matter for communities and affronted parties. We might even speculate that this process provoked the development of rules defining who was allowed to perform specific legal procedures.[18]

In the eleventh century, then, there are some rather limited hints that fundamental long-standing assumptions about law and order were beginning to change. Just as we cannot be wholly sure about the extent to which the ideas implicit in

---

[16] Chapter 3, pp. 114–36.   [17] Chapter 6, pp. 274–6.
[18] Chapter 7, pp. 346–7.

Ine's and Wihtred's laws were rooted in earlier periods, we must acknowledge that there is a degree of uncertainty about the period separating Cnut's conquest from 1066. It is highly probable that there was considerable continuity at both ends of our period, but it may be that the key aspects of the Anglo-Saxon legal order did not all coalesce until the late seventh century, and that it was beginning to fray around the edges in the half-century before the Norman Conquest. In the periods for which our evidence is strong, however, the basic continuities are striking.

This is not to deny the existence of important changes but to argue that those changes worked with the grain of the established legal order, respecting the assumptions on which it was founded. Seventh-century kings have the best claim to have brought about a legal revolution: a plausible case can be made for kings having radically changed their own legal role. As we have seen, however, the role they claimed essentially involved overseeing the operation of an existing legal order, protecting the interests of the community as a whole as they were traditionally understood. In practical terms this primarily meant the proliferation of fines payable to the king. However, it may be that the novelty here was not punitive fines themselves but the king's right to receive them: it is possible that at least some communities had developed punitive practices independently, and that our evidence actually reveals kings co-opting these practices rather than establishing something entirely new. Nonetheless, even if royal punitive claims were inspired by existing communal arrangements, the significance of kings' attempts to ensure that those practices were implemented by assemblies throughout their kingdoms should not be underestimated. Punishment may well have made sense within Anglo-Saxon legal culture long before kings became interested in it, and it may even have been part of established legal practice, but it is difficult to doubt that it became a more prominent feature of legal practice because of the efforts of ideologically motivated kings in the late seventh century. Even if we remain sceptical about the idea of a late seventh-century legal revolution, we should give serious consideration to the idea that kings in this period brought about a significant legal shift, improving the operation of their legal systems in line with existing assumptions.[19]

The significance of tenth-century reforms is much easier to assess. The laws make it clear that this was a period in which most kings took their legal responsibilities seriously, often attempting to bring about positive social change using their power to legislate. Their most prominent aim was the improvement of their people's *frið* (peace), which they clearly understood to require the rigorous suppression of theft.[20] Though this was a well-established royal legal priority—visible in Æthelberht's laws and probably referenced specifically in the ritual for the inauguration of kings—the lengths to which tenth-century kings went in pursuit of it were unprecedented. Æthelstan's attempt to increase the severity of punishment for theft, which may well have failed in the long term, is in fact something of a distraction here.[21] The main way kings attacked the problem of theft was by trying

[19] See Chapter 2.   [20] Chapter 5, pp. 207–10.
[21] Chapter 4, pp. 174–7.

to shape local legal procedure; they insisted on much more stringent implementation of traditional legal practices. Standing suretyship arrangements, the witnessing of transactions, communal pursuit of thieves, communal enforcement expeditions, procedural disqualifications for the untrustworthy—all seem primarily to have been targeted at thieves. Seemingly because of frustration with their ability to mould such local legal practices through existing structures, in the third quarter of the tenth century kings enacted a major top-down reform of local communal assemblies, establishing a standardized network of districts known as hundreds (wapentakes in some Scandinavian-influenced regions).[22] Tenth-century kings' commitment to the improvement of *frið* is quite remarkable, as indeed is the sheer ambition of some of their reforms.

Yet for all their ambition there is little to suggest late Anglo-Saxon kings had any desire to alter the fundamental assumptions on which their legal order was based or even to follow their seventh-century predecessors by making significant changes to their own role. Royal punishment remained confined to theft, religious misconduct, and procedural offences, just as is had been in the late seventh century.[23] Though later kings, perhaps beginning with Edmund, used their power to offer protection to enable them to penalize certain forms of violence (notionally avenging the personal affronts caused by their breach) their agenda was a familiar one—to encourage men to pursue feuds in a measured way rather than hastily resorting to violence—and broadly analogous experiments with royal protection can be found in the seventh century.[24] The establishment of hundreds may well have increased kings' capacity to mould legal practice, enabling them to demand that all local assemblies adhere to their template of how a hundred should operate, but it did not challenge its basic communality. Indeed, laws about hundreds emphasize communities' responsibility for the practical implementation of law significantly more than any previous legislation, perhaps deliberately bypassing the rural reeves and relatively minor lords on whom kings had previously relied for local oversight of legal practice.[25]

It would be easy to assume that the allure of new sources of revenue was part of what motivated kings to engage in legal reforms but for most of the Anglo-Saxon period there is little to support this reading. Kings routinely gave their legal revenues away as part of a standard package of non-military rights that also included food renders and labour services, and it appears that the right to receive unpredictable windfalls from legal cases was traditionally regarded as the least valuable part of this package. Tenth-century laws show no inclination to reserve legal revenues to the king; indeed, the only times we find them devoting serious attention to the destination of revenues are when they are asserting the local community's right to take a cut, seemingly in return for their role in the processes that generated them.[26]

---

[22] Chapter 6, pp. 243–50.   [23] See Chapter 4.
[24] Chapters 1, 2, and 4, pp. 54–7 (agenda implicit in Æthelberht's laws), 83–4, 90–4 (seventh-century experiments), 183–90 (Edmund's use of protections).
[25] Chapter 6, pp. 246–50.
[26] Chapters 3 and 7, pp. 152–6, 315–17.

Royal legislation seems generally to have been ideologically rather than financially motivated. (Seventh-century laws even envisage kings choosing to pay out their own money in exchange for the right to execute captured thieves).[27] Even Edgar's insistence that every man have standing sureties guaranteeing his ability to pay punitive fines, a measure with profound implications for fines as a source of revenue, could have been intended primarily as a means of bringing about improvements to legal practice: a way of both isolating suspected thieves (who could be punished for failing to find sureties even if no specific charge could be proven) and dealing with the problem of flight (it gave sureties a strong financial motivation to track down fugitives).[28]

Economic growth and the introduction of sheriffs towards the end of the tenth century may have changed this, however. From the early eleventh century onwards, writs provide strong evidence that aristocrats felt the need to defend their right to receive specific legal revenues from usurpation, and Cnut's laws betray a similar concern to protect royal revenues.[29] At roughly the same time that these signs of a more mercenary attitude to royal legal rights start to appear, our best evidence for kings' idealistic approach to their legal responsibilities, their legislation, comes to an end. This evidence is not conclusive but if it is correct to infer that kings' commitment to traditional legal ideals diminished after Æthelred's reign, and that they came to value their position in the legal order more for the revenue it allowed them to raise, this could have had significant consequences. The basic shape of Anglo-Saxon law had remained stable for centuries because kings and their elites were committed to its underlying vision of an ideal order. Their legal reforms had always been designed to bring about a society of free men who, though they were at liberty to harm and insult one another, were able to resolve the potentially dangerous conflicts this caused through compensation settlements precisely calibrated to leave everyone's honour intact. They aimed to mould a community of socially responsible men who conducted in themselves in ways that risked neither dividing society against itself (through secret wrongs which sowed suspicion among neighbours or rash disregard for communal conflict-resolution processes) nor bringing divine wrath down upon it (through reckless impiety).[30] If in the early eleventh century this vision was becoming less important and royal priorities were shifting instead to the maximization of legal revenues, we might well suspect that England had set off down a path towards fundamental change— that the future held financially orientated legal developments and the gradual erosion of traditional ideals.

We cannot know whether or not this is an accurate assessment of the likely trajectory of English legal developments from the mid-eleventh century because the Norman Conquest intervened. The legal shifts of the century that followed 1066 are so fundamental and our evidence for law between Cnut's reign and Henry II's so fraught with interpretative difficulties that securely identifying the later

---

[27] Chapter 2, pp. 84–5, 90.   [28] Chapter 6, pp. 273, 276–82.
[29] Chapter 7, pp. 308–10.
[30] Chapters 1, 2, and 5, pp. 54–7, 95–102, 216–27.

consequences of these early eleventh-century changes is probably impossible.[31] It would be hard to deny that the installation not just of a new king but of a new ruling elite, all of whose assumptions about law and order owed little to Anglo-Saxon tradition, had the potential to bring about significant legal shifts regardless of the newcomers' conscious intentions.[32] This is not the place to work through the changes of the late eleventh and twelfth centuries in detail but a brief review of what, from an early medieval perspective, seem the most salient signs of change is a useful way of throwing the basic continuity that characterizes the Anglo-Saxon period into relief.

The clearest signs that Norman assumptions about law and order differed substantially from those of the Anglo-Saxons relate to the rights of free men. Whereas Anglo-Saxon laws had always protected the right of free men with unblemished legal records to clear themselves of charges using collective oaths, the mode of proof the Normans seem to have favoured was trial by combat: the accuser and accused fought and the victor, having been favoured by God, won his case.[33] This, of course, did not confer a significant advantage on free defendants in good standing in the way that Anglo-Saxon oath procedures traditionally had. Trial by battle was not initially imposed on Englishmen except in cases when their accuser was French, but a reduced respect for the free man's right to deny charges on oath would fit with the story that fifty Englishmen charged with stealing the king's deer were forced to undergo the ordeal by William II, and perhaps with the *Anglo-Saxon Chronicle* account of the royal justice, Ralph Basset, executing forty-four thieves and mutilating a further six in a single session in 1124.[34] By the end of the twelfth century collective oaths had ceased to be an option for free men accused of significant forms of wrongdoing.[35]

It is also worth emphasizing that Normans do not seem to have had fixed wergilds, or at least they are conspicuously absent from post-Conquest legal treatises.[36] One of the most basic aspects of Anglo-Saxon legal culture was the

---

[31] A succinct review of the available evidence covering a slightly broader period can be found in John Hudson, *The Oxford History of the Laws of England*, vol. 2: *871–1216* (Oxford, 2012), pp. 865–80.

[32] On the Norman background: Gilduin Davy, *Le Duc et la Loi: Héritages, Images et Expressions du Pouvoir Normatif dans le Duché de Normandie, des Origines à la Mort du Conquérant* (Paris, 2004); David Bates, *Normandy before 1066* (London, 1982), pp. 162–72; Julius Goebel, *Felony and Misdemeanor: A Study in the History of English Criminal Procedure* (New York, 1937), chs. 3–5.

[33] See Hudson, *Oxford History*, pp. 327–8.

[34] Wl lad 2 explains that, when accused by a Frenchman, an Englishman was entitled to refuse trial by battle and undergo the ordeal of red-hot iron, if that was what he preferred. This must, in effect, have imposed trial by battle in such cases. For William II, see R. C. Van Caenegem, *English Lawsuits From William I to Richard I*, 2 vols. (Selden Society 106–7, London, 1990–1), no. 150. For Ralph Basset: *Anglo-Saxon Chronicle*, s.a. 1124E.

[35] Hudson, *Oxford History*, pp. 731–2, 739–40.

[36] The most striking evidence for this is the extended discussion of various types of homicide in Hn 68–77:2, which runs to twenty-eight pages in its modern edition: L. J. Downer, ed., *Leges Henrici Primi* (Oxford, 1972), pp. 214–42. Across this passage the author provides precise values for wergilds at several points (Hn 69:2, 70:1–70:2, 70:6–70:7, 74:1a–74:1b, 76:3a–76:4b, 76:6a–76:7) and even alludes to the possibility of a slain Frenchman's kinsmen receiving compensation (Hn 75:6); if the author had known of a fixed Norman wergild, he would certainly have included it at some point here.

assumption that in cases where someone affronted a free man it was possible, and highly desirable, to come to a balanced compensation settlement which allowed both sides to emerge with their honour intact, thus ending a conflict with the potential to destabilize the community as a whole. The absence of a Norman wergild suggests that, for homicide cases and quite possibly more generally, England's new elite were not committed to the same compensatory ideal: they may have paid and accepted compensation in practice, but the notion that precisely calibrated compensation could rectify violent affronts, allowing all parties to emerge with their honour intact, was not emphasized in the legal discourse of the incomers in the same way as that of the natives. (The possibility that the Normans' feuding ethic was distinctly more vengeful than the Anglo-Saxons' would be worth exploring in greater depth.) It is highly unlikely that compensation for homicide disappeared quickly in the wake of 1066, but we can be confident that it had ceased to be part of formal legal practice by the late twelfth century; the text known as *Glanvill*, composed in the 1180s, makes it plain that killers were now subject to severe royal punishment: execution or mutilation.[37] Indeed, as John Beckerman has shown, from the thirteenth century onwards English law was remarkable in a European context for refusing to recognize affronts to honour, allowing compensation only for material loss or harm.[38]

This development was clearly related in some way to a shift in how the king's place within the legal order was understood. Anglo-Saxon kings had two distinct legal roles. They existed within the legal system as its highest-ranking free males and were thus entitled to compensation when they were affronted. But they were also representatives of the community, responsible for overseeing the proper functioning of the legal system and thus set apart from it; in this capacity they had the right to receive punitive legal revenues. These roles are not always sharply defined, but the basic distinction is implicit throughout the Anglo-Saxon evidence: the laws show kings taking a punitive approach to theft, religious misconduct and procedural offences, and engaging with violent offences through the extension of their protection.[39] By the end of the twelfth century these roles had ceased to be separable. The king's peace was no longer a protection extended to specific individuals who requested it; it covered everyone at all times. The notion that offences breached

---

See Hudson, *Oxford History*, pp. 409–12; Frederick Pollock and Frederic William Maitland, *The History of English Law Before the Time of Edward I*, 2 vols. (2nd edn, Cambridge, 1898), i. 81.This absence is notable given the tendency of Anglo-Saxon texts which discuss inter-ethnic legal relations explicitly to establish the equivalence of wergilds: AGu 2; II Atr 5–5:1; Duns 5.

[37] G. D. G. Hall, ed., *The Treatise on the Laws and Customs of the Realm of England Commonly Called Glanvill* (Oxford, 1965), i. 2, xiv. 3. For a review of the evidence for the prohibition of homicide during this uncertain period, see T. B. Lambert, 'Protection, Feud and Royal Power: Violence and Its Regulation in English Law, c.850–c.1250' (University of Durham PhD thesis, 2009), ch. 4.

[38] John S. Beckerman, 'Adding Insult to *Iniuria*: Affronts to Honor and the Origins of Trespass' in Morris S. Arnold et al., eds., *On the Laws and Customs of England: Essays in Honour of Samuel E. Thorne* (Chapel Hill, 1981), pp. 159–81. However, note also the compelling case for tacit acceptance of extra-judicial compensation settlements constructed in Roger D. Groot, 'The Jury in Private Criminal Prosecutions Before 1215', *American Journal of Legal History* 27 (1983), pp. 113–41.

[39] See Chapters 2 and 4, and Chapter 1, pp. 57–62.

the king's peace, affronting his honour, became a central part of the legal theory
underpinning royal punishment of wrongdoing generally, not just in cases involving violence. The king's roles as affronted party and representative of society had
merged into one.[40]

These changes had an effect on the dynamics of local justice. Most strikingly, the
emergence of severe royal punishment for homicide by the late twelfth century, and
eventually the establishment of the notion that all significant acts of violence
constituted breaches of the king's peace, presumably meant that affronted individuals could no longer legitimately threaten offenders with violence to enforce their
legal claims: independent feuding ceased to be part of legitimate legal practice,
though wronged parties were sometimes the ones who executed or mutilated
offenders.[41] The agency of free males was reduced in more subtle ways as well.
Late Anglo-Saxon hundreds were communal forums for local politics: there was
always a powerful lord who stood to profit from an individuals' conviction—the
landhlaford in tenth-century terminology, often the king himself or a great magnate
represented by a reeve—but accused men could call on their connections to help in
their defence: their kinsmen, friends, fellow guild members and, in particular, their
personal lords. Lords by commendation could intervene on behalf of their men,
perhaps using their influence to muster the oath-helpers required to deny a charge,
to ensure that procedural rulings fully respected the defendant's rights, or to
negotiate a good deal with the prosecuting party.[42] The decline of collective
oaths eventually removed one of these options entirely but it is also important to
note shifts in judicial structures. Again, the early evidence is thin, but by the early
twelfth century it was clearly normal practice for lords to hold assemblies in which
cases involving their own men were judged.[43] The dynamics of assemblies in which
all present were men of the same lord must have been rather different from those of
hundreds, in which several important local political patrons could be present. It was
probably significantly more difficult for accused men to persuade others to support
them, or to involve a lord other than the one who stood to profit from their
punishment.

Furthermore, the signs of a reduction in the importance and autonomy of local
communities extend beyond the establishment of assemblies for the men of
particular lords. The Anglo-Saxon legal tradition seems to have envisaged kings
providing support and leadership to local communities in their attempts to deal
with selfish, apathetic, or irresponsible individuals. Royal laws gave orders as to how
communities ought to conduct their legal affairs, specifying punishments for
individuals who undermined communal efforts. Corrupt or incompetent reeves
and *landhlafords* who failed to guide assemblies properly in the application of the

---

[40] The historiography of the development of 'the king's peace' in this period is reviewed in Lambert,
'Protection, Feud and Royal Power', ch. 5.

[41] Hudson, *Oxford History*, p. 509.

[42] See Chapter 6, pp. 258–60. The best discussion is Stephen Baxter, 'Lordship and Justice in Late
Anglo-Saxon England: The Judicial Functions of Soke and Commendation Revisited', in Stephen Baxter
et al., eds., *Early Medieval Studies in Memory of Patrick Wormald* (Farnham, 2009), pp. 383–419.

[43] See Hn 9:4, 20:1a–20:2, 25:1, 55:1; Hn Com 3–4.

law were held personally responsible for unjust judgements. Similarly, men who refused to do their communal duty and ride in enforcement expeditions were to pay fines, which in some texts are clearly destined for the local community rather than the king or a lord. Communal activity remained an important feature of law after 1066 but the relationship between local communities and royal authority shifted. Rather than seeking to help communities punish individuals who failed to cooperate with local legal procedures, royal law increasingly held communities collectively responsible for ensuring that justice was done properly, punishing entire communities when local mechanisms failed. The most striking example of this is the rapid introduction in the wake of 1066 of the *murdrum* fine—a large collective fine imposed on any hundred in which someone of French ancestry was killed, if the local community failed to arrest the killer—but the rise of collective punishment is a much broader trend in post-Conquest evidence.[44] The *Leges Henrici Primi*, for instance, envisage the men of hundreds being fined collectively for issuing unjust judgements: a clear reversal of tenth-century English laws' policy of holding reeves and privileged lords personally responsible.[45] The imposition of collective fines for neglect of legal procedures would become a routine feature of local justice under the common law.[46] While this development should probably be understood to have been built on foundations laid by of Anglo-Saxon suretyship reforms, and though it could plausibly have been underway in the decades before 1066, driven by revenue-hungry sheriffs, the shift in emphasis between pre- and post-Conquest evidence is striking.

An associated development was the expanding network of royal officials (many of whom had aristocratic counterparts) with increasingly specific legal functions. Again, the evidence makes charting the early stages of this difficult, but there may have been experiments with roving royal prosecutors in the early twelfth century, and it is clear that a system of itinerant royal justices was established under Henry II, based on what may have been more ad hoc arrangements under Henry I.[47] As Paul Brand has shown, the evidence seems to imply that the assemblies held by these justices initially applied the customs of the relevant shires, but that by the end of Henry II's reign the itinerant justices were issuing judgements on their own authority: the right to interpret the law shifted from shire communities (applying their own customs albeit under the guidance of royal officials) to a central group of legal experts employed by the king (applying an

[44] Lambert, 'Protection, Feud and Royal Power', pp. 171–7, reviews the early evidence and the historiographical debate about origins, arguing for its establishment after 1066 on the basis of Wl art 3–4, and thus agreeing with George Garnett, '*Franci et Angli*: The Legal Distinction between Peoples after the Conquest', *Anglo-Norman Studies* 8 (1985), pp. 109–37 at 117. For the opposing view: Bruce R. O'Brien, 'From *Morðor* to *Murdrum*: The Preconquest Origin and Norman Revival of the Murder Fine', *Speculum* 71 (1996), pp. 321–57. See also, Hudson, *Oxford History*, pp. 405–9.
[45] Hn 29–29:1b, 29:4. III Atr 13:2 suggests that arrangements were slightly different in the Danelaw.
[46] Hudson, *Oxford History*, pp. 717, 745–6; Pollock and Maitland, *History of English Law*, i. pp. 587–8, 593–7, 642–4.
[47] See R. C. Van Caenegem, 'Public Prosecution of Crime in Twelfth-Century England', repr. in and cited from R. C. Van Caenegem, *Legal History: A European Perspective* (London, 1991), pp. 1–36.

increasingly standardized body of law common to the entire realm).[48] To the sheriffs and rural reeves of the Anglo-Saxon period were added not just such royal justices but also (somewhat obscure) lesser figures known as serjeants, and in 1194 officials with shire-wide responsibilities known as coroners.[49] Jurisdictional rules evolved demarcating the roles of at least the higher ranking officials, and the rights of privileged lords came to be measured in these terms: rights to perform some or all of the duties of the sheriff, or to appoint their own coroners. By the 1190s, at least, we have evidence for disputes over the right to maintain a gallows: conflicts which must on some level have been about legal revenues are framed in jurisdictional terms.[50] By this point we have moved from a world in which the right and duty to perform major legal functions was assumed to belong to all free men, to one which assumed this right naturally belonged to the king and could legitimately be exercised by others only with his licence.

There can be no doubt English legal culture changed fundamentally in the century and a half after 1066. How and why (even when) the various developments just surveyed took place are difficult issues which I have no intention of trying to resolve here. I would suggest, however, that the Norman Conquest is likely to have been significant even if its effects were not immediate. William's declared policy was legal continuity—to uphold the laws of Edward the Confessor—and we need not think this insincere, but he and his new Norman elite may well have come to Anglo-Saxon legal structures with different assumptions about what good order was and what role the king, and indeed the aristocracy, ought to play in its maintenance. Major changes affected the English legal system both before and after 1066, but those which took place beforehand respected the basic assumptions on which the Anglo-Saxon legal order was founded, whereas those which took place afterwards often did not. It is possible that the period between Cnut's conquest and William's, extremely obscure in legal terms, saw the origins of some of these shifts, that 1066 did not start the processes which led to fundamental change so much as accelerate them. However, the main concern of this book is not later changes and their causes, but the forces which kept the Anglo-Saxon legal order stable for so long; the key factor must surely be the commitment of Anglo-Saxon kings and elites to a set of socio-legal ideals rooted, for the most part, in the pre-Christian past. The signs of royal investment in this traditional vision of an ideal order, unmistakeable up to Æthelred's reign, become scarce and ambiguous afterwards, and this may be significant. But if there was a key moment in the process by which England's ruling elite abandoned these basic assumptions—a moment which ensured future developments would fundamentally reshape its legal culture—it must surely have been the wholesale replacement of the native aristocracy in the wake of 1066.

---

[48] See Paul Brand, '"Multis Vigiliis Excogitatam et Inventam": Henry II and the Creation of the English Common Law', repr. in and cited from Paul Brand, *The Making of the Common Law* (London, 1992), pp. 77–102.
[49] Hudson, *Oxford History*, pp. 507–8.   [50] Hudson, *Oxford History*, p. 562.

To argue that the Norman Conquest represents a key turning point in the development of English law, initiating a period of revolutionary change, is not to argue for a complete break in 1066. This book has made no attempt to identify the Anglo-Saxon roots from which the common law would later develop—such an agenda would have been distinctly at odds with the goal of understanding Anglo-Saxon legal ideas and structures on their own terms—but I have no doubt that Wormald was right to argue that these roots existed and were important.[51] I hope it will be clear to readers of this book that my intention here has not been to diminish the legal achievements of Anglo-Saxon kings but to redefine the standards by which historians assess them. It is anachronistic to imagine that tenth-century kings were aiming to suppress 'crime' in roughly the same way as their thirteenth-century successors; their understandings of what constituted good order, and what role royal law was meant to play in ensuring it, were very different and deeply engrained in their culture. Although these ideas are much more alien to modern readers than those of the thirteenth-century common law, and therefore more difficult for us to grasp, it would be a mistake to regard them as any less coherent. The Anglo-Saxons' legal order made sense on its own terms and kings were aiming to perfect it with their laws. They did not try to outlaw feuding, nor did they try to bring local communal justice directly under the administrative control of a network of royal officials, but this is because doing so was not part of their vision. It is not a sign of weakness, still less of failure. Modern scholarship emphasizes the remarkable ingenuity and success of the systems by which late Anglo-Saxon kings ruled their kingdoms, and—in spite of taking issue with some points of detail that currently underpin that interpretation in a legal context—this book does the same. Tenth-century kings made ambitious attempts to realize deeply traditional socio-legal ideals through their legislation and seem likely to have met with considerable success. We can and should be impressed, but we should not imagine them as the architects of a modern state-like legal order.

---

[51] The clearest statement is to be found in his unpublished papers: Patrick Wormald, *Papers Preparatory to the Making of English Law: King Alfred to the Twelfth Century*, vol. 2: *From God's Law to Common Law*, ed. Stephen Baxter and John Hudson (University of London, 2014) <http://www. earlyenglishlaws.ac.uk/reference/wormald/>, ch. 7B.

Bibliography

PRIMARY SOURCES

Alfred the Great: Asser's Life of King Alfred *and Other Contemporary Sources*, ed. Simon Keynes and Michael Lapidge (London, 1983).

Anglo-Saxon Charters, ed. A. J. Robertson (Cambridge, 1956).

Anglo-Saxon Charters: An Annotated List and Bibliography, ed. P. H. Sawyer (London, 1968). Consulted in the updated online version: <http://www.esawyer.org.uk>.

The Anglo-Saxon Chronicle: A Collaborative Edition, ed. David Dumville, Simon Keynes, et al., 9 vols. (Cambridge, 1983–).

The Anglo-Saxon Chronicle: A Revised Translation, trans. D. Whitelock, D. C. Douglas, and S. I. Tucker (London, 1961).

The Anglo-Saxon Chronicles, trans. Michael Swanton (revised edn, London, 2000).

Anglo-Saxon Writs, ed. Florence E. Harmer (1989).

Asser's Life of King Alfred Together With the Annals of St Neot's Erroneously Ascribed to Asser, ed. W. H. Stevenson (2nd edn, Oxford, 1959).

Bede, *Ecclesiastical History of the English People*, ed. Bertram Colgrave and R. A. B. Mynors (Oxford, 1969).

The Beginnings of English Law, ed. Lisi Oliver, ed., (Toronto, 2002).

Bracton: De Legibus et Consuetudinibus Anglie, ed. Samuel E. Thorne, 4 vols. (Cambridge, Mass., 1968–77).

Capitularia Regum Francorum, ed. Alfred Boretius, 2 vols. (Monumenta Germaniae Historica, Legum sectio II, Hanover, 1883–97).

Charlemagne: Translated Sources, ed. P. D. King (Kendal, 1987).

The Charters of Abingdon Abbey, ed. S. E. Kelly, 2 vols. (Oxford, 2000–2001).

The Charters of Christ Church Canterbury, ed. S. E. Kelly and N. P. Brooks, 2 vols. (Oxford, 2013).

The Charters of New Minster, Winchester, ed. Sean Miller (Anglo-Saxon Charters 9, Oxford, 2001).

The Chronicle of Hugh Candidus, A Monk of Peterborough, ed. W. T. Mellows (London, 1949).

Chronicon Abbatiae Rameseiensis, ed. W. Dunn Macray (Rolls Series 83, London, 1886).

Councils and Synods with other Documents Relating to the English Church I: A.D. 871–1204, ed. D. Whitelock, M. Brett and C. N. L. Brooke, 2 vols. (Oxford, 1981).

The Crawford Collection of Early Charters and Documents, ed. A. S. Napier and W. H. Stevenson (Oxford, 1895).

The Cult of St Swithun, ed. Michael Lapidge (Winchester Studies 4.ii, Oxford, 2003).

Diplomatarium Anglicum Ævi Saxonicum: A Collection of English Charters from the Reign of King Æthelberht of Kent to That of William the Conqueror, ed. Benjamin Thorpe, (London, 1864).

Domesday Book, ed. John Morris et al., 39 vols. (Chichester, 1975–86).

The Early Charters of the West Midlands, ed. H. P. R. Finberg (2nd edn, Leicester, 1972).

English Historical Documents, vol. 1: *c. 500–1042*, ed. Dorothy Whitelock (2nd edn, London, 1979).

English Historical Documents, vol. 2: *1042–1189*, ed. D. C. Douglas and G. W. Greenaway (2nd edn, London, 1981).

English Lawsuits from William I to Richard I, ed. R. C. van Caenegem 2 vols. (Selden Society 106–7, London, 1990–1).

Die Gesetze der Angelsachsen, ed. Felix Liebermann, 3 vols. (Halle, 1898–1916).

God's Peace and King's Peace: The Laws of Edward the Confessor, ed. Bruce R. O'Brien (Philadelphia, 1999).

Heimskringla, ed. Bjarni Aðalbjarnarson, 3 vols. (Reykjavik, 1941–51).

Heimskringla, trans. Alison Finlay and Anthony Faulkes, 3 vols. (London, 2011–).

Inquisitio Comitatus Cantabrigiensis, ed. N.E.S.A. Hamilton (London, 1876).

The Kalendar of Abbot Samson of Bury St. Edmunds and Related Documents, ed. R. H. C. Davis (Camden Society Third Series 84, London, 1954).

King Alfred's Version of St. Augustine's Soliloquies, ed. Thomas A. Carnicelli (Cambridge, Mass., 1969).

The Laws of the Earliest English Kings, ed. F. L. Attenborough (Cambridge, 1922).

The Laws of the Kings of England from Edmund to Henry I, ed. A. J. Robertson (Cambridge, 1925).

Leges Henrici Primi, ed. L. J. Downer (Oxford, 1972).

The Leofric Missal, ed. Nicholas Orchard, 2 vols. (London, 2002).

Liber Eliensis, ed. E. O. Blake (Camden Society Third Series 92, London, 1962).

Liber Eliensis: A History of the Isle of Ely from the Seventh Century to the Twelfth, trans. Janet Fairweather (Woodbridge, 2005).

Pactus Legis Salicae, ed. Karl Augustus Eckhardt (Monumenta Germaniae Historica, Legum sectio I, Leges Nationum Gemanicarum 4.2, Hanover, 1962).

Pseudo-Cyrprianus De XII Abusivis Saeculi, Siegmund Hellmann (Leipzig, 1909).

Select Charters and Other Illustrations of English Constitutional History, ed. William Stubbs and H. W. C. Davis (9th edn, Oxford, 1921).

Sermo Lupi ad Anglos, ed. Dorothy Whitelock (rev. edn, Exeter, 1976).

The Treatise on the Laws and Customs of the Realm of England Commonly Called Glanvill, ed. G. D. G. Hall (Oxford, 1965).

Two Ælfric Texts: 'The Twelve Abuses' and 'The Vices and Virtues': An Edition and Translation of Ælfric's Old English Versions of 'De duodecim abusiuis' and 'De octo uitiis et de duodecim abusiuis', ed. Mary Clayton (Cambridge, 2013).

Walter Map, *De Nugis Curialium: Courtiers' Trifles*, ed. M. R. James, C. N. L. Brooke, and R. A. B. Mynors (Oxford, 1983).

SECONDARY WORKS

Abels, Richard. '*Trinoda Necessitas*', in Michael Lapidge et al., eds., *The Wiley-Blackwell Encyclopedia of Anglo-Saxon England* (2nd edn, Chichester, 2014), p. 475.

Abels, Richard P. *Lordship and Military Obligation in Anglo-Saxon England* (London, 1988).

Adams, Henry. 'The Anglo-Saxon Courts of Law', in Henry Adams et al., *Essays in Anglo-Saxon Law* (Boston, 1876), pp. 1–54.

Ammon, Matthias. '"Ge mid wedde ge mid aðe": The Functions of Oath and Pledge in Anglo-Saxon Legal Culture', *Historical Research* 86 (2013), pp. 515–35.

Aston, T. H. 'The Origins of the Manor in England', *Transactions of the Royal Historical Society* 8 (1958), pp. 59–83.

Baker, Peter S. *Honour, Exchange and Violence in Beowulf* (Cambridge, 2013).

Banham, Debby and Rosamond Faith. *Anglo-Saxon Farms and Farming* (Oxford, 2014).

Barnwell, P. S. 'The Early Frankish *Mallus*: Its Nature, Participants and Practices', in Aliki Pantos and Sarah Semple, eds., *Assembly Places and Practices in Medieval Europe* (Dublin, 2004), pp. 233–46.

Barrow, Julia. 'Demonstrative Behaviour and Political Communication in Later Anglo-Saxon England', *Anglo-Saxon England* 36 (2007), pp. 127–50.

Bartlett, Robert. *Trial by Fire and Water: The Medieval Judicial Ordeal* (Oxford, 1986).

Bartlett, Robert. 'Symbolic Meanings of Hair in the Middle Ages', *Transactions of the Royal Historical Society*, sixth series, 4 (1994), pp. 43–60.

Bassett, Steven. 'In Search of the Origins of Anglo-Saxon Kingdoms', in Steven Bassett, ed., *The Origins of Anglo-Saxon Kingdoms* (Leicester, 1989), pp. 3–27.

Bates, David. *Normandy before 1066* (London, 1982).

Baxter, Stephen. *The Earls of Mercia: Lordship and Power in Late Anglo-Saxon England* (Oxford, 2007).

Baxter, Stephen. 'Lordship and Justice in Late Anglo-Saxon England: The Judicial Functions of Soke and Commendation Revisited', in Stephen Baxter et al., eds., *Early Medieval Studies in Memory of Patrick Wormald* (Farnham, 2009), pp. 383–419.

Baxter, Stephen and John Blair. 'Land Tenure and Royal Patronage in the Early English Kingdom: A Model and a Case Study', *Anglo-Norman Studies* 28 (2006), pp. 19–46.

Beckerman, John S. 'Adding Insult to *Iniuria*: Affronts to Honor and the Origins of Trespass', in Morris S. Arnold et al., eds., *On the Laws and Customs of England: Essays in Honour of Samuel E. Thorne* (Chapel Hill, 1981), pp. 159–81.

Bedingfield, Brad. 'Public Penance in Anglo-Saxon England', *Anglo-Saxon England* 31 (2002), pp. 223–55.

Bennett, M. 'Military Masculinity in England and Northern France, c.1050–c.1225', in D. M. Hadley, ed., *Masculinity in Medieval Europe* (London, 1999), pp. 71–88.

Blair, John. *The Church in Anglo-Saxon Society* (Oxford, 2005).

Blair, John. 'The Dangerous Dead in Early Medieval England', in Stephen Baxter et al., eds., *Early Medieval Studies in Memory of Patrick Wormald* (Farnham, 2009), pp. 539–59.

Blair, John. *The British Culture of Anglo-Saxon Settlement* (H. M. Chadwick Memorial Lectures 24, Cambridge, 2013).

Blattman, Marita. '"Ein Unglück für sein Volk": Der Zusammenhang zwischen Fehlverhalten des Königs und Volkswohl in Quellen des 7.–12. Jahrhunderts', *Frühmittelalterliche Studien* 30 (1996), pp. 80–102.

Bonnaud Delamare, Roger. *L'Idée de Paix a l'Époque Carolingienne* (Paris, 1939).

Joseph Bosworth and T. Northcote Toller, eds., *An Anglo-Saxon Dictionary* (London, 1898): <http://bosworth.ff.cuni.cz/>.

Boynton, Mark and Susan Reynolds. 'The Author of the Fonthill Letter', *Anglo-Saxon England* 25 (1996), pp. 91–5.

Brand, Paul. '"Multis Vigiliis Excogitatam et Inventam": Henry II and the Creation of the English Common Law', repr. in and cited from Paul Brand, *The Making of the Common Law* (London, 1992), pp. 77–102.

Brookes, Stuart and Andrew Reynolds, 'The Origins of Political Order and the Anglo-Saxon State', *Archaeology International* 13 (2011), pp. 84–93.

Brooks, Nicholas P. 'England in the Ninth Century: The Crucible of Defeat', *Transactions of the Royal Historical Society* 29 (1979), pp. 1–20.

Brooks, Nicholas P. 'The Development of Military Obligation in Eighth- and Ninth-Century England', in Peter Clemoes and Kathleen Hughes, eds., *England before the Conquest: Studies in Primary Sources Presented to Dorothy Whitelock* (Cambridge, 1971), pp. 69–84.

Brooks, Nicholas P. 'The Laws of King Æthelberht of Kent: Preservation, Content and Composition', in Bruce O'Brien and Barbara Bombi, eds., *Textus Roffensis: Law, Language and Libraries in Medieval England* (Turnhout, 2015), pp. 105–36.

Brooks, Nicholas P. 'The Fonthill Letter, Ealdorman Ordlaf and Anglo-Saxon Law in Practice', in Stephen Baxter et al., eds., *Early Medieval Studies in Memory of Patrick Wormald* (Farnham, 2009), pp. 301–17.

Brown, Warren C. and Piotr Górecki, 'What Conflict Means: The Making of Medieval Conflict Studies in the United States, 1970–2000', in Warren C. Brown and Piotr Górecki, eds., *Conflict in Medieval Europe: Changing Perspectives on Society and Culture* (Aldershot, 2003), pp. 1–35.

Bullough, D. A. 'Anglo-Saxon Institutions and Early English Society', repr. in and cited from David E. Pelteret, *Anglo-Saxon History: Basic Readings* (New York, 2000), pp. 1–19.

van Caenegem, R. C. 'Public Prosecution of Crime in Twelfth-Century England', repr. in and cited from R. C. van Caenegem, *Legal History: A European Perspective* (London, 1991), pp. 1–36.

Cam, Helen M. *The Hundred and the Hundred Rolls* (London, 1930).

Cam, Helen M. 'The Evolution of the Mediaeval English Franchise', *Speculum* 32 (1957), pp. 427–42.

Cam, Helen M. 'The Private Hundred in England Before the Norman Conquest', repr. in and cited from Helen M. Cam, *Law-Finders and Law-Makers in Medieval England* (London, 1962), pp. 59–70.

Cam, Helen M. 'Early Groups of Hundreds', repr. in and cited from Helen M. Cam, *Liberties and Communities in Medieval England* (London, 1963), pp. 91–106.

Cameron, Angus, Ashley Crandell Amos, and Antonette diPaolo Healey, eds., *Dictionary of Old English: A-G Online* (Toronto, 2007): <http://www.doe.utoronto.ca>.

Campbell, James. 'Bede II', repr. in and cited from James Campbell, *Essays in Anglo-Saxon History* (London, 1986), pp. 29–48.

Campbell, James. 'Bede's *Reges* and *Principes*', repr. in and cited from James Campbell, *Essays in Anglo-Saxon History* (London, 1986), pp. 85–98.

Campbell, James. 'Observations on English Government from the Tenth to the Twelfth Century', repr. in and cited from James Campbell, *Essays in Anglo-Saxon History* (London, 1986), pp. 155–70.

Campbell, James. 'The Significance of the Anglo-Norman State in the Administrative History of Western Europe', repr. in and cited from James Campbell, *Essays in Anglo-Saxon History* (London, 1986), pp. 171–89.

Campbell, James. *The Anglo-Saxon State* (London, 2000).

Campbell, James. 'The Late Anglo-Saxon State: A Maximum View', repr. in and cited from Campbell, *The Anglo-Saxon State* (London, 2000), pp. 1–30.

Campbell, James. 'Some Agents and Agencies of the Late Anglo-Saxon State', repr. in and cited from James Campbell, *The Anglo-Saxon State* (London, 2000), pp. 201–25.

Campbell, James. 'Archipelagic Thoughts: Comparing Early Medieval Polities in Britain and Ireland', in Stephen Baxter et al., eds., *Early Medieval Studies in Memory of Patrick Wormald* (Farnham, 2009), pp. 47–63.

Chadwick, H. M. *Studies on Anglo-Saxon Institutions* (Cambridge, 1905).

Chaney, William A. *The Cult of Kingship in Anglo-Saxon England: The Transition from Paganism to Christianity* (Manchester, 1970).

Charles-Edwards, Thomas. 'Kinship, Status and the Origin of the Hide', *Past and Present* 56 (1972), pp. 3–33.

Charles-Edwards, Thomas. 'The Distinction between Land and Moveable Wealth in Anglo-Saxon England', in P. H. Sawyer, ed., *Medieval Settlement: Continuity and Change* (London, 1976), pp. 180–7.

Charles-Edwards, Thomas. 'Honour and Status in some Irish and Welsh Prose Tales', *Ériu* 29 (1978), pp. 123–41.

Charles-Edwards, Thomas. 'Early Medieval Kingship in the British Isles', in Steven Bassett, ed., *The Origins of Anglo-Saxon Kingdoms* (Leicester, 1989), pp. 28–39.

Charles-Edwards, Thomas. *Early Irish and Welsh Kinship* (Oxford, 1993).

Charles-Edwards, Thomas. 'Law in the Western Kingdoms between the Fifth and Seventh Centuries', in Averil Cameron, Bryan Ward-Perkins, and Michael Whitby, eds., *The Cambridge Ancient History*, vol. 4: *Late Antiquity: Empire and Successors, AD 425–600* (Cambridge, 2001), pp. 260–87.

Charles-Edwards, Thomas. 'Social Structure', in Pauline Stafford, ed., *A Companion to the Early Middle Ages: Britain and Ireland, c.500–1100* (Oxford, 2013), pp. 107–25.

Charles-Edwards, Thomas. *Wales and the Britons, 350–1064* (Oxford, 2013).

Charles-Edwards, Thomas. 'Nations and Kingdoms: A View from Above', in Thomas Charles-Edwards, ed., *After Rome* (Oxford, 2003), pp. 23–58.

Clanchy, Michael. 'Law and Love in the Middle Ages', in John Bossy, ed., *Disputes and Settlements: Law and Human Relations in the West* (Cambridge, 1983), pp. 47–68.

Clanchy, Michael. *From Memory to Written Record: England 1066–1307* (3rd edn, Chichester, 2013).

Clayton, Mary. 'The Old English *Promissio Regis*', *Anglo-Saxon England* 37 (2008), pp. 91–150.

Clayton, Mary. 'Suicide in the Works of Ælfric', *Review of English Studies* 60 (2009), pp. 339–70.

Clayton, Mary. '*De Duodecim Abusiuis*, Lordship and Kingship in Anglo-Saxon England', in Hugh Magennis and Stuart McWilliams, eds., *Saints and Scholars: New Perspectives on Anglo-Saxon Literature and Culture* (Cambridge, 2012), pp. 141–63.

Collins, Roger. 'Law and Ethnic Identity in the Fifth and Sixth Centuries', in Alfred P. Smyth, ed., *Medieval Europeans: Studies in Ethnic Identity and National Perspectives in Medieval Europe* (Basingstoke, 1998), pp. 1–23.

Colman, Rebecca V. '*Hamsocn*: Its Meaning and Significance in Early English Law', *American Journal of Legal History* 95 (1981), pp. 95–110.

Comaroff, John L. and Simon Roberts. *Rules and Processes: The Cultural Logic of Dispute in an African Context* (Chicago, 1981).

Cooper, Alan. 'The King's Four Highways: Legal Fiction Meets Fictional Law', *Journal of Medieval History* 26 (2000), pp. 351–70.

Cooper, Alan. 'The Rise and Fall of the Anglo-Saxon Law of the Highway', *Haskins Society Journal* 12 (2002), pp. 39–69.

Cowdrey, H. E. J. 'The Peace and Truce of God in the Eleventh Century', *Past and Present* 46 (1970), pp. 42–67.

Crick, Julia. 'St Albans, Westminster, and Some Twelfth-Century Views of the Anglo-Saxon Past', *Anglo-Norman Studies* 25 (2003), pp. 65–83.

Cubitt, Catherine. 'Bishops, Priests and Penance in Late Saxon England', *Early Medieval Europe* 14 (2006), pp. 41–63.

Cubitt, Catherine. '"As the Lawbook Teaches": Reeves, Lawbooks and Urban Life in the Anonymous Old English Legend of the Seven Sleepers', *English Historical Review* 124 (2009), pp. 1021–49.

Cubitt, Catherine. 'The Politics of Remorse: Penance and Royal Piety in the Reign of Æthelred the Unready', *Historical Research* 85 (2012), pp. 179–92.

Darby, H. C. *The Domesday Geography of Eastern England* (3rd edn, Cambridge, 1972).

Dark, K. R. *Civitas to Kingdom: British Political Continuity 300–800* (Leicester, 1994).

Davies, Rees. 'The Medieval State: The Tyranny of a Concept?', *Journal of Historical Sociology* 16 (2003), 280–300.

Davies, Wendy. *Small Worlds: The Village Community in Early Medieval Brittany* (Berkeley, 1988).

Davies, Wendy. 'Adding Insult to Injury: Power, Property and Immunities in Early Medieval Wales', in Wendy Davies and Paul Fouracre, eds., *Property and Power in the Early Middle Ages* (Cambridge, 1995), pp. 137–64.

Davies, Wendy and Hayo Vierck. 'The Contexts of the Tribal Hidage: Social Aggregates and Settlement Patterns', *Frühmittelalterliche Studien* 8 (1974), pp. 223–93.

Davis, Donald R. Jr. 'Centres of Law: Duties, Rights, and Jurisdictional Pluralism in Medieval India', in Paul Dresch and Hannah Skoda, eds., *Legalism: Anthropology and History* (Oxford, 2012), pp. 85–113.

Davis, Donald R. Jr. 'Rules, Culture and Imagination in Sanskrit Jurisprudence', in Paul Dresch and Judith Scheele, eds., *Legalism: Rules and Categories* (Oxford, 2015), pp. 29–52.

Davy, Gilduin. *Le Duc et la Loi: Héritages, Images et Expressions du Pouvoir Normatif dans le Duché de Normandie, des Origines à la Mort du Conquérant* (Paris, 2004).

Dresch, Paul. *Tribes, Government and History in Yemen* (Oxford, 1989).

Dresch, Paul. 'Aspects of Non-State Law: Early Yemen and Perpetual Peace', in Paul Dresch and Hannah Skoda, eds., *Legalism: Anthropology and History* (Oxford, 2012), pp. 145–72.

Dresch, Paul. 'Legalism, Anthropology and History: a view from the Part of Anthropology', in Paul Dresch and Hannah Skoda, eds., *Legalism: Anthropology and History* (Oxford, 2012), pp. 1–37.

Dresch, Paul. 'Outlawry, Exile and Banishment: Reflections on Community and Justice', in Fernanda Pirie and Judith Scheele, eds., *Legalism: Community and Justice* (Oxford, 2014), pp. 97–124.

Dumville, David. 'The Tribal Hidage: An Introduction to its Texts and their History', in Steven Bassett, ed., *The Origins of Anglo-Saxon Kingdoms* (Leicester, 1989), pp. 225–30.

Dyer, Christopher. *Making a Living in the Middle Ages: The People of Britain 850–1520* (New Haven, 2002).

Esmonde-Cleary, A. S. *The Ending of Roman Britain* (London, 1989).

Esmonde-Cleary, A. S. 'The Ending(s) of Roman Britain', in Helena Hamerow, David A. Hinton, and Sally Crawford, eds., *The Oxford Handbook of Anglo-Saxon Archaeology* (Oxford, 2012), pp. 13–29.

Evans-Pritchard, E. E. *The Nuer: A Description of the Modes of Livelihood and Political Institutions of a Nilotic People* (Oxford, 1940).

Faith, Rosamond. *The English Peasantry and the Growth of Lordship* (London, 1997).

Faith, Rosamond. 'Hide', in Michael Lapidge et al., eds., *The Wiley-Blackwell Encyclopedia of Anglo-Saxon England* (2nd edn, Chichester, 2014), pp. 243–4.

Fell, Christine. 'A "Frewif Locbore" Revisited', *Anglo-Saxon England* 13 (1984), pp. 157–66.

Fell, Christine. *Women in Anglo-Saxon England* (Oxford, 1984).

Fell, Christine. 'An Appendix to Carol Hough's Article "A Reappraisal of Æthelberht 84"', *Nottingham Mediaeval Studies*, 37 (1993), pp. 7–8.

Fischer, Andreas. 'Lexical change in late Old English: from *æ* to *lagu*', in Andreas Fischer, ed., *The History and the Dialects of English: Festschrift for Eduard Kolb* (Heidelberg, 1989), pp. 103–14.

Fleming, Robin. *Domesday Book and the Law: Society and Legal Custom in Early Medieval England* (Cambridge, 1998).

Fleming, Robin. *Britain After Rome: The Fall and Rise* (London, 2010).

Flower, Robin. 'The Text of the Burghal Hidage', *London Medieval Studies* 1 (1937), pp. 60–4.

Foot, Sarah. *Æthelstan: The First King of England* (New Haven, 2011).

Frantzen, Allen J. *The Literature of Penance in Anglo-Saxon England* (New Brunswick, 1983).

Fruscione, Daniela. 'Beginnings and Legitimation of Punishment in Early Anglo-Saxon Legislation from the Seventh to the Ninth Century', in Jay Paul Gates and Nicole Marafioti, eds., *Capital and Corporal Punishment in Anglo-Saxon England* (Woodbridge, 2014), pp. 34–47.

Fruscione, Daniela. '*Drihtinbeag* and the Question of the Beginnings of Punishment', in Bruce O'Brien and Barbara Bombi, eds., *Textus Roffensis: Law, Language and Libraries in Medieval England* (Turnhout, 2015), pp. 157–74.

Ganshof, François Louis. *Frankish Institutions under Charlemagne* (Providence, 1968).

Garnett, George. '*Franci et Angli*: The Legal Distinction between Peoples after the Conquest', *Anglo-Norman Studies* 8 (1985), pp. 109–37.

Garnett, George. 'The Third Recension of the English Coronation *Ordo*: The Manuscripts', *Haskins Society Journal* 11 (2003), pp. 43–71.

Gates, Jay Paul and Nicole Marafioti. 'Introduction: Capital and Corporal Punishment in Anglo-Saxon England', in Jay Paul Gates and Nicole Marafioti, eds., *Capital and Corporal Punishment in Anglo-Saxon England* (Woodbridge, 2014), pp. 1–16.

Gilsenan, Michael. *Lords of the Lebanese Marches: Violence and Narrative in an Arab Society* (Berkeley, 1996).

Gluckman, Max. 'Peace in the Feud', in Gluckman, *Custom and Conflict in Africa* (Oxford, 1955), pp. 1–26.

Godden, M. R. 'Ælfric's changing vocabulary', *English Studies* 61 (1980), pp. 206–23.

Godden, Malcolm. 'Apocalypse and Invasion in Late Anglo-Saxon England', in Godden, D. Gray and T. Hoad, eds., *From Anglo-Saxon to Early Middle English: Studies Presented to E.G. Stanley* (Oxford, 1994), pp. 130–62.

Goebel, Julius Jr. *Felony and Misdemeanor: A Study in the History of English Criminal Procedure* (New York, 1937).

Goody, Jack, ed. *The Myth of the Bagre* (Oxford, 1972).

Goody, Jack. 'Memory in Oral Tradition', in Patricia Fara and Karalyn Patterson, eds., *Memory* (Cambridge, 1998), pp. 73–94.

Groot, Roger D. 'The Jury in Private Criminal Prosecutions Before 1215', *American Journal of Legal History* 27 (1983), pp. 113–41.

Groot, Roger D. 'Proto-Juries and Public Criminal Law in England', in Dietmar Willoweit, ed., *Die Entstehung des öffentlichen Strafrechts: Bestandsaufnahme eines europäischen Forschungsproblems* (Cologne, 1999), pp. 23–39.

Hadley, D. M. 'Introduction: Medieval Masculinities', in D. M. Hadley, ed., *Masculinity in Medieval Europe* (London, 1999), pp. 1–19.

Hadley, D. M. *The Northern Danelaw: Its Social Structure, c. 800–1100* (London, 2000).

Hadley, Dawn M. and Jo Buckberry. 'Caring for the Dead in Late Anglo-Saxon England', in Francesca Tinti, ed., *Pastoral Care in Late Anglo-Saxon England* (Woodbridge, 2005), pp. 121–47.

Halsall, Guy. 'Violence and Society in the Early Medieval West: An Introductory Survey', in Guy Halsall, ed., *Violence and Society in the Early Medieval West* (Woodbridge, 1998), pp. 1–45.

Hamerow, Helena. 'The Earliest Anglo-Saxon Kingdoms', in Paul Fouracre, ed., *The New Cambridge Medieval History*, vol. 1: *c.500–c.700* (Cambridge, 2005), pp. 263–88.

Hamilton, Sarah. 'Rites for Public Penance in Late Anglo-Saxon England', in Helen Gittos and M. Bradford Bedingfield, eds., *The Liturgy of the Late Anglo-Saxon Church* (London, 2005), pp. 65–103.

Harvey, Sally. *Domesday: Book of Judgement* (Oxford, 2014).

Hatch, Elvin. 'Theories of Social Honor' *American Anthropologist* 91 (1989), pp. 341–53.

Head, Thomas. 'Peace and Power in France Around the Year 1000', *Essays in Medieval Studies* 23 (2006), pp. 1–17.

Hedges, Robert. 'Anglo-Saxon Migration and the Molecular Evidence', in Helena Hamerow, David A. Hinton, and Sally Crawford, eds., *The Oxford Handbook of Anglo-Saxon Archaeology* (Oxford, 2012), pp. 79–90.

Hehl, Ernst-Dieter. 'War, Peace and the Christian Order', in David Luscombe and Jonathan Riley-Smith, eds., *The New Cambridge Medieval History*, vol. 4: *c.1024–c.1198*, Part I (Cambridge, 2004), pp. 185–228.

Higham, Nicholas J. 'The Five Boroughs', in Michael Lapidge et al., eds., *The Wiley-Blackwell Encyclopedia of Anglo-Saxon England* (2nd edn, Chichester, 2014), pp. 191–2.

Higham. Nicholas. J. and Martin Ryan. *The Anglo-Saxon World* (New Haven, 2013).

Hills, Catherine. *The Origins of the English* (London, 2003).

Hines, John. 'Units of Account in Gold and Silver in Seventh-Century England: *Scillingas, Sceattas* and *Pæningas*', *Antiquaries Journal* 90 (2010), 153–73.

Hollister, C. Warren. *Anglo-Saxon Military Institutions on the Eve of the Norman Conquest* (Oxford, 1962).

Holt, Richard. 'The Urban Transformation in England, 900–1100', *Anglo-Norman Studies* 32 (2010), pp. 57–78.

Hough, Carole. 'Alfred's *Domboc* and the Language of Rape: A Reconsideration of Alfred, ch. 11', repr. in. and cited from Carole Hough, *An Ald Recht: Essays on Anglo-Saxon Law* (Newcastle upon Tyne, 2014), pp. 169–202.

Hough, Carole. 'Legal and Documentary Writings', repr. in and cited from Carole Hough, *An Ald Recht: Essays on Anglo-Saxon Law* (Newcastle upon Tyne, 2014), pp. 2–24.

Hough, Carole. 'Numbers in Manuscripts in Anglo-Saxon Law', repr. in and cited from Carole Hough, *An Ald Recht: Essays on Anglo-Saxon Law* (Newcastle upon Tyne, 2014), pp. 251–71.

Hough, Carole. 'Palaeographical Evidence for the Compilation of *Textus Roffensis*', repr. in and cited from Carole Hough, *An Ald Recht: Essays on Anglo-Saxon Law* (Newcastle upon Tyne, 2014), pp. 216–50.

Hough, Carole. 'A Reappraisal of Æthelberht 84', repr. in and cited from Carole Hough, *An Ald Recht: Essays on Anglo-Saxon Law* (Newcastle upon Tyne, 2014), pp. 150–7.

Hough, Carole. 'The Structure of English Society in the Seventh Century: A New Reading of Æthelberht 12', in Carole Hough, *An Ald Recht: Essays on Anglo-Saxon Law* (Newcastle upon Tyne, 2014), pp. 74–86.

Hough, Carole. 'Two Kentish Laws Concerning Women: A New Reading of Æthelberht 73 and 74', repr. in and cited from Carole Hough, *An Ald Recht: Essays on Anglo-Saxon Law* (Newcastle upon Tyne, 2014), pp. 87–110.

Hough, Carole. 'Women and the Law in Seventh-Century England', repr. in and cited from Carole Hough, *An Ald Recht: Essays on Anglo-Saxon Law* (Newcastle upon Tyne, 2014), pp. 46–72.

Hough, Carole. 'The Earliest English Texts? The Language of the Kentish Laws Reconsidered', in Bruce O'Brien and Barbara Bombi, eds., *Textus Roffensis: Law, Language and Libraries in Medieval England* (Turnhout, 2015), pp. 137–56.

van Houts, Elisabeth. 'The Vocabulary of Exile and Outlawry in the North Sea Area around the First Millennium', in Laura Napran and Elisabeth van Houts, eds., *Exile in the Middle Ages: Selected Proceedings from the International Medieval Congress, University of Leeds, 8–11 July 2002* (Turnhout, 2004), pp. 13–28.

Hudson, John. *The Formation of the English Common Law: Law and Society in England from the Norman Conquest to Magna Carta* (London, 1996).

Hudson, John. '*The Making of English Law* and Varieties of Legal History', in Stephen Baxter et al., eds., *Early Medieval Studies in Memory of Patrick Wormald* (Farnham, Surrey, 2009), pp. 421–32.

Hudson, John. 'Feud, Vengeance and Violence in England from the Tenth to the Twelfth Centuries', in Belle S. Tuten and Tracey A. Billado, eds., *Feud, Violence and Practice: Essays in Medieval Studies in Honour of Stephen D. White* (Farnham, 2010), pp. 29–53.

Hudson, John. 'From the *Leges* to *Glanvill*: Legal Expertise and Legal Reasoning', in Stefan Jurasinski, Lisi Oliver, and Andrew Rabin, eds., *English Law Before Magna Carta: Felix Liebermann and Die Gesetze der Angelsachsen* (Leiden, 2010), pp. 221–49.

Hudson, John. *The Oxford History of the Laws of England*, vol. 2: *871–1216* (Oxford, 2012).

Hurnard, Naomi. 'The Anglo-Norman Franchises', *English Historical Review* 64 (1949), pp. 289–327, 433–60.

Hyams, Paul R. 'Maitland and the Rest of Us', in John Hudson, ed., *The History of English Law: Centenary Essays on 'Pollock and Maitland'* (Proceedings of the British Academy 89; Oxford, 1996), pp. 215–41.

Hyams, Paul R. *Rancor and Reconciliation in Medieval England* (Ithaca, 2003).

Hyams, Paul R. 'Afterword: Neither Unnatural nor Wholly Negative: The Future of Medieval Vengeance', in Susanna A. Throop and Paul R. Hyams, eds., *Vengeance in the Middle Ages: Emotion, Religion and Feud* (Farnham, 2010), pp. 203–20.

Innes, Matthew. *State and Society in the Early Middle Ages: The Middle Rhine Valley, 400–1000* (Cambridge, 2000).

Innes, Matthew. 'Charlemagne, Justice and Written Law', in Alice Rio, ed., *Law, Custom, and Justice in Late Antiquity and the Early Middle Ages: Proceedings of the 2008 Byzantine Colloquium* (London, 2011), pp. 155–203.

Insley, Charles. 'Southumbria', in Pauline Stafford, ed., *A Companion to the Early Middle Ages: Britain and Ireland, c.500–c.1100* (Oxford, 2009), pp. 322–40.

Jenkins, Dafydd. 'Crime and Tort and the Three Columns of Law', in Thomas Charles-Edwards and Paul Russell, eds., *Tair Colofn Cyfraith: The Three Columns of Law in Medieval Wales. Homicide, Theft and Fire* (Bangor, 2005 [i.e. 2007]), pp. 1–25.

John, Eric. *Land Tenure in Early England* (Leicester, 1960).

Jones, S. R. H. 'Transaction Costs, Institutional Change, and the Emergence of a Market Economy in Later Anglo-Saxon England', *Economic History Review* 46 (1993), pp. 658–78.

de Jong, Mayke. *The Penitential State: Authority and Atonement in the Age of Louis the Pious, 814–840* (Cambridge, 2009).

Jurasinski, Stefan. 'The Continental Origins of Æthelberht's Code', *Philological Quarterly* 80 (2001), pp. 1–15.

Jurasinski, Stefan. '*Reddatur Parentibus:* The Vengeance of the Family in Cnut's Homicide Legislation', *Law and History Review* 20 (2002), pp. 157–80.

Jurasinski, Stefan. *The Old English Penitentials and Anglo-Saxon Law* (New York, 2015).

Kaeuper, Richard. 'Vengeance and Mercy in Chivalric *Mentalité*', in T. B. Lambert and David Rollason, eds., *Peace and Protection in the Middle Ages* (Toronto, 2009), pp. 168–80.

Karn, Nicholas. 'Rethinking the *Leges Henrici Primi*', in Stefan Jurasinski, Lisi Oliver and Andrew Rabin, eds., *English Law Before Magna Carta: Felix Liebermann and Die Gesetze der Angelsachsen* (Leiden, 2010), pp. 199–220.

Keefer, Sarah Larratt. '*Ðonne se Cirlisca Man Ordales Weddigeð*: The Anglo-Saxon Lay Ordeal', in Stephen Baxter et al., eds., *Early Medieval Studies in Memory of Patrick Wormald* (Farnham, 2009), pp. 353–67.

Keene, Derek. 'Text, Visualisation and Politics: London, 1150–1250', *Transactions of the Royal Historical Society* 18 (2008), pp. 66–99.

Kelly, Fergus. *A Guide to Early Irish Law* (Dublin, 1988).

Kennedy, A. G. 'Cnut's Law-Code of 1018', *Anglo-Saxon England* 11 (1982), pp. 57–81.

Kennedy, A. G. 'Disputes about *Bocland*: The Forum for their Adjudication', *Anglo-Saxon England* 14 (1985), pp. 175–95.

Kershaw, Paul J. E. *Peaceful Kings: Peace, Power, and the Early Medieval Political Imagination* (Oxford, 2011).

Keynes, Simon. *The Diplomas of Æthelred 'the Unready', 978–1016: A Study in their Use as Historical Evidence* (Cambridge, 1980).

Keynes, Simon. 'Royal Government and the Written Word in Late Anglo-Saxon England', in Rosamond McKitterick, ed., *The Uses of Literacy in Early Mediaeval Europe* (Cambridge, 1990), pp. 226–57.

Keynes, Simon. 'Crime and Punishment in the Reign of King Æthelred the Unready', in Ian Wood and Niels Lund, eds., *People and Places in Northern Europe, 500–1600: Essays in Honour of Peter Hayes Sawyer* (Woodbridge, 1991), pp. 67–81.

Keynes, Simon. 'The West Saxon Charters of King Æthelwulf and His Sons', *English Historical Review* 109 (1994), 1109–49.

Keynes, Simon. 'England, *c.*900–1016', in Timothy Reuter, ed., *The New Cambridge Medieval History*, vol. 3: *c. 900–c.1024* (Cambridge, 1999), pp. 456–84.

Keynes, Simon. 'An Abbot, an Archbishop, and the Viking Raids of 1006–7 and 1009–12', *Anglo-Saxon England* 36 (2007), pp. 151–220.

King, Vanessa. 'St Oswald's Tenants', in Nicholas Brooks and Catherine Cubitt, eds., *St Oswald of Worcester: Life and Influence* (London, 1996), pp. 100–16.

Lambert, Tom. 'Spiritual Protection and Secular Power: The Evolution of Sanctuary and Legal Privilege in Ripon and Beverley, 900–1300', in Tom Lambert and David Rollason, eds., *Peace and Protection in the Middle Ages* (Toronto, 2009), pp. 121–40.

Lambert, Tom. 'Royal Protections and Private Justice: A reassessment of Cnut's "Reserved Pleas"', in Stefan Jurasinski, Lisi Oliver, and Andrew Rabin, eds., *English Law Before Magna Carta: Felix Liebermann and Die Gesetze der Angelsachsen* (Leiden, 2010), pp. 157–75.

Lambert, Tom. 'Theft, Homicide and Crime in Late Anglo-Saxon Law', *Past and Present* 214 (2012), pp. 3–43.

Lambert, Tom. 'Compensation, Honour and Idealism in the Laws of Æthelberht', in Stefan Esders, Han Nijdam and Lukas Bothe, eds., *Wergild, Compensation and Penance: The Monetary Logic of Early Medieval Conflict Resolution* (Leiden, forthcoming 2017).

Lancaster, Lorraine. 'Kinship in Anglo-Saxon Society', *British Journal of Sociology* 9 (1958), pp. 230–50, 359–77.

Lavelle, Ryan. 'Ine 70.1 and Royal Provision in Anglo-Saxon Wessex', in Gale R. Owen-Crocker, ed., *Kingship, Legislation and Power in Anglo-Saxon England* (Woodbridge, 2013), pp. 259–73.

Lawson, M. K. 'The Collection of Danegeld and Heregeld in the Reigns of Æthelred II and Cnut', *English Historical Review* 99 (1984), pp. 721–38.

Lawson, M. K. *Cnut: England's Viking King* (2nd edn, Stroud, 2004).

Lendinara, Patrizia. 'The Kentish Laws', in John Hines, ed., *The Anglo-Saxons from the Migration Period to the Eighth Century: An Ethnographic Perspective* (Woodbridge, 1997), pp. 211–30.

Lewis, C. P. and A. T. Thacker. eds., *A History of the County of Chester*, vol. 5, Part 1: *The City of Chester: General History and Topography* (London, 2003).

Leyser, Henrietta. *Medieval Women* (London, 1995).

Loyn, Henry. 'Gesiths and Thegns in Anglo-Saxon England from the Seventh to the Tenth Century', *English Historical Review* 70 (1955), pp. 529–49.

Loyn, Henry. 'Kinship in Anglo-Saxon England', *Anglo-Saxon England* 3 (1973), pp. 197–209.

Lupoi, Maurizio. *The Origins of the European Legal Order*, trans. Adrian Belton (Cambridge, 2000).

Lyon, Stewart. 'Historical Problems of Anglo-Saxon Coinage – (3) Denominations and Weights', *British Numismatic Journal* 38 (1969), pp. 204–22.

Maddicott, John. 'Plague in Seventh-Century England', *Past and Present* 156 (1997), pp. 7–54.

Maitland, Frederic William. *Domesday Book and Beyond: Three Essays in the Early History of England* (Cambridge, 1897).

Marafioti, Nicole. 'Punishing Bodies and Saving Souls: Capital and Corporal Punishment in Late Anglo-Saxon England', *Haskins Society Journal* 20 (2008), pp. 39–57.

Meens, Rob. 'Politics, Mirrors of Princes and the Bible: Sins, Kings and the Well-Being of the Realm', *Early Medieval Europe* 7 (1998).

Meens, Rob. *Penance in Medieval Europe, 600–1200* (Cambridge, 2014).

Miller, William Ian. 'Choosing the Avenger: Some Aspects of the Bloodfeud in Medieval Iceland and England', *Law and History Review* 1 (1983), pp. 159–204.

Miller, William Ian. *Bloodtaking and Peacemaking: Feud, Law and Society in Saga Iceland* (Chicago, 1990).

Miller, William Ian. *Eye for an Eye* (Cambridge, 2006).

Miller, William Ian. *Why is Your Axe Bloody? A Reading of Njál's Saga* (Oxford, 2014).

Molyneaux, George. 'Why Were Some Tenth-Century English Kings Presented as Rulers of Britain?', *Transactions of the Royal Historical Society* 21 (2011), pp. 59–91.

Molyneaux, George. 'The Ordinance Concerning the Dunsaete and the Anglo-Welsh Frontier in the Late Tenth and Eleventh Centuries', *Anglo-Saxon England* 40 (2012), pp. 249–72.

Molyneaux, George. 'Did the English Really Think They Were God's elect in the Anglo-Saxon Period?', *Journal of Ecclesiastical History* 65 (2014), pp. 721–37.

Molyneaux, George. *The Formation of the English Kingdom in the Tenth Century* (Oxford, 2015).

Morris, William Alfred. *The Frankpledge System* (London, 1910).

Morris, William Alfred. *The Medieval English Sheriff to 1300* (Manchester, 1927).

Mumby, Julie. 'The Descent of Family Land in Later Anglo-Saxon England', *Historical Research* 84 (2011), pp. 399–415.

Murray, Alexander. *Suicide in the Middle Ages,* II: *The Curse on Self-Murder* (Oxford, 2000).

Naismith, Rory. 'The English Monetary Economy, c.973–1100: The Contribution of Single-Finds', *Economic History Review* 66 (2013), pp. 198–225.

Naismith, Rory. 'H. M. Chadwick and the Anglo-Saxon Monetary System', in Michael Lapidge, ed., *The Life and Writings of Hector Munro Chadwick* (Aberystwyth, 2015), pp. 143–56.

Nelson, Janet L. 'The Earliest Royal *Ordo*: Some Liturgical and Historical Aspects', repr. in and cited from Janet L. Nelson, *Politics and Ritual in Early Medieval Europe* (London, 1986), pp. 341–60.

Nelson, Janet L. 'The Rites of the Conqueror', repr. in and cited from Janet L. Nelson, *Politics and Ritual in Early Medieval Europe* (London, 1986), pp. 375–401.

Netterstrøm, Jeppe Büchert. 'Introduction: The Study of Feud in Medieval and Early Modern History', in Jeppe Büchert Netterstrøm and Bjørn Poulsen, eds., *Feud in Medieval and Early Modern Europe* (Aarhus, 2007), pp. 9–67.

O'Brien, Bruce R. 'From *Morðor* to *Murdrum*: The Preconquest Origin and Norman Revival of the Murder Fine', *Speculum* 71 (1996), pp. 321–57.

O'Brien, Bruce R. *God's Peace and King's Peace: The Laws of Edward the Confessor* (Philadelphia, 1999).

O'Brien, Bruce R. 'The *Instituta Cnuti* and the Translation of English Law', *Anglo-Norman Studies* 25 (2003), pp. 177–98.

O'Brien, Bruce R. '*Textus Roffensis*: An Introduction', in Bruce O'Brien and Barbara Bombi, eds., *Textus Roffensis: Law, Language and Libraries in Medieval England* (Turnhout, 2015), pp. 1–16.

Oliver, Lisi. '*Cyninges Fedesl*: The King's Feeding in Æthelberht, ch. 12', *Anglo-Saxon England* 27 (1998), pp. 31–40.

Oliver, Lisi. 'Protecting the Body in Early Medieval Law', in T. B. Lambert and David Rollason, eds., *Peace and Protection in the Middle Ages* (Toronto, 2009), pp. 60–77.

Oliver, Lisi. *The Body Legal in Barbarian Law* (Toronto, 2011).

Oliver, Lisi, ed. *The Beginnings of English Law* (Toronto, 2002).

Orchard, Andy. 'Oral Tradition', in Katherine O'Brien O'Keefe, ed., *Reading Old English Texts* (Cambridge, 1997), pp. 101–23.

Pantos, Aliki. '*In medle oððe an þinge*: The Old English Vocabulary of Assembly', in Aliki Pantos and Sarah Semple, eds., *Assembly Places and Practices in Medieval Europe* (Dublin, 2004), pp. 181–201.

Pelteret, David A. E. *Slavery in Early Medieval England: From Alfred the Great until the Twelfth Century* (Woodbridge, 1995).

Pirie, Fernanda. *Tribe and State in Eastern Tibet: Feuding, Mediation and the Negotiation of Authority among the Amdo Nomads* (Working paper no. 72. Halle: Max Planck Institute for Social Anthropology, 2005).

Pirie, Fernanda. 'Order, Individualism and Responsibility: Contrasting Dynamics on the Tibetan Plateau', in Keebet von Benda-Beckmann and Fernanda Pirie, eds., *Order and Disorder: Anthropological Perspectives* (Oxford, 2007).

Pirie, Fernanda. 'From Tribal Tibet: The Significance of the Legal Form', in Michael Freeman and David Napier, eds., *Law and Anthropology* (Current Legal Issues 12; Oxford, 2009), pp. 143–61.

Pirie, Fernanda. *The Anthropology of Law* (Oxford, 2013).

Pirie, Fernanda. 'Rules, Proverbs and Persuasion: Legalism and Rhetoric in Tibet', in Paul Dresch and Judith Scheele, eds., *Legalism: Rules and Categories* (Oxford, 2015), pp. 105–28.

Pirie, Fernanda and Judith Scheele. 'Justice, Community, and Law', in Fernanda Pirie and Judith Scheele, eds., *Legalism: Community and Justice* (Oxford, 2014), pp. 1–24.

Pollock, Frederick. 'The King's Peace', in Frederick Pollock, *Oxford Lectures and Other Discourses* (London, 1890), pp. 65–90.

Pollock, Frederick and Frederic William Maitland. *The History of English Law Before the Time of Edward I*, 2 vols. (2nd edn, Cambridge, 1898).

Pratt, David. *The Political Thought of Alfred the Great* (Cambridge, 2007).

Pratt, David. 'Written Law and the Communication of Authority in Tenth-Century England', in David Rollason, Conrad Leyser and Hannah Williams, eds., *England and the Continent in the Tenth Century: Studies in Honour of Wilhelm Levison (1876–1947)* (Turnhout, 2010), pp. 331–50.

Pratt, David. 'Demesne Exemption from Royal Taxation in Anglo-Saxon and Anglo-Norman England', *English Historical Review* 128 (2013), pp. 1–34.

Rabin, Andrew. 'Ritual Magic or Legal Performance: Reconsidering an Old English Charm Against Theft', in Stefan Jurasinski, Lisi Oliver, and Andrew Rabin, eds., *English Law Before Magna Carta: Felix Liebermann and Die Gesetze der Angelsachsen* (Leiden, 2010), pp. 177–95.

Renna, Thomas. 'The Idea of Peace in the West', *Journal of Medieval History* 6 (1980), pp. 143–67.

Reuter, Timothy. 'The Insecurity of Travel in the Early and High Middle Ages: Criminals, Victims and their Medieval and Modern Observers', in Timothy Reuter, *Medieval Polities and Modern Mentalities*, ed. Janet L. Nelson (Cambridge, 2006), pp. 38–71.

Reuter, Timothy. 'Plunder and Tribute in the Carolingian Empire', repr. in and cited from Timothy Reuter, *Medieval Polities and Modern Mentalities*, ed. Janet L. Nelson (Cambridge, 2006), pp. 231–50.

Reynolds, Andrew. *Anglo-Saxon Deviant Burial Customs* (Oxford, 2009).

Reynolds, Susan. 'The Historiography of the Medieval State', in Michael Bentley, ed., *Companion to Historiography* (London, 1997), pp. 117–38.

Reynolds, Susan. *Kingdoms and Communities in Western Europe, 900–1300* (2nd edn, Oxford, 1997).

Reynolds, Susan. 'The Emergence of Professional Law in the Long Twelfth Century', *Law and History Review* 21 (2003), pp. 347–66.

Reynolds, Susan. 'There Were States in Medieval Europe: A Response to Rees Davies' *Journal of Historical Sociology* 16 (2003), pp. 550–5.

Reynolds, Susan. 'Government and Community', in David Luscombe and Jonathan Riley-Smith, eds., *The New Cambridge Medieval History*, vol, 4: *c.1024–c.1198*, Part 1 (Cambridge, 2004), pp. 86–112.

Richards, Mary P. 'I-II Cnut: Wulfstan's *Summa?*', in Stefan Jurasinski, Lisi Oliver, and Andrew Rabin, eds., *English Law Before Magna Carta: Felix Liebermann and Die Gesetze der Angelsachsen* (Leiden, 2010), pp. 137–56.

Richardson, H. G. and G. O. Sayles. *The Governance of Medieval England from the Conquest to Magna Carta* (Edinburgh, 1963).

Richardson, H. G. and G. O. Sayles. *Law and Legislation from Æthelberht to Magna Carta* (Edinburgh, 1966).

Rio, Alice. 'Freedom and Unfreedom in Early Medieval Francia: The Evidence of the Legal Formulae', *Past and Present* 193 (2006), pp. 7–40.

Rio, Alice. 'Introduction', in Alice Rio, ed., *Law, Custom, and Justice in Late Antiquity and the Early Middle Ages: Proceedings of the 2008 Byzantine Colloquium* (London, 2011), pp. 1–22.

Rio, Alice. 'Self-Sale and Voluntary Entry into Unfreedom', *Journal of Social History* 45 (2012), pp. 661–85.

Rio, Alice. '"Half-Free" Categories in the Early Middle Ages: Fine Status Distinctions Before Professional Lawyers', in Paul Dresch and Judith Scheele, eds., *Legalism: Rules and Categories* (Oxford, 2015), pp. 129–52.

Rio, Alice. 'Penal Enslavement in the Early Middle Ages', in Christian Giuseppe de Vito and Alex Lichtenstein, eds., *Global Convict Labour* (Leiden, 2015), pp. 79–107.

Roach, Levi. 'Public Rites and Public Wrongs: Ritual Aspects of Diplomas in Tenth- and Eleventh-Century England', *Early Medieval Europe* 19 (2011), pp. 182–203.

Roach, Levi. 'Penance, Submission and *Deditio*: Religious Influences on Dispute Settlement in Later Anglo-Saxon England', *Anglo-Saxon England* 41 (2012), pp. 243–71.

Roach, Levi. *Kingship and Consent in Anglo-Saxon England, 871–978* (Cambridge, 2013).

Roach, Levi. 'Law Codes and Legal Norms in Later Anglo-Saxon England', *Historical Research* 86 (2013), pp. 465–86.

Roach, Levi. 'Penitential Discourse in the Diplomas of King Æthelred "the Unready"', *Journal of Ecclesiastical History* 64 (2013), pp. 258–76.

Roach, Levi. 'Apocalypse and Atonement in the Politics of Æthelredian England', *English Studies* 95 (2014), pp. 733–57.

Roberts, Simon. 'The Study of Disputes: Anthropological Perspectives', in John Bossy, ed., *Disputes and Settlements: Law and Human Relations in the West* (Cambridge, 1983), pp. 1–24.

Sawyer, Peter. *The Wealth of Anglo-Saxon England* (Oxford, 2013).

Sbriccoli, Mario. 'Legislation, Justice and Political Power in Italian Cities, 1200–1400', in Antonio Padoa-Schioppa, ed., *Legislation and Justice* (Oxford, 1997), pp. 37–55.

Scheele, Judith. 'Rightful Measures: Irrigation, Land, and the Sharī'ah in the Algerian Touat', in Paul Dresch and Hannah Skoda, eds., *Legalism: Anthropology and History* (Oxford, 2012), pp. 197–227.

Scheele, Judith. 'Community as an Achievement: Kabyle Customary Law and Beyond', in Fernanda Pirie and Judith Scheele, eds., *Legalism: Community and Justice* (Oxford, 2014), pp. 177–200.

Scheele, Judith. 'In Praise of Disorder: Breaking the Rules in Northern Chad', in Paul Dresch and Judith Scheele, eds., *Legalism: Rules and Categories* (Oxford, 2015), pp. 153–76.

Seebohm, Frederic. *Tribal Custom in Anglo-Saxon Law* (London, 1911).

Sharpe, Richard. 'The Use of Writs in the Eleventh-Century', *Anglo-Saxon England* 32 (2003), pp. 247–91.

Simpson, A. W. B. 'The Laws of Ethelbert', in M. S. Green et al., eds., *On the Laws and Customs of England: Essays in Honor of Samuel E. Thorne* (Chapel Hill, 1981), pp. 3–17.

Sims-Williams, Patrick. *Religion and Literature in Western England, 600–800* (Cambridge, 1990).

Sims-Williams, Patrick. 'Kings of the Hwicce (act. c.670-c.780)' *Oxford Dictionary of National Biography* (Oxford University Press, 2004; online edn, Sept 2011).

Stafford, Pauline. 'The Laws of Cnut and the History of Anglo-Saxon Royal Promises', *Anglo-Saxon England* 43 (1981), pp. 173–90.

Stafford, Pauline. *Unification and Conquest: A Political and Social History of England in the Tenth and Eleventh Centuries* (London, 1989).

Stafford, Pauline. 'Kings, Kingships and Kingdoms', in Wendy Davies, ed., *From the Vikings to the Normans* (Oxford, 2003) pp. 11–39.

Stafford, Pauline. 'King and Kin, Lord and Community: England in the Tenth and Eleventh Centuries', in Pauline Stafford, *Gender, Family and the Legitimation of Power: England from the Ninth to the Early Twelfth Century* (Aldershot, 2006), VIII, pp. 1–33.

Stafford, Pauline. 'Ealdorman', in Michael Lapidge et al., eds., *The Wiley-Blackwell Encyclopedia of Anglo-Saxon England* (2nd edn, Chichester, 2014), pp. 156–7.

Stafford, Pauline. 'Reeve', in Michael Lapidge et al., eds., *The Wiley-Blackwell Encyclopedia of Anglo-Saxon England* (2nd edn, Chichester, 2014), pp. 397–8.

Stenton, F. M. *Types of Manorial Structure in the Northern Danelaw* (Oxford, 1910).

Stenton, F. M. *Anglo-Saxon England* (3rd edn, Oxford, 1973).

Stewart, Frank Henderson. *Honor* (Chicago, 1994).

Stubbs, William. *The Constitutional History of England in its Origin and Development*, 3 vols. (6th edn, Oxford, 1903–6).

Stuntz, William J. *The Collapse of American Criminal Justice* (Cambridge, Mass., 2011).

Sutherland, Donald W. *Quo Warranto Proceedings in the Reign of Edward I, 1278–1294* (Oxford, 1963).

Tanner, Norman and Sethina Watson, 'Least of the Laity: the Minimum Requirements for a Medieval Christian', *Journal of Medieval history* 32 (2006), pp. 395–423.

Taylor, Alice. 'Crime Without Punishment: Medieval Scottish Law in Comparative Perspective', *Anglo-Norman Studies* 35 (2013), pp. 287–304.

Taylor, Alice. '*Lex Scripta* and the Problem of Enforcement: Anglo-Saxon, Scottish and Welsh Law Compared', in Judith Scheele and Fernanda Pirie, eds., *Legalism: Community and Justice* (Oxford, 2014), pp. 47–75.

Taylor, Alice. *The Shape of the State in Medieval Scotland, 1124–1290* (Oxford, 2016).

Thompson, Victoria. *Dying and Death in Later Anglo-Saxon England* (Woodbridge, 2004).

Þorláksson, Helgi. 'Feud and Feuding in the Early and High Middle Ages: Working Descriptions and Continuity', in Jeppe Büchert Netterstrøm and Bjørn Poulsen, eds., *Feud in Medieval and Early Modern Europe* (Aarhus, 2007), pp. 69–94.

Vansina, Jan. *Oral Tradition as History* (Oxford, 1985).

Vinogradoff, Paul. *English Society in the Eleventh Century: Essays in English Mediaeval History* (Oxford, 1908).

Walker, H. E. 'Bede and the Gewissae: The Political Evolution of the Heptarchy and its Nomenclature', *Cambridge Historical Journal* 12 (1956), pp. 174–86.

Wallace-Hadrill, J. M. *The Long-Haired Kings* (London, 1962).

Wallace-Hadrill, J. M. *Early Germanic Kingship in England and on the Continent* (Oxford, 1971).

Ward-Perkins, Bryan. 'Why Did the Anglo-Saxons Not Become More British?', *English Historical Review* 115 (2000), pp. 513–33.

Ward-Perkins, Bryan. *The Fall of Rome and the End of Civilization* (Oxford, 2005).

Warren, W. L. 'The Myth of Norman Administrative Efficiency', *Transactions of the Royal Historical Society* 34 (1984), pp. 113–32.

Warren, W. L. *The Governance of Norman and Angevin England, 1086–1272* (London, 1987).

White, Stephen D. 'Kinship and Lordship in Early Medieval England: The Story of Cynewulf and Cyneheard', *Viator* 20 (1989), pp. 1–18.

White, Stephen D. 'Protection, Warranty, and Vengeance in *La Chanson De Roland*', in T. B. Lambert and David Rollason, eds., *Peace and Protection in the Middle Ages* (Toronto, 2009), pp. 155–67.

White, Stephen D. '"The Peace in the Feud" Revisited: Feuds in the Peace in Medieval European Feuds', in Conrad Leyser and Kate Cooper, eds., *Making Early Medieval Societies: Conflict and Belonging in the Latin West, 300–1200* (Cambridge, 2016), pp. 220–43.

Wickham, Chris. *Courts and Conflict in Twelfth-Century Tuscany* (Oxford, 2003).

Wickham, Chris. *Framing the Early Middle Ages: Europe and the Mediterranean, 400–800* (Oxford, 2005).

Wickham, Chris. *The Inheritance of Rome: A History of Europe from 400–1000* (London, 2009).

Wickham, Chris. 'Consensus and Assemblies in the Romano-Germanic Kingdoms: A Comparative Approach', in Verena Epp and Christoph H. F. Meyer, eds., *Recht und Konsens im frühen Mittelalter* (Vorträge und Forschungen 82; Konstanz, 2016), pp. 387–424.

Williams, Ann. *Æthelred the Unready: The Ill-Counselled King* (London, 2003).

Williams, Ann. 'Eadric of Laxfield (d. in or after 1066?)', *Oxford Dictionary of National Biography* (Oxford, 2004).

Williams, Ann. *The World Before Domesday: The Anglo-Saxon Aristocracy 900–1066* (London, 2008).

Wood, Ian. 'The North-Western Provinces', in Averil Cameron, Bryan Ward-Perkins and Michael Whitby, eds., *The Cambridge Ancient History*, vol. 14: *Late Antiquity: Empire and Successors, AD 425–600* (Cambridge, 2001), pp. 497–524.

Wood, Ian. '"The Bloodfeud of the Franks": a Historiographical Legend', *Early Medieval Europe* 14 (2006), pp. 489–504.

Wormald, Patrick. 'The Uses of Literacy in Anglo-Saxon England and Its Neighbours', *Transactions of the Royal Historical Society* 27 (1977), pp. 95–114.

Wormald, Patrick. 'Introduction', in Wendy Davies and Paul Fouracre, eds., *The Settlement of Disputes in Early Medieval Europe* (Cambridge, 1986), pp. 1–5.

Wormald, Patrick. 'Archbishop Wulfstan and the Holiness of Society', repr. in and cited from Patrick Wormald, *Legal Culture in the Early Medieval West: Law as Text, Image and Experience* (London, 1999), pp. 225–51.

Wormald, Patrick. 'Charters, Law and the Settlement of Disputes in Anglo-Saxon England', repr. in and cited from Patrick Wormald, *Legal Culture in the Early Medieval West: Law as Text, Image and Experience* (London, 1999), pp. 289–310.

Wormald, Patrick. 'Engla Lond: the Making of an Allegiance', repr. in and cited from Patrick Wormald, *Legal Culture in the Early Medieval West: Law as Text, Image and Experience* (London, 1999), pp. 359–82.

Wormald, Patrick. 'Frederic William Maitland and the Earliest English Law', repr. in and cited from Patrick Wormald, *Legal Culture in the Early Medieval West: Law as Text, Image and Experience* (London, 1999), pp. 45–69.

Wormald, Patrick. 'Giving God and King Their Due: Conflict and Its Regulation in the Early English State', repr. in and cited from Patrick Wormald, *Legal Culture in the Early Medieval West: Law as Text, Image and Experience* (London, 1999), pp. 333–57.

Wormald, Patrick. 'A Handlist of Anglo-Saxon Lawsuits', repr. in and cited from Patrick Wormald, *Legal Culture in the Early Medieval West: Law as Text, Image and Experience* (London, 1999), pp. 253–87.

Wormald, Patrick. 'In Search of King Offa's "Law-Code"', repr. in and cited from Patrick Wormald, *Legal Culture in the Early Medieval West: Law as Text, Image and Experience* (London, 1999), pp. 201–23.

Wormald, Patrick. '"Inter Cetera Bona Genti Suae": Law-Making and Peace-Keeping in the Earliest English Kingdoms', repr. in and cited from Patrick Wormald, *Legal Culture in the Early Medieval West: Law as Text, Image and Experience* (London, 1999), pp. 179–98.

Wormald, Patrick. '*Laga Eadwardi*: The *Textus Roffensis* and its Context', repr. in and cited from Patrick Wormald, *Legal Culture in the Early Medieval West: Law as Text, Image and Experience* (London, 1999), pp. 115–38.

Wormald, Patrick. '*Lex Scripta* and *Verbum Regis*: Legislation and Germanic Kingship from Euric to Cnut', repr. in and cited from Patrick Wormald, *Legal Culture in the Early Medieval West: Law as Text, Image and Experience* (London, 1999), pp. 1–43.

Wormald, Patrick. 'Lordship and Justice in the Earliest English Kingdom: Oswaldslow Revisited', repr. in and cited from Patrick Wormald, *Legal Culture in the Early Medieval West: Law as Text, Image and Experience* (London, 1999), pp. 313–32.

Wormald, Patrick. *The Making of English Law: King Alfred to the Twelfth Century*, vol. 1: *Legislation and Its Limits* (Oxford, 1999).

Wormald, Patrick. 'The *Leges Barbarorum*: Law and Ethnicity in the Post-Roman West', in Hans-Werner Goetz, Jörg Jarnut and Walter Pohl, eds., *Regna and Gentes: The Relationship Between Late Antique and Early Medieval Peoples and Kingdoms in the Transformation of the Roman World* (Leiden, 2003), pp. 21–53.

Wormald, Patrick. *The First Code of English Law* (Canterbury, 2005).

Wormald, Patrick. 'Kings and Kingship', in Paul Fouracre, ed., *The New Cambridge Medieval History*, vol. 1: *c. 500–c. 700* (Cambridge, 2005), pp. 571–604.

Wormald, Patrick. 'Bede and the Conversion of England', repr. in and cited from Patrick Wormald, *The Times of Bede: Studies in Early English Christian Society and its Historian*, ed. Stephen Baxter (Oxford, 2006), pp. 135–66.

Wormald, Patrick. 'How Do We Know So Much About Anglo-Saxon Deerhurst?', repr. in and cited from Patrick Wormald, *The Times of Bede: Studies in Early English Christian Society and its Historian*, ed. Stephen Baxter (Oxford, 2006), pp. 229–48.

Wormald, Patrick. 'Pre-Modern "State" and "Nation": Definite or Indefinite?', in Stuart Airlie, Walter Pohl and Helmut Reimitz, eds., *Staat im frühen Mittelalter* (Vienna, 2006), pp. 179–89.

Wormald, Patrick. 'Frankpledge', in Michael Lapidge et al., eds., *The Wiley-Blackwell Encyclopedia of Anglo-Saxon England* (2nd edn, Chichester, 2014), pp. 197–8.

Wormald, Patrick. *Papers Preparatory to the Making of English Law: King Alfred to the Twelfth Century*, vol. 2: *From God's Law to Common Law*, ed. Stephen Baxter and John Hudson (University of London, 2014): <http://www.earlyenglishlaws.ac.uk/reference/wormald/>.

Yorke, Barbara. *Wessex in the Early Middle Ages* (London, 1995).

Yorke, Barbara. *Kings and Kingdoms of Early Anglo-Saxon England* (London, 1990).

UNPUBLISHED THESES

Barrett, Graham. 'The Written and the World in Early Medieval Iberia' (University of Oxford DPhil Thesis, 2015).

Breen, Aidan. 'Towards a Critical Edition of De *XII Abusivis*: Introductory Essays with a Provisional Edition of the Text Accompanied by an English Translation' (Trinity College Dublin PhD thesis, 1988).

Joy, C. A. 'Sokeright' (University of Leeds PhD thesis, 1972).

Lambert, T. B. 'Protection, Feud and Royal Power: Violence and Its Regulation in English Law, c.850–c.1250' (University of Durham PhD thesis, 2009).

Index